White Collar and Corporate Crime

A Case Study Approach

White Collar and Corporate Crime

A Case Study Approach

Laura Pinto Hansen

Associate Professor in Criminal Justice
Department of Criminal Justice and Sociology
Western New England University

Published by Wolters Kluwer in New York.

Wolters Kluwer Legal & Regulatory U.S. serves customers worldwide with CCH, Aspen Publishers, and Kluwer Law International products. (www.WKLegaledu.com)

Cover image: iStock/Pol Maria-stock.adobe.com

To contact Customer Service, e-mail customer.service@wolterskluwer.com, call 1-800-234-1660, fax 1-800-901-9075, or mail correspondence to:

 Wolters Kluwer
 Attn: Order Department
 PO Box 990
 Frederick, MD 21705

Printed in the United States of America.

1 2 3 4 5 6 7 8 9 0

ISBN 978-1-5438-1721-8

Library of Congress Cataloging-in-Publication Data

Names: Hansen, Laura L. (Laura Lynn) author.
Title: White collar and corporate crime : a case study approach / Laura Pinto Hansen, Associate Professor in Criminal Justice, Department of Criminal Justice and Sociology, Western New England University.
Description: New York : Wolters Kluwer, [2021] | Series: Criminal justice series | Includes bibliographical references and index. | Summary: "Introductory criminal justice book on white collar crime"—Provided by publisher.
Identifiers: LCCN 2020029783 | ISBN 9781543817218 (paperback) | ISBN 9781543823295 (ebook)
Subjects: LCSH: White collar crimes. | Political corruption. | White collar crime investigation. | White collar crimes—Law and legislation.
Classification: LCC HV6768 .H367 2021 | DDC 364.16/8—dc23
LC record available at https://lccn.loc.gov/2020029783

About Wolters Kluwer Legal & Regulatory U.S.

Wolters Kluwer Legal & Regulatory US delivers expert content and solutions in the areas of law, corporate compliance, health compliance, reimbursement, and legal education. Its practical solutions help customers successfully navigate the demands of a changing environment to drive their daily activities, enhance decision quality and inspire confident outcomes.

Serving customers worldwide, its legal and regulatory portfolio includes products under the Aspen Publishers, CCH Incorporated, Kluwer Law International, ftwilliam.com and MediRegs names. They are regarded as exceptional and trusted resources for general legal and practice-specific knowledge, compliance and risk management, dynamic workflow solutions, and expert commentary.

Summary of CONTENTS

CONTENTS

CHAPTER **ONE**

THE "IDEAL" ORGANIZATION   1

How organizations are supposed to run (in theory)

CHAPTER **TWO**

HOW ORGANIZATIONS REALLY RUN 25

What can go wrong that can lead to white collar or corporate crime

CHAPTER **THREE**

CHAPTER **FOUR**

CHAPTER **FIVE**

CORPORATE CRIME AND SCANDALS   123

When the whole barrel is rotten

CHAPTER **SIX**

CYBER WHITE COLLAR CRIME   153

What's my password?

CHAPTER **SEVEN**

FRAUD AGAINST CONSUMERS   181

Caveat emptor (buyer beware)

CHAPTER **EIGHT**

HEALTH CARE FRAUD AND CRIMES   **207**

Tell me where it hurts

CHAPTER **NINE**

RELIGION, CRIME, AND MISCONDUCT 241

Preying on the faithful

CHAPTER **TEN**

ENVIRONMENTAL CRIME 275

What harm is a little dumping?

CHAPTER **ELEVEN**

POLITICAL WHITE COLLAR CRIME 305

When clever people do stupid things

CHAPTER **TWELVE**

WHITE COLLAR CRIME AND TERRORISM   343

Follow the money

CHAPTER **THIRTEEN**

THE MEDIA AND WHITE COLLAR CRIME   373

Nothing like a juicy scandal to sell ad space

CHAPTER **FOURTEEN**

INVESTIGATING AND PROSECUTING WHITE COLLAR CRIME   401

When it pays to have a good defense attorney on retainer

CHAPTER **FIFTEEN**

DIAGNOSIS AND TREATMENT OF WHITE COLLAR AND CORPORATE CRIME   **437**

Eating the elephant one bite at a time

PREFACE

This book has been a labor of love, that has been over 20 years in the making. I started my professional life working in a number of financial occupations, including in banking, mortgage banking, personal and small business taxes, and as a financial paraplanner in the investments industry. When I walked away from Corporate America to pursue an academic career, it has led to an abundance of intrinsic rewards.

I had no intention of focusing on my scholarship on crime, much less white-collar crime. But as I got further into my graduate school experience, it became abundantly clear that studying financial crime would be a natural fit, as I had already worked extensively on the legitimate side of the finance industry and understood a lot about the nuances. What more fun could I have in research than to explore the underbelly of Wall Street?

Since beginning my exploration into the reasons why people break laws and regulations in the financial sector, I have always been curious as to why people in elite occupations and positions of power will risk it all to commit white collar crimes. *Fortune Magazine* (Kelleher, 2018) reported that the average Wall Street salary rose by 13 percent in 2017 and is now seven times as much as the average salary in the United States!

Since Sutherland proclaimed in 1939 that "white collar" crime is a different beast not to be confused with "conventional" crime, scholars have scratched their heads as to motivations, beyond money, for committing crimes that no doubt could result in the ruination of people's personal, financial, and professional lives. Even the money motive doesn't always make sense, because in some cases, the money that white collar criminals have stolen is really not that much, as compared to the legitimate salaries of many of the criminals we are introduced to in this book. We will see evidence of this throughout this book, in a number of case studies.

In my research with a colleague, Siamak Movahedi, at University of Massachusetts Boston, we proposed that one explanation for white collar crime is collective behavior, where individual greed is a myth (Hansen and Movahedi, 2010). I still largely believe that is true in many cases, including Watergate, Enron, and the conspiracies that are currently alleged, investigated by the Mueller team and in the impeachment investigations of President Trump. Some white collar crime is instigated by an "everybody is doing it, wink, wink, nod, nod" mentality, where crime becomes part of "doing business as usual" in certain professional environments in which case, it's difficult for regulators and policy makers to curb the behavior.

In order for readers to get a better grasp in understanding the environments in which white collar crimes are committed, I have included a chapter in the beginning that will familiarize you with how organizations *are supposed to work*, in theory, if they plan on functioning within legal boundaries. I follow this chapter with others that discussed some of the cultural and structural reasons why white collar crime happens, even in the most regulated of industries, including financial markets and medicine.

There are a number of types of white collar crime we will be exploring in this textbook. Some of the ploys in which to rob individuals of their hard earned money have been around for a long time, as in the case of Ponzi schemes. Others are newer types, primarily due to rise of technological innovation in recent decades, making some types of crimes easier to commit, as in the example of the use of email to commit fraud.

More recently, I have become interested in the intersection of cybercrime and white collar crime. You will see the evidence of this in Chapter 7, Cybercrime, an addition that is sometimes missing from other textbooks in white collar crime. As we become more technologically sophisticated, it means that the "bad guys" (and gals) have even more creative methods to steal from individuals, governments, and corporations, including sensitive employee information. The threat is no longer that an employee will stick their hands in the proverbial cookie jar as in the case of stealing cash or merchandise; they are becoming increasingly more likely to steal through electronic means.

The good news is that technology has also created a number of great tools in order to capture both conventional and white collar criminals, including the use of social network analysis. It is because social network analysis, or SNA, is now more commonly used in a variety of criminal investigations, that I have included a chapter on basic SNA theory and terminology in this book.

Whether you ever need to know the information contained between the covers of this book in your profession or if you simply have some of the same curiosities I have about the world of white collar crime, I suspect that the cases will spark interest to do your own research. Also, as I like to teach my own students, I hope to instructed you on how to be a better skeptic and informed consumer. Plus, how to spot a scam artist. If a deal sounds too good to be true, it probably is! No doubt you have heard the expression, "buyer beware," *caveat emptor* in Latin. Hopefully this book will help you to be able to sniff out fraud before you fall victim to it yourself.

In this day and age of media savvy, I have also included a chapter on how the media treats the investigation and prosecution of white collar criminals, including a discussion of the very public "perp walk." For those of you not familiar with this, unlike most cases of white collar criminals volunteering to turn themselves in to a police station, on the heels of an indictment and arrest warrant, law enforcement makes a very public arrest that amounts to a bit of media circus.

We should not forget that in most cases, elite white collar criminals are treated differently than the common, garden variety criminal, from arrest through to incarceration.

The book is organized so that you will have exposure to a wide variety of white collar crimes. In each chapter, I've included both well-known and lesser known examples of white collar criminals. In some cases, the perpetrator is a single person. In many of the cases in this book, there is a whole cast of characters committing a particular crime or crimes. These are presented in the *Law in the Real World* sections of each chapter.

At the end of each chapter, I have included a more comprehensive *case study analysis*. This is an opportunity to dive deeper into a single white collar crime case related to the specific chapter content. As in the words of Robert Ronstadt (1977), the way case studies are approached in this text book is not *the only way* by which to analyze crime. They are designed to offer a suggested way by which to study white collar crime through both a criminological and sociological lens.

The case study analyses are organized in the same way that I have organized the research papers that I assign my students, with five major sections covered for each crime, with the exception of Chapter One where we discuss what organizations *get right*:

1. *Classification of the crime* — legal and scholarly definitions are given for the type of crime or crimes committed in each case.
2. *Theories to help explain why the crime took place*—Classic and contemporary theories in criminology, sociology, economics, and other related disciplines that might help explain why the crime took place. These theories will be based on the information that we have available and by no means includes a comprehensive list. You are encouraged to think about alternative explanations not give in each case.
3. *Criminal justice system and/or policy responses to the crime*—In this section, we will discuss the case as it goes through the criminal justice system, from investigation, arrest, prosecution, courts, and sentencing. If the case has resulted in policy or changes in laws in an effort to prevent the crime or crimes from being committed in the future, then these will be discussed as well.
4. *Social response to the crime*—With a number of media sources in which to exhaustively explore any particular crime that outrages the public, it should be of interest to see just how invested the media is in reporting the crime. I have included everything from magazine articles, books, blogs on the Internet, and movie deals, where they apply in any particular case.
5. *Unanswered questions and unresolved issues related to the case*—As a final wrap up to the case study, I also include a discussion of some of the questions or issues that have not been answered in each case. After all, there is a lot of information that never comes out in the courts,

because both prosecutors and defense attorneys are laser-focused on only presenting evidence that will help win the case for their side.

For each case study analysis, you are encouraged to think about a number of your own unanswered questions and alternative theories.

I am hoping that you, the reader, will find great value in the inclusion of real cases of white collar crime. Perhaps not as always as sensational or chaotic as the cases you might read in a standard criminology or criminal justice textbook, each of the types of crimes described in this book will have had a direct or indirect effect on your own lives. As you will soon learn by reading this book, you are far more likely to be the victim of white collar crime than of common garden variety street crime.

Laura Pinto Hansen, Ph.D.
Associate Professor in Criminal Justice
Western New England University

ACKNOWLEDGMENTS

Within my journey in graduate school and beyond, there are a number of people that I wish to acknowledge who were instrumental in shaping the scholar that I am today. In my undergraduate program at University of California Riverside, Raymond Russell was the first to introduce me to the study of large-scale organizations, including corporations. It was under his tutelage I learned how companies are supposed to look like in theory and how they function (or malfunction) in the "real world". In graduate school, Robert Hanneman taught me how to be a critical thinker in research. Austin Turk and Kirk Williams were instrumental in helping me make the leap from criminological theory to applications in studying corporate life.

I would be remiss in not including dedication to some of my family members. I would like to acknowledge the influences of my parents, most importantly, my mother, Irene. She faithfully took us to the library during our childhood, instilled the love of reading, plus the value of learning and curiosity, whether one is self-taught or possesses a formal education. For that, I will forever be grateful. My father, a man who dropped out of high school and went on to be a brilliant design engineer, taught me the value of pursing education tenaciously. I would also like to thank my brother, John Pinto, for the very friendly sibling rivalry throughout our lives that contributed greatly to my drive to live an intellectually productive life. Finally, I want to thank my maternal great-grandmother, Hannah Wilson (nee Hansen), who bravely left Norway at age 16 to start a new life in America, and started the long line of strong women in my family, including 1920s flappers and 1970s feminists. Without their guts and determination, I may not have had to the courage to take my own less conventional path in life.

Laura Pinto Hansen
Monson, Massachusetts and Edgewood, New Mexico

White Collar and Corporate Crime

A Case Study Approach

Chapter ONE

The "Ideal" Organization

How organizations are supposed to run (in theory)

> "One of the enduring truths of the nation's capital [Washington, D.C.] is that bureaucrats survive."
>
> —Gerald Ford, 38th President of the United States of America

Chapter Objectives

- Introduce the characteristics of the "ideal" organization briefly, in advance of studying white collar crime.
- Learn about what scholars say about how legitimate organizations were/are run in the 19th into the 21st century.
- Learn what business managers say about how they would like to see their organizations run, in an ideal world.
- Introduce the characteristics of organizational structures that might explain why white collar crime occurs.
- Explore employee/employer relationships, in an ideal organization.

Key Terms

Bureaucracy
Bureaucratic control
Chain of command
Employee Stock Option Program (ESOP)
Extrinsic reward
Financial markets
Formal organizational structure
Hierarchy

Informal organizational structure
Intrinsic reward
Jurisdictional roles
Markets
Multinational corporation
Simple control
Technical control
Workers' compensation

INTRODUCTION

To borrow from Richard Edwards (1979), the workplace and organizations are contested terrains. There is a push/pull on a number of levels, between workers and between employers and their employees. This is true whether it is a small business or a great big *multinational corporation*. As much as organizations attempt to be impersonal and efficient, as we shall see in the next chapter, there are a number of things that stand in the way of these goals, including personalities, political climate, and the economic environment.

As much as any organization in the public or private sector may attempt to run like well-oiled machinery, they are made up of human beings who are inherently flawed. That is not to say that all workers or volunteers are self-serving, nor are they incompetent. They simply come to the organization with their own personal and professional histories.

In some cases, individuals or groups within organizations cross the line into criminal behavior, whether they do so intentionally or are just clueless when it comes to laws and regulations in their industry. There would be absolutely no need for a textbook like this one if everyone working, volunteering, or taking up space in an establishment operated 100 percent above board, following a strict professional, moral, or ethical compass.

As Meyer and Rowan (1977, p. 340) noted, "formal organizations are generally understood to be systems of coordinated and controlled activities . . . ." This, of course, is in theory, as we will see later on in this textbook where systems are not necessarily coordinated or controlled. In some cases it is utter chaos, resulting in ruined finances, ruined companies, and ruined reputations.

In order to better understand what goes wrong in organizations that might lead to white collar crime, it is helpful to have some working knowledge of how they are expected to run. We should note that the most recent "heyday" of organizational theory was in the 1980s and 1990s, and research has somewhat hit a bit of a dry spell since, save a handful of scholars. For any of you budding scholars with an eye on graduate school, this is an area that might be of interest to pursue.

MAX WEBER AND BUREAUCRACY

For obvious reasons, no organization can function for long without some form of structure. In fact, organization is the very definition of structure. There are two types of structures in organizations, both fraught with challenges. The first type is the *formal organizational structure*. In organizational theory, formal structures have everything explicitly, and in most cases legally, spelled out as to the roles and responsibilities of each employee. Formal structures also come with rules and company policies, as we might find in an employee handbook.

The second structure is less visible. In every organization there is the *informal structure*, which includes social networks. These social networks can include friends, alliances, or groups of individuals who share a common role or goal in the organization. However, the informal structure does not come with strict written rules or policies. We will see later in Chapter 3 why the informal structure has much to do with the things that can lead to white collar criminal behavior.

The most commonly seen structure in both private and public sector industries, including the university or college you are now attending, is *bureaucracy*. First clearly defined by Max Weber (1922), bureaucratic structures have clear division of labor, where individuals are hired based on their experience, credentials, and expertise, rather than because of nepotism.

Though Weber viewed bureaucracy as the perfect organizational structure, he did not believe that it could be perfectly replicated in the real world and it had its limitations. His typology simply stands as a template by which organizations can be compared to see how close they come to the ideal. Weber's identification of the imperfections of bureaucracy are further discussed in Chapter 3.

CHARACTERISTICS OF BUREAUCRACY

Weber (1922) identified a number of defining features of bureaucracy. Much of what Weber spoke to was the characteristics of the employee. In Weber's world, workers should be hired based on their training and experience. This also requires specialization, as demonstrated by the auto industry prior to robotic automation, where each component of the car is handled by someone who has expertise in the one part they add along the assembly line. For instance, if you were responsible for installing the seatbelts, you had better be really, really good at that one task! Otherwise it is a lawsuit waiting to happen from some unfortunate customer against the auto manufacturer.

Here is an abbreviated example of hiring people with specializations, from an advertisement for a police officer position for the Town of Manchester, Connecticut (retrieved from http://www.manchesterpolice.org/index.cfm/recruitment/):

Education: Must possess an Associate's Degree in law enforcement, or related field, 60 college credits or two years of full-time active military service with honorable discharge.

Character: Candidates must be of good moral character, with no record of dishonorable discharge from any police or fire department or the armed forces of the United States.

Physical: Must have considerable agility and endurance.

A Police Officer of the Town of Manchester represents the town and performs duties affecting safety and security of the community. The process of selecting people for employment as Police Officers is extremely important and includes several parts.

- Written Examination
- Oral Panel Examination
- Background Investigation
- Post-Offer Physical Examination
- Post-Offer Polygraph

Of course, the position of police officer requires serious background checks and civil service exams, even for smaller jurisdictions. We should note that the college degree requirements for the Manchester police position is not necessarily uniform in every town or city. In some places, you can have any undergraduate degree and be hired by a department, assuming you have all the other qualifications.

In this day and age of Big Data, it is much more difficult for people to fake their credentials or qualifications. Many employers, including police departments, require an official transcript from the university or college that you attended, along with criminal background checks, in most cases. Some employers are even asking for copies of prospective employees' credit reports. They do so to make sure that job candidates are not having some kind of financial difficulty that puts them at risk for committing white collar crimes, including embezzlement.

When you think of the average time that a face-to-face job interview takes, around 45 minutes, in many cases the employer has little information about the candidate except what is on their resume and recommendations when they hire them. In academia, professors generally have interviews that last up to 24 hours or longer, with a number of people that they must meet with on a university campus. However, in the academic setting, full-time faculty are historically hired with the expectation that they will stay at the university for the entirety of their working career, except at the most aggressively competitive research schools. This means that college administrators want to make absolutely sure that their prospective colleague will be a good fit for the needs of the department they are interviewing in and for the school.

The more complex the profession is, the more specific the specializations will be and the more that the employer has to scrutinize a candidate's credentials. A medical practice would not hire someone trained as a veterinary doctor unless it is a vet practice, even though technically, the basics of mammalian anatomy are pretty similar across species.

Some years ago, there was a movie depicting the true story of Frank Abagnale, Jr. (*Catch Me If You Can*, 2002, DreamWorks Pictures), who, as a young man in his late teens during the 1960s, impersonated different professions that require extensive training and licensing. In a couple of these professions, Abagnale, Jr. passed himself off as a doctor and a Pan American World pilot with counterfeit credentials. He obviously had enough intelligence and skills to be hired for the jobs and keep them for some time before being detected as a fraud, and was eventually being caught by the FBI. Most, if not all, people would agree that whether it is your doctor or the pilot of the commercial jet you are traveling on, you would want the people who hired them to make sure that they had the necessary credentials and skills for the job. It is far more difficult to falsify college degrees and credentials now than it was in the 1960s.

In addition to possessing expertise in their field, workers are structured in a clear *hierarchy*, where everyone knows their position in the organization. This also requires that their work is confined to *jurisdictional roles*. In theory, you are only responsible for your duties and responsibilities and no others. So if it is NOT in your job description to go fetch coffee for a boss, you are NOT required (in theory) to do so, unless you want to do so as a courtesy. But this is one of those contested terrains in the workplace gender wars, particularly for women, who have historically been asked to serve as secretaries and waitresses in meetings even if they hold credentials and positions equal to their male counterparts.

Because everyone is supposed to know their responsibilities, job descriptions can be pretty specific as far as what is expected of workers. Job descriptions contain the duties and responsibilities of workers and are pretty much interchangeable with jurisdictional duties. Here is a general job description for attorneys (retrieved from https://www.myplan.com/careers/lawyers/description-23-1011.00.html):

> Represent clients in criminal and civil litigation and other legal proceedings, draw up legal documents, or manage or advise clients on legal transactions. May specialize in a single area or may practice broadly in many areas of the law.

Probably one of the best examples of bureaucratic structure is the military, where the hierarchy of ranks is made very clear. In fact, the military is such a great template that Max Weber (1905; 1922) used it as an example while researching the characteristics of an "ideal" organizational structure.

For as much as we complain about bureaucratic structures, they can be the most efficient way in order to move large quantities of data, procedures, people, services, and products along in orderly fashion. We should note that there was a break down in the supply chain during the COVID-19 pandemic, so bureaucratic structures don't always anticipate the unexpected. Can you imagine if people were allowed to get on an amusement park ride willy-nilly without any well-organized line? You would certainly have to call the police or the paramedics if there wasn't the requirement to wait in a queue. This is much like the way computer work has to be sequenced while waiting for processing, otherwise chaos may ensue.

A recent article in *Harvard Business Review* (Chung and Bechky, 2018) claims that for all the complaints of inefficiencies, depending on the industry, bureaucracy really works. Instead of feeling like they have less control, the supposed rigidity of bureaucracy allows some specialists more control over their work, so much so that sometimes people in different technical capacities work together to solve bureaucratic crises as they arise before management is even aware there is a problem (Chung and Bechky, 2018).

As Weber (1922) proposed, this adherence to allowing workers more control over their work should hold true if workers are hired for impersonal reasons and for technical expertise, rather than because of nepotism — where they know or are related to the right people. You are expected to be hired based on what you know, not who you know.

Law in the Real World: The Blockbuster Movie

There is a myth that because the film industry is creative, that there is less structure. That is far from the truth. Movie studios, like other economic organizations, are required to pay close attention to the bottom line. At Disney Studios, Walt Disney was always viewed as the creative force behind cartoons, feature films, and theme parks. However, Roy Disney, Walt's brother, provided balance in the company, keeping an eye on the financial side of operations.

There is room in the film industry for most larger studios to release films that are not anticipated to make a huge profit but will be well received by critics. An Oscar nomination brings new fame and respect to actors, directors, and studios. However, in order to remain a viable competitor in a crowded field of film studios, there is the goal of producing blockbuster films even if they are not critically acclaimed movies. The real magic happens when a blockbuster is also a critical success.

In order to be a blockbuster, a film has to have a certain amount of predictability to it. In other words, once a film becomes a blockbuster, many films to follow will be formulaic, trying to imitate the success of the original movie. This is demonstrated by Hickey's (2014) study of data on blockbuster movies in the graph below.

**Top 10 Genres of Blockbuster Movies
1975–2013**

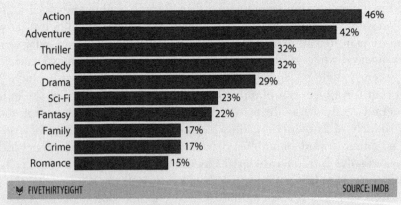

Genre	%
Action	46%
Adventure	42%
Thriller	32%
Comedy	32%
Drama	29%
Sci-Fi	23%
Fantasy	22%
Family	17%
Crime	17%
Romance	15%

FIVETHIRTYEIGHT   SOURCE: IMDB

EXHIBIT 1.1 ‖ **Top 10 Genres of Blockbuster Movies** *Source:* https://fivethirtyeight.com/
‖ features/the-11-defining-features-of-the-summer-blockbuster

It may require shelling out big salaries to well-established movie or television stars, which coincides with Weber's admonishment that only experts with the right resume should be hired for positions in an organization. The thought process is that then you have hired people who see their job as a vocation, rather than as a job with no future. No doubt that with the exception of lower level employees, key personnel on a film that is expected to be a blockbuster, including lead actors and directors, are known quantities with extensive resumes.

Of course, as in any case, there are exceptions. *Crouching Tiger, Hidden Dragon* was a huge sleeper hit from Columbia Pictures even though there were no big Hollywood names attached to the film at the time. Ang Lee was a relatively unknown director in the United States, as were the actors in the film.

A second departure from convention was that *Crouching Tiger, Hidden Dragon* was a foreign film with a cast of Chinese actors who had yet to be widely introduced to the American film-going public. However, the film did stick to formula for blockbuster films as it was an adventure film, and it followed on the heels of the very popular *The Karate Kid* franchise, also produced by Columbia Pictures. Both *Crouching Tiger, Hidden Dragon* and *The Karate Kid* movies featured the martial arts that appealed to both children and adults alike. Even though the film was a gamble and the studio hoped for a critical success, they could not anticipate the broad appeal that pulled in blockbuster-size revenue.

Discussion Questions

1. Why might a film studio gamble on an adventure film rather than romantic comedies?
2. Is it possible to completely remove nepotism in the film industry, or any industry, as Weber proposed is ideal?
3. Once upon a time in Hollywood, film studios signed on movie stars for multi-film deals, the so-called "studio system." Why would film studios no longer use the studio system if they don't want to take chances with a relatively unknown actor or director?
4. What effect might the demise of the studio system have on the loyalty that stars or directors may have for a studio?

JOBS vs. CAREERS

The best way to describe a job is that it is an occupation that is nothing more than a means to an end. It provides a paycheck that will keep the roof over one's head, put food on the table, and keep the car running or pay for public transportation to get to the job. In other words, people are working to live and focused on the *extrinsic rewards* of the job.

For most of you here in this university or college course, your expectation is that you will earn a degree that will lead to a meaningful career. This is consistent with Weber's view of bureaucracy, where individuals should be choosing their professions based on "a calling." In fact, that is why careers are also called vocations. Borrowed from religious clergy, people should be drawn to their professions because they have a strong desire to do that type of work or they believe that they have the potential to be skilled at it. For instance, a social worker generally knows that they are going into a career with little promise of monetary reward in their paycheck, but still pursue the profession because they have a strong desire to help people.

This is not to say that somewhere out there is the licensed doctor, or accountant, or other financially rewarding person, who went into their chosen professions because of pressure from the parental units or by society in general. For some, the prestige or desire to please others' expectations might overshadow any desire to pursue a different career path. Again, this chapter is focused on the ideal and the same holds true for careers. For a career to be meaningful, the expectation is that it will bring *intrinsic rewards* where one is living to work, rather than the other way around.

For all the meaningfulness of careers, in Weber's bureaucratic world, the person occupying a position in an organization is not as important as the position itself. There is very good reason for this. As much as charismatic leadership will motivate workers, it is equally important to make sure that the position is preserved in the event that the leadership resigns or falls apart for some reason, such as in the case of the death of a president of a company. If organizations are to survive, they must have clear plans in place for succession of leadership. For example, most governments have codified plans in place after a president leaves office, either due to death, an election, or removal from office.

Law in the Real World: Steve Jobs and Apple, Inc.™

(Source: Isaacson, 2011)

It is unlikely that anyone in your class, much less your university, has not heard of Apple™ computers, cell phones, and tablets. Steve Jobs, a driven visionary in the infancy of personal computers, embodies the mythology of the American Dream. Starting his life as an adopted child, and one of the co-founders of Apple, Inc.™ (along with Ronald Wayne and Steve

Wozniak), was a drop out of Reed College, not unlike many trailblazers in the computer science and IT world in the 1970s. He no doubt inherited some of his drive from his adoptive father, Paul Jobs, who in 1946 had wagered with his Coast Guard crewmates that he would find himself a wife within two weeks…which he did. Clearly Jobs' position at Apple, Inc.™ was not a job, but a career, with a lot of personal investment and emotions poured into the company.

Apple, Inc.™ flourished and the company began to launch a series of even more compact personal devices, including the iPod in its various forms, iPads, and the ubiquitous iPhone. Much of this was under the direction of Steve Jobs, as president and CEO of the company.

Jobs passed away in 2011 from pancreatic cancer, leaving some to wonder if the company would be the same without him. Yet the company did not fold with his death, and instead continued to thrive under the new leadership of Tim Cook. When Apple, Inc.™ had its initial stock offer in 1980, it opened at $22 per share. Today one share of Apple is around $277 (as of April 20, 2020). The death of Jobs in 2011 did little to stop the momentum, as to be expected with any change of leadership in a well-organized structure.

Discussion Questions

1. What characteristic or characteristics of bureaucracy do you believe allowed the company to continue on?
2. In the case of Apple, Inc., if Steve Jobs was one of key driving forces behind the company, besides bureaucratic structure, why do you think it was able to survive and even thrive after his death?
3. What challenges would you expect to see in a company that has bureaucratic structure, but also has a charismatic leader (though reportedly a difficult person at times) like Steve Jobs?
4. What challenges might there be for a tech company when leadership changes?

PROFESSIONAL ASSOCIATIONS AND ORGANIZATIONS

In order to maintain the integrity of some professions, organizations have been established to provide guidance on industry standards. Doctors and dentists in the United States are encouraged to be board certified through the American Board of Physician Specialties (ABPS) and to follow the strict guidelines set out by the American Medical Association (AMA). Lawyers are expected to pass exams and to follow the professional ethics that are outlined by the American Bar

Association. As a sociologist and criminologist, the author of this book is expected to adhere to the principles of the American Sociological Association (ASA) and the American Society of Criminology (ASC).

Professional organizations play a valuable role in keeping industries consistent with laws and regulations. Some professional organizations, such trade unions, are advocates for workers to protect them from unreasonable demands of employers, unsafe working conditions, and unfair wages. Perhaps one of the most important roles of professional organizations is to keep their members up to date on latest developments in their industries. Many hold annual conferences allowing for networking opportunities among contemporaries in the same field.

CONTROL OF WORKERS AND MANAGEMENT STYLES

In economic organizations that are driven by profit, the management control varies. Edwards' provocative book, *Contested Terrain* (1979), proposed three ways by which you get employees to do what you want them to do, even if they don't want to do whatever they are being asked to do. The first proposed by Edwards is *simple control*. You tend to see this in small family businesses, where control of workers is very personal, subjective, and at times, inconsistent.

Edwards' second type is *technical control*, where workers are required to pace their work with others or with machinery, as in the case of assembly lines. Of course, we see less traditional assembly lines with increased automation displacing workers, along with globalization. However, technical control still can be found in the workplace. An example would be cashiers at grocery stores where the number of items that they scanned per hour/day and dollar amount spent by customers is stored digitally in cash registers. In the modern office building, it is not unusual to see workers in cubicles to discourage them from socializing with each other. This could be considered yet another form of technical control, where control is built into the physical structure of the organization.

The last type of control is in Edwards' estimation (and Weber's) the most impersonal, but effective because it is more predictable: *bureaucratic control*. Here the control of workers is built into the rules and policies of the organization. In the next chapter we will further discuss how workers circumvent the restrictions of bureaucratic structures.

Bureaucratic control is designed to offer permanency to organizations, where the positions within them are more important and lasting than the people who occupy them. Big corporations would never survive if they were solely dependent on the leadership of a chief executive officer (CEO) or president who might leave at any time due to retirement, illness, better job offer, or more drastically, death. This is why bureaucratic control is the most effective way to run governments, no matter what the political ideology might be. If not for the stable structure of at least some semblance of bureaucracy, you would find countries failing left and right.

Depending on which scholar you speak to (or read), there are different supervisory typologies. This can sometimes be specific to an industry. For instance, you may find by-the-book correction officers in a prison, but you may also find some who are more parental, taking on more informal mentoring roles. The success of either type is dependent on the prison facility and how well the correction officer functions overall in their profession.

The three most commonly recognized management types are the *autocratic, democratic*, and *laissez-faire* leader. All three types have their strengths and weaknesses, and the chosen leadership need can be dependent on the type and size of the industry. They range from the most restrictive — the autocratic — to the most permissive — the laissez-faire manager. All three types can be found in all industries due to industry standards and because much has to do with the personalities and training of managers and supervisors.

For the autocratic, it's their way or the highway — their authority is not to be questioned. They have absolute power (or at least believe they do) over every aspect of their domain. One common historical example of autocratic leadership is Adolf Hitler and Nazi Germany during the 1930s. As a refresher of what happened between WWI and WWII in Germany, the country suffered economically, struggling to gain footing in the new world order. Germany could not afford war reapportions to members of the Ally countries, including France and Britain, who were victorious in WWI. Historians largely believe that Hitler rose to power in the 1930s with almost unquestioned authority because the people of Germany were looking for a leader to bring them back to their past glory and financial stability. In their desperation, they turned a blind eye to the atrocities of the Third Reich or were unaware of them due to propaganda.

A more contemporary example of autocratic leadership, essentially a dictatorship, would be Saddam Hussein, who ruled in Iraq from 1979-2003. Had he not taken the bold move to invade Kuwait to the south of Iraq, he might have continued to rule on in Iraq unchecked. Kuwait is an oil-producing country with close allies in the West, including the United States. In response to Iraq's invasion of Kuwait, the First Gulf War was launched (1990-1991). Ultimately Hussein was forcibly removed from office and executed during the Second Gulf War (2003).

There are a number of other dictators that we can turn to as examples of absolute power, but with the understanding that this type of autocratic authority is the extreme and somewhat unusual in the Western world. If we use the position of a military officer as an example, their authority is absolute when it comes to the officers and enlisted men who serve below them in the *chain of command*. Military leaders and officers are expected and required to lead with integrity and respect for their subordinates, though this is not always the case, as we will see in our discussions of political white collar crime, later in Chapter 12.

The second leadership type is the democratic manager. In this case, though the manager has final oversight over decisions made, they are consulting with their teams and workers in the decision-making process. In some cases, others in equal or superior power positions in the hierarchy may have the authority to over-turn decisions made by the democratic manager.

The way the government was established in the United States was to include a system of checks and balances between the three branches of government: the president, Congress, and the Supreme Court. This is similar to democratic management in private or non-profit industries, where no one part of the organization has absolute authority over the others. However, as we will see in other chapters on dysfunction, such as in Chapter 3, the system of checks and balances does not always work, as in the case of one political party controlling all three branches of the United States government.

The laissez-faire form of leadership is the most informal. Some managers are confident in the abilities of their employees and, aside from what is minimally mandated by the organization, pretty much leave workers alone to do their jobs. This is most useful in technology industries, where workers are highly specialized and managers may not fully understand all aspects of the workers' jobs. However, researchers have noted that this is a leadership style that lends itself to less productivity. In some cases, the leadership style is perceived as avoidance of responsibility on the part of managers and workers struggle to find guidance or mentoring (Skogstad, 2014).

Added to the management types are the two management styles. For the *micro-manager*, which is not the most efficient way to manage an organization, the manager will want to have their hands in every corner of the operations. For the *macro-manager*, tasks are delegated to various members of the organization with the understanding that in a perfect world, you only give tasks to those who are best qualified to handle them. Both styles have their merits and can be found in many different types of organizations. Management styles have more to do with individual characteristics of the manager and not on the demands of the position.

McDONALDIZATION OF ORGANIZATIONS

Since Weber's theories of the ideal organization may be somewhat outdated for some industries, we should also give recognition to theorists who have contributed to organizational theory that might be more relevant in today's world. One of these is George Ritzer, who coined the term "McDonaldization" in his book, *The McDonaldization of Society* (1993). Ritzer proposed that society in general had come to expect the same characteristics that exist in fast food restaurants in other aspects of their everyday lives.

Ritzer identified four components of McDonaldization: efficiency, calculability, predictability, and control (Ritzer, 2011). Ritzer (2011, p. 55) defines efficiency as "choosing the optimum means to a given end." Generally considered a good thing, managers and owners want their workers to perform their tasks efficiently as efficiency represents greater profits (Ritzer, 2011). But as we will see in upcoming chapters, working fast does not translate to working within legal limits or industry standards.

Calculability means that the creation of goods and services can be measured quantitatively in order to assure that workers are moving production along swiftly and in the most cost-effective means possible. Again, Ritzer (2011) notes that this is a good thing, as given in the example of a fast food restaurant where the goal is to get customers in and out quickly while making sure that there is a standard for the size of everything from hamburger patties to beverages.

As much as things can be automated to achieve calculability, it reduces the chances of human error. For instance, workers at fast food restaurants are not responsible for timing the frying, as fry machines now have timers that loudly go off when some fried food item is ready. Or the beverage machines that, at the push of a button, will dispense the exact amount of beverage into a cup. Any spillage or burnt food represents loss of profit to the owner and/or shareholders.

Predictability is beneficial to both owners and customers. As Ritzer (2011) explains, when you go to a McDonald's restaurant anywhere in the world (with some exceptions where cows are believed to be sacred, as in parts of India), you pretty much expect a Big Mac hamburger to look and taste like one ordered in the states. This also means that with a loyal customer base, owners do not necessarily have to rely on costly innovative changes to their product or service lines, making their day-to-day operations predictable.

Because of consumer demands, there is an awful lot of pressure on for-profit organizations to deliver on promises. Ritzer identifies a number of places where the characteristics of the fast food restaurant model has been applied outside of the food service industry. One of the most outlandish examples he provides is from a three-story pornographic center in New York City, described by an official as having "cookie-cutter cleanliness and compliance with the law." (Ritzer, 2011, p. 13).

The biggest focus of employers, as far as control goes, is the control of employees. Close, personal control of workers is difficult and costly (Ritzer, 2011). As Edwards (1979) pointed out, a more efficient way to control workers and the flow of work is to have it built into the physical structure. In more recent decades, one way of controlling office workers is to have cubicles instead of an open concept room. Cubicles represent barriers between workers so that more time is spent on work and less on socializing. Of course, in this day and age of communication technology, this does not prevent workers from "talking" to one another by way of instant and text messaging.

Even the university setting, once believed to be one of the least controlled places to work, has employed non-human ways to control professors (Ritzer, 2011). Most universities require that professors turn in grades within a couple days of giving exams and also require course evaluations, which may result in professors adjusting their teaching style in order to garner higher ratings. Ratings of professors in themselves are somewhat subjective, but they can be the basis of promotion within the tenure systems.

For those unfamiliar with the promotion system in universities, a brand-new junior faculty member is typically required to work six years at one school before they will be considered for tenure, the closest to permanent employment and job security that there is. Similar systems exist in public primary and secondary schools. Again, this is not necessarily a bad thing, as less experienced teachers are held accountable for the content of their courses.

Probably one of the best examples of employee control is the current health-care system in the United States. With the rise of health maintenance organizations (HMOs) and preferred provider organizations (PPOs), which are essentially insurance companies, they are the "gatekeepers" of medical care. Physicians may provide diagnoses and suggested treatment, but ultimately insurance companies have the final say on what treatments, procedures, surgeries, and prescription drugs will be paid for by insurance. As we will see in discussion of medical white collar crime, physicians, insurance companies, and even patients themselves can be involved in insurance fraud.

Subsequent theorists, including Alan Bryman (1999; 2004), took Ritzer's concept further to claim that society is not only McDonaldized, but also Disneyfied. In other words, besides consumers expecting things to be fast and predictable, they also are looking for a theme park experience everywhere, including on cruises, where every form of entertainment and dining experience is at their fingertips. As we will see in the next chapter, this might result in alienated workers who feel like they are responsible for satisfying every whim of the customer, even the demands unreasonable.

Law in the Real World: Southwest Airlines

(Source: Srinivasan, 2005)

Once upon a time, air travel was fairly glamorous. But with security concerns and rising operating costs, particularly after the 1970s gas crises, airlines had to become more efficient to protect the bottom line of profit. Advertised as a no-frills airline, Southwest Airlines was one of the first to go ticketless with e-tickets, as well as a number of other cost-saving strategies. Being one of the very first airlines to create a website where customers could book their own tickets, online booking cut out the need for having many people working in reservations.

In running such a lean operation, there is the risk of alienating workers and making for less enthusiastic passengers. By making air travel less glamorous, in turn, it made the profession less glamorous as well. To counter this, Southwest Airlines was the first airline to offer an *employee stock ownership plan (ESOP)*. The philosophy behind this is that if employees are essentially part-owners of the operations, they will be more invested in their work.

Even Southwest Airlines' mission statement has the worker in mind. "We are committed to provide our Employees with a stable work environment with equal opportunity for learning and personal growth. Creativity and innovation are encouraged for improving the effectiveness [and efficiency?] of Southwest Airlines." (Srinivasan, 2005). We should note that employees of Southwest Airlines are represented by the Transport Workers Union, so they do have some bargaining power.

For the consumer, there was savings, but some drawbacks as well. With unassigned, first come, first served seating, the experience of flying can be a bit like taking the subway, with people jostling for the best seats. However, it has not seemed to deter people from flying with Southwest Airlines, as the airline continues to be in business and was thriving at least until the 2020 COVID-19 pandemic adversely affected all airlines. Plus, Southwest Airlines was one of the first airlines to compensate loyal customers with frequent flier programs.

Discussion Questions

1. Similar to the question about loyalty in the case study of Hollywood blockbuster films, how might Southwest Airline's ESOP program offer more than extrinsic (financial) rewards to employees?
2. Since we will find out in upcoming chapters how unhappy employees may become criminal employees, how might Southwest Airlines' philosophy of encouraging personal growth and creativity from their employees help workers to remain happy in their jobs or careers?
3. How might a labor union, along with the employer, help employees to stay within compliance of their professions?

LABOR MARKETS

In some cases, it is far more expensive to hang on to a full-time employee. Some of the associated costs are health insurance, sick time or leave time, *workers' compensation*, retirement plans, and other employee benefits. We will discuss in future chapters how some of these benefits can be abused and result in white-collar crime or malfeasance. For now, it is important to understand why not all employees are salaried or full-time. In some cases, it is less expensive for a company to hire someone who owns their own business and hires themselves out for work in their field.

For example, if a doctor's office is struggling with the business end of the practice, they might hire a consultant to come in temporarily to help train office personnel on management and marketing. That consultant would be an independent contractor, responsible for their own self-employment taxes and health insurance. The doctor would only be responsible for paying the consulting fees.

One of the most seminal pieces of scholarship on when it is better to hire someone who is an independent contractor vs. hiring a full-time employee comes from William G. Ouchi (1980). Ouchi (1980) believed that even though hiring experts outside of an organization is costly and might result in less loyalty than from a salaried employee, there are times when it is more cost-effective. One case where it is less expensive to hire an independent contractor is when the work needed is temporary, as in the case of designing a new building for a college campus. A university wouldn't necessarily need to keep an architect around as a full-time employee for building design.

Another reason to hire an independent contractor is that full-time employees expect to be retained by a company, even when there is a downturn in the economy. This isn't to say that there are not layoffs. We certainly witnessed this through the COVID-19 virus crisis in 2020 where employers were forced to let their workforce go, sometimes permanently. Some industries are more vulnerable to the whims of the economy and workers within these industries come to expect layoffs from time to time. Aerospace is an example of a less secure place to work, even though it is historically one of the largest industries. This is largely due to some dependence on government contracts. Restaurants are likewise vulnerable to economic conditions, when customers can no longer afford to go out and eat.

If a company is afraid to lose employees when sales are down because they don't want to lose their expertise, it means that the company may have to incur the continued costs of their salaries and benefits even when profits are down. Companies may also have to deal with changes in employee morale in the event of temporary layoffs or reductions in employee benefits as cost-saving strategies in tough economies.

LAWS AND REGULATION IN ORGANIZATIONS

For the very reason this book even exists, organizations and the people who work in them cannot always be trusted to control themselves. This is true within industries as well. It is because of this that a number of laws, rules, and regulations exist to make sure that they are operating in compliance. In some industries, these change on a regular basis as new information or research results are made available. This protects both employees and customers, as well as protecting the reputation of the industry in general.

Law in the Real World: California's SB 1342

(Source: California Legislative Information, retrieved from https://leginfo.legislature. ca.gov/faces/billTextClient.xhtml?bill_id=201720180SB1343)

California has historically been on the leading edge of labor laws. In the "Me Too"[1] era, employers are increasingly working to prevent sexual harassment or assault from happening in the workplace. In 2018, then-Governor Jerry Brown signed Senate Bill 1342 stating that businesses employing five or more employees, including temporary employees, are required to provide at least two hours of training and education on sexual harassment, abusive conduct, and harassment based on gender. The training is required for all supervisors within six months of employment, with additional training every two years.

It makes sense that California would be one of the first states to aggressively tackle the problem of sexual harassment in the workplace. California is the home of Hollywood, long notorious for being a city where actors and actresses have to face the "casting couch" — a euphemism for providing sexual favors — in exchange for movie or television roles.

There are a few important things to note in this case study, as it applies to white collar crime. First, where the accused and the alleged victim are in the organizational hierarchy is critical. Even when a social or sexual relationship is consensual, it is assumed that if one of the people is a supervisor and the other is a subordinate, there is concern about the inequality of their power. It is one of the reasons why companies and organizations discourage people from dating coworkers. There can be the question as to whether the subordinate is being coerced into the relationship by their supervisor.

The second thing to note is that sexual harassment and assault in and out of the workplace can happen to people of all gender and sexual orientations. Though women are disproportionately more likely to be a victim of a sexual predator in the workplace, men have also reported having been harassed or assaulted.

Where sexual harassment and sexual assault is most closely tied to white collar crime is when there is a bribe or payoff to the victim to keep them quiet. It is bad enough when the funds for a payoff is coming out of the

---

[1] "Me Too," a term which initially was used in social media in 2006 by a sexual harassment survivor, became a movement in 2017 with accusations of sexual misconduct and assault by Hollywood movie mogul, Harvey Weinstein. The phrase came to represent the growing number of men and women in a number of industries who are survivors of sexual violence in the workplace.

personal pocket of the perpetrator. It is criminal (and a white collar crime) when money is coming out of funds that do not belong to perpetrator, as in the case of using campaign funds to payoff someone with damaging information on a politician.

California's SB 1343 legislation is one means by which businesses and public organizations help inform supervisors of what exactly is legally inappropriate behavior in the workplace. The question is whether it will prevent bribes and payoffs when inappropriate sexual behavior does take place.

Discussion Questions

1. Why do you think that the movie and television industries might be slow to respond to allegations of sexual harassment or assault?
2. Why might victims not want to come forward with accusations?
3. This will take a little bit of research. What other states are actively working to require training for supervisors, like in California SB 1343?
4. What might happen to the reputation of a company if they are found to have documented cases of sexual harassment?

As Weber noted, rule-bound organizations avoid a number of problems and function more efficiently. Some of the problems are logistical, others are social, and both types are kept in check. In the "ideal" organization, rules and compliance to them minimizes the risks of things going wrong that might lead to civil or criminal actions in the courts.

SUMMARY

No organization is perfect. Because organizations are made up of people, there will always be things that go wrong. However, there are a number of things that organizations can do to minimize the damage when things do not go according to plan.

In Weber's world, organizations should possess five key characteristics: (1) Workers who are specialized, with a clear division of labor; (2) A clear hierarchy where everyone knows their role; (3) Clearly spelled out rules and regulations that are written down; (4) Workers who are technically competent with the appropriate degrees, licenses, or credentials; and (5) Formal and standardized means by which to communicate between workers and divisions. The closest we come to an ideal organization, in Weber's estimation, is the military.

Within the organizational structure, there are a number of management styles and personalities. The choice of which one to use is dependent on the industry as well as the individual. This can be a result of formal training or mentoring in the workplace.

Organizations and professionals do not operate alone in self-regulation. There are a number of laws and regulations, for all professions that deal in goods and services, that have been legislated by the federal, state, and local governments. Both public and private organizations have to comply with these laws and regulations. Otherwise they may face civil lawsuit or criminal prosecution, depending on which law or regulation they might have broken.

A second layer of protection for professions are professional organizations. Most, if not all, professions have organizations or associations, like the American Medical Association, that set standards for the industry. Some of the standards duplicate what has already been made into laws or regulations. Others are mutually exclusive. Even though professionals are not legally bound to follow these standards, they may be morally or ethically required to do so in order to be respected within their profession.

Most organizations strive to work within legal and ethical guidelines. As we will see in the coming chapters, it is not always easy for organizations to live up to the ideal. When they do stray, whether intentionally or unintentionally, it puts them in danger of a number of consequences, including their demise.

Case Study ▪ Keeping Employees Happy: Twitter®

Because this chapter addresses what organizations get right, or at least get right in theory, our case study is written in a classic business school model. In the case of Twitter®, we will examine how the culture of the company makes for happy employees. As we will learn in this book, one key way to prevent employees from committing crimes is if they are delighted with the work they do in their positions, satisfied with their salaries or other compensations in their job, and have a sense of loyalty to the organization.

Background

Twitter® came into being as many ideas that catch on to become Horatio Alger stories. For those less familiar with the premise of the stories, Alger wrote in the 19th century about boys who came from poverty who, through hard work and integrity, raised themselves into financial security. Twitter® is the brainchild of Jack Dorsey, plus a development team at the podcast company he worked for at the time in 2006, who devised an SMS-based system online that would allow people to communicate with one another without going through the formality of email or in real time, as in chat rooms.

What Twitter® Gets Right for Employees

Beginning with a 140-character limit, Twitter® continued to keep current with the way people interacted on the website, increasing the limit of tweets to 280 characters in 2017, to adapt to increased use of smart phone technology (MacArther, 2019). Love or hate the website, Twitter® created a whole new online culture that includes changing the way people settle disputes. Today, few people are unaware of the concept of Twitter® wars, where individuals, companies, and politicians use the platform to sling mud at one another. However controversial these disputes and the subsequent fallouts may be, Twitter® has also proven to be one of the best places in the United States to work. *Glassceiling.com* ranked the company as receiving the highest ratings of any company in an anonymous survey, based on its corporate culture and values (Huddleston, 2014).

So, what have been some of the company's strategies for keeping their employees happy? According to Patel (2015) and Huddleston (2014), Twitter® employees benefit from the following perks at the San Francisco headquarters:

- Rooftop meetings
- Team-oriented environment
- Free meals (at San Francisco headquarters only)
- Yoga classes
- Unlimited vacation for some employees

We should note that tech companies, in general, offer much higher than average salaries, along with perks beyond generous benefit packages (e.g., retirement, health, etc.). The fact that Twitter® rose above other tech companies in employee ratings is an indication that they are doing something very right in the area of employee satisfaction.

Possible Threats to Employee Happiness

For anyone familiar with a SWOT analysis (strengths, weaknesses, opportunities, threats), the biggest risk to Twitter® culture and the happiness of its workers is in getting too big. It may be impossible to sustain the current intimate corporate environment. This in itself represents both weaknesses and threats to Twitter®. As we will see in the next chapter, when organizations become too bureaucratic, something that can come with rapid corporate growth, the company can get too weighed down by red tape. Worse yet, it becomes so impersonal that company loyalty becomes nonexistent. This in turn puts the organization at risk for bad behavior on the part of employees, including members of the management team.

The other risk the company faces is that online forums, like Twitter® have a shelf life. It is likely that many of you reading this book, as we head into the third decade of this century, never possessed a Myspace® account. Yet at one time in the early 21st century, this was THE social media website, quickly overtaken by Facebook® and Twitter®. If Twitter® begins losing a substantial amount of their revenue, primarily raised through advertising, all those perks that employees currently enjoy may go away.

Sources

Huddleston, T. (2014) Twitter tops all in culture and values, employees say. *Fortune*. Aug 22. Retrieved from https://fortune.com/2014/08/22/twitter-tops-list-company-culture/.

MacArthur, A. (2019) The real history of Twitter, in brief: How the micro-messaging wars were won. *Lifewire*. Nov 12. Retrieved from https://www.lifewire.com/history-of-twitter-3288854.

Patel, S. (2015) 10 examples of companies with fantastic cultures. *Entrepreneur*. Aug 6. Retrieved from https://www.entrepreneur.com/article/249174

GLOSSARY

Bureaucratic control   A system by which an organization is impersonally organized, where workers' behavior and employers' expectations are controlled through formal rules.

Bureaucracy   Described by Max Weber as a merit based, impersonal organizational structure that is characterized by written rules, organizational hierarchy, and the promise of promotion within a career for the deserving.

Chain of command   Synonymous with hierarchy, ranks or positions are clear as to who are in leadership positions (e.g., CEO, midlevel managers) and who is subordinate (e.g., entry-level employees).

ESOP   Employee Stock Option Plans became popular beginning in the 1970s, giving employees stock shares in the company they work for. The philosophy behind ESOPs is that a worker will work harder if they own part of the company.

Extrinsic reward   A reward that can be measured in salary, income, bonuses, or material goods that might motivate workers to be more productive in their jobs.

Financial markets   Used to buy and trade a number of securities and futures, along with other types of financial investments. Examples of securities are stocks, bonds, precious metals that have monetary value. Future markets are places where individuals can invest, and to some extent gamble on, in goods that will have true market value at a future date. An example of a future investment would be in an agricultural crop that will not have a specific monetary value until it is harvested.

Formal organizational structure   Any organizational structure that has been formally adopted, generally with all aspects of how the organization is to be operated written down in mission statements, employee handbooks, and company charters.

Hierarchy   Synonymous with chain of command, the hierarchy is a clear organizational chart indicating who gives orders in an organization and who follows orders. An example of a hierarchy or chain of command is the organizational structure in the military.

Informal organizational structure   The informal structure includes the friendships, alliances, and enemies that form between workers outside of the formal, written structure, that may enhance or undermine an organization.

Intrinsic rewards   Unlike extrinsic rewards, there is no monetary value attached to them and included feelings of accomplishment and well-being in the work one does or the position one has in an organization.

Jurisdictional roles   Within the formal structure of a bureaucratic organization, written instructions that spell out exactly what work that each employee is responsible for. Jurisdictional roles can many times be found in employee handbooks or the organizational chart showing the chain of command.

Markets   Generally associated with, but not limited to free market economies where investments, goods, and services are bought and sold.

Multi national corporation   A company or corporation that has an international presence, with factories, stores, or restaurants throughout the world. Examples of a multi-national corporation would be Coca Cola® or McDonald's® fast food restaurants.

Nepotism   Hiring and promotion practices within an organization, based on family or friendship ties and not necessarily on the merit or credentials of the individual.

Simple control   Type of worker control found in smaller operations, like a family-owned restaurant. Rules and roles for employees may not be written down and could be arbitrary, personal.

Technical control   A company that has the control of workers built into the physical structure. Examples would be offices with cubicles that discourage workers from socializing or factory assembly lines.

Workers' compensation   Insurance policies that provide employees who have been injured or fall ill as a direct result of their job with medical benefits and income while recovering, required by law to be provided by employers with five or more employees. Workers' compensation does not have to be provided for independent contractors hired by a company.

REFERENCES AND SUGGESTED READINGS

Abolafia, M. Y. (1996) *Making markets: Opportunism and restraint on Wall Street*. Cambridge, MA: Harvard University Press.

Bryman, A. (2004) *The Disneyization of society*. London: Sage Publishing.

Chung, D. E. and B. (2018) When bureaucracy is actually helpful, according to research. *Harvard Business Review*. Jan 3. Retrieved from https://hbr.org/2018/01/when-bureaucracy-is-actually-helpful-according-to-research.

Edwards, R. (1979) *Contested terrain*. New York: Basic Books (Hachette Books).

Geisst, C. R. (2018) *Wall Street: A history*. New York: Oxford University Press.

Harvey, R. (2002) *A few bloody noses: The realities and mythologies of the American Revolution*. New York: Abrams Books.

Isaacson, W. (2011) *Steve Jobs*. New York: Simon and Shuster.

Horowitz, I. L. (2003) The cult of dictatorship vs. the culture of modernity. *Society*. Jul/Aug, 40, 5:9-19.

Meyer, J. W. and B. Rowan. (1977) Formal structure as myth and ceremony. *The American Journal of Sociology*. Sept, Vol 83, No 2:340-363.

Ouchi, W. G. (1980) Markets, bureaucracies, and clans. *Administrative Science Quarterly*. 25, 1: 129-141.

Ritzer, G. (2011) The *McDonaldization of society*. Thousand Oaks, CA: Pine Forge Press. 6th ed.

Skogstad, A., J. Hetland, L. Glasø, and S. Einarsen. (2014) Is avoidant leadership a root cause of subordinate stress? Longitudianl relationships between laissez-faire leadership and role ambiguity. *Work & Stress*. Oct-Dec, 28, 4:323-341.

Srinivasan, M. (2005) Southwest Airlines operations – A strategic perspective. *Airline Industry Articles*. Retrieved from http://airline-industry.malq.net/southwest-airlines-operations-a-strategic-perspective/.

Weber, M. (1922, 2013) Bureaucracy. *Economy and Society*. Vol. 2. Oakland, CA: University of California Press. Ch 11.

Chapter TWO

How Organizations Really Run

What can go wrong that can lead to white collar or corporate crime

---

Major Major: Sergeant, from now on, I don't want anyone to come in and see me while I'm in my office. Is that clear?

Sgt. Towser: Yes, sir. What do I say to people who want to come in and see you while you're in your office?

Major Major: Tell them I'm in and ask them to wait.

Sgt. Towser: For how long?

Major Major: Until I've left.

Sft. Towser: And then what do I do with them?

Major Major: I don't care.

—*Catch-22 (Paramount Pictures, 1970)*

Chapter Objectives

- Introduce the human side of organizations, with all its imperfections.
- Describe the realities of issues that arise in modern organizations.
- Identify the problems that have the potential of leading to employee or company misconduct.
- Introduce the two key motivations behind white collar and corporate crime: greed and fear.

Key Terms

Alienation of workers

Autocrat

Bankruptcy

Bounded rationality

Corporate violence
Espionage Act of 1917
Fiduciary responsibility
Gender politics
Iron Cage of Bureaucracy
Malfeasance
Micromanagement

Organizational death
Span of control
"Whistleblowers"
Whistleblower Protection Act, 1989
White collar crime
White collar malfeasance

INTRODUCTION

The reality of organizations is that they are made up of people. As a species, we have our imperfections and this spills over into the organizations that we are a part of. Most of the time these minor hiccups will not result in long term effects. However, there are some mistakes that are so big they may mean the end of a company. In extreme cases, they may result in injury or death to customers, employees, or people who just happen to be in the path of some tragic corporate disaster.

Though the goal of individuals and organizations should be to seek the best means in which to make sure that things are running smoothly, excessively seeking perfection is irrational. Striving for a flawless organization creates its own organizational problems, causing stagnation and disorder. As we will see in Weber's *Iron Cage of Bureaucracy* (1922), there is such a thing as being over-regulated or having way too many rules. Think of it being like a teenager who rebels against overly strict parents. This in turn can stifle creativity, or as John Ruskin mused, "To banish imperfection is to destroy expression .... to paralyze vitality." (Ruskin and Rosenberg, 1964, p. 184). So in some industries, like in the tech sector, innovation and thinking outside the box of organizational order is encouraged, even if it results in a series of trials and errors. In fact, risk taking has been the hallmark of innovation.

Beyond the chaos of technology running amok, office politics are inescapable. Any time you throw in a mix of individuals with their own personal and professional histories, there is bound to be friction from time to time. Personalities and management types won't always get along. When this friction escalates to resentment and anger, it can be a recipe for rebellion and possibly criminal behavior. In other cases, it results in apathy and careless mistakes can happen.

We should note that the cases in this chapter do not all represent ethical or illegal wrongdoing, but rather organizations that have made decisions resulting in temporary or long-term distrust or chaos. In all cases, it took time for these organizations to regain the trust of the public. One way or another, whether these were cases of neglect, ignorance, or general organizational recklessness, they demonstrate that what we have read in Chapter 1 reflects an unrealistic ideal of how an organization can or should operate.

DEFINING MALFEASANCE AND WHITE COLLAR CRIME

When we are examining the things that go wrong in organizations, we have to understand the differences between consciously committing crime, ignorance, and misguidance. Most of what we see in organizations that is defined as unethical or unconventional behavior can be defined as *malfeasance*. It's a great term to have in our organizational vocabulary while looking at *white collar crime*. Malfeasance means that some type of unacceptable behavior has occurred that can either be illegal or simply unacceptable by industry and regulatory standards. It can also mean any employee misdeeds that go against specific organizational policies. To put this in simple terms, all white collar crime is malfeasance, but not all malfeasance is criminal.

Malfeasance can happen in a number of different organizational settings, as we will see in the upcoming chapters of this textbook. It can happen in government arenas, educational settings, or religious institutions. It can occur in both non-profit and for-profit organizations. And it can be committed by people at the top of the organizational chart, like a CEO, or by the lowest paid employee.

Criminal behavior and malfeasance are not always a result of individual behavior or collective behavior. Sometimes it is simply the structure or culture of the organization that fails to provide adequate safeguards against employee crimes. In the fast pace world of finance, it has only been in recent decades that compliance officers have taken more significant roles in making sure that regulations are followed. Even quality assurance in health care has only made significant progress in the past half century (Marjoura and Bozic, 2012).

White collar crime is a little more difficult to define. What we do know is that it is distinctly different from ordinary, conventional street crime. We can thank Edwin Sutherland for introducing the concept of white collar crime in a keynote speech to the American Sociological Association in 1939. Sutherland initially restricted his definition of who is likely to commit white collar crimes to those who are otherwise respectable individuals of high social status. Though his definition has subsequently been criticized because of limiting the classification of white collar crime to elite individuals, we still turn to his definition as being a good starting point to understanding how individuals who are otherwise making decent incomes turn to crime to further enhance their bank accounts or power.

We should keep in mind that white collar crimes can be committed by people in a number of different occupations, including both "white collar workers" and "blue collared workers." Men are more likely to commit white collar crimes at higher levels of organizations, partially due to the fact they are more likely to occupy positions of power. However, we cannot disregard women who commit white collar crimes within occupations that are more femininized, or "pink collar" careers.

The distinction between white collar and blue collar occupations came from dividing the labor force into those who generally work in an office and those who are manual laborers, where their livelihood is made by using their hands, as in the case of a construction worker. However, regardless of whether an individual who embezzles money or materials from their employer or customers is working in an office building or out on a construction site, we classify the theft as "white collar crime."

FEAR AND GREED

As we will see in upcoming chapters, there are two very powerful motivators for committing any wrongdoing in organizations: fear and greed. In Max Weber's ideal organization, discussed in Chapter 1, a career is counted on to provide security and the promise of promotions if one does an excellent job in their current position in the hierarchy. In reality, when we look at the classic organizational chart, there is only so much room for promotion. Hence one factor for fear.

There are a couple of different types of employees when it comes to fear. There is the person who is extremely loyal to the company or institution, and will do anything to cover up something that might embarrass the company. For instance, perhaps an automobile has been heavily advertised before being available at dealerships. The engineers and managers are aware that there is a potential problem, but fail to report it for fear that the company will lose sales, profits, and reputation.

The second type of fear stems from anxiety over whether one's own work performance can only be enhanced through criminal behavior. An example of this second type of fear would be in the case of a financial planner who attempts to sell stock that doesn't exist to unsuspecting clients, for fear that their legitimate transactions for their clients are not enough to keep them employed.

On the individual level, there are a number of reasons why someone is fearful about their own place in an organization. In a competitive job market, individuals may feel like they are disposable labor, easily replaceable. Sometimes it is simply due to personal insecurities, where individuals feel like they are unable to live up to their reputation or credentials. In other cases, it may be a matter of hiding some mistake the employee has made that they don't want anyone to find out about.

Sometimes the fear is coming from the competitive environment. Change can be fast in coming, as in the case of when Amazon® became an attractive and cheaper alternative to traditional shopping. Malls have been closing at a steady pace as their anchor stores become obsolete. This was never so evident as when customers had to rely primarily on online shopping, including for groceries, during the COVID-19 pandemic when people around the world were ordered to stay home. Retailers who had been in business for decades were forced to close a number of their brick and mortar stores in malls, like in the case of Nordstrom, a once popular department store (Peterson, 2020). It is similar to what happened to locally owned stores on any Main Street in the United States when big box stores like Walmart® and Target® started sprouting all over rural, suburban, and urban landscapes. This may force companies and corporations, both small and large, to take drastic measures to stay afloat, sometimes tiptoeing into questionable legal territory.

In some cases, fear and greed can intersect. Some individuals, depending on their socioeconomic status in their formative years (childhood or young adulthood), may be afraid that they might be plunged back into poverty. Even if they have had career success and great financial compensation, they may live in dread of ever being poor again. This in turn might motivate them to become greedy, as no amount of money in the bank and investment is ever enough.

It is important to note that there is a difference between real, biological poverty, where you cannot keep a roof over your head or food on the table, and relative poverty. With relative poverty, you may feel like you are impoverished compared to those around you. For example, you may be able to afford a home in Beverly Hills, California, but it may be the least expensive property. In this case, if you have the least expensive property in Beverly Hills and it's the only thing you can afford in that pricy zip code, you may very well feel like the poor relations.

We cannot discount the cultural environment as a source of both fear and greed. In some industries, the competition for customers and profits is so fierce it sets up a "dog-eat-dog" culture. Wall Street is notorious for gobbling up new MBA graduates and putting them through grueling workdays to prove their worth. As Rosoff et al.'s book *Profit Without Honor* (2013) implies, white collar crime may be "business as usual" rather than a rare occurrence. Financial institutions are a good example of places where the culture doesn't exactly discourage malfeasance if it means big profits (Hansen and Movahedi, 2010), as we will see in our chapter of financial white collar crime and discussions of Wells Fargo® Bank.

One of the biggest fears that companies have is the real or perceived loss of profits, a fear that is exacerbated in publicly traded companies. This means that there are shareholders who have invested in the company with the expectation that there will be a return on their money. Between the "Go-Go" years of the 1960s and the mergers and acquisitions rush in the 1980s, profits bordered on the obscene. Unfortunately, many investors get accustomed to unusually high profits and mistakenly believe that it is the new normal. The reality is that the stock market at times can look like a rollercoaster ride. Again, this can represent the intersection of companies' fears and investors' greed, which can result in questionable business practices.

IRON CAGE OF BUREAUCRACY

Think about how it feels when you go get your driver's license or state identification card at the Department of Motor Vehicles (or Registry of Motor Vehicles — the name may be different depending on where you live). Though things have been somewhat streamlined since the Age of the Dinosaurs, it can still be an all-afternoon ordeal to get your license or identification card. You go to one window for one thing, get sent to another window for something else, and then move on to possibly a third or fourth window to get your picture taken.

To make matters more sluggish, with digital photography, you may be offered a choice of which photo will appear on your license or identification card. If you have someone in front of you in line who is posing for their photo as if for an Instagram® posting, the waiting time can be even longer! Thankfully motor vehicle departments have kept up with technology and there are a lot of things that you can accomplish online instead of going to a local office.

Or perhaps you are unfortunate enough to have to go to an emergency room or urgent care center. Hospital and medical personnel are trained to triage, taking the most critical cases first, and there is the inevitable paperwork to fill out. So no matter how panicked you may feel about your medical condition in the moment, the wait to get in to see a doctor or nurse practitioner can be excruciatingly long. Time feels like it comes to a standstill, particularly if you are surrounded by others who are in various states of misery. A hospital has to staff for predicted patient needs and cannot always anticipate a sudden influx of new patients, as in the case of a sudden flu epidemic or a major automobile pileup on the highway. This was part of the reasons why hospitals in the United States were overwhelmed in the beginning for the COVID-19 crisis.

Max Weber, for all of his praises for bureaucratic structure, was also one of its harshest critics. He cautioned his readers that organizations can get so rule-bound that it becomes difficult to accomplish anything. As rational as bureaucratic organizations are, they may eventually become irrational, following a growing number of rules and regulations or by being stuck in old habits.

When you hear the word "bureaucracy" or "bureaucrat," it should not come as a surprise if the first thing you think of is mounds of red tape in order to get anything accomplished. Bureaucratic structures are fraught with inertia — a term used in physics to mean that things are in a state of rest and sluggishness and basically will not move. It takes some external force to nudge it along.

For example, a company may be required to adapt due to changes in customer tastes, market forces, or technological changes after running their operations the same way for a great number of years. The old saying "if it ain't broke, don't fix it" applies here. However, what if a company isn't aware that something is broken? What if some of the ways that a company gets things done are not exactly broken, but outdated? Sometimes they choose to avoid shifting gears and modernizing their advertising, products, or operations until it is too late.

The Coca-Cola Company is a good example of being able to successfully run operations smoothly for a number of decades with relatively little change to its product. In the 1980s, it was confronted with rising competition from other cola companies. The company's response was to launch a new product, New Coke®. It was advertised as having improved taste that would keep customers from drinking products from the competitors, like Pepsi®. Unfortunately, this was not a successful campaign, as the customer loyalty to "old" Coke® was underestimated. The company quickly returned "Classic Coke®" to grocery store shelves. To some extent we are seeing the same phenomenon with the company in recent history, with the launching of a number of Diet Coke® flavors, with far more successful outcomes. One key feature of survival is the ability to change direction and learn from past mistakes, as Coca Cola® has in recent years.

The major concern with the "iron cage" is that if management and/or workers get frustrated enough, they might cut corners to get things done. Worse yet, they may feel compelled to do something unethical or illegal. For instance, a lobbyist in Washington might resort to bribery in order to secure a vote favorable to their cause if they are not willing to take the time to legitimately woo a Congress member into their way of thinking. It is one of the main reasons that there are legal limitations on gifts and contributions to political campaigns by lobbyists.

CHAIN OF COMMAND ISSUES

In most cases, a hierarchy, sometimes called the chain of command, functions well as long as everyone has a clear picture of their place in the organization. A chain of command implies that you should only go to your immediate supervisor with questions or concerns. This allows those higher up in the hierarchy to not be tied down to every detail of day to day operations.

Much as in the case made by Weber in his description of the Iron Cage of Bureaucracy, the chain of command slows things down. When things go wrong, there might be a reluctance to admit to your superiors that a mistake has been made. When problems are reported, people higher up in the hierarchy might not act on the information readily or, in some cases, at all.

There is also the issue of the *span of control*. The span of control is the number of employees that a supervisor has directly beneath them in the chain of command (or organizational chart) that they can effectively manage. The standard size of the span of control is different, depending on the industry and use of technology. For instance, because an assembly line mechanically controls the flow of work being done by employees, there is less need for supervision, as control is built into the physical structure. A doctor who is supervising new medical school graduates, either interns or residents, will not be able to supervise as many newly minted doctors.

There are a number of things that will determine the size of the span of control of a supervisor. The key determinants are (1) actual span of control (number of supervisors divided by the number of workers at any particular level), (2) how routine the work is and how easily understood by workers, and (3) the complexity of the work, including how specialized workers' roles are (Dewar and Simet, 1981).

The size of a span of control may be restricted by regulations or industry standards. There is some evidence that how specialized workers are affects how many employees can be managed at any given time. For good reason, because if there are too many people who have to directly report to you, supervisory control will be compromised. Think of the example of the elementary school teacher who has 20 students in their class, as compared to the teacher who has to manage 40 students. It is easier to control smaller classes of students at every level of education, from pre-school through college. If workers (or students) are not adequately supervised, they will not be able to perform as well at their tasks and are at more risk of getting into mischief, including malfeasance and crime.

INNOVATION

Innovation is one key factor for any organization to survive in a competitive marketplace, but innovation can be a costly process and doesn't always result in successes. A drug company could be working for some time to find a remedy for some medical condition. The company may only come to find out that after drug trials that they have to go back to the drawing table, sometimes starting from scratch.

For other companies, in particular those in Silicon Valley, California, innovation means getting a product out on the market before competitors come up with a cheaper alternative. Plus, anything associated with computer technology becomes obsolete very quickly. There might be frustration when the world of fast paced Silicon Valley meets the slow processes of regulatory agencies in either the state of California or in Washington, D.C. For instance, Uber, the taxi service where drivers use their own cars, is in the research and development stages of introducing flying cars. As National Public Radio (NPR) and New England Public Radio (NEPR have reported, the one challenge for Uber is the regulatory waters they still have to navigate (McDonald, 2017). The Federal Aviation Agency (FAA) regulations will no doubt have to be followed, as there has to be consideration for air space with flying cars. The concern is that if there are any corners cut or any overlooked safety features, the potential for multiple car pileups in the skies above is real.

Law in the Real World: Challenger Shuttle Disaster

(Source: Vaughn, 2016)

A classic case of things going terribly wrong within a hierarchy is the Challenger space shuttle disaster. The Challenger was set to launch with the first teacher to ever travel to space, Christa McAuliffe. Within moments of the launch, the shuttle exploded, killing all seven astronauts, including McAuliffe. Needless to say, it was a major public relations disaster for NASA beyond the tragedy of lost lives. The subsequent Rogers Commission determined that decisions were made based on management rationale instead of technical rationale. It was determined that the launch proceeded over the protest of Thiokol engineers, the makers of the O-rings, a type of gasket used on the shuttle. The Thiokol engineers were rightfully concerned that there was a risk of the O-rings failing in the unusually cold winter weather that day at the Kennedy Space Center in Cape Canaveral, Florida, where the launch was taking place. One NASA management argument for proceeding with the launch was that there had already been a number of delays due to weather and technical glitches. To delay yet again would be a public relations nightmare in an era of waning interest in space programs.

Of course, the Challenger disaster did not spell the end of NASA or space programs. NASA came under the microscope once again in 2003 when the Columbia space shuttle, returning from a mission, failed to land in one piece. The shuttle disintegrated upon reentry, killing the seven astronauts on board. The final determination of the cause was that a loose piece of foam from the external tank flew into one of the wings of the spacecraft (Howell, 2019). The potential problem had been known for years by engineers, but didn't stop decisions being made to launch space shuttles even after the Challenger tragedy. It may have been the final blow to fully the space shuttle program, with the program retired in 2011. NASA has yet to regain its footing and, in some administrations, funding to continue space exploration. They have more recently had to join with SpaceX, a private company, in order to bring supplies up to the International Space Station (ISS).

Discussion Questions

1. What reasons might management have for proceeding with the launch against the advice of Thiokol engineers?
2. As we are squarely in the technological age, how can traditional managers of technology employees balance the "bottom line" (profit) with the concerns of the tech personnel?
3. In light of the Challenger disaster, what role, if any, has the privatization of space (e.g., SpaceX) exploration to further tarnished NASA's reputation?

BOUNDED RATIONALITY

As we continue to note in this chapter, humans are not perfect. In fact, as a species, we can be pretty flawed. Yet we are required to make all kinds of important decisions that may have long term consequences, including where to go to school, if and whom we might marry, etc. When we make these decisions, we can only base them on the information that we have at hand. Sometimes the information itself is misunderstood or limited. In these situations, we find ourselves left with the dilemma of *bounded rationality* (Simon, 1957).

Sometimes the information that decision makers have is incorrect or incomplete. As we saw in the Challenger disaster case study, because the upper echelon management at NASA did not see the complete picture about the O-rings' performance in cold temperatures, as they were not engineers, they felt that they could not necessarily act on yet another recommendation to scrap the mission. In some cases, not having the right information results in the loss of life. In most cases, it means missed opportunities to take corrective action or increase profit margin. For some companies, keeping an eye on details may preserve their reputations in the long run.

Other things that might interfere with decision making include being influenced by others who might be equally clueless of all the facts. Sometimes there is the risk of "doing things as we have always done them" when a new, different direction might be better in a given situation. There is also the concern that individuals will make decisions that are in their own best interest and not that of the group or the organization.

CEREMONIAL EVALUATIONS

In recent years there has been a lot of discussion around formal employee evaluations, which generally are conducted once a year. In fact, there is a growing trend to do away with formal performance reviews all together, as they take considerable time, money, and effort (Cunningham, 2015). In studies conducted by CEB, a company that specializes in best business practices, 95 percent of managers are dissatisfied with formal evaluations and 90 percent of Human Resources professionals believe the evaluations to be inaccurate (Smith, 2018).

In some industries, particularly in the tech sector, because managers do not necessarily fully understand the work their employees do, they may not know when employees are doing a good job or failing miserably unless something obvious goes wrong. Think of it like when you are expecting a guest and don't have enough time to clean up. You might resort to shoving everything into a drawer, sweeping dust under the rug, throwing things haphazardly into a closet. As long as your guest doesn't snoop around the house, they may think that you are an immaculate housekeeper based on what they can see on the surface. In an organization that isn't looking too closely under the proverbial rug, they may not be able to capture an accurate picture of an employee's performance in the annual evaluation.

In formal organizations that are larger and complex, evaluations may be superficial because formal evaluations are time consuming, costly propositions. Those organizations that don't do away with employee evaluations do so because it gives the organizational work legitimacy, increasing their prospects for surviving, particularly in a competitive environment (Meyer and Rowan, 1977).

However, as witnessed in times of war, these standards are not always upheld, as in the case of the My Lai massacre during the Vietnam War, where a number of U.S. servicemen, including officers, sexually assaulted and killed unarmed South Vietnam civilians. The offenders, soldiers in Charlie Company, encountered no resistance from My Lai villagers on March 16, 1968, and were ultimately held accountable for their actions after a cover-up had been exposed (Gray and Martin, 2008).

LEADERSHIP GONE HAYWIRE: THE AUTOCRAT AND MICROMANAGER

Not all leaders, managers, or supervisors are benevolent. Some manage people through fear and intimidation. What they all have in common is that they have the power, in most cases, to hire and fire at will. But this is not describing a ruler within a restrictive country that is ruled by dictatorship. You were first introduced to these leadership types and styles in Chapter 1. You can just as easily find a boss in a bureaucratic structure who runs operations as if they were a dictator.

A dictator is defined as an individual who has total power and control over their domain. You are more likely to see the term *"autocrat"* to describe someone who supervises this way in an organization, regardless of what industry it is. This can sometimes be the "bad boss" who intimidates employees into doing what they want them to do, by threatening to fire them or worse, if employees question their authority.

There are instances, particularly in emergency management, when there is need for autocratic leadership. Decisions have to be made quickly and there may not be time to come to a democratic consensus. The problem occurs when autocratic or dictatorship management continues over long periods of time and outside the context of emergency situations. Workers are more likely to quit, to take their skills and resources with them, under autocratic leadership, leading to organizational instability (Van Vugt et al., 2004).

A companion leadership type to the autocratic that can be a threat to an organization is the micromanager. In *micromanagement*, the supervisor will have their hands in every aspect of operations. This leadership type is common among leaders who want or need complete control over work processes and workers. Again, as in our example of emergency management, when there temporarily needs to be a micromanager.

Though it has a somewhat more benign reputation than a dictatorship, micromanagement can be detrimental to an organization over time. It is exhausting for both the micromanager and the employees directly being supervised by them. It is doubly difficult if an employee has more than one supervisor and they have different management styles. For example, it is not uncommon for part-time workers in fast food services to have different supervisors on different shifts. The worker then has to make constant adjustments to their workflow depending on what supervisor they have at any given time.

Micromanagers may be a product of individual personality traits or work conditions. If a supervisor finds that they cannot trust their workers, they feel like they have to increase their control. But this can become a vicious cycle of supervisors not trusting employees and employees losing faith in their management in turn, as demonstrated in Exhibit 2.1.

EXHIBIT 2.1 ‖ **Cycle of Mistrust** *(Source:* SherpaDesk, retrieved from https://www.sherpadesk.com/
‖ blog/how-to-end-micromanagement-to-improve-your-team)

Whether we are talking about citizens living under a dictatorship or employees working under a micromanager, there will be the concern that rebellion will happen. Some of this rebellion might be passive aggressive, where workers purposely slow down the pace of their work without directly confronting their supervisor. A second issue is that micromanagement stifles creativity, innovation, and growth (Austin and Larkey, 1992). Workers are less likely to take risks that could benefit an organization as they will have little to no autonomy. On the flip side, to work around their restrictive supervisor, they may end up engaging in risky activities that can be unethical, illegal, or generally bad for the organization.

ALIENATED WORKERS

Within the last few decades, there have been increasingly more corporate scandals. Whether it is due to more reporting of crime and malfeasance of companies or whether there is indeed a significant increase in white collar crime, one explanation is that many workers are just not happy in their jobs. We define an alienated worker as one who is not engaged in their work, nor necessarily cares about the end product of their efforts. They may only put in enough effort to not get fired and to justify the collection of a paycheck. There are a number of reasons why a worker might become disillusioned and frustrated in their job.

In a recent poll conducted by The Conference Board, reported by CNBC (2019), 88 percent of American workers are generally satisfied in their jobs. However, other research contradicts this, including a 2017 Gallup poll reporting that a large percentage of people in the world actually hate their jobs, including bosses (Clifton, 2017). Academic research is more supportive of the latter contention that there are a lot of unhappy workers, including in the United States.

What is contributing to the *alienation of workers*? There are several factors that will create an employee who no longer cares about their job or the organization they work for. One of the more obvious reasons is burnout. As reported regularly in the news regarding public school teachers, burnout from a demanding job can result in emotional exhaustion, illness and associated absenteeism, and feelings of low personal accomplishment (Garcia-Carmona, 2019).

If workers are unhappy enough and part of a union, the most drastic means by which to get the attention of management is to go on strike. This may not be disruptive to the general public if it is a smaller company with workers on strike, but if it is a company that provides crucial goods or services, this can cause considerable inconvenience and concern. For instance, when public school teachers or nurses go on strike, parents are concerned about whether their children are getting an adequate education and patients will not trust that they are getting the best health care.

Law in the Real World: The U.S. Postal Strike, 1970

(Source: Rubio, 2018)

People in towns and cities depend on basic government services in order to go about their daily business. One of the services that they expect to run without disruption is the postal service. A city the size of New York City processes millions of pieces of mail on a daily basis, including letters and packages, even in the computer age where correspondence is more speedily achieved by email.

In March 1970, starting in New York City, postal workers in 12 cities, 671 postal offices across the country walked off the job. Postal workers are represented by a number of different unions including the National Association of Letter Carriers, the National Postal Union, the United Federation of Postal Clerks, and the National Alliance of Postal and Federal Employees, along with a number of smaller, local unions (Rubio, 2018). The union national leaders did not endorse the strike, further complicating matters. Because it wasn't supported by the unions, it was described as a "wildcat strike," one of the largest of its kind in the United States. We should note that unions, including postal service workers' unions, have historically faced public relations issues, as some have been steeped in charges of bribery, blackmail, and corruption.

The striking postal workers were demanding similar changes to those demanded in legitimate strikes. They were asking for better wages, benefits, and working conditions. Postal workers complained that offices were outdated, described as dungeons that were either too hot or too cold depending on the season of the year (Rubio, 2010). There was also the ongoing fight of trying to address the continued racial injustices in the workplace, a problem that was publicly brought to light by Civil Rights movements in the 1950s and 60s as more African-Americans were hired by the postal service (Rubio, 2010).

At the time, the unions were in the process of collective bargaining with the United States government that runs the postal service. Because the post office is government-funded, changes are slow to happen, as it requires oversight from Congress. Even if it is given priority in any given Congressional session, the demands of government workers may not be met quickly (think Iron Cage of Bureaucracy again).

Ultimately, then-President Nixon (of Watergate fame, discussed later in this book) ordered the National Guard to restore order and break up the strike. The strike lasted 18 days in total, disrupting the government, organized labor, and the private and public sectors. Some labor union historians believe that Nixon's response to the strike set up contentious conditions between management and labor, with repercussions felt well into the air traffic controllers' strike in the 1980s and the weakening of labor union power.

The strike, though a notable case in labor studies, did not result in improved working conditions. As Rubio (2018, p. 66) has noted, "Internal strife became missed with insurgency within postal unions.... The NPMHU [National Postal Mail Handlers Union] remained mired in issues of corruption and non-democratic representation." In Rubio's estimation, the postal workers' unions have strong cultural differences even today, though they have formed a "frenemy" alliance (to borrow from the slang contraction of friend and enemy). Today, postal workers continue to ask for better working conditions as their lighter letter load due to more email correspondences have been replaced with more package deliveries, even on Sundays, with the rise in Internet sales.

Discussion Questions

1. If labor unions are not as powerful as they once were prior to the 1970s, under what conditions might workers strike today?
2. What might have been the motivation for postal workers to strike, even though the strike was not endorsed by their labor unions?
3. What other industries might be places that are at risk for workers' strikes? Why?

Though not a topic generally discussed in white collar crime books, in extreme cases, worker alienation can turn deadly. There have been a number of cases where disgruntled or fired workers have brought weapons to their former places of employment, opening fire on employees. In some cases, the shootings are specifically targeting bosses or hated coworkers. In other cases, the workplace shootings are random, with no specific target. In the context of whether employers should be on the lookout not only for general employee unhappiness and alienation, they need to also be aware of those employees who might pose a serious threat to the well-being of themselves and others.

IRRATIONALITY OF McDONALDIZATION

One contributing factor to the alienation of workers is that with automation, the worker is dehumanized. Even in Ritzer's first discussions of the McDonaldization of society (2011), he warns that the very things that make production efficient for the owner is irrational from the perspective of employees. One example of the irrationality of efficiency is in education.

Widespread use of standardized testing for undergraduate college admissions has been around since the 1920s. The idea behind standardized testing, historically the SAT and ACT, made sense. Because colleges couldn't be assured that the grades and grade point averages reflected in high school transcripts were equally unbiased from school to school and region to region, the standardized admissions tests were intended to give a more objective measure of whether a potential student could succeed at the college level. Even with revisions to the tests to reflect changes in school curriculum, in recent decades critics of the tests have been making the argument that they are subjectively biased and not a true reflection of applicants' abilities.

The idea of standardized testing trickled down to primary and secondary education in the "Leave No Child Behind" campaign under the presidency of George W. Bush. Though well-meaning, a consequence of standardized testing in public schools is that in making school curriculums uniform and efficiently preparing students for work or school after graduation, teachers feel compelled to teach to the test. This in turn has made it difficult for teachers to train students in other, unmeasurable skills such as socialization and critical thinking.

In 2019 we saw the indictment of a number of affluent parents who paid college admissions consultants, including William Rick Singer, to fraudulently inflate test scores. Among those indicted were celebrities and well-known business people. This brought to the forefront of public opinion the notion that that test scores become meaningless if they could be fraudulently altered or if wealthy parents could pay for their children to take extra time on the exams even though they did not have documented learning disabilities to warrant the extra time.

An additional, timely example of irrationality in McDonaldization is the way we communicate. It may seem rational and efficient to have mobile phones used to conduct business. However, this has resulted in some employers believing that their employees are available 24/7, even when they are on vacation.

Efficiency, calculability, predictability, and control, all characteristics of McDonaldization (Ritzer, 2012), should in theory make customers happy, work life better for employees, and more profits for owners. The reality is that customers can be made to feel like they are being rushed in and out of places, including fast food restaurants. Workers are made to feel that they can be easily replaced by machinery, and employers may become out of touch with whether or not both customers and employees are satisfied. This is again a recipe ripe for white collar crime such as sabotage of machinery, illegitimate work "sick outs" when employees are unhappy, and embezzlement.

GENDER POLITICS

Though not generally discussed in context of white collar crime, the "Me Too" movement of the 2010s is a good indication that not all of what we see go wrong in organizations has to do with finances and profit. However, we should note that there have been criminal offenses associated with sexual harassment or predatory behavior, as in the case of television evangelist Jim Bakker and hush money paid to one of his church's secretaries, Jessica Hahn, for an alleged rape. We certainly have to address the issue of any accounting irregularities and crimes associated with hush money when discussing white collar crimes.

Most of what we see in *gender politics* has more to do with general malfeasance and organizational environment than necessarily criminal behavior. However, as sexual assault and/or coercion in the workplace is part of the dark figure (unreported cases) of crime, we do not have a clear idea of the true statistics for victimization, nor to what extents payoffs are happening.

WHISTLEBLOWERS

We cannot assume that everyone within an organization where white collar crime is taking place are aware that it is taking place. We also cannot assume that everyone who knows that a crime is happening will allow it to go unreported. If law enforcement and regulatory agencies are unaware of malfeasance, it may come to their attention by way of a *whistleblower.*

A "whistleblower" is generally an individual or group of individuals within an organization who, for moral or ethical reasons, shines light on a problem that others would prefer to remain hidden from the public, law enforcement, and regulatory agencies and the public eye. Whistleblowers' motives have been historically suspect and places them at risk of being fired from their job when they step forward. Worse yet, they fear that they might be held criminally libel for their actions. In the case of Edward Snowden, a former contractor with the National Security Agency and of Wikileaks fame, he was criminally charged under the *Espionage Act.* Fear is probably one of the key reasons that people do not report criminal or questionable behavior that is occurring within their place of employment.

There are four types of whistleblowers, as identified by Smaili and Arroyo (2019). Their reasons for whistleblowing are similar to the reasons given for committing white collar crimes in the first place, but we do not want to imply that whistleblowers in general are criminals. The first type is *protective*, seeking to protect the reputation of the company or the industry. The second type is *skeptical*, with skepticism born of suspicions of possible misrepresentation of a product or service or general distrust of management. In *role-prescribed*, the third type, an individual is required as part of their job to report misconduct or irregularities, but may be discouraged to do so by management. In the last type, *self-interest*, the whistleblower is calling attention to a problem in order to receive monetary compensation or to enhance their own reputation.

Sometimes the whistleblower is so intimidated by the prospect of confronting their coworkers and supervisors that they will go to the media. There is also the fear of retaliation from employers or fellow employees (Smaili and Arroyo, 2019; Near and Miceli, 1996; Miceli and Near, 1994). Smaili and Arroyo (2019, p. 95) contend that "most whistleblowers opt for external channels when they fail to receive an adequate response from management, seeking media exposure, are interested in financial benefits resulting from the act of whistleblowing (short sellers), or are interested in protecting their investment." It is safe to say that not all whistleblowers will come forward strictly on the basis of moral or ethical reasons.

One of the more famous political crime cases that we will be discussing in our political crime chapter is Watergate. In this case the whistleblower, W. Mark Felt, met covertly with Bob Woodward and Carl Bernstein of *The Washington Post* to help guide them to the criminal abuses of the Nixon administration in the early 1970s (Woodward, 2005). Felt had served as the Assistant Director of the Federal Bureau of Investigation (FBI) during the time the Watergate scandal took place. It is ordinarily unheard of for law enforcement, much less the second in command at the FBI, to leak information to the press during an ongoing investigation.

The *Whistleblower Protection Act* (WPA, 1989, 5 U.S.C. §2302(b)(8)) makes it somewhat easier for people to come forward when they find crime or malfeasance in their organizations. Under the act, individuals are protected from harassment or firing when they come forward with claims of law or regulation violations, gross mismanagement, financial mismanagement, abuses of authority, or anything that represents a danger to public or employee health and safety (Office of the Inspector General, n.d.). This has allowed advocacy groups such as the Government Accountability Project (whistleblower.org) and Whistleblower Aid (whistlebloweraid.org) to actively represent and protect whistleblowers. According to John Tye, a former government official currently working with Whistleblower Aid, several dozens of whistleblowers have come forward on the heels of the Ukrainian and Russian scandals currently rocking Washington, D.C. (Bilton, 2019).

Law in the Real World: Jeffrey Wigand and Big Tobacco

(Source: National Whistleblower Center, retrieved from https://www.whistleblowers.
org/members/jeffrey-wigand/)

One upon a time, advertising agencies representing tobacco companies used doctors in their ad campaigns. In their defense, in the 1940s and the early 1950s, the medical community did not yet fully comprehend the harm that tobacco products caused, including cancer and contributing to heart disease. It wasn't until comprehensive research in the 1950s that a possible link between smoking and lung cancer was made (American Cancer Society, 2019). At the same time, scientists were just beginning to understand the addictive characteristics of tobacco, including nicotine.

So why, after clear evidence and major public education campaigns on the dangers of smoking, would a tobacco company manipulate chemicals such as ammonia in cigarettes, increasing the addictive effects of nicotine? This is precisely what tobacco companies were accused of doing, including Brown and Williamson as discussed in this case study.

It is understandable during the heyday of Madison Avenue advertisement in the 1960s, so aptly portrayed in the popular show *Mad Men* (Lionsgate Television), that tobacco companies would scramble to make cigarette smoking appear to be not only harmless, but in fact glamorous, as witnessed in a number of movies from the 1940s and '50s. The advertising blitz of tobacco companies in the 1960s and 1970s was in reaction to mounting scientific evidence that cigarette smoking could be deadly. New marketing strategies had to be used to create new customers, as well as keeping existing ones, as more and more people quit smoking in response to medical reports. However, unbeknownst to the public, the nicotine manipulation by tobacco companies occurred in the 1990s.

Jerry Wigand was a vice president at Brown and Williamson, an American tobacco company. Possessing both a Masters and Ph.D. in biochemistry and endocrinology (Wigand, 2019), he was not the stereotypical executive at a tobacco company with a business school education. Prior to working for Brown and Williamson, Wigand worked in the health care sector.

After no doubt a lot of soul searching, weighing the risks of biting the hand that paid his salary, Wigand blew the whistle on the tobacco industry's alleged blatant disregard for consumer health. He was a witness in lawsuits that the States of Mississippi and Kentucky brought against Brown and Williamson for the costs of medical care for illnesses and diseases associated with cigarette smoking. In spite of failed attempts by Brown and Williamson's lawyers attempts to interrupt Wigand's testimony during the trials, he revealed the company's practice of manipulating the nicotine levels in their cigarettes.

Discussion Questions

1. Why do you think that it took so long for tobacco companies to come forward with or agree with the scientific evidence that cigarettes are harmful to health?
2. What have tobacco companies been required to do as a result of scientific evidence that tobacco products are addictive and can lead to certain cancers?
3. In what other industries might whistleblowers sound the alarm about unsafe, unethical, or illegal activities?

In some cases, the whistleblower can be compensated for coming forward with information of wrongdoing. The Securities and Exchange Commission (SEC) can reward whistleblowers between 10 percent to 30 percent of recovered assets or fines in successfully prosecuted cases. In March 2019, the SEC announced that they were awarding $50 million (USD) to two whistleblowers who came forward with "smoking gun" evidence in a case that was invaluable in protecting investors and the markets (SEC, 2019). If not for moral reasons, there is monetary reason for whistleblowers in the financial sector to come forward with information about crimes being committed in banks and financial institutions.

We cannot underestimate the value of whistleblowers in helping to uncover criminal or unethical behavior in organizations. In a study conducted by the Association of Certified Fraud Examiners (ACFE, 2016), 39.1 percent of fraud cases are first detected by whistleblowers. Of whistleblowing cases, employees are reported as being the source of almost half of cases that lead to successful detection of fraud (ACFE, 2016). For all the vilification of whistleblowers within their organizations, they appear to be one of the best means by which organizational crime reaches the eyes and ears of the public.

UNFORESEEN DISASTERS

It has only been fairly recently that companies and organizations have turned their attention to disaster preparedness. The 9/11 terrorist attacks on the Twin Towers in New York City and the Pentagon in Washington, D.C. brought focus on humanmade disasters, but we are still slow to prepare for natural disasters like tornadoes, hurricanes, and wildfires.

In July 2019, Louisiana faced the aftermath of yet another weather-related disaster, Tropical Storm Barry. Fourteen years after Hurricane Katrina devasted the city in August of 2005, New Orleans has yet to fully recover. Disasters are not only taxing on local first responders and rescue teams, it impacts local businesses. Following Hurricane Katrina, some businesses failed to recover, and tourism in particular fell off by several million visitors a year between 2004 and 2006 (Rosenberg, 2017).

Unfortunately, disasters create conditions ripe for a number of fraud schemes. These consist of fake charities soliciting for donations and insurance schemes. As we have noted (and will again in Chapter 8, Consumer Crimes), the most vulnerable in the population will fall prey to these.

In some cases, the fallout from a disaster can be predicted but preventative measures are not put in place. This is largely due to cost saving strategies, but can also be out of ignorance. It is expensive to prepare for a disaster that might or might not even happen. This author had a well-outfitted earthquake kit while living in Southern California that never needed to be put into use. The kit wasn't even used after the 1987 Whittier Narrows earthquake in San Gabriel Valley that measured 5.9 on the Richter magnitude scale, though there was considerable damage reported, 200 plus injuries, and two related deaths (Lloyd, 2018). The more recent earthquakes, in and around Ridgecrest, in June and July of 2019 are yet another reminder to residences and businesses to be prepared. To date, earthquakes occur at fairly unpredictable intervals, though scientists continue to search for tools to better predict them.

There are some places where a disaster is somewhat predictable, if not cyclical or seasonal. For instance, those who live in states that are within what is described as "Tornado Alley," seen in the map on page 45, are instructed frequently on how to survive a tornado event. Schools, public and private companies, and medical facilities are for the most part well-prepared in advance.

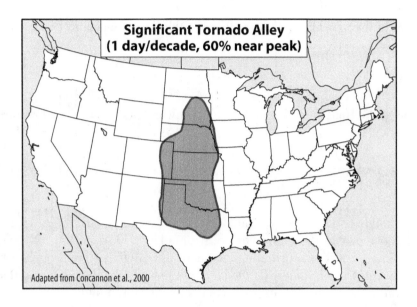

EXHIBIT 2.2 | **Tornado Alley** *(Source:* NOAA, National Centers for Environmental Information https://www.ncdc.noaa.gov/climate-information/extreme-events/us-tornado-climatology/tornado-alley)

As we will mention throughout this book, the COVID-19 virus pandemic left many in business and government caught off guard and ill-prepared to handle the financial consequences of the global illness. There will be debates for decades to come as to what could have been done to prepare for millions of people falling ill to the virus, not to mention the hundreds of thousands who have died.

From an economic standpoint, the COVID-19 virus pandemic represented millions of people out of work globally for the unforeseeable future, with businesses ill-prepared to handle the safety protocols of social distancing recommended by the Center for Disease Control and Prevention and the World Health Organization. Restaurants were forced to offer curbside pickup or delivery, if they could. Theme parks, sports arenas, and movie theaters, all representing billions of dollars of entertainment revenue, were forced to shut down all together, placed into a holding pattern until the virus was fully managed or a vaccine could be found.

In the context of white collar crime, there are disasters that could be avoided or at least settled with reduced tragic consequences. When a company fails to prepare for a disaster or fails to take measures to prevent a disaster from happening in the first place, they can be held criminally responsible. At the very least, they leave themselves open for civil lawsuits. Again, much of the reason that companies fail to prepare is that they are trying to save money and resources, crossing their fingers that disaster never happens. In some cases, they are so ill-prepared that when disasters do hit, it ultimately is far more costly than if they had prepared for them in the first place, as we will see in the Pacific Gas and Electric *bankruptcy* case.

Law in the Real World: Pacific Gas and Electric (PG&E) Bankruptcy

---

(Source: CNN, Ayer and Glover, 2018, retrieved from https://www.cnn.com/2018/
12/19/us/camp-fire-pge-invs/index.html)

In the fall of 2017, Northern California was hit with devastating wildfires, killing two people and destroying approximately 8,900 homes (CNN, Ayer and Glover, 2018). Contributing factors to the wildfires were drought and subsequent dry conditions. Of the large number of fires that occurred that autumn in California, 11 are suspected of being caused by Pacific Gas and Electric (PG&E), California's largest public utility. As Ayer and Glover (2018) noted in their reporting, PG&E did not purposely start the fires, but rather it was a perfect storm of a serious drought in California and PG&E's alleged failure to clear brush around power lines, violating utility safety codes.

PG&E is a publicly traded company. This means that the company is dependent on people investing in their stocks. When the wildfires hit Northern California and suspected liability fell on the shoulders of PG&E, stock prices dropped 50 percent in value practically overnight. Hundreds of civil lawsuits from wildfire victims had been filed against the company. Without investment in the company, management at PG&E believed they had no alternative but to file for Chapter 11 bankruptcy protection in 2019.

In a bankruptcy case, the debts owed by an individual, or in this case, a company, can be reduced or forgiven. In some cases, payment is consolidated or postponed. This allows the company to reorganize itself so it can get back on its feet financially. Filing for bankruptcy in court is a public relations nightmare that can further drive down the value of stock, even if investors somewhat cautiously have faith that the company can turn itself around. In any bankruptcy case involving a publicly traded company, shareholders can expect price volatility and lost dividends, making the stock less attractive to some investors. In the 2001 PG&E bankruptcy, investors were estimated to have lost $1.7 billion in dividends alone (KGO-TV, 2019).

A company as large as PG&E can't simply close its doors to business when there are setbacks. As a utility company, PG&E provides services to millions of people in California and employs thousands of workers. To simply shut operations down completely is a near impossibility as it would be extremely disruptive to people's day-to-day lives. It would be ruinous to the California economy as well.

Customers had to be reassured that their gas and power would remain on. As in the case of the 2001 energy crisis when they filed for bankruptcy protection, PG&E may be forced to charge more for services for the foreseeable future, making for unhappy customers. Under bankruptcy protection, workers at PG&E may find their health benefits and retirement plans at risk, though we should note that utility workers are generally represented by unions. No matter what is ultimately determined in civil courts as far as PG&E's liability, for long term viability, the company has to work fast to calm the nerves of customers, investors, and employees.

Discussion Questions

1. In the case of PG&E, is the company acting out of fear, greed, or both?
2. Should bankruptcy be an option for a company that has been found guilty of violating laws?
3. What issues, particularly in management, might the company have that led them to overlook some safety precautions?

CORPORATE VIOLENCE

We ordinarily associate violence with conventional crimes like assault, rape, and murder. Conventional crime and white collar crime are not mutually exclusive when it comes to the consequences of criminal behavior. When injuries or death occur in the commission of a white collar crime as a result of intended neglect, we describe this as *corporate violence*.

It is a popular myth that white collar criminals are essentially harmless (Michel, 2017). As people tend to do when someone has been robbed but not physically harmed, they breathe a sigh of relief, reminding the victim that at least they walked away with their life. In most cases of white collar crime, the worst thing that happens to the victim is that they may lose their life's savings. This in itself is devastating. But when calculated neglect results in the injuries and deaths of employees, customers, or civilians, the devastation can last for generations. We cannot also discount the emotional fallout of financial victimization, including anxiety and depression.

In cases of corporate violence, the harm may not even be identified until days, months, or even years later. We certainly saw this in the case of tobacco products, where the negative long-term effects were downplayed by tobacco companies even after irrefutable evidence that smoking can lead to a number of chronic and fatal diseases. This is also common in cases of environmental crimes, like dumping toxic materials into rivers, where the effects might not be obvious until wildlife has been genetically altered in some way, or similarly, when there are an unusually high number of cancer cases in communities where there has been illegal discarding of harmful chemicals.

One more famous case of corporate violence was that of a chemical leak that happened in 1984 at the Union Carbide pesticide plant in Bhopal, India. Approximately 26 to 40 tons of methyl isocyanate gas leaked over the course of three days, resulting in the death of at least 3,000 people and exposing an estimated 569,000 people to long-term health effects (Satgunam and Chindelevitch, 2017). The culprit behind the leak was a number of organizational deficiencies in the plant, including operating errors, design flaws, maintenance failures, poor training, and cost-cutting strategies (Diamond, 1985).

Over three decades later, there are still symptoms felt by victims of the Union Carbide gas leak, including a number of ophthalmic issues. Common eye-related symptoms that can be linked to the 1984 gas leak included poor vision, noncancerous growths, watery eyes, cataracts, and headaches (Satgunam and Chindelevitch, 2017). The Bhopal plant gas leak is perhaps one of the most dramatic instances of corporate violence.

We should note that part of the reason why corporate violence may be more likely to occur in developing countries, where transnational corporations set up shop with factories is that regulations are not uniform around the globe for customer and worker safety. One of the reason why companies will build factories outside of Europe and the U.S. is that they can find cheaper labor and more corporate friendly regulation elsewhere. In the Union Carbide case, though the cause was overall neglect, it was not necessarily a matter of violating industry regulations in its host country, India.

ORGANIZATIONAL DEATH

All organizations, no matter how well run, will from time to time be at risk for organizational death. *Organizational death* can be natural, as when a product or service is obsolete. Take the example of Blockbuster© video stores. The company had to shift gears when videos were replaced by DVDs. Once online streaming services like Netflix® became popular, the company was faced with the end of the very technology that created a vast empire of stores in the 1980s. Blockbuster© is still in business with its own streaming service, but is not nearly as popular as it once was. Other organizational deaths are unnatural and avoidable when an event is so big, as in the case of a company found guilty of criminal wrongdoing, that it rattles the confidence of regulators, investors, and customers.

Some types of industries are at greater risk for organizational death within them. For instance, new restaurants have high mortality rates as they can be expensive to start up, require constant attention to labor laws and food handling regulations, and are dependent on the loyalty of customers. Though a restaurant may be novel to begin with, repeat customers, along with word of mouth, will help establish them as neighborhood favorites. We have yet to see just how many restaurants will go out of business as a result of the COVID-19 pandemic.

Age seems to be a determining factor in whether an organization will survive or not. Too new, as in our restaurant example, a company might be run financially into the ground and heavily into debt before it has a chance to really take off. Without new investors to have faith in them and see them through the uncertainty in the beginning of a venture, companies can quickly fade away. The second age related "illness" that organizations can experience is inertia due to being older and obsolete in product or business practices (Freeman et al., 1983). Sometimes the death is slow and agonizing, as in the newspaper publishing business. Other times, death comes swiftly.

For some companies, their attitude of "if it isn't broken, why fix it?" causes the inertia in the first place. In this case, a company may ultimately stagnate, and as a result fail to act fast enough when there is a threat from a competitor. IBM, which has been around for over 100 years, is an example of a company that has off and on faced the possibility of failure due to stagnation. One more recent resurrection was in 2015, when it introduced new products and announced plans for a hybrid cloud environment (Lau, 2015).

We cannot discount the death throes of an organization as contributing to the risk for white collar crime or malfeasance. Out of fear, owners may turn to fraudulent accounting, including false information to banks in order to secure loans, to keep their businesses afloat. Workers may commit crimes if they believe that their company is the proverbial sinking ship, taking advantage of the chaos. When we come to the case of the energy broker company Enron in this book, we will see that people will resort to desperate measures if they feel threatened with the possible demise of their company.

SUMMARY

Though most organizations do their utmost best to make sure that they are following the letter of the law and good industry practices, inevitably things can and do go wrong. Best case scenario, the problem is minor and solutions are easily found. In worse case scenarios, people's lives and livelihoods are jeopardized. If the problem is made public, it may result in organizational death.

There are two primary motivators behind organizational malfeasance and crime: fear and greed. These motivators are not restricted to free market economies but can occur in any type of economy, including traditional economies more dependent on farming and command economies with centralized power, as in the example of communist countries. The fear can be of losing money, as in cases of falling profits, or of being found out when something has gone wrong with a product. Greed can be the inexplicable desire to make even more money even though it appears that an individual or company has more than enough resources to live on for the foreseeable future. In some cases, individuals and corporations are motivated by both fear and greed.

White collar malfeasance and crime are far from being victimless. Their repercussions to customers, employees, and the general public might be felt for decades to come. At the very least, people lose faith in institutions, as witnessed with the effect that the Challenger space shuttle disaster had the space shuttle program and NASA. In the most devasting cases there are injuries and losses of life, as witnessed in the corporate violence case of the Bhopal, India gas leak.

For all their flaws, most organizations will not experience large-scale scandals. But every organization is at risk for a number of things to go wrong, some of which are reparable and others that will result in ruined careers and the end of the organization itself. It is the reason why the list of characteristics we see in Weber's bureaucracy (Chapter 3), for all of its own flaws, continues to be one of the most common templates for efficient management along with laws and regulations.

Case Study ▪ What Happens in Hollywood (and New York) Doesn't Necessarily Stay in Hollywood: The Weinstein Scandal

From this chapter and throughout the rest of the book, we will be looking at what goes terribly wrong that results in either crime or malfeasance in organizations. This case study, as in subsequent chapters, will identify the type of crime, theories to explain why the crime may have occurred, social responses to the crime such as from the media, and how the criminal justice or civil court system addressed the crime.

We should note that the theories offered in this textbook in each case study are not exhaustive. There may be other explanations, including those coming from other disciplines such as economics and psychology. The cases will offer an excellent opportunity to spark discussion in class and with your fellow students on all the possible explanations for crime and bad behavior in organizations.

Background

There are few examples in recent decades of companies or company presidents that are as loathed as The Weinstein Company and one of its co-founders, Harvey Weinstein (Stebbins et al., 2018). During the 1990s there were a number of film companies emerging from the old studio system ran by only a handful of companies, with independent films gaining momentum. Whereas older studios seemed to be afraid to break barriers as social life changed in America, independent films were beginning to gain box office popularity, taking on controversial topics such as sexuality, race, and social inequality. The Weinstein Company was viewed as innovative and ahead of the curve when it came to independent film distribution.

Defining the Crime(s)

Sexual harassment and assault are legally defined differently, being physical or verbal, and may or may not result in sexual intercourse, consensual or otherwise. According to the U.S. government Equal Employment Opportunity Commission (n.d., retrieved from https://www.eeoc.gov/laws/types/sexual_harassment.cfm), "It is unlawful to harass a person (an applicant or employee) because of that person's sex. Harassment can include 'sexual harassment' or unwelcome sexual advances, requests for sexual favors, and other verbal or physical harassment of a sexual nature."

We do not ordinarily think of sexual harassment and sexual assault as white collar crimes. Indeed, they are more likely to be categorized as conventional crimes. However, in the case of Weinstein, his alleged crimes occurred in the workplace or in the course of conducting business. As a result, his alleged actions and subsequent camouflage, by himself and possibly by some of his employees, blurs the lines between conventional and white collar crimes.

Theories to Explain the Crime

Though there are many theories that we could turn to, including those that address the culture of organizations, in this case, Routine Activities Theory, or RAT for short (Cohen and Felson, 1979), is a good starting point. We will return to this theory again as we work our way through examples and cases elsewhere in this book.

In RAT, Cohen and Felson (1979) proposed that the way by which crimes occur requires three elements:

1. A motivated offender — You have to have a criminal willing to take a chance on committing the crime in the first place.
2. A suitable target — Unless you have a potential victim or an item to be harmed, vandalized, or stolen, it makes logical sense that a crime is unlikely to be committed.
3. Absence of someone to stop the crime — White collar and conventional criminals are much less likely to commit a crime if the target is being protected in some way, either by the presence of barriers, bystanders, or law enforcement.

Based on the evidence to date, Weinstein allegedly lured young women into various compromising acts of non-consensual sex. He has pleaded not guilty to all charges. Weinstein was found guilty, with the evidence pointing to his choice of victims based on their vulnerability. Weinstein was a powerful co-head of a successful film company and as a result had contact with a number of current and rising stars. Without anyone to protect some of them from the proverbial casting couch of Hollywood, they may have fallen prey to the promise of fame in exchange for sexual favors.

To further support this theory, there has been a number of reports of public outrage not directed solely at Weinstein, but also at the management at The Weinstein Company, including its board of directors, for allegedly protecting Weinstein's reputation for decades from the scandals (Stebbins et al. 2018). As Weinstein's crimes prove to be true in a court of law, management in companies could certainly be prove to be a guardian to the victims in the workplace and could have prevented further sexual mistreatment from occurring.

Social and Media Responses

The media attention surrounding the Weinstein case has resulted in a number of additional women coming forward and accusing him of sexual harassment or assault. As of 2017, 87 alleged victims have accused Weinstein of sexual misconduct ranging from harassment to rape, including some of Hollywood's most respected actors — Rosanna Arquette, Kate Beckinsale, Salma Hayek, and Ashley Judd, to name a few (Moniuszko and Kelly, 2017). Whether Weinstein will be charged and convicted in all the criminal cases is yet to be seen and somewhat improbable.

The company was forced to distance itself from the Weinstein name. Shortly after the scandal broke, the company went into a financial tailspin. The Weinstein Company ultimately had to be sold to a private equity firm, Lantern Capital Partners (Isidore, 2018; Sperling, 2019), after filing bankruptcy in 2018. With the sale and company reorganization, the company is now being advertised as being more pro-female, with Maria Contreras-Sweet, part of an investor group that bought the company, leading the charge stating in a press statement that it would now be built on best practices of governance and transparency (Desta, 2018).

Weinstein's brother, Bob, is an unfortunate victim of the collateral damage that the Weinstein scandal has created in the press. When the company was sold, both brothers were equity owners who owned a sizable portion of stock, all of which became devalued as a result of the scandal. Bob Weinstein was also forced to step down from the company's board. However, it is unknown at this time as to whether Bob was equally complicit in covering up his brother's alleged sexual misconduct. He has not been charged with any criminal wrongdoing. In 2019, it was reported that he was launching a new production company, Watch This Entertainment, in the hopes that he could revitalize his career away from his brother's alleged crimes (Sperling, 2019). Interesting to note that the first film currently planned to be distributed by the new company is an animated feature, with female actress Tea Leoni staring and co-producing (Sperling, 2019). This is certainly a departure from the more "edgy" films distributed by the Weinstein Company. It is important to note that the Weinstein case was instrumental in launching the #MeToo movement. The publicity surrounding this case brought to light a workplace problem that has largely been either resolved behind closed doors or unfortunately shrugged off as "business as usual" with people in powerful positions.

In academia, the Weinstein case, as well as the #MeToo movement, has in turn sparked a new round of inquiry into sexual harassment in the workplace, as well as new attention to discrimination. For example, Lawhon (2018) examines the issues that happen within higher education, once a bastion of hypermasculinity where the greater majority of professors were male and sexual harassment was less likely to be reported.

Criminal Justice and Policy Responses

Law enforcement is not always the first to get wind of possible crimes in the workplace. In the Weinstein case, it was investigative reporters who first made the alleged sexual harassment, sexual assault, and sexual abuse allegations public (McBain, 2019). Though there had been rumors for a number of years about Weinstein's questionable behavior, there was little in the way of substantiated stories.

It is not uncommon in the case of the victims of sexual abuse in the workplace to be reluctant to come forward with their stories. For women in particular, there is the concern that if they do tell, it may very well make it difficult for them to find work again in a particular industry. The same can be said about whistleblowers in general. Weinstein is certainly not the first Hollywood executive to be suspected of abusing women in the film industry. However, he has certainly been found, at least in the media, one of the worst alleged offenders.

Once victims started coming forward, law enforcement had no choice but to conduct their own investigation. Originally indicted in 2018 with six counts of sexual assault in New York, one of the counts was dropped due to inconsistencies in the story of one alleged victim (BBC, 2019). The Los Angeles District Attorney's Office may be considering adding additional charges to the current list of indictments against Weinstein after their own two-year investigation (CBS News, 2019). If new charges are brought against Weinstein and if he is found guilty on all charges in both New York and California, he runs the risk of spending the rest of his life in prison. With Weinstein currently 67 years old, even receiving 25 years in prison is potentially a life sentence as it is.

Civil judgment against Weinstein and former board members as the Weinstein Company is still pending, with lawyers for the plaintiffs and respondents in negotiations for a settlement. Weinstein is still in negotiations as of December 2019 (BBC, 2019). A civil judgement by no means assumes criminal guilt.

Weinstein's trial began in January 2020, hence the use of the term "alleged" at the beginning of this case study. We do have to be reminded that in the American criminal justice system, the indicted is assumed to be not guilty until found otherwise in a court of law. Even if Weinstein was found innocent on all charges, as American actor Tom Hanks told the British Broadcasting Company (BBC), there is little chance that he can come back from the scandal in a similar fashion as his brother, with his name forever being associated with workplace sexual misconduct and the proverbial Hollywood casting couch (BBC, 2019).

Whereas cases of sexual harassment are more likely to end up in civil court, the more serious crime of sexual assault is more likely to be handled within the jurisdiction of criminal court. In both types of cases, they are challenging in either court, as there needs to be witnesses and/or physical evidence to strengthen the case against the alleged offender. One might suspect that even though Weinstein is suspected of committing these types of offenses against women for decades, it is only recently that alleged victims have come forward.

Weinstein, was ultimately convicted of a number of charges of sexual assault in 2020 and sentenced to 23 years in prison (Levenson et al., 2020). His case launched an avalanche of discussion about sexual misconduct in the workplace. It resulted in human resources departments everywhere to be even more diligent in their compliance with Title IV as it applies to sexual harassment and reporting of misconduct.

In a twist of fate, Weinstein tested positive for the COVID-19 virus while serving time in prison at the Wende Correctional Facility, near Buffalo, New York (BBC News, 2020). His extradition to California in 2020 to face charges was been delayed due to the pandemic.

Unanswered Questions and Unresolved Issues Related to the Case

This case is still unfolding at the writing of this book. In the meantime, as in the case of alleged employee abuses, whether general harassment or sexual assault by superiors, it is still too early to know if all of Weinstein's alleged victims have been identified. An additional unanswered question and possibly unresolved issue is whether the Weinstein case is only the tip of the iceberg when it comes to Hollywood executives covering up criminal behavior, either committed by one of their own or by famous movie or television stars.

Again, we have to question how much the conspiracies and cover ups can be considered white collar crimes, even if the accusations of sexual harassment, assault, or abuse fall more clearly under the umbrella of conventional crime. The key to solving the problem may lie in appealing to the financial sensibilities of companies, even if they do not proactively address problems of sexual harassment. As in the case of the Weinstein Company, it had to scramble after the scandal broke, to the extent that it was forced to rebrand itself altogether in order to remain viable.

Sources

British Broadcasting Company. (2019) Harvey Weinstein timeline: How the scandal unfolded. *Entertainment and Arts.* Dec 20. Retrieved from https://www.bbc.com/news/entertainment-arts-41594672.

British Broadcasting Company. (2020) Coronavirus: Harvey Weinstein tests positive. US & Canada. March 23. Retrieved from https://www.bbc.com/news/world-us-canada-52000173.

CBS News. (2019) More charges against Harvey Weinstein? Video. Dec 26. Retrieved from https://www.cbsnews.com/video/more-charges-against-harvey-weinstein-possible/.

Desta, Y. (2018) $500 million deal saves Weinstein Company – but Harvey's reportedly getting nothing. *Vanity Fair.* March 2. Retrieved from https://www.vanityfair.com/hollywood/2018/03/the-weinstein-company-500-million-deal-harvey-bob.

Isidore, C. (2018) Remains of the Weinstein Company sold to the only real bidder. *CNN Business.* May 2. Retrieved from https://money.cnn.com/2018/05/02/media/weinstein-company-bidder/index.html.

Lawhon, M. (2018) Post-Weinstein academia. *ACME: International E-journal for Critical Geography.* Vol 17, Issue 3:634-642.

Levenson, E., L. del Valle and S. Moghe. (2020) Harvey Weinstein sentenced to 23 years in prison after addressing his accusers in court. *CNN.* March 11. Retrieved from https://www.cnn.com/2020/03/11/us/harvey-weinstein-sentence/index.html.

McBain, S. (2019) The making of #MeToo: How Harvey Weinstein was exposed. *New Statesman.* Nov 1. Vol 148, Issue 5495:42-43.

Moniuszko, S. M. and C. Kelly. (2017) Harvey Weinstein scandal: A complete list of the 87 accusers. Oct 27. Retrieved from https://www.usatoday.com/story/life/people/2017/10/27/weinstein-scandal-complete-list-accusers/804663001/.

Sperling, N. (2019) Bob Weinstein, brother of disgraced mogul, starts new production company. *The New York Times.* Oct 12. Retrieved from https://www.nytimes.com/2019/10/12/business/media/bob-weinstein-production-company.html.

Stebbins, S., E. Comen, M. B. Sauter, and C. Stockdale. (2018) Bad reputation: America's top 20 most-hated companies. *USA Today.* Feb 1. Retrieved from https://www.usatoday.com/story/money/business/2018/02/01/bad-reputation-americas-top-20-most-hated-companies/1058718001/.

U.S. Equal Employment Opportunity Commission. (n.d.) Sexual harassment. Laws, Regulations, Guidance & MOUs: Types of Discriminations. Retrieved from https://www.eeoc.gov/laws/types/sexual_harassment.cfm.

GLOSSARY

Alienation of workers   A topic that is particularly popular among Marxist and Neo-Marxist scholars, proposes that the nature of work in contemporary life creates workers who are not connected with the work they produce.

Autocrat   Leadership in which the manager, supervisor has absolute power over workers.

Bankruptcy   Lacking the necessary funds or finances to repay debt; sometimes results in filing for bankruptcy with civil court in order to consolidate, reduce, or eliminate debt.

Bounded rationality   First identified by Herbert Simon (1982), bounded rationality model proposes that decisions are made on the limited amount of information and time available to make those decisions.

Corporate violence   Injury or death that happens to customers, employees, or civilians as a result of calculated neglect, usually as a cost-saving measure, by a company or corporation.

Espionage Act of 1917   United States bill passed to make it a punishable offense to speak, write, or act against the government or military, including submitting false reports or interfering with war efforts. The bill was passed while the United States was still involved in WWI.

Fiduciary responsibility   An individual's responsibility through their occupation, whether employed or self-employed, to secure the finances and/or material goods, including intellectual property of clients, customers, and their employer.

Gender politics   The ongoing politics and debate about roles people are supposed to have in and out of the workplace, depending on their biological sex.

Iron Cage of Bureaucracy   Weber's (1922) cautionary tale about the downside of bureaucratic structures where they become so rule-bound, nothing gets accomplished.

Malfeasance   Any ethical or illegal wrongdoing by an individual or organization.

Micromanagement   Leadership style where the manager takes charge of every aspect of day-to-day operations.

Organizational death   Conditions where internal or external forces result in the end of an organization, company, or corporation.

Span of control   The number of employees that a supervisor has working directly below them and that they are responsible for.

Whistleblowers   Individuals who bring to the attention of management or the public activities within their organizations that might be unethical or illegal.

Whistleblower Protection Act (WPA), 1989   Along with the False Claims Act passed by Congress, these acts assure that whistleblowers cannot be retaliated against or fired when they come forward to report mismanagement, malfeasance, or crime in the organization they work for. The act also provides the whistleblower with anonymity and immunity from prosecution.

White collar malfeasance   Ethical or illegal wrongdoing within the context of white collar occupations (e.g., attorneys, accountants, doctors).

White collar crime   First identified in Edwin Sutherland's 1939 address at the annual conference of the American Sociological Association, defined as a crime that is committed by individuals with respectable and high social statuses within their occupations.

REFERENCES AND SUGGESTED READINGS

American Cancer Society. (2014) The study that helped spur the U.S. stop-smoking movement. Jan 9. Retrieved from https://www.cancer.org/latest-news/the-study-that-helped-spur-the-us-stop-smoking-movement.html.

Ayer, M. and S. Glover. (2018) California's largest utility provider's role in wildfires is under scrutiny. *CNN*. Dec 19. Retrieved from https://www.cnn.com/2018/12/19/us/camp-fire-pge-invs/index.html.

Bernstein, C. (2005) *The secret man: The story of Watergate's Deep Throat*. New York: Simon and Schuster.

Bilton, N. (Host) (2019, Nov 22) Can a whistleblower really bring down Trump? *Inside the Hive by Vanity Fair* [Audio podcast] Retrieved from https://podcasts.apple.com/us/podcast/inside-the-hive-with-nick-bilton/id1232383877.

Clifton, J. (2017) The world's broken workplace. *Gallup*. Retrieved from https://news.gallup.com/opinion/chairman/212045/world-broken-workplace.aspx.

Cunningham, L. (2015) In a big move, Accenture will get rid of annual performance reviews and rankings. *The Washington Post*. July 21. Retrieved from https://www.washingtonpost.com/news/on-leadership/wp/2015/07/21/in-big-move-accenture-will-get-rid-of-annual-performance-reviews-and-rankings/?utm_term=.b7bff359321a.

Dewar, R. D. and D. P. Simet. (1981) A level specific perdition of spans of control examining the effects of size, technology, and specialization. *Academy of Management Journal*. Vol 24, No 1:5-24.

Diamond, S. (1985) The Bhopal disaster: How it happened. *The New York Times*. Jan 28.

Freeman, J., G. R. Carroll, and M. T. Hannan. (1983) The liability of newness: Age dependence in organizational death rates. *American Sociological Review*. Oct Vol 48, No 5:692-710.

Garcia-Carmona, M., M. D. Marin, and R. Aguayo. (2019) Burnout syndrome of secondary school teachers: A systematic review and meta-analysis. *Social Psychology of Education*. Vol 22:189-208.

Hansen, L. L. and S. Movahedi. (2010) Wall Street scandals: The myth of individual greed. *Sociological Forum*. Vol 25, No 2:367-374.

Howell, E. (2019) Columbia disaster: What happened, what NASA learned. *Spaceflight, Space.com*. Feb 1. Retrieved from https://www.space.com/19436-columbia-disaster.html.

KGO-TV. (2019) PG&E Chapter 11 Bankruptcy: Here's how it will affect customers, employees, and shareholders. Jan 29. Retrieved from https://abc7news.com/business/pg-e-bankruptcy-heres-how-itll-affect-customers-employees-shareholders/5076360/.

Lau, C. (2015) IBM's stagnation is ending. *IT World Canada*. April 28. Retrieved from https://www. itworldcanada.com/blog/ibms-stagnation-is-ending/374115.

Marjoua, Y. and K. J. Bozic. (2012) Brief history of quality movement in US healthcare. *Current Reviews in Musculoskeletal Medicine*. Dec, 5 (4): 265-273. Retrieved from https://www.ncbi. nlm.nih.gov/pmc/articles/PMC3702754/.

Miceli, M. P. and J. P. Near. (1994) Relationships among valued congruence, perceived victimization, and retaliation against whistleblowers. *Journal of Management*. Vol 20 No 4:773-794.

Michel, C. (2018) Cognitive dissonance resolution strategies after exposure to corporate violence scenarios. *Critical Criminology*. Mar, Vol 26, No 1:1-28.

Meyer, J.W. and B. Rowan. (1977) *Institutionalized organizations: Formal structure as myth and ceremony. American Journal of Sociology*. Sept, Vol. 83, No. 2: 340-363.

McDonald, G. (2017) Flying cars are (still) coming: Should we believe the hype? All Tech Considered, NPR. April 25. Retrieved from https://www.npr.org/sections/alltechconsidered/2017/04/ 25/525540611/flying-cars-are-still-coming-should-we-believe-the-hype.

Near, J. P. and M. P. Miceli. (1996) Whistle-blowing: Myth and reality. *Journal of Management*. Vol 22, No 3:507-526.

Office of the Inspector General. (n.d.) Whistleblower Protection Act (WPA). United States Consumer Product Safety Commission. Retrieved from https://www.cpsc.gov/About-CPSC/Inspector-General/Whistleblower-Protection-Act-WPA.

Peterson, H. (2020) Nordstrom is permanently closing 16 stores in 9 states. Here's the list. *Business Insider*. May 8. Retrieved from https://www.businessinsider.com/nordstrom-will-close-16-stores-list-2020-5

Ritzer, G. (2011) *The McDonaldization of society*. Thousand Oaks, CA: Pine Forge Press. 6th ed.

Rosenberg, J. M. (2017) After a Katrina or Harvey, businesses suffer long after water recedes – many never recover. *Associated Press, NOLA.com*. Sept 6. Retrieved from https://www.nola.com/ news/business/article_06c0e4bb-0061-5a30-b099-c40e8519231b.html

Rosoff, S., H. Pontell, and R. Tillman. (2013) *Profit without honor: White collar crime and the looting of America*. New York: Pearson Education. 6th ed.

Rubio, P. F. (2010) *There is always work at the Post Office: African-American Postal workers and the fight for jobs, justice, and equality*. Chapel Hill: University of North Carolina Press.

Rubio, P. F. (2018) After the storm: Postal politics and labor relations following the 1970 U.S. Postal wildcat strike, 1970-1981. *Employee Responsibilities and Rights Journal*. March 1. Vol 30:65-80.

Satgunam, P. N. and L. Chindelevich. (2017) Vision screening results in a cohort of Bhopal gas disaster survivors. *Current Science*. May 25. Vol 112, No 10:2085-2088.

Securities and Exchange Commission (SEC). (2019) SEC awards $50 million to two whistleblowers. Press Release. March 26. Retrieved from https://www.sec.gov/news/press-release/2019-42.

Simon, H. A (1982) *Models of bounded rationality*. Cambridge, MA: MIT Press.

Smaili, N. and P. Arroyo. (2019) Categorization of whistleblowers using the whistleblowing triangle. *Journal of Business Ethics*. Vol 157:95-117.

Smith, A. (2018) More employers ditch performance appraisals. SHRM. May 18. Retrieved from https://www.shrm.org/resourcesandtools/legal-and-compliance/employment-law/pages/more-employers-ditch-performance-appraisals.aspx.

Vaughn, D. (2016) *The Challenger launch decision: Risky technology, culture, and deviance at NASA*. Chicago: The University of Chicago Press.

Van Vugt, M., S. F. Jepson, C. M. Hart, and D. De Cremer. (2004) Autocratic leadership in social dilemmas: A threat to group stability. *Journal of Experimental Social Psychology*. Vol 40:1-13.

Wigand, J. S. (1995) Testimony transcript, *The State of Mississippi v. Brown and Williamson*. June 25, 2019. Retrieved from http://www.jeffreywigand.com/pascagoula.php.

Chapter THREE

What You Know vs. Who You Know

The role of social networks in white collar crimes

> Six degrees of separation doesn't mean that everyone is linked to everyone else in just six steps. It means that a very small number of people are linked to everyone else in a few steps, and the rest of us are linked to the world through those special few.
>
> —*Malcom Gladwell, The Tipping Point:*
> *How Little Things Can Make a Big Difference (2000)*

Chapter Objectives

- Introduce the reader to basic social network analysis theories and terminology.
- Connect social network theory with conventional theories that explain white collar crimes.
- Identify when white collar crime and organized crime networks are connected.
- Demonstrate how criminal behavior can be learned within social networks.
- Define the social pressures that social networks exert on individuals to conform, either to legitimate or illegitimate behavior.

Key Terms

Agency	Forbidden triad
Black market	Formal social networks
Broker	Free-rider
Clique	Hegemony
Coercive isomorphism	Informal social networks
Differential Association Theory	Mimetic isomorphism
Directional ties	Network boundaries
Embeddedness	Network noise

Node   Social network actor
Normative isomorphism   Social Network Analysis (SNA)
Peer pressure   Social network tie
Reciprocal ties   Structural hole
Social contagion

INTRODUCTION

Most of what people think of today when we hear the term *"social networks"* is what we find in social media by way of Facebook®, Instagram®, Twitter®, and other Internet platforms. Though these networks can be conduits in which crimes are committed, we will first identify the more traditional social networks, those that are created in and out of the workplace. We will also be discussing the differences between *formal* and *informal social networks*.

Social network analysis (SNA) in the social sciences was first explored in the 19th century by sociologists and anthropologists, though anthropologists didn't historically describe what they did in research as SNA. Nevertheless, that was what they were doing whenever they attempted to construct tribal kinship ties. In fact, family, defined as people who you are related to by blood, marriage, or adoption, is the very first social network you belonged to. Though sociologists have used social network methodology, grounded in mathematical and qualitative narrative telling social science for decades, anthropologists are just now coming around to using some of the same formal technology, including computer programs specifically for SNA.

SNA is yet another tool in understanding white collar crime offending that compliments traditional criminological theories. It isn't enough to understand the formal network structure in organizations, as we defined in Chapter 2. It is perhaps more critical to identify the characteristics of the informal structure, as that is more likely where criminal white collar behavior will take place.

BASIC SOCIAL NETWORK TERMS

There are a number of terms that we can use to describe the social dynamics in a network. Some of these you may be more familiar with, as some of the language used in SNA has crept into common every day vocabulary. For instance, we understand a *clique* in school to be a group of students who hang out together on the basis of similar interests and lifestyles. As this is not a course textbook for SNA, we will stick to some of the more basic terminology.

For starters, when we describe people or things in a network, we usually refer to them as *nodes* or *actors*. *Node* is a term that is used in social network graft theory, which is beyond the scope of this textbook, and is interchangeable with the term "actor." We will stick to the terms "actor" or "actors" to refer to an individual or group of individuals in a social network.

When we say that two actors are connected in a social network, we say that they have a *tie*. Without going into too much detail, there can be different kinds of ties. We will look at the two most common ones that we will find in a criminal network: *directional ties* and *reciprocal ties*. A *directional tie* is one where the action/feelings/transaction is identifiably going in one direction. For instance, someone might feel like they can confide in you, but you do not feel like you can share your secrets so readily with them.

Reciprocal ties are when action/feelings/transaction go in both directions between actors. It is what we see in friendship networks where everyone likes everyone else. Of course, this may not always be the case, so you may possibly find both directional and reciprocal ties in the same network.

Putting this into context of a criminal conspiracy, you might find that some people are willing to co-offend, others might be trying to gain membership to the network, and others may be trying to create new alliances. If you examine organized crime families or gangs, you will find people on the fringes of the network who do favors for established members in order to be accepted. Think of it as a type of initiation. After all, people who want to join criminal networks are more than likely going to have to prove their loyalty to the group in some fashion. This is very common in street gangs and similarly so among Wall Street elites who commit crimes (Hansen, 2014).

A *broker* is a very powerful position in a network. The role of the broker is to connect two parts of a network that wouldn't otherwise be connected. Take the example of a sustainability expert. These are individuals who understand the needs of both the business community and of the engineers working on a project. Because the business community and scientific community many times do not speak the same technical language, nor have the same goals, the sustainability expert acts as a translator. But as translation goes, how well the information gets passed from one end to the other end of a network is only as good as the translator.

Where the broker position plays an important role in white collar crime or in any criminal network is that it is both a very financially lucrative position, but the most dangerous one to be in. Think of the role of a drug dealer who has to not only work with the drug supplier, but also with the customer. The drug dealer is left more exposed on the street to law enforcement and rival dealers than the drug supplier. In order to maintain this powerful position, it also requires maintaining *structural holes.*

A concept introduced by Burt (1992), a *structural hole* is the gap between two people or networks who would not ordinarily be connected except for the *broker* between them. If you consider the way that secrets have a way of getting out, *structural holes* are very valuable to maintain in order to have fewer people involved who possess full knowledge of a conspiracy.

According to Granovetter (1973), a structural hole will not stay that way forever. He described this as the *forbidden triad*. It is exhausting to maintain a structural hole in a network, especially in criminal networks, if it is strategic to hang onto it in order to remain competitive. There might be others in the network who are trying to gain more power, willing to step over whomever they have to in order to do so. *If A has strong ties to B and A likewise has strong ties to C, sooner or later B and C, at the very least, will be aware of each other's existence.*

Take the example of infidelity. It is rare for an extramarital affair to go on forever undetected without the spouse and the girl/boyfriend finding out about one another, which can become an expensive proposition in some divorce proceedings. Like in the case of extramarital affairs, if a broker loses their advantage of keeping people away from one another, it may result in a financial loss. In extreme cases, it might even cost someone their life if this occurs within organized crime circles and there is any sense of betrayal requiring retribution.

TRIADS

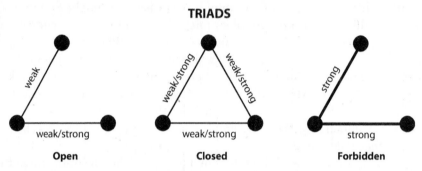

| Open | Closed | Forbidden |

EXHIBIT 3.1 ‖ **"Forbidden Triad" (Granovetter, 1973)** *Source:* Central European University, Retrieved from https://networkdatascience.ceu.edu/article/2016-11-11/secret-power-forbidden-triads

Sometimes there are actors in a social network who are more powerful than others. When an actor has more or the most ties in a network, as compared to everyone else, we say that they have *hegemony*. The term hegemony implies that someone has more power or is dominant within the network. In theory, the more actors that you know within a network, the more powerful you will be. It's even better if you also possess a lot of ties to other networks as well. Of course, we have to say something about the quality of ties.

Just because there is a connected tie between two actors doesn't necessarily mean that the connection is strong. There is a difference between casual acquaintances and close friends. We can say the same thing about coworkers. You may work at the same place, but that doesn't mean that all employees feel equally close to one another, though we know that friendship ties do come out of work ties (Hansen, 2014; Hansen and Movahedi, 2010).

One way to get around the deficiencies of network analysis, where it is a challenge to measure the strength of a tie, is to measure how many times the actors interact. In criminological terms, it's the difference between whether two Wall Street bankers exchange illegal insider trader information once or if it is an ongoing exchange of information, or whether someone defrauds a customer once, by selling a faulty product, or continues to defraud the same customer over and over again. Likewise, if someone purchases drugs from a drug dealer once, or has ongoing transactions, there is a distinct difference in how strong that tie is between the actors.

Network noise is something we have all experienced within our friendship networks, workplaces, and communities where we live. The noise we refer to is all the misinformation and interruptions that happen between people as something is being transmitted through the network. Certainly, unsubstantiated rumors can be considered network noise. *Social contagion* can happen very quickly in social networks, where news, whether true or not, spreads like wildfire. We can certainly find plenty of examples from social media websites, where deceptive news is reposted again and again, even when it has been proven to be based on falsehoods.

Law in the Real World: GoFundMe Crowdsourcing

(Sources: Simko-Bednarski, CNN, Retrieved from https://www.cnn.com/2019/01/09/us/gofundme-bobbitt-arrest-warrant/index.html; Alsup and Simon, CNN Retrieved from https://www.cnn.com/2017/11/24/us/couple-raises-money-for-homeless-man/index.html*)*

The GoFundMe website (*gofundme.com*) is a well-meaning way by which to raise money for a number of worthy causes, plus help individuals and families who are in dire need due to any number of life's setbacks. Crowdfunding is the 21st century equivalent of passing the hat around for donations. Unfortunately, it has become one more way for criminals to commit fraud.

In 2017, a story circulated on the Internet about a good Samaritan, Johnny Bobbitt, Jr., who had supposedly given his last $20 to a stranded motorist. Kate McClure was allegedly almost out of gas on Interstate 95 in Philadelphia. At the time, Bobbitt was reported to be a homeless veteran, further making the story poignant.

The story quickly spread through social media, attracting news agencies, who aired the story. Kate McClure and her boyfriend, Mark D'Amico, set up a fundraiser through the GoFundMe website, supposedly in order to help Bobbitt to get back on his feet and off the streets. The fundraiser resulted in more than $400,000 in donations within days after the news story became viral through a news article published online. Almost instantaneously donations poured in from all over the world, demonstrating just how far viral news can spread in a relatively short amount of time. The donations were all deposited into McClure's bank account.

Things turned ugly when Bobbitt sued McClure and D'Amico in civil court, accusing them of using the greater part of donations, approximately $300,000, for their own benefit, alleging that they squandered funds on luxury items. By November 2018, prosecutors accused Bobbitt, McClure, and D'Amico of taking part in a fraudulent fundraiser, criminally charging them with second-degree theft by deception and conspiracy to commit theft by deception.

At the time of this writing, McClure has pleaded guilty and has been convicted, admitting that she and her now ex-boyfriend had made up the story. She faces four years in state prison. Bobbitt has also pleaded guilty. Both McClure and Bobbitt claimed that D'Amico was the mastermind of the scheme. D'Amico is currently awaiting trial after pleading not guilty to the charges. GoFundMe refunded most of the money that people donated once they became aware that the fundraiser was more than likely fraudulent.

Discussion Questions

1. Why do you think that this story in particular touched so many people's hearts in this day and age of endless "feel good" stories on social media?
2. Why did the news travel so fast through Internet sources if it was a story originally reported locally by television news?
3. As the U.S. court system assumes innocence before conviction, why do you think that GoFundMe felt compelled to issue refunds to donors even before the court cases were decided?

If you recall from the last chapter, we talked about bounded rationality. The decisions people make are only as good as the information that they have to make those decisions. If there is a lot of false information floating around through a network, whether it is intended to be spread or not, it can have consequences on decision making processes.

When we discuss *network boundaries*, we are talking about all the actors who are identifiable within a network. For the researcher, this is very similar to snowball sampling, where you ask everyone that you have already identified to be members of a network who else should be included in the membership list. This is, of course, a challenge when we are looking at criminal conspiracies. Even law enforcement has a difficult time identifying everyone who has taken part in criminal activities within a network, whether examining organized crime groups, gangs, or links between white collar criminals.

One term that is important to understand in white collar crime is the concept of *embeddedness*. As we will see later in this chapter in defining formal and informal social networks, sometimes there is a network embedded within another network. Generally, we find that people who have professional ties will sooner or later form friendship networks.

For instance, you might find that people are connected because they work at the same place. If they in turn form friendships that result in spending time socializing outside of work, you now have a friendship network that is embedded within the formal work network. Or in the case of white collar crime, people who you start hanging out with socially outside of work may become your co-conspirators. We will see this theme again in Chapter 4, when we further discuss embedded networks and financial crimes.

Given the example of coworkers who decide to go to lunch together on a regular basis or out for drinks on Friday nights, they might start liking one another outside the context of work relationships as they find out what else they have in common. It might be that they have similar family dynamics or they share the same passion for sports. This can also create problems if in turn there is a falling out between people who have formed relationships outside of work, as in the case of office romances. A couple may no longer be romantically involved, but still have to work with one another professionally. It's the very reason why many companies now have "nonfraternization" clauses in contracts, where coworkers risk being fired if they fail to disclose that they are dating each other. In some companies, dating between coworkers is completely forbidden, though in some states (e.g., California) employers cannot legally do so. Where it is the most problematic is when a boss attempts to date a subordinate.

Finally, we should have some discussion about *agency*. As close as people are in a social network, we can never be sure if they are acting in the best interest of the network or acting out of their own self-interest. They may do so in order to minimize any social or financial cost. Within the theory, it is proposed that actors may be more afraid to take risks, may be more rational, and may be more narrowly self-interested (Bosse and Phillips, 2016).

Self-interest theories also dictate that individuals are still bounded by social norms of reciprocity and fairness, even when they are acting out of self-interest (Bosse and Phillips, 2016). It is difficult to understand that any of this is true in the case of white collar crimes, as criminals tend to be risk-takers with little thought to the consequences to others (Hansen, 2011). In the case of white collar crimes that occur on Wall Street, the professions within the financial sector tend to attract risk-takers (Hansen, 2011). Agency and self-interest are best used in discussions of white collar crimes happening within networks and the process of plea bargaining with prosecutors when criminals are indicted.

FORMAL SOCIAL NETWORKS

The most common understanding of the formal network is through the hierarchy in an organizational chart, discussed in both Chapters 1 and 2. Though not all organizational charts have quite the same vertical and horizontal structures, they share common characteristics. One thing that is a concern in any organizational chart is the span of control. As we found in Chapter 2, this is effectively the number of individuals that a manager can supervise without everything becoming chaotic. The reality is that organizations do not always adhere to logic when it comes to putting a number of employees under the control of a manager.

We can examine an example of a span of control that was somewhat unmanageable during a major construction project in Southern California. While one of the toll roads was being constructed, one of the supervisors was responsible for both day and night shift operations. There were a number of foremen on both shifts working under the direction of the supervisor. However, the supervisor was essentially required to be on call 24 hours a day, six days a week. The supervisor reported putting in anywhere from 72 to 90 hours a week of work and ultimately was in charge of hundreds of pieces of earth-moving machinery during the three-year construction of the toll road. Thankfully no major issues developed during the construction of the toll road, a credit to the supervisor and the company he worked for. But the supervisor, a married father with two elementary school-aged children, at the time ultimately was overwhelmed in both his personal and professional lives.

In the case above, the company may have had too few bosses. The opposite, or as *Psychology Today* termed it, "multiple boss madness" (Taylor, 2011), can happen as well. It is difficult to report to a number of bosses, resulting in on-the-job stress. This in itself can lead to workplace deviance, as one easygoing boss may be played off against a more "by the rules" one. This is not unlike a set of parents with distinctly different parenting styles, where children can learn to manipulate them, particularly in the case of divorce.

Taylor notes that there are a number of red flags associated with "multiple boss madness" (2011, *Psychology Today*, available at https://www.psychologytoday.com/us/blog/tame-your-terrible-office-tyrant/201102/how-deal-multiple-boss-madness):

- There is in-fighting among members of management. This in turn can lead to deviance in the work place if bosses are fighting among themselves for employee loyalty.
- Employees don't know whom to please or when. This can lead to confusion as to when work needs to be completed and can result in sometimes illegal corners being cut to satisfy ambiguous deadlines.
- Employees are confused as to whether they should handle the conflict on their own or get Human Resources involved. If they point out that there is a problem with management, it might be turned back on them and they could be accused of wrongdoing.

There are a number of ways to determine what the span of control should be, including the level of expertise that is required for a job, as well as concerns for safety. These numbers can range on average, from 5 people to upwards of

20 individuals per supervisor. In reality, there are managers who are responsible for far too many workers. A picture of an organizational chart with some indication of what a normal span of control should look like is depicted in Exhibit 3.2.

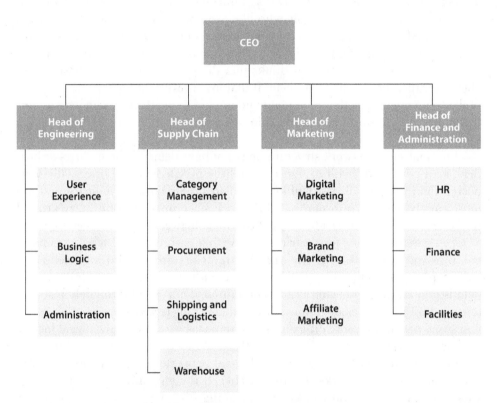

EXHIBIT 3.2 | **Example of an Organizational Chart.** *Source:* https://www.lucidchart.com/pages/templates/org-chart

Another formal network is one that is created between companies or organizations. In supply chain economics, the relationships between manufacturer, distributor, buyer, and ultimately the consumer are formal relationships that generally leave some type of paper trail. Many times, these network ties between companies and organizations are further formalized by legal contracts.

If we go back to Weber's definition of bureaucracy and the hierarchy, the relationships within and between formal networks are supposed to be impersonal. The purpose of this is to maintain stability. Consequently, because we are really talking about human beings, these relationships can become informal, including strong friendships forming. This runs counter to the transactions between actors in formal networks that should take place "through loose connections of individuals who maintain impersonal and constantly shifting exchange ties." (Uzzi, 1997, p 35; Powell, 1990). This in turn can lead to informal social networks forming between people with the same goals, in some cases criminally focused.

INFORMAL SOCIAL NETWORKS

In some instances, the informal social network is more effective in getting things accomplished than the formal network. Informal social networks are those that form organically between people who like each other, want to work with each other, or find it advantageous to form an alliance outside of the formal, hierarchical structure. This is common with social ties that are based on nepotism. Say, for example, a lower level employee thinks that there is a problem and hasn't been able to get their boss to listen to them. If that lower level employee is the offspring of the company owner, they just might end up discussing the problem over a family dinner. This in turn might move things along much more quickly in resolving the problem.

Informal social network structures may not have definable boundaries or borders, as it is more difficult to figure out all the people who are informally connected than the formal ties. Unlike formal social network boundaries that are more clearly defined, informal social network structures are a bit fuzzy around the edges. Generally, there are no legal contracts between informal social ties.

You wouldn't enter into a friendship with someone with a legal document spelling out the terms of the friendship. Certainly, criminals who are co-conspirators would not intentionally have a legal contract spelling out the details of a crime that is going to be committed. That could ultimately result in a paper trail that traces the crime back to them. This is why the size of an informal social network is more difficult to determine, as we see with the illegal insider trading networks during the 1970s and 1980s on Wall Street (Hansen, 2011).

It is important to note that informal social networks are many times embedded within formal networks (Hansen, 2011). It is commonly said that "it's not what you know, but who you know," meaning that the person holding power may not be the person you think it is. Many times, when you wish to get something accomplished or need information, the best person to speak to in an organization is an administrative assistant or executive secretary, who might have eyes and ears everywhere compared to their more myopic boss.

It is critical in understanding white collar crime to understand embeddedness of informal networks within formal networks. Our next case study involves this very situation, where Dennis Levine, a Wall Street executive working in finance, created complex informal networks of sources of insider information within and outside of his company during the 1970s and 1980s.

PEER PRESSURE AND INFLUENCE IN SOCIAL NETWORKS

When we generally think about *peer pressure*, we automatically think about the pressure to fit in during our teen years. However, we can experience peer pressure throughout our lives. The term "peer" means nothing more than someone who possesses the same status as we do. Your fellow students are your peers.

Within competitive industries, like finance, our peers may also be our greatest competition. Whether it is competition for sales or for new customers, it may be that the very people we work with are chasing after the same professional goals. If you look at most organizational charts, there is only so much room for promotion.

Much is said about team building and "team spirit," particularly in sales, so that members of the team are working towards the betterment of the organization. This works, in theory, if compensation, like job performance bonuses, are dependent on team efforts. However, in many positions involving sales, including in the financial industry, people are individually compensated with commissions and bonuses. They may have a 100 percent commission-based income, a salary that is drawn against commission, or commission paid above their set guaranteed salary. In any case where there are commissions and bonuses, there will be competition, even between friends.

The encouragement of teamwork is a double-edged sword. On one end, the peer pressure to perform may indeed motivate individuals to do better working in groups instead of individually. However, within the context of white collar crime, any pressure to use deviant means to reach common goals results in the possibility of the whole network being corrupted. Conversely, team work may result in the discouragement of deviant behavior through peer pressure to perform within ethical guidelines.

One way that peer pressure works is through shaming. To distinguish between guilt and shame, sociologists define guilt as something that is internal to the individual, whereas shame is coming from external forces, in this case our peers (Kandel and Lazear, 1992). But this means that individuals can be shamed into behaving ethically or criminally. It is like the playground dare — if you don't follow through on whatever dare it is, you might be labeled a " 'fraidy cat" or whatever derogatory name is popular at the time. Unfortunately, some adults can be blameworthy of the same type of behavior in the workplace as children on a playground.

We can't underestimate the free-rider effect as well. A *free-rider* is an individual who, while not putting forth much effort in a group, will nevertheless benefit from the victories, financial and otherwise, of that group. Some of you may have worked on group projects during high school or college. You may have at times been frustrated by members of the group who have not contributed as much to the project as you have, but have earned the same grade as others in the group who carried the lion's share of the work.

There are also two powerful social dynamics that can contribute to people or networks conforming to the expectation of others. Dimaggio and Powell (1983) identified these as *normative isomorphism* and *coercive isomorphism*. We will discuss their third type, *mimetic isomorphism*, in the section on conflicts of interest in this chapter. The term isomorphism simply means the practice of trying to act like everyone else so as to fit in. In *normative isomorphism*, you pretty much act like everyone else within your profession because it is pretty much expected of you. For example, if you are a professor teaching in a classroom, you are expected by students to deliver a lecture from the front of the classroom, though you might wander up and down the aisles from time to time to get students' attention. You are certainly going to be labeled unconventional if you deliver your lecture at the back of the room, to the backs of students' heads. Or the example of the surgeon who is expected to wash his hands and put gloves on before performing surgery. There would be plenty of other people, including other doctors and nurses, who would be reporting the surgeon if they refused to follow sterile protocol in the operating room.

Coercive isomorphism, on the other hand, is when we are forced to behave like others, not because it is necessarily the right behavior, but because there is a lot of pressure to conform. Sutherland certainly discussed this type of conformity in his *Differential Association Theory* (1939, 1947), where you will not necessarily be rewarded for good behavior in a criminal network. You may already be familiar with this theory from other criminology courses you have taken. Members of the network are coerced into criminal behavior because, in the same vein as children and teens might claim, "everyone else is doing it."

POWER IN SOCIAL NETWORKS

In any group, sooner or later leaders emerge. Think about any reality television show that you might have watched. Even though the cast members are more or less on equal footing in the beginning (e.g., *Big Brother* or *Survivor*, CBS), stronger personalities will inevitably overshadow weaker ones. As we have discussed elsewhere in this book, the higher one goes, the farther one has to fall. Because of this principle, power and leadership positions in social networks carry both risks and rewards.

We can consider that membership in the right social network is a form of social capital, making it easier for us to accomplish life goals, everything from getting into the best school and graduating college to landing the first job in your profession. A leader in an important network has additional social capital for the fact that they can more easily exert power and influence over others. Going back to our reality television example, leaders are not always the loudest voice in the room. Recently one of the winners of the TV reality television show *Love Island* (ITV2, currently streaming on Hulu®), coming out of the United Kingdom, appeared to be unlucky in her quest for love (and prize money?). Up until the very last minute, she did not appear to be a frontrunner to win. But win she did, as part of a power couple.

What we do know from research is that in many cases leaders and their immediate followers are more likely to come from the elite class, going all the way back to the early theories of C. Wright Mills. These are individuals who already have a considerable amount of social capital to begin with, by way of their disproportionate ownership of social and material resources (Cornwell and Dokshin, 2014), sometimes bestowed on them at birth.

If we use the example of the Kennedy family, led by patriarch Joe Kennedy, the origins of the family wealth came from bootlegging liquor during Prohibition in the 1930s. By the 1950s and '60s, the family had amassed considerable social and political capital as well. Like the Robber Barons in the 19th century, the Kennedy family members were able to clean up their tarnished reputations from the Prohibition era by using some of their wealth in philanthropic ventures that only increased their legitimate, elite social ties, including in politics.

The very survival of a social network, including those that are centered around criminal activity, depends on the extent to which leaders can create cohesion within the network. Criminal enterprises are highly dependent on faith in leadership. But like in legitimate business, criminal enterprises can be arenas for power struggles between and within networks. If you consider organized crime during Prohibition, it was one of the bloodiest times in American crime history, where mob bosses ordered each other killed for control over the illegal distribution and sale of liquor, plus other illegal activities such as gambling and prostitution.

Even once a leader has been disgraced, or in the case of white collar crime, convicted, the social capital that they have amassed may not entirely go away. No doubt being in a powerful position in a powerful network has its advantages, even after someone has had to serve prison time for their white collar crime. We will see more evidence of this when we look more closely to some of the more notorious financial crimes in our next chapter (Chapter 4).

Law in the Real World: George Steinbrenner, New York Yankees Owner

(Source: Santini, 1989; New York Daily News, 2016)

Anyone familiar with baseball will be aware that the New York Yankees have a long and illustrious history in the game. The Boston Red Sox and Yankees team rivalry is infamous. Between the well-publicized rivalry and 27 World Series wins to date, the Yankees franchise has become extremely lucrative, including ticket sales and merchandise.

As the Yankees have few rival teams for popularity, it holds a powerful place within Major League Baseball (MLB). Because of this, any owner of the Yankees would likewise be in a powerful position. George Steinbrenner, owner of the team from 1973 until his death in 2010, who had already created a fortune in a number of business enterprises, became one of the most powerful people within the MLB. He also had ties to Washington, D.C., with a history of contributing to both Democrat and Republican candidate election campaigns (Grier, 2010).

In 1972, Steinbrenner was accused of making illegal campaign contributions. Steinbrenner defended his actions, claiming that he was unfamiliar with campaign contribution laws.

Steinbrenner was eventually charged with funneling $100,000 in illegal corporate funds into Nixon's reelection campaign, which in itself is a bit of irony, as President Nixon ultimately was accused of orchestrating the break-in at the headquarters of the Democratic National Committee in the Watergate Hotel. As we will see in Chapter 11, Political Crimes, the Watergate scandal resulted in impeachment proceedings and Nixon's resignation.

In 1974, Steinbrenner pleaded guilty to one felony count of violating federal campaign laws and was ordered to pay a $15,000 fine, escaping a prison sentence. As a basis of comparison, John Junker, former executive director and CEO of college football's Fiesta Bowl, served 11 months in federal prison on similar charges in 2011, even though he pleaded guilty (Woods, 2014). Steinbrenner's sentence was relatively light. After Steinbrenner's conviction, he was also suspended from the MLB until 1976, which meant that even though he was the owner of the Yankees, he was prohibited from being involved with day-to-day operations.

As they say, it pays to have friends in high places. In 1989, during the end of his second term in office and exercising his presidential privilege, President Reagan pardoned Steinbrenner of his crime. As a footnote, Steinbrenner was eventually permanently banned from the management of the Yankees by the MLB after yet another unrelated scandal.

Discussion Questions

1. What social network benefits might there be in owning a professional sports team?
2. Why might Steinbrenner's fame bring attention of his illegal contributions to campaign regulatory agencies?
3. As Steinbrenner had to have used legitimate social networks in order to make illegal campaign contributions, why might Steinbrenner be the only person who was prosecuted in the case?

Within the last two decades, social network scholars have been rethinking the importance of a single leader in social networks. In particular, the importance of centralized leaders in illegal networks is being questioned. Given the example of attitudes towards the potential for terrorism in the United States since 9/11, "we have become accustomed to the idea that the West is battling against a decentralized 'network of terrorist cells' that lacks any hierarchical command structure and is distributed throughout the world." (Buchanan, 2002, p 21) We cannot discount that in a well-connected global economy, we might find more than one decentralized leader in a complex white collar crime network, with clusters located throughout the world.

TRUST IN SOCIAL NETWORKS

Just as in friendships, the ties within networks are only as strong as the trust between *actors* in them. Part of that trust is already established, as networks where membership is voluntary tend to be made up of like-minded people (Scheran et al., 2013). You wouldn't be likely to continue hanging out informally with a bunch of people for any length of time, at least by choice, if you find out that you have absolutely nothing in common.

If you have ever seen the movie *The Godfather* (1972, Paramount Pictures), Don Corleone ruled his crime empire ruthlessly, relying on surrounding himself with people he trusted, including his own children. Employing his children was not merely a question of nepotism. With family as the oldest and many times most trusted social network, it is not uncommon to find in criminal conspiracies to have family members involved. However, we have to preface that with the fact that it is less commonly found in criminal white collar crime networks.

In many legitimate business transactions, a contract may be entered before you fully know what the direct benefits and risks are to you. Sometimes decisions are made quickly without having all the necessary information, largely due to the fear of missing out on a good thing. From a network standpoint, you may not have time to verify information with other people you know in a network before a decision has to be made.

Under the best of circumstances, you might have ample time to make a valid decision. However, that is not in every case, so the logical thing to do is to hold off making any decision altogether until you gather more facts. Realistically, that is not even an option. Many times, decisions have to be made immediately and can at times result in disastrous outcomes. In crime, rash decisions made by criminals may very well be good news for law enforcement.

We generally don't make decisions with people that we haven't already established some rapport with. However, we don't always have the luxury of establishing a strong relationship with the person first. As Burt (2005, p. 93) notes, trust, including trust in others to help you make decisions, requires "you commit to a relationship before you know how the other person[s] will behave." Distrust, on the other hand, is a normal reluctance to enter into any relationship, including a criminal conspiracy, without some guarantees of how others will hold up their end of the bargain (Burt, 2005).

Think about what happens when you go out on the job market, which some of you may be doing soon, in advance of graduation from college. Depending on the prospective employers, you may not have ample time to weigh the pros and cons of the job if you are offered a position in a company. Most job interviews do not offer enough time to ask all the right questions or talk to people who might become your colleagues. In the case of successful job interviews, it is a mutual decision—the employer's decision to hire you and your decision to accept the position. Both are trusting the limited amount of information you have on one another. Internet searches can only take you (and the prospective employer) so far to learn all you need to know to make the right decision.

Let's take the same scenario of a job interview, with a few different variables thrown in. You are being offered a job at a company and you also have a strong network of people you can consult who are in the same industry. This could include professors in your department or at your university. You will then be armed with more information than you might ordinarily have if you had not already built a good professional network in advance of going on the job market. For criminals, particularly career criminals, they will only be as successful as the trust they have in the networks that they have formed in advance of committing crimes, including those made while serving time in prison.

Trust is a complicated thing in illegitimate networks. As we have already seen, social networks tend to be gossipy. That means that disagreement and all-out feuds play out with the risk of people taking sides. As we have also seen, people may make decisions based on limited information. If the gossip flying through a social network is untrue or distorted, as it tends to be, trust in individuals can be tested.

If gossiping becomes a chronic condition, the whole network is at risk of falling apart. We can see this in small, localized youth street gangs (Hansen, 2005). It doesn't take much in the way of rumors to spread around for the gangs to disband, whether it is disagreements over turf or romantic love interests. In worse cases, whether we are looking at street gangs or more established organized crime groups, rumors leading to distrust can become deadly.

In white collar criminal conspiracies, like Dennis Levine's insider trading network, trust in confidentiality is crucial so as to not be detected. Law enforcement personnel trained in network analysis are well aware of this. When one suspected criminal is caught, law enforcement hope to use any breakdown in trust among network members in order to gain evidence and additional information on crimes and co-offenders.

As we have discussed with social capital, we need to view trust in social networks as yet one more valuable asset. We can also see it as a commodity that can be bought, sold, and traded. It may be the person most trusted in the network who is in possession of the most critical information that can allow that person to gain or retain power.

BROKERS IN CRIMINAL NETWORKS

One of the more interesting arguments in social networks is whether you have greater advantage if everyone is tied to everyone else versus gaps between network actors that can be exploited. Earlier, in our section on basic social network definitions, we had a discussion of structural holes and how valuable they are for those trying to maintain a broker role in a network.

But being a broker in a criminal network can be a dangerous position to be in. Sometimes the broker is the one who puts together criminals to pull off some big caper. In the *Ocean's* movie franchise (1960, Warner Bros.; 2001 to 2018, Warner's Bros., Village Roadshow Pictures, NPV Entertainment), the criminal characters in the movies were brought together by the lead character, Danny Ocean, who chose them because of their specialized skills and his trust in them. In the later 2018 film, *Ocean's Eight,* with a female crew led by Danny's sister, Debbie, the same network premise was used where she brought together criminal minds she could trust to pull off a diamond heist.

Unfortunately for real-life criminals, things are not so neatly pieced together as in the movies. In white collar crime networks, the broker may only know individuals based on their legitimate professional skills, and it requires considerable interaction before trust is built up enough to bring them into a criminal conspiracy (Hansen and Movahedi, 2010). The broker has to depend on collective greed or collective fear in order to pull any crime off with less risk for detection (Hansen and Movahedi, 2010).

CONFLICTS OF INTEREST: OVERLAPPING NETWORKS

For any criminal conspiracy, there is always a concern that the individuals who are taking part in it may have conflicting loyalties. Take, for instance, youth street gangs. Because some of the communities that have more gang activity also have more transient populations due to more rental properties and fewer homeowners, some gang members feel compelled to join the gang in wherever is their current neighborhood. This means that they might technically have membership in more than one neighborhood gang (Hansen, 2005). This mostly becomes problematic when they are rival gangs.

There is a similar network dynamic that happens in company boardrooms. It is not uncommon for members of one board to be members of a board at another company, even in the same industry. However, this will pose the problem of conflicts of interest, when companies that interlocking directors are affiliated with are in direct competition with one another. For example, you might have a board member that sits on both executive boards of PepsiCo® and Coca Cola®. Where do the loyalties of the board member lie? This is not an uncommon problem and certainly opens the door for the possibility of white collar crime in the form of corporate espionage.

Besides conflicting loyalties, one benefit of interlocking directorates and networks can also be their curse. On one hand, individuals who are connected to different networks become valuable sources of information. However, this also becomes a problem of mimetic isomorphism (Krause et al., 2019, Dimaggio and Powell, 1983). Minetic isomorphism occurs when in order to stay ahead of competition, companies and products begin to look too much alike. As networks become more connected, no real innovation is going on. There emerges a redundancy of information. This can hold true as well for white collar crime networks as well, as demonstrated by Dennis Levine's continued scramble to find new people in new networks in order to obtain new insider information that few people might have.

CRIMINAL SOCIAL NETWORKS

The tricky thing about criminal social networks, particularly when we discuss financial white collar crime, is that they are tangled webs with the informal, criminal network embedded within legitimate formal and informal social networks. Because they are embedded, there is sometimes confusion between what is legitimate and what is illegitimate in transactions that are taking place. How an illegitimate network can emerge from a legitimate one can be a mystery to scholars, regulators, and law enforcement alike.

One of the most useful explanations of the mechanics of criminal networks is Sutherland's *Differential Association Theory* (1939, 1947), introduced earlier in this chapter. One of the theory's key features is that criminal behavior is proposed to be learned in the company of other criminals. For any criticism of the theory by Burgess and Akers (1966) that simply having contact with criminals does not necessarily lead to criminal behavior, it is profoundly true that the behavior is learned when the members of a criminal network are already agreeing to commit to criminal behavior. This is particularly true in white collar crime networks. Few white collar criminals unwittingly execute their crimes, even though they may not fully understand the consequences.

One key feature of white collar criminal behavior that happens within a social network is that there is a certain element of collective denial on the part of the criminals. The behavior is excused by claims of ignorance or, as children may exclaim when caught red handed, "I didn't know!" When it is the near unanimous consensus of the network that there was no wrongdoing, the blame may be deflected onto the victim.

Another useful concept in white collar crime is neutralization. There are a number of ways by which to neutralize a victim and minimize the severity of a crime. We can identify eight of those ways here (Sykes and Matza, 1957; Coleman, 1985; Smallridge and Roberts, 2013), as they apply to white collar criminals:

- Denial of responsibility
- Denial of injury
- Denial of victim
- Condemning the condemners
- Appealing to higher loyalties
- Claims of normalcy
- Claim of entitlement
- Defense of necessity

A more comprehensive explanation of each of these different types of strategies for neutralization can be found in Table 3.1. Each one of these forms of neutralization can happen individually or in conjunction with others, to the extent that all eight (and other strategies) may be happening for the same crimes. It is much easier for neutralization to take place when most members of a criminal network are on the same page with the same commitment to the crime, as we see with terrorist networks.

TABLE 3.1: Neutrality Theory Strategies (Sykes and Matza, 1957; Coleman, 1985; Smallridge and Roberts, 2013)

Types	Definitions	Examples
Denial of responsibility	Behavior is rationalized as being beyond the deviant's control.	A car part fails and the manufacturer claims that it was an unanticipated design flaw.
Denial of injury	Rationalized that the injury is minimal with no real or lasting damage.	Customers have been sold a ten-dollar cell phone dock that is proven to be worthless.
Denial of victim	The victim is deserving or to blame for their injury.	Victims did not fully read directions before assembling a DIY TV cabinet that collapses.
Condemning the condemners	Condemners are hypocrites who are likely to be engaged in some criminal behavior.	Claiming that the politicians making regulatory policy are receiving suspicious campaign donations from banks.
Appealing to higher loyalties	Criminal behavior was intended to benefit the group or organization.	If a company doesn't lie on financial reports, the company may lose investors.
Claims of normalcy	The deviance is condoned by group or management.	A finance company regularly offers insider information to clients.
Claim of entitlement	The individual or group is entitled to the rewards coming from the deviant or criminal behavior.	Top executives in a company receive year-end bonuses while the company is in bankruptcy.
Defense of necessity	The "good" coming from the behavior outweighed the "bad."	A questionable medical procedure that has not been fully tested might save lives.

When deviance and crime happen in a whole industry, which is essentially one big social network, the victims may be blamed for not reading the fine print. We saw evidence of this in the mortgage banking meltdown in 2008. We will see this theme again in discussions of consumer fraud, in Chapter 7. This deflection and victim blaming are forms of neutralization.

We ordinarily think of white collar criminals and organized crime networks as separate entities. However, to dispel that myth, we only need to examine what finally brought Al Capone to justice. Though law enforcement knew that Capone had directly or indirectly been involved in a number of homicides during the hey-day of Prohibition, he was finally arrested and convicted for the more mundane (but white collar) crime of income tax evasion.

Organized crime groups cannot function without corrupting some law enforcement personnel and politicians. We will see this theme emerge again in Chapter 11, on political crime. It also makes perfect sense that because organized crime groups cannot merely stuff their illegally earned money under the prover-bial mattress, they would have to know people who work in financial institutions and are willing at times to turn a blind eye to irregularities. Perhaps nowhere do we better see the overlap of white collar crime and organized crime than in post-Soviet era Russia.

Law in the Real World: Post-Communist Russia, White Collar and Organized Crime

(Source: Gerber, 2000)

Many (if not most) of you reading this book were not born yet when the Soviet Union collapsed under former soviet leader, Mikhail Gorbachev, in the late 1980s. This was largely due to Soviet political and economic systems falling apart. The former Soviet Union, along with its satellite countries that pulled away from the republic, attempted to create more open economic systems.

With the subsequent social and economic upheavals, the underground *black market* shadow economy in Russia flourished more than ever. From what historians and economists can tell, the current black market first emerged in the 1950s and had been around for a number of decades before the fall of communism in Russia. An underground economy can be traced even further back to before the Russian Revolution in 1917, at a time when vast numbers of Russians lived in poverty under the ruling by czars. As Russian-organized crime groups largely control the black market, they in turn have managed to profit immensely from the economic changes occur-ring in the past few decades.

Until the fall of communism in Russia, the only real competition that organized crime had in the Soviet Union was the Communist Party. Old bosses of the Communist Party and the *Vory* (organized crime networks) competed for power in the emerging new economy. Added to this was the emergence of a better educated class of crime bosses, the *authorities*.

Eventually the two networks, old Soviet bosses and organized crime bosses, began to overlap with interlocking membership. With high unemployment, organized crime could attract former KGB members, law enforcement, military, and even scientists—essentially a number of individuals occupying white collar professions (Gerber, 2000; Handelman, 1999). In contemporary Russia, it is now difficult to tell the differences between legitimate business, crime, and political networks, by most reports: "Consequently most new Russian capitalists operate mainly in the so-called 'gray zone' that exists between the underground and the official [legitimate] world." (Gerber, 2000, p. 332; Voronin, 1997)

Discussion Questions

1. Why might the relationship between organized crime and white collar crime be largely ignored by the media?
2. What enticements (or threats?) might there have been that attracted people working in legitimate white collar professions to work with organized crime networks?
3. What social network dynamics that we have learned in this chapter might explain why the black market economy could flourish in post-Communist Russia?

Perhaps there is no better example of the blurring of legitimate business, white collar crime, and organized crime networks than in the early days of Las Vegas. Las Vegas began as a railroad town, but like similar towns, had been all but deserted in the early 20th century. During the building of Hoover Dam in the 1930s, which is in close proximity to Las Vegas in Nevada, men working on the dam project would travel to the dusty desert town and spend money on what few amenities that were available there, including prostitutes and liquor. This created a booming underground economy, not unlike that which emerged in Russia after communism, and where there is an underground economy, organized crime is not far behind. By the 1950s and '60s, Las Vegas, sometimes not-so-affectionately called "Lost Wages" because of gambling establishments, became a town that the Mob built. But they couldn't do so without the blessing or at least the promise from politicians that they would turn a blind eye to the corruption and crime associated with the Mafia. Mobsters, including Meyer Lansky and Benjamin "Bugsy" Siegel, were the power behind building the now famous Las Vegas Strip (Fischer, 2007). They could not have done so without networking with people in legitimate professions, including accountants, financiers, and local politicians.

CRIME, SECRECY, AND SOCIAL NETWORKS

If a white collar criminal is smart, they will make sure that their criminal network is what we would describe as "stringy," with lots of gaps between actors. One of the ways that criminal social networks are detected is that there are just too many people who know everyone else. In order for any conspiracy to work or a criminal network to last, there has to be secrecy.

As any of you who have ever lived in a college dorm knows, secrets have a way of getting out, circulate, and become distorted. Humans are just inherently prone to gossip, some more so than others. During WWII, there were a number of public service campaigns with the slogan "loose lips sink ships." The same can be said about criminal networks, whether they are made up of terrorists, organized crime mobsters, or white collar professionals.

Because secrets have a way of leaking out, it is very difficult for any criminal conspiracy, including white collar crime, to continue undetected. Whether anyone acts on the information is a different matter — the very culture of a network or industry may discourage whistleblowing when crimes are detected (Hansen, 2009). We do see a few rare cases, like Bernie Madoff's pyramid scheme (Chapter 4), where secrets are so well-hidden it just takes an unforeseen turn of events to have the crime suddenly become detected after decades of deception.

SUMMARY

As we have seen in this chapter, social network analysis (SNA) theories and methods are extremely useful tools in understanding white collar crime. Though they are more commonly used by law enforcement to detect co-offending in conventional crime cases, we are certainly seeing more use of social network analysis, particularly using social media websites and examining email exchanges between criminals, to uncover criminal networks.

While we have historically thought of white collar criminals and organized crime to be somewhat mutually exclusive, we are now understanding how these two worlds interact with one another. Organized crime groups are dependent on legitimate business in order to conduct their illegitimate enterprises, including transfer of illicit funds into banks. As we saw in the example of what happened after the fall of communism in Russian, under the right circumstances, people working in legitimate professions might be easily recruited into organized crime networks. We also saw this with the example of Dennis Levine.

There are a number of classic crime theories that compliment SNA. Sutherland's Differential Association Theory allows us to understand how criminal behavior is learned and reinforced within social networks. Likewise, theories of victim neutralization can be explained as criminal network members may remind one another that 1) the criminal behavior is not that bad and everyone else is doing it and 2) it is the victim's own fault for being duped.

All of the dynamics that we see in our personal and professional social circles can also be applied in studying white collar crime networks. Leaders will emerge, strategic alliances and cliques will form, and broker positions will be made between networks. More importantly, because criminal networks are made up of people who are inherently prone to gossip, secrets do get leaked. In some cases, law enforcement can act on the information. In other cases, where whistleblowing is discouraged, it may take a long time for law enforcement and regulatory agencies to even be aware that crimes have been committed.

Case Study ▪ The Dominos Fall—The Informal, Criminal Network of Dennis Levine

Background

Wall Street is notorious for highs and lows, where investors vacillate between being wonderfully optimistic about stock markets ("bull market") and being pessimistic and risk-adverse ("bear market"). Both extremes can create chaos for Wall Street professionals. Unfortunately, along with new opportunities for investment come new opportunities for white collar crime. Ivan Boesky is one of those household names that is associated with crime on Wall Street, but perhaps the more interesting criminal to study is Dennis Levine, a lesser-known character in the drama of insider trading crimes during the 1980s.

Defining the Crime(s)

The central crime committed in this case was insider trading. As we will explore more extensively in the next chapter, illegal insider trading occurs when individuals either buy or sell stock based on information that has not been made public yet. It is primarily regulated by the Securities and Exchange Commission (SEC) and can be prosecuted within the criminal court system. The belief behind the law is that insider information is an unfair advantage over other investors who do not have the same knowledge in order to make informed decisions about their investments. By having the unfair advantage, the theory is that investors will lose confidence in the market and might invest their money elsewhere.

A second criminological theme associated with illegal insider trading is that there has to be some conspiracy to hide the money. The criminals committing these acts are many times working within the financial industries and will, by habit, want their money to work for them, collecting interest in bank accounts or dividends in other investments. One way that criminals, including white collar criminals, hide money they illegitimately make is to place it in offshore accounts, in countries that have more secrecy around who is making deposits into their banks. Switzerland has historically been one of these countries, though their banks are not completely without regulation and do cooperate when crimes have been detected. However, we should note that some banks in some countries are more willing to turn a blind eye to regulation.

Theories to Explain the Crime(s)

Dennis Levine came on the scene on Wall Street at a time when financial institutions began to hire on the basis of talent, not on what alma mater that prospective brokers graduated from. Levine was one of the first in his family to go to college, eventually earning an MBA from CUNY Baruch College, a well-regarded business school that doesn't possess the same prestige as Ivy League colleges like Harvard or Yale. In the '70s, Wall Street was more likely to hire only graduates from MBA programs offered at Ivy League colleges with ties to elites already working in finance. In his book on the scandals that rocked Wall Street during the 1980s, *Den of Thieves*, Steward (1992) speculates as to whether Levine felt that he had to work doubly hard to prove himself because he did not attend an Ivy League MBA program.

As Levine was working his way up through the dog-eat-dog world of Wall Street, he did so during a mergers and acquisitions frenzy. Mergers and acquisitions (or M&A) is a specialization within the financial sector that focuses on the buying and selling of companies. Sometimes these are companies that are struggling for various reasons and forced to be sold. Simply put, arbitrage, an integral part of mergers and acquisitions, is the goal of buying low, then turning around and selling high—that is where the profit is made, along with associated fees for brokering the deal. It is a very lucrative place in finance for both the brokers and investors, with moderate to high risk.

Because arbitrage involving mergers and acquisitions carries greater risk than other types of investments, there can be great gains but also the risk of great losses as well. The people who work in arbitrage can be some of the biggest risk-takers in the business. It is also a cutthroat business, with many of the mergers and acquisitions a direct result of hostile takeovers. The companies that are involved can see their stock prices fluctuate radically once the news is out.

One theory we might use, borrowed from sociology, is the Social Exchange Theory (Blau, 1964), to explain why Levine and his co-conspirators took the risks they did. Generally used in discussions of legitimate social or economic relationships, the theory can be equally applied to criminal networks. Within the theory, Blau proposed that social exchanges, in this case information, can be used to create trust and social bonds between participants. As there was a dependence on secrecy within Levine's network, those bonds could also be doubly built because of the faith that others would not give the operation away, either to their employer or to regulators.

During its early conception, exchange theories focused on the relationship between two people, or as they are called in social network theory, dyads. Emerson (1976) expanded on Blau's earlier theory to include exchanges within larger social networks where there are not simply two actors. Emerson's theory is further legitimized by his proposal that there is inequality within exchanged relationships when we move between the interactions of only two people, with power either being balanced or imbalanced (Emerson, 1976), in this case, within the network. Behavioral change as a consequence of imbalanced relationships, is inevitable. Levine and Ivan Boesky were to a large extent powerful by the number of individuals they brought into the network, but also by their level of expertise on both the legitimate and illegitimate sides of financial markets. It might also suggest that a certain amount of social Darwinism was occurring, where only the socially adept and agile could survive on Wall Street, on either side of the law.

To further support this theory, we only need to examine how Levine set himself up to be a powerful network player. Levine made mergers and acquisitions his specialization early on in his career. This meant that during his career, he had considerable knowledge of what was going on in companies on the verge of being sold or merging with other companies. This in turn has an effect on their stock prices as investors scramble to buy or sell their stock in those companies once the news had been made public.

Because so much of what happens in financial markets is dependent on the latest information, this also required Levine to cultivate an extensive professional network with other Wall Street elites in this specialization. Most of the ties he established were completely legitimate and expected in his profession, in order to remain competitive. By the time Levine was in his late 20s, he was beginning to put together a plan to create an illegitimate network of insider traders, exploiting the news he learned about companies being bought and sold for his own gain, in advance of public disclosure.

By the late '70s, Levine was making a healthy salary by Wall Street standards in his positions, first with Smith Barney, then with Lehman Brothers, eventually ending up as a merger specialist at Drexel Burnham Lambert.

Whether due to his own insecurities or the pressures and culture of Wall Street, Levine began cultivating a network of people who were willing to risk breaking law and finance regulations in order to make even more money on the side.

Other theories we might consider applying in the Levine case comes from cognitive behavioral science. Like in gambling, the excitement plus fear that might be associated with making money illegitimately by using insider information may trigger the pleasure/reward systems of the brain.

The people involved in Levin's illegal network made money outside of their legitimate salaries primarily by committing insider trading crimes. Insider trading is when individuals sell or buy stock based on information they have that hadn't been released to the public yet. We will go into more detail on the crime of insider trading in the next chapter (Chapter 4) on financial crimes, including other, more familiar convicted white collar criminals such as Martha Stewart, Ivan Boesky, and Michael Milken.

The Bahamas, a series of islands in the Caribbean, is also a country that has bank secrecy laws that can help criminals have their illegal banking transactions go undetected. One motivation is to hide even legitimate assets from taxation. We should note that when they do detect irregular transactions, authorities in those countries are not held to the same secrecy regulations and will report the suspicious activity to the Securities and Exchange Commission in the U.S. or other similar regulatory agencies in other countries.

One of these banks that Levine deposited illegal funds into and made stock market trades through, Bank Leu, was not without its own set of deviant employees who overlooked Levine's suspicious transactions. The employees who were willing to turn a blind eye to regulation were able to make their own hefty profits from the transactions. Some bank officials at Bank Leu went so far as destroying evidence, leading to criminal charges.

Thus, Bank Leu, a legitimate bank, had an informal network of deviant, criminal actors embedded within the legitimate, formal network of employees, most of whom were going about their jobs legitimately. This was on top of the already tangled web of Wall Street's criminal network, constructed by Levine and embedded within financial institutions that were operating within legitimate regulatory standards.

Levine's network continued to grow throughout the early '80s, making it more difficult to maintain structural holes needed to preserve secrecy. His strategy for hiding his illegitimate stock transactions reads like a spy novel, where he would use pay phones to make his trades. One of his biggest mistakes was to create a Bahamian account in the name "Diamond," easily traced back to him as it was his wife's maiden name.

Social and Media Responses

We should look at the Levine case in context of the era when it occurred. Without the vast online media sources that we are both privileged and cursed to have, few outside of the financial industry were paying attention to the events that were unfolding on Wall Street in the Levine case. Newspapers and nightly television broadcasts were certainly reporting the news, but the average person was much less likely to be aware back in the 1980s of the social ramifications of the insider trading crimes. At least with CNN's conception, there was more media response to the crimes as the network, still in its infancy, scrambled to fill 24 hours with news broadcasts.

As the news of the vastness of the network spread, some of the banks involved, including Drexel Burnham Lambert and Bank Leu, had their reputations permanently tarnished as well. Beyond the insider trading scandals of Levine, Drexel Burnham Lambert was equally damaged by other questionable business practices involving high yield "junk" bonds. Never fully recovering, the investment bank that employed Levine filed for bankruptcy in 1990 and went out of business by 2015. Bank Leu closed its doors in 2007. Similarly, as in the Weinstein Company discussed in the previous chapter, these investment banks never could fully recover from the scandal.

Ultimately, it was a relatively small number of criminals operating in an illegal, informal network, embedded within legitimate investment banking networks, that resulted in the collapse of a number of longstanding financial institutions.

Criminal Justice and Policy Responses

As we always note in white collar crime, it is generally regulators who first get wind that anything is going wrong, who in turn alert law enforcement when warranted.

Levine's network continued to grow throughout the early '80s, making it more difficult to maintain structural holes needed to preserve secrecy. His strategy for hiding his illegitimate stock transactions reads like a spy novel, where he would use pay phones to make his trades. One of his biggest mistakes was to create a Bahamian account in the name "Diamond," easily traced back to him as it was his wife's maiden name.

The whole scheme fell like a line of domino tiles. In 1986, one of Levine's suspicious stock trades was detected because it was too coincidently tied to others in his criminal network who were making the same trade in advance of public announcement of a merger deal. It was a series of events, including Bank Leu's use of a Merrill Lynch broker to carry out some of his trades, that led to his downfall. A broker reported the irregularities to the Merrill Lynch compliance department, which in turn reported the suspicious trades to the SEC (Teachout, 1987). According to indictments, Levine had been operating an insider trading network from 1979 through mid-1986, before he was caught (Steward, 1992). For Levine, if not for a series of unfortunate events and somewhat foolish decisions on his part, we can only speculate how much longer his network would have operated.

After an indictment on several charges in May 1986, one month later Levine pleaded guilty to securities fraud and insider trading, tax evasion and perjury. His conviction resulted in a sentence of two years in federal prison, forfeiture of illegal profit, fines, and a lifetime ban from the securities business (Teachout, 1987). Levine, after serving time in Lewisburg Federal Prison in Pennsylvania, launched a financial consulting business (McCartney, 1991).

Unanswered Questions and Unresolved Issues Related to the Case

As in the case of any criminal conspiracy involving a social network, it is difficult for investigators to see the entire network. It is unknown just how many people benefited from the insider information that Levine shared. Whether we are examining terrorist networks, street gangs, or the "bad people" on Wall Street, the so-called outer limits of these networks are fuzzy at best. If we put this in the context of exploring the universe, telescopes can only see so far out into space. The rest becomes theoretical. The same can be true for investigators trying to uncover large criminal conspiracies operating within sophisticated social networks.

A second unresolved issue in this case is regulation. Little has been done since the 1980s insider trading scandals to prevent insider trading from happening in the first place. As we will discuss further in the next chapter, the crime of insider trading is ambiguous. Those who study regulation and instances of insider trading agree that what we do see of insider trading is only a small fraction of what actually occurs. Regulations are only as good as they are enforced, whether by regulatory agencies or self-regulation within professions. With as profitable as the financial industry is, it is difficult to say whether government regulations is enough. There is just too much incentive to take risks, some of which may be illegal.

Sources

Blau, P. (1964) *Exchange and power in social life*. New York: Wiley Publishing.

Emerson, R. M. (1976) Social exchange theory. *Annual Review of Sociology*. Vol. 2: 335-362.

Hansen, L. L. (2004) The "Bad Boys of Wall Street": A Social Network Analysis of Insider Trading, 1979-1986. Doctoral dissertation. University of California Riverside.

Hansen, L. L. (2011) Les coûts sociaux des délits d'initiés sur les marchés financiers (à traduire) (Tearing at the Social Fabric: Social Costs of Insider Trading as Informal Economy) in *Shadow Economies and Their Paradoxes*. N. Barbe and F. Weber, eds. Paris: Editions de la Maison des Sciences de l'Homme.

Hansen, L. L. (2014) "Gossip boys": Insider trading and regulatory ambiguity. *Journal of Financial Crimes*. Vol. 21, No. 1: 29-43.

McCartney, R. J. (1991) New clouds loom over Dennis Levine. *The Washington Post*. Sept. 24. Retrieved from https://www.washingtonpost.com/archive/business/1991/09/24/new-clouds-loom-over-dennis-levine/e27d58d6-b539-4c7b-a3dd-96273b64ae90/?utm_term=.e4925608c755

Steward, J. B. (1992) *Den of thieves*. New York: Touchstone.

Teachout, T. (1987) Inside Dennis Levine: He was a formidable operator who had his insider-trading ring planned when he was all of 27. *CNN Money*. Sept. 28. Retrieved from https://money.cnn.com/magazines/fortune/fortune_archive/1987/09/28/69569/index.htm.

GLOSSARY

Agency   The extent to which an individual is acting in their own best interest.

Black market   The illegal economic system that functions underground. Law enforcement and regulatory agencies are aware of its existence but find it difficult to prevent. Example: the illegal prescription drug market.

Broker   An individual who is between two actors who do not have ties in a network or acts as a conduit between two separate networks.

Clique   A subgroup of a network, made up of three or more closely connected individuals.

Coercive isomorphism   Dimaggio and Powell's (1983) terms to mean the social and economic pressure to conform to an industry standard, not because of choice, but due to competition.

Differential Association Theory   Edwin Sutherland's (1939, 1947) theory that criminal behavior is learned when people associate with criminals.

Directional ties   These are social network ties between actors where things may flow in one direction between them. Example: Information.

Embeddedness   Within a social network, the degree to which people are well connected on the individual level. Can also refer to the extent that two or more social networks are connected to one another through mutual ties.

Forbidden triad   Condition identified by Granovetter (1973) where in a triad of three people, if there are strong ties between two of the actors, a third will inevitably form and all three actors will be connected.

Formal social networks   These are the generally sanctioned social networks that are part of an organization. Examples: Chain of command, hierarchy.

Free-rider   An individual who benefits from the work of a group or network, without putting in the same efforts as other members of the group.

Hegemony   The degree to which an individual or a group of individuals have power in a network, generally measured by the number and quality of social ties they possess.

Informal social networks   The natural social network that forms within formal social networks, due to friendship, mutual dependency, or expediency.

Mimetic isomorphism   The phenomenon identified by Dimaggio and Powell (1983) where people or companies will start looking like one another, by imitating each other's structure.

Network boundaries   The extent to which we can identify all members belonging to a social network.

Network noise   False information or events that happen, that disrupt the flow of factual information through a social network.

Node   Another term for "actor" in SNA that can refer to a thing (e.g., a company) or a person.

Normative isomorphism   The type of conformity that is expected within a profession (Dimaggio and Powell (1983).

Peer pressure.   The pressure to conform to the behaviors and expectations of a group of people that you consider to be your equals.

Reciprocal ties   Social ties where the action/feelings/transaction are identifiably going in both directions between actors. Example: One broker will offer information on possible leads to another broker, in exchange for information, an exchange that is beneficial to both parties.

Social contagion   Any piece of information, whether factual or falsehood, that is passed around quickly within and between networks.

Social network actor   Another name for an individual who is a member of a social network.

Social Network Analysis (SNA)   A set of theories and research methodologies that are grounded in mathematical and qualitative sociology within criminology, that helps in understanding how individuals, organizations, and things are socially connected.

Social network tie   A definable connection between actors within a social network.

Structural hole   The gap between two actors, identified by Burt (1992) as being a competitive edge, where there is a broker who connects the two of actors together where they are not personally connected to one another. Example: The buyer and seller of a home do not ever meet and the transaction between them is handled by a real estate agent.

REFERENCES AND SUGGESTED READINGS

Alsup, D. and D. Simon. (2017) Couple raises thousands for homeless veteran to thank him for self-less act. *CNN*. Nov. 24. Retrieved from https://www.cnn.com/2017/11/24/us/couple-raises-money-for-homeless-man/index.html.

Bosse, D. A. and R. A. Phillips. (2016) Agency theory and bounded self-interest. *Academy of Management Review*. Vol. 4, No. 2: 276-297.

Buchanan, M. (2002) *Nexus: Small worlds and the groundbreaking science of networks*. New York: W.W. Norton and Co., Inc.

Burgess, R. and R. L. Akers. (1966) A differential association-reinforcement theory of criminal behavior. *Social Problems*. Vol. 14: 363-383.

Coleman, J. W. (1985) *The criminal elite: The sociology of white collar crime*. New York: St. Martin's Press.

Cornwell, B. and F. A. Dokshin. (2014) The power of integration: Affiliation and cohesion n a diverse elite network. *Social Forces*. Vol. 93, No. 2: 803-832.

Dimaggio, P. J., & Powell, W. W. (1983). The iron cage revisited: Institutional isomorphism and collective rationality in organizational fields. *American Sociological Review*. Vol. 48, No. 2:147–160.

Fischer, S. (2007) *When the mob ran Las Vegas: Stories of money, mayhem, and murder*. New York: MJF Books. 3d ed.

Gerber, J. (2000) On the relationship between organized and white collar crime: Government, business, and criminal enterprise in post-Communist Russia. *European Journal of Crime, Criminal Law, and Criminal Justice*. Apr, Vol. 8, No. 4: 327-342).

Granovetter, M. S. (1973) The strength of weak ties. *American Journal of Sociology*. May, Vol. 78, No. 6:1360-1380.

Grier, P. (2010) George Steinbrenner spent big on politics, too. *The Christian Science Monitor*. Retrieved from https://www.csmonitor.com/USA/Politics/Decoder/2010/0716/George-Steinbrenner-spent-big-on-politics-too.

Handelman, S. (1999) Russia's rule by racketeers. *The Wall Street Journal*. Sept. 20.

Hansen, L. L. (2011) Les coûts sociaux des délits d'initiés sur les marchés financiers *(à traduire)* (Tearing at the Social Fabric: Social Costs of Insider Tradin g as Informal Economy) in *Shadow Economies and Their Paradoxes*. N. Barbe and F. Weber, eds. Paris: Editions de la Maison des Sciences de l'Homme.

Hansen, L. L., & Movahedi, S. (2010). Wall Street scandals: The myth of individual greed. *Sociological Forum*. Vol. 25, No. 2: 367-374.

Kandel, E. and E. P. Lazear. (1992) Peer pressure and partnerships. *The Journal of Political Economy*. Aug, Vol. 100, No. 4: 801-817).

Krause, R., Z. Qu, G. D. Bruton, and S. Carter. (2019) The coercive isomorphism ripple effect: An investigation of nonprofit interlocks on corporate boards. *Academy of Management Journal.* Feb, Vol. 62, Issue 1: 283-308.

New York Daily News. (2016) Yankees owner George Steinbrenner is pardoned by Ronald Reagan in 1989 for his illegal contributions to Nixon. Originally published Jan. 20, 1989, M. Santini. Retrieved from https://www.nydailynews.com/sports/baseball/yankees/george-steinbrenner-pardoned-ronald-reagan-article-1.2478639.

Sherchan, W., S. Nepal and C. Paris. (2013) A survey of trust in social networks. *ACM Computing Surveys.* Aug. Vol. 45, No. 4, Article 47:1-33.

Simko-Bednarski, E. (2019) Homeless man in GoFundMe case arrested. *CNN.* Jan. 10. Retrieved from https://www.cnn.com/2019/01/09/us/gofundme-bobbitt-arrest-warrant/index.html.

Skyes, M. and D. Matza. (1947) Techniques of neutralization: A theory of deviance. *American Sociology Review.* Vol. 22, No. 6: 664-670.

Smallridge, J. L. and J. R. Roberts. (2013) Crime specific neutralizations: An empirical examination of four types of digital piracy. *International Journal of Cyber Criminology.* Dec., Vol. 7, No. 2: 125-140.

Taylor, L. (2011) How to deal with "multiple boss madness": Learn "multiple boss mastery" and reduce job stress. *Psychology Today.* Feb. 23. Retrieved from https://www.psychologytoday.com/us/blog/tame-your-terrible-office-tyrant/201102/how-deal-multiple-boss-madness.

Voronin, Y. (1997) The emerging criminal state: Economic and political aspects of organized crime in Russia. In *Russian Organized Crime: The New Threat?*, P. Williams, ed. London: Frank Cass Publishers. pp. 53-62.

Woods, C. D. M. (2014) Do campaign finance violations warrant jail time? A question of ethics. *Roll Call.* Retrieved from https://www.rollcall.com/news/do-campaign-finance-violations-warrant-jail-time-a-question-of-ethics.

Chapter FOUR

Financial Crime

The bad boys (and girls) of Wall Street

"I will tell you the secret to getting rich on Wall Street. You try to be greedy when others are fearful. And you try to be fearful when others are greedy."

—*Warren Buffett*

Chapter Objectives

- Offer a brief history of how financial markets work and how they can be abused.
- Define and identify what is meant by "financial crime."
- Familiarize the reader with the terms most commonly used in discussions of financial crime.
- Introduce the reader to some of the more common forms of financial crime committed by individuals.
- Present some of the more infamous cases of corporate financial crime.

Key Terms

Audit

Conservatorship

Control fraud

Earned income

Embezzlement

Endowment

Federal Deposit Insurance
  Corporation (FDIC)

Fiduciary responsibility

Insider tipping

Insider trading

Mutual funds

Ponzi schemes

Pyramid sales structures

Racketeering

RICO Act of 1970

Securities

Shell companies

Stocks

Unearned income

Wire fraud

INTRODUCTION

As the biblical adage goes, "money is the root of all evil." The impetus behind financial crimes is perhaps the easiest to understand. If we focus primarily on the motive of greed, rather than fear, the drive to increase one's wealth by any means, to a large degree, provides us a very good explanation for why seemingly respectable professionals steal from employers and customers.

Early definitions of white collar crime focused on the violation of one's *fiduciary responsibility*, where individuals are charged with protecting their employer's or clients' assets. These assets can include money, investments, or material goods. For instance, a financial planner is expected to make sure that they are acting in their clients' best interests when recommending investment strategies. If they are simply selling investment products to earn the commission or fees associated with the sales, they are more interested in their own bank accounts than the financial affairs of their clients.

Financial white collar crime is in many respects the most difficult to detect and regulate. What might appear on the surface to be perfectly legitimate financial arrangements can ultimately be devastating to investors and borrowers. We will see this in our discussion of sub-prime mortgages. Other crimes, like the Ponzi schemes we discuss in this chapter, may take years to detect, as in our case of Bernie Madoff.

The challenge is in determining whether a financial arrangement is criminal or simply unethical. In a free market society, people who invest or borrow money are expected to understand that there is risk involved. Whether you are making an investment or borrowing money from a lending institution, there are a number of documents that you must sign that essentially say you understand the risks you are undertaking. It is the responsibility of the investor or borrower to do their due diligence in understanding all the details of the contract that they are entering into with a financial institution. Realistically, as in the example of anyone who has ever signed mortgage documents to purchase a home, few will read all the fine print of contracts.

THE "FUNCTIONING" OF MARKETS AND REGULATION

If we look at the means by which to accumulate wealth in early America, it was primarily in land and slaves (Geisst, 2018). Slavery, besides being incredibly inhumane and immoral, proved to be an unreliable source of income, with limitations. Land has always been speculative as well, with value dependent on a number of factors. In addition, land is not necessarily revenue-generating unless it is rented out.

Money, and eventually financial markets, emerged to be a more impersonal, reliable medium for economic exchange. This became particularly handy with the growth of capitalism during and after the Industrial Revolution. As impersonal as money may be theorized to be by Simmel (1978), the management of money is a whole different proposition. Even money has not been demonstrated as a completely predictable investment, as witnessed by the mid-18th century slump when trade was decaying, credit was impossible to obtain, and debtors were ruined.

Though financial markets have also been proven to be unpredictable, as more recently witnessed by the up-and-down roller coaster of 2018 and 2019, money still represented a different, more controllable kind of wealth once currency stabilized. However, with money having a property of more invisibility and secrecy (Simmel, 1978), financial markets became ripe environments for a whole new set of crimes to emerge, which means that unlike other types of property, money that criminals make can be more easily hidden.

Wall Street and financial markets are now extremely interdependent in today's world economy. Ideally, they need to function cooperatively even though they are expected to be competitive, otherwise chaos would ensue and investors would be jittery. As Abolafia (2001) discovered in his ethnographic study of Wall Street, financial markets are normatively regulated and there is a lot of peer pressure to conform to its culture. This is in spite of cycles of individuals acting in their own self-interest and collective self-restraint.

More importantly, financial markets are regulated by law, particularly since the Great Depression (1929-1939). The Roosevelt administration (1933-1945) was instrumental in seeking out new laws to regulate the stock exchanges (Geisst, 2018). This was met with resistance that continues today. It may be why so many laws that deal with financial markets are purposely ambiguous, as we shall see when we cover the topic of insider trading. It is always a tug-of-war between those who believe in a free market economy and those who believe that financial markets should be heavily regulated. The reality is somewhere in between.

This all runs counter with one of the primary driving forces of economies: innovation. Innovators tend to be deviant, and we do not mean to imply this in a negative way—remember that all crime is deviant, but not all deviance is crime! Innovators will work outside of currently accepted practices that may or may not become the new norm (Abolafia, 2001). However, innovation also leaves open opportunities to commit crimes, as we shall see in the case of insider trading and new pharmaceutical developments.

THE ROLE OF INTERNATIONAL MARKETS IN FINANCIAL CRIME

There are a number of ways that the world is connected by financial markets. Even global currencies are interdependent, with the value of a currency in one country dependent on the currency of another. For instance, in 2019 China undervalued its currency, the Chinese yuan, in response to Trump's trade war. By doing so, China can in turn boost its exports and further the trade gap between the United States and China.

One instrument that global investors can invest in is currency futures. In the early 1970s, the International Monetary Market (IMM) began trading in currency futures. This made speculating on world currency values as lucrative (and as risky) as any other type of investment in commodity futures like corn, soybeans, or live hogs (Geisst, 1997). However, this in turn offered another market in which white collar criminals can hide their illegal earnings by purchasing currency other than from their own country.

During the "go-go years" of the 1960s, the Asian economies ("Asian Tiger"), including South Korea and Taiwan (Wright and Hope, 2019) were booming, in spite of a decade of social strife and the Vietnam War. The 1990s brought a whole stock market in Malaysia. It was an attractive place for white collar criminals to park their money and a place where insider traders could stock purchases that would be deemed illegal in the United States, boldly violating security laws on the Malaysia stock exchange (Wright and Hope, 2019).

Another market that is internationally connected is real estate, which is ripe for criminal activity. Most of you are familiar with purchases of homes or commercial property for dual purposes of personal use and investment. There is a far larger speculative real estate market, by the amount of money invested, that attracts international investors. For instance, California home prices have gone up exponentially within the last decade.

Part of the reason behind the rise in home prices, beyond California's favorable climate and mystique, is an increase in foreign investors. In many cases they are coming in with cash offers, sometimes over asking price when there are bidding wars on desirable properties. This becomes very difficult to compete with for the homeowner who needs to take out a mortgage on a property. Real estate is still a speculative market for both the regular garden variety homeowner and the investor, as the real estate market can change dramatically like it did during the 2008 economic meltdown.

Again, within the context of white collar crime, we see the intersection of organized crime and white collar crime when proceeds from criminal acts are invested in legitimate markets, including in real estate. To combat money laundering (discussed later this chapter), real estate brokers are required to report any large cash purchase over $10,000 (USD) to the United States Internal Revenue Service (IRS).

There is little in the way of restrictions of who can invest in global markets. Even when there are restrictions, many times there are backdoors and loopholes around regulations. Though this chapter doesn't specifically address political crimes, the degree to which there is regulation in financial markets is a function of just how ethical or corrupt any given government is.

Law in the Real World: Jho Low and 1MDB Scandal

(Source: Wright and Hope, 2019)

Once a darling of the 2000s "in crowd," Low Taek Jho, more commonly known as Jho Low, became the center of international financial intrigue that included political corruption and luxury goods including expensive artwork, private jets, and yachts. His escapades included a vast money laundering scheme that spanned the globe. There was even an alleged murder on the peripheral of Low's white collar criminal activities.

As Wright and Hope describe him (2019), anyone who might have read F. Scott Fitzgerald's *The Great Gatsby* will recognize similarities between the title character of the novel and Low in their love of an extravagant life-style. Where Gatsby and Low part ways is in their beginnings: Whereas Gatsby came from poverty, Low's family had modest wealth thanks to his self-made grandfather.

Like many pre- and young teens in the 1990s (as well as today), Low spent considerable time on the computer exploring the new social forum of chat rooms. Like most teens, he wanted to be perceived to be cool, advertising himself as a model, though by modeling standards Low was ordinary in appearance. In Low's case, he may not have outgrown this phase going into his adulthood as he continued to paint a picture of himself as an affluent international playboy. He was able to live out his fantasy to a great extent, spending time with hip-hop artists, Hollywood actors, and socialites, including Paris Hilton.

Like his father who made part of his own fortune in the new Malaysian market and property investment, Low became a financial risk-taker. Educated in London and the United States, attending the University of Pennsylvania, Low quickly gained a reputation for his financial schemes, partying, and awkward attempts at approaching women. On entering the Wharton School of Business, he did not dispel rumors that he was a "prince of Malaysia," though fellow Malaysian students scoffed at the idea (Wright and Hope, 2019).

Through his position as CEO of Jynwel Capital Limited and *shell companies*,[1] Low became involved with 1Malaysia Development Berhad (1MDB), a state-owned investment fund and development company.

---

[1] Shell companies can be used for both legitimate or illegitimate business transactions. Shell companies do not occupy physical space, nor do they employ workers. They are a vehicle where financial transactions can be conducted with more anonymity. For example, in order to prevent other businesses from crowding into Orlando, the Disney Co. legitimately used shell companies to purchase land when building Walt Disney World, so as to do so with a certain degree of anonymity.

1MDB, as a government company, was under the political patronage of the then Prime Minister Najib Razak (Adam et al., 2018). 1MDB raised part of its capital through bond funds. Despite claims that Low had no official position at 1MDB, he, along with Razak, allegedly siphoned off billions of dollars from the company, including from the bond funds directly. Both Low and Razak, along with others charged in the scandal, used these illegally obtained funds to live lavish lifestyles.

In another plot twist, at the height of his criminal activities, Low help bankroll the movie *Wolf of Wall Street* (2013, Red Granite, Warner Bros.), starring Leonardo DiCaprio. This was no coincidence, as Low's own father was a fan of Hollywood movies that portrayed white collar crime, including the original *Wall Street* film (1987, 20th Century Fox). Hence, a movie about white collar crime was most likely partially funded with money that was made through white collar crime.

Jho Low is currently a fugitive from the United States, Malaysia, and Singapore justice systems. He has so far escaped prosecution, and is thought to currently be somewhere in China (Sukumaran, 2018). He was initially charged with a number of counts of money laundering, funneled through a Swiss bank account (Latiff, 2018).

More recent criminal charges against Low and four others include 13 counts of money laundering, criminal breach of trust, and losses of 1MDB funds to the tune of $1.17 billion USD, or 4.2 billion Malaysian ringgit (Latiff, 2018). Former Prime Minister Najib Razak is currently on trial in Malaysia for his part in the embezzlement of 1MDB and money laundering. In an unusual move in the world of financial crime, the Malaysian government has filed charges directly against Goldman Sachs Group, Inc., after several of its employees faced criminal charges. Ordinarily, banks and corporations involved in crime are sued in civil court. Goldman Sachs Group, Inc., is currently defending the charges.

Along with criminal charges, Low was slapped with a civil asset forfeiture suit to reclaim luxury items that had been purchased with his illegal funds, including his 91-meter (approximately 300 ft.) yacht, *Tranquility*, reportedly purchased for $250 million. Leonardo DiCaprio, in cooperation with the U.S. Justice Department, handed over a Basquiat collage worth $9 million, a Picasso painting (*Nature Morte au Crâne de Taureau*, 1939) worth $13 million, and Marlon Brando's Oscar statue, all said to be gifts from Low to DiCaprio, paid for with illegal funds. DiCaprio has not been accused of any wrongdoing in accepting the gifts from Low, and is cooperating fully with U.S. authorities (Kinsella, 2017).

Discussion Questions

1. As in the case of Low, why might there be an impulse to purchase luxury items with illegal funds, even though it might increase the chances of crimes being detected?
2. The IRS requires banks and brokers to report deposits or purchases with cash over $10,000. What might criminals do differently to avoid IRS detection?
3. Why might it be difficult for authorities to find a paper trail for things purchased with illegal funds?

EMBEZZLEMENT

The legal definition of *embezzlement* comes closest to the legal definition of financial crime. As we noted, earlier definitions of financial crime include any case in which a fiduciary responsibility has been violated. If a bank teller pockets a package of twenties out of the vault, that is considered embezzlement, punishable by firing at the very least and more likely treated as a criminal offense. The penalties for embezzlement vary from state to state based on the value of stolen money or goods.

Likewise, if a store employee goes home with merchandise from their place of business without paying for it, that is considered embezzlement, an offense less likely to result in criminal prosecution depending on the cost of the theft to the employer. Embezzlement is the most common type of crime that employees commit and when it happens, the white collar criminal tends to be a repeat offender who just hasn't been caught as yet.

Technically, there are very few employees who haven't embezzled at one time or another. Mostly this is unintentional. Think about the number of employees who take office supplies (e.g., pens, etc.) for their own personal use. It may seem like an innocuous offense, but if you think about companies with large numbers of employees, the cost of pilfered pens can add up. Employers have come to expect that, more or less, and it is unrealistic to chase after, reprimand, or fire every employee who has taken a pen from work. Employers and law enforcement will take disciplinary and legal action when the theft is too large to ignore (unlike the occasional pen being "borrowed"). CNBC reports that employee theft results in costs of up to $50 billion (USD) to employers each year (Pofeldt, 2017).

If we go back to our store employee example, if it becomes a common habit among employees at that store, it can cost a substantial amount of lost revenue for the owner. It would also be considered a form of embezzlement if the store employee is giving out their employee discounts to all their friends. If the store owner doesn't designate that employee discounts are allowed to be extended to friends and family, they are within their legal rights to have that employee fired and prosecuted for embezzlement, though the latter is rarely pursued.

Unless the theft of merchandise is a sizeable amount, generally stores take care of these types of employee thefts by simply firing the employee. In some cases, a business wishes to avoid any negative publicity and will not necessarily call in law enforcement. We should note that the greater bulk of merchandise loss to theft is not happening because of shoplifting, but due to employee theft. We should also note that when shoplifting occurs, it is generally treated as larceny-theft, which is a conventional crime. When employee theft occurs, it is considered embezzlement and therefore a white collar crime. Of course, much depends on how prosecutors want to charge the crime and the concerns of the store owner.

An embezzler does not necessarily have to be an employee of a company. They can be self-employed and, as part of their profession, are the court-appointed managers of other people's money, possessions (an "estate"), and in some cases, medical decisions. For example, when someone is unfortunately in a coma due to an injury or illness, they can no longer take care of their day-to-day affairs, including paying bills and making financial decisions on their own.

When an individual is unable to take care of their own finances or manage their own business affairs, a court may appoint someone to be their conservator. This means that individual is responsible for paying bills and making financial decisions on behalf of their client for a fee. In some cases, they may also be making medical decisions for the incapacitated individual. It is becoming more common for people to designate a health care proxy. Any personal possessions that a conservatoree might own has to be inventoried as part of the process of accounting for everything that conservatoree may have at the time that they can no longer handle their affairs. This is similar to the procedures an executor of an estate has to follow after an individual is deceased.

Often if the person who is responsible for a conservatorship is not an attorney, they will have one on retainer (fees paid in advance of legal work) or hire a lawyer from time to time as needed. *Conservatorships* are most commonly court ordered for individuals who are either severely disabled or elderly with diminished cognitive abilities, as in the case of Alzheimer's or dementia patients. Conservatorships can be temporary while an individual recovers, if the disability is temporary, or permanent legal arrangements.

Sometimes a family member acts as the conservator. In the now famous case of Britney Spears, her father took over her financial affairs during a period of her life when her judgement was called into question over her ability to handle her multimillion-dollar fortune. If the conservatorship is temporary, the individual whose name the conservatorship is in can petition the court to restore their rights to manage their financial affairs.

Most people who take on the responsibilities of conservatorships do so with no intention of stealing from their client. Unfortunately for some clients, sometimes the conservator's temptation is too great due to a number of reasons, including greed or character flaws, to take money or possessions that do not belong to them. In these cases, if they do take funds or material items away from the client's estate, it is considered embezzlement.

Though these cases don't generally make the headlines, most cases of embezzlement are low-level thefts, anywhere from a few dollars to a few thousand. The logic behind having smaller amounts stolen is that it is less detectable that larger sums. The other argument is "go big or go home." In some cases, the embezzlement is small amounts from different sources by the same individual, as in our examination of the Girl Scouts of America (GSA) and their annual cookie sale.

We should also note, as in the GSA case, that embezzlement does not only occur in for-profit corporations and companies. Unfortunately, it also occurs in the nonprofit sector, as in the case of leaders and laypeople in religious organizations skimming off the top of contributions. Over the course of a number of years, Barry Herr embezzled an estimated $1 million from his church, allegedly to purchase classic cars (*Christian Century*, 2009). A former president of the United Way of America, William Aramony, was jailed in 1995 for embezzlement and fraud amounting to over $1 million. In the past couple of decades of nonprofit scandals, there has been more demand for increased accountability (Keating and Frumkin, 2003), though it is a sensitive topic in organizations that are assumed to be populated with employees and volunteers devoted to philanthropy.

Law in the Real World: Patricia Cascione and Girl Scout Cookies

(Source: Granda, 2019; Mejia, 2019)

The Girl Scouts of America (GSA) have been selling cookies to raise funds for more than a century. Once upon a time, before the age of "helicopter parents," Girl Scouts would scour their neighborhoods, wagon in tow full with boxes of cookies, peddling them door-to-door. In recent decades, you are more likely to place an order with a parent/guardian of a scout or purchase the cookies at a table in front of a big box store or grocery market. Even more recently, GSA has taken to selling cookies in cyberspace. When there are virtual, face-to-face sales, it requires the girls or the parent/guardian to collect the funds. When the collection of funds in larger GSA local council is sizable, as it is in metropolitan areas, it requires the volunteer services of financial experts.

In the more affluent community of Santa Clarita, just north of Los Angeles, California, Girl Scout cookie sales can be expected to be robust. From 2013 to 2017, Patricia Cascione, a certified public accountant (CPA), volunteered her services as a treasurer for two local GSA chapters. In 2018, after a 15-month investigation of suspected fraud, she was arrested for allegedly embezzling over $90,000 from GSA troop bank accounts she had control over. She was initially charged with suspicion of theft and theft by false pretense.

What makes this case appear doubly unethical is that Cascione is also being accused of embezzling from the Beverly Hills Cancer Center where she was employed as their chief financial officer (CFO). Like the GSA, the Beverly Hills Cancer Center also functions as a nonprofit organization. She is being accused of funneling money from the cancer center to GSA accounts to embezzle. In March 2019, Cascione entered a not guilty plea to the charges and faces possible prison time if convicted. The investigation is still ongoing. Cascione was also offering her volunteer services to other nonprofit organizations, including fundraising for the Saugus High School girls' soccer team and managing a GoFundMe page for a young man who had been struck and killed by a vehicle. These are not mentioned in the current criminal complaint, but other charges may yet to be brought against Cascione.

Discussion Questions

1. In your estimation, do volunteers who embezzle from nonprofits purposely offer their services in order to have the opportunity to commit crimes, or initially begin volunteering in order to give back to their community?
2. What might drive an individual to steal from a nonprofit organization?
3. In what ways might these cases motivate donors to give less money to nonprofits when cases are made public?

MONEY LAUNDERING

When the cash starts rolling in from criminal activity, there are only a few ways to get rid of it: invest it, give it away, or start buying shiny objects. One of the biggest mistakes that conventional and white collar criminals do is start buying a lot of fancy things like cars, jewelry, and real estate that is obviously beyond the means they can legitimately make. This immediately draws attention to them, particularly if they start making purchases with large sums of cash. And it isn't like criminals are unaware of this fact. It is a common trope used in crime movies, where the criminal gets caught after driving around in some fancy car that attracts the interest of law enforcement.

One way to get rid of large sums of cash is to funnel it through a legitimate business, preferably one that deals primarily in cash transactions. The Italian Mafia traditionally owned cash-based businesses including restaurants, laundromats, and dry cleaners, hence the name "money laundering." It is still a very common practice for large scale drug dealers, prostitution rings, and other organized crime groups. The legitimate business then reports sales that are inflated to account for the cash flow. This is accomplished by creating fraudulent sales receipts, as in fake restaurant tabs. It is always suspicious when a restaurant that doesn't appear to have a lot of customers is depositing large sums of cash at the bank.

These days it is far less common to find cash-only businesses, but they can still be found. We should caution that not all cash-based businesses are money laundering operations. Some smaller business will only accept cash from their customers because they don't wish to incur the cost of allowing them to pay with credit or debit cards. If you have ever been to a store that had a point of sale (POS) terminal that can read your card strip or chip, those businesses pay fees to the card companies in order to accept credit or debit cards. Of course, we can't discount the businesses that dishonestly fail to report all of their cash sales in order to avoid paying taxes, which brings us to a topic coming up in this chapter, income tax evasion.

MAIL AND WIRE FRAUD

White collar criminals can be charged with mail or *wire fraud* if they use one or both of those vehicles to commit crimes. Mail fraud is any use of the U.S. Postal Service or private mail service to engage in illegally obtaining money or property. Mail fraud can also include the sale or distribution of counterfeits. Mail fraud is more closely related to consumer crimes than financial crimes, but it is not unusual for indictments for financial crimes include mail and/or wire fraud as well.

An example from consumer crime would be if someone is selling jewelry through a website such as Craigslist©, eBay© or Etsy© that they claim is solid 14-karat gold, when in fact it is gold-plated, which is far less expensive. As much as these websites fight fraud as much as they can, unscrupulous people do show up on from time to time. Depending on the scale of the offense, this crime example could be classified as both mail fraud and cybercrime.

Wire fraud, on the other hand, is the use of telecommunications, wires (as in wiring money between banks), and telegrams to commit financial crimes. For instance, in the case of *Pasquantino v. United States* (2005), the Supreme Court decided in favor of using a wire fraud charge in a case of buying alcohol in the U.S. and smuggling it into Canada to avoid Canadian excise taxes (Friedman, 2006).

INCOME TAX EVASION

In any country that collects taxes from individual or business income, there is the risk that people are not honestly reporting what they are really making. If an employee is working for a company, in the United States employers are required by law to collect payroll taxes, including federal income tax, Medicare, and Social Security taxes (FICA). If a state also requires state income tax, this too has to be taken out of the employees' paychecks. It is why when you are told what your gross income will be for a job, you may be very surprised at how much is taken out for taxes in your first paycheck.

If an individual is self-employed or an independent contractor working for an employer, they are responsible for their own payroll taxes. Depending on their income, these are sent to the IRS on a quarterly basis. According to CPA Practice Advisor (2018), 32 percent of self-employed workers underreport their income. This is most definitely a place where white collar criminal malfeasance can occur, when a small businessperson underreports their income. This crime is called income tax evasion because you are essentially avoiding paying all the taxes that you are legally obligated to pay to the government. We should note that self-employed individuals are more likely to be *audited* by the IRS.

Businesses can likewise fraudulently underreport their income. One way that businesses can do this, again possibly fraudulently, is to keep their bank deposits of cash under $10,000 (USD). Of course, small businesses can have faulty accounting practices, as most self-employed individuals are not CPAs, nor do they necessarily employ them for their day-to-day business. Accounting mistakes do happen. But if there is a consistent pattern of red flags, the IRS can and will investigate, sometimes resulting in criminal charges of income tax evasion.

One notorious case of income tax evasion is Al "Scarface" Capone. A Chicago mobster during Prohibition, he was believed to be directly or indirectly involved in a number of gangland homicides, he was never convicted of murder or other violent crimes. After Eliot Ness's failed attempts at capturing Capone red-handed, he took another tactic and with the help of his team, uncovered Capone's underreporting of his income. He was ultimately convicted of this crime and served prison time in the Eastern State Penitentiary in Philadelphia as well as in infamous Alcatraz prison, located on an island in San Francisco Bay. Though the IRS is certainly concerned about any crimes associated with income generation, they are primarily charged with collecting income taxes on any or all income, *earned* or *unearned*.

On the subject of unearned income, money that you make at your occupation is not the only type of funds that are taxable. You are required to pay taxes on some forms of returns on investments, including any profit you may have made on selling a home, depending on current tax laws. Any dividends earned on investments you might earn may be subject to capital gains taxes as well. It is much more difficult to underreport investment income, as most of this is reported to the IRS through financial institutions.

BANK FRAUD

There are a number of types of fraud against consumers, including defective products, failure to deliver on contracts or promises, and fraudulent use of donations in nonprofits, including donations collected in religious organizations. In this chapter we are focusing on the type of fraud that occurs within banking institutions. In some cases, the transactions appear to be completely legitimate, as in mortgage loan origination, in which case it is very difficult for the consumer and investors to know whether they are being deceived.

When examining bank fraud, we have to look at two sides of the coin. It is not always a bank or the bank industry that is doing the swindling. Consumers can likewise commit banking fraud as well. Overall, bankers can be the worst offenders, as we will see with the Wells Fargo Bank case discussed later in this chapter. As Black's 2005 book title claims, the best way to rob a bank is to own one.

If we begin with how people commit fraud against a bank, the most common form is lying on loan applications. Generally, where they are most apt to lie is about their income. It is a bit more difficult to lie about how much debt you have, as you are required to have a credit check run to check your FICO score, one measure of your credit worthiness and financial "health." Even with low interest rates on mortgage loans, with house prices rising exponentially in some areas (e.g., California and Massachusetts), there has been a sharp increase in mortgage fraud where borrowers "juice their incomes" in order to qualify for a loan (Olick, 2018).

RACKETEERING

Some of you who have studied organized crime may already be familiar with the term *racketeering*. What we see as charges for racketeering in organized crime cases are likely to fall under *Racketeer Influenced and Corrupt Organizations (RICO)* act, passed in 1970. Though originally used to target syndicate crime groups, prosecutors have found the law useful in prosecuting other types of corruption, including in law enforcement agencies and politicians, as the use of RICO was extended to civil cases where financial damages can be recouped (Coppola and DeMarco, 2012).

We also see charges of racketeering in white collar crime; less commonly known as RICO charges, except when there is an intersection of organized crime figures with white collar criminals working with them. Racketeering charges are used when there are a broad range of business crimes and malfeasances. Racketeering charges may not result in criminal prosecution, but rather warnings from regulators when detected. We are introducing the term here as there are a number of white collar criminals that have been convicted on racketeering charges, including in the case of Michael Milken, discussed later in this chapter.

2008 "DEEP RECESSION" AND WHITE COLLAR CRIME

One of the things that economists and politicians fear is whether we might slip into another economic downturn like the United States witnessed in 1929. On

October 29, 1929, after a period of economic expansion and overly inflated stock prices, the New York Stock Exchange witnessed a steep crash, with billions of dollars lost in one day. The Great Depression that followed lasted a decade. Since the Great Depression, there have been a number of regulatory precautions put into place to assure that there would never be another stock market crash like 1929.

For all these precautions, the United States very nearly had a second Great Depression when on September 29, 2008, the Dow Jones Industrial Average, the barometer of all stock exchanges around the world, fell 778 points on the heels of Congress failing to pass a bill that would bail out banks. It is not unusual for the U.S. government to bail out banks when they are faltering. It is one of the safeguards put in place following the stock market crash of 1929. One of the reasons that Congress did not vote to subsidize banks is that they were primarily in trouble due to questionable subprime mortgage lending practices.

During the 1990s and early 2000s, subprime mortgages were very popular so as to allow borrowers who would not ordinarily qualify for a mortgage to purchase a home. A subprime mortgage basically allows the borrower to start with a greatly reduced interest rate, making their monthly payments lower than if they had a standard mortgage interest rate. Mortgage interest rates are based on whatever the Federal Reserve has set, plus a bit more so that banks can make a profit on the loan.

The lower interest rate offered on a subprime mortgage is not indefinite. Eventually it will go up or down based on prevailing interest rates and a number of other factors. Some of these loans allowed borrowers to pay back only interest, never making a dent in the original loan amounts. If mortgage rates went up, the new rate on the subprime mortgage would go up, sometimes putting the borrower in a position of owing more than the original loan amount.

Both the bank and borrower are gambling that the borrower's income will go up to meet the demands of higher mortgage payments. However, in the last few decades wages have been fairly flat, not keeping up with inflation in most professions. There came a point where so many borrowers were defaulting on their mortgage loans, falling into foreclosure on their homes, that banks had an unmanageable number of properties that they now owned and loans that they had to charge off as losses.

The subprime mortgages were only the tip of the iceberg. What ultimately led to the mortgage mess was financial deregulation, allowing banks to devote more resources to hedge funds that were risky but more profitable. This in turn caused banks to require more mortgage loans, supposed to be a more stable income, to offset the volatility of hedge funds.

The reason we are spending so much time in discussion of what was essentially legal banking practices is that the 2008 stock market crash put into motion a number of things that ultimately led to the detection of white collar crime that had been going on just prior to the crash. These crimes, including Bernie Madoff's Ponzi scheme, discussed later in this chapter, and the case study of Iceland at the end of this chapter, only came to light when the stock market and world economy were sent into a tailspin.

PONZI SCHEMES

Pyramid sales structures in business, of which *Ponzi schemes* are one type, can be difficult to define as criminal. We have previously noted in this book that direct sales organizations (DSOs) are built on a pyramid structure, where people towards the top will make income off of people they manage below them. In some cases, directors in DSOs are actually earning commissions off of the inventory that people below them are purchasing from the company, not on their actual sales. Though it may not seem ethical, as many people fail while operating as independent contractors in direct sales when they cannot sell the product for whatever reason, it is not considered illegal. It is simply considered controversial by some people's standards.

Pyramid schemes, whether legitimate or illegitimate, are highly dependent on social network ties. More importantly, they are dependent on trust in social ties, plus as opportunity theories in criminology will tell us, someone to encourage people from parting with their money (Nash et al., 2018). Using our DSOs as an example, unless a friend or family member cautions us against investing in inventory, we might be tempted to take on credit card debt in order to pay for it, with no guarantee of actually selling than inventory.

Where a pyramid scheme is clearly criminal is when earlier investors are seemingly being paid dividends on their investments, when they are actually being paid with funds coming in from new investors. These investment instruments are usually sold as being very lucrative with fast and high returns on investments. If this is the case, we call this a Ponzi scheme.

Named after Charles Ponzi, a con artist who dangled big returns on investors' money in the early part of the 20th century, Ponzi schemes represent one of the oldest swindles in financial crimes. According to Rosoff et al. (2013), Ponzi convinced approximately 20,000 investors to give him nearly $10 million through his Boston company, Financial Exchange Company. He did so by promising an unheard of 50 percent return on investments within 45 days (Rosoff et al., 2013). His promises of outrageous returns caught the attention of *The Boston Post*. Once the newspaper began investigating Ponzi's scheme, his clients became nervous and began to pull out of the investment (Rosoff et al., 2019). As we will see in the following case of Bernie Madoff, these schemes can play out for a long time before being detected. In Ponzi's case, it was a newspaper exposé that was his undoing. For Bernie Madoff, it was the events in 2008 that ultimately set off a global financial crisis.

Law in the Real World: Bernie Madoff

(Source: Committee of Financial Services, U.S. House of Representatives, 2009; Dangremond, 2017)

Perhaps the granddaddy of all Ponzi schemes was Bernie Madoff's 26-year escapade, which he almost got away with but for the stock market crash of 2008. Swindling investors out of billions of dollars, Madoff would attract new clients while paying existing investors "dividends" with the money that new investors brought in. There were no real investments being made on behalf of clients. Madoff was illegally pocketing large sums of investors' money to spend on himself and keep him and his family in the lap of luxury.

Some of Madoff's list of victims reads like a who's who of Hollywood royalty, including director Steven Spielberg, actors Kevin Bacon and Kyra Sedgwick, and talk show host Larry King. Politicians including former New York governor Eliot Spitzer, himself disgraced by a prostitution scandal, invested with Bernie Madoff, only to lose money. Even Holocaust survivor, college professor, and writer Elie Wiesel was among his victims. These were not unintelligent, naïve investors, a tribute to just how clever and deceitful Madoff's scheme was.

Individual investors were not the only ones who lost large amounts of money with Madoff. Investment banks in the U.S. and abroad were among his victims as well. Yeshiva University and Stony Brook University in the U.S. invested their *endowments*, funds that are mainstays of university finances, in Madoff's scheme. Of all people to practice due diligence, the number of financial wizards in banks and universities who were taken in by Madoff's scheme was a surprise.

In all fairness, the SEC was not completely unaware of Madoff's activities. However, with a notoriously limited budget and staffing, they were limited as to how fast they could investigate his financial dealings. The grossly understaffed agency oversees thousands of *mutual funds* and tens of thousands of financial advisors.

Additionally, Madoff would mislead government examiners from the SEC with documents that were doctored to look legitimate. As Representative Kanjorski (Pennsylvania, 11th congressional district) noted in the Congressional hearing looking into the Madoff affair, it was like sending a mouse to conduct an audit on an elephant.

As art (and Hollywood) can imitate life, a number of books, films, and documentaries came out after the Madoff scandal, including

- *Chasing Madoff* (MPI Media Group, 2012)
- *Madoff* (Series, Amazon Prime, 2016)

- *The Wizard of Lies* (Cleon Movies, HBO, 2017)

Unfortunately, many investors do not follow through with the due diligence in fully researching an investment opportunity (Nash et al., 2018), particularly if they get word of a "good opportunity" through their friends and family members. Certainly when it comes to investments, if it sounds too good to be true, having greater returns than what we would ordinarily expect from any given market, it is either an extremely risky investment or it might be a Ponzi scheme.

Discussion Questions

1. Why might investors fail to investigate potential investments?
2. Why did Madoff get away with his scheme for so long?
3. On average, do investors trust their friends and family more than financial advisors?

INSIDER TRADING AND TIPPING

For those of you who are unfamiliar with stock markets and *securities*, a brief tutorial on how they work might be helpful in understanding the crime of *insider trading*. When companies need to raise capital (e.g., cash) in order to start up or continue to stay in business, they may decide to go "public." What we mean by that is they will open opportunities to investors to buy stock in their company.

The stock entitles the investor to receive returns on their investments (most commonly dividends) by sharing in any profits the company might make in selling their product or services. Investors can also make money on their investments when the price of the stock goes up and they sell it. There is also the risk of stock losing value. The stock prices used to determine their value will go up and down; any experienced investor knows to weather bad markets and not get too optimistic in good ones. The price of the stock is dependent on the demand for the stock, meaning that investors do risk losing their original investment if a company falls apart due to bad management or decreased demand.

When a company first offers stock to the public, it is called an initial public offering (IPOs). Depending on the company, it can mean a very lucrative return on the investment, though these investments are riskier to the investor than more established company *stocks*. Buying stock in the right IPO can be profitable as well, as early investors in Google® and Apple® can attest to.

Other securities can include a number of investments, including debt securities (bonds) where the investor is actually lending money. Unlike stocks, where the company is under no obligation to pay back the initial investment, bonds are a commitment by a company or government to not only pay back the original investment amount, but guarantee a set amount of interest to be paid as well. In bond funds, the investment return may fluctuate.

For example, a city wants to build a new subway system. One way of raising funds is to offer government bonds to investors, where they lend money to the government. Bonds have a maturity date, with a specific date as to when the loan is to be paid back to investors with interest. This was a common practice during WWII, when the U.S. government sold war bonds where the government borrowed money from investors to fund the war effort with a promise to pay back the bond loan.

Government bond investments are for the most part extremely safe investments, at least when the government is of a country with a stable economy and leadership. However, like some individuals, the company or government might become insolvent, go broke, and end up defaulting on the loan. This means that there is still the risk that the bond will go unpaid, along with the interest due to the investor.

Other types of securities, including derivatives, futures, and mineral securities, are beyond the scope of this book. However, the reader should be made aware that all types of securities, including these, may be tools in which insider traders can commit crimes. With any investment, there is the risk that it will provide a means by which white collar criminals and organized crime can make incredibly large sums in illegitimate profits.

Insider trading, one of the most ambiguous financial crimes that we will discuss, is when an individual buys or sells stock or other securities based on information that has not been made public yet. In theory, this gives that individual an unfair advantage over the general population of stock market investors and runs counter to free market enterprise. In a market economy, there are a lot of questions as to whether insider trading should even be considered a crime. The whole philosophy behind a free market is for there to be unrestricted supply and demand of things we purchase and sell, with little to no government interference or regulation including in investments. This is impractical in practice, as there are real concerns for the safety and financial wellbeing of investors.

We should make a clear distinction between legitimate and illegitimate stock trading. If you work for a company and are part of the management team, in all likelihood, if that company offers stock to investors, you will own some. It is perfectly legitimate to invest money in one's place of employment, otherwise employee stock options (ESOPs) would be illegal. However, the Securities and Exchange Commission (SEC), a government regulatory agency, is charged with making sure that all securities purchases and sales, including stock, are conducted within legal guidelines.

A legitimate insider trader is an employee or company owner who buys and sells their company stock based on information that has already been made public. This requires a lot of moral fortitude in legitimate insider traders. Remember, one of the most famous pieces of advice (right or wrong) given to investors is to buy low, sell high. If an individual is working for a company that is about to put out a new product that may revolutionize a whole industry, like what we saw in the 1980s and computer technology, it would take a lot of willpower not to purchase large amounts of stock in that company based on information that has not been made public.

Conversely, if an investor becomes aware by a company insider that a stock is going to plummet based on bad news that hasn't been made public yet, it would be ever so tempting to dump that stock, selling it before the stock price drops. However, it can be confusing as to whether the stock sale is legitimate when this happens, as experienced investors will often have standing orders with their brokers to sell if a stock drops to a certain price. This way the investor can at least minimize their losses with more risky investments.

Take, for instance, an auto manufacturer who has advertised a new model car to be ready for purchase in spring. Because it is being advertised publicly, someone who works for that company can legitimately purchase company stock if they think they would like to gamble on the popularity of the new car. However, if engineers suddenly find a design flaw that needs to be addressed, pushing back the date for when the car will be ready for the showroom floor, that can be a whole different story.

If it looks like there might be a rush to market with the car before it really isn't ready, risking vehicle recalls, and this has not been announced to the general public yet, it is considered to be insider information. Company employees are prohibited by law to buy or sell stock in advance of the information being released to the public, at which time the announcement may very well have an effect on stock prices as investors lose confidence in the company.

Law in the Real World: Martha Stewart

(Source: SEC, 2003; New York Times, 2004)

One more famous case of stock dumping was Martha Stewart, who at one point was accused of acting on insider information. Stewart, a household name in home décor and culinary skills, had by the early 2000s amassed a vast business empire, including a popular magazine, *Martha Stewart Living*. Within her investment portfolio, Stewart owned stock in ImClone Systems, a pharmaceutical company specializing in oncology and cancer treatments. Yet there are a lot of misconceptions about what Stewart was ultimately convicted of.

In 2001, allegedly on a tip from her broker, Peter Bacanovic, Stewart sold 4,000 shares of stock in the company in advance of a public announcement that a promising cancer drug being tested by the company was not going to receive FDA approval (Hays, 2004). Stewart and her broker, Bacanovic, were charged by the SEC with securities fraud (SEC, 2003). Lesser charges filed by the States Attorney for the Southern District of New York against Stewart and Bacanovic included providing false statements to investigators, a criminal offense (SEC, 2003).

As we have noted with elite crimes and prosecution, Stewart was in an enviable position for an alleged offender, as she had the means to hire highly qualified criminal lawyers. Stewart's defense was that she had a standing understanding with her broker to sell ImClone Systems in a "stop-loss" order. Though the urban myth is that Stewart was convicted on insider trading, in reality she was found guilty of the four lesser counts of obstruction of justice and lying to investigators, but not on the more serious charge of insider trading (Eaton, 2004).

Stewart could have conceivably been sentenced to years in prison. Instead she received the minimum sentence of five months in prison, five months of home confinement with an ankle monitor, and was ordered to pay a $30,000 USD fine and court costs (Hays, 2004). If you compare this to the typical 1-year minimum sentence for drug possession, Stewart got off relatively lightly.

Technically, Stewart could have appealed her conviction. As stock prices in her own publicly traded company, Martha Stewart Living, Inc. (now Martha Stewart Living Omnimedia, Inc.) had become erratic, Stewart made the decision to serve her sentence in order to put the scandal behind her as quickly as possible. She served her sentence at a minimum-security prison for women, in Alderson, West Virginia, nicknamed "Camp Cupcake" for its relative freedom for inmates as compared to more secure facilities.

Once released, Stewart was able to resume running her company during house confinement in her Connecticut home and permission to travel to her corporate offices in New York City. During the period of house confinement, she was ordered to wear an ankle monitor for the remainder of her sentence. It proved to be a smart business decision to not appeal her conviction, as the stock in her company recovered quickly and Stewart continues to be a successful businessperson to this day in spite of her conviction and prison time.

Discussion Questions

1. Martha Stewart was reportedly worth over a billion dollars when she committed insider trading. She only stood to lose approximately $60K had she waited to sell her ImClone stock when the news went public. What might motivate her to take this risk?

2. Why might her crime hurt her product name, even though most of her customers were no doubt unfamiliar with the complexity of the case?

3. Why do you think that some famous people survive crime scandals, whereas some never recover their reputations?

Martha Stewart is by far not the worst offender when it comes to insider trading. In the last chapter, you were introduced to the case of Dennis Levine and his insider trading network. One of the most notorious people within Levine's inner circle was Ivan Boesky, who started his own stock brokerage firm in the 1970s, Ivan F. Boesky and Company. If you recall, Wall Street was in the middle of a mergers and acquisition frenzy in the 1980s, and Boesky's company was legitimately exploiting this contagion. The legitimacy of Boesky's company was quickly overshadowed by his shameless illegal insider trading, uncovered in 1986 (Hansen, 2004).

Insider trading is the most difficult for regulators to detect when it happens. There are several reasons for this, the least of which is that regulatory agencies, like the SEC are notoriously understaffed. The funding of regulatory agencies is closely tied to the political climate. It ebbs and flows with whatever way the political wind is blowing, dependent on who is currently holding office in both the executive and legislative branches of the government. To a lesser extent, who occupies the court benches within the judicial branch also will have an effect on agencies' abilities to regulate insider trading.

The person who illegally sells or buys stock based on insider information is not the only one in trouble. The person who leaks insider information can also be held criminally responsible for *insider tipping*. Any time someone tells someone else information that has not been made public and can affect stock prices in a publicly traded company, there is the potential for the information to be be used to commit insider trading.

JUNK BOND MARKET, SAVINGS AND LOANS, AND CONTROL FRAUD

The definition of *control fraud* is similar to the definition of white collar crime. Essentially, it is a case in which people in positions where they have a responsibility to act in the best interest of their clients, customers, or constituents will engage in fraudulent activity for their own personal gain, at the expense of those they are expected to serve. Control frauds can be committed by individuals, entire corporations, or government agencies. The Savings and Loan banking sector is particularly vulnerable to control fraud (Black, 2005, pp. xiii-xiv):

"In the 1980s, a wave of control frauds ravaged the savings and loan industry.... Several factors make control frauds uniquely dangerous. The person who controls a company (or country) can defeat all internal and external controls because [s]he is ultimately in charge of these controls."

Junk bonds are exactly what they sound like and are one vehicle used in control fraud schemes. Investments in what could ultimately be worthless in the long run, junk bonds offer extremely high risk, but high reward if they pay off. Most people who invest in these riskier investments are well aware of the risks. However, that is not always the case, as we shall see with Lincoln Savings and Loan in the 1980s. Continuing the theme in this chapter of regulations failing to prevent crimes, regulations surrounding junk bonds have ebbed and flowed between permissive and restricting depending on which way the political wind is blowing.

The junk bond market itself was largely built during the 1970s and 1980s by another notorious white collar crime offender, Michael Milken. Milken operated out of the posh Beverly Hills offices on Wilshire Boulevard of Drexel Burnham Lambert, an investment firm. Diving into the madness of the mergers and acquisitions frenzy in the 1980s, Milken developed the low-rated bond market with so called "fallen angels," companies that had once been prosperous but had fallen on hard times and needed capital to survive (Teitelman, 2016). Though Milken was reputed to fly under the radar, avoiding publicity, he almost singlehandedly created the environment in which Charles Keating and other nefarious investment professionals defrauded their customers. We should note that in 2020, President Trump pardoned Milken for his white collar crimes, as allowed within the executive privileges of the office of the President of the United States (*Wall Street Journal*, 2020).

Law in the Real World: Lincoln Savings and Loan

(Source: Black, 2005)

In 1984, Charles "Charlie" Keating bought Lincoln Savings and Loan through his company, American Continental Corporation. A savings and loan bank is different from a commercial bank in that there is more focus on lending, including mortgages. Savings and loan banks are under the same types of regulations as commercial banks for deposits, but with an additional set of regulations exclusive to them in mortgage lending.

Keating ultimately took unethical and illegal risks with depositors' money at Lincoln Savings and Loan, aggressively recommending that they invest largely in the unsecured junk bond market. As many of these depositors were retirees on fixed incomes, they could little afford to take gambles with their savings. He ended up defrauding approximately 23,000 investors out of about $250 million (Black, 2005). We should note that during this time, Keating was reportedly living a lavish lifestyle, receiving $19.4 million in salary, stock options, and a number of other forms of compensation, over the course of five years before his crimes were discovered (Christie, 2014).

Keating could not have gotten away with peddling the risky investments by himself. After Keating purchased the bank and began running into trouble in 1987 with auditors who were questioning his risky investments, he scrambled to keep the federal government from seizing the bank. It is important to note that Lincoln Savings and Loan used the accounting firm of Arthur Andersen, the same company in the Enron scandal discussed later in this book (Black, 2005).

When a bank is so badly managed as a result of serious crimes or malfeasance perpetrated by its owners or managers that the government can seize the bank, it puts the whole banking industry at risk. Keating convinced a group of senators, the "Keating 5," to relax the regulations around savings and loans institutions. The "Keating 5" included Senators Alan Cranston (D-California), John Glenn (D-Ohio), Dennis DeConcini (D-Arizona), John McCain (R-Arizona), and Don Riegle (D-Michigan), all of whom Keating had given generously to their election campaigns (Nowicki and Muller, 2018).

Ultimately, Lincoln Savings and Loan failed by 1989. Thousands of retired pensioners were left with worthless bonds and lost, in some cases, their life's savings. Keating was convicted in state and federal courts on several wire and bankruptcy fraud charges, some of which he pleaded guilty to. Initially sentenced to 10 years in prison, of which he served a little over 2 years; prosecutors impressed by his cooperation with the investigation were convinced to advocate for a lighter sentence.

Discussion Questions

1. There was a bit of political fallout for the five senators involved in helping with deregulation of the bond market but most of them survived, including John Glenn and John McCain, who went on to be well-respected members of Congress. In this day and age of social media, would it be as easy to rehabilitate their reputations after a scandal as large as the junk bond crisis?
2. Should there be additional penalties to white collar criminals when their activities result in the failure of the companies that they work for?
3. As we have seen in a number of white collar crimes in this chapter, why might it be that federal regulatory agencies may be slow to respond to evidence pointing to criminal activity in banks?

As a postscript to the Lincoln Savings and Loan scandal, there were a number of other people involved in selling junk bonds that ended up being prosecuted, though none quite as bold in their crimes. For his part in creating a junk bond crisis in the first place, as well as his involvement with insider trading as a part of Denise Levine's network, Michael Milken likewise was indicted and charged with racketeering. Charges were also filed against Drexel Burnham Lambert. By 1990, Drexel Burnham Lambert filed for bankruptcy as a result of its criminal activity, ultimately collapsing in 1994 (Rosoff et al., 2013). Milken was sentenced to 10 years in prison but released after 2 years for good behavior. He was also fined $600 million, which gives a pretty good indication of just how wealthy he was as well as how seriously the courts took his offenses.

Like other white collar criminals who have the financial means to start over after serving time in prison, Milken continued work as cofounder of a charitable foundation (Milken Family Foundation, available at https://www.mff.org/) and launched a nonprofit think tank and consulting firm, the Milken Institute (https://www.milkeninstitute.org/). Though he has been barred from selling securities or any other investment product, Milken has managed to reinvent himself after his fall from grace.

SUMMARY

Financial crimes give us closest to the original definition of crime, where respectable people in respectable occupations steal from their employers or clients. Whereas we are all likely to fall victim to consumer crime some time in our life, we are somewhat less likely to be taken advantage of a financial crime perpetrated by individuals in companies. Most of the damage is done against employers, in some cases irreparably ruining the reputations of companies, corporations, and in some cases a whole industry, as we saw with Lincoln Savings and Loan.

Financial crimes cannot occur without some complacency in regulation. Like in the case of insider trading, the regulation itself is ambiguous and there are philosophical differences as to whether a crime has even been committed. We also noted in this chapter that in most cases the regulatory agencies, including the SEC, are understaffed, overwhelmed, and left with few resources to combat financial crimes. Funding and attitudes towards regulation is highly dependent on the political environment.

We have only scratched the surface of financial crimes in this chapter. In 2018 alone, the SEC brought 821 actions against offenders and obtained court orders for more than $3.9 billion (USD) in penalties and restitution (SEC, 2018). Because not all employee theft is reported to law enforcement, there are untold billions of dollars' worth of cash and merchandise stolen every year by employees and in some cases, when banking fraud occurs, an untold number of victims.

Case Study ▪ **Iceland Financial Meltdown**

(Source: Grettisson, 2018; Benediktsdóttir et al., 2017; Hofverberg, 2014)

Background

For those who are unfamiliar with the geographic location of Iceland, it is a relatively small island nation in the North Atlantic Ocean northwest of the U.K, and a bit southeast of Greenland. Like Hawaii, Iceland was built from volcanos, some of which are still active today. Iceland is considered to be part of western Europe, having once been a part of Denmark's empire, and has an approximate population of 340,000 (2019). Relatively speaking, the country has a fairly non-diverse economy, where the primary industries prior to 2008 were fishing, geothermal energy, and banking. Unfortunately for Icelanders, its banking industry was built on a house of cards. Some speculate that the global banking crisis occurred not solely because of the U.S. mortgage mess, but began in Iceland, this otherwise unassuming tiny island nation.

Iceland had not historically been a major player in world markets, but in the 1990s it grew to be a formidable competitor within the banking sector. Originally state-owned, Icelandic banks became private enterprises in the 2000s. Similar to Wall Street oversight, once Icelandic banks were no longer under state control, regulation became laxer and more ambiguous. Icelandic banks under privatization were largely unregulated, more likely to give into market pressures for risky lending.

Defining the Crime(s)

Much of what we saw with the 2008 financial meltdown felt around the world could be classified as bank fraud. As this was an international event and financial crimes are defined differently globally, we will stick to the broader terms of lending irregularities in banks. The difficulty in defining bank fraud is that if lending practices are widespread and legitimate, as in the case of subprime mortgage loans, it is a question of whether it is illegitimate (or should be) or simply immoral.

Bank fraud can happen in a number of ways. Under 18 U.S. Code §1344, bank fraud is defined as any successful or attempted act to defraud financial institutions or to obtain money from financial institutions under false pretenses, e.g., providing false proof of ability to repay a loan (Legal Information Institute, n.d.).

When all three Icelandic banks collapsed during the 2008 financial crisis, Icelanders, along with thousands of global stakeholders, suffered large losses. The krona, the currency of Iceland, fell sharply in value. The Central Bank of Iceland, functioning similarly to the Federal Reserve in the United States, was unable to take over as a lending institution, further contributing to Iceland's financial crisis. Banks in Britain and the Netherlands, where Icelandic banks filtered some of their debt securities market, mistakenly thought their money was protected with insurance, similar to the *Federal Deposit Insurance Corporation (FDIC)* insurance in the United States. Unfortunately for these investors, there were no such safeguards in Icelandic banks. This resulted in years of litigation against Iceland banks.

One of the contributing factors in Iceland's financial crisis was that some of the loans being made after privatization constituted banking fraud. In one instance alone, the CEO and chairman of the board of Kaupþing Bank were indicted for extending a loan to Qatar investor Sheikh Mohammed Bin Khalifa Bin Hamad Al Thani, who in turn used the money to buy shares in the bank. This is considered to be market abuse and fraud under Iceland's Securities Act.

Theories to Explain the Crime

One of the best theories that we might use to explain not only the Iceland financial meltdown but also the worldwide financial crisis in 2008 is Donaldson's (2012; Kvalnes and Nordal, 2019) *Normalization Theory*. Within the theory, there is a question as to when less than moral behavior becomes normative. In other words, we go back to that age-old explanation for bad behavior, given to parents when their offspring have been caught doing something wrong: "But everyone is doing it!" As Donaldson (2012) describes it, when the whole group has neutralized the moral code, it is difficult to get anyone to return to more ethical behavior.

Similar to other criminological theories, the normalizing of bad behavior can bring about a number of forms of denial. According to Kvalnes and Nordal (2019), these can include denial of injury to the victim or victims and denial that victims even exist, claiming that they themselves are to blame for what has befallen on them. The opus often sung by corporations, including financial institutions, is "buyer beware!" You are responsible for your own financial mistakes, even if the financial institution can legitimately be blamed.

An additional theory we might suggest to add is one that comes by way of the psychology of consumer behavior from Sigmund Freud. Like a child, adults can sometimes fall prey to magical thinking. If you wish very hard for something, then it will appear. However, in the case of financial fraud, it is more like wishing very hard for unethical behavior to magically become acceptable because the financial rewards continue to be too great as compared to the rewards for moral behavior. If this is done collectively, as in the case of Icelandic bankers all acting together, then it is difficult to return to what had previously been morally acceptable behavior.

As psychologists suggest, magical thinking can be an obstacle to making good, sound, and ethical decisions (Stavrova and Meckel, 2017).

Social and Media Responses

The reactions to the Iceland crisis were less a reaction to the immediate impending financial doom than they were a testament to the sturdiness of the Icelandic people. Known to be politically vocal, if not charmingly eccentric at times, Icelanders demanded immediate attention to the problem as economic development came to a standstill and jobs were lost. After all, Iceland was the country that brought the Pirate Party, once a tiny social movement based on Swedish and German idealisms (Leurth, 2016), into serious political consideration. The Pirate Party may have only gained such popularity, particularly with younger voters, because of the financial crisis (Leurth, 2016), but Iceland is a unique country that will easily throw an individual or party out of power and replace them with, in their uniquely collective estimation, a better alternative.

There has also been more worldwide attention on how Iceland bounced back and less, at least in popular, mainstream media, on the financial crisis. Even though Iceland was arguably one of the first dominoes to fall in 2008, setting off a chain reaction of financial crises around the world, they were largely ignored in the media as one of the primary catalysts.

Criminal Justice and Policy Responses

Though the types of investments and loans that banks were making were questionable and unethical because there was little in the way of regulation, they were not technically illegal. It is rare for bankers to be prosecuted for their deeds that help create financial crises. This was not the case in Iceland. In total, 36 bankers were convicted on various bank fraud charges and sentenced collectively to 96 years in prison. The director of Kaupþing Bank received the harshest sentence of a total of 7 years.

We should note the significance of these convictions for two reasons. First, all of the bank directors in Iceland were convicted for their part in contributing to the financial crisis, unheard of in any other western country. Second, Iceland, being a small, homogenic country, functions on reliance on strong societal norms, and does not have a large prison population to begin with. To incarcerate 36 white collar criminals has been significant by Icelandic criminal justice standards.

Unlike government reactions in the United States and elsewhere to similar financial crises, Iceland did not resort to direct bailout of their banks. Benediktsdóttir et al. (2017, p. 194) suggest that the Iceland example serves as a case study in what to do in the event of a banking crisis: "let the banks go bust!" As a direct result of the crisis, the Icelandic legislature passed laws immediately for government control of the banks. The Icelandic government also put in place deposit guarantees in hopes of regaining faith in the financial institutions. The government also created a Special Investigation Commission (SIC) in 2008 to get to the bottom of the crisis and to help prevent similar bank failures in the future. The newly formed SIC concluded that the crisis was first created by the rapid growth of the financial sector, which overtook the bulk of Gross Domestic Product (GDP). Because of this rapid growth, the SIC concluded that the banks became too large, with balance sheets and lending portfolios mismanaged and out of control.

Unanswered Questions and Unresolved Issues Related to the Case

Iceland, like the rest of the world, has somewhat bounced back from the 2008 financial crisis. In recent years, Iceland has become a very popular tourist destination, attracting over 2 million people a year to its glaciers, Blue Lagoon hot springs, and a variety of outdoor adventures. However, Iceland has been cautioned to not depend on tourism indefinitely, as like the banking bubble, it too can come crashing down due to a number of factors, including volcanic activity that disrupts air travel and the rising costs of travel to Iceland because of its current popularity. How much that Iceland has heeded this warning remains to be seen, in light of the disruption of travel worldwide due to COVID-19 pandemic.

Sources

Benediktsdóttir, S., G. B. Eggertsson, and E. Þórarinsson. (2017) The rise, fall, and resurrection of Iceland: A postmortem analysis of the 2008 financial crisis. Brooks Papers on Economic Activity. Fall: 191-308.

Donaldson, T. (2012) Three ethical roots of the economic crisis. *Journal of Business Ethics*. Vol. 106, No. 1: 5-8.

Grettisson, V. (2018) 36 bankers, 96 years in jail. The Reykjavík Grapevine. Feb 7. Retrieved from https://grapevine.is/news/2018/02/07/36-bankers-96-years-in-jail/.

Hofverberg, E. (2014) Iceland: Icelandic bankers jailed for fraud. *Global Legal Monitor, The Law Library of Congress*. July 30. Retrieved from https://www.loc.gov/law/foreign-news/article/iceland-icelandic-bankers-jailed-for-fraud/.

Kvalnes, Ø. and S. Nordal. (2019) Normalization of questionable behavior: An ethical root of the financial crisis in Iceland. *Journal of Business Ethics*. Vol. 159: 761-775.

Legal Information Institute. (n.d.) U.S. Code §1344. Bank fraud. Cornell University Law School. Open access. Retrieved from https://www.law.cornell.edu/uscode/text/18/1344.

Leurth, B. (2016) Iceland's Pirate Party: What is it—and how did it become so popular? *The Conversation*. Oct. 28. Retrieved from http://theconversation.com/icelands-pirate-party-what-is-it-and-how-did-it-become-so-popular-67879.

Spicer, A. (2009) The normalization of corrupt business practices: Implications for Integrative Social Contracts Theory (ISCT). Journal of Business Ethics. Vol. 88: 833-840.

Stavrova, O. and A. Meckel. (2017) The role of magical thinking in forecasting the future. British Journal of Psychology. Vol. 108: 148-168.

GLOSSARY

Audit   An internal or external review of accounting and financial practices of an organization that may or may not be required by law.

Conservatorship   Either a court-appointed family member or guardian who oversees the personal and business affairs of individuals. Those individuals are deemed by the court to be temporarily or permanently mentally or physically limited and cannot care for their own affairs.

Control fraud   Any financial malfeasance or criminal act that is committed by a person for personal gain, who is highly placed in an organization, including a company, corporation, nonprofit, or government office, agency.

Earned income   Income you make by selling your labor, either as an independent contractor or employee, often subject to state and federal taxes, depending on income level.

Embezzlement   Theft of property or money by employees, trustees, or other individuals who are paid to safeguard them.

Endowment   Generally charitable donations in the form of money or property given to nonprofit causes. Endowments can be given while donor is alive or can be bequeathed in a will after their death.

Federal Deposit Insurance Corporation (FDIC)   Created after the Great Depression, the Federal Deposit Insurance Corporation insures deposits in banks, credit unions, and thrifts that are insured by the FDIC that is backed by the U.S. government. Depositors are insured up to $250,000 per account, with some exceptions. *See* https://www.fdic.gov/deposit/deposits/brochures/deposit-insurance-at-a-glance-english.html for more details on FDIC insurance.

Fiduciary responsibility   The responsibility of an individual to act in the best interest of their employer or client while entrusted with their money or other assets, including property.

Insider tipping   Telling someone information that has not been made public about a publicly traded company that might result in their stock going up or down.

Insider trading   Selling or buying stocks or other market investments on information that has not been made public. Example: A pharmaceutical executive buys stock in a company before there is an FDA announcement that a new drug will be approved.

Mutual funds   An investment fund that trades in a diversified portfolio and is managed by a certified financial professional.

Ponzi schemes   Pyramid schemes that often offer unrealistic returns on investments where people who first invested in them are being paid dividends from new investors contributions rather than from a legitimate investment product.

Pyramid marketing   All Ponzi schemes are pyramid schemes, but not all pyramid marketing structures are Ponzi schemes that are illegitimate. *See Ponzi schemes.*

Racketeering   Broad category of crimes that involve deceptive or fraudulent business transactions. First used in prosecution of organized crime figures, now commonly used in charging white collar criminals.

RICO Act of 1970   Racketeer Influenced and Corrupt Organizations Act (RICO) is a federal law that was initially passed to target organized crime, allowing for greater criminal or civil penalties if crimes are committed as part of an established criminal enterprise. In recent decades, it is used to prosecute street gangs and white collar criminals.

Securities   Tradable and sellable investments that can result in profit or loss for its owner and are not insured by the FDIC, like bank deposits. Example: stocks.

Shell companies   Companies that do not have a physical location, employees, or assets, but are used to raise money, conduct hostile takeovers, start a new business, or add additional businesses to an already established company. Shell companies are not illegal per se, but can be used to hide criminal activities.

Stocks   Investments in companies that give the investor the potential to share in the profits of those companies. There is also the risk of losing some or all of the investment if a company goes out of business with no take over or buyer.

Unearned income   Income that is generated by investments, including stock dividends, and profits made in the sale of assets, including stocks, real estate, collectables (e.g., art works).

Wire fraud   Any financial fraud where telecommunications, including cable, telegraph, or information technology is used to commit the crime.

REFERENCES AND SUGGESTED READINGS

Abolafia, M. Y. (2001) *Making Markets: Opportunism and Restraint on Wall Street.* Cambridge, MA: Harvard University Press.

Adam, S., L. Arnold, and Y. Ho. (2018) The story of Malaysia's 1MDB, the scandal that shook the world of finance. *Bloomberg.* Dec 17. Available at https://www.bloomberg.com/news/articles/2018-05-24/how-malaysia-s-1mdb-scandal-shook-the-financial-world-quicktake.

Benediktsdóttir, S., G. B. Eggertsson, and E. Þórarinsson. (2017) The rise, fall, and resurrection of Iceland: A postmortem analysis of the 2008 financial crisis. *Brooks Papers on Economic Activity.* Fall:191-308.

Black, W. K. (2005) *The Best Way to Rob a Bank is to Own One.* Austin, TX: University of Texas Press.

The Christian Century. (2009) Church embezzlers also rob congregations of trust. Sept. 22, Vol. 126, Issue 19:16.

Christie, B. (2014) Swindler Keating dies at 90. *Associated Press, Daily Hampshire Gazette.* April 10. Retrieved from https://www.gazettenet.com/Archives/2014/04/keating-hg-040214.

Dangremond, S. (2018) The most famous victims of Bernie Madoff's Ponzi scheme. *Town and Country.* Nov. 20. Retrieved from https://www.townandcountrymag.com/society/money-and-power/g13797624/bernie-madoff-victims/.

Eaton, L. (2004) The Martha Stewart verdict: The overview; Stewart found guilty of lying in sale of stock. *The New York Times.* March 6. Retrieved from https://www.nytimes.com/2004/03/06/business/martha-stewart-verdict-overview-stewart-found-guilty-lying-sale-stock.html.

Friedman, J.S. (2006) Whiskey and the wires: The inadvisable application of the wire fraud statute to alcohol smuggling and foreign tax evasion. *The Journal of Criminal Law and Criminology.* Vol. 96, No. 3: 911-945.

Gorman, T. (1999) Bookkeeper in estate fraud case enters guilty plea. *Los Angeles Times.* Nov. 11. Retrieved from https://www.latimes.com/archives/la-xpm-1999-nov-11-me-32277-story.html.

Granda, C. (2019) Embezzlement suspect accused of stealing more than $88,000 from Girl Scout troops, Beverly Hills Cancer Center. *ABC Channel 7.* Retrieved from https://abc7.com/woman-accused-of-embezzling-more-than-$88k-from-nonprofits/4285406/.

Grettisson, V. (2018) 36 bankers, 96 years in jail. *The Reykjavík Grapevine.* Feb 7. Retrieved from https://grapevine.is/news/2018/02/07/36-bankers-96-years-in-jail/.

Hays, C. L. (2004) Martha Stewart's sentence: The overview; 5 months in jail and Stewart vows, "I'll be back." *The New York Times.* July 17. Retrieved from https://www.nytimes.com/2004/07/17/business/martha-stewart-s-sentence-overview-5-months-jail-stewart-vows-ll-be-back.html.

Hofverberg, E. (2014) Iceland: Icelandic bankers jailed for fraud. *Global Legal Monitor, The Law Library of Congress.* July 30. Retrieved from https://www.loc.gov/law/foreign-news/article/iceland-icelandic-bankers-jailed-for-fraud/.

Keating, E. K. and P. Frumkin. (2003) Reengineering nonprofit financial accounting toward a more reliable foundation for regulation. *Public Administration Review.* Jan-Feb, Vol 63, Issue 1:3-16.

Kinsella, E. (2017) Leonardo DiCaprio surrenders $3.2 million Picasso and $9 million Basquiat to US government. *Art and Law, artnet®news.* Retrieved from https://news.artnet.com/art-world/leonardo-dicaprio-gives-pack-jho-low-picasso-basquiat-996377.

Latiff, R. (2018) Malaysian fugitive Jho Low, four others hit with fresh 1MBD charges. *World News, Reuters.* Retrieved from https://www.reuters.com/article/us-malaysia-politics-1mdb-financier/malaysian-fugitive-jho-low-four-others-hit-with-fresh-1mdb-charges-idUSKBN1O40AW.

Mejia, L. (2019) Santa Clarita Girl Scout treasurer charged with embezzlement returns to court. Radio station *KHTS.* March 2019.

Nash, R., M. Bouchard, and A. Malm. (2018) Twisting trust: Social networks, due diligence, and loss of capital in a Ponzi scheme. *Crime, Law, and Social Change.* 69: 67-89.

Nowicki, D. and B. Muller. (2018) John McCain gets into 'a hell of a mess' with the Keating Five scandal. *The Republic.* April 2. Retrieved from https://www.azcentral.com/story/news/politics/arizona/2018/04/02/john-mccain-keating-five-scandal-arizona-senator/538034001/.

Olick, D. (2018) Mortgage fraud is getting worse as more people lie about their income to qualify for loans. *CNBC.* Oct. 3. Retrieved from https://www.cnbc.com/2018/10/03/mortgage-fraud-is-getting-worse-as-more-people-lie-about-their-income.html.

Polfeldt, E. (2017) This crime in the workplace is costing US businesses $50 billion a year. *CNBC.* Sept. 12. Retrieved from https://www.cnbc.com/2017/09/12/workplace-crime-costs-us-businesses-50-billion-a-year.html.

Rosoff, S. M., H. N. Pontell, and R. Tillman. (2013) *Profit without Honor: White Collar Crime and the Looting of America.* Upper Saddle River, NJ: Pearson Education. 6th edition.

Securities and Exchange Commission. (2003) SEC charges Martha Stewart, broker Peter Bacanovic with illegal insider trading. Press Release. Retrieved from https://www.sec.gov/news/press/2003-69.htm.

Securities and Exchange Commission. (2018) Annual Report. *Division of Enforcement.* Retrieved from https://www.sec.gov/files/enforcement-annual-report-2018.pdf.

Sukumaran, T. (2018) What's the deal with Jho Low, Malaysia's most wanted man? *South China Morning Post.* Nov. 2. Retrieved from https://www.scmp.com/news/asia/southeast-asia/article/2171428/whats-deal-jho-low-malaysias-most-wanted-man.

Teitelman, R. (2016) Michael Milken and the birth of junk bonds. *Mergers and Acquisitions: The Dealermaker's Journal.* May. Vol. 51, Issue 5: 44-50.

U.S. House of Representatives. (2009) Meeting on assessing the Madoff scheme and the need for regulatory reform. Committee of Financial Services. 111 Congress, First Session. Jan. 5.

Wall Street Journal (online). (2020) The Michael Milken pardon: Trump's act of clemency recalls an era riff with the politics of envy. Feb. 19. *ProQuest.* Web. 23 Feb. 2020.

Wright, T. and B. Hope. (2019) *Billion Dollar Whale: The Man Who Fooled Wall Street, Hollywood, and the World.* New York: Hachette Books.

Chapter FIVE

Corporate Crime and Scandals

When the whole barrel is rotten

Too many crooks spoil the Roth [IRA][1]

—*Brian Spelling*

Chapter Objectives

- Distinguish between crimes that are committed by corporations vs. crimes committed by individuals in corporations.
- Identify some of the more notorious types of crimes committed by corporations.
- Introduce corporate crimes from a global perspective.
- Characterize some of the industries more susceptible to white collar offenses.

Key Terms

Bank Secrecy Act of 1970 (BSA)
Conglomerate
Consumer Financial Protection
    Bureau (CFPB)
Corporate espionage
Corporate Social Responsibility (CSR)

Dodd-Frank Act of 2010
Monopolies
Multinational corporations
Sarbanes-Oxley Act of 2002
Sherman Antitrust Act of 1890
World Bank (WB)

---

[1] A Roth IRA is a retirement investment. This quote is basically saying that rogue, criminal companies can make a mess of one's retirement portfolio, as we saw in Chapter 4 with Enron and Lincoln Savings and Loan.

INTRODUCTION

There is a saying that a few rotten apples can ruin the whole barrel. In our last chapter, we saw acts of individuals that brought down banks and companies. What is unfair about individuals committing crimes in corporations is that often the corporation is fined with little consequence happening to the individual save reprimand or firing (Gilchrist, 2018). In this chapter we are taking the focus off the individual offender and turning our attention to cases where there were a number of people in the organization who were to blame for workers laid off, investors bilked, dishonesty, or good, old-fashioned fraud running rampant.

There are times when a corporation's culture is so questionable, the whole barrel can be considered rotten through and through. We do have to preface this statement with the fact that with some exceptions, corporations are not in the business of breaking the law. Just as wealthy white collar criminals have access and resources to commit crimes and conceal them (Gottschalk, 2019), corporations are likewise in a position to keep their less ethical practices hidden from public view. There might be several people involved, or the whole company is essentially riddled with unethical or illegal behavior. Sometimes the malfeasance is conducted out of fear, as in the case of covering up faulty product design. The focus of this chapter is financial crime, so we can assume, with few exceptions, that the primary motivation is greed and include fraud and accounting irregularities.

We have discussed how regulation, which is dependent on the political environment, has much to do with how corporate executives can run amok. Think of it as a bunch of elementary school children at recess with no adult supervision. They may start out behaving, but eventually some will run a bit wild, forgetting their manners, as they test the limits of what they can get away with. The only social control in place, unless there is a grownup around, is what they impose on themselves. This is why professions, to a large extent, are self-regulating, sometimes to their determent. It is a challenge to create regulations that protect consumers but don't stifle the creativity and profitability of companies.

There have been such an extraordinary number of corporate scandals in the past forty years that it would take an entire textbook in order to do each one justice. Any one of the examples presented in this chapter could be a case study by itself. We will only present the ones that made it into the headlines for months, if not years, and created the most damage to customers and employees.

Our focus will be on financial scandals, not cases that involve some other type of crimes as in the cases of Hewlett Packard's spying scandal in 2006[2] or Facebook's data breach in 2019.[3] We will additionally save any discussion of crimes

---

[2] In 2006, Hewlett Packard's chairperson, Patricia Dunn, was accused of hiring private investigators to spy on board members and journalists.

[3] In 2019, Facebook was accused of leaking data on millions of users of the social network website and failing to warn them of the data breach.

committed in the health care field, even if they are financial, for Chapter 8. It is important to remember that one of the reasons it feels like there have been more scandals in recent years is because of the immediacy of online news. Plus, more whistleblowers are willing to step forward. Corporations have a much more difficult time hiding their flaws in this day and age.

We will also make a slight departure in this chapter from the structure of previous and future chapters. The focus will be more on the stories in specific business sectors and less on the crime typologies and theories, as we did in previous chapters. These are cases where a number of crimes we discuss in this book were committed, including financial and consumer crimes, where blame can be spread around throughout an organization, instead of focusing on solitary white collar criminals or small conspiracies. Many, if not all, of the theories discussed so far in this book can apply. Hence this chapter is loaded with more than the usual number of examples to discuss in class compared to other chapters in this book.

What follows in this chapter are brief summaries of the biggest corporate financial scandals within the last couple of decades, listed in chronological order within each industry sector. You should note that not all of these scandals originated in the United States. However, as some of these companies were multinational corporations, most, if not all, of these scandals had worldwide repercussions whether they were located in the United States or not.

This is also not an exhaustive list of all business sectors that are susceptible to white collar crime, nor is it a complete list of companies that have gotten themselves into trouble. What we have tried to accomplish is to present cases that are not only interesting, but also represent some of the worst offenders in corporate America and beyond.

INDENTIFYING CORPORATE CRIME

We should first identify what we mean by a corporation. A company and corporation are not synonymous, having subtle differences. Both are businesses that are more likely to be for-profit operations, but can in some instances be nonprofit. Companies tend to be smaller, whereas corporations tend to be much larger. By law, both are defined as individuals, not unlike you and I, with certain rights and obligations. In other words, instead of the government viewing a corporation as being made up of a bunch of people, it is treated as one entity. There are advantages to this, with the exception that if one person messes up in a company, they could all fall.

Corporate crime is not a new thing. We are just made more acutely aware of it because news travels fast in this age of social media and 24-hour news cycles, both of which we discuss in more detail later in the book. We only need to go back to the 19th century and the heyday of the robber barons (J. P. Morgan and the lot) to see that corporate crime has been around as long as there have been corporations. Since the 19th century, and certainly since the Great Depression and more recently the Great Recession that began in 2008, regulations are designed to prevent corporations from committing wrongdoings.

CONTROLLING CORPORATE CRIME

Deterrence theories of crime control are difficult to apply to corporate crime. It is also a difficult thing to bring down a corporation that has committed criminal acts. The challenges are threefold. First, there is always the concern that in bringing down a corporation that has been misbehaving, you may punish the innocents, including employees and shareholders. Second, larger corporations have contributed the lion's share of economic growth, industrial development, and commercial development of the United States and other Western countries (Clinard and Yeager, 1980). Third, there are really no good statistics on the number of corporations that commit crimes, as not all of them get caught red-handed (Pollman, 2019).

Depending on how big the corporation is, any announcements of criminal behavior or even mildly disturbing news can have an effect on the stock market, sometimes in a whole industry. For example, if there is a major military operation that is being planned requiring the use of non-government contractors, if for some reason the operation is cancelled, it can send ripples throughout the defense industry.

For the most part, in order for corporations to function and survive, they are required to change as demand and technology change. In not changing with the times, corporations run the risk of running into trouble and, in some cases, organizational death. We certainly have witnessed this with our previously mentioned example of Blockbuster, LLC, which had numerous stores renting and selling videos. When entertainment technology made the rapid transition to DVDs, Blockbuster responded by switching over to the new medium and expanding their video game rentals. But the company could not keep up with the age of online streaming services and has all but gone out of business. Whenever there is technological change, there is the risk of an increase in corporate crime. Corporations may cut corners from regulatory standpoint in order to beat the competition to market.

We cannot ignore the fact that corporations are in the business of making money. In recent decades, there has been increasingly more pressure to bring in obscene and in some cases unrealistic returns to investors. The other side of the squeeze on corporations is regulation. While corporations are not in a position to push back against unrealistic demands from investors, they are notorious for pushing for less regulation. As Clinard and Yeager (1980, p. 57) noted during the beginning of Wall Street's most aggressive decade, "[c]orporations also constantly press for changes in existing laws, attempting to weaken controls currently in effect" and government officials have little stomach for increased regulation, with "little desire to provide more controls over the expansion and exercise of corporate power." (Clinard and Yeager, 1980, p. 57).

It is because of these dynamics that corporations are at risk for committing crimes, particularly in times of uncertainty, such as when the economic environment becomes volatile. If you will recall, in Chapters 2 and 3 we discussed the phenomenon of bounded rationality. People, or in this case corporations, will make decisions that are based only on the information that is available to make those decisions. For better or worse, these decisions can sometimes result in corporate misbehavior.

BANK FRAUD

For consumers, there is perhaps no more important decision to be made, beyond the doctors they choose, than the financial institutions that they entrust with their money. The whole purpose of putting money into a bank is to keep it safe. Within the last decade, however, there have been an extraordinary number of banking crises. Next to the Great Depression in the 1930s, the banking industry has witnessed some of the worst periods and is to a large extent still recovering from the 2008 "Great Recession" (Agarwal and Sharma, 2014).

One contributor to a general banking crisis is that consumers having so many more choices. Even though there are still only a handful of big banks, there are a number of local banks and credit unions that they can deposit money into, make investments, and secure credit cards and loans. Add to the mix a number of virtual banks that offer a range of deposit options, though there are fewer online banks that offer mortgages or personal, unsecured loans. The movement of the banking industry is towards a virtual financial world that is paperless. In theory, online banking, though with an unearned reputation for being riskier, is reported to provide faster detection of fraud and identity theft than offline banking (Dykman and MoneyBuilder, 2011).

Usually the threat of fraud is coming from outside of a bank, perpetrated by individuals targeting one or more accounts. As we saw in the Lincoln Savings and Loan scandal cooked up primarily by Charles Keating and Michael Milken, sometimes the fraud is coming from inside the institution. Our next case about Wells Fargo is a situation where there were several individuals responsible within the bank who contributed to an overall environment of unethical and criminal behavior. The Wells Fargo scandal has certainly earned its place in this chapter.

Law in the Real World: Wells Fargo & Co. (U.S., 2016-2017)

(Source: Mims, 2017; Gottschalk, 2019)

Wells Fargo & Co., specializing in banking and other financial services, is hardly the new kid on the block. The bank opened its doors for business in 1852 and to this day is recognizable by its logo of a stage coach "thundering across the American West, loaded with gold" (*History of Wells Fargo*, retrieved from https://www.wellsfargo.com/about/corporate/history/).

Wells Fargo & Co. is considered to be the biggest retail bank, with over 6,300 branches and offices (Reckard, 2013).

Like other financial institutions in the wake of the 2008 global financial meltdown, even though it was a well-established company and one of the largest banks in the United States, Wells Fargo had to assure themselves that they would remain profitable through the worst of the turmoil in markets and mortgage banking.

As most bank employees are compensated by salary, depending on the bank, the income that tellers and other frontline personnel earn may not be all that competitive. The average base pay for a Wells Fargo teller is $14/hour, or an *average* pay of $30,000 per year (*Glassdoor.com*, 2019). Considering that the poverty level income in the United States for families with four members living together is around $26,000 per year, these are difficult wages to live on. We should also consider that banks are increasingly requiring their entry level employees to have already earned a Bachelor's degree.

A common practice that banks have to help increase their employees' take-home pay is to push them to sell products such as new accounts and credit cards to new and existing customers, and the bank will in turn give the employees bonuses on top of their salaries. To prevent these incentive programs from getting out of hand on the heels of the mortgage banking mess in 2008, Congress acted under public pressure to address the unethical behavior of banks, particularly in mortgage lending. One stipulation in the *Dodd-Frank Wall Street Reform and Consumer Protection Act (Dodd-Frank Act) of 2010* requires any financial institution with over $1 billion outlined in the act to disclose the structure of any incentive-based programs that they might have for their employees.

Somewhere in the Wells Fargo & Co. incentive scheme, things started going terribly wrong. It began to be abundantly clear that the company incentive program was in all probability violating the Dodd-Frank Act. Wells Fargo & Co. was reporting a number of accounts per household that was almost four times the industry average. In a 2013 Los Angeles Times article, Scott Reckard described Wells Fargo Bank as a pressure cooker. The anxiety was coming from the threat of being fired if employees did not meet certain new account quotas. "'We were constantly told we would end up working for McDonald's,' said Murillo, who later resigned [from Wells Fargo]." (Reckard, 2013, retrieved from https://www.latimes.com/business/la-fi-wells-fargo-sale-pressure-20131222-story.html/.)

Behind the scenes, sales managers were instructing their workers to inflate their sales numbers. With the pressure to meet quotas under draconian conditions, new accounts were opened, including credit card accounts, without customers' knowledge or permission. Reckard (2013) reported that when customers complained about the unwanted credit cards, bank managers would fabricate stories about computer glitches or mistakes made because some other customer had the same or similar name. When one bank manager did sound the alarm after some of her employees talked a homeless woman into opening six accounts with fees adding up to $39, there was no response from the bank manager's superiors as to whether any action had ever been taken.

Eventually there was a fraud investigation after enough complaints, which uncovered just how widespread the fraud was within Wells Fargo. As Gottschalk (2019) claims, most white collar criminals do not understand what is so wrong with what they did, in some cases denying any crime had been committed. It was difficult for Wells Fargo employees to understand exactly what they did wrong, as in some cases they were receiving training from their managers on how to increase sales. To their credit, some employees, including tellers and personal bankers, left the company once the fraud came to light.

Wells Fargo & Co. had to pay almost $600 million to settle claims, as they violated state consumer laws. Besides settling claims, the bank was fined $185 million by the *Consumer Financial Protection Bureau (CFPB)*, the Los Angeles City attorney's office, and the Office of the Comptroller of the Currency (Blake, 2016). The company reportedly fired 5,300 employees (1 percent of their workforce) who had been identified as taking part in the fraud (Blake, 2016). To date, no Wells Fargo & Co. employee has been charged and tried for a criminal offense in association with this case of banking fraud. Thanks to the Wells Fargo mess, the tables have turned and financial institutions are now under pressure to change their incentive programs in order to reduce the risk of employees opening fraudulent accounts for new and existing customers.

Discussion Questions

1. Besides incentive programs, in what other ways could financial institutions offer compensation to employees for their sales activities?
2. Does it seem, in light of the Wells Fargo & Co. case, that the Dodd-Frank Act has been an effective measure to prevent banking fraud?
3. Why might it be that in the Wells Fargo case, it is very unlikely that anyone will be charged with a crime?

GLOBAL BANKING SECTOR CRIMES

We cannot ignore the fact that with the exception of small, local banks, larger banks have a global footprint. For instance, Bank of America has offices in a number of countries. This makes perfect sense when you consider that there are American citizens scattered all over the globe for a number of reasons, including the military. Plus, American banks have foreign investors, just as Americans invest in foreign banks. There are some limitations, and the first concern is always whether money is being hidden in foreign banks in order to avoid paying capital gains taxes. One way or another, as Clinard and Yeager (1980, p. 3) reminded us, "the giant corporations [banks included] possess such awesome aggregates of wealth and such vast social and political powers that their operations vitally influence the lives of virtually everyone, from cradle to grave." Nowhere is this truer than in banking. The world has become more dependent on consumer lending to finance everything from our college educations to the cars we drive and homes we have or hope to purchase one day.

In addition to concerns about hiding investment income that could potentially be taxable, the second concern in banking is money laundering. Organized crime groups do not hide the total sum of their illicit funds under the proverbial mattress. We have already seen in the previous chapters that there can be an overlap between organized crime and legitimate business.

A third banking threat is funding to terrorist groups. Just as financial crimes intersect with political crime and organized crime, terrorist organizations have to raise money for their operations. They also need a place to park the money and a means to transfer funds around the globe to terrorist cells and operatives. According to the U.S. Treasury (2018), the most common terrorist financing activity is identified as individuals or financial institutions who knowingly fund terrorists.

There have been a number of measures in combating the most serious concerns outlined here. The *Bank Secrecy Act of 1970 (BSA)* requires U.S. financial institutions, including banks and investment companies, to actively combat money laundering operations. They are also required to cooperate with government agencies who investigate irregularities, including the S.E.C. and the F.B.I.

There are certainly plenty of banking crimes we could discuss in this book that took place in the United States. In fact, an entire book on the subject would probably not completely do the subject justice. But in all fairness to U.S. banks, we should pay some attention to foreign banks as well. The next case is more about professional inexperience but lends itself well to companies that do not fully monitor their employees, particularly early in their careers. In this case, it really was the fault of the company for not seeing the warning signs until it was too late.

Law in the Real World: Barings Bank (U.K., 1990s)

(Source: Monthe, 2007)

Barings Banks, established in the 18th century and counting Queen Elizabeth II of England as a customer, came to its demise because of one man.

Nick Leeson, possessing no college degree, moved up the ranks of the bank at a time when a degree was not a requirement for employment. In 1992, just 25 years old, Leeson, by that time a broker operating out of Singapore for the bank, began making risky investment decisions. He made unauthorized speculative trades that at first provided the bank with as much as 10 percent of its profits in 1993 (Monthe, 2007).

Unfortunately for Leeson and for Barings Bank, his speculations did not continue to pay off. He began to incur losses and falsified records to regulatory authorities to cover the fact that he was fraudulently placing trade orders on behalf of the bank.

In 1995 when the losses became too great to escape detection, Leeson fled. He left Singapore for Malaysia, Thailand, and eventually Germany, leaving a note behind simply saying "I'm sorry." (Monthe, 2007). The fallout of his crimes resulted in the firing of a number of bank officers for incompetency for their part in not discovering his criminal behavior. The bank eventually folded, closing its doors in 1995. In the U.S., the Federal Reserve Board, in a move to avoid the same type of scandal happening in American financial institutions, demanded that the banking industry conduct more internal and external audits (Seiberg, 1996).

For all of his attempts to flee, Leeson was ultimately captured and arrested. Leeson was apprehended when he landed in Germany, then extradited back to Singapore where he stood trial for his crimes (Monthe, 2007). He was convicted and sentenced to 6.5 years in prison, released early in 1999 due to a diagnosis of colon cancer (Monthe, 2007).

In some respects, this was more a case of inexperience than greed. To record, Leeson was not aggressively making illegitimate trades to pad his bank account, but to inflate his reputation at Barings Bank. Once he started making mistakes that led to massive losses for the bank, he attempted to hide them by faking documents. Ironically, he ultimately did make money with the scandal, writing a book, *Rogue Trader* (Little, Brown, and Company, 1996), which became a movie in 1999 (Pathé, U.K. and Cinemax) (Monthe, 2007).

Discussion Questions

1. In their hiring practices, are financial institutions depending too heavily on the credentials of their employees (e.g., college degrees and connections) and not on maturity or actual experience?
2. What type of training might a financial institution require for new employees that might help to avoid these types of outrageous crimes?

3. Why might a financial institution turn a blind eye to possible white collar crimes if their employees appear to be productive and making money for them?

ENERGY SECTOR CRIMES

We all more or less expect that when we flip a light switch, the light will go on, at least in developed countries. Even in poorer nations, electricity and natural gas are available, even if it is supplied to a small portion of the population. Anyone who has ever lived through a blackout or failed to pay the electric bill and had their electricity shut off knows how terribly inconvenient life becomes in short order. Our dependency on electricity and natural gas leaves us vulnerable to the whims of the energy sector corporations that control their distribution.

Our next example, though an accounting scandal, involves so much more than simple accounting malfeasance. There are some people in the population who are especially dependent on electricity for medical reasons, as in the cases of the elderly, patients on home ventilators, and insulin-dependent diabetics who have to keep their drugs refrigerated. When electric brokers like Enron artificially manipulate supply and demand in addition to pricing, resulting in outrageous utility bills or unnecessary brownouts or rolling blackouts,[4] the public sees this as morally wrong.

Law in the Real World: Enron and Arthur Andersen (U.S., 2001)

(Source: McKlean and Ekland, 2004)

As anyone who has ever lived in California knows, it is not the most afford-able place to live. Beyond the sky-high housing prices, utilities can run higher than in other parts of the country as well, particularly in the summer months. Most places in California require air conditioning to survive the heat during July and August, even going into fall. During some years it has been known to reach the 80s Fahrenheit (high 20s Celsius) on New Year's Day in Southern California.

With little in the way of regulation at the time, the energy costs in the state surged in the early 2000s. This meant many California residents (this

---

[4] A "brownout" is when the electrical power supply is reduced on purpose in order to handle increased demand on electrical grids. An example would be when there is higher than normal air conditioning use in extreme hot weather that puts too much strain on the supply of electricity. Electricity is not completely shut off in a brownout. A "rolling blackout" is used in extreme cases when electrical power supply is intentionally shut down, rotating through regions in order to deal with increased demand.

author included) were required to choose between paying their electric bill or other household expenses, including rent, food, and medication. It was predominantly a burden on low-income residents and senior citizens on fixed incomes.

Though it may seem that way as we confidently turn on our lights and run our appliances, electricity is not in endless supply. Along with soaring prices, California began experiencing an unusual number of rolling black-outs, in which power is intentionally shut down when it appears that the demand will exceed the supply available through electric grids. This meant that residents could lose power during peak hours in the hot summers, resulting in the loss of valuable air conditioning. This was particularly diffi-cult on senior citizens on fixed budgets and those with frailer health who require air conditioning in the heat. The culprit behind the rising costs and unusually high number of rolling blackouts was Enron, a Houston-based energy company.

Enron had the makings of a lucrative investment in the energy sector in the late 1990s. The company was considered to be one of the most forward thinking at the start of the 21st century, named the most innovative com-pany in America from 1995 to 2000 by *Fortune* magazine (McLean and Elkind, 2006). The façade of Enron in the 1990s looked impeccable, a sound investment that stock market analysts raved over. As a broker in energy commodities, there were few real competitors to Enron in energy bro-kerage at the time. But it became abundantly clear that the company was built on fraud. The key figures in the fraud case at Enron were (Black, 2004, p. xi):

- Kenneth Lay, Founder, Chairman, and Chief Executive Officer
- Jeffrey Skilling, President and Chief Operations Officer
- Andrew Fastow, Chief Financial Officer
- Rebecca Mark, Chief Executive Officer of Enron International

In 2000 there was a devastating forest fire raging, threatening power-lines and ultimately shutting down a major transmission line leading into California (Roberts, 2004). In the documentary *Enron: The Smartest Guys in the Room*, Enron traders were heard saying, "Burn, baby, burn. That's a beautiful thing." (2929 Entertainment HDNET Films, Magnolia Pictures, 2005). As a result of the fires and lost power, the traders (along with untold others) cashed in on the resulting surge in stock prices. Further dialogue between the traders connected Enron executives Ken Lay and Jeffrey Skil-ling to a scheme to exploit the power transmission crisis in California (Roberts, 2004). In the meantime, with power prices soaring, hundreds of thousands of lower income Californians, including pensioners, were left with electric bills they could ill-afford to pay. When the tapes of the Enron traders talking were made public, it showed the world just how heartless Enron executives could be.

Something very wrong was happening behind the scenes, and accounting irregularities began to show up in 2001. Management kept informing Enron employees, who had their retirement pensions invested in the company, that the company was on sound financial footing. But unbeknownst to employees, upper level management personnel were dumping their own investment in the company and committing insider trading crimes. This included Ken Lay, the founder, chairperson, and CEO, who sold his Enron stock as fast as he possibly could. Yet employees, many of whom had their entire retirement savings invested in the company, were being told that everything was rosy. Something didn't add up. An audit immediately turned up all kinds of accounting irregularities and the company was in deep financial trouble.

After the Enron debacle was uncovered, Andrew Fastow, chief financial officer (CFO), claimed that he was completely unaware of any accounting irregularities. Possessing a Master's degree in Business Administration (MBA) from Northwestern University, a well-respected institution, it was highly unlikely that Fastow could be completely in the dark about the accounting irregularities at Enron. Evidently prosecutors agreed, and Fastow was charged in 2004 with a number of crimes, including conspiracy, securities fraud, and money laundering. Fastow pleaded guilty to wire and securities fraud, accepting a plea deal of 10 years in federal prison. He became an informant in the case, greatly reducing the number of years he could have been sentenced to.

As in the Urban Bank case, discussed at the end of this chapter, Enron represented one catastrophe after another. John Baxter, who had briefly served as a CEO in Enron, shot himself to death while sitting in his Mercedes Benz. Speculation was that he felt compelled to commit suicide after inquiring phone calls from a congressional committee and the expectation that the FBI and SEC would soon be reaching out to him as well to possibly testify against his friends (McLean and Elkind, 2004).

If there is one critical lesson, as far as accounting practices go, it is that a company should not have the same accounting firm handle both their day-to-day needs and external audits. The whole purpose of having an external audit is to have fresh, objective pair of eyes look at financial statements and ledgers. Enron's use of Anderson as both inside and outside auditor represented a conflict of interest.

One regulatory change that came about from the Enron scandal was the passing of the *Sarbanes-Oxley Act* in 2002. The legislation was passed overwhelmingly in the U.S. Congress in order to hold executives accountable for their actions, ban company loans made to executives, and offer job protection to whistleblowers (Amadeo, 2018). We should note that since the

Sarbanes-Oxley Act passed, there have been attempts to amend it or eliminate it altogether, as critics of the act claim that it resulted in stifling accounting practices and duplicates regulation that was already in place before Enron (Tucker, 2018).

Ultimately over 85,000 workers lost jobs in both companies, pensions were lost, and one of the top 5 accounting firms in the world, Arthur Andersen, went out of business. Up to the time of its collapse, Arthur Andersen maintained its innocence, claiming to be yet another victim of Enron (McLean and Elkind, 2006). As big as the Enron scandal was, it is rapidly becoming a footnote in the history of financial crime as other corporate crimes capture the spotlight.

For their crimes, there were a number of Enron executives who received prison sentences. For his part in the Enron scandal, former CEO Kenneth Lay never served a day in prison. Lay died of a heart attack at his vacation home in Colorado less than six weeks after his conviction (Horsley, 2006).

Discussion Questions

1. Thinking back to previous chapters of this book, why might there be a callous disregard to how price hikes and rolling blackouts might affect children, the elderly, and people with certain health conditions that require electricity to treat (e.g., ventilators)?
2. How might an accounting company learn a lesson from Arthur Andersen's demise to prevent from going under when there is a scandal?
3. Beyond the arguments given here, why might energy companies prefer less regulation, not more, as in the case of objections to the Sarbanes-Oxley Act?

ACCOUNTING SCANDALS

As we noted earlier in this chapter, corporations have the financial means to hide accounting messes from their customers and employees. Employees may cooperate in hiding these messes because they are afraid of losing their jobs. The early part of the 21st century found us in the middle of a rash of accounting scandals. In some cases, billions of dollars disappeared with no explanation for where they had gone to.

We should try to put the organizational chart in perspective to understand each executive's role in a company and their culpability if something goes wrong. The president of a company is many times tasked with being more environmentally focused, keeping an eye on competition and changes within an industry (Mintzberg, 2001). With this more outward focus, a president has to trust that the more internally focused executives are keeping an eye on the bottom line while making sure that operations are running smoothly. A CEO is responsible for maintaining the principles of a company's mission statement, which can be somewhat ambiguous and vague, open to interpretation. The CFO is the head of all financial operations within a company, charged with the management of day-to-day financial decisions including planning, accounting, and financial filings with agencies including the SEC and IRS.

When things run afoul financially, one or all of these executives and the employees that work under them can be held personally and criminally responsible. After the Sarbanes-Oxley Act of 2002, executives can no longer claim innocence, even if they have been truly kept in the dark. CFOs are particularly under fire and held to more accountability after Enron. As Howell (2002, p. 20) observed, "the role of the CFO and finance organization must change from being primarily an accountant and controller (the catchy terms applied were 'compliance' and 'cop') to that of 'business partner' and 'strategist'."

Law in the Real World: WorldCom (U.S., 1999-2002)

(Source: Tran, 2002; Giroux, 2008)

The business world tends to choose to practice selective amnesia when it comes to scandals. No sooner had Enron started fading from headlines than along comes WorldCom, which in many ways overshadowed Enron in the audacity of the fraudulent accounting. The second largest long-distance telephone service provider after AT&T, WorldCom looked to be on solid financial ground with a reported $104 billion in assets in 2001.

What was really happening was that CEO and founder Bernard Ebbers had been taking the company rapidly into debt through a large number of acquisitions in an alarmingly short amount of time. Stepping away from day-to-day operations in 2000, Ebbers entrusted the company to director John Sidgmore. Sidgmore was abruptly announced as head of WorldCom in 2002 when Ebbers suddenly left the company.

On closer examination, the assets reported were an illusion. Included in the total was a sizeable amount that was really goodwill, an asset that is intangible and difficult to accurately measure. The amount of debt the company had was being downplayed in SEC filings. The actual cash value of the company was $1.5 billion, an amount that for a company the size of World-Com was of great concern. An internal audit in 2002 found that there was double counting of revenues and debt, which in SEC and IRS reporting would be fraudulent. In other words, they were reporting expenses as investments, artificially inflating assets, which is a great big accounting no-no. Conceivably, the company could fraudulently apply and get loans on falsified reports of company assets.

Accounting firm Arthur Andersen of Enron fame was fired and new auditor KPMG was called in to review the books. In turn, WorldCom was forced to announce in 2002 that there were $3.8 billion in accounting errors after an internal audit, mainly attributed to fees charged to other telecom companies. That figure would later be revised to $11 billion. Instead of the supposed profits reported in 2001 and 2002, both years actually had losses that went unreported. On top of this, there was a suspicious personal loan made to CEO Bernard Ebbers.

WorldCom officer and director John Sidgmore blamed the finance team. With this and other accounting irregularities that were discovered in KPMG's audit, CFO Scott Sullivan and controller David Myers were immediately fired. The two former executives faced up to 65 years in prison, having been charged with securities fraud and conspiracy.

Just weeks after the SEC filed civil fraud charges against WorldCom in 2003, Sidgmore, age 52 at the time, died suddenly from kidney failure (Feder, 2003). In 2005, former CEO Ebbers was convicted of a number of crimes, including securities fraud and making false regulatory filings to the SEC, and sentenced to 25 years in federal prison. The now 77-year-old Ebbers is currently serving his sentence in Texas. Former controller Myers, also pleading guilty, was sentenced in 2005 to one year and one day in prison. WorldCom went into bankruptcy, with debtors, many of whom had been financially devasted by the company's deception, only receiving back 35 cents on the dollar(Giroux, 2008).

Discussion Questions

1. Why does it seem like companies fail to learn from the crimes of others or, as we stated at the beginning of this case, practice selective amnesia?
2. Do some types of industries, in this case telecommunications, have greater risk for accounting fraud?
3. What type of message are the SEC and federal prosecutors sending with the unusually long sentence for former executive Bernard Ebbers?

In many respects, the WorldCom case represents collective greed, as the executives hid losses as a direct result of aggressive acquisitions. It also represents collective fear, as accurate reports of losses over the course of 2001 and 2002 would result in investor defection and inability to acquire more debt for any new acquisitions.

Greed is often the primary reason behind accounting fraud, primarily in the act of hiding embezzlement when executives dip into profits to enhance their already wealthy lives. In our next case, it was an extravagant lifestyle that helped bring down a company's CEO. Though this case may seem like it should belong in Chapter 4 with crimes committed by individuals, the Tyco case is a reflection of the high-flying days of general corporate excesses from the 1980s to the early 2000s.

Law in the Real World: Tyco International (U.S. 2002)

(Source: Bandler and Guidera, 2002; Sweeney, 2002)

Dennis Kozlowski, CEO of Tyco International Ltd., a publicly traded security and fire protection company, wanted to do something special for his second wife's 40th birthday. Staging an over-the-top, Ancient Rome-themed party on the Italian island of Sardinia, Kozlowski pulled out all the stops on party planning. Every attention was given to authenticity, including toga-wearing waiters, rented fig trees adorned with lights, and chalices replacing wine glasses on linen covered tables. Singer-songwriter Jimmy Buffet was on hand to entertain guests, as well as a described bevy of dancing women and half-naked models (Williams, 2002). As CEO, Kozlowski had earned a reported $1.6 million in salary, with an additional $4 million in bonuses in the fiscal year 2001 (Williams, 2002), and it appeared on the surface that this was a luxury he could well afford.

Joining Tyco International Ltd. in 1992, the party reflected Kozlowski's reputation as having the Midas touch. Tyco was not flashy, selling rather mundane products, but its CEO had far from modest tastes. Having aggressively taken the company to new heights during the acquisition frenzy of the 1990s, Kozlowski built Tyco into a massive *conglomerate*. But with aggressive accounting practices, high debt loads, and unnaturally inflated stock prices, there were a number of red flags even before the party.

With around 100 guests, the estimated $2.1 million extravaganza caught the attention of investigators in the Manhattan D.A.'s office. Sold as a party that combined Tyco business with pleasure, investigators suspected that the party was disproportionally being paid for with Tyco money. The party was just the top of the iceberg. Kozlowski was evidently using company money to support his lavish lifestyle, including a $30 million apartment in New York City filled with high end luxury furnishings. Court documents revealed that he even had a $6,000 shower curtain.

From what investigators could tell, borrowing money illegally to support luxury lifestyles was pandemic at Tyco. The company's CFO, Mark Swartz, got in hot water with the IRS. In an abuse of the company's loan program, Swartz helped himself to $12.5 million of Tyco's money, which he didn't appear to intend to pay back. Together, Kozlowski and Swartz were held accountable for a number of corporate fraud and grand larceny charges, and each was sentenced to 8.5 to 25 years in prison in 2005. By 2013, both men were in work release programs and eventually paroled well in advance of the 25-year limit on their sentences.

Kozlowski and Swartz were not alone in their financial chess games with Tyco. Belnick, an attorney, was hired as the company's general legal counsel in 1998 after the company had grown too large to not have a more seasoned legal department. Offered a lucrative salary, Belnick was also offered an interest-free loan for relocation to New York City, which was 25 miles away from his home. Belnick took out a $4 million relocation loan from the company, purchasing a luxury apartment in the city.

It is not unusual for companies to assist with relocation costs, but Tyco's policy at the time was only for existing employees, not new hires. When the stock market took a dangerous dip in 2001, Belnick made the fatal mistake of dipping into company funds to give himself another illegal interest-free relocation loan of $10 million to fund a second home in Utah. Kozlowski approved the loan but Belnick never filled out the necessary paperwork. Belnick was eventually criminally charged and prosecuted for corporate corruption in 2004 for both illegitimate relocation loans, but was acquitted in that case.

Belnick did not escape a civil lawsuit. The SEC subsequently filed a civil case against Kozlowski, Swartz, and Belnick (*SEC v. L. Dennis Kozlowski, Mark H. Swartz, and Mark A. Belnick*) in 2002, settling the case in 2006 (SEC, 2006). Belnick was ordered in the settlement to pay a fine of $100,000 and, under the terms of the agreement, banned from serving as an officer or director of a public company (SEC, 2006).

Discussion Questions

1. Why is it more difficult to be a whistleblower in a company like Tyco, when the top executives appear to have no watchdogs?
2. Should companies even have loan programs for top executives after the Tyco mess?
3. Is it unethical to mix business with pleasure? Why? Why not?

MALFEASANCE IN THE AUTOMOTIVE INDUSTRY

Similar to other industries, there are a number of types of crimes that can occur in the automotive industry, including fraud and corruption. Most of the time when automakers cut corners, it is to save money. The buying public's taste and financial ability in buying cars is dependent on the economic climate, including prevailing interest rates. When automakers take shortcuts, even in order to save customers money, it can turn deadly.

Law in the Real World: Ford *Pinto*[5] "Leaving You with that Warm Feeling"

(Source: American Museum of Tort Law, 2019; Gray and Grimshaw v. Ford Motor Company, 1981)

Automakers in America were building great big gas guzzling cars into the 1970s. In the meantime, foreign companies like Volkswagen (VW) had started selling models in the United States that quickly became popular because of their gas efficiency and smaller size, including the popular VW bug. The American auto industry for the most part was slow to respond with more compact models, and there were fairly inexpensive foreign automobiles that could meet that demand.

Famous for its sporty *Mustang* car that came out in the 1960s and is still collectable today, in 1970 the Ford Motor Company rushed to get a smaller hatchback model, the *Pinto*, to the market in response to the shift in changing customer preferences. In doing so, Ford Motor Company made a fatal decision. In a cost-savings measure for both the company and the consumer, the Ford company decided to not install a firewall between the gas tank and the passenger cab of the car.

In 1972, Lilly Gray was merging onto a California freeway with a passenger, 13-year-old Richard Grimshaw, when her Ford *Pinto* suddenly stalled. She was rear-ended, resulting in her gas tank rupturing and fumes reaching the passenger cab where they were then ignited into flames by a spark. Gray died of horrific burns within hours of the accident. Grimshaw suffered from extensive, disfiguring burns, requiring a number of painful surgeries during his recovery.

Gray's exploding gas tank was not an isolated incident. There were some 180 known accidents similar to Gray's. As one would expect, the Gray and Grimshaw families sued the Ford Motor Company. During the trial, internal company documents revealed that in safety trials, the gas tank exploded in every test where rear impact happened at speeds over 25 miles per hour.

---

[5] You may have noticed that one of your authors' surnames is Pinto. When the Ford *Pinto* came out, the author's father, who was a mechanical engineer, wrote a scathing letter to the Ford Company about the quality of the car with our name on it. As far as we know, that letter was never answered.

The car that rear-ended Gray's car was traveling at an estimated 30 miles per hour.

This was not a mere oversight or design flaw. Under pressure to bring the *Pinto* to market weighing no more than 2,000 lbs. and costing no more than $2,000, the company under Lee Iacocca's direction decided to forgo any of the engineers' suggestions for safety features, estimated to cost no more than $8 per vehicle to add on. In a terrible coincidence, some ad campaigns for the *Pinto* claimed that the car left you "with that warm feeling" and advertised it as "Ford's new *Pinto*. The little carefree car."

Ironically, and perhaps in a twist of fate, the automobile, which had a brief period of popularity, quickly became the brunt of late-night talk show comedy jokes and would have faded into obscurity but for a resurgence in interest by car collectors in recent years. There are currently kits available online to purchase to correct the firewall omission in the original models.

Discussion Questions

1. Is the Ford Motor Company story one of greed or one of fear?
2. This question may take a bit of research. How does the debacle of the *Pinto* model compare with the failure of Ford Motor Company's *Edsel* model?
3. Why, if it was an executive decision, was no executive held accountable for making the decision to omit the firewall in the *Pinto*?

America automakers are not the only ones to cut corners at the cost of buyers' peace of mind and safety. This is only criminal if automakers are not meeting regulatory standards. We rarely get disclosure of industrial mishaps or crimes from China. However, as an exception, news leaked that as China's economy was weakening, the Chinese were choosing to purchase the more economic domestic sports utilities vehicles (SUVs), some of which were missing key safety features. For example, a critical component that should be standard in any SUV, the electronic stabilizing control (ESC), was only offered as an expensive add on option in China (CNBC, 2016).

Unlike the U.S. where safety standards of vehicles and all fatal automobile accidents are made public, China guards these figures as state secrets (CNBC, 2016). The World Health Organization (WHO) has stated that the traffic fatalities reported by China may only represent 25 percent of all actual fatalities (CNBC, 2016). Again, regulatory agencies are key in providing guidelines that meet both ethical and legal standards. But that does not mean that companies necessarily follow them.

MONOPOLIES AND ANTITRUST LAWS

Since the 1890 *Sherman Antitrust Act*, regulators have been on the lookout for companies that have become so big that they have crowded out the competition. In a free market economy, proponents would say, "so what?"—let the marketplace determine who will survive and who will perish; it's Darwinian economics. Where the concern lies is not so much in one company becoming more powerful than others. It is in the abuses that might come about as a result of that unchallenged power.

The biggest trepidation concerning *monopolies* is that these companies in turn will charge whatever they want to for their goods or services, because they can. Take, for example, if Starbucks® were the only coffee shop in a city, they could pretty much charge whatever they wanted for their products as long as people were willing to pay the price. As expensive as some might think a cup of Starbucks® coffee is (part of which is for the services of a barista), if the company did not have competition in the less pricy option of Dunkin'® Donuts[6], prices might very well be much higher.

Though companies can be criminally charged with violating antitrust laws, generally investigations result in civil settlements. Some of the bigger cases have involved telecommunication companies like AT&T in the tech industry ("Big Tech") and more recently with Google® and Amazon®. Antitrust trials can seem like classic David and Goliath combat, with companies possessing deep pockets for litigation, but the Sherman Antitrust Act has so far proven to be a powerful tool in breaking up companies that are getting too big and are edging out all other competitors.

MULTINATIONAL CORPORATIONS

The difficulty in regulating *multinational corporations* is that they are required to follow the laws and regulations in their host countries. There a number of advantages to opening branch offices and factories overseas. The first and most obvious one is that labor can be cheaper elsewhere than in the United States. The second advantage is that not all countries are as rulebound as the United States.

In an exposé tell-all book by John Perkins, *Confessions of an Economic Hitman* (2004), he shares his experiences of working as the advance man for companies that are seeking to establish themselves in poorer countries. He claims that these underdeveloped countries took out loans from the *World Bank* (WB) that they could ill-afford to build necessary infrastructures, including paved roads and utilities. In theory, these improvements, including the jobs that multinational companies bring to poor countries, are beneficial to local the population. If the companies are forced to leave, as in the case of political upheaval, the country is now on the hook for loans that they cannot pay back without some revenue

---

[6] Dunkin'® Donuts is located primarily in the Northeast.

stream coming from the companies (e.g., taxes) that have by that time left the country. And of course, this is all legal.

So, we have to assume that if multinational companies do walk a fine line ethically, they are also at risk for committing widespread global crime and mayhem. Of course, this is not always their fault as in the case of civil war, but it's a questionable practice to leave one poor country for another if it is only being done out of the interest of finding cheaper labor.

Law in the Real World: Parmalat (Italy, 2002-2005)

(Source: Weeke, 2019)

Few countries have a history as long and illustrious in dynasties, where families rule for centuries, as Italy. Making strategic business and marriage alliances, these families operated like modern day corporations. The Medici family of Florence and Tuscany (c. 1434-1737 B.C.E.) is but one, finally losing power after 300 years of control. The Tanzi family was one in a long line of Italian families building dynasties in the 20th century. The Tanzi family story in the Northern Italy town of Parma was viewed as being out of a fairy tale by the townspeople. Though somewhat exaggerated, it was a rags to riches tale. In 1960, Calisto Tanzi, as the third generation to join the family business that dealt primarily in prosciutto, a dried Italian ham, began selling the product door to door.

One of the companies under the direction of the Tanzi family was Parmalat, a name derived from the city name, Parma, and the primary product, milk. The Tanzi family turned its attention to milk when technology was introduced that would give milk products a longer shelf life. Started in 1961, Parmalat quickly became one of the largest and richest multinational companies in Italy after the Italian government privatized dairies in the 1980s (Heller, 2003).

With products now having a longer shelf life, it was possible for the company to ship the product far and wide, including attracting contracts with NATO to supply troops with milk products. By 2003, the company was on the verge of collapse and began the process of seeking bankruptcy protection. The bankruptcy filing was reported as one of the largest in Europe's history. In the process, it was soon discovered that there were a lot more things wrong with the company than crushing debt. Decades after helping to start the company, Calisto Tanzi was removed as CEO, eventually ending up in jail in Milan, Italy currently, awaiting charges and potentially a trial for a number of white collar crimes.

So, what exactly happened to contribute to Calisto Tanzi's fall from grace? The company had some failed projects in the 1990s, but that is not unusual for companies. They can survive these failures as long as they are diversified enough, which Parmalat was. Plus, the company went public, selling shares of stock in the company beginning in the early 1990s and shifting some of the financial burden to investors. What ultimately created the biggest financial scandal in Italian history was that Parmalat's true financial troubles were being hidden between false financial statements and shady offshore bank accounts.

Fausta Tonna, Chief Financial Officer for Parmalat and a close confidante of Tanzi, was initially identified as the orchestrator of an elaborate scheme to hide the real financial state of the company. One of the first to be arrested when the scheme was uncovered by investigators, Tonna cooperated with law enforcement, making the claim that he was just following orders, assumedly from Tanzi. In total, 11 people of Parmalat's management were arrested, including Tanzi. Once an audit by Price Waterhouse Coopers was conducted, it was discovered that the company was $17.6 billion USD (14 billion euros) in debt, a figure that was eight times the size reported on the falsified financial documents.

To date, the executives who were arrested have yet to be charged with crimes. More recently, Alessandro Bassi, who had served as an aide to Fausto Tonna, committed suicide by throwing himself off a bridge in Parma.

In addition to the accusations that Tanzi falsified financial statements, he is also being accused of treating Parmalat as his own, even after the company went public in the 1990s. It has been suggested that Tanzi might have been dipping into company funds he was no longer entitled to once the company went public. For someone with a reputation of being conservative, this is somewhat of mystery. There are still billions of dollars unaccounted for. As Weeke writes (2019, retrieved from http://www.nbcnews.com/id/4030254/ns/world_news/t/parmas-god-falls-sky/#.XXq1H5NKhN1), "But for the people of Parma the fairy tale is being washed away forever in a tidal wave of 'spilt milk.'"

The Parmalat story is one of the rare occasions where a huge corporate scandal has a somewhat happy ending, at least for the innocent employees working for the company. The company was resuscitated after the scandal and is alive and well today, though now under the leadership of the Lactilas Group that took over the control of the company in 2011 (Parmalat website, retrieved from http://www.parmalat.com/en/about_us/). It continues to be a thriving multinational company.

Discussion Questions

1. Why might a family business be more or less susceptible to white collar crime and malfeasance?
2. Why do you think it took so long to discover that there were financial irregularities and only after the bankruptcy filing?
3. Where might there be a contradiction between Tanzi's presumably conservative lifestyle, avoiding the flashiness that can come from wealth, and the alleged missing billions of dollars from the company?

CORPORATE SOCIAL RESPONSIBILITY

The good news is that there has been a paradigm shift in the corporate world where companies are increasingly pressured to take the high road. Many companies have departments that are devoted to *social responsibility*, with a business strategy of working with communities and nonprofits to take greater responsibility for their actions. This includes the way they treat their employees and how their companies might impact stakeholders. Of course, it is still all in the name of sound business practice and not necessarily only out of generosity, as social responsibility adds to the intangible of a company's reputation. Taking a *mea culpa*[7] stance after scandals can go a long way to repair damage, as witnessed in BP's public relations campaign after the 2010 Deepwater Horizon oil spill in the Gulf of Mexico. We certainly see our fair share of buildings, especially in New York City (e.g., Carnegie Hall), with the last names of robber barons, as they used charitable giving as a means to improve their image in the public eye. In many respects, it's a win-win. The companies get positive PR and the public many times get cultural enhancements in their cities.

SUMMARY

Though most of the time we can point to one individual or a handful of people who are causing the chaos and mayhem in a company, in the cases presented in this chapter, we have to ask ourselves what it is about the corporate culture that companies risk far more than just their reputations when cutting corners with what they might not even realize is criminal behavior. It certainly says a lot about the legal teams of these companies if they were aware of the crimes that were being committed. At the very least, one would think that even unethical behavior would be questioned, even if it doesn't lead to lawsuits or criminal charges.

We see corporate crime in a number of industries, but some seem to be more vulnerable than others. Perhaps some are more tempted by crime as well in the

---

[7] *Mea culpa* is Latin for an apology that is an admission of one's guilt, fault, or error.

endless quest for profits. These include tech companies and the pharmaceuticals industry. Wherever innovation is fast in coming and the competition is fierce, it is likely that there will be times that executives get so caught up in the game, so to speak, that they forget the bigger ramifications of their actions.

There have been a number of measures that have been made in order to stem corporate crime. Unfortunately, new laws tend to be reactive rather than preventative. We have seen examples in this chapter, from the Sherman Antitrust Act of 1890 to more recent legislation in response to the mortgage lending crisis of 2008.

Case Study • Garbage Loans, Deceit, and Suicide in Urban Bank (Philippines, 2000)

Background

As we noted in the beginning of this book, rarely do we see violence associated with white collar crime. But suicide[8] can certainly be considered to be a form of violence, even if it is self-inflicted. In theory, justice is not served when the accused commits suicide, as it is the responsibility of the courts and corrections to dispense punishment on the convicted. On April 12, 2005, news headlines read that the former president of Urban Bank in the Philippines, Teodoro Borlongan, under the shadow of indictment and conviction, had committed suicide using a .45 caliber Glock automatic pistol to shoot himself in the left temple (Torres, 2005).

During his tenure at Urban Bank, Borlongan and his colleague, Arsenio Bartolome, concocted an illegal scheme of placing depositors' money in "garbage receivables" (Porcalla, 2000)—dubious lines of credit—to the tune of billions in Philippine pesos. "Garbage receivables" occur when investors put money in the bank that they expect to be used in bank loans that will ultimately make a profit for the investor. To make them "garbage" and basically extremely risky for investors means that the loans are dubious, given to underqualified borrowers with the considerable risk of the loans never being paid back (Bangko Sentral NG Philipinas, 2000). This is similar to the junk bonds we discussed in Chapter 4 and are illegal, as investors generally are clueless as to where their money is being invested.

The garbage receivables resulted in ₱1 billion (Philippine pesos, or $19,727,000 USD in today's dollars) lost in defaulted Urban Bank loans (Philstar, 2009). With Borlongan and Bartolome seeking help from the Philippine government to deal with banking irregularities unrelated to their

---

[8] National Suicide Prevention Lifeline—1-800-273-8255 (available 24 hours a day, 7 days a week)

own crimes, they covertly began misusing bank funds. The greater concern was that while they were defrauding customers, they were also defrauding the Philippine government, as the necessity to bail out Urban Bank came about because of criminal mismanagement. This ultimately brought criminal charges of economic sabotage against Borlongan.

As far as Urban Bank itself, it was already in financial deep water before Borlongan and Bartolome's crimes. The bank never did recover. After the bank went into receivership, it ultimately failed, which is as we see a common story when financial scandals are just too big to bounce back from.

Defining the Crime(s)

Economic sabotage, as defined in Philippine law, is an umbrella term for a number of financial crimes including price fixing, smuggling, and profiteering:

> 'Economic sabotage' is an act or activity which undermines, weakens or renders into disrepute the economic system of the country or tends to bring about such effects and shall include inter alia, price manipulation to the prejudice of the public especially in the sale of basic necessities and prime commodities. (Section 3 of *Republic Act 7581*, Sen. Ejercito, Senate of the Philippines, 2014)

Borlongan and Barolome were accused of victimizing customers in amounts in excess of the equivalent to $960 thousand USD, in Philippine pesos (Porcalla, 2000). Convictions for economic sabotage carry the death penalty in the Philippines.

Theories to Explain the Crime

It does not appear that corporate greed is enough to explain the audacity of Borlongan's crimes. In the absence of a psychological profile of Borlongan and Bartolome, it is a challenge to use theories of individual psychopathology to explain these crimes as well, though in light of Borlongan's suicide, psychological explanations cannot be completely discounted.

A relatively newcomer to leadership theories is the concept of "dark" or "dark-side" leadership. In the theory, as spelled out by Marshall et al. (2013; Paulhus and Williams, 2002), "dark leaders" are destructive, with a tendency to possess three key personality characteristics: Machiavellianism, psychopathology, and narcissism. Machiavellianism refers to the writings of Niccolo Machiavelli (*The Prince*, 1513), a fictional accounting of the Medici family in Florence, who ruled the city for approximately 300 years by economic and social manipulation. Narcissism is defined as the blatant disregard of other people's feelings or needs, where the individual's primary occupation is on themselves. In combination, a leader possessing all three characteristics may not take into consideration the consequences of their criminal behavior or if they do, they dismiss them as unimportant in comparison with their own needs. If we have a case of more than one "dark" leader in an organization, as in the case of Urban Bank, we can surmise that this is another route to corporate crime.

If anything, this case supports the argument that there are many instances when the threat of the death penalty does not prevent crime. Deterrence theories argue that if the punishment is severe enough, in this case execution, it should be enough to prevent criminals to follow through on their premeditated plans. For some criminals this might be the case, though research has been generally inconclusive as to the effectiveness of deterrence punishments.

Opponents of the death penalty and critics of deterrence theories argue that criminals are not stopped, even if the penalty is death for their crimes. If Silberman (1976) is correct, then the key for deterrence policies to work is if there is a moral imperative to not commit the crime, besides the possible punishment. In other words, something like a strong faith in one's religious doctrine (e.g., the Ten Commandments) may be a stronger deterrence than law to prevent crime from happening, though the blurred lines of what is morally acceptable within corporations when profit is the number one motivator for behavior is always brought to question.

Social and Media Responses

As white collar crime goes, this case, at least from a standpoint of financial fallout, is pretty massive. However, there was little attention to it outside of international financial market circles. Unlike the antics of Jordan Belfort, the so-called "wolf of Wall Street" that resulted in a memoir and movie both named after Belfort's nickname, the Urban Bank case got relatively little attention. It was only when Borlongan committed suicide that the crimes receive more widespread media attention, yet the financial losses were far greater than any associated with Belfort.

There was somewhat of a scramble for other banks, including U.S. investment banks, to make clear to the public that the Urban Bank scandal was unusual. Merrill Lynch, a U.S.-based investment company, stated in the media that the problems at Urban Bank were not systemic and that customers should not likewise be suspicious of their own investment bankers (Ebias, 2000).

Criminal Justice and Policy Responses

Borlongan was in the appeals process for the criminal convictions, having already had civil lawsuits dismissed at the time of his suicide (Torres, 2005; Porcalla, 2000). In spite of winning the civil lawsuits, Borlongan had been left financially devastated. Others charged in the case, including Bartolome and corporate secretary Corazon Bejasa, had their lesser swindling charges cleared by the courts in 2001.

Other bank officials at the former Urban Bank have distanced themselves from the crime. In testimony in Philippine court, ten top officials argued that they had been kept in the dark by Borlongan and Bartolome about the real financial disaster that was looming (Philstar Global, 2001). However, the garbage receivables were only the tip of the iceberg for mismanagement at Urban Bank. Other scandals were uncovered in the process of investigating Borlongan's crimes, including the alleged embezzlement of ₱73 million ($1,441,868 USD) from the sale of property in 1994 (Punay, 2012). A number of bank officials, including Borlongan, were accused of taking kickbacks in the real estate transaction.

As ambiguous as regulation is, it continues to be the best, if not the only, solution to corporate crime such as economic sabotage. With even the threat of the death penalty in countries like the Philippines for certain financial crimes not providing adequate deterrence, criminal justice responses appear to be inadequate for prevention.

There was a call to tighten up rules, policies, and procedures of banks in what services can be legitimately offered to customers, or at least a demand from U.S. investment banks that operate in the Philippines to have stricter regulation (Ebias, 2000). Generally, after big scandals in banking, as what we witnessed after the 2008 worldwide banking crisis, there is a sizable demand for tighter regulation to prevent them from happening again.

Unanswered Questions and Unresolved Issues Related to the Case

The biggest unanswered questions from this case center around Borlongan's suicide. If we could get inside the minds of white collar criminals, are they more afraid of the devastation of financial ruin or possible criminal conviction? We also have to ask what responsibilities financial institutions should take when there is obvious criminal behavior being committed by one of their key executives, even if the malfeasance is not company-wide. For no other reason than to regain the respect and trust of customers, it appears that the banks that are more likely to survive are those that address the issues face on, as in the case of Wells Fargo. Sadly, Urban Bank, once one of Philippine's larger banks, like Barlongan himself, did not survive the scandal.

Sources
Bangko Sentral NG Pilipnas. (2000) Urban Bank case on track. Media Releases. Oct. 13. Retrieved from http://www.bsp.gov.ph/publications/media.asp?id=1332&yr=2000.
Ebias, J. (2000) Urban Bank collapse note systemic—Merrill Lynch. *Philstar Global.* May 4. Retrieved from https://www.philstar.com/business/2000/05/04/98900/urban-bank-collapse-not-systemic-merrill-lynch.
Ejercito, J. V. G. (2014) Senate Bill No. 2050. Senate of the Philippines Sixteenth Congress, First Regular Session. Retrieved from https://www.senate.gov.ph/lisdata/1850815678!.pdf.

Marshall, A., D. Baden, and M. Guidi. (2013) Can an ethical revival of prudence within Prudential Regulation tackle corporate psychopathy? *Journal of Business Ethics*. Oct. Vol. 117, Issue 3: 559-568.

Paulhus, D. L. and K. M. Williams. (2002) The dark triad of personality: Narcissism, Machiavelianism and psychopathy. *Journal of Research in Personality*. Vol. 36: 556-563.

Philstar Global. (2001) Urban Bank directors testify versus Bartolome, Borlongan. March 19. Retrieved from https://www.philstar.com/business/2001/03/19/96455/urban-bank-directors-testify-versus-bartolome-borlongan.

Porcalla, D. (2000) Economic sabotage a 'dead law'. *Philstar Global*. March 9. Retrieved from https://www.philstar.com/headlines/2000/03/09/95267/economic-sabotage-dead-law.

Punay, E. (2012) P73-M kickback for Urban execs? *The Philippine Star*. ABS/CBN. Apr 30. Retrieved from https://news.abs-cbn.com/business/04/30/12/p73-m-kickback-urban-execs.

Silberman, M. (1976) Toward a theory of criminal deterrence. *American Sociological Review*. Vol. 41: 442-461.

Torres, T. P. (2005) Urban Bank president commits suicide. *Philstar Global*. April 12. Retrieved from https://www.philstar.com/headlines/2005/04/12/273586/urban-bank-president-commits-suicide.

GLOSSARY

Bank Secrecy Act of 1970 (BSA)   Enacted by Congress in order to prevent money laundering, requiring businesses to keep records and file reports to regulatory agencies with transparency of cash flow, income sources, etc.

Conglomerate   A number of companies in different industries that are under one corporate entity. Example: Johnson & Johnson products include pharmaceuticals, baby products, and over the counter medications.

Consumer Financial Protection Bureau (CFPB)   Created in 2011, the CFPB has the responsibility of assuring that credit cards, mortgages, and other loan products are fair and transparent for consumers so that they can make informed choices in their financial decisions. *See* https://www.consumerfinance.gov/.

Corporate espionage   Also called industrial espionage and corporate spying, it is the act of either infiltrating a company or working for a company, stealing trade secrets and intellectual property that can be used by competitors or sold on the black market to foreign governments.

Corporate Social Responsibility (CSR)   A business model that is a fairly new trend of companies to self-regulate their activities, so that they are in the best interest of employees, customers, and business partners. Viewed as a smart part of the public relations functions of companies.

Dodd-Frank Act of 2010   Also known as the Dodd-Frank Wall Street Reform and Consumer Protection Act that helped create the CFPB and was intended to address many of the problems in the financial industry, including mortgage lending, that resulted in the 2008 financial crisis in the United States.

Monopolies   Companies that have essentially squashed any competitors with the intention of controlling products or trade in a specific industry. Side note: The goal of the board game *Monopoly* (Parker Brothers) is to own as much property as possible so that other players go broke paying you rent on the properties you own (e.g., railroads, real estate).

Multinational corporations   Companies and corporations that have a number of offices, factories, or retail locations around the globe. Example: McDonald's® fast food restaurants.

Sarbanes-Oxley Act of 2002   Federal law passed in response to Enron intended to tighten auditing and financial regulations for publicly traded companies (i.e., companies that sell stock to investors).

Sherman Antitrust Act of 1890   First law in the United States to outlaw monopoly companies.

World Bank (WB)   International banking group that provides loans and funding to poorer, developing countries.

REFERENCES AND SUGGESTED READINGS

Agarwal, N. and M. Sharma. (2014) Fraud risk prediction in merchant-bank relationship using regression models. *Vikalpa: The Journal of Decision Makers.* July-Sept., Vol. 39, Issue 3: 67-75.

American Museum of Tort. (2019) The Ford Pinto. *Famous Cases.* Retrieved from https://www.tortmuseum.org/ford-pinto/.

Bush, M. (2014) 10 CEOs brought down by greed. *MSN News.* Oct. 23. Retrieved from https://www.msn.com/en-ca/news/other/10-ceos-brought-down-by-greed/ss-BBaHOLt.

Dykeman, A. and MoneyBuilder. (2011) Are online banks safe? *Forbes.* Retrieved from https://www.forbes.com/sites/moneybuilder/2011/03/30/are-online-banks-safe/#5ced1ac5017.

Feder, B. J. (2003) John Sidgmore, 52, dies; Headed WorldCom. *The New York Times.* Dec. 12. Retrieved from https://www.nytimes.com/2003/12/12/business/john-sidgmore-52-dies-headed-worldcom.html.

Giroux, G. (2008) What went wrong? Accounting fraud and lessons from recent scandals. *Social Research.* Winter, Vol. 75, Issue 41205-1238.

Heller, R. (2003) Parmalat: A particularly Italian scandal. *Forbes.* Dec. 30. Retrieved from https://www.forbes.com/2003/12/30/cz_rh_1230parmalat.html#49f969d95162.

Horsley, S. (2006) Enron founder Kenneth Lay dies of heart attack. *NPR.* July 5. Retrieved from https://www.npr.org/templates/story/story.php?storyId=5534705.

Keneally, M. (2019) Man who spent 36 years in prison for stealing $50 from a bakery to be freed. *ABC News.* Aug. 29. Retrieved from https://abcnews.go.com/US/man-spent-36-years-prison-stealing-50-bakery/story?id=65264675.

McLean, B. and P. Elkind. (2006) *The Smartest Guys in the Room: The Amazing Rise and Scandalous Fall of Enron.* New York: Penguin Books.

McLean, B. and P. Elkind. (2006) The guiltiest guys in the room. *CNN Money.* July 5. Retrieved from https://money.cnn.com/2006/05/29/news/enron_guiltyest/.

Mims, J.H. (2017) The Wells Fargo scandal and efforts to reform incentive-based compensation in financial institutions. North Carolina Banking Institute. Article 21, Vol. 21, Issue 1: 428-467.

Mintzberg, H. (2001) The yin and yang of managing. *Organizational Dynamics.* Spring, Vol. 29, Issue 4: 306-312.

Monthe, P. (2007) How Nick Leeson caused the collapse of Barings Bank. *NextFinance.* Retrieved from https://www.next-finance.net/How-Nick-Leeson-caused-the.

Pollman, E. (2019) Corporate disobedience. *Duke Law Journal.* Jan., Vol. 68, Issue 4: 709-765.

Roberts, J. (2004) Enron traders caught on tape. *CBS Evening News.* June 1. Retrieved from https://www.cbsnews.com/news/enron-traders-caught-on-tape/

Seiberg, J. (1996) Fed to order more audits of foreign banks in wake of Daiwa and Barings scandals. *American Banker.* Vol. 161, Issue 45:3.

Sweeney, P. (2002) The travails of Tyco. *Financial Executive.* June, Vol. 18, Issue 4: 20-22.

Tran, M. (2002) WorldCom accounting scandal. *The Guardian.* Aug. 9. Retrieved from https://www.theguardian.com/business/2002/aug/09/corporatefraud.worldcom2.

Tucker, G. (2018) Sarbanes-Oxley is suffocating our essential capital market. *Real Clear Markets.* May 11. Retrieved from https://www.realclearmarkets.com/articles/2018/05/11/sarbanes-oxley_is_suffocating_our_essential_capital_markets_103255.html.

U.S. Congress. (2004) *Hearing Before the Committee on Banking, Housing, and Urban Affairs, United States Senate.* June 3. 108 Congress, Second Session.

U.S. Securities and Exchange Commission. (2006) SEC settles litigation with former Chief Corporate Counsel of Tyco International Ltd. *Litigation Release No. 19678.* May 1. Retrieved from https://www.sec.gov/litigation/litreleases/2006/lr19678.htm.

U.S. Treasury Department. (2018) *National Terrorist Financing Risk Assessment.* Retrieved from https://home.treasury.gov/system/files/136/2018ntfra_12182018.pdf.

Weeke, S. (2019) Parma's god falls from the sky: An Italian city mourns as a dynasty collapses over financial scandal. *World News on NBCNEWS.com.* Retrieved from http://www.nbcnews.com/id/4030254/ns/world_news/t/parmas-god-falls-sky/#.XXp0_utKjOQ

Wells Fargo Bank. (2019) History of Wells Fargo. Retrieved from https://www.wellsfargo.com/about/corporate/history/.

Williams, L. (2002) Tyco CEO receives $1.65 mln salary. *Market Watch.* Jan 28. Retrieved from https://www.marketwatch.com/story/tyco-ceo-kozlowski-gets-hefty-salary-bonus-hike.

Chapter SIX

Cyber White Collar Crime

What's my password?

> "You are so paranoid, you are paraparanoid."
>
> —*Silicon Valley, Season 2, Episode 8 (HBO)*

Chapter Objectives

- Distinguish between cybercrime that is distinctly white collar offending from other forms of cybercrime, including cyberterrorism.
- Understand the "typical" cybercriminal.
- Explore organizational, social, and psychological conditions that raise the risks for cybercriminal offending.
- Introduce theories to explain cybercrimes.
- Examine current measures to prevent and prosecute cybercrimes.

Key Terms

Blockchain
Botnets
Computer coding
Computer hacking
Computer Fraud and Abuse Act, 1986
Computer worms
Corporate espionage

Cyber fraud
Cybercrime
Dark Web
Electronic Crime Task Force (2001)
Malware
Phishing

INTRODUCTION

As we march further into the 21st century, what we define as *cybercrime* is rapidly evolving. Everything from alleged election tampering to cyberbullying falls under its umbrella. However, so as to be clear in our definitions for this book, the focus will be on cybercrimes that are clearly under the heading of white collar criminal behavior. The earliest and most common forms that we will explore are *computer hacking* and fraud.

There is some confusion, as in the case of other types of white collar crime, as to whether the cybercriminals themselves really should be classified as a white collar criminal. If we are to embrace Sutherland's first definitions of white collar criminality, the discussion should be isolated to only include individuals who commit cybercrimes within their occupations.

It is worth noting the overlap between those who commit cybercrimes through avenues available in their occupations, including training for legitimate purposes, with those who solely commit cybercrimes as their primary occupation. Sutherland could not have anticipated the technological revolution that would ultimately challenge his definition of the white collar criminal. We pretty much call someone who makes crime their full-time job a "career criminal." This can be the case with cybercriminals. We will try to confine our discussions in this chapter to the former type, who commit cybercrimes while working in a legitimate job.

Another misconception is that a great deal of cybercrime is associated with national security. The protection of highly classified information and computer infrastructure that is associated with the military, energy, transportation, and telecommunications is paramount. However, a good portion of cybercrime is associated with fraud and financial white collar crime. Here we might find some overlap with crimes against consumers, found in Chapter 7.

The threat of a foreign country or terrorist organization infiltrating our cyberspace through social media brings on a greater degree of societal anxiety. The reality is that financial cybercrime costs individuals, organizations, governments, and businesses billions of dollars annually. This is outside of the costs of putting safeguards in place in the form of cybersecurity, not to mention the overhead costs for maintenance of systems and paying for specialized cybersecurity personnel.

Simply using a computer as a tool in the commission of a crime, as in the case of spam mail in Nigerian schemes, is not enough to be technically classified as cybercrime. Definitions do generally include the use of computers vis-à-vis the Internet within this category. However, those who perpetrate these types of fraud can be, on the most part, computer-illiterate because it only requires knowledge of the use of email and ability to obtain email lists. These are openly available publicly, as in the example of faculty and staff email addresses on a university website. Other lists are available for sale on the "Dark Web," discussed in this chapter.

THE MORALITY OF CYBERCRIMES AND THE NARCISSISTIC CRIMINAL

Cybercrimes, whether for financial or intrinsic reasons, represent a different type of criminal than in the case of conventional crime or white collar crime in general. Unlike many street crimes (e.g., assaults, homicides), the criminal act is not necessarily personal. When cybercrime is committed just for fun or thrill-seeking, the criminal most times is not out to target a specific victim. In fact, as the act offers a certain amount of anonymity (until detected), cybercrimes happen in the shadows. This begs the questions: Is it simply a matter of the cybercriminal able to hide their identity that they also do not put a face to the victim? Or is there something morally corrupt in the cybercriminal, even if the crime is presented as being committed for the right reasons? One explanation is narcissism, where the criminal's focus is on their own gratification, with little regard for others.

Though it can be present in the general social and psychological makeup of a person, narcissism rarely exists without comparison of self with other people's lives and accomplishments. In the highly competitive world of high-tech, the usual institutional and legal means by which to control criminal behavior may be inadequate to prevent cybercrime. Pathological narcissists have a difficult time in self-regulating as it is; shaming will not work if the crimes are not easily detected. And sanctions, including the threat of being fired from a job, do not seem to stop cybercriminals from committing the crimes in the first place.

It may take innovation beyond the usual sanctions imposed in the case of "conventional" white collar crime, ordinarily fines imposed by civil courts, in order to serve as a deterrence. However, in the case of the narcissistic actor, it becomes an enormous challenge to prevent them from offending or reoffending, as seen in the case of Julian Assange of Wikileaks notoriety. Again, this is largely due to little regard as to who the narcissist might hurt with their actions.

Law in the Real World: Julian Assange

(Source: Whitmire, 2015)

It's not uncommon for a narcissist to have a larger than life personality and lifestyles to match them. There can be a certain amount of mythology surrounding them and they can be very charismatic. The narcissist is above all looking for constant attention and reassurance that they are as wonderful as they believe themselves to be.

For those who are unfamiliar with it, Wikileaks is a nonprofit organization whose mission is to uncover and release classified government information. Its founder and former editor-in-chief, Julian Assange, is in the center of several controversies surrounding sensitive information that was leaked through Wikileaks' website.

Wikileaks is a really difficult case in white collar crime to classify. Is the website a public service to the international community? Is it political crime? Is it cybercrime? To be accurate, it is the intersection of all three.

As there has been so much debate on Assange's dedication to revealing government information he believes is in the public's best interest to know, Assange's motivations make this case a good one to include in our discussions of the narcissistic cybercriminal.

We should note that to date, Assange has yet to be convicted of any cybercrimes and is to be presumed innocent unless proven guilty of his alleged crimes in a court of law. Assange is, however, facing a number of criminal charges. In 2012, he was out on bail in a case where he stood to be extradited to Sweden on crimes unrelated to his Wikileaks activities, when he sought asylum in the Ecuadorian Embassy in London. By 2019, Assange had overstayed his welcome and was evicted, taken into custody by British police. Though the Swedish government dropped criminal charges against him, he currently faces charges in the U.K. and in the United States.

The primary criminal complaint against Assange is that he agreed to receive transmitted classified documents from Chelsea Manning (born Bradley Edward Manning) while she was serving in the U.S. Army in Iraq. He has been convicted in the U.K. to 50 weeks in prison for violating the terms of his bail.

Manning was ultimately court-martialed, charged, and convicted for her role in hacking into sensitive military files. In 2010 she leaked these files to Assange and the Wikileaks organization, leading to her conviction in 2012, carrying a prison sentence of years for her crimes. President Obama commuted her sentence in 2017, shortening her sentence to seven years. Like Assange, Manning believes that her role is that of a whistleblower, not a criminal.

In many respects, Assange represents the trickster archetype in mythology and Jungian psychology, possessing exceptional intelligence and a habit of ignoring rules and laws to suit himself (Whitmire, 2015). "Assange plays both deceiver and inventor of his own record.... has a very free and easy relationship with the truth." (Whitmire, 2015, p. 84; Domscheit-Berg, 2011, p. 65) Though not clinically diagnosed as a narcissist, he is largely viewed as an attention seeker, one of the characteristics of pathological narcissism (BBC, 2019; Dashineau et al., 2019).

Discussion Questions

1. What motive might Julian Assange have to leak sensitive government and military documents, even if it might endanger personnel?
2. Can Assange's alleged criminal activities be part of his legitimate occupation or could he be classified a career criminal?

3. What challenges might governments have in protecting classified information in this day and age of public demand for transparency?

In the organizational setting, say in Silicon Valley where information technology lives somewhat in its own bubble, there are legends of the self-made tech people like Steve Jobs. Unlike in some other industries, there is no necessity to even appear to conform to what is normative in business. The very nature of technological innovation dictates that the industry attracts and socializes a different brand of employee to "good practices."

As Steven John observed, high-tech companies are islands with their own species of "flora and fauna": "Silicon Valley . . . . [has]developed different life-forms than anywhere else." (Harris and Alter, 2014). Add to that the stereotype of laid-back California, in tech-land, ready for action, workers in the high-tech industry are a blend of innovation, entrepreneurship, and excitement (Harris and Alter, 2014). In this Petri dish, it makes sense that combined with questionable moral character and narcissism, the "right" individual may be motivated to operate at the margins or outside the boundaries of cyber laws.

The culprit behind "good" workers turning "bad" may be that workplace morality and ethics have changed over the past few decades since the rise of the information economy that is dependent on computers. We saw this in our discussions of financial crimes on Wall Street where online trading is so instantaneous. As in Bauman's observation (1993) that postmodern destruction of people generally follow norms, the individual may be operating in their own moral autonomy and efficacy, as we see in financial white collar crime (Hookway, 2018).

Perhaps contributing to only following moral code when it is convenient, is the perception that younger generations of workers, including Millennials, are less likely to stay at the same company for very long. "Job-hopping" — leaving a job in less than two years in a company — is of greater concern for security of trade secrets, when workers bounce around between competitors. It is perfectly understandable in the technological fields that workers would want to take advantage of any opportunities that come their way to further their education.

The loyalty then seems to be to the career building experience than to a single company. Workers in the tech industry in Silicon Valley reportedly jump from companies with inferior technologies to those that have more superior innovation (Fallick et al., 2006).

This perception of workers' lack of loyalty has not necessarily been accurately measured empirically, as the Bureau of Labor Statistics, one of the best resources for flow of workers in and out of industries, has never attempted to estimate how many times people might change employers, much less careers, in the course of their lives (BLS, available at https://www.bls.gov/nls/nlsfaqs.htm#anch43, accessed October 2, 2018). It should be noted that there is higher than average changeover in the tech industry, as supply and demand volatility is facilitated by the fast cycles of new technologies and products.

Moral fluidity is not limited to the individual criminal. There is considerable debate underway as to the morality of shifting from conventional war to cyberwarfare. Tactics in conventional war have been exhaustively debated by themselves. The argument for cyberwarfare is the perception that cyberattacks are less likely to result in the killing of human beings or cause lasting physical or infrastructure damage (Dipert, 2010). The alleged interference in the 2016 presidential election by Russia is being held up as an example of a means by which to undermine a rival country without a single shot fired. Within the context of white collar crime, cyberattacks weaken rival companies and individual competitors, with questionable moral implications.

THE ROLE OF SOCIAL NETWORKS

If we view cybercrimes as being similar to organized crime, the characteristics of secrecy and covert operations can certainly be applied to cybercriminal networks. Actors are not only connected by cyberspace, but also by complex social networks that are dependent on trust. Trust is intimately connected to the extent by which that we can count on those we are close to to keep our secrets. First explored by Georg Simmel, the ability to maintain secrets is a function of how many are privy to them. Simmel predicted that the more people that know a secret, the more likely it is going to be leaked (Simmel, 1906).

Organized crime, whether operating on the streets or in cyberspace, functions similarly to legitimate businesses, including the establishment of norms, codes of conduct, and being loosely held together with some common goals. As in the case of organized crime or legitimate cross-national companies, cyber conspirators can be scattered across the globe, offering more flexibility in operations and provide social support (Fielding, 2017).

Cyber forums are another conduit by which potential co-conspirators can connect. In fact, there might even be active recruitment of forum members to join *phishing* and *malware* groups (Leukfeldt et al., 2017). This may be attractive to "wannabe Black Hats," discussed later in this chapter, much like individuals who are actively attempting to join a street gang.

If these networks can be viewed as secret societies where membership is limited to only the most trustworthy, the structural processes are similar to those of any exclusive, legitimate organization. Secret societies are far from being new phenomena. Noel Gist (1938, p. 349) observed that "secret societies constitute one of the important culture patterns both of primitive and of modern civilizations . . . . The numerous benevolent and protective societies bear witness to the social significance of institutionalized secrecy in the western world." Covert, criminal enterprises are no different and are subject to the same vulnerabilities of exposure. Secret societies are particularly vulnerable these days to exposure with the immediacy of social media.

Though keeping secrets can be the glue that holds conspiracies together, for some individuals, it is exhausting to continually monitor their behavior, including what they say and who they talk to. This leaves them tempted to either cooperate with authorities when networks start to crumble or to expose previously undetected networks either for fear of detection or as an attempt to extract themselves from the conspiracy.

THE DARK WEB

Since the launching of the Internet, it became a vehicle by which criminals are allowed free rein to set up shop with full anonymity. The Internet is structured in such a way that even though anyone can access the Dark Web with specialized software, the generators of the websites are largely untraceable and go undetected.

The *Dark Web* is a conduit in which illicit commerce is not limited to white-collar crimes. It is certainly a means by which to market violence and extremism, but it also offers brokerage for child pornography and money laundering operations (Janis et al., 2018). Cryptomarkets within the Dark Web also offer opportunities for drug traffickers to hide operations (Garcia Sigman, 2017).

COMPUTER HACKING

Cybercrime in the form of *computer hacking* is motivated by a number of reasons: political ideology, financial gain, and testing the limits of abilities to do so are a few of the more salient reasons. This chapter focuses on the latter, the hacker who is largely not motivated by the act of sabotage, possible information, or financial gain from the act but by the act itself, perhaps the most common of hackers. More specifically, the focus of this chapter is to better understand the division between legitimate hacking and illegitimate, unauthorized access to programs and systems. In order to commit the quasi- or fully illegitimate crime of hacking, one must also be intimately knowledgeable of *computer coding* as well as the vulnerabilities of computer systems.

What makes hacking "for the heck of it" interesting, as a follow up to the insider trading described in this book, is that this appears to be a crime with not so fuzzy legal edges, as in the case of a number of white collar crimes. Just as company executives in publicly traded companies must disclose if they are legitimate insider traders, some hacking activities are done in the open, as illustrated by DEF CON® conferences which, though advertised as being "underground," are actually conventions that are conducted within the public sphere, to the extent that these are not held in some secret location. This is exemplified by the DEF CON® conference in Las Vegas in 2018 (https://www.defcon.org/index.html). Certainly, most large-scale tech companies, as well as organizations who are keepers of sensitive and private information, including government agencies, have on site employees who are devoted to cyber security. To work in this field, individuals have to have serious working knowledge of both sides of legality, including regulation and the ways by which cybercriminals access unauthorized information.

In 2004, Voiskounsky and Smyslova noted that the motivation behind cyber hacking was largely ignored in psychology. Though we have come a long way technologically within information technology and computer science in understanding this crime, this remains an area also largely ignored in criminal justice and sociology research. The focus has been more on the means than the motive. Even within criminal justice circles, the focus on cybercrime has just come to the forefront of law enforcement efforts in recent years, on the heels of high-profile cases. However, even here, the focus is on the hacker who is motivated by personal financial gain or "hacktivism" (e.g., Wikileaks) (Kopfstein, 2013).

What about the hacker who is motivated by the act itself? Is it simply a matter of trying to broaden the computer amateur's or expert's knowledge base? Or, as in some other cases of conventional or white collar crime, is it more about the intrinsic thrill of the act? As in previous chapters, cases that have been recently highlighted in the news have been examined and debated as to whether theories of low self-control (Bossler and Burrus, 2011) are most applicable. Another paradigm suggests that the intersection of collective narcissism and thrill-seeking behavior has more merit when explaining cybercrime, particularly illegal hacking. What makes this type of computer activity so fascinating is that not all hackers are criminals, nor do all criminal hackers view themselves as acting maliciously, as the term, "hacker," itself is up for debate.

More recently, individuals within the CS and IT communities have been attempting to regain the legitimacy of the label "hacker." When the division between legitimate and illegitimate hackers began, the community borrowed terms from the wild, wild west: "White Hats" to denote those who were looking for openings in programs/systems in order to assist in patching them up and "Black Hats" who were doing so in order to gain entry into the "White Hats" world or for general mischief. This dichotomy has been so popularized, it was depicted in a television show, *Silicon Valley* (Lyons, HBO, 2015, Season 2, Episode 8). A "Gray Hat," on the other hand, is someone who skirts around laws or possible ethical standards, but does not have the malicious intent of someone who is defined to be a "Black Hat." Like the "Black Hat," the "Gray Hat" may be attempting to make entry into legitimate employment within the high-tech field by demonstrating their talent, albeit quasi-legally.

This is where the conundrum lies. How can one make the transition from Black Hat to White Hat without drawing attention to one or more criminal acts? As in the case of insider trading, hacking is an activity that can be conducted within the context of one's occupation or a "recreational" sideline. However, more commonly it is the Black Hat hacker who begins in illegitimacy who will cross over to the White Hats when they begin reporting the vulnerabilities of a system. We should note here that these are the old school hackers: Historically, criminal hackers were looking for admiration and recognition from their peers, in addition to media attention (Decary-Hetu and Dupont, 2015). The latest generation of hackers are very much aware of their power to infiltrate the Internet and secured computers and are more likely to see it as an opportunity to enter illegal markets.

In some cases, the organizations or website managers inadvertently leave themselves vulnerable for attack or infiltration. In September 2018, CNN reported that an attack exposed 50 million Facebook users to the potential of having their accounts taken over. Facebook responded by immediately contacting the FBI and law enforcement, finding that the vulnerability was a result of three distinct bugs first appearing in 2017 (CNN, available at https://money.cnn.com/2018/09/28/technology/facebook-breach-50-million/index.html, retrieved September 26, 2018). Even with Facebook's diligence to respond once the problem was detected, investigations may take months, sometimes years, to fully understand what exactly was executed by the perpetrator(s) and how it was executed, as witnessed by the protracted time between implementation and full disclosure to the public. The same can be said about the National Security Agency security breach discovered in 2017, discussed in further detail later in this chapter.

On a larger scale than isolated incidents of infiltrating computers or systems, hackers can create massive networks of infected computers, with the use of *computer worms* through *botnets* or other means by which to glean personal or financial information from unsuspecting victims (Decary-Hetu and Dupont, 2015). What is of greatest concern is that the use of botnets greatly reduces the amount of experience and knowledge that the participant needs to sell stolen personal and financial information on the black market (Decary-Hetu and Dupont, 2015). Any minimally qualified individual can easily initiate illegal transactions with the use of software found online in the Dark Web.

THE LONE HACKER vs. THE SOCIAL HACKER

Within the context of this chapter, we are looking primarily at two types of actors who might not be mutually exclusive. The first type of hacker can be described as the "lone hacker," the individual who is covertly working by themselves. The second fits more neatly within the confines of social network theory discussed earlier in this chapter.

The use of the analogy of golf when describing differences between the lone hacker and the social hacker might be helpful in distinguishing the two. Like in golf, there are two types of enthusiasts when it comes to the learning curve and competition. Though golf has been described as a solo competition sport, where the amateur's goal, in theory, is to beat their own average scores, in reality, as demonstrated by amateur leagues and tournaments, for many people the game is motivated by trying to beat other players. Like in golf, both types of competition, against oneself and against others, are at the same time frustrating and rewarding for the individual hacker.

The concerns of assuming that a hacker is acting alone is that unless co-conspirators are detected, it may actually be a criminal network that is at work trying to gather sensitive information illegally. In some cases, the goal is to create havoc within an organization or beyond. Certainly, with the case of Julian Assange, he continues to be portrayed in the media as if he is a solo actor. However, in order to be as extensively damaging as he has been, other guilty parties have to be involved, including people leaking information to him. Law enforcement and regulators should view a single illegitimate hacker as possibly the tip of the proverbial iceberg, that we continue to refer to in this book, as in the case of detecting the full extent of terrorist conspiracy in the 9/11 Twin Towers tragedy in New York City (September 11, 2001).

There is even newer technology than the Dark Web that may either be a bane or a blessing to law enforcement and regulators. According to Don and Alex Tapscott (2016), the *blockchain* is a digital ledger of economic transactions, including a vehicle for bitcoins.

As blockchain technology decentralizes networks, they may become "stringy." As borrowed from social network analysis and described by less densely packed networks, the blockchain may result in even more difficulty detecting illegal activity that is being conducted through the blockchain than in the case of greater network cohesion where detection might be more likely to occur (Wasserman and Faust, 1994; Hubbell, 1965; Katz, 1947). Cryptocurrency can conceivably be used for illegal financial exchanges. And again, the blockchain offers the same anonymity as the Dark Web.

Law in the Real World: Ashley Madison Database Hack

One of the more headline-grabbing cases happened in 2015 when the Ashley Madison database, an online dating service for married people looking to conduct extramarital affairs (Wiemann, 2015), was hacked for information on users. In this case, there did not appear to be a motive to merely collect financial data, but also an opportunity to gather intimate details on individuals' sexual fantasies. What makes this case interesting is that there is double duplicity: the perpetrator(s) were anonymous, as well as some of the website's users who created fictitious profiles with phony names. However, between the hacking and media attention, plus the ability to access leaked information on users of the website, a number of Ashley Madison customers were publicly exposed and humiliated.

Discussion Questions

1. If the purpose of hacking a website to gain personal information is solely to humiliate individuals (which was not the case with Ashley Madison), does this constitute a white collar crime?
2. Why are law enforcement and regulators not more aggressively finding ways to protect consumers, even if it is something like the Ashley Madison website, where there is a possibility of elite clientele?
3. What are the challenges and limitations in attempting to find ways to protect consumers?

CORPORATE ESPIONAGE

Corporate espionage is generally separated into three categories: spying and piracy practiced (1) by companies, (2) by financial institutions, and (3) by foreign governments (Javers, 2011). Increasingly, the type of corporate espionage that we are witnessing is state-sponsored, meaning it is being conducted by governments. Because of this, depending on the perpetrator, the crime can be corporate white collar crime or state-sponsored white collar crime initiated for the purposes of not only stealing corporate secrets, but also undermining a global adversary in the form of a foreign government.

In some cases, corporate espionage involves complex spy networks. One attractive industry is finance, where criminal networks can be embedded within legitimate financial institutions (Hansen, 2009). As in cases of insider trading, the espionage is not readily detected. We don't ordinarily associate insider trading with espionage, but it might require covert operations to get insider information for purposes other than stock purchase or sale.

Criminal white collar networks can operate for a number of years, in some cases decades, before they are finally discovered. Generally, the discovery happens when someone within the network makes a foolish mistake or becomes a whistle blower, or regulators and law enforcement finally detect an irregularity. However, in the case of corporate espionage that is happening through computer access, there are some safeguards in today's security technology to somewhat prevent probes into sensitive data archives.

Once upon a time, if a company wanted to steal trade secrets from a competitor, they would hire someone to infiltrate that company. The corporate spy would apply for a position that afforded them the opportunity to have access to anything from sensitive financial information to insider information on research and development. Of course, this would require hiring a corporate spy who was technically qualified and possessed the credentials for a position at a competitor company that allowed them free access to corporate secrets. In some cases, the purpose is to sabotage operations rather than to gather intelligence on a competitor. Though this tactic of espionage is still used today, the more efficient method to infiltrate a company is to do so electronically. A company insider could also be recruited as in the case of the employee who is disgruntled or is being blackmailed with information that might be embarrassing, compromising to their position in the company, or a threat to their family in some way.

The watchdogs themselves are vulnerable to hacking. A group that called themselves the Shadow Brokers stole a number of disks that held sensitive NSA data in 2013 (Schneier, 2017). The leaked information not only embarrassed the NSA, but it revealed the vulnerabilities of one of the most critical agencies charged with protecting government information.

In a highly connected global economy, corporate espionage is more likely to take place via the use of hacking. Ordinarily corporate espionage that is occurring between U.S. corporations is handled through criminal and/or civil courts. However, when corporate espionage involves a foreign government, the U.S. National Security Agency (NSA), will get involved in the investigation. One common ploy by cyber criminals is to send out spam emails, much in the same vein as Nigerian advance-fees scams, for the purpose of trying to gain sensitive technologies from American executives (Javers, 2011). There are also well-documented cases of organized attacks on Google and Gmail by Chinese operatives (Dipert, 2010).

Law in the Real World: Chinese Espionage

In 2008, a supposed executive recruiting firm called Fox Adams began circulating emails to executives at American companies hinting at lucrative job opportunities. The executives were instructed to reply with contact information. If a "potential job recruit" responded to the email, they were instructed to provide a number of pieces of information, including details of their work, access to technology, and work experience. As it was eventually discovered and investigated by security experts and U.S. intelligence agents, the spam emails were actually coming from Chinese intelligence — Fox Adams did not exist. As Javers (2011, p. 53) observed, "the Fox Adams ploy [is] a routine China intelligence probe of U.S. corporate infrastructure...." acting as a means to gather industrial secrets.

More commonly, China, like other world economic competitors, is accused of hacking into U.S. and other countries' computer systems to collect intellectual property and confidential business records. These hackers may or may not be connected to the Chinese government and it is a challenge for investigators to figure out the difference. However, there are times when the connection is clear.

There have been a number of criminal cases in recent decades brought against Chinese nationals. In 2018, two Chinese hackers were accused of attempting to hack into American companies and government agencies, with suspected criminal activities allegedly beginning in 2006 (U.S. Department of Justice, 2018). Within the indictment against members of the Advanced Persistent Threat 10 Group (APT10), the prosecution accused them of waging a campaign to infiltrate the computer systems of 45 technology companies and U.S. government agencies (U.S. Department of Justice, 2018).

As they were suspected of hacking from 2006 through 2018, until the arrest of two main defendants, Zhu Hua and Zhang Shilong working for APT10, immeasurable amounts of intellectual property were successfully stolen, including targeted finance, pharmaceutical, communications, and transportation technologies (U.S. Department of Justice, 2018; U.S. District Court, Southern District of New York, 2018). In the indictment, Hua and Shilong, along with APT10, were believed to be operating on behalf of the Chinese government. Historically, since the creation of People's Republic of China, all companies were owned by the government. With economic reform beginning in the late 20th century, some companies were allowed to be private or publicly traded. However, there is still deep-rooted institutionalized connections to the Chinese government, even with reform.

Of greater concern, per Javer's account (2011), there is always the question as to whether any former CIA-trained agents are taking part in cyber corporate espionage, even unwittingly. "What is astonishing about the private spy industry is how little the U.S. government seems to know about it. The CIA says it does not know where its former agents are working today and argues that tracking where they are employed would violate the civil rights of those agents; it surely behooves the U.S. intelligence community to have some sense of where its alumni are plying their trade, however, and whose payrolls they join when they enter the private the private sector." (Javers, 2011, p. 58) Though we would like to assume that no former CIA agent is committing corporate espionage, but there is no means by which to track if any might be working for a foreign government, including China, that is infiltrating cyber systems worldwide.

Kevin Mallory is an example of a former CIA employee who became involved in espionage on behalf of the Chinese government. He was convicted of conspiring to pass on sensitive U.S. defense intelligence to a

Chinese intelligence officer, and sentenced to 20 years in prison (U.S. Department of Justice, n.d.).

The U.S. Department of Justice has increased its efforts in countering China's industrial espionage efforts, including economic cyberwarfare. Assistant Attorney for National Security John C. Demers, who was named to lead the Department of Justice's China initiative in 2018, warned that China's goal in committing corporate espionage is to further gain economic dominance in the world (U.S. Department of Justice, n.d.). Mallory's name is added to a list of others, including retired Army officer Ron Hansen[*], who leave U.S. government employment only to sell state secrets to a foreign government (U.S. Department of Justice, 2019).

Discussion Questions

1. How might companies take precautions against corporate espionage that takes place through electronic means?
2. China and the United States have historically been "frienemies" (advisories or competitors who put up a front of being friendly). What motivation might a "friendly" nation have to hack into a supposed ally nation's corporate computers?
3. What would motivate a former government employee to sell government secrets to foreign governments, even though they were likely asked to take an oath to protect and defend their countries?

HEALTHCARE AND MEDICAL RECORDS HACKING

As every industry has entered the digital age, medical records are now more likely to be stored electronically. Healthcare and medical care providers are required by law to securely store records, with a limited number of personnel allowed access. Additional protection of records is provided through the Health Insurance Portability and Accounting Act (HIPAA, 2003). However, as in the case of even the most sensitive information, however well-protected, healthcare and medical records are vulnerable to hacking.

---

[*]No relation to this book's author.

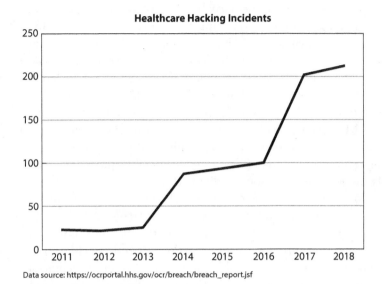

Healthcare Hacking Incidents

Data source: https://ocrportal.hhs.gov/ocr/breach/breach_report.jsf

EXHIBIT 6.1 | **Healthcare Hacking Incidents** (*Source:* Cynerio Research, available at https://cynerio.co/ healthcare-hacking-medical-record-fraud/)

According to NetStandard, a company in the business of advising companies on how to protect their sensitive data, health data is more valuable than credit card information. In fact, Phelps (2016) makes the claim that hacking medical records is relatively easy. The most common motivation is to gather information to steal individuals' identities, including addresses, contact information, recent medical history, and access to Social Security numbers. A second reason for stealing individuals' medical information is to commit insurance fraud.

CYBER FRAUD

Cyber fraud is a different kind of beast than mere hacking, though some hacking is done for the purposes of committing fraud. What they have in common is that the means by which potential victims are targeted is becoming more sophisticated as computer technology becomes more advanced. The most common types of cyber fraud include online shopping fraud, online fraud banking/payment schemes, advanced fee fraud, cyber threats/harassment, and malware (Reep-van den Bergh and Junger, 2018). Where they part ways in similarities is that cyber fraud is purely a business proposition with little in the way of political ideology or intrinsic thrill at the ability to commit the act itself, financial gains aside.

In discussions of cyber fraud, it is helpful to turn more attention to the victim than we have previously explored in this chapter. But before we completely ignore the perpetrator, the motives should be explained first. Goffman (1974) discussed a type of social interaction where only one party has control over the interaction, a reframing process he described as fabrication (Burgard and Schlembach, 2013). The role of the fraudster is to convince the victim to voluntarily take part in the fraud scheme.

Unlike the case of the passive hacking victim, the cyber fraud victim actively engages with the criminal, though they are unwitting to the fact that they are being victimized. Burgard and Schlembach (2013) use a fishing analogy: The perpetrator throws out the bait in hopes that the victim will be hooked. Generally, the victim is swayed to be hooked by an offer that on closer scrutiny is often too good to be true.

One common means by which to commit identity theft is through dating websites. The websites themselves (e.g., Match.com, OkCupid) may be legitimate, but online dating lends itself to some individuals hiding their true identities, much as in the case of the Ashley Madison website. The lonely or the naïve may be swayed to send money, gifts, or goods to the perpetrator (Rege, 2009).

The most likely victim of cyber fraud, as in the case of fraudulent phone solicitations on land lines, are the divorced, widowed, and the elderly. Because these populations are more likely to be older, they might not be as technically savvy, but the good news is that older people are becoming more adept at using computer technology as it becomes necessary in their professions. Senior advocacy groups actively work to educate this demographic on the risks of computer fraud (e.g., AARP). However, grooming can take place over months, as the targeted victim is swayed by hard luck stories and being taken into the supposed confidence by the scammer.

Nice to Know You

◂ Naomi Surugaba [azlin@moa.gov.my]   ↩ ↩ ↪   Actions

Inbox   Monday. March 10, 2014 1:18 PM

Dear Beloved Friend,
I know this message will come to you as surprised but permit me of my desire to go into business relationship with you.
I am Miss Naomi Surugaba a daughter to late Al-badari Surugaba of Libya whom was murdered during the recent civil war in Libya in March 2011, before his death my late father was a strong supporter and a member of late Moammar Gadhafi Government in Tripoli. Meanwhile before the incident, my late Father came to Cotonou Benin republic with the sum of USD4, 200,000.00 (US$4.2M) which he deposited in a Bank here in Cotonou Benin Republic West Africa for safe keeping .
I am here seeking for an avenue to transfer the fund to you in only you're reliable and trustworthy person to Investment the fund. I am here in Benin Republic because of the death of my parenf's and I want you to help me transfer the fund into your bank account for investment purpose.
Please I will offer you 20% of the total sum of USD4.2M for your assistance. Please I wish to transfer the fund urgently without delay into your account and also wish to relocate to your country due to the poor condition in Benin, as to enable me continue my education as I was a medical student before the sudden death of my parenf's. Reply to my alternative email:missnaomisurugaba2@hotmail.com, Your immediate response would be appreciated. Remain blessed,
Miss Naomi Surugaba.

EXHIBIT 6.2 ‖ **Cyber Scam Example** *Source:* Eichelberger, E. (2014) What I learned hanging out with Nigerian email scammers. Mother Jones. Retrieved from https://www.motherjones.com/politics/2014/03/what-i-learned-from-nigerian-scammers/

Identity fraud is much more nuanced than mere identity theft. Finch (2007) and Rege (2009) identify three ways by which identity fraud is committed: It is one thing to steal one's financial information, but quite another to steal someone's social identity, as sometimes happens in the practice of catfishing where people are lured into relationships with stolen social media content, including photographs, many times without the intent of meeting face-to-face.

COVID-19 CYBERSCAMS

As we have mentioned previously in this book, the COVID-19 pandemic left the door wide open for different forms of cybercrimes. These scams preyed on the fear of people coping with a vast array of social changes, including working from home, home schooling children, and social distancing. This was on top of the real fear of contracting the virus.

One type of scam uncovered by the Federal Trade Commission (FTC) involved unsolicited text messages. As there were more genuine efforts to do contact tracing — a method by which public health officials can trace who infected people have been in contact with — these crucial efforts were stymied by criminals. According to the FTC (Tressler, 2020), scammers pretended to be contact tracers, and if the unsuspecting victim takes the bait, criminals could access personal and financial information off of devices, including smart phones and tablets.

From the beginnings of the pandemic, the FBI and other investigative agencies began receiving complaints about illicit website activity, including fake charities. This was not unlike what is witnessed following any national emergency, including 9/11. According to the Department of Justice, by April 2020, the FBI had received complaints about the following types of cybercrimes (DOJ, 2020, retrieved from https://www.justice.gov/opa/pr/department-justice-announces-disruption-hundreds-online-covid-19-related-scams)

- An illicit website pretending to solicit and collect donations to the American Red Cross for COVID-19 relief efforts.
- Fraudulent websites that spoofed government programs and organizations to trick American citizens into entering personally identifiable information, including banking details.
- Websites of legitimate companies and services used to facilitate the distribution or control of malicious software.

An additional type of scam emerged during the distribution of stimulus payments by the IRS. Look-alike websites mimicking the official government website for the IRS were suspected to have been created in order to assist in phishing schemes (DOJ, 2020). To their credit, the FBI, in coordination with the Department of Justice, have been able to thwart a number of these schemes, primarily through the cooperation of the public and private sectors (DOJ, 2020).

Bottom line, it didn't take long for cybercriminals to exploit the virus for their own personal gain. It made it difficult both for legitimate agencies and American citizens to fight off both the threat of the virus and the associated cybercrimes. There were added concerns as people needed to work from home, using their personal computers for work-related business, making people more susceptible to cybercrime attacks (Taunton, 2020).

CYBERCRIME PREVENTION AND REGULATION

As in the case of many white collar crimes, the Achilles' heel is in prevention of cybercrimes. The challenge is in keeping up with the technology itself because cybersecurity requires specialized training and education[1], as well as complex computer software. When companies fail to protect customer or employee sensitive information, they run the risk of being held responsible, including for criminal sanctions and civil liability (Rishikof and Lunday, 2011). As such, companies, organizations, and agencies are highly motivated to invest in cybersecurity, but some may be limited by resources available to them.

Because regulation is a function of legislation, it is difficult for regulators to stay ahead of the "bad guys." With the fast pace of technological advances — for instance, our phones and computers become obsolete practically the moment we purchase them — when a crime is committed in cyberspace, criminals move on to more sophisticated methods before legislation is passed to prevent further victimization. However, effective regulation is written in broad enough terms to capture a number of types of offenses. And unlike financial regulation, cybercrime regulation is far more transparent and enforceable.

An additional challenge to enforcing cybercrime laws is that the victims may be too embarrassed to come forward. The National Consumers League (NCL) estimated an average loss of $2000 per victim in 2009 (Rege, 2013). More recent estimates are close to $50 million in the United States, with the average amount closer to $9,000 attributed to Internet romance scams alone, with scammers spending time looking for targets in chatrooms and dating websites. (Bindley, 2012, Available at https://www.huffingtonpost.com/2012/05/15/online-romance-scams-cost-50-million-in-2011_n_1518162.html, retrieved September 29, 2018). Similar to what we will see with telemarketing schemes discussed in Chapter 7, scammers use well-rehearsed scripts, preying on the vulnerability of people looking to connect with others through legitimate websites promising romance and companionship.

---

[1] It is anticipated that growing demand (faster, on average, than other professions) for employees in the information security sector will outpace the number of trained professionals (Bureau of Labor Statistics, available at https://www.bls.gov/ooh/computer-and-information-technology/information-security-analysts.htm).

COMPUTER FRAUD AND ABUSE ACT, 1986

A "protected computer" is a computer that is "used in or affecting interstate or foreign commerce. . . . used by the federal government and financial institutions." (Section 1030, Computer Fraud and Abuse Act, 1986, DOJ). Additional definition that is key in understanding hacking is "authorization," where it is a criminal offense, under the CFAA, to access a computer without authorization or exceeding authorized access. (18 U.S.C. §§1030(a)(3), (a)(5)(B), (a)(5)(C) and 18 U.S.C. §§1030(a)(1), (a)(2), (a)(4), CFAA, 1986, DOJ).

ELECTRONIC CRIME TASK FORCE, 2001

As part of the broader preventative measures after 9/11, the USA Patriot Act (2001) called for the creation of the *Electronic Crime Task Force*. As in the case of other types of crime that cross jurisdictional lines, it is not always clear as to whose responsibility it is to investigate a suspected cybercrime. Along with the NSA and FBI, the U.S. Secret Service is playing a greater part in assisting in providing training in computer forensics and network analysis, as well as coordinating with international law enforcement agency partners (Secret Service, available at https://www.secretservice.gov/investigation/#, retrieved September 29, 2018).

TABLE 6.1 Computer Fraud and Abuse Act (CFAA), 1986

STATUTE	CRIME	SUMMARY
§1030(a)(1)	Obtaining National Security Information	Knowingly access computer without or in excess of authorization; obtain national security information, communication, delivery, transmission (or attempt to transmit) information could injure the U.S. or benefit a foreign nation; OR willful retention of the information
§1030(a)(2)	Accessing a Computer and Obtaining Information	Misdemeanor: Intentionally access a computer without or in excess of authorization; obtain information from financial records of financial institution or consumer reporting agency OR the U.S. government OR protected computer Felony: Committed for commercial advantage or private financial gain OR committed in furtherance of any

STATUTE	CRIME	SUMMARY
		criminal or tortious act OR the value of the information obtained exceeds $5000
§1030(a)(3)	Trespassing in a Government Computer	Intentionally access without authorization a nonpublic computer of the U.S. that was exclusively for the use of U.S. or was used by or for U.S.
§1030(a)(5)	Damaging a Computer or Information	Misdemeanor: Knowingly cause transmission of a program, information, code, or command; intentionally cause damage to protected computer without authorization; recklessly cause damage or cause loss Felony: Results in loss of $5000 during 1 year OR modifies medical care of a person OR causes physical injury OR threatens public health or safety OR damages systems used by or for government entity for administration of justice, national defense, or national security OR damages affect 10 or more protected computers during 1 year.

Source: Department of Justice, 2015

SUMMARY

Like many white collar crimes, cybercrimes may happen for a long, protracted time before they are detected. Sometimes the detection is a fluke, other times it is due to some error on the perpetrator(s), and in yet other cases, it is due to the diligence of people in the cybersecurity professions, one of the fastest growing career paths in CS and IT.

However, the complexity and the anonymity of the Dark Web makes detection of both the crimes and the perpetrator difficult until the damage is done. Though law enforcement is rapidly catching up with technologies to detect cyber-criminal activity, prevention continues to be the biggest challenge, as in the case of other types of organized crime.

We will continue to see, as we did in this chapter, that there are some populations who are more vulnerable to cybercrimes, including children, the elderly, recent immigrants, and the disabled. Criminals who use chatrooms and dating sites to find possible targets are also preying on the lonely.

As cyberwarfare becomes more commonplace, and the newest weapon since the creation of nuclear weapons and intercontinental missiles (Dipert, 2010), cybercrime will continue to be the biggest challenge in fighting white collar crimes. Cyberwarfare is not limited to adversaries in business, but is perhaps the biggest weapon unleashed by nations on businesses and other countries' governments moving forward into the mid-21st century.

Case Study ▪ Massachusetts Teenager Running Amok in Cyberspace

Background

We rarely discuss white collar crimes that are committed by juveniles. However, juveniles, in particular teenagers who are working, do on occasion steal from their employers when given the motivation and opportunity. What is more likely to happen since the computer age is that teens may be tempted to illegally hack into computer systems or the Internet, if for no other reason than to prove that they can do it. A popular movie during the 1980s, *War-Games* (MGM, 1983), depicted the worst-case scenario where a gamer hacks into the Pentagon mainframe and initiates what could be WWIII, a global nuclear war. Justifiably, in real life, it is becoming increasingly possible for motivated black hat hackers to run amok in supposedly secure computer systems.

Juveniles, when they do offend, are a special class of criminal. First, there is always a question as to how culpable parents or guardians might be when a child commits a crime. Second, as more current research suggests that the frontal lobes of the brain, the center for impulse control, is not fully developed until early adulthood (Johnson et al., 2009), there is always the question of whether children are mature enough to even understand the consequences of their action. It becomes particularly problematic when there is the somewhat detached reality of committing a crime in cyberspace as compared to, say, robbing a convenience store.

In 2004 and 2005, a juvenile in Massachusetts was discovered running amok and hacking into the Internet and telephone providers over the course of 15 months (Press release, Department of Justice, District of Massachusetts, 2005). In this case, the juvenile was not doing so simply for the fun of it. They were doing so to steal personal information and broadcast it over the Internet. Celebrity Paris Hilton reportedly was one of the victims who had information stolen from her cell phone and broadcasted publicly online, having been hacked by the juvenile in this case, though prosecutors did not confirm this as is the common practice in sealed juvenile cases (Associated Press, 2005).

The juvenile also used the information from the telephone providers to set up accounts for himself and his friends without paying for the accounts (Press release, Department of Justice, District of Massachusetts, 2005). Secondary to the computer hacking crimes, they were also making bomb threats by email to Florida and Massachusetts high schools, plus to emergency services (Press elease, Department of Justice, District of Massachusetts, 2005).

The juvenile in this case did not act alone, as he also had help in data storage. At one point, when one of the juvenile's friends had their fraudulent phone service cut off, they called the phone company, threatening to shut down the telephone service's online operations if the account was not reactivated (Press release, Department of Justice, District of Massachusetts, 2005). When the telephone service did not comply with the request, he did just that, creating havoc for the company and for customers.

Defining the Crime(s)

There were a number of crimes committed in this case. The crime best associated with white collar crime was computer hacking. We have noted in this chapter that not all computer hacking is malicious, as in the examples of "grey hat" and "white hat" hackers. But the teenager in this case clearly falls in the category of "black hat" hacker, as his intent was solely malicious and outside of common, garden variety teenage curiosity. Under the Computer Fraud and Abuse Act (18 U.S.C. §1030), under which this case falls, computer hacking consists of any illegal attempts, successful or otherwise, to use a computer with the intent to commit fraud or to cause harm (Computer Crime and Intellectual Property Section, Criminal Division, U.S. Department of Justice, 2015).

Secondary to the hacking crimes, and not technically considered white-collar crimes, are the emailed bomb threats. In the United States, freedom of speech is limited to the extent that any verbal or written threats that result in public fear or panic is considered illegal. Even if the threat does not turn out to be real, the U.S. federal government considers these to be serious crimes. As FBI Deputy Director Bowich noted (FBI, 2018, retrieved from https://www.fbi.gov/news/stories/hoax-threats-awareness-100518), "Issuing a threat — even over social media via text message, or through e-mail is a federal crime (threatening interstate communication).... Hoax threats disrupt school, waste limited law enforcement resources, and put first responders in unnecessary danger." Beyond the monetary costs to responding to bomb threats, even if they are found to be hoaxes, is the societal costs, including psychological trauma to students, school personnel, and parents and guardians (FBI, 2018).

Theories to Explain the Crime

David Aucsmith, a cybersecurity expert, proposed that there were five different types of hackers that provide various levels of cyberthreats. These include the vandal, author, trespasser, thief, and spy, the classification based on the level of motivation and skill level of the hacker (Shoemaker et al., 2018).

Based on these typologies, we can assume that in the case of this teenager, this was not mere curiosity, but rather a malicious attempt to steal information and illegally access free Internet and telephone service. Though we do not know the extent to which the teenager was a skilled hacker, it is safe to assume that he was somewhere within the categories of "undergraduate" and "expert." There is also an overlap between "trespasser" and "thief," where the teenager may have first sought fame, supported by the fact that outside of the hacking activities he had sent the emailed bomb threats to high schools and emergency services. Somewhere along the way he also segued to "thief," as he and his associates used the hacked information to not only cause mischief for the victims but to also illegally obtain services for free.

As the teenager in this case is alleged to have had "associates," one might also consider social learning theories as well to explain his behavior. If computer hacking was normative within his social circles, there might have been the peer pressure, if not the competitive environment, to test the limits of what he could do effectively in hacking. One social learning theory to consider, which is apt in a number of white collar crime cases and in juvenile delinquency, is Sutherland's Differential Association Theory, where deviant behavior is learned by hanging out with others who are themselves committing deviant acts. Keeping in mind, again, that if the offenders in this case were juveniles, they may not yet have the maturity to realize that what they were doing was harmful. More importantly, they might not fully appreciate the financial costs to victims associated with their actions.

Social and Media Responses

In the case studies in this book, we ordinarily focus on the social or media attention on the case. We will somewhat deviate here and begin by discussing the widespread emotional and monetary damage to the victims. As the offender was a juvenile at that time of his crimes, media attention was legally prohibited from reporting the juvenile's name. We rarely learn the name of juvenile offenders, except in cases of truly horrific homicide cases. An example of juvenile names being released to the public was when then-12-year-olds Morgan Geyser and Anissa Weier stabbed a classmate in 2014, inspired by the online fictional character Slender Man.

The U.S. Attorney Sullivan emphasized the seriousness of the crimes committed by the juveniles in this case:

> Computer hacking is not fun and games. Hackers cause real harm to real vic-
> tims as graphically illustrated in this case.... Would-be hackers, even juve-
> niles when appropriate, should be put on notice that such criminal activity
> will not be tolerated and that stiff punishment awaits them if they are caught.
> (Press release, Department of Justice, District of Massachusetts, 2005,
> retrieved https://www.justice.gov/archive/criminal/cybercrime/press-
> releases/2005/juvenileSentboston.htm)

The bomb threats alone in Florida and Massachusetts, which were proven
to be false alarms, burdened emergency management resources, and there
was reportedly $1 million (USD) worth of damage done to identity theft vic-
tims in this case (Associated Press, 2005).

Criminal Justice and Policy Responses

Except in cases where juveniles are prosecuted in adult court or, like in our
example, some homicides committed by minors, most children under the
age of 18 who commit crimes and are being adjudicated in juvenile court will
not have their court records available to the public, including the media. They
are protected by law with anonymity even if they are adjudicated, the equivalent of a guilty finding in adult court. There simply is limited access to juvenile criminal records, even when an adult offender has a juvenile record.

The teenager in this case ultimately pleaded guilty to nine counts of juvenile delinquency and was adjudicated in the U.S. District Court in Boston to
11 months in juvenile detention (Associated Press, 2005). Among the charges
that he pleaded guilty to were hacking into both Internet and telephone service providers, theft of customers' personal information with the purposes of
posting it on the Internet, and making bomb threats to high schools (Associated Press, 2005).

As a basis of comparison, if the juvenile in this case had been an adult, he
would have faced slightly different charges. Among them would be three
counts of making bomb threats, three counts of causing damage to a protected computer system, two counts of aggravated identity theft, and additional charges related to illegally obtaining information (Press release,
Department of Justice, District of Massachusetts, 2005). In other words, if
he had been an adult offender, he would have had far graver charges leveled
against him, with much more severe penalties, as compared to being tried as a
juvenile.

As part of his sentencing, the teenager was prohibited from possessing
any computer, cell phone, or any equipment that can access the Internet once
released from juvenile custody (Associated Press, 2005). When you stop and
think about these prohibitions, it no doubt was a difficult task for juvenile
probation officers to monitor these stipulations, as the teenager could have
access to computers and cellphones through his friends.

Unanswered Questions and Unresolved Issues Related to the Case

When juveniles offend, once they are in the custody of the juvenile justice system, they are at greater risk of aging into the adult system. As it is an impossibility to keep individuals away from Internet resources, it is also a challenge to prevent reoffending by computer hackers, whether they are juveniles or adults. When we also consider that a number of professions require the use of computers that have access to the Internet, it becomes doubly problematic.

As the offender in this case was a juvenile at the time of his crimes, and is now an adult with juvenile records sealed, it is unknown whether he has reoffended or not. One possible route this individual could have taken out of the criminal justice system was to become a white hat hacker, using his skills to help companies, including telephone service providers, understand the vulnerabilities of their systems.

Beyond the publicity surrounding the individual teenager who was prosecuted in juvenile court, the extent to which he was part of a larger network of cybercrime offenders is unknown. If some of his so-called "associates," as mentioned in Department of Justice press releases, were also juveniles, they may have escaped prosecution if they had turned state's evidence, in which case they would have had their own juvenile records sealed.

Sources

Associated Press. (2005) Paris Hilton hacker gets 11 months. CBS News. Sept. 14. Retrieved from https://www.cbsnews.com/news/paris-hilton-hacker-gets-11-months/.

Federal Bureau of Investigations (FBI). (2018) Think before you post: Hoax threat are serious federal crimes. *News*. Oct. 5. Retrieved from https://www.fbi.gov/news/stories/hoax-threats-awareness-100518.

Johnson, S. B., R. W. Blum, and J. N, Giedd. (2009) Adolescent maturity and the brain: The promise and pitfalls of neuroscience research in adolescent health policy. *Journal of Adolescent Health*. Sept. Vol. 45, No. 3: 216-221.

Shoemaker, D., A. Koehnke, and K. Sigler. (2018) *How to Build a Cyber-Resilient Organization*. Boca Raton, FL: CRC Press, Taylor and Francis.

U.S. Department of Justice. (2005) Massachusetts teen convicted for hacking into Internet and telephone service providers and making bomb threats to high schools in Massachusetts and Florida. U.S. State Attorney's Office, District of Massachusetts. Sept 8. Retrieved from https://www.justice.gov/archive/criminal/cybercrime/press-releases/2005/juvenile Sentboston.htm.

U.S. Department of Justice. (2015) *Prosecuting Computer Crimes*. Computer Crime and Intellectual Property Section, Criminal Division. Jan. 14. Published by Office of Legal Education, Executive Office for United States Attorneys. Available at https://www.justice.gov/sites/default/files/criminal-ccips/legacy/2015/01/14/ccmanual.pdf.

U.S. Department of Justice (2020) Department of Justice announces disruption of hundreds of COVID-19 related scams: Hundreds of domains disrupted through public and private sector cooperative efforts. *Justice News*, Office of Public Affairs. April 22. Retrieved from https://www.justice.gov/opa/pr/department-justice-announces-disruption-hundreds-online-covid-19-related-scams.

GLOSSARY

Blockchain   A supposedly incorruptible digital ledger of economic transactions.

Botnet   A network of private computers infected with malicious software and controlled as a group without the owners' knowledge. Example: Spam mail.

Computer coding   Also program coding, is a set of instructions forming a computer program which is executed by a computer.

Computer hacking   To use a computer to gain unauthorized access to data in a system.

Computer Fraud and Abuse Act, 1986   United States cybersecurity bill that is an amendment to existing computer fraud as part of the Comprehensive Crime Control Act of 1984.

Computer worms   Malware computer program that replicates itself in order to spread to other computers, much like a computer virus.

Corporate espionage   Also referred to as industrial espionage, is intellectual property theft committed for commercial purposes, but increasingly includes foreign countries infiltrating commercial enterprises.

Cyber fraud   Fraud committed by using the Internet as a means by which to perpetrate online scams.

Cybercrime   Criminal activities that are cared out by means of computers or the Internet.

Dark Web   World Wide Web content that exists on overlaying networks that use the Internet but require specific software, configurations, or authorization to access. Users and crimes committed on the Dark Web are difficult to detect.

Electronic Crime Task Force (2001)   One function of the United States Secret Service tasked to provide surveillance of illegal activity on the Internet, as part of the USA Patriot Act, 2001.

Phishing   The fraudulent practice of sending emails purporting to be from reputable companies or individuals in order to obtain personal information, including passwords and credit card numbers.

Malware   Software that is intended to damage or disable computers.

REFERENCES AND SUGGESTED READINGS

Bauman, Z. (1993) *Postmodern ethics.* Cambridge, U.K.: Polity Press.

Bindley, K. (2012) Internet romance scams cost victims $50 million in 2011. *Huffington Post.* Retrieved from https://www.huffingtonpost.com/2012/05/15/online-romance-scams-cost-50-million-in-2011_n_1518162.html.

Bossler, A. M. and G. W. Burruss. (2011) The general theory of crime and computer hacking: Low self-control hackers? *Corporate hacking and technology-driven crime: Social dynamics and implications,* T. J. Holt and B. H. Schell, eds. UK: IGI Global.

Broadhurst, R., P. Grabosky, M. Alazab, B. Bourhours, S. Chon. (2014) Organizations and cyber crime: An analysis of the growing nature of groups engaged in cyber crime. *International Journal of Criminology.* Vol. 8 (1): 1-20.

Dalins, J., C. Wilson, and M. Carman. (2018) Criminal motivation on the dark web: A categorization model for law enforcement. *Digital Investigation.* Vol. 24: 62-71.

Dashineau, S.C., E. A. Edershile, L. J. Simms, and A. G. C. Wright. (2019) Pathological narcissism and psychosocial functioning. Personality Disorders: Theory, Research, and Treatment. July 1. Advance online publication. http://dx.doi.org/10.1037/per0000347.

Dipert, R. R. (2010) Ethics of cyberwarfare. *Journal of Military Ethics.* 9(4): 384-410.

Domscheit-Berg, D. (2011) *Inside WikiLeaks: My time with Julian Assange at the world's most dangerous website.* London: Jonathan Cape.

Fallick, B., C. A. Fleischman, and J. B. Rebitzer. (2006) Job-hopping in Silicon Valley: Some evidence concerning the microfoundations of high-technology cluster. *The Review of Economics and Statistics.* Vol. 33, No. 3: 472-481.

Fielding, N.G. (2017) The shaping of covert social networks: Isolating the effects of secrecy. *Trends in Organized Crime.* 20: 16-30.

Garcia Sigman, L. I. (2017) Narcotrafico en la Darkweb: Los criptomercados. *URVIO.* Dec. (21): 191-206.

Gist, N. P. (1938) Structure and process in secret societies. *Social Forces.* Vol. 16(3): 349-357.

Hansen, L. L. (2009) Corporate financial crime: Diagnosis and treatment. *Journal of Financial Crime.* Vol. 16, No. 1: 28-40.

Harris, J.G. and A. E. Alter. (2014) Corporate culture: California dreaming. Accenture *Outlook,* retrieved from https://www.accenture.com/t20150522T061601Z__w__/us-en/_acnmedia/Accenture/Conversion-Assets/Outlook/Documents/1/Accenture-Outlook-California-Dreaming-Corporate-Culture-Silicon-Valley.pdf#zoom=50

Hookway, N. (2018) The moral self: Class, narcissism and the problem of do-it-yourself moralities. *The Sociological Review.* Vol. 66(1): 107-121.

Hutchings, A. (2014) Crime from the keyboard: organized cybercrime offending, initiation and knowledge transmission. *Crime, Law and Social Change.* Vol. 62 (1): 1-20.

Hubbell, C. (1965) An input output approach to clique identification. *Sociometry.* 28(4):377-399.

Javers, E. (2011) Secrets and lies: The rise of corporate espionage in a global economy. *Georgetown Journal of International Affairs.* Winter-Spring, 12 (1):53-60.

Jones, C. M. (2014) Why persistent offenders cannot be shamed into behaving. *Journal of Offender Rehabilitation.* 53: 153-170.

Katz, L. (1947) On the matric analysis of sociometric data. *Sociometry.* 10: 233-241.

Kelly, H. (2018) Facebook says attack exposed info of 50 million users. Retrieved from https://money.cnn.com/2018/09/28/technology/facebook-breach-50-million/index.html.

Kopfstein, J. (2013) Hacker with a cause. *The New Yorker.* November 21. Retrieved from http://www.newyorker.com/tech/elements/hacker-with-a-cause.

Long, A. L. (2012) Profiling hackers. SANS Institute. Retrieved from https://www.sans.org/reading-room/whitepapers/hackers/profiling-hackers-33864.

Lyons, D. (2015) "White Hat/Black Hat," Silicon Valley. HBO. Season 2, Episode 8.

Phelps, T. (2016) Why hackers want your medical records. NetStandard. 17 Nov. Retrieved from http://www.netstandard.com/hackers-want-medical-records/.

Reep-van den Bergh, C. M. M. and M. Junger. (2018) Victims of cybercrime in Europe: A review of victim surveys. *Crime Science*. 7 (1): 1-15.

Rishikof, H. and K. Lunday. (2011) Corporate responsibility in cybersecurity: Building international global standards. *Georgetown Journal of International Affairs*. Vol. 12 (1): 17-24.

Schneier, B. (2017) Who are the Shadow Brokers? *The Atlantic*. May 23. Retrieved from https://www.theatlantic.com/technology/archive/2017/05/shadow-brokers/527778/.

Simmel, G. (1906) The sociology of secrecy and of secret societies. *American Journal of Sociology*. Vol. 11(4): 441-498.

Tapscott, D. and A. Tapscott. (2016) *Blockchain revolution*. Brilliance Audio (MP3), May 2.

Taunton, Y. (2020) Coronavirus and cybercrime – hackers use COVID-19 as phishing bait. UAB News, The University of Alabama at Birmingham. April 3. Retrieved from https://www.uab.edu/news/research/item/11219-coronavirus-and-cybercrime-hackers-use-covid-19-as-phishing-bait.

Tressler, C. (2020) COVID-19 contact tracing text message scams. Consumer Information, Federal Trade Commission. May 19. Retrieved from https://www.consumer.ftc.gov/blog/2020/05/covid-19-contact-tracing-text-message-scams?utm_source=govdelivery&fbclid=IwAR3zGRvy1b0ZWXDTwYw5wEqVZwEY7-5fJniyuqu11ksnjkl4vaZcNks8wDU.

U.S. Department of Justice. (n.d.) Information about the Department of Justice's Attorney General China Initiative, AAG Demers bio and compilation of China related criminal cases since Jan. 2018. Press release. Retrieved from https://www.justice.gov/opa/press-release/file/1179321/download.

U.S. Department of Justice. (2018) Two Chinese hackers associated with the Ministry of State Security charged with global computer intrusion campaigns targeting intellectual property and confidential business information. Press release, Office of Public Affairs. Dec. 20. Retrieved from https://www.justice.gov/opa/pr/two-chinese-hackers-associated-ministry-state-security-charged-global-computer-intrusion.

U.S. Department of Justice. (2019) Former defense intelligence officer pleads guilty to attempted espionage. Press Release, Office of Public Affairs. Mar. 15. Retrieved from https://www.justice.gov/opa/pr/former-defense-intelligence-officer-pleads-guilty-attempted-espionage.

U.S. Department of Justice (2020) Department of Justice announces disruption of hundreds of COVID-19 related scams: Hundreds of domains disrupted through public and private sector cooperative efforts. *Justice News*, Office of Public Affairs. April 22. Retrieved from https://www.justice.gov/opa/pr/department-justice-announces-disruption-hundreds-online-covid-19-related-scams.

U.S. District Court. (2018) *United States of America v. Zhu Hua, a/k/a/ "Afar," a/k/a "CVNX," a/k/a "Alayos," a/k/a "Godkiller," and Zhang Shilong, a/k/a "Baobeilong," "a/k/a "Zhang Jianguo," a/k/a "Atreexp"*. Southern District of New York. Dec. 1, file date. https://admin.govexec.com/media/china_case.pdf.

U.S. Secret Service. (2018) Cyber operations. United States Government. Retrieved from https://www.secretservice.gov/investigation/#.

Voiskounsky, A. E. and O. V. Smyslova. (2004) Flow-based model of computer hacker's motivation. *CyberPsychology and Behavior*. July, 6(2): 171-180.

Wasserman S. and K. Faust. (1994) *Social network analysis: Methods and applications*. Cambridge University Press.

Weimann, G. (2015) Going dark: Terrorism on the dark web. *Studies in Conflict and Terrorism*. Vol 39(3):195-206.

Whitmire, N. (2015) Julian Assange, Wikileaks, and the trickster: A case study of archetypal influence. *ReVision*. Winter, Vol. 32, Issue 2/3: 84-93.

Chapter SEVEN

Fraud Against Consumers

Caveat emptor (buyer beware)

> "If you live for having it all, what you have is never enough."
>
> —*Vicki Robin, Your Money or Your Life (2018)*

Chapter Objectives

- Review of history of consumer fraud.
- Familiarize reader to the more common forms of consumer fraud.
- Introduce some of the regulatory and consumer protection agency responses to consumer fraud.
- Examine new technologies, including applications ("apps"), used to commit consumer fraud crimes.

Key Terms

Apps
Children's Online Privacy Protection
  Act (COPPA)
Class action lawsuits
Federal Trade Commission
FICO® credit score
Forgery
Fraud

Mobile medical applications (MMAs)
Provenance
Refund Anticipation Loans (RALs)
Robocalls
Telemarketing
Upfront fee
Usury lending

INTRODUCTION

Though there is some question as to whether he originated the saying, P.T. Barnum of circus fame has been quoted as saying, "there is a sucker born every minute." No matter the origins of the saying, in a consumer-driven economy like we are presenting living in, there will always be criminally motivated entrepreneurs ready to hoodwink the buying public. In some countries, like China, there is limited regulation. In others, there is a conscious effort to protect consumers. After all, a consumer economy is not sustainable as long as people are not buying products out of fear of being taken advantage of, beyond the costs of goods and services.

In this chapter we will be exploring cases where the perpetrators knew exactly what they were doing, as in the case of counterfeit art objects. We will also explore whether some of the offenses committed were simply business ventures that had not been carefully thought through before executing, as in the 2014 Amazon case discussed in this chapter.

Whether the seller consciously or unconsciously hoodwinks the buyer, consumer *fraud* accounts for, based on prosecution records, approximately 3 percent of all white collar crimes (TRAC Reports, 2019; Durney and Proulx, 2011). However, this does not account for the number of crimes that go unreported, the number of cases with insufficient evidence, nor the number of civil cases tried involving consumer fraud.

One of the best theoretical explanations for why consumer fraud takes place is the Routine Activities Theory (Felson and Cohen, 1979; Pratt et al., 2010). In Routine Activities Theory, three elements need to be present in order for a crime to take place: a motivated offender, a suitable target, and no barriers (e.g., regulation, law enforcement) to prevent the crime from happening. Pratt et al. (2010) argue that with technological advances, particularly the Internet, there are even more motivated offenders.

LIKELY VICTIMS OF CONSUMER FRAUD

As in the case of financial crimes, there are certain classes of people who are more vulnerable to falling victim to fraud. Elderly individuals are particularly vulnerable to being victimized, though children can also be defrauded. Since children can fall prey to fraud or deceptive marketing, their parents or legal guardians are likewise victimized.

Another vulnerable population is disabled persons. The degree to which a disabled person is at risk depends on whether the disability is physical or mental (Lichtenberg et al., 2015). In the case of the elderly, they can be doubly vulnerable if they have been disabled due to neurological deterioration that can occur in old age, including deterioration caused by strokes, dementia, or Alzheimer's.

TELEMARKETING FRAUD

Though *telemarketing*, the practice of making unsolicited calls to potential customers, has a shady reputation, not all telemarketing is fraud. However, as the practice more commonly happens by way of phone calls, mostly on landlines, it is a business practice that lends itself to criminal activity, damaging the reputation of companies who are legally making calls, however unsolicited.

Companies can legitimately use "cold calling" — either telephone calls or face-to-face solicitation of goods and services to customers who are not necessarily seeking them out. Once upon a time, cold calling was done by door-to-door sales personnel, which was time consuming. Today it is far less common for salespeople to knock on doors.

Increasingly *robocalls*, telemarketing phone calls that are automated, are being made to cell phones. Fortunately, as annoying as telemarketing calls are, the phone numbers they are being generated from are easily blocked on most smart phones.

Because older people are more likely to have a landline, they are more likely to be victimized by fraudulent telemarketing. Experienced, legitimate telemarketers will generally use lead lists bought from businesses that buy and sell consumer information (Shover et al., 2017). But both legitimate and illegitimate telemarketers are aware that they are more likely to reach an elderly person than a younger individual on a landline.

The types of fraud that are common among criminal telemarketers targeting the elderly include Medicare and health insurance scams, and extorting money from grieving widows or widowers with claims of unpaid funeral costs. There are also fake lottery schemes, where "winners" can only claim their prize if they submit a "small" fee.

Another common telemarketing scheme is to impersonate a charity. The caller always sounds like they are coming from a legitimate organization, like fundraisers that appear to be calling on behalf of law enforcement or firefighter charities. They might ask for credit card information over the phone. The unwitting donor to a fake charity may be doubly victimized: Once by giving to a fraudulent organization, and again if the donation is claimed on an income tax return form and the IRS detects that it is fake. The donor then has to defend themselves against any claim by the IRS that they are filing a fraudulent tax return.

The FTC instructs the public to do a little research before giving to any charity. Is it a legitimate charity, or does it just sound like one? There are a number of places where you can find out if a charity is legitimate or is really doing the type of philanthropic work that you want to support. These include the Better Business Bureau (BBB, www.give.org) and the American Institute of Philanthropy (https://www.charitywatch.org/home).

Both legitimate and illegitimate telemarketers work with scripts. Scripts, are written sales pitches that are rarely deviated from when found to be successful in enticing people to buy products or services. The scripts can also include prompts for salespeople if the potential customer is showing reluctance, using a number of tactics in order to keep the person on the line listening to the sales pitch.

One of the most diabolical schemes, though not telemarketing per se, is the "grandparent scam." As described by the National Council on Aging (available at https://www.ncoa.org/economic-security/money-management/scams-security/top-10-scams-targeting-seniors/#intraPageNav8), when a scammer detects an older person on a call, they start a conversation by asking, "Grandma (or Grandpa), do you know who this is?" When the grandparent guesses the name of a grandchild that might be calling, the scammer then proceeds to claim that they (the alleged grandchild) have a financial problem, and "please don't tell my parents; they would kill me." The older person is then instructed where and how to send funds to the financially troubled "grandchild." As the National Council on Aging notes, what makes this scheme so diabolical is that it tugs at the heartstrings of grandparents.

Once someone has been victimized by a telemarketing scheme, they run the risk of being victimized again by the same set of criminals. There is a lot of incentive to return to the same victims, as in many cases, they are unaware that they have been victimized. Criminal telemarketers often use aliases and operate out of countries where it is difficult for law enforcement to come after them (Georgia Department of Law, 2019).

ADVANCE FEE SCHEMES

It is very likely that in the past, you have been sent an email promising you great riches for a small *upfront fee*. The public is much more aware of the use of email to commit fraud, as in the now more widely known Nigerian scams. The emails typically open with some sad story of a relative who has passed away and left a fortune, that cannot be transferred to the heirs without intervention from the targeted victim.

The email recipient is often asked to help with the transfer or with legal fees, in exchange for a percentage of the funds. The target may then be asked to provide some personal information, like Social Security number and bank account number with passwords, that will allow the criminal to draw from accounts. In other cases, the target may be asked to wire funds into a fraudulent account, then never hear again from the perpetrators.

This is certainly one of those cases where if it sounds too good to be true, it probably isn't legitimate. It is one of the reasons why consumers are protected from sweepstakes or lottery schemes by regulations stipulating that entrants of legitimate contests are not required to purchase anything in order to enter or win, hence the statement, "No purchase necessary to win," that is posted to contests that are complying with prize promotion laws.

Contest marketing is so effective and prevalent as a means to attract new customers, that it is difficult for an unsuspecting consumer to know what is legitimate and what is not. But sweepstakes and lotteries are not the only places where customers might be asked to pay an upfront fee. Until regulation prohibited it, it was not uncommon for tax preparation services to charge an unusually high fee in order for the customer to receive their tax refund faster than the government would send it, in the form of a *refund anticipation loan.*

The *Federal Trade Commission* also warns customers to beware of companies that are offering to eliminate or consolidate consumer debt, including from credit cards. Though there are companies that legitimately help with debt repair and consolidation, because there are so many offers out there, it is difficult to tell the difference between legitimate and illegitimate companies.

Debt reduction scammers will ask for an upfront fee or require the consumer to purchase a "membership," sometimes charged to the very credit cards that the debtor wants to pay down in the first place! In some cases, because no real debt consolidation takes place, a person who is already in financial trouble may incur additional debt, risking loss of property or legal action (Bureau of Consumer Protection, Federal Trade Commission, available at https://www.ftc.gov/about-ftc/bureaus-offices/bureau-consumer-protection)..

We should note that *usury lending*, the practice of charging unusually high interest rates for loans or consumer debt, is illegal. Usury laws were created to protect consumers from predatory lending.

Unfortunately, the people who must pay higher interest rates are those who can least afford it. Lending, by most institutions, whether in loans or credit cards, is based on the ability for the borrower to pay back a loan. Individuals with average or poor credit ratings, usually measured by their *FICO® credit score* along with documented income, are typically (and legitimately) charged much higher interest rates, sometimes as much as over 30 percent interest on personal loans.

Law in the Real World: Instant Tax Service

(Source: D. Herrera, 2014) https://www.sfcityattorney.org/wp-content/uploads/2015/07/Instant-Tax-lawsuit-presskit.pdf

Though not specifically an advance fee scheme, high interest rates paid by consumers who request income tax refund advances from their tax preparation provider can also be victims of consumer fraud. In the case of Instant Tax Service, a California based franchise, it operated similarly to payday cash advance operations, collecting large sums in return for quick refunds. The rapid refunds, which were really short term loans borrowed against the taxpayer's anticipated income tax refund, included high fees, that represents inflated interest on the loan.

The rapid refund loans (RALs), in exchange for high fees, were marketed by well-respected companies including H&R Block™ and began to be offered in the 1980s. The loans were typically funded by third-party lending institutions, including banks and credit unions. The benefits of rapid refund loans were that the customer got their refund faster than if they waited for it to be sent in the mail from the IRS, plus they help to pay the fees for customers' tax preparation as well.[1]

When rapid refund loan programs were first introduced in the 1980s, because old, established tax preparation companies offered this service, the fees were not initially perceived to be suspiciously high. These were considered to be legitimate until consumer groups called for investigation. For tax preparation services, RAL programs proved to be highly profitable, bringing in new customers. Once rapid refund loans were called into question during the 1990s, H&R Block™ and other established tax preparation companies quickly changed their programs so as to avoid usury lending practices. The RAL has been largely replaced by the Rapid Anticipation Check (RAC). However, not all tax preparation companies followed new regulations, such as Instant Tax Service.

Even though Instant Tax Service was not the only company offering loans in advance of anticipated tax refunds, their marketing practices were objectionable. Instant Tax Service targeted poorer customers in a number of lower income areas of California and other states. In one usury lending scheme, the company took advantage of the Earned Income Credit. The Earned Income Credit is a program that offers a refundable credit on income tax returns to lower income workers who qualify. The program was designed to encourage people to work, even in low income jobs, instead of depending on welfare programs. San Francisco City Attorney Dennis Herrera claimed that Instant Tax Service would collect as much as $1,500 (USD) for loans as low as $50.

As we have discussed throughout this book, most of what we see in white collar crimes, in particular consumer crimes, are settled in civil court. Instant Tax Services were sued in *class action lawsuits* in St. Louis and Kansas City, Missouri. Depending on the number of the number of people in a class action lawsuit, individuals may only receive a small fraction of the amount of money that they have lost.

Though Instant Tax Services had been one of the fastest growing companies in the United States, early in this century, they were finally forced to close by federal courts. The owner, Fesum Ogbazion, was indicted in

---

[1] The process is much faster these days with the capability of electronically filing an income tax return and with direct deposit into your bank account by the IRS of any refund you're due. Any refund of overpaid taxes generally is received within two weeks, depending on whether the electronic return has been accepted by the IRS and what time of the tax season you file your return.

2015 on a number of fraud charges beyond usury lending, including tax evasion related to business operations.

Discussion Questions

1. Why might customers agree to pay a high fee in order to receive their income tax refund faster than the IRS can mail them a check or make a direct deposit to their bank?
2. What reasons would individuals with lower income be targeted for rapid refund loans or checks?
3. If the rapid refund loan programs began in the 1980s, what might have contributed to their being in use until the 1990s, when it was determined that the fees associated with them were usury lending?
4. What other products or services might put customers at risk of paying high fees?

CASHIER'S CHECK AND MONEY ORDER SCAMS

Not only do criminals want you to part with your money, they can also want you to part with your property. A real cashier's check will be issued and guaranteed by a bank because the purchaser has used real currency to purchase one, sometimes for a small bank fee. Money orders can be issued by other places besides banks, including some grocery stores, again purchased with real currency. Along with currency and personal checks, cashier's checks and money orders can be counterfeit.

Unlike the other frauds that are described in this chapter, there are times when it is the seller who is the victim. When individuals try to sell something privately, they stand the chance of not getting paid. For instance, if someone ships an item they are selling on eBay® (an online service that allows people to list new and used items for sale for a fee), but they have not received payment in advance of shipping, there is a chance they will lose the item forever if the buyer fails to pay them or provides payment with a fraudulent check.

Cashier's checks and money orders are commonly used in transactions that involve the sale of second-hand goods. Because they are as good as cash, it protects a seller from a personal check from the purchaser that might be returned to the seller's bank for non-sufficient funds ("bounced check"). For example, if you have a used car that you want to sell, you may try to do so through a third party, like Craigslist, in hopes of getting more for the vehicle than you might get from a dealership. It would be much safer to accept a cashier's check, guaranteed by a bank, than to accept a personal check that might bounce with the buyer nowhere to be found.

ONLINE CONSUMER FRAUD

Though we extensively cover cybercrimes in Chapter 6, this chapter addresses the issues of the use of the Internet to commit fraud. In the case of online consumer fraud, the computer is merely a tool to commit crimes that were once primarily done through face-to-face transactions, mail, or telephone marketing. The old adage "buyer beware" is never so apt as when purchasing an item online, essentially basing buying decisions on photos or previous customer reviews. As in the case of previous methods of defrauding customers, it is not a difficult task to alter photographic images or provide fake customer reviews.

There are several means by which criminals will commit consumer fraud. We should note that both fraudulent mail and telephone sales do still occur, but older individuals less familiar with computer and mobile phone technology are more likely to fall prey to those schemes. Increasingly many, if not most, consumer transactions, at least for small ticket items such as clothing and electronics, are being purchased online. The Census Bureau of the U.S. Department of Commerce (2019, https://www.census.gov/retail/mrts/www/data/pdf/ec_current.pdf) reported, "the estimate of U.S. retail e-commerce sales for the first quarter of 2019, adjusted for seasonal variation.... was $137.7 billion, an increase of 3.6 percent (±0.7 percent) from the fourth quarter of 2018." And e-commerce rose exponentially during the COVID-19 pandemic in 2020.

We should establish that not all e-commerce is generated by companies, fraudulent or not. Some scams are perpetrated by individuals on websites like Craigslist (www.craiglist.org), eBay (www.ebay.com), and Etsy (ww.etsy.com). Like the social network website Facebook, websites that offer a platform for online, person-to-person sales, do offer extensive instruction on how to avoid scams. And if you are a victim of fraud, websites like Craigslist offer a list of government agencies that should be alerted, including the FTC (available at https://www.craigslist.org/about/scams).

Online commerce has further escalated by the introduction of smart phones with not only Internet capability, but also applications ("*apps*") that offer instantaneous purchasing. In some ways, apps encourage impulse buying without necessarily encouraging comparison shopping or cautious purchase habits. This in itself is not criminal, but as applications for computers and mobile devices are still in their infancy, regulation is slow to catch up with new uses. In the case of *mobile medical applications* (*MMAs*) that are more likely to receive more scrutiny, the FDA was fairly quick to respond with regulation (Terry and Gunter, 2017). Of greatest concern for the FDA are the self-assessment tools in MMAs that might not adequately address mental health issues, as compared to working directly with a psychologist or psychiatrist. However, beyond MMAs, applications are loosely regulated.

Of biggest concern are the phone apps that masquerade as legitimate, known retailers. According the FTC (2016), the motivation for the creation of fake phone apps is to steal consumer credit card or bank information or to install malware, then demanding the unwitting person pay money in order to unlock it. The FTC offers a number of tips to avoid fraudulent apps (Retrieved from https://www.consumer.ftc.gov/blog/2016/12/theres-app-it-might-be-fake):

- If not sure whether a shopping app is legit, go directly to a retailer's website to see if the app is being promoted there.
- Search on the web for the brand name, plus "fake app" to see if the company has reported its brand is being spoofed.
- Read reviews for the app before downloading it, both in app stores and on the web. If there are no reviews, the app is more than likely recently created and may be a fake.
- Don't download apps with misspelled words in their description. The creators of real apps will have taken the time to carefully edit any description before release. Fake apps are more likely to be created in a hurry.
- Keep records of transactions; monitor credit card statements frequently for charges that you don't recognize.

Law in the Real World: Amazon in-App Purchases

(Source: Federal Trade Commission, 2014; 2016)

One upon a time, with the invention of 900 telephone numbers ("premium-rate") where the caller was charged a fee for any number of services, a parent's nightmare was to open a phone bill with a number of unauthorized calls made by their child. The phone numbers are used for a number of services, including horoscopes and psychics or, more commonly, adult chat lines (phone sex). The author of this book had this very experience where there was a number of calls made from the home phone to a 900 number, made by one of her children who were 12 and 15 at the time. The resulting phone bill was over $900 USD, deviating from the usual charges of less than $100 USD. We never did establish which child committed the indiscretion, but at the time, there was little recourse for parents except to complain to the phone company that their underaged child made unauthorized calls.

More commonly now, parents will note unauthorized purchases being generated by the phone apps their children are using. These transactions are called "in-app purchases," where the user may be using a free app, but in order to fully continue using the app they might have to make purchases. For example, any fans of the *Angry Birds* game apps, of which there are several variations (Rovio Entertainment), will find that they can't successfully complete several levels of the games with certainty.

Depending on the skill of the player, users may have to resort to purchasing in-app add-ons in order to continue playing. For instance, as in many games, when a player fails to complete a level, they will "lose a life." These so-called lives are finite and are generally restricted to around five lives. When the player has exhausted their supply of lives, they can either purchase more or have to wait a protracted period of time (e.g., 12 to 24 hours) in order to continue playing.

Instead of using real money directly on a game, non-real money enticements are purchased within the app, further distancing the player, particularly children, from thinking that add-ons cost real currency. For example, in some fashion apps, your model will not be dressed (in virtual space, of course) in fancier choices without paying real money for computer generated clothing. FTC noted in their case against Amazon (2014) that by using virtual items, it blurs the lines between virtual and real money.

By law, children (minors under the age of 18 in the United States) cannot enter legal contracts without the permission and signature of parents or legal guardians. With the Children's Online Privacy Protection Act (COPPA, 1998, 16 CFR Part 312), the definition of minor is challenged when it comes to consumer behavior. *COPPA* requires that websites or online services must protect personal information that is collected from a child under the age of 13.

As the FTC scrambled to keep up with the new ways that consumers could be defrauded by computer and phone apps, the parental public outcry against unauthorized in-app charges made by children led to a lawsuit in 2014 against Amazon (FTC, 2016).

According to the case details, Amazon had received a number of complaints by parents, including inadequate disclosures about the possibility of in-app charges from otherwise free apps. The FTC had previously reached settlements with Apple, Inc. and Google, Inc. "related to unauthorized in-app charges incurred by children requiring the companies to fully refund consumers for such charges, resulting in refunds to consumers totaling over $50 million." (FTC, 2016, retrieved from https://www.ftc.gov/news-events/press-releases/2016/04/federal-court-finds-amazon-liable-billing-parents-childrens).

As charged by the FTC in the 2014 lawsuit, Amazon's in-app system had no safeguards to prevent children from making unlimited in-app purchases, such as including adequate use of passwords in order to make the purchase. FTC Chairwoman Edith Ramirez accused Amazon of turning a blind eye to the problem as "even Amazon's own employees recognized the serious problem its process created." (FTC, 2014, retrieved from https://www.ftc.gov/news-events/press-releases/2014/07/ftc-alleges-amazon-unlawfully-billed-parents-millions-dollars). As early as 2012, internal emails within Amazon indicated that the consumer complaints could best be described as a "house on fire" situation.

After being found liable for in-app purchase made by children without their parents' authorization after a two-year court battle that included judgements and appeals on both sides, Amazon settled for up to $70 million USD in refunds to affected customers (Stevens, 2017). The courts determined that to their credit, Amazon implemented more safeguards immediately at the onset of the lawsuit, not waiting for a final judgement to take corrective action (Stevens, 2017).

Discussion Questions

1. Why wouldn't Amazon anticipate a problem with the in-app purchase offers?
2. Can a child over the age of 13 also be victimized by in-app purchases, more importantly, their parents?
3. How might Amazon make sure that there is adequate protection of passwords for purchases?

ART(ISAN) AND ANTIQUITIES FORGERY

The art world is one that is ripe for fraudulent behavior. To the frustration of artisans, collectors, investors, and art museums, the art market lacks transparency (Durney and Proulx, 2011). Because the buying and selling of art is emotionally charged for many, the art collector is defenseless against fakery and *forgery*.

With artwork being so unique to an artist, you would think that it would be difficult to duplicate a famous painting or sculpture. But with the right training, formal or self-taught, a talented artist can duplicate some masters' work effortlessly. In fact, most students learn studio art by duplicating the techniques of famous artists before they develop their own style. It was not uncommon for the great masters to have a fleet of young apprentices, including artists who went on to become masters themselves. Leonardo da Vinci started out as an apprentice painter and no doubt learned his craft by imitating the works of others who came before him.

It is one thing to claim that a painting or any artwork is inspired by and completed in the style of another artist. It is a completely different thing to make the claim that the work has been done by the artist himself when it is a forgery. According to Durney and Proulx (2011), fakery resembles, but not perfectly, the original artwork, whereas forgery attempts an exact copy.

In some cases, artwork is difficult to imitate given the materials that are used today as compared to even a century ago. Attempting to create a fraudulent masterpiece from the Renaissance period (1300s-1600s Europe) is a particular challenge, as there are far better means today by which to date materials, including frame, canvas, and paints. But art museums have purchased fraudulent artworks that they thought were painted by masters, even after careful examination by experts.

Even if a forgery is well-executed and in itself fine art, it does not have the same commercial value as original pieces of art. There are rare cases where the forgers themselves are so infamous, that their forgeries become cultural curiosities with monetary value (Durney and Proulx, 2011). In the case of the Spanish Forger operating in the late 19th to early 20th century, a criminal whose illuminated manuscripts replicated the style of the 14th to 16th centuries, his/her[2] works were given a solo exhibition at the Morgan Library (Durney and Proulx, 2011), indicating that even forgeries can have monetary, historical, and artistic significance.

Artwork is not the only thing that can be a forgery. Due to rising interest in antiquities, popularized by archaeological discoveries beginning in the 19th century, this has been yet another opportunity to fool the consumer. Collectors of contemporary folk art and primitive art have also been taken advantage of, as these are relatively easy art forms to imitate. When these types of art forms are forgeries, it not only robs collectors of their money, but robs cultural groups of their heritages and, in many cases, a means by which to make a living.

As is common in the case of many white collar crimes, art crimes tend to be handled in civil court (Durney and Proulx, 2011).

Law in the Real World: H.H. Tammen Company, Denver, Co.

(Source: Inez Guzman, 2019)

In the mid to late 19th century, with the expansion into Southwest United States, explorers and tourists alike became fascinated with Native American culture, including artifacts. The skills of native artisans had been passed down through many generations. The richness of materials available to make jewelry to sell to outsiders, including turquoise and silver, provided a means by which to make a living among desperately impoverished people.

As the demand for Native American crafts increased with the opening of the Southwest to easterners, it also resulted in non-Native Americans fraudulently recreating art that was far from authentic, ultimately diluting the value of the real thing. Some of the fakes are really good imitations; others

---

[2] More than likely the Spanish Forger was male, as the art world, like now, was dominated by men in the 19th and 20th century. However, as the identity of the Spanish Forger remains a mystery, we cannot be certain of their gender.

are obviously fraudulent to the trained eye. Even good facsimiles of turquoise can be made that can fool all but a certified gemologist.

As Inez Guzman (2019) explains, the mail order company, H.H. Tammen, operating out of Denver, Colorado in the late 1800s, created knockoff jewelry that had questionable Native American motifs, which were actually made from coin silver. Wholesalers like H.H. Tammen would hire Pueblo and Navajo men to work in shops to work on-site, offering demonstrations to make it seem that all the jewelry was native made.

For the uninitiated, "handmade" indicates that the jewelry was made, start to finish, by the artisan, including stonecutting. "Handcrafted" means that some components of the piece have been purchased from a craft or jewelry supply store, including pre-cut stones. The artisan is then assembling the piece, which is also considered to be authentic, though not necessarily as valued in the marketplace as handmade goods. Unfortunately, the fake market sells itself as *"authentic enough,"* at prices well below those of truly authentic art, making it an attractive alternative to the average or uneducated buyer (Inez Guzman, 2019).

As the demand over the years has increased exponentially, going through phases of resurgence in popularity, some of the so-called "native made" jewelry available on the market, including on websites, is actually made in overseas factories, in countries like the Philippines where sweatshop conditions exist. In order to be truly authentic, the jewelry must be completely handcrafted by a member of a Native American or First Nations tribe, or at least assembled by one, using materials purchased.

Early in the 20th century, when authentic and fake jewelry flooded the market, pro-Native American groups and regulators began to lobby for stricter control of the Native American jewelry market. Secretary of the Interior Hubert Work mandated the creation of the Indian Arts and Crafts Act in 1935.[3] The purpose of the act was to protect the interests of Native Americans who had few means to become economically independent after their mass displacement in the 19th and early 20th centuries. The initial act was further fortified by the passing of the Indian Arts and Crafts Act of 1990, a truth-in-advertising law prohibiting the sale of anything, including jewelry, pottery, rugs, clothing, and artwork in general, as being Native-made when it is not. Even with the passage of these acts, they are difficult laws to regulate, as there are limited experts out there, outside of Native American

---

[3] In the 1970s, use of the term "Indian" to refer to the indigenous people of North America was found to be offensive and a misrepresentation of the tribes that occupied the continent long before white explorers and settlers. Canada changed the name to "First Nations" people, followed by the United States where the term "Native American" became popularized. Today there are still references to "Indians" in Southwest jewelry, including "Indian pawn" to refer to used pieces that are in many cases popularly vintage, depending on the age of the jewelry.

artisans themselves, who can tell the difference between what is real and what is fake Native American jewelry.

Even today, with H.H. Tammen jewelry authenticity being called into question, the so-called "Fred Harvey jewelry," named after the famous Fred Harvey string of hotels and restaurants that served the tourists and travelers on the railroads, is highly collectable. However, because of the use of non-native artisans, plus the fact that the jewelry was mass-produced, it is difficult to determine if a piece of Fred Harvey jewelry is truly Native American-made, much less handcrafted.

Today, according to Inez Guzman (2019), an estimated 50 to 80 percent of jewelry marketed and sold as "Native American-made" in the United States is actually fake and most probably made by a non-Native American person. It is a difficult task for the buyer to determine if the jewelry they are buying is the real thing.

Discussion Questions

1. Why should it matter whether a piece of art is fake or not, if it gives pleasure to the owner?
2. What roadblocks do you see that prevent Native Americans from having a bigger voice in regulating so-called Native-made goods?
3. How might consumers still be fooled by catalogues in this day and age of Internet sales?
4. Who might be the most likely victim to fall prey to fake jewelry and watches (e.g., fake Rolex)?

Art fraud and forgery not only deplete investors and collectors of funds, it they can ruin careers when brokers are unaware that they have been duped. In order to make sure that what they are purchasing is real, collectors, brokers, and dealers ask for *provenances*, documentation that what they have in their hands is authentic. However, even provenances can be faked. An old, respected, and well-established New York gallery, Knoedler and Company, was reduced to ruin in 2011 after the gallery's head, Ann Freedman, became embroiled in an art forgery ring that began in the 1990s (Amore, 2015).

Freedman had purchased a number of fake abstract expressionist paintings for the gallery attributed to famous artists, like Jackson Pollock. Abstract expressionist paintings are some of the easiest to imitate because of the abstract use of color and design. Some of the fakes that ended up in galleries were painted by a very gifted forger, Pei-Shen Qian, whose imitations of master artists were convincing not only for technique, but for the use of period-appropriate canvases (Amore,

2015). It is one thing to be able to replicate a famous artist's work. It is another to do so on canvases that are the right age, in order to get away with the con.

As artwork can cost up to several million dollars for paintings by masters, it is an attractive place for talented art forgers. Scientific methods today are making it increasingly more difficult to pass off forged art and antiquities as real. Beyond careful research to determine if supporting documentation, including provenances, are authentic, microscopic examination and x-rays of artwork has greatly helped as well. Paint samples can be taken without harming a piece of art, and new 3D visual technology helps the researcher get a better look at the layers of paint that are commonly present in older artwork.

FOOD FRAUD AND SAFETY

We don't ordinarily think of "fake food" as constituting white collar crime. However, when you think in terms of some food items being not only gourmet, but pricy, it makes sense that this is one place where illicit profit can be made.

One common area of food fraud is in the sale of diluted or fraudulent alcoholic beverages. Restaurants make a considerable amount of their revenue from beverage sales, including fountain drinks, like Coca-Cola® products. An estimated profit margin for alcoholic beverages is around 80 percent on mixed drinks, so it makes sense that these are items that are readily solicited to customers.

Some bars and restaurants will illegally add water or cheaper liquor to the bottles of more expensive alcoholic beverages to further increase their already bloated profit margin. To further complicate regulating the authenticity of liquor served at restaurants, cheap wine can be substituted for more expensive vintages. Because there is a certain amount of snobbery in ordering wine, the customer might be embarrassed to point out a fraudulent wine or may not even be knowledgeable enough to tell the difference.

In the Wansink et al. field study of wine promotions at restaurants (2006), they point out that for the novice connoisseur, there is a certain amount of peril in ordering wine. "Ordering wine can be both financially and socially risky. Even if a diner is reasonably knowledgeable about wines, there are wide variations between varieties, vineyards, countries, and years." (Wansink et al., 2006, p 328). Whether purchased at a bar, restaurant, or store, the consumer runs the risk of purchasing fraudulent wine. Counterfeit wines have become a multi-billion dollar (USD) illegitimate business within an otherwise legitimate industry (Micallef, 2018).

The beer industry is not immune to fraud as well. As an article in *The Economist* (2018) and any fan of trendy micro-breweries and craft beers will tell you, description of boutique beers have become as flowery (pun intended) as those for wines. Terms attached to a particular brew, like "hoppy," "smoky," or "floral" will give the beer enthusiast false confidence that what they are purchasing is really a quality product using the ingredients that the brewer claims are in it.

But the beer could just as easily be a mixture of both high and low quality hops (*The Economist*, 2018).

What is interesting to note is that the detection of both wine and beer fraud is not coming from law enforcement, though they will step in once fraud has been detected. A diverse number of scientists are involved in fraud detection. In the case of fraudulent beer, researchers in Slovenia have come up with a solution. Miha Ocvirk and Iztok Kosir of the Institute of Hop Research and Brewing in Slovenia use fraud detection methods used for other types of expensive foods. By tracking carbon, nitrogen, and sulfur isotopes in hops, they can determine whether the hop flowers present in a beer are really those that are being advertised (*The Economist*, 2018).

Law in the Real World: Fake Extra-Virgin Olive Oil

Source: Olmsted (2017) Real Food/Fake Food

It is one thing to go to a wine or beer tasting and for the expert to detect what is fake and what is real. It is another thing for the average consumer to walk into the grocery store and know that the olive oil they are purchasing is really extra-virgin, as advertised. Olive oil is one of the most commonly counterfeited food products. As Fuller (2017) explains, you can't simply go to the cooking oil aisle of the grocery store and sample the olive oils.

The label itself is not helpful in detecting fraudulent food products. In fact, like fake wine and beer, this can be counterfeit or misleading as to the contents of the bottle. Some of the questionable practices are legal, like mixing last year's harvest with this year's harvest in making the oil, even if it's considered to be subpar with diminished health benefits (Olmsted, 2017). The difference between extra-virgin olive oil and regular olive oil is the latter is a blend and less processed to remove any impurities, making the blend less desirable.

Passing off blends as the more desirable extra-virgin olive oil is not a new thing. Corruption within the olive oil industry has been around since the days of ancient Rome (Mueller, 2011). More recently, olive oil has begun to be cut with less valuable oils such as hazelnut and sunflower seed (Mueller, 2011).

If "extra-virgin" olive oil isn't confusing enough, claims of "truffle essence" or "truffle aroma" on labels are dubious at best to the more knowledgeable connoisseur. Truffle, which comes in white and black varieties, is a fungus that is a precious commodity in culinary circles and has a distinct flavor. This flavor can be captured synthetically and added to olive oil relatively inexpensively, but with "truffle" on the label, it drives up the price largely due to its reputation of being a luxury food item. Producers can get away with the labeling, as was decided in a 2017 court case against the Monini olive oil company. Judge Stanton concluded that the ingredient label described the truffle essence as "substance-flavored" rather than actual truffles (Bone, 2017). It is perfectly legal to advertise an olive oil as being truffle-flavored as long as it doesn't advertise that there are real truffles in it.

Because following the USDA standards for olive oil is voluntary, there is little financial incentive to import and sell the costlier-to-process extra-virgin version. A cheaper, inferior blend can be passed off as the real thing. It is only recently that the FDA started to test imported olive oil in the United States (Fuller, 2017). Olmsted (2017) suggests that you are more likely to avoid purchasing fake olive oil if you shop at specialty shops or reputable markets. But by doing so, you pay for authenticity and will not necessarily avoid fakery all together. If you do want the real extra-virgin olive oil, Omstead (2017; Fuller, 2017) makes the following recommendations:

1. Do not buy olive oil that doesn't have "extra-virgin" on the label. Without it, you are pretty much guaranteed that it is an inferior product.
2. Look for the "harvest date," plus the name of the estate or mill. Only the best oils will have "pressed on" date or "harvest date."
3. Ignore "best by" and "bottled on" dates. These are arbitrary without legal standards.
4. Look for a third-party certification seal. If coming from California, look for the seal from the California Olive Oil Council ("COOC Certified Extra Virgin"). If the product is imported, look for a seal from the EU, the European Union's Protected Designation of Origin (PDO), or the Italian *Denominazione d'Origine Protetta* (Protected Designation of Origin or DOP).
5. If the extra-virgin olive oil is made in Australia or Chile, it can be considered fresh and legitimate as these countries have more stringent standards and testing systems.
6. Don't fall for fancy packaging or high price tags. This is a red flag that it may be a fake masquerading as real extra virgin-olive oil and probably has an artificial "use by" date.
7. Trust your senses. Fake oil is more likely to smell rancid or unpleasant, whereas good olive oil should smell and taste fresh.

Italy is perhaps the most proactive country to go after fake olive oil. We should consider the selling of fake foods, however minimally regulated they might be elsewhere, as part of white collar crime. Though Italy is not at the top of the list of olive oil-producing countries (Spain is), olive oil perhaps has the greatest reputation as a staple in Italian cuisine. Between 2014 and 2016 Italian authorities seized more than 2,000 tons of fake olive oil, launching an investigation into the manufacturing practices of some of the leading olive oil producers in the country (Fuller, 2017).

Discussion Questions

1. If it smells good and tastes good, why does it matter if you purchase fake food instead of an authentic product?
2. Other than the products mentioned in this chapter, what other products might be at risk for being counterfeit?
3. Why might there be little incentive for regulatory agencies to go after fake products as compared to regulating food safety?

Beyond fake food is dangerous food that might cause illness, injury, or in extreme cases, death. The Federal Food and Drug Administration (FDA) is tasked with assuring that tainted or unadulterated foods are yanked from store shelves when there have been complaints or questions about their safety for consumption (Bazley, 2008). They likewise do this for drugs and medical devices, but we will save further discussion of the FDA's role in those cases for the next chapter on medical fraud (Chapter 8).

There have been a number of recalls of baby food over the years. Nothing strikes fear or brings on a more emotional response than when discussing the safety of food or formula fed to infants, toddlers, and children. Because of their size, younger children are particularly vulnerable to the harmful effects of poisonous substances.

Unfortunately, food recalls in general are not always effective, as not all consumers pay attention to news reports of recalls. However, in this day and age of the Internet, the word gets out quickly (and virally), which helps to pull tainted food items off consumers' kitchen shelves and into the trash.

CONSUMER PROTECTION AND EDUCATION

In the United States, there are a number of state and federal agencies responsible for consumer protection. As the funding of these agencies are tied to the political climate locally and nationally, these agencies are only as effective as the resources they have on hand at any given time. The agencies that are most likely to handle consumer complaints about fraud are the Federal Trade Commission (FTC) and state consumer protection offices.

There are a number of organizations and publications that work in conjunction with federal and state law enforcement agencies to assist in educating the public on the risks for consumer fraud. Among these in the United States are the Better Business Bureau (BBB), Consumer Reports, American Coalition of Citizens with Disabilities, and Consumer Watchdog. There are also a number of consumer protection organizations and agencies elsewhere in the world, including the European Association for the Co-ordination of Consumer Representation in Standardisation (ANEC) and Consumers International.

Because the elderly population is one of the biggest targets for fraud schemes, along with the National Council on Aging, the American Association of Retired Persons (AARP) offers a number of resources. AARP provides a free hotline (877-908-3360) to seniors and their loved ones if they suspect that they have been victimized (AARP, 2019, available at https://www.aarp.org/money/scams-fraud/).

Under President Barack Obama, the Consumer Financial Protection Bureau (CFPB) was created. It is the brainchild of Senator Elizabeth Warren (Massachusetts), having been a consumer advocate for many years before she served in Congress. The bureau was authorized by Dodd-Frank Wall Street Reform in 2010 after the mortgage lending crisis in 2008. The responsibilities of the CFPB, in conjunction with other government agencies, is to lobby for new laws to protect consumers from questionable financial services and products that could potentially be fraudulent or unethical. This included lending practices by financial institutions. For more information about Dodd-Frank Wall Street Reform refer to Chapter 4, Financial Crime.

SUMMARY

There is a reason why early in this book, we noted that not all of us will fall victim to conventional crime but most, if not all, of us will fall prey to consumer fraud. Next to financial crimes, this is most likely to be the type of crime that will happen to us in our lifetimes. The greatest protection against consumer fraud is consumer education.

That is the good news. Government attempts to regulate product safety and prevent fraud. The bad news is that in a free market society, the buyer assumes a lot of responsibility as to the authenticity and reliability of products. This isn't to say that countries that have other types of economic systems don't have their own share of unsafe or fraudulent products. And regulatory agencies are only as good as they are funded to go after offenders, working hand in hand with prosecutors as well.

We saw in this chapter a number of ways that the consumer can be hoodwinked. Some of these include income tax refund loans, phony contests, and telemarketing schemes. To add to the confusion for regulators and the public alike, telemarketing isn't always illegal, hence the sales calls and spam emails, some of which are completely legitimate, if not annoying. Whether legitimate or illegitimate, sales solicitations tend to play on the emotions on the targeted, many times working with a carefully crafted script designed to best get the desired response of a sale.

Lesser known types of consumer frauds include counterfeit artifacts and art. The individual collector is not the only one victimized. Museums have on occasion purchased items that came with provenances that have fooled even the most seasoned art or archeological expert.

The consumer is not always the victim. Sellers of products can also be victimized, if they are paid with counterfeit cashier's checks or money orders. They can also be victimized by buyers knowingly writing bad checks on bank accounts with non-sufficient funds. The product sold is long gone, along with the criminal.

We have also seen that there are some people who are more vulnerable to fraud, including the elderly and the disabled. Though increasingly we see fraud being committed online, older people are more likely to still have a landline phone, making it an attractive way to find new victims, particularly if the criminal purchases a phone list. With online options, including phone apps, there is the increase possibility of being fooled by phony app that will become available, looking like legitimate apps, and disappear just as quickly with consumers' money before authorities can arrest the culprits.

Bottom line, it is becoming increasingly important that the consumer and not governmental agencies have to help with the prevention of victimization with consumer education. This has become ever more critical with the rise of online fraud. So the old adage, "buyer beware", has never been as important as in the complexity of buying and selling options in the 21st century.

Case Study ▪ You Have a Virus! Fleecing the Elderly in Tech Service Schemes

Background

We have already established that young people, older adults, and immigrants are among the more common victims of consumer fraud. According to the U.S. Federal Trade Commission (FTC), younger people are more likely to fall victim to fraud but older people in their 70s have greater losses per victim (Witt, 2018; Fair, 2019).

A Massachusetts couple, Shalu and Vishal Chawla, are currently accused of running a tech support company that targeted senior citizens in the state and across the country (Weisman, 2019). Similar to auto repair shop scams where customers are charged for nonexistent repairs, allegedly the Chawlas' company, Vtech Software Solutions, Inc., would send pop-up ads to their computers warning of viruses, then would promise to repair the supposed problem for a fee (Weisman, 2019). In a statement to the press,

Massachusetts Attorney General Healey stated that "This couple preyed upon residents in our state — many of them elderly — and tricked them into paying for computer repairs that didn't exist." (Weisman, 2019).

Defining the Crime(s)

Elder fraud is a special type of consumer crime where senior citizens, generally defined as 65 years old or older, are specifically targeted. Among the types of crimes that seniors are likely to fall prey to is deceptive advertising and promises of the delivery of goods, services, or financial investments that do not exist, or were never intended to be delivered (Stopfraud.gov, n.d.). One of the types of fraudulent services targeting seniors is in technical support, as is being alleged of the Chawlas.

Theories to Explain the Crime

When we are examining the victimization of the elderly, we have to take into consideration, particularly when it comes to tech services fraud, that older people may not be as tech savvy as younger people who grew up in the Computer Age. According to the American Association of Retired Persons (AARP), only 66 percent of elderly over the age of 70 own a desktop computer; 56 percent own a laptop (Anderson, 2017).

One theory that might help to explain victimization of the elderly by tech service fraud is an offshoot of Routine Activities Theory (RAT, Cohen and Felson, 1979). If we also add the possibility that one's lifestyle may also contribute to victimization, we can more seriously consider lifestyle-routine activities theory or L-RAT (McNeeley, 2015; Cohen and Felson, 1979; Hindelang et al., 1978) as a more thorough explanation.

In L-RAT, it proposes that it is the day-to-day activities of the individual, coupled with the fact that there is no capable guardian available, that puts them at risk of being victimized. Demographic variables such as age can be a factor on the type of lifestyles people live (McNeeley, 2015), putting them at greater or lesser risk for victimization. If we consider that as early as at the first part of this century, computers allowed the elderly to comfortably stay home more often, as those with computers increasingly were able to access information and shop online (Hilt and Lipschults, 2010).

Older Americans may have had more access to computers in recent decades, but this does not mean that they were necessarily adept at figuring out basic computer skills, including simple coding or troubleshooting. Younger people are more likely to have had exposure to basic computer classes in their education, some as early as elementary school. If you consider that the average person in their 70s in 2020 was already in their 30s when personal computers became commonplace in the 1980s, it is less likely that they would have had formal computer education unless their careers demanded it.

We may also consider abundance theories of crime to explain the victimization of the elderly. Historically, abundance theories propose that there are more thefts of things because, well, there are just more things to steal. Consider that the average household now possesses a number of electronics, so there are more items of value to steal from homes. Extend that to service plans for electronics, and there is greater potential for tech service fraud because of the prevalence of electronics used in the household.

Social and Media Responses

There are a couple of things to take into consideration in the discussion of responses to crimes committed against the elderly. One, the Western world continues to be more youth-oriented, as compared to Eastern cultures. For example, it is not unusual for older parents to live with their adult children and their families in Asian countries. It is far less common in the United States. As a result, there isn't as much public or media attention when the elderly fall prey to fraud schemes. However, we need to remind ourselves that white collar crime has never received the same attention as conventional crimes, particularly violent ones. There is far more likely to be public outcry if a grandmother had been strangled in her home than if someone had stolen her pension or Social Security check.

The strongest responses and advice given has come from the Federal Trade Commission (FTC) and from organizations that serve to protect the interests of the elderly, like AARP.

Criminal Justice and Policy Responses

The Massachusetts Attorney General's Office first got wind of the alleged tech service scheme after a number of customer complaints were reported to the Federal Trade Commission (FTC). The FTC in turn referred the case to the Attorney General's Office. The Attorney General's Office determined, after its investigation, that the Chawlas have allegedly violated the Massachusetts Consumer Protection Law[4].

A part of Massachusetts General Laws Chapter 93A states broadly that any unfair or deceptive practices are illegal (Mass.gov, n.d.). Under the law, the state or individuals can sue for damages if a business has been found liable in civil court. This is yet another example of when a white collar crime case, though clearly one that involves theft, generally will not end up as state or federal criminal charges.

Rather than charged in criminal court, the Chawlas are being sued in a civil case. Accused of stealing up to $2.4 million for unwarranted computer repairs (Weisman, 2019), technically the couple could also face civil litigation

---

[4] The details of the law are available from the 191st General Court of the Commonwealth of Massachusetts, at https://malegislature.gov/Laws/GeneralLaws/PartI/TitleXV/Chapter93A/.

by individual victims or in a class action lawsuit. In the state's civil complaint, the Chawlas, along with Vtech Software Solution, Inc., violated the Massachusetts Consumer Protection Law (Wickedlocal.com, 2019). The Chawlas are also being accused of cashing consumer checks without authorization (Wickedlocal.com, 2019).

If found liable, the Chawlas could face paying restitution of the $2.4 million alleged to have been stolen, as well as to additional civil damages. As we caution in examining the outcome of any case, criminal court must find the defendant guilty beyond a shadow of a doubt. In civil court, there only needs to be substantial evidence of wrongdoing, not complete confidence in the guilt or innocence of the respondent(s) in the case.

Unanswered Questions and Unresolved Issues Related to the Case

As this is an ongoing case, there is always the question of how many victims are out there. The Attorney General's Office has already determined that there has been close to or over $2.4 million of losses to the victims. As AARP reports, it continues to be a problem of the elderly being less likely to report victimization when it comes to consumer crime (Anderson, 2017). It is unknown how much of this is a case of being ignorant as to whether one is a victim or not, or, as in some crimes, the fear of being viewed as foolish for having fallen for a fraud scheme.

Sources

Anderson, O. (2017) Technology use and attitudes among mid-life and older Americans. *AARP Research*. Dec. 20. Retrieved from https://www.aarp.org/content/dam/aarp/research/surveys_statistics/technology/info-2018/atom-nov-2017-tech-module.doi.10.26419%252Fres.00210.001.pdf.

Fair, L. (2019) Scams and older consumers: Looking at the data. *Consumer Information*, Federal Trade Commission (FTC). Oct. 23. Retrieved from https://www.consumer.ftc.gov/blog/2019/10/scams-and-older-consumers-looking-data.

Hilt, M. L. and J. H. Lipschultz. (2004) Elderly Americans and the Internet: E-mail, TV news, information and entertainment websites. *Educational Gerontology*. Vol. 30, No 1: 52-72).

Mass.gov (n.d.) The Massachusetts Consumer Protection Law. Retrieved from https://www.mass.gov/service-details/the-massachusetts-consumer-protection-law.

Stopfraud.gov. (n.d.) Elder fraud and financial exploitation. Archive, Financial Fraud Enforcement Task Force. Retrieved from https://www.justice.gov/archives/stopfraud-archive/elder-fraud-and-financial-exploitation.

Weisman, R. (2019) AG charges Melrose couple with running a tech support scam targeting seniors. The Boston Globe. Dec. 10. Retrieved from https://www.bostonglobe.com/metro/2019/12/10/charges-melrose-couple-with-running-tech-support-scam-targeting-seniors/Nz488NwCMbzWdKJjYl6zEJ/story.html.

Wickedlocal.com. (2019) Melrose couple sued by AG's Office for scamming consumers through tech support scheme. Melrose, MA. Dec. 11. Retrieved from https://melrose.wickedlocal.com/news/20191211/melrose-couple-sued-by-ags-office-for-scamming-consumers-through-tech-support-scheme.

Witt, P. (2018) Top frauds of 2018. U.S. Federal Trade Commission (FTC). Retrieved from https://www.ftc.gov/news-events/blogs/business-blog/2019/02/top-frauds-2018.

GLOSSARY

"Apps"   Applications, or as they are more commonly known as, "apps," are software that can be installed on a computer or mobile phone.

Children's Online Privacy Protection Act (COPPA)   Legislation passed by the U.S. Congress in 1998 to give parents more control of what information can be collected from children who are using the Internet.

Class action lawsuits   Civil cases where a number of people who have been harmed or defrauded by a company can sue the company collectively instead of suing individually.

"Cold Calling"   Marketing strategy that include unsolicited telephone calls to or face-to-face encounters with potential customers.

Federal Trade Commission   One of the key U.S. agencies charged with protecting consumers.

FICO® credit score   The Fair Isaac Corporation (FICO®) provides creditors with credit scores of potential borrowers to demonstrate credit worthiness, typically ranging from 300 (poor) to 850 (excellent).

Forgery   A forgery is any fake replication or reproduction, without legal permission, of signatures, currency or checks, or work of art.

Fraud   Criminal deception that is intended to obtain money from unsuspecting victims, with no compensation with goods or services.

Mobile Medical Applications (MMAs)   Applications that can be downloaded to a computer or mobile device that provide users with medical and health care information. MMAs are regulated by the Federal Drug Administration to ensure that the information is accurate and that they are legitimate sources.

Provenance   Documents that provide proof of authenticity of artwork and history of ownership.

Refund Anticipation Loans (RALs)   Popular in the 1980s and 1990s, RALs offered tax filers the opportunity to receive their income tax refunds faster than the IRS could process the return and send out a check. The loans provided payment out of the tax refund for tax preparation services. They have been replaced with Refund Anticipation Check (RAC) programs.

Robocalls   Automated phone calls, typically from telemarketing companies.

Telemarketing   Generally unsolicited telephone calls to potential customers. These can be automated calls or "cold calling" by operators at telemarketing companies.

Upfront fee   A fee charged by a company in advance of a product or service being provided to a customer. The fee can be a deposit towards final payment or a separate fee for providing a product or service in advance of payment.

Usury lending   The practice of illegally charging unusually high interest rates on personal and consumer loans.

REFERENCES AND SUGGESTED READINGS

Amore, A. M. (2015) *The Art of the Con.* New York: St. Martin's Press.

Bone, E. (2017) 'Truffle oil' without any actual truffles. *The New York Times.* Sept. 15. Retrieved from https://www.nytimes.com/2017/09/15/opinion/truffle-oil-chemicals.html.

Cohen, L. and M. Felson. (1979) Social Change and crime rate trends: A routine activities approach. *American Sociological Review.* 44: 589.

Durney, M. and B. Proulx. (2011) Art crime: A brief introduction. *Crime, Law, and Social Change.* Sept. 56: 115-132.

Federal Trade Commission. (2014) FTC alleges Amazon unlawfully billed parents for millions of dollars in children's unauthorized in-app charges: No password or other indication of parental consent was required for charges in kids' apps; internal e-mail referred to situation as "house on fire". Press release, July 10. Retrieved from https://www.ftc.gov/news-events/press-releases/2014/07/ftc-alleges-amazon-unlawfully-billed-parents-millions-dollars.

Federal Trade Commission. (2016) Federal Court finds Amazon liable for billing parents for children's unauthorized in-app charges. Press release, April 27. Retrieved from https://www.ftc.gov/news-events/press-releases/2016/04/federal-court-finds-amazon-liable-billing-parents-childrens).

Federal Trade Commission. (2019) How to donate wisely and avoid charity scams. Retrieved from https://www.consumer.ftc.gov/features/how-donate-wisely-and-avoid-charity-scams.

Fuller, J. R. (2017) Seven ways to tell if your olive is fake. *Epicurious.* May 25. Retrieved from https://www.epicurious.com/ingredients/seven-ways-to-tell-the-difference-between-real-and-fake-olive-oil-article

Georgia Department of Law. (2019) Telemarketing fraud. Consumer Protection Division. Retrieved from http://consumer.georgia.gov/consumer-topics/telemarketing-fraud.

Inez Guzman, A. (2019) Faked out: Counterfeit Native jewelry, has flooded the market, fooling buyers and harming authentic makers. *New Mexico Magazine.* July. Pp 38-45.

Jorna, P. (2016) The relationship between age and consumer fraud victimization. *Trends and Issues in Crime and Criminal Justice.* Nov, Issue 519:1-16.

Lazarus, A. (2016) There's an app for that (but it might be fake). U.S. Federal Trade Commission Consumer Information. Dec. 22. Retrieved from https://www.consumer.ftc.gov/blog/2016/12/theres-app-it-might-be-fake.

Lichtenberg, P.A., M. A. Sugarman, D. Paulson, L. J. Ficker, and A. Rahman-Filipiak. (2015) Psychological and functional vulnerability predicts fraud cases in older adults: Results of a longitudinal study. *Clinical Gerontology.* Vol. 39, No. 1: 48-63.

Micallef, J. V. (2018) What's in your cellar? Counterfeit wines are a multi-billion dollar business. Forbes. Dec. 1. Retrieved from https://www.forbes.com/sites/joemicallef/2018/12/01/whats-in-your-cellar-counterfeit-wines-are-a-multi-billion-dollar-problem/#7ae741ac1c83.

Mueller, T. (2011) *Extra Virginity: The Sublime and Scandalous World of Olive Oil.* New York: W.W. Norton & Co.

National Council on Aging (2019) Top ten financial scams targeting seniors. Retrieved from https://www.ncoa.org/economic-security/money-management/scams-security/top-10-scams-targeting-seniors/#intraPageNav8.

Olmsted, L. (2017) *Real Food/Fake Food: Why You Don't Know What You're Eating and What You Can Do About It.* New York: Algonquin Books.

Pratt, T.C. K. Holtfreter, and M.D. Reisig. (2010) Routine online activity and internet fraud tartgeting: Extending the generality of Routine Activity Theory. *Journal of Research in Crime and Delinquency.* Vol. 47, No. 3: 267-296.

TRAC Reports, Inc. (2019) White collar crime prosecutions for April 2019. Syracuse University. Retrieved from https://trac.syr.edu/tracreports/bulletins/white_collar_crime/monthlyapr19/fil/.

Stevens, L. (2017) Amazon, FTC end legal battle, clearing the way for up to $70 million in refunds. *The Wall Street Journal.* April 4. Retrieved from https://www.wsj.com/articles/amazon-ftc-end-legal-battle-clearing-the-way-for-up-to-70-million-in-refunds-1491337565.

U.S. Census Bureau. (2019). Quarterly retail e-commerce sales, 12st quarter 2019. U.S. Department of Commerce. May 17. Retrieved from https://www.census.gov/retail/mrts/www/data/pdf/ec_current.pdf.

Wansink, B., G. Cordua, E. Blair, C. Payne, and S. Geiger. (2006) Wine promotions in restaurants: Do beverage sales contribute or cannibalize? *Cornell Hotel and Restaurant Administration Quarterly.* Nov. Vol. 47, Issue 4: 327-336.

Chapter EIGHT

Health Care Fraud and Crimes

Tell me where it hurts

"Any system that values profit over human life is a very dangerous one indeed."

—*Suzy Kassem, in Rise Up and Salute the Sun:*
The Writings of Suzy Kassem

Chapter Objectives

- Introduce medical terminology associated with health care crimes and malfeasance.
- Identify the specializations in health care most at risk for the occurrence of white collar crime.
- Distinguish where health care crimes and financial crimes intersect.
- Familiarize the reader with the basics of medical ethics.

Key Terms

Administrative court
Federal Drug Administration (FDA)
Belmont Report
"Big Pharma"
Chapter 11 bankruptcy
Controlled substances
Hippocratic Oath
Informed consent

Institutional Review Board (IRB)
Kickbacks
Malpractice
Medicaid
Medicare
Price gouging
Price hiking
Tort law

INTRODUCTION

There is perhaps no more confusing area in white collar crime studies than crimes that are committed by health care professionals. Physicians, at least in some medical schools in the United States, ritualistically take the *Hippocratic Oath*, summarily vowing to above all, do no harm to their patients. Though realistically some doctors go into the profession for the potential earnings, ideally most do so in order to help people.

We also must remind ourselves that health care today is essentially set up after the corporate model. Health care insurance companies are not in the business of losing money. In fact, as publicly traded companies, insurance companies are expected to generate profits for their investors, though modest in comparison to some other industries like petrochemicals. Some insurance companies are still nonprofit, but most now function as for-profit enterprises.

Because there is a broad range of crimes committed by doctors, nurses, ancillary services personnel (e.g., respiratory therapy, physical therapy, etc.), and administrative staff, we will focus primarily on financial crimes such as insurance fraud, plus unethical practices that clearly fall under white collar crime. We will discuss bad or unethical decisions that result in patient harm or death. We will not include obvious homicides committed by health care professionals, as those fall under "conventional" crime. For example, it would not be appropriate to include cases of the so called "Angels of Death," serial killer nurses who murder patients, some doing so in the mistaken belief that they are entrusted to put them out of their misery.

We cannot engage in a discussion about medical crime without talking about the pharmaceutical industry. We should remind ourselves once again that much of white collar crime is handled in civil court with lawsuits. In the situation of *malpractice*, the malfeasance may not be due to intentional neglect, but from exhaustion, inexperience, laziness, or outright foolishness. Not all medical personnel are equal in their expertise. Somewhere out there is the doctor who graduated at the bottom of their class in medical school, at the least respected university or teaching hospital, yet was still able to obtain a medical license. All things equal, the concerns that we discussed in Chapter 7 on consumer crimes apply equally here: Patients should do their homework if they are able and find out a bit about their doctors and hospitals before blindly using their services. Unfortunately, in an emergency, the patient doesn't always have that luxury.

We should also be reminded of the discussion in Chapters 2 and 3 about professional organizations helping with keeping health care professionals in line. The American Medical Association (AMA) and American Psychological Association (APA) have from their inception been the watchdogs for ethical behavior in medicine and psychology. Each specialization in medicine also has its own organizations to keep physicians current on best practices, including medical boards (e.g., American Board of Ophthalmology). The gold standard in medicine is to be board certified.

The topics we will be discussing in this chapter are focused on the health care system in the United States. In the growing debate centered around socialized medicine vs. a free market system, there has always been the question as to whether some of the problems introduced here might go away or might be replaced with new problems if the U.S. went to a universal health care program. The biggest argument has more to do with economics and the fate of insurance companies. The health care industry makes up 17.9 percent of the money in the U.S. Gross Domestic Product (GDP) that is represented by the overall healthcare industry. 34 percent of that is spent on private insurance alone, or $1.2 trillion per year (DHHS, CMS, 2019). Unfortunately, health care insurance, whether it is through private insurance or government programs like *Medicare* and *Medicaid*, is an industry hit with fraud on a frequent basis.

With the current state of affairs in medicine, at least in the United States, insurance companies are the gatekeepers to what physicians, psychiatrists, and psychologists, plus hospitals can offer in the way of health care. Those in the health care professions, to some extent, have their hands tied in what they can or cannot do in the way of diagnosis and treatment. The cases in this chapter are about crime and malfeasance that was well within the control of health care professionals and has little to nothing to do with the restrictions they live under by insurance companies.

MALPRACTICE

The search for justice and restitution in cases of inept physicians and incompetent psychiatrists has been a part of civilization for millennia. In the ancient world, punishment in cases of malpractice ranged from losing one's professional reputation to capital punishment (Flemma, 1985). To this day, as in the case of conventional crimes, there is the consideration as to whether the malpractice is an event that happened intentionally (*tort law*) or unintentionally (*neglect*).

American jurisprudence and medical malpractice cases are still in their relative infancy, dating just to the early 18th century. As far back as 1750 B.C.E., the Code of Hammurabi in ancient Babylon was used in cases of serious neglect and carelessness by surgeons, where they were met with severe punishment; in ancient Egypt, the penalty could be death (Flemma, 1985). In post-Colonial America, physicians were somewhat more likely to be held criminally responsible when something went wrong with a patient. We should remind ourselves that until the early 1900s, except when physicians cared for the very wealthy, they were not held in as high regard as they are today. In some cases, the only qualifications were to be handy with a saw, knife, needle, and thread.

In the current era of medicine, patients are required to sign consent forms before procedures, including surgery, that spell out the risks involved. Except in the case of an unconscious patient in a life-threatening condition, as in the example of an automobile accident, no procedure will be done without the patient or the patient's guardian's signature (e.g., parent). Even in emergencies, a guardian or parent will be asked to sign the consent form if they are available to do so, before doctors will proceed with treatment.

To fully understand the origins of the litigation of malpractice, it might be best to go back to one of the earliest malpractice cases tried in court in the western world. In *Stratton v. Swanlond*, in 14th century England, a physician bungled the repair on an injured hand. The case was dismissed due to a legal technicality, but the court agreed that this was an avenue by which physicians could be held liable in the event that there was negligence (Field, 2011). In 14th century England, the relationship between the patient and doctor was based on the theory of contract, where wealthy patrons could sue the physician for neglect and the physician could sue for payment when the patient refused to pay the retainer fee (Flemma, 1985).

Though we do not ordinarily think of the patient-doctor relationship as one that is based on a contract, to a large extent it is. If you have to have repairs on your home you sign a good faith contract on the estimate of the cost and what type of repairs the contractor will do. In the event that the contractor fails to provide the services that they promised or overcharges, the customer has the option of suing the contractor in civil court. Same goes for the contract relationship between physicians, psychiatrists and their patients.

There are a variety of types of malpractice identified today. It can be treated as a civil matter or as a criminal offense. Though perhaps more subjective to measure, the story behind why a health care professional is negligent will determine which court system it will be handled in. Of course, there is always the option of suing a health care professional in civil court, even if they have already been brought to justice in the criminal court system.

There are four criteria in determining whether medical malpractice or negligence has occurred, also known as "the four Ds": *duty, dereliction, damages,* and *direct cause* (Preskorn, 2014). *Duty* refers to the responsibility of a doctor to follow best practices and protocol for their specialization. *Dereliction* is when a physician has failed to follow those best practices and protocol, whether they intended to do so or not. *Damages* are measured by the extent to which the dereliction has resulted in preventable physical or emotional harm. Finally, *direct causation* refers to whether the damage done can be proven to be as a direct result of the physician's actions or inactions.

Beyond "the four Ds," any medical or psychiatric professional can be criminally charged with malpractice if they are in charge of direct patient care. For example, if medical students are taking part in a surgery, the surgeon who is supervising them is ultimately responsible. Though rare, when there are criminal charges, they are only brought directly against the individual who is criminally negligent.

Hospitals and clinics, like corporations, can be part of civil malpractice lawsuits. If enough patients are harmed, it can result in a class action lawsuit, meaning everyone harmed sues the doctor or hospital together. This generally does not end up with a sizable judgement for each victim as the awarded compensation will be divided between all the plaintiffs. Keep in mind as well that the litigation attorney can get as much as 30 percent of the settlement funds, plus there can be court costs.

There are two types of damages that can be paid in malpractice cases. The first are the more obvious expenditures, including the medical costs, legal fees, and potential loss of earning capacity. The second type of damages paid in cases is more difficult to measure. These are noneconomic costs that are the proverbial "pain and suffering" awards, as well as any psychological harm to the victim being financially compensated.

The most commonly tried malpractice cases, according to Meinhart, Smith, and Manning, PLLC (https://www.bluegrassjustice.com/famous-medical-malpractice-cases/), a law firm specializing in malpractice, are as follows:

- Foreign objects left inside of patients after surgery, including needles, scalpels, clamps, scissors, sponges[1], electrical equipment, and knife blades.
- Surgery on incorrect body part (e.g., wrong arm or leg)
- Birth injury
- Stroke
- Medication errors
- Anesthesia errors
- Misdiagnosis

As we do not want to neglect discussions of white collar crimes elsewhere in the world, we should note that in countries that have socialized medicine, medical neglect cases can be handled somewhat differently. In the example of the Danish health care system, cases of neglect do not exist in the local court systems, with less chance of lessons being learned throughout the medical community. Unlike the U.S., in the Danish system, beyond compensating the victim, the focus is on collecting data from claims to help identify health care providers with track records of repeated mistakes (Pierce and Allen, 2015). In Japan, which also has a universal health care insurance system, patients file few malpractice claims (Ramseyer, 2010).

In the Spanish legal system, whether a medical accident happens in a public hospital or private hospital will determine whether the case will be filed in an *administrative court* or civil court (Amaral-Garcia, 2019). There is some argument for higher financial compensation in administrative court cases because not only has a patient been mistreated in a public hospital, but taxpayers' contributions to them have been misused as well (Amaral-Garcia, 2019). Judges evidently tend to be more lenient in these cases, as compared to civil cases against private hospitals.

There is little that is as emotional for juries to hear than when it comes to malpractice lawsuits involving infants or children. Parents have sued doctors, seeking damages for the cost of childbirth and raising a child when they have

---

[1] In the 1960s, when malpractice cases were less common, the author's father had hernia repair surgery where the surgeon accidently left a surgical sponge in the body cavity, resulting in an infection. He was required to have a second emergency surgery to remove the sponge. Thankfully, her father recovered from both surgeries and infection. No malpractice lawsuit was filed in this case.

failed to provide adequate genetic testing before a disabled child is born (Paul, 1984). Under these circumstances, it is considered a *wrongful birth*. When a sterilization procedure fails due to neglect during surgery and a pregnancy results, it is called a *wrongful pregnancy*. Courts do not always distinguish between the two, even if they are distinctly different outcomes and some use the terms interchangeably, as in the Illinois Supreme Court case, *Cockrum v. Baumgarten*, 1984 (Paul, 1984).

Law in the Real World: Wrongful Pregnancies

(Source: Barrell, Will, Lewellyn and Edwards, PLC, 2016)

One of the biggest controversies and debate issues in politics and medicine has been birth control, primarily for religious reasons. Whether it is someone who is trying to prevent a pregnancy from happening outside of marriage, postponing pregnancy until they are more financially stable, or deciding to never have children, there have only been a few legal, effective ways to do so. In the early 1970s, gynecological methods took one step closer to a more predictable means by which to prevent pregnancy permanently with the introduction of safe and effective tubal ligations (Greenberg, 2008). A tubal ligation requires the surgeon to essentially tie off the woman's fallopian tubes, preventing ova[2] from entering the uterus with the potential of becoming fertile. The surgery can be done by laparoscopy with small incisions in the abdominal wall, through transcervical sterilization which is minimally invasive, or after a Cesarean section ("C-section") delivery of a baby while the lower abdominal cavity is still open (Greenberg, 2008).

As much as tubal ligations are as close to being 100 percent effective as possible, there are odd times when the surgery fails. If this happens, a woman could potentially become pregnant. As the choice to have surgical sterilization through tubal ligation is generally not taken lightly, this is understandably of great concern. There is failure in an estimated 0.1 to 0.8 percent of cases within the first year after surgery (Date et al., 2014). So, the probability of a pregnancy is extremely low. However, in a study of 140 cases of sterilization failure, 27 cases or 19.29 percent were the result of improper surgical procedure (Date et al., 2014).

---

[2] An ovum (plural, ova) is a mature female egg that will become an embryo once fertilization occurs with male sperm.

One of the largest settlements in a wrongful pregnancy case resulted in a jury verdict for $1.8 million in 2016. The lawsuit was filed in Virginia state court after a patient became pregnant following a tubal ligation procedure. The plaintiff's attorneys, Lewellyn and Dunnigan, argued that the surgical procedure had been improperly done, failing to sterilize the patient. Though the surgeon's defense attorney argued that no damages were done, as the mother loved her unplanned child, the jury agreed with the plaintiff's attorneys that the mother was entitled to additional noneconomic compensation for emotional distress and mental anguish: "..... The mother's love for her child did not excuse the doctor's medical negligence." (Davies et al., 2016, Retrieved from https://www.dbwle.com/firm-news/2016/august/-1-8-million-jury-award-in-wrongful-pregnancy-ca/)

Discussion Questions

1. What factors do you think juries take into consideration in wrongful birth or wrongful pregnancy cases?
2. What emotional costs might there be in raising an unplanned child after a failed sterilization?
3. How does a case like this compare to a case in which an individual has been accidentally sterilized because of medical neglect?

There are a lot of obvious and hidden costs to malpractice cases. Health care providers, including physicians, psychiatrists, hospitals, and clinics, must carry malpractice insurance policies. Depending on the specialization, some malpractice insurance policies are more expensive than others. For example, one of the most expensive types of malpractice insurance policies covers obstetrics and gynecology (OBGYN), as compared to insurance costs for general practitioners. Likewise, there are some riskier procedures that logically are more at risk of lawsuits when things go wrong (Ramseyer, 2010). And for obvious reasons, surgeons have to carry more liability insurance than non-surgeons. The annual medical liability system costs in the U.S. are estimated to be 2.4 percent of all health care spending, representing billions of dollars (Mello et al., 2010).

For physicians, the American Medical Association (AMA) malpractice insurance premiums can cost over $200,000 annually as indicated in Table 8.1, depending on the specialization (Guardado, 2018).

TABLE 8.1 Medical Professional Liability Insurance Premiums for $1M/$3M Policies, Selected Insurers, 2008-2017

Medical Professional Liability Insurance Premiums for $1M/$3M Policies, Selected Insurers, 2008–2017

	\$									
Obstetrics/Gynecology	2008	2009	2010	2011	2012	2013	2014	2015	2016	2017
California (Los Angeles, Orange)	63,272	49,804	49,804	49,804	49,804	49,804	49,804	49,804	49,804	49,804
Connecticut	170,389	170,389	170,389	170,389	170,389	170,389	170,389	170,389	170,389	170,389
Florida (Miami-Dade)	238,728	201,808	201,808	201,808	201,808	190,829	190,829	190,829	190,829	190,829
Illinois (Cook, Madison, St. Clair)	178,921	178,921	177,441	177,441	177,441	177,441	177,441	177,441	177,441	177,441
New Jersey	117,340	117,340	109,189	109,189	109,189	109,189	109,189	90,749	90,749	90,749
New York (Nassau, Suffolk)	194,935	194,935	204,864	206,913	204,684	227,889	214,999	214,999	214,999	214,999
Pennsylvania (Philadelphia)	171,813	169,336	168,317	163,793	165,657	124,627	124,627	112,289	117,415	119,466
General Surgery										
California (Los Angeles, Orange)	54,505	41,775	41,775	41,775	41,775	47,595	47,595	47,595	41,775	41,775
Connecticut	65,803	65,803	65,803	65,803	65,803	65,803	65,803	65,803	65,803	65,803
Florida (Miami-Dade)	213,054	190,088	190,088	190,088	190,088	190,829	190,829	190,829	190,829	190,829
Illinois (Cook, Madison, St. Clair)	119,334	119,334	118,909	118,909	118,909	118,909	118,909	118,909	118,909	118,909
New Jersey	78,484	78,484	73,074	73,074	73,074	73,074	73,074	60,810	60,810	60,810
New York (Nassau, Suffolk)	104,054	104,054	114,770	128,542	114,770	148,454	134,923	134,923	134,923	134,923
Pennsylvania (Philadelphia)	137,227	135,986	134,084	130,026	131,274	90,802	90,802	80,154	84,280	85,930
Internal Medicine										
California (Los Angeles, Orange)	14,237	10,343	10,343	10,343	10,343	8,274	8,274	8,274	8,274	8,274
Connecticut	34,700	34,700	34,700	34,700	34,700	34,700	34,700	34,700	34,700	34,700
Florida (Miami-Dade)	54,710	46,372	46,372	46,372	46,372	47,707	47,707	47,707	47,707	47,707
Illinois (Cook, Madison, St. Clair)	40,726	40,726	40,865	40,865	40,865	40,865	40,865	40,865	40,865	40,865
New Jersey	20,200	20,200	18,900	18,900	18,900	18,900	18,900	15,900	15,900	15,900
New York (Nassau, Suffolk)	30,692	30,692	32,288	32,611	32,288	35,883	33,852	33,852	33,852	33,852
Pennsylvania (Philadelphia)	37,380	37,190	37,353	36,469	37,360	26,037	26,037	23,335	24,433	24,873

Notes:

1. Sources: Annual Rate Survey (October) issues of the Medical Liability Monitor , 2008–2017. The numbers in this table are manual premiums reported by a liability insurer selected on the basis of data availability in every year. Premiums reported for Connecticut pertain to $1 million/$4 million limits, and Pennsylvania premiums include Patient Compensation Fund surcharges.

2. Counties to which the premiums refer are in parentheses. Counties in California (CA), Illinois (IL) and Pennsylvania (PA) changed slightly over time. However, CA counties always include Los Angeles, IL counties always include Cook and PA counties always include Philadelphia.

Source: Table 2 from pg. 5, AMA report https://www.ama-assn.org/sites/ama-assn.org/files/corp/media-browser/public/government/advocacy/policy-research-perspective-liability-insurance-premiums.pdf—Guardado, AMA, 2018).

There is also the added expense of the loss of the health care professional's productivity, as they are often suspended from practicing medicine or psychiatry until civil or criminal cases are resolved (Mello et al., 2010). Similarly, as in the case of divorce, there is the option for a malpractice lawsuit to go to mediation in advance of litigation, possibly resolving the issue faster, compensating the patient faster, and expediting any reform that is needed in a physician or psychiatrist's practice or in hospitals. In mediation, a neutral party hears both sides and helps the two parties, the plaintiff and respondent, to come to a compromised settlement without going to a jury trial. If mediation fails, it then goes to the more expensive option of a civil trial.

So far, we have been discussing cases that have been more about malfeasance and not technically criminal. There is one area within the OB/GYN, fertility specialization, that has clearly been demonstrated as being currently criminal. When a doctor performing *in vitro* fertilization (IVF) misrepresents the viability of the sperm, ovum, or embryo used in the procedure, this is not only unethical, it can also result in a criminal complaint. If that isn't bad enough, there have been incidents where the doctor has used their own sperm without their patients' knowledge, as in our next case, which is particularly reprehensible in the public eye.

Law in the Real World: Donald Cline, Baby Maker

(Source: Zhang, 2019)

In the 1970s, the IVF procedure was still relatively new. It was first used on a patient in 1977, resulting in the first baby born by IVF in 1978, a so-called "test tube baby" in the U.K. Since 1977, there have been more than 8 million babies born by IVF (Scutti, 2018). Basically, the procedure involves introducing sperm to ova in a laboratory and inserting any resulting embryo into a woman's uterus. Some of the cases that we have seen of multiple births (e.g., twins, triplets, etc.) are due to IVF, where the doctor implants more than one embryo in hopes that at least one will result in a successful pregnancy.

Fast forward to the current popularity of DNA testing with the National Geographic® genome project, Ancestry.com (ANCESTRYDNA®), and 23andMe®. In 2014, there were a number of people in Indiana that discovered through 23andMe® that they were related in an illogical way. Donald Cline, a fertility doctor, turned out to be the connecting relative, who had been secretly impregnating his patients with his own sperm during IVF procedures in the 1970s and 1980s. Though the number of children he sired is unknown, as DNA testing become more popular, more biological children of Cline were identified. By 2018, there were over 50 offspring. The parents in these cases thought that Cline was using sperm from a sperm bank.

At the time that IVF was developed, there were few, if any, laws that prohibited doctors from using their own sperm during the procedure. As a consequence of the Cline case, new laws were introduced and passed in Indiana to make it a criminal offense for doctors to use their own sperm without their patients' knowledge. At the very least, Cline acted unethically by misrepresenting where sperm came from for his IVF procedures.

What makes the Cline case particularly confusing is that it was not the first time a doctor had been discovered to have fathered children illegally within their fertility practices. In an earlier case, *United States v. Jacobson*, court documents indicate that Dr. Cecil Jacobson, though promising to impregnate women with anonymous donor sperm, instead used his own sperm. It would seem that there has historically been no uniformity in state laws and that may explain why the practice of using one's own sperm in IVF procedures only became prohibited recently.

Discussion Questions

1. Why would doctors using their own sperm in IVF procedures be criminally charged?
2. What harm can you see happening if DNA testing had not discovered people being closely related to one another unbeknownst to them, particularly in a smaller community?
3. Would it be ethical for a doctor to use his own sperm in IVF, if his patient was aware of it? What legal issues might there be in doing so?

MEDICAL EXPERIMENTATION

There are a lot of ethical codes that have to be followed in any research, especially in experiments using human subjects. There are even ethical codes for treatment of animals in research. An extra layer of protection and protocol is needed and followed for research participants who fall in the category of a "special population." These include prisoners, children, pregnant women, and institutionalized people, including those in medical or psychiatric hospitals. The most common criminal charges to happen as a result of unethical research practices are when no consent was given by research subjects or there is failure to report obvious risks in participating in a research project.

Historically, medical and psychological research has been far from ethical. If you have taken an introductory psychology class or a class in social science research methods, you may recall horror stories of the Milgram experiment and the Stanford Prison experiment. Both of those projects have become the models for what not to do in research that can potentially cause long-term harm to the research participants, and more so the potential of physical *and* psychological damage that can occur in medical research. Yet currently, the criminal justice system is slow to respond to cases of criminal medical experimentation. Or, as Richardson (2009, p. 89) noted, "Medical researchers engaged in human experimentation commit criminal acts seemingly without consequence."

Under federal law, colleges and universities, including your own, are required to have an *Institutional Review Board (IRB)* that has oversight with research projects. This is to make sure that they follow the principles of the *Belmont Report*, published in 1978. Without research oversight, colleges and universities expose themselves to the risks of lawsuits. It is an additional reason why research subjects are asked to sign an *informed consent* form, which spells out the purposes of a study and possible risks.

One of the worst cases of unethical medical experiments on human subjects happened in the 1930s with the Tuskegee syphilis study, which lasted 40 years. The research subjects included black men, some of whom had the socially transmitted disease and others didn't. The study took place in an era before the

Belmont Report and there was no informed consent of the research subjects (Davis et al., 2012; Center for Disease Control).

By the 1940s, while the study was still being conducted, penicillin proved to be effective in the treatment of syphilis. However, the infected Tuskegee study participants were not being offered treatment. Unfortunately, though this study was highly immoral and unethical, there were no laws or Belmont Report to prevent the researchers from withholding treatment from the infected. It wasn't until the 1970s, when the experiment that was supposed to only last 6 months came to light and was still ongoing, did public outrage put a stop to the research.

It is important to note that research ethics protocol is not universal. For those of us who do international research, we have to follow whatever types of regulations are standard in the countries we conduct research in, along with the Belmont Report requirements here in the U.S. There are international organizations that try to create some ethical conformity across the globe, including the International Conference on Harmonization (ICH) (Ekmekci, 2016). Turkey, for example, is rapidly becoming an attractive location for clinical trials in spite of political unrest in the last few years. But according to Ekmekci (2016), Turkey still has a long way to go in passing regulatory policy that will minimize risk to human subjects.

ADDICTION AND HEALTH CARE PROFESSIONALS

Discounting alcohol addiction, rates of prescription drug abuse in the health care workforce is alarming. Though actual numbers are unknown, as not all drug abuse by health care professionals is detectable, it is generally understood that doctors and nurses represent higher rates of addiction compared to other professions. This is largely due to easier access to prescription drugs. Similar to alcoholics who can still hold down jobs and family life, many drug abusing health care professionals are highly functioning addicts who can hide their addiction for a period of time without it being detected (Ready, 2019). The most commonly abused drugs by health care professionals are prescription opioids.

As health care professionals, particularly doctors, are fairly well-compensated financially in their careers, it may seem improbable that they would risk their jobs by stealing and/or using drugs. We should note that some Wall Street professionals have had their own share of addiction stories, including cocaine use in the 1980s and 1990s, and more recently Adderall abuse (Swab, 2014). Adderall is a drug used in the treatment of attention deficit hyperactivity disorder (ADHD). It has rapidly become the drug of choice on Wall Street. Adderall reportedly allows the user to have heightened concentration. For Wall Street professionals who do use prescription or street drugs, they are seeking to enhance job performance in sometimes 12+ hour work day professions.

Unlike Wall Street professionals seeking to stay awake and increase their concentration, health care professionals are more likely to self-medicate in order to cope with and escape from the demands of the job. There are some identifying characteristics of health care professionals who abuse drugs. These include histories of anxiety or depression, reported stress at home, sexual disorders, and personality difficulties resulting in neurosis (Bennett and O'Donovan, 2001; Brooke et al., 1993). There are telltale signs that indicate that a health care worker, or any worker for that matter, has a drug or alcohol problem (Recovery Worldwide, LLC., Addiction Center, 2019, retrieved from https://www.addictioncenter.com/addiction/medical-professionals/):

- Changing jobs frequently
- Preferring night shift work, with less supervision, more access to medication
- Falling asleep on the job
- Volunteering to administer narcotics to patients
- Anxiousness about working overtime or extra shifts
- Taking frequent bathroom breaks or unexplained absences from their work station
- Smelling of alcohol, excessive use of breath mints or mouthwash
- Extreme financial, relationship, or family stress
- Glassy eyes or small pupils
- Unusually friendly relationship with doctors who write prescriptions
- Incomplete charting or repeated errors in paperwork

There are some medical specializations that are at greater risk for drug abuse and addiction. Understandably, work in acute care hospitals can be more stressful than working in the clinic setting. The specializations that have been discovered to carry the greatest risks for worker burnout, addiction, and alcohol abuse include emergency medicine, psychiatry, anesthetics, and nurses in high stress nursing specialties, including intensive care (e.g., ICU, NICU) (Bennett and O'Donovan, 2001).

PRESCRIPTION DRUG ABUSES AND THEFT

There are a couple of ways that prescription drugs can be abused within the health care community. The first is when doctors or psychiatrists overprescribe, possibly receiving incentives such as luxury vacations or money, and "swag"[3] from pharmaceutical representatives. There are now laws preventing drug companies from excessively gifting physicians and pharmacists in order to entice them to prescribe and dispense their products. Though bribery by pharmaceutical

---

[3] "Swag," in this context, is slang for any free items that pharmaceutical or medical supply companies give to health care professionals in order to entice them to carry their products. Examples of swag that doctors are legally allowed to accept, based on the Physician Payments Sunshine Act (2010), are company-sponsored meals, drug samples, and educational gifts (e.g., anatomical models by law) worth less than $100 (USD). (Source: https://www.mdlinx.com/internal-medicine/article/3715).

companies is of concern, more worrisome is the drug addicted health care professional. A health care professional doesn't even have to be drug addicted yet to become a threat to themselves and to patients if they start using prescribed or street drugs.

Most of the prescription drug abuses we see involve *controlled substances*. These are drugs that hospitals and pharmacies can only distribute in limited supplies, primarily due to their perceived risks for addiction. There are five types of controlled substances regulated by the federal government in the U.S., under the Controlled Substance Act of 1970:

- *Schedule I*—Drugs or substances identified by the federal government as having no medical purpose and having high potential for addiction (e.g., heroin, cannabis[4], peyote)
- *Schedule II*—Drugs or substances identified by the federal government as having high potential for addiction or abuse. Some, but not all are available by prescription. (e.g., cocaine, methamphetamine, methadone[5], oxycodone, fentanyl, Adderall, Ritalin)
- *Schedule III*—Drugs or substances identified by the federal government as having low to moderate potential for physical and/or psychological dependence (e.g., ketamine, anabolic steroids, testosterone).
- *Schedule IV*—Drugs or substances identified by the federal government as having low potential for abuse or dependence (e.g., Xanax, Darvon, Valium, Ambien).
- *Schedule V*—Drugs or substances that are identified by the federal government as having lower potential of abuse or addiction than Schedule IV, containing limited quantities of narcotics (e.g., prescription cough suppressants, Lyrica, Parepectolin).

For a comprehensive list of controlled substances, visit the U.S. Department of Justice Drug Enforcement Administration page at https://www.deadiversion. usdoj.gov/schedules/orangebook/c_cs_alpha.pdf.

When we look at drug addicted doctors, pharmacists, and nurses, in a lot of cases, we may be looking at the intersection of medical and financial crimes. If you will recall from Chapter 4 on financial crimes, stealing drugs from a hospital or pharmacy by employees can be considered embezzlement. We can think of the intersectionality of medicine and financial greed, where physicians may be amply compensated for turning a blind eye to their patients' addictions, in some cases illegally supplying the drugs themselves.

---

[4] Currently cannabis, more commonly known as marijuana, is illegal at the federal level but is legal for recreational or medical use in some states in the U.S., including Alaska, California, Colorado, Illinois, Maine, Massachusetts, Michigan, Nevada, Oregon, Vermont, and Washington, along with the District of Columbia. Several other states have decriminalized marijuana for recreational use.

[5] Ironically, methadone treatment is used to treat heroin addiction. So essentially you are using a controlled substance to counteract a controlled substance.

Law in the Real World: The Death of Michael Jackson

(Sources: Richards, 2016; Memmott, 2011; Bitsoli, 2018, https://thecrimereport.org/
2018/05/02/opioid-deaths-whom-should-we-blame/*)*

Michael Jackson, the "King of Pop," and Prince Rogers Nelson, otherwise known as Prince and "The Artist Formerly Known as Prince," were arguably two of the most creative musicians spanning five decades between them. They had earned a combined 24 platinum and multi-platinum albums, representing billions in sales. Though both men died of drug overdoses, the circumstances around their deaths were different. Prince died from counterfeit Vicodin pills that contained fentanyl, a powerful opioid, that were sold on the black market. Jackson died from a prescription drug administered by a licensed physician.

Similarly, as in circumstances of patients who have experienced an accident that leaves residual pain and discomfort, Jackson suffered a couple of serious misfortunes that resulted in a dependency on prescription medications. The first of his injuries occurred in 1984 when his hair was set on fire during the filming of a Pepsi Co. commercial when pyrotechnics were set off, resulting in second and third degree burns to his scalp (Richards and Langthorne, 2016). The second of his mishaps occurred in 1999 when he injured his back during a concert (Richards and Langthorne, 2016). In addition to his injuries, Jackson had had extensive plastic surgery to alter his appearance. To treat his chronic pain, concert promoter AEG Live hired Dr. Conrad Murray, a cardiologist, to act as Jackson's personal physician for an upcoming concert tour. Dr. Murray was expected to receive a reported $150,000 (USD) per month for his services. Within weeks of Dr. Murray's employment, Jackson was dead.

In June 2009, Jackson was at his home in Los Angeles, preparing to go on tour. The tour never took place. Instead, on June 25 he died of a cardiac arrest under suspicious circumstances. At 50 years old, it isn't unheard of for a man of Jackson's age to have cardiac problems, though the average age for a first heart attack in males is 65 (*Harvard Men's Health Watch*, 2009). Jackson came into the emergency room by ambulance after an odd call from Dr. Murray to 911, with reports that Jackson was unconscious and not breathing. One of the paramedics who attended to him stated that Jackson looked pale and emaciated, thinking at first that Jackson might be a hospice patient.

It was the events leading up to his death that caught the attention of the paramedics and doctors who attempted to revive him at the UCLA Medical Center. Ultimately, the circumstances around his death caught the attention of law enforcement.

After a criminal investigation, Dr. Murray admitted to giving Jackson small doses of propofol intravenously (IV) at night, allegedly to treat his insomnia. It was an unheard-of treatment for the disorder, much less administered in a home setting. Dr. Murray had virtually no medical equipment on hand to treat an overdose in Jackson's rented home, even though it is a common side effect of propofol (Memmott, 2011). The State of California subsequently charged Dr. Murray with involuntary manslaughter when it was determined in the autopsy that he had administered a massive overdose of the drug, resulting in Jackson's death. During the trial, evidence pointed to Dr. Murray ordering massive quantities of the drug, having it delivered to an apartment he shared with his girlfriend (Memmott, 2011).

In 2011, Dr. Murray was found guilty of the charges of involuntary manslaughter and received the maximum sentence of four years in prison. The judge in the case, Superior Court Judge Michael Pastor stated during sentencing that Dr. Murray's defense was to blame the victim, Jackson, for the overdose (Memmott, 2011), which was shameful and, based on his conviction, not a very effective defense. In Judge Pastor's estimation, Dr. Murray showed no remorse. Dr. Murray completed only half of his sentence before being released from prison. In a civil lawsuit decision, the company that hired Dr. Murray, AEG Live LLC, was not found to be liable in Jackson's death. Jackson's father, Joe Jackson, dropped a wrongful death lawsuit against Dr. Murray after his criminal conviction.

Never fully recovering his reputation or finances from the trial and subsequent incarceration, Dr. Murray published a book in 2016, titled *This Is It!: The Secret Lives of Dr. Conrad Murray and Michael Jackson*, using a self-publishing company (BookBaby). As Dr. Murray has a history of financial problems, including failure to pay child support and difficulty paying back school loans, we might speculate that the motive behind publishing a "tell-all" book was an attempt to recover financially, since his medical career was essentially ruined.

The outcome in the aftermath of Prince's death was decidedly different than in Jackson's case. Sadly, investigators in Prince's case were unable to identify the person or persons who supplied him with the counterfeit pain medication that resulted in his death, and no criminal charges were ever brought against anyone who might be responsible for his death at age 57 in 2018 (Flanagan, 2018).

Discussion Questions

1. Why might a celebrity have an easier time obtaining drugs for their addiction, as compared to the ordinary person?

2. How does a case of a doctor supplying drugs to an addict differ from a bartender serving an alcohol to a known alcoholic, from a standpoint of white collar crime?

3. This one will take a bit of research. How does the sentencing in Dr. Murray's involuntary manslaughter case, four years, compare to other involuntary manslaughter cases (e.g., vehicular manslaughter)?

It is extremely important to note that illicit drug use and abuse is increasingly being viewed as a public health problem. Where we have to emphasize the importance in discussing drug use and addiction within the context of white collar crime are the professional consequences of abuse. It can result in drug theft from clinics, hospitals, and pharmacies, plus malpractice.

THE OPIOID CRISIS

After the 1990s and the Internet revolution, more doctors were seeing patients who were self-diagnosing, some with unrealistic expectations for medical outcomes. Going online and conducting dubious research, patients increasingly were looking for 100 percent pain relief after surgery or accidents. This is a promise that is difficult to deliver on, as there are few drugs that can completely eliminate pain without being dangerously addictive or having a higher potential for overdose. Physicians, faced with more demanding patients, felt pressured to do their best to treat pain symptoms, even if it wasn't always in the best interest of the patient in the long run. This was largely due to the fear of lawsuits, particularly after the jump in the number of malpractice claims paying out over $500,000 each in the early 2000s (Belk, 2019).

The powerful pain reliever drug oxycodone, a semisynthetic opioid, was first available on the market in 1996. In 1998, when the *Federal Drug Administration (FDA)* certified the drug to be a "minimally addictive" pain reliever (Hansen and Netherland, 2016), it seemed like physicians had found a wonder drug that effectively killed pain and could appease demanding patients. It quickly became abundantly clear that the drug was highly addictive and there was high risk for both addiction and overdose. It also put physicians at risk of unwittingly or unethically (and illegally, in some cases) prescribing the opioid to drug-seeking patients. Addicts can be clever in their abilities to shop for doctors that are willing to prescribe opioids or will go to a number of different physicians. Emergency rooms see the same phenomenon.

According to the CDC, there were a record 48,000 deaths in the U.S. during 2017 attributed to opioid use, primarily with heroin and prescription drugs, including oxycodone (STAT, 2019). This is representative of an overall steady increase in overdose deaths since 2013 (CDC, 2019). Once the FDA's initial review of the drug's addiction properties were found to be vastly underestimated, physicians were instructed to cut back on the number of prescriptions they gave patients. Not all did so, and some doctors began prescribing or distributing oxycodone illegally.

Law in the Real World: "Dr. Johnny"

(Source: U.S. Drug Enforcement Administration, 2019)

Dr. Johnny Di Blasi, a physician with weight-loss clinics in Georgia, was arrested on Christmas Eve, 2018 by DEA agents at the Miami International Airport. Di Blasi was preparing to board a flight to Colombia. "Dr. Johnny," as he was known, was attempting to flee prosecution. There was a nine-count indictment against him for "Conspiracy to Unlawfully Dispense Controlled Substances (Oxycodone), Unlawful Dispensation of Controlled Substances (Schedules II and IV), and False Statements Related to Health Care Matters." (Department of Justice, U.S. Attorney's Office, South District of Georgia, 2019, retrieved from https://www.justice.gov/usao-sdga/pr/doctor-charged-prescribing-narcotics-non-patients-ordered-detained-until-trial).

Acknowledging that most doctors take the Hippocratic Oath seriously, Everett Ragan, the Counter Narcotics Team Director in Chatham-Savannah, Georgia, set this as an example as to why the DEA "'will seek all drug dealers no matter if they wear a white coat or what their day job or title is.'" (DEA, 2019, retrieved from https://www.dea.gov/press-releases/2019/06/13/doctor-sentenced-prison-prescribing-narcotics-non-patients).

Overprescribing drugs to patients is one thing. Prescribing to friends and families, or to people who are not even your patients, is another ethical thing all together. For a little over a year, "Dr. Johnny" was prescribing a number of drugs to non-patients, including for narcotics, opioids and amphetamines. He would write his prescriptions through his clinics, but people were traveling from at least 11 states that the DEA was aware of to collect these prescriptions from him. He also prescribed controlled substances, including opioids and amphetamines, to people he met in restaurants and bars. This was highly irregular and illegal, with no medical records and no formal evaluation conducted in a clinic setting. In court proceedings, "Dr. Johnny" was described as a common drug dealer, peddling prescriptions for non-medical use.

During the case, U.S. Attorney Bobby L. Christine stated that "a key component of the opioid crisis gripping our nation is the supply chain provided by unscrupulous profiteering medical professionals who violated the law while breaking their oath of to 'do no harm'." (Department of Justice, U.S. Attorney's Office, South District of Georgia, 2019, retrieved from https://www.justice.gov/usao-sdga/pr/doctor-charged-prescribing-narcotics-non-patients-ordered-detained-until-trial). The court decided that Di Blasi was indeed part of this problem. The case resulted in Di Blasi in pleading guilty to the one count of conspiracy to unlawfully dispense controlled substances, sentenced to 33 months in prison.

Discussion Questions

1. "Dr. Johnny" owned and operated weight-loss clinics. As amphetamines have been used (though questionably) for weight loss, what possible ethical use might there be for oxycodone, a pain reliever?
2. Weight-loss clinics and programs can be lucrative operations. What motive might "Dr. Johnny" have for risking the possible loss of his clinics and his professional reputation by handing out illegal prescriptions?
3. In what ways is "Dr. Johnny" different from or similar to a street corner drug dealer, considering he was writing prescriptions in bars and restaurants?

By the time physicians were warned to cut back on oxycodone prescriptions, it was too late. Too many patients were already addicted and when they could no longer obtain it legally through their doctors and pharmacy, some resorted to buying the drug on the black market. Legally, one 10 mg dose of oxycodone costs $1.25; illegally, the same dose costs between $5 and $10 on the street (Wheeler, 2019).

A much cheaper option to oxycodone obtained through drug dealers is heroin, with lower cost and easier access. There has been growing evidence within the past decade that the legal peddling of oxycodone has contributed substantially to a rising global public health, blamed on heroin. One way or another, the current opioid crisis is proving to be both costly and deadly. An estimated 68,000 overdose deaths per year in the U.S. are attributed to opioid use (Haworth, 2019). Many of these deaths are due to abuse of street drugs, including heroin, but a great number of them can also be traced back to prescription drug abuses.

Increasingly within the past decade, the FBI and Drug Enforcement Agency (DEA), have busted drug rings that include pharmacists and physicians. What became particularly suspicious was that over half of the oxycodone sold in the

U.S. was being bought by only 15 percent of pharmacies, leading to investigations of the biggest offenders (The Crime Report, 2019, https://thecrimereport.org/2019/08/13/15-of-pharmacies-handled-nearly-half-of-opioids/):

> In a federal database tracking every pain pill sold in the U.S. at the height of the opioid crisis, one Albany, Ky. [Kentucky] pharmacy, has come into sharp focus: Shearer Drug. [Between 2006 and 2012] Shearer Drug procured more opioid pills on a per capita basis per county than any other retail pharmacy in the U.S.... Shearer operated his pharmacy out of a building he shared with a doctor who plead guilty in federal court in March [2019] to illegally prescribing opioids.

As in the Kentucky case, federal and state agencies started seeing patterns of co-offending between pharmacists and doctors.

"BIG PHARMA"

Pharmaceutical companies, or as they are commonly referred to collectively, *"Big Pharma,"* are argued to be among the worst corporate criminal offenders. Some of these opinions are based on the number of civil lawsuits in recent decades brought against pharmaceutical companies, with sizeable judgements awarded to plaintiffs.

Among the types of common offences that pharmaceutical companies commit is the illegal marketing of drugs for uses that they were not intended for, questionable research, hiding possible harmful side effects, and *price hiking* (Gøtzsche, 2013). Yet as we saw in Chapter 7, pharmaceutical companies are more likely to be sued in civil court than having individuals responsible for fraud or financial crime prosecuted in criminal court.

As "Big Pharma" has increasingly been in the news in recent years, we will present two different cases, one of which involves unethical marketing practices by Purdue Pharma that resulted in civil damages. The second case involves criminal charges brought against pharmaceutical executive Martin Shkreli for additional financial crimes to his blatant price hiking of one effective treatment for HIV/AIDS that he has yet to be prosecuted for.

Law in the Real World: Purdue Pharma

(Source: Van Zee, 2009; Spector and DiNapoli, 2019; Joseph, 2019)

One of the most serious concerns about any drug, especially with controlled substances, is that there are stringent requirements on the dispensing of addictive drugs by pharmacies. Regulation fails when the Food and Drug Administration (FDA) offers little oversight on the marketing of controlled substances (Van Zee, 2009). In recent years, some pharmaceutical companies have taken advantage of seemingly lax regulation and enforcement.

Purdue Pharma, makers of oxycodone under the commercial name OxyContin, is currently in legal hot water. With more than 70 million doses of the drug sold by the company in Massachusetts alone since 2007, the Sackler family, owners of Purdue Pharma, have been charged with aggressive marketing tactics in the distribution of OxyContin. Dr. Art Van Zee (2009) identified early on that the promotion of the drug was posing a serious public health risk. Purdue Pharma had downplayed the seriousness of the addictive properties of the drug in their marketing campaign, along with the risk for drug overdoses, even after the concerns came to light.

Among their marketing tactics, between 1996 and 2001, Purdue Pharma recruited physicians and nurses to essentially be trained as unofficial spokespeople for the company (Van Zee, 2009). They did so by conducting all-expenses paid conferences for doctors and nurses that were held at resorts in the vacation and sunshine meccas of Florida, Arizona, and California (Van Zee, 2009). By recruiting physicians to act as spokespeople, they were also creating a vast network of doctors who may influence one another to prescribe the drug to their patients.

Once the drug was found to be highly addictive and contributing to some patients turning to street drugs, including heroin, when they could no longer obtain legitimate prescriptions, the Sackler family down played their role in the crisis: "'We have to hammer the abusers in every possible way.... They are the culprits and the problem. They are reckless criminals." (Joseph, 2019, retrieved from https://www.statnews.com/2019/01/15/massachusetts-purdue-lawsuit-new-details/).

For their part in contributing to the opioid crisis, Purdue Pharma is facing liability in over 2,000 lawsuits filed against them to date. Purdue Pharma is not the only alleged offender in the opioid crisis. But what makes them unique is that it is a privately owned company. Unlike Endo International and Insys Therapeutics Inc., two publicly traded pharmaceutical companies that are facing similar lawsuits, the members of the Sackler family who own Purdue Pharma are also personally under the specter of civil lawsuits. The Sackler family is also being accused by the New York Attorney General's Office of hiding up to $1 billion of their financial assets taken from the company in order to keep a portion of their wealth away from possible liability in additional civil or criminal cases (Gonzales, 2019).

In March 2019, Purdue Pharma began to explore the option of filing for *Chapter 11 bankruptcy* protection. The family predicts that the fallout of the oxycodone scandal will result in the demise of the company altogether.

Discussion Questions

1. How might the FDA tighten regulation of pharmaceutical company marketing practices?
2. How successful might a public health campaign be, aimed at educating physicians on the dangers of aggressive marketing?
3. Is it even possible to enforce restrictive regulation on marketing for a multi-billion-dollar industry like pharmaceuticals, in a free-market economy?

FAULTY MEDICAL DEVICES

We have already discussed when medical procedures fail due to negligence. What we also need to discuss is when medical devices (e.g., pacemakers, artificial joints) fail. In failure, they may result in greatly harming the patient and even death. Of course, these devices can be absolutely sound with no defects and still fail due to the incompetency of surgeons. There are a number of regulations that help maintain the integrity of medical devices. In this section, we are going to focus on the liability of manufacturers of the defective devices, not on the failure of doctors to use them properly when treating patients.

The FDA defines the following as medical devices (FDA, 2019):

- Can range from a tongue depressor and bedpans to complex programmable equipment (e.g., pacemakers)
- General purpose lab equipment and test kits
- Electronic radiation emitting equipment (e.g., x-ray, ultrasound)
- Any device used in diagnosis or in the cure, prevention of disease
- Any device intended to affect or replace any function/structure of the body (e.g., total hip replacement joint)

There are several points where a medical device can fail or be badly manufactured. The potential for a medical device failure can originate at the factory or be caused by damage in transit, in the operating room, or doctor's office. Where the failure is identified to have occurred will make a difference as to whether a company or doctor is found to be at fault.

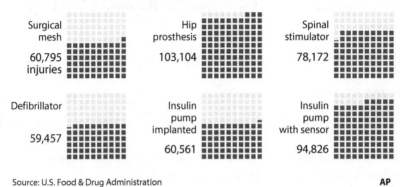

Many Device Injury Reports Stem from a Few Devices

▪ = 10,000 injury reports between 2008–2017

Surgical mesh
60,795 injuries

Hip prosthesis
103,104

Spinal stimulator
78,172

Defibrillator
59,457

Insulin pump implanted
60,561

Insulin pump with sensor
94,826

Source: U.S. Food & Drug Administration

AP

EXHIBIT 8.1 ‖ **Device injuries 2008-2017** *Source:* U.S. FDA, from https://www.statnews.com/2018/11/25/medical-devices-pain-other-conditions-more-than-80000-deaths-since-2008/.

As in the case of your car, when something is found to be defective due to faulty engineering, medical devices can be recalled. In this case, it is generally determined that it was unforeseen or honest human error, in which case the company is not held criminally negligent. But occasionally there is more than human error involved, where it is clear that the intent is to purposely ignore the harm a device might cause or flagrantly break the law.

In *United States v. ACell, Inc.* (2019), a maker of the contaminated medical dressing product, MicroMatrix, pleaded guilty to one misdemeanor count of failure and refusal to report the removal of the product to the FDA, which is required by law (U.S. Department of Justice, 2019). At least the company recalled the product when found to be contaminated, but it was a costly mistake for them to ignore reporting the recall to the FDA, as it resulted in having to pay a fine of $3 million (U.S. Department of Justice, 2019). ACell, Inc. was required to pay an additional $12 million in the civil judgement (U.S. Department of Justice, 2019), for a total of $15 million. A costly mistake, indeed.

MEDICARE AND MEDICAID FRAUD

Once upon a time, medical care, though not cheap, was still within the means of the average American to afford without going into crushing debt. In the 1950s and early 60s, a trip to a pediatrician generally cost under $10 and could be easily paid out of pocket by the average person, except for lower income families. A hospital birth without complications cost around $50 per birth to the patient in the early 1950s—this at a time when new mothers were kept in the hospital up to a week after a normal delivery. Today, a birth without complications can cost patients on average out of pocket cost of $3,500, and mothers and babies without complications are sometimes sent home within 24 hours after birth.

By the mid-1960s, as insurance and pharmaceutical companies became more prevalent with powerful lobbyists in Washington, D.C., health insurance and health care costs started to be out of reach for lower income families and for senior citizens on fixed incomes. As part of several laws that came into effect during the 1960s when health care costs became too much for these populations, President Lyndon Johnson signed the Medicare Law (1965) as part of the Social Security Act, in order to provide health insurance to senior citizens who are 65 years or older. Medicaid, passed at the same time as the Medicare Law, is a similar program that provides government paid health care to low income people who are not yet eligible for Medicare.

Once insurance companies and insurance programs became lucrative operations, it also quickly became an opportunity for disreputable doctors and clinics to play the system. Medicare and Medicaid, as government programs, became particularly vulnerable. This meant that doctors and clinics could conceivably be charging for services that were never given, or submit claims for patients that don't exist or are deceased, essentially defrauding the U.S. government. Unfortunately, these abuses can amount to billions in losses to the government, which indirectly come out of the pockets of taxpayers and require exhaustive resources to combat.

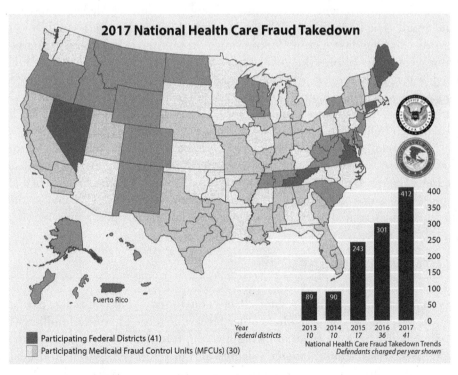

EXHIBIT 8.2 ‖ **Health Care Fraud** *Source:* https://oig.hhs.gov/newsroom/media-materials/2017/2017-
‖ takedown.asp.

229

In one of the most flagrant Medicare schemes in Miami, Florida, a doctor defrauded the federal government out of $1.3 billion. Philip Esformes, owner of 30 nursing and assisted-living facilities, along with hospital administrator Odette Barcha and physician assistant Arnaldo Carmouze, were indicted for running a scheme of billing Medicare and Medicaid for unnecessary services (Teichert, 2016). During the trial, (*United States v. Esformes et al.*, 2019), there was evidence that Esformes and his co-conspirators were not only improperly billing Medicare and Medicaid, they were also bribing visiting inspectors and regulators with *kickbacks* (U.S. Department of Justice, 2019).

Assistant Attorney General Benczkowski stated during the trial that this was "one of the largest health care fraud schemes in U.S. history," while Special Agent in Charge Denise Stemen of the F.B.I. commented that "Philip Esformes is a man driven by almost unbounded greed." (U.S. Department of Justice, 2019, retrieved from https://www.justice.gov/opa/pr/south-florida-health-care-facility-owner-convicted-role-largest-health-care-fraud-scheme-ever). Esformes was ultimately convicted of his crimes in 2019. Carmouze pleaded guilty to conspiracy to commit health care fraud for his part in the scheme and sentenced to 6.5 years in federal prison; Barcha pleaded guilty to one count of conspiring to violate an anti-kickback statue, sentenced to 15 months in federal prison followed by three years of supervised release and ordered to pay $704,516 in restitution to the U.S. government (U.S. Department of Justice, 2019). Esformes is currently awaiting sentencing.

The U.S. government has one powerful tool in combating Medicare and Medicaid fraud. The Federal False Claims Act (or "Lincoln Law"), passed by Congress in 1863, made it a crime to knowingly present the government with a false claim, essentially billing the government for services that were never fulfilled. The law originally was intended to keep the government from fraud from military contractors and being charged for military equipment or services that didn't exist. With increases in insurance fraud, the focus of enforcing the False Claims Act has shifted from military to health care since the 1990s (Helmer, 2013).

If you recall, earlier in this book we have talked about the role of the whistleblower. In the case of defrauding the government, the vast majority of cases using the False Claims Act are due to filings by whistleblowers (Hesch, 2012). The False Claims Act has one of the strongest whistleblower protections in U.S. law, so there are fewer concerns about retaliation against the whistleblower.

MENTAL HEALTH ABUSES

Trust in your physician is one thing. Being able to trust your counselor, psychiatrist, or psychologist is on a whole other level. For those of you unfamiliar with the distinctions between types of mental health professionals, a counselor is more likely to have a terminal master's degree and have a license in mental health counseling. A licensed psychologist has a doctorate degree (e.g., Ph.D.). Neither counselor nor psychologist can prescribe drugs for their patients. A licensed psychiatrist has completed medical school and is allowed to prescribe drugs, meaning that the unscrupulous psychiatrist may be subject to the same temptations to overprescribe and abuse prescription privileges. There is also the question of malpractice, in the event that the therapist neglects the mental well-being of the patient they are responsible for treating.

In theory, therapy only works if there is a good working, trusting relationship between the therapist and the patient. There are two common ethical issues surrounding therapy: (1) sexual relations between therapist and patient and (2) confidentiality in the so-called double loyalty of the therapist (Zaki, 2014). "Double loyalty" refers to the responsibilities that the therapist has to both the patient and to the employer. In this day and age of health management organizations (HMOs), the therapist may be limited to the amount of therapy they can provide, depending on the health insurance company the patient is insured with.

There is also the somewhat dubious and unethical practice of urging patients to continue therapy even after they have recovered from their psychological issues, if they have more allowed hours of treatment from their insurance company. As it is somewhat subjective and different from case to case, it is impossible to measure how much of this type, if any, of insurance abuse occurs. As we note in Medicare/Medicaid fraud, this is more likely to be the type of dishonestly that occurs in dishonest therapists, not in the larger population of mental health care professionals who follow both ethical and legal protocols.

The therapists themselves are subject to considerable emotional stress within their professions. It unknown how much professional burnout in the mental health care professions can contribute to abuses, but burnout certainly explains cases of self-medication with alcohol, prescription, or non-prescription, illicit drugs of any health care professional.

Though it is difficult to do in this day and age of licensing, certificates, and electronic background checks, every once in a while, a person attempts to impersonate a psychologist, hanging out a sign and seeing patients. Of course, any psychologist who is being paid directly by insurance, including Medicare and Medicaid, will have been carefully vetted to make sure that they are legitimate. However, there are some psychologists in private practice whose patients pay directly out of pocket for their treatment. This is largely due to some insurance companies offering only minimal coverage for mental health care. The vast majority of these psychologists possess the necessary credentials, some do not, and unless something goes wrong, they might never be detected as frauds.

SUMMARY

As we noted early in this chapter, there are few types of white collar crime that are as worrisome as crimes connected to health care. Just like financial crime on Wall

Street chips away at investors' confidence, medical crimes undermine patients' faith in their health care providers.

There are several ways that health care professionals can be negligent or criminal, many of which we introduced in this chapter. The list here is not exhaustive, but the cases are among the more common ways that doctors and pharmaceutical companies can fail their patients. Some of these failings include medical devices that are known to be faulty or defective. In this case, it could be the doctor or the manufacturer that is held criminally liable or held accountable in civil court.

By far the most common and expensive offense is fraudulent billing. Since the Medicare and Medicaid bill was enacted in the 1960s, there have been numerous cases amounting to billions and billions of fraudulent claims filed with the government. These include billing for services that were never done on patients.

There are a few options when health care workers misbehave. In some cases, being fired from their jobs is the least of their worries. In the case of criminal neglect or fraud, they could be charged with a criminal offense. More often, as in the case of corporate crime, the offense will be handled as a civil matter with a malpractice lawsuit. This is why malpractice insurance is so expensive, though there are greater efforts by courts to toss out frivolous lawsuits.

No matter how a medical crime is handled, careers and reputations can be ruined, perhaps more so than in the case of corporate crime. The public wants to have faith in their health care professionals and when that is shaken, it is far more difficult to redeem themselves, as we saw in the case of Michael Jackson and Dr. Murray. But as we said early on in this chapter, health care is big business, and beyond patient care, the importance placed on profit margin ("the bottom line") cannot be ignored in understanding why medical crimes occur.

Case Study • "Pharma Bro"

Background

For the past decade, there has been public outcry against the rising costs of prescription drugs. There are a number of cases we could point to, including the recent controversies over the cost of EpiPens,® the lifesaving injectable drug for patients who are experiencing a sudden allergic reaction, as in the example of someone who is allergic to bee stings. The controversy can lie in what drug company owns the patent on a drug, so as to elbow out the competition when they cannot produce the same drug without paying royalties to the manufacturer holding the patent. This is why generic drugs are far less expensive, even though the active ingredients in them are generally the same. Once a patent expires, then any company can make the same drug at the greatly reduced cost of the generic to the consumer.

Perhaps one of the most offensive crimes in the pharmaceutical sector having to do with prescription drug prices is the case of Martin Shkreli, nicknamed "Pharma Bro" (Chapelle, 2019). Shkreli was the CEO of Turing Pharmaceuticals, a publicly traded company based out of Switzerland. In 2015, Shkreli raised the price of Daraprim, a drug used in the treatment of HIV, (Chappelle, 2019). Raising the price from $13.50 per pill to $750 each, there was the potential of hundreds of thousands of dollars in costs for this one single drug alone to patients who were dependent on it to help prevent the disease to progress to full blown AIDS.

Ultimately, it was not the *price gouging* that landed Shkreli in prison. Along with a New York attorney, Evan Greebel, Shkreli was accused of conspiring to steal millions from Retrophin, another pharmaceutical company that Shkreli had been associated with (U.S. Attorney's Office, Eastern District of New York, 2017).

Defining the Crime(s)

There were a number of possible crimes that Shkreli could have been charged with. The obvious one is price gouging. Price gouging, simply put, is when a company raises the price of a commodity, in this case prescription drugs, to a price much higher than what the market would warrant.

We should note that most HIV/AIDS patients take a number of drugs to help keep the disease at bay. Once a diagnosis that meant a death sentence in the 1980s, HIV/AIDS symptoms can be effectively treated today, with better drug "cocktails" discovered each year. Shkreli's cavalier and unethical price hiking can easily be described as price gouging, where individuals or companies take advantage of crisis situations (in this case, an HIV/AIDS diagnosis) to unethically raise the price astronomically on essential drug treatments. This is similar to the public outrage against the drug company Mylan when they raised the price of EpiPens,® used by people with certain allergies, who carry them in case they start going into anaphylactic shock, by six-fold.

As an example, if there is a sudden demand for bottled water due to an impending hurricane and retailers hike the price per bottle from $1.50 to $3, it can certainly be argued that the principles of supply and demand economics applies here. We saw this with disinfectant products during COVID-19 pandemic. However, whether it makes sense from an economic standpoint or not, most people (and sometimes regulatory agencies) can agree that this is unethical price gouging. Outrageously, Shkreli raised the price of Daraprim dosage by an unthinkable 5,000 percent (Chappelle, 2019).

The other crimes that Shkreli was accused of and convicted on were financial crimes that were unrelated to his alleged price gouging on HIV/AIDS medications. In fact, they were not medical crimes at all. At the time of his arrest, Shkreli was accused of running a Ponzi-like scheme, where he defrauded investors (Smythe and Geiger, 2015).

Theories to Explain the Crime

Though we have dispelled theories of individual greed in favor of collective greed, there are times when we can depart from the criticisms of blaming crime on one individual's lack of self- control. Greed itself has some basis in biology, in response to self-preservation.

Greed is a term that is somewhat challenging to define. Within economic theories, greed is suggested to be the "invisible hand" that drives markets, as first proposed by Adam Smith (Zhou, 2013). To some extent, theories on greed can be paired with rational choice theory within criminology, assuming that individuals will weigh the pros and cons of committing the crime. In Shkreli's case, it is difficult to believe that he was unaware of the consequences of his actions. But weighing them against the financial rewards he would reap, both with the outrageous drug pricing and the financial malfeasance, greed appears to have won out.

We could also make the argument that the pharmaceutical industry is greedy. The pharmaceutical manufacturing business is immense, not only in the United States, but in other countries as well, including India (Jacobs, 2016). We consider that when medication is costly to patients, it may result in their cutting back on dosage, to the detriment of their health. Jacobs (2016) cautions that as a result of patients taking as little as 50 percent of their prescribed dosages, as many as some 125,000 preventable deaths occur, as well as 10 percent increase in hospitalizations.

Social and Media Responses

Prior to his arrest for financial crimes, Shkreli did a round of television and video interviews, including on *NPR*, defending the price hikes of Darapin, claiming that half of the drugs that Turin dispenses is given away for free, including to Medicaid patients (Seper, 2015). One of his arguments was that Darapin, though charged to patients' insurance companies at $750 per pill, was only needed by approximately 2,000 patients (Seper, 2015). He also placed some of the blame on the fact that, according to him, health care costs are a political issue (Seper, 2015).

The public, at least in the United States, has been grumbling for years about the rising cost of medical care in general, more so the cost of prescription drugs. Though the Bureau of Labor Statistics reports a steady drop in prices (Bartash, 2019), if the platforms on which some 2020 presidential candidates were running on are to be believed, they are not falling fast enough. Overall, Shkreli's arguments fell on all but deaf ears.

Described as "the most hated men in America," once the public got wind of the dramatic increases in the HIV/AIDS medication manufactured by

Shkreli's company, there was immediate widespread outrage. Overnight, Shkreli became the face and poster child for the perceived greed of pharmaceutical companies.

Criminal Justice and Policy Responses

Though Shkreli earned his greatest notoriety from raising the price on Daraprim, he was ultimately arrested and charged with a number of counts of fraud, stemming from cheating investors, resulting in $10.5 million in a securities scheme and financial irregularities during his time running Retrophin, a biopharmaceutical company. He was found guilty of those charges and is currently serving a 7-year sentence in federal custody.

Shkreli's co-conspirator, Greebel, who served as legal counsel at Retrophin, was convicted on two counts of conspiracy to commit securities fraud and conspiracy to commit wire fraud (Department of Justice, 2017). In announcing the verdict in the case, then Acting United States Attorney Bridget M. Rohde stated,

> "By helping Retrophin CEO Martin Shkreli steal millions of dollars and cover up Shkreli's fraud, the defendant Evan Greebel betrayed the trust placed in him by Retrophin's board of directors to represent the company's best interests...." (Department of Justice, 2017, retrieved from https://www.justice.gov/usao-edny/pr/new-york-attorney-convicted-securities-fraud-and-wire-fraud-conspiracies).

As offensive as the price gouging at Turin Pharmaceuticals was, in the end, the Department of Justice was far more interested in convicting Shkreli and his associate, Greebel, on the financial fraud associated with the Retrophin drug company. Whereas Shkreli received a 7-year sentence, Greebel was given the far more modest sentence of 18 months in prison (Morris, 2018). Neither Shkreli nor Greebel have been successful yet in appeals to overturn or reduce their sentences. Greebel has lost his law license and is currently serving the remainder of his sentence in a halfway house (Newsham, 2019). For both, it is a long road to redemption in any industry, much less in pharmaceuticals.

Unanswered Questions and Unresolved Issues Related to the Case

In the Shkreli case, he was charged and convicted only on financial crimes, which begs the question of why he had not been charged for price hiking or price gouging. It is very possible that prosecutors led with the more serious charges, which is not entirely uncommon. Much has to do with just how strong a case can be built for any or all charges.

One of the biggest questions coming out of this case is whether Shkreli and Turing Pharmaceuticals are exceptions in charging unusually high prices for prescription drugs in the United States or elsewhere in the world. It has also brought up a moral dilemma. Drug companies, as primarily publicly traded corporations, have an obligation to their investors to make every effort to offer a return on their stock investments. However, at what cost to the consumer? With rising drug costs, there have been several discussions in political circles, including Congress, on where the solutions lie. As yet, no clear answers or solutions have been found, at least within countries that run on a market economy without socialized medicine.

Sources

Chappell, B. (2019) "Pharma Bro" Martin Shkreli loses appeal, will stay in prison. *NPR.* July 18. Retrieved from https://www.npr.org/2019/07/18/743130735/pharma-bro-martin-shkreli-loses-appeal-will-stay-in-prison.

Jacob, H. E. (2016) Pharmaceutical greed and its consequences. *Connecticut Medicine.* May. Vol. 80, No. 5: 315-316.

Jin, H. and X. Y. Zhou. (2013) Greed, leverage, and potential losses: A prospect theory perpective. *Mathematical Finance.* Jan. Vol. 23, No. 1: 122-142.

Morris, D. Z. (2018) Martin Shkreli's lawyer sentenced to 18 months in prison. *Fortune.* Aug 18. Retrieved from https://fortune.com/2018/08/18/martin-shkreli-lawyer-sentenced-prison/.

Newsham, J. (2019) Shkreli lawyer Evan Greebel has conviction upheld by Second Circuit. *New York Law Journal,* LAW.COM. Oct. 30. Retrieved from https://www.law.com/newyorklawjournal/2019/10/30/shkreli-lawyer-evan-greebel-has-conviction-upheld-by-second-circuit/?slreturn=20200002180413.

Seper, C. (2015) Martin Shkreli: Not sorry. Video interview, NPR. Sept. 25. Retrieved from https://medcitynews.com/2015/09/martin-shkreli-not-sorry/?rf=1.

Smythe, C. and K. Geiger. (2015) Shkreli, drug price gouger, denies fraud and posts bail. Bloomberg. Dec 17. Retrieved from https://www.bloomberg.com/features/2015-martin-shkreli-securities-fraud/.

U.S. Department of Justice. (2017) New York attorney convicted of securities fraud and wire fraud conspiracies. U.S. Attorney's Office, Eastern District of New York. Dec 27. Retrieved from https://www.justice.gov/usao-edny/pr/new-york-attorney-convicted-securities-fraud-and-wire-fraud-conspiracies.

GLOSSARY

Administrative court   The civil court that specializes in administrative matters, as in the case of malfeasance with public hospital administration.

Federal Drug Administration (FDA)   The U.S. agency that is charged with the responsibility of regulating prescription distribution and safety, as well as the safety of medical devices.

Belmont Report   A 1970s report written by the National Commission for the Protection of Human Subjects of Biomedical and Behavioral Research that provides ethical guidelines in conducting research on human subjects.

"Big Pharma"   The nickname for the pharmaceutical industry.

Chapter 11 bankruptcy   A bankruptcy option for corporations or partnerships that are in financial trouble, giving them time to reorganize and work with creditors so as to assure that their companies can survive.

Controlled substances   A list of drugs and substances that the U.S. government identifies as either having no medical use and/or having some level of risk for addiction. Doctors are only allowed to prescribe a limited number of doses to patients of prescription drugs identified as controlled substances. Patients are required to show ID in order to purchase these drugs.

Hippocratic Oath   Written by Hippocrates, who was a medical practitioner in the 4th century B.C.E. Some physicians still take a modified version of this oath when they graduate from medical school, essentially promising to put their patients first and to practice medicine ethically.

Informed consent   A form that research subjects sign that spells out the purposes of the study, possible risks, if any, confidentiality, and the participant's rights.

Institutional Review Board (IRB)   A committee charged with making sure that any research conducted at their institution is following the principles in the Belmont Report.

Kickbacks   A bribe or payment paid, usually to someone who is a co-conspirator in a criminal scheme. Example: Paying regulators a bribe to turn a blind eye to malfeasance or crime.

Malpractice   Any type of misconduct, neglect, or harm committed by a health care provider that results in harm or death to a patient.

Medicaid   U.S. health care program that provides government assistance to lower income individuals or families. Was part of health care reform in the 1960s.

Medicare   U.S. health care program that provides government assistance to senior citizens, age 65 and older.

Price gouging   When a seller raises the prices of products or services higher than is considered to be fair or ethical.

Price hiking   An increase in prices of products or services, usually measured by a percentage. See *price gouging*.

Tort law   Civil law that is used to measure the degree to which an individual has been harmed or injured and the monetary reward that is considered fair as compensation.

REFERENCES AND SUGGESTED READINGS

Amaral-Garcia, S. (2019) Medical malpractice appeals in a civil law system. Do administrative and civil courts award noneconomic damages differently? *Law and Society Review*. June, Vol. 23, Issue 2: 386-419.

Bartash, J. (2019) Prescription drug prices aren't rising—they're falling for the first time in 47 years. Market Watch. March 12. Retrieved from https://www.marketwatch.com/story/prescription-drug-prices-arent-rising-theyre-falling-for-the-first-time-in-47-years-2019-03-12.

Belk, D. (2019) True cost of healthcare. *Malpractice statistics*. Retrieved from http://truecostofhealthcare.org/malpractice_statistics/.

Bennett, J. and D. O'Donovan. (2001) Substance misuse by doctors, nurses, and other healthcare workers. *Current Opinion in Psychiatry*. Vol. 14, Issue 3: 195-199.

Brooke, D., G. Edwards, and T. Andrews. (1993) Doctors and substance misuse: types of doctors, types of problems. *Addiction*. Vol. 88: 655-663.

Centers for Disease Control and Prevention. (2019) U.S. Public Health Service Syphilis Study at Tuskegee. Retrieved from https://www.cdc.gov/tuskegee/timeline.htm.

Centers for Disease Control and Prevention. (2019) Opioid overdose. Retrieved from https://www.cdc.gov/drugoverdose/data/statedeaths.html.

Center on Media, Crime, and Justice, John Jay College. (2019) 15% of pharmacies bought nearly half of opioids. *Crime and Justice News*, The Crime Report. Aug. 13. Retrieved from https://thecrimereport.org/2019/08/13/15-of-pharmacies-handled-nearly-half-of-opioids/.

Date, S. V., J. Rokade, V. Mule, and S. Dandapannavar. (2014) Female sterilization failure: Review over a decade and its clinicopathological correlation. *International Journal of Applied Basic Medical Research*. July-Dec., Vol. 4, No 2: 81-85.

Davies, Barrell, Will, Lewellyn and Edwards, PLC. (2016) $1.8 million jury award in wrongful pregnancy case. *Firm News*. August. Retrieved from https://www.dbwle.com/firm-news/2016/august/-1-8-million-jury-award-in-wrongful-pregnancy-ca/.

Davis, J. L., B. L. Green, and R. V. Katz. (2012) Influence of scary beliefs about the Tuskegee Syphilis Study on willingness to participate in research. *ABNF Journal*. Summer, Vol. 23, No. 3: 59-62.

Ekmekci, P. E. (2016) Main ethical breaches in multicenter clinical trials regulation in Turkey. *Medicine and Law*. Vol. 35: 491-508.

Federal Drug Administration (FDA). (2019) Is the product a medical device? Device Regulation. Retrieved from https://www.fda.gov/medical-devices/classify-your-medical-device/product-medical-device.

Field, R. I. (2011) The malpractice crisis turns 175: What lessons does history hold for reform? *Drexel Law Review*. Vol. 4: 7-39.

Flemma, R. J. (1985) Medical malpractice: A dilemma in the search for justice. *Marquette Law Review*. Winter, Vol. 68, Issue 2: 237-258.

Gonzales, R. (2019) New York AG says Sacklers transferred $1 billion from Pharma accounts to themselves. *NPR*. Retrieved from https://www.npr.org/2019/09/13/760688886/new-york-ag-says-sacklers-transferred-millions-from-pharma-accounts-to-themselves.

Greenberg, J. A. (2008) Hysteroscopic sterilization: History and current methods. *Reviews in Obstetrics and Gynecology*. Summer, Vol. 1, No 3: 113-121.

Guardado, J. R. (2018) Medical professional liability insurance premiums: An overview from 2008-2017. *Policy Research Perspectives*, American Medical Association. Retrieved from https://www.ama-assn.org/sites/ama-assn.org/files/corp/media-browser/public/government/advocacy/policy-research-perspective-liability-insurance-premiums.pdf.

Hansen, H. and J. Netherland. (2016) Is the prescription opioid epidemic a white problem? *American Journal of Public Health*. Dec, Vol. 106, Issue 12: 2127-2128.

Harvard Health Publishing. (2009) Premature heart disease. *Harvard Men's Health Watch*, Harvard Medical School. Retrieved from https://www.health.harvard.edu/heart-health/premature-heart-disease.

Haworth, J. (2019) 41 charged in opioid ring allegedly responsible for distribution of 23 million pills. ABC News. Retrieved from https://abcnews.go.com/US/41-charged-opioid-ring-allegedly-responsible-distribution-23/story?id=65265173.

Helmer, Jr., J. B. (2013) False Claims Act: Incentivizing integrity for 150 years for rogues, privateers, and patriots. *University of Cincinnati Law Review*. Vol. 81, Issue 81: 1261-1282.

Joseph, A. (2019) 'A blizzard of prescriptions': Documents reveal new details about Purdue's's marketing of OxyContin. *Boston Globe, STAT*. Jan 15. Retrieved from https://www.statnews.com/2019/01/15/massachusetts-purdue-lawsuit-new-details/.

Mello, M. M., A. Chandra, A. A. Gawande, and D. M. Studdert. (2010) National costs of the medical liability system. *Health Aff.* Sept., Vol. 29, No. 9: 1569-1577.

Memmott, M. (2011) Michael Jackson's doctor gets four-year sentence. *NPR*. Nov. 29. Retrieved from https://www.npr.org/sections/thetwo-way/2011/11/29/142895015/michael-jacksons-doctor-gets-4-year-sentence.

Paul, R. G. (1984) Damages for wrongful pregnancy in Illinois. *Loyola University Chicago Law Journal*. Summer, Vol. 15, Issue 4: 799-842.

Pierce, O. and M. Allen. (2015). How Denmark dumped medical malpractice and improved patient safety. *ProPublica*. Retrieved from https://www.propublica.org/article/how-denmark-dumped-medical-malpractice-and-improved-patient-safety.

Preskorn, S. H. (2014) Clinical psychopharmacology and medical malpractice: the four Ds. *Journal of Psychiatric Practiae*. Sept., Vol. 20, No. 5: 363-368.

Ramseyer, J. M. (2010) The effect of universal health insurance on malpractice claims: The Japanese experience. *Journal of Legal Analysis*. Vol. 2: 621-686.

Recovery Worldwide, LLC. (2019) Substance abuse in healthcare. Addiction Center. Retrieved from https://www.addictioncenter.com/addiction/medical-professionals/.

Richards, M. (2016) *83 Minutes: The Doctor, The Damage, and the Shocking Death of Michael Jackson*. New York: Thomas Dunne Books.

RxList. (2019) Diprivan: Side effects. Retrieved from https://www.rxlist.com/diprivan-drug/patient-images-side-effects.htm.

Scutti, S. (2018) At least 8 million IVF babies born in 40 years since historic first. *Health, CNN*. July 3. Retrieved from https://www.cnn.com/2018/07/03/health/worldwide-ivf-babies-born-study/index.html.

Spector, M. and J. DiNapoli. (2019) Exclusive: OxyContin maker prepares 'free-fall' bankruptcy as settlement talks stall. *Business News*, Reuters. Sept. 3. Retrieved from https://www.reuters.com/article/us-purdue-pharma-opioids-exclusive/exclusive-oxycontin-maker-prepares-free-fall-bankruptcy-as-settlement-talks-stall-idUSKCN1VO2QN/.

Swab, A. (2014) Adderall not cocaine: Inside the lives of the young wolves of Wall Street. WGBY, *PBS News Hour*. Feb. 18. Retrieved from https://www.pbs.org/newshour/economy/adderall-cocaine-inside-lives-young-wolves-wall-street.

U.S. Department of Health and Human Services. (2019) *National Health Expenditures 2017 Highlights*. Centers for Medicare and Medicaid Services. Retrieved from https://www.cms.gov/Research-Statistics-Data-and-Systems/Statistics-Trends-and-Reports/NationalHealthExpendData/downloads/highlights.pdf.

U.S. Department of Justice (2019) Doctor charged for prescribing narcotics to non patients ordered detained until trail. *Press release*, Office of Public Affairs, The U.S. Attorney's Office, Southern

District of Georgia. Jan. 28. Retrieved from https://www.justice.gov/usao-sdga/pr/doctor-charged-prescribing-narcotics-non-patients-ordered-detained-until-trial.

U.S. Department of Justice. (2019) Medical device maker ACell Inc. pleads guilty and will pay $15 million to resolve criminal charges and civil false claims allegations. Press Release, Office of Public Affairs, The U.S. Attorney's Office, U.S. District Court, Maryland. Retrieved from https://www.justice.gov/opa/pr/medical-device-maker-acell-inc-pleads-guilty-and-will-pay-15-million-resolve-criminal-charges.

U.S. Department of Justice. (2019) South Florida health care facility owner convicted for role in largest health care fraud scheme charged by The Department of Justice, involving $1.3 billion in fraudulent claims. Press Release, Office of Public Affairs. Retrieved from https://www.justice.gov/opa/pr/south-florida-health-care-facility-owner-convicted-role-largest-health-care-fraud-scheme-ever.

Van Zee, A. (2009) The promotion and marketing of OxyContin: Commercial triumph, public health tragedy. *American Journal of Public Health*. Feb, Vol. 22, No. 2: 221-227.

Zaki, M. (2014) The ethical issues in the relationship between the psychologist as therapist and the patient. *Medicine and Law*. Oct, Vol. 33, No. 3: 3-12.

Zhang, S. (2019) A decades-old doctor's secret leads to new fertility fraud law. *The Atlantic*. May 7. Retrieved from https://www.theatlantic.com/science/archive/2019/05/cline-fertility-fraud-law/588877/.

Chapter NINE

Religion, Crime, and Misconduct

Preying on the faithful

> "There is a sucker born every minute."
>
> —*Allegedly P.T. Barnum, 19th-century showman*

Chapter Objectives

- Reintroduce readers to common white collar crimes as they apply to religious organizations and ministries.
- Discuss who is most likely to be victimized by charlatans.
- Introduce some of the more outrageous cases of crime committed in the name of religion.

Key Terms

1st Amendment, U.S. Constitution	Megachurches
Affinity fraud	Ministerial exception
Charlatans	Misappropriation
Cults	Y2K bug
Establishment and Free Exercise Clauses	

INTRODUCTION

There is perhaps no other place within white collar crime prosecution where district attorneys want to be doubly sure that a crime has been committed than when it occurs in a religious organization. At the bottom of this is religious freedom. However, donors want to be assured their money will be well-spent. As Fleckenstein and Bowes (2000, p. 112) remind us, "There is a relationship of trust between the [religious] organization and donor who must believe that the values are sacrosanct and that the donated funds will be used for the purpose stated."

However, religious charities and organizations do not always operate above-board. It is principally disconcerting when the faithful are solicited to donate money to a fraudulent religious ministry with the promise that they can be spiritually redeemed if they simply open their wallets. Approximately $18 billion is given to religious organizations and ministries each year (Barborak, 2014). Out of that, a portion can be assumed to have been fraudulently solicited. Of course, taking into consideration cash donations, this figure might be an underestimation.

To some extent, stealing from both religious organizations and faithful followers is a byproduct of capitalism, though crimes committed in the name of religion are not exclusive to capitalist economies. Weber proposed in *The Protestant Ethic and the Spirit of Capitalism* (1905) that as capitalism took hold, focus in religion shifted from looking for heavenly rewards after death, and more attention was given to secular rewards. If someone has wealth on Earth, whether by inheritance or earned, then a spiritual, superior being has blessed you during your lifetime, instead of in the afterlife. Unfortunately, some religious groups and leaders have translated this to mean "my money is my money; your money is my money" literally, all fraudulently in the name of God (or whatever deity the group worships).

Because some of the groups we are discussing in this chapter are quasi-religious or *cults*, including NXIVM, we will focus on the characteristics that place them in the category of religious organizations. Durkheim (1912; 1995) proposed that religion acts as a social glue, involving rituals and beliefs that primarily serve to satisfy the basic human need to be social and to belong. Though Durkheim was speaking primarily of rituals and beliefs directed at spiritual objects, we will expand his definition in our discussion of white collar crime to include religious-like devotion to charismatic leaders who commit crimes.

1ST AMENDMENT, UNITED STATES CONSTITUTION

One of the liberties that is afforded to Americans under the U.S. Constitution is the freedom to practice whatever religion that one wishes to follow. This makes prosecuting religious fraud tricky. If people are free to follow a religion, should they also be protected from making contributions to a religious organization when questionable? And is this any different than when people make foolish purchases as we saw in the case of consumer crimes? As there is the concern of overstepping the state's authority in religious matters, religious misdeeds are rarely prosecuted.

Subsequent legislation, including the Establishment and Free Exercise Clauses of the 1st Amendment (1972), demands that the U.S. government is not allowed to favor one religion over another. This has been tested in a number of court cases, as in the example of protests over nativity scenes or other religious objects displayed on government property during the holiday seasons. In *Allegheny County v. Greater*

Pittsburgh ACLU, where both Christian and Jewish religious symbols were displayed by the city in a private park, the District Court concluded that this was not in violation of the Establishment Clause (Legal Information Institute, 1989). However, this decision was overturned later by The Court of Appeals, citing *Lynch v. Donnelly* where even though the displays were on private property, because the city provided them, it was viewed as an endorsement of the religions, which was in violation of the Establishment and Free Exercise Clauses (Legal Information Institute, 1989).

Religious broadcasting in the United States is allowed fairly liberal interpretation of the freedom of speech guaranteed in the 1st Amendment of the Constitution. And the content of television religion has changed since the 1980s, with the use of religious broadcasting to shape American politics even though there is, at least in principle, separation of church and state. As an example, the fundamentalist organization, Moral Majority, has used its religious platform to try and influence politicians to overturn *Roe v. Wade*, the abortion law, and to oppose the Equal Rights Amendment (Bivins, 2003). Religious broadcasting continues to be a means to influence social and political change, as well as solicit for funds to support their missions, causes, and organizations.

LIKELY VICTIMS

If we look at the functions of religion, it acts as a means of social support in communities. This is certainly apparent when natural disaster strikes. Religious groups many times are the first on the scene to help with disaster recovery. Religious faith is intended to ease the pain and loneliness of some members of society (Senn, 1990).

The concern is that in seeking solace in religion, do people then leave themselves vulnerable to victimization? We can certainly point to evidence of this in some religious cults, as in the example of Heaven's Gate in San Diego, California. In that case, the founder of the cult, Marshall Applewhite, himself a self-described lost soul, attracted other disenfranchised individuals who were seeking religious meaning outside of conventional sects (e.g., Protestant churches, etc.). In extreme cases, including the Heaven's Gate and The People's Temple, located in Jonestown in Guyana, victims were not only asked to donate all their worldly goods and money to a religious organization, but followers were swayed into dying by mass suicide.

Law in the Real World: Heaven's Gate

(Source: Zeller, 2014)

As we were on the cusp of the 21st century, there were a number of upcoming events that caused some trepidation. In the Computer Age, there was an unfounded fear that all electronics and communications, dependent on cyber technology, would cease to function at midnight, January 1, 2000. Called the "*Y2K bug*," programmers had been working for a few years in advance of the time and date change to correct the issue of shortsighted coding, where the year was only denoted by the last two digits (e.g., 1/1/00 for the date, instead of 1/1/2000). Computers would then register the date changes as reverting back to the beginning of the 20th century all over again.

The Y2K bug created an impending disaster mentality for some, and not just for the computer illiterates. Even some highly intelligent people irrationally believed that the new century would bring on the "end of days," a universal theme in religion. Similar to what happened after the launch of Sputnik by the Russians in the 1950s, the definition of the heavens was redefined and some followers of traditional religions became disillusioned. Religious cults that resembled science fiction began to emerge within the last decades of the 20th century, offering a more appealing explanation of spiritual life for some. The arrival of Comet Hale-Bopp in 1997 on a 4,000-year pass by of Earth, added with the anxiety over the approaching Y2K, triggered a number of "Doomsday" prophecies.

One such group, Heaven's Gate, had a fateful date with Comet Hale-Bopp in March 1997. Founded in 1974 by Marshall Applewhite, a failed actor and music professor, and Bonnie Nettles, a psychiatric nurse, the cult proved to be deadly for some members. By 1976, Applewhite and Nettles had implemented a strict hierarchy with themselves at the top of the organizational chart, sending recruiters out on their behalf to find new members around the United States. They demanded absolute obedience from their followers and took complete control over their religious, financial, and social lives.

The name of the new religion evolved under a number of different titles, including Human Individual Metamorphosis, before settling on the name, Heaven's Gate. On the heels of social change in the 1960s, the 1970s ushered in a number of alternative religious movements, so conditions were ripe for this new religion to take hold.

The basic premise of Heaven's Gate, according to their website (heavensgate.com/misc/intro.htm), is that two thousand plus years ago, members of the Kingdom of Heaven determined that a percentage of humans in the late 20th century had advanced enough to become, as termed by Applewhite, "containers for soul deposits." The religion was a blend of the New Age Movement, science fiction themes, and Evangelical Christianity.

Applewhite, without using the exact words, implied in writings and videos that he was essentially Jesus Christ reincarnated. This is a common claim of cult leaders, either that they are godlike, divine beings, or are the offspring of a superior being. Applewhite further spread this claim after

Nettle's death from liver cancer in 1985, when he was left to evolve the religion on his own.

According to Applewhite, he had been tasked by his heavenly father to lead members to casting off all of their worldly connections, including family, sensuality (e.g., sex), selfish desires, and their minds and bodies. This again is straight out of the playbook of most cults that require members to turn their backs on family and friends if they cannot be recruited into the fold. The premise of doing so is that loved ones who might discourage them from joining, alarmed by demands to give up all of their savings and possessions to a religious group, will not interfere in their conversion.

The group had settled in Rancho Santa Fe, an upscale, primarily affluent community in North San Diego County, California. According to *Zillow*, in 2019 terms, the median price of a home in Rancho Santa Fe is $2,469,000 (Retrieved from https://www.zillow.com/rancho-santa-fe-ca/home-values/). The members of Heaven's Gate were not without means or employment, as they were expected to contribute to the $7,000/month rent on the property. This ran in contrast with how recruiters in the cult lived — sent out into American and Canadian cities destitute, required to sleep on the streets, and dependent on panhandling in order to support themselves. By joining the group, members voluntarily gave up a number of personal liberties. Reportedly, some of the male members of Heaven's Gate even underwent castration in their quest for androgynous immortality (Lindlaw, 1997). Members were convinced by Applewhite that the only way to be fully committed is to live a monastic life.

When the Comet Hale-Bopp was scheduled to make its brightest appearance in the skies in 1997, Applewhite convinced followers that this was the time to die by group suicide. The purpose of doing so, according to Applewhite, was to leave their human bodies and be reunited with an unidentified flying object (UFO) or a spacecraft that was supposedly trailing behind Comet Hale-Bopp.

Just as Comet Hale-Bopp was at its closest distance to Earth in March 1997, Applewhite, along with 17 men and 21 women, each took a lethal dose of phenobarbital and vodka, taking their own lives in shifts. Each shift was charged with cleaning up and arranging the bodies of each group of deceased members until all 39 members were dead. They were found on bunkbeds, wearing matching outfits of black sweats and brand-new Nike® sneakers. Tucked in their pockets were rolls of quarters and five-dollar (USD) bills, as if they might need currency in their afterlives. At their sides were packed duffle bags, like they were headed off for a vacation instead of into some eternity. Their faces were covered with purple shrouds.

It would be easy to jump to the conclusion that the members were brainwashed or mentally unstable. As Zeller (2014) proposes, the followers found the message believable, and willingly complied with the demands of giving up their possessions and ultimately their lives. We should note that this is in contrast with Jonestown, where some of the members, including children, were forced to drink drug-laced Kool Aid™ in what was essentially mass murder and suicide.

There is some speculation that Applewhite suffered from mental illness himself, allegedly suffering from schizophrenia and delusions, which would make his fantastical religion all the more explainable (Zeller, 1997). Applewhite had met Nettles in a psychiatric hospital during a period of crisis in his life. But this does not explain why supposedly sane people, Nettles included, would follow Applewhite into the great beyond. And as we will speculate in other cases, it also fails to explain why some members of the cult would live on the streets, in poverty, in order to recruit new members.

The Heaven's Gate website (http://www.heavensgate.com/) is still up and functioning, though for all intents and purposes, the cult died along with its founder in 1997.[1]

Discussion Questions

1. Why might supposedly sane people follow a decidedly unconventional religion?
2. In what ways do supposed apocalyptic events create white collar criminals and victims?
3. How might law enforcement or regulatory agencies help to prevent this type of extreme victimization?

There are a number of characteristics of people who are attracted to new religious movements, some of which are unscrupulous, as in the case of cults. There is the mistaken idea that someone who joins a non-traditional religion is suffering from mental illness (Buxant, et al., 2007). Non-traditional religions and cults are perceived as brainwashing organizations that might do psychological harm to their members. This may be largely due to not fitting into the standard mold of mainstream religions.

Religious organizations themselves can be victimized. The most common offense committed against religious organizations is some form of embezzlement or *misappropriation* by clergy, volunteers, or employees. In 1991, the comptroller of the Diocese of Buffalo, New York, for the Catholic Church, was forced to resign when he used the church's tax-exempt status for his own purchases, including $9,000 worth of landscaping at his home (Fleckenstein and Bowes, 2000). This

---

[1] Allegedly there were two surviving members after 1997, one of whom subsequently later died by suicide (Dougan, 1997).

not only robbed the state of legitimate tax revenue had the comptroller reported the money as income, but it was yet one more public relations nightmare for the scandal-ridden Catholic Church. Anthony Franjoine, the comptroller, was entrusted with the financial health of the Diocese and violated his responsibilities to the church (Fleckenstein and Bowes, 2000).

We have discussed Felson and Cohen's Routine Activities Theory elsewhere in this textbook. If you will recall, the theory suggests that a crime will be committed if there is (a) a target, (b), a motivated offender, and (c) no one or nothing that is preventing a crime from happening, like law or regulatory enforcement. The victims themselves may not even be aware that they are being victimized until it is too late. This theory can be applied in our discussions of white collar crime involving religious organizations and leaders.

There are certain populations that are at greater risk for being victims of religious fraud and bad behavior. Outside of white collar crime, there have been a number of cases of child molestation crimes reported to have been committed by religious leaders in the past few decades. The focus on victimization in this book is outside of those cases and is concentrated primarily on cases of people who have been asked to part with their hard-earned money to fund questionable religious organizations.

Of even greater concern is the growing practice of religious organizations accepting credit cards for donations. Some organizations will only allow donations made using debit cards, which is essentially the same as cash. The practice of prohibiting the use of credit cards for donations may have more to do with the fees that credit card companies charge to vendors, or in this case, a church, synagogue, mosque, etc. However, some religious organizations do accept credit cards for donations. The faithful may be convinced by unscrupulous *charlatans* to go into crippling consumer debt if they charge their donations to credit cards, under the delusion that by doing so, they will be "saved."

Beyond the lonely or disenfranchised, the likely victim is on either end of the age spectrum. Younger people are more likely to be victimized because of their financial naivety; older people are more likely to be victimized because they are more willing to listen to a sales pitch (Spann, 2017). Once recruited into a questionable religious organization, it can become difficult for family members and loved ones to convince the converted to leave:

> The [new] belief is often relished, amplified, and defended by the possessor of the belief and should be differentiated from an obsession or a delusion. The belief grows more dominant over time, more refined and more resistant to challenge. The individual has an intense emotional commitment to the belief and may carry out violent behavior in its service. (Rahman, 2018, p. 11; Rahman et al., 2016; Weiss, 2016)

As Rahman stresses (2018), for people who join questionable religions, even if they are skeptical before recruitment, unusual behaviors and requests such as relinquishing one's possessions become normalized over time. The speculation is that in contemporary society, some people feel disconnected from religious life in a secular world. They might reject the religion that they have been brought up with or, in some cases, try to find their spiritual home in the absence of any religious training in childhood. When individuals join non-traditional religions or cults, they will rationalize anything that may seem unorthodox as a price for joining, in exchange for a community that will welcome them with open arms (Barker, 1986).

PREDATORY RELIGION

Most, if not all, religious organizations are primarily economic organizations. They cannot remain in business without donations, which requires growing congregations and soliciting for funds. It is a tricky thing to point to fundraising and proselytization as being fraudulent. Part of the hands-off approach of prosecutors is due to the continued challenge of a secular government staying out of the affairs of religious organizations. To a large extent, there is a "buyer beware" mentality we see in consumer transactions that we have discussed in Chapter 7.

Though most, if not all, religious organizations ask for money from their followers, cults are more likely to be predatory in their solicitation. They can play on the fear of people with a promise of redemption or everlasting life, both powerful motivators. The rituals themselves reinforce this, with a focus on religious objects or charismatic leaders. From a white collar crime standpoint, once victims have been wooed and won over, the next logical step for charlatans is to ask them to open up their wallets, encouraging them to give generously.

AFFINITY FRAUD

Closely related to predatory religions is *affinity fraud*. One common type of affinity fraud that is committed by criminals in religious organizations are Ponzi schemes. As we discussed in Chapter 4, the premise of a Ponzi scheme is to pay early investors with money that is being stolen from new investors. As we saw with Bernie Madoff, these schemes fall down like a house of cards when the stock market is volatile or the economy is shaky, as in a recession when a lot of investors want to pull their money out to put into "safer"[2] investments.

The reason why Ponzi schemes are so successfully executed in religious organizations is that relationships in these groups are based on trust. The perpetuators of Ponzi schemes are dependent on exploiting their social networks. Religious

---

[2] Except for certain bank deposits (e.g., checking accounts, savings accounts), money invested in the stock market is not guaranteed by FDIC insurance, in case the stock market crashes or there is a deep recession. Even bonds are risky, except for municipal or U.S. backed savings bonds.

leaders, including laypersons, are held up on pedestals, viewed as being charitable, selfless, and compassionate (Spann, 2017). In all reality, most do their best to live up to this image. It's the few who betray this trust and take advantage of their social networks that law enforcement are interested in prosecuting.

We are including in our definition of religious leaders people who volunteer their time in helping to run the organization (e.g., church elders). It isn't always a religious leader that is exploiting social networks in religious organizations. For example, fellow members in a church are viewed as part of the flock, and are assumed to trustworthy. People who belong to religious group tend to hire the services of people that they know from their congregation, like attorneys, doctors, plumbers, etc.

Law in the Real World: Ephren Taylor II and Wendy Connor

(Source: The United States Attorney's Office, Northern District of Georgia, 2015; The Economist, 2012) https://www.economist.com/business/2012/01/28/fleecing-the-flock

The New Birth Missionary Baptist Church in Lithonia, Georgia, is part of a new, hip revolution in churches founded in the African-American Pentecostal tradition. With dynamic leadership, the megachurch has attracted over 27,000 members. What better location to find new investors interested in socially conscious investments?

Touring the country giving popular talks on how to build personal wealth, Ephren Taylor II had been a guest on NPR, CNN, and even spoke at the 2008 Democratic National Convention. When he came to Georgia, he was invited to speak at The New Birth Missionary Baptist Church. When Eddie Long introduced him to the congregation, he stated "[God] wants you to be a mover and shaker" referring to the congregants, "....To finance you well to do His will." (*The Economist*, 2012, retrieved from https://www.economist.com/business/2012/01/28/fleecing-the-flock) To any scholar of Weber, this echoes the foundation of Protestantism under capitalism.

But as these things go, Taylor's scheme was nothing more than smoke and mirrors. While Taylor and his accomplice, Wendy Connor, served as officers at City Capital Corporation, they managed to swindle over 400 investors out of $16 million USD. They specifically targeted church congregations, including the New Birth Missionary Baptist Church. In Georgia alone, investors lost more than $2 million.

Selling an investment plan that was too good to be true, he was running a classic Ponzi scheme. Like in the case of Bernie Madoff, his investment was suspicious, promising returns that were impossibly inflated. Claiming to invest in small businesses including laundromats, juice bars, and gas stations, Taylor and Connor falsified the revenues of these business that in truth were unprofitable.

In addition to small business investments, Taylor and Connor peddled investments in sweepstake machines, computers that have various games in which players can win cash prizes. In their investment advertisements, Taylor and Connor made the claim that the sweepstake machines investment would generate an impossible 300 percent return and were 100 percent risk-free. If you recall, there are no guarantees with any investment, save those made in conventional checking and savings accounts at banks or in government backed savings bonds.

Worse yet, investors were encouraged to transfer their retirement accounts, specifically IRAs[3], that were directed to the pay for the ongoing expenses of City Capital but went into the pockets of Taylor and Connor instead of being invested. To add salt to the wound, Taylor and Connor made the claim that their "'low-risk investment[s] with high performances' [were] chosen with guidance from God." (*The Economist*, 2012, retrieved from https://www.economist.com/business/2012/01/28/fleecing-the-flock).

After a number of investigations initiated by the IRS and the U.S. Attorney's office, as well as the United States Secret Service, with assistance from the U.S. Securities and Exchange Commission, Taylor and Connor were arrested. In the court case, Special Agent in Charge Veronica Hayman-Pillot, an IRS investigator, stated "'These defendants are fraudsters and world-class manipulators.... Taylor and Connor knew that the investment they were touting were based entirely on deception and lies, which is driven by their insatiable greed.'" (The United States Attorney's Office, Northern District of Georgia, 2015, retrieved from https://www.justice.gov/usao-ndga/pr/ephren-taylor-sentenced-federal-prison).

In a plea bargain, Taylor was convicted of conspiracy to commit wire fraud and sentenced to 19 years, seven months in federal prison. He will have three years of supervised release after he serves his sentence and was ordered to pay restitution to the tune of over $15 million to his victims. At 36 years old, Taylor will be close to 60 before he has finished his sentence, hardly an age to kickstart a new career, particularly if he is barred for life from selling or managing the investments of others.

---

[3] An IRA is an individual retirement account that employees may have in lieu of a traditional pension plan. They do not guarantee income for life, like pensions. Nor are the investments guaranteed, unless invested in a defined plan.

For her part, Connor pleaded guilty to interstate transportation of money taken by fraud and was sentenced to five years in federal prison, three years of supervision, and required to serve the first 18 months of her post-incarceration sentence in house arrest. She was ordered to pay over $5 million in restitution to her victims. They could both be, conceivably, subject to civil class action lawsuits as well.

Discussion Questions

1. We hear these types of stories time and time again in white collar crime cases. Why would someone chance all of their retirement savings on a "too good to be true" investment?
2. What fallout, if any, could happen to membership and donations when religious organizations, however innocently, open the door to people like Taylor and Connor?
3. Compared to other crimes we have studied in this book, were Taylor and Connor's sentences proportional to the crimes they pleaded guilty to?

MISAPPROPRIATION OF FUNDS OR ASSETS

Misappropriation is a slightly different crime from embezzlement. Whereas embezzlement is more often than not intended to directly line the pockets of an embezzler, misappropriation involves the channeling of money or assets to somewhere other than their intended uses. Even if the money or assets are being used within the organization, strict accounting principles dictate that they go only where they are designated to go.

Donors to religious organizations have the discretion to have their donations directed to specific projects or causes. For instance, if a church needs a new building, parishioners may be asked to donate specifically to a building fund. When those funds do not go to their intended purposes, it is considered to be misappropriation of funds.

EMBEZZLEMENT

We have spent some time examining the white collar crime of embezzlement in other chapters. In religious organizations, clergy and volunteers may be tempted to pocket donations. This, of course, runs counter with most religious teachings. It is one thing to scratch one's head over a Wall Street executive stealing from their company. But when individuals are within religious organizations, the greed and temptation to steal from them is doubly puzzling.

One of the oldest established Christian sects is the Catholic Church. In a study reported in 2007, based on data collected from about half of dioceses in the United States, the church was alarmed to discover that embezzlement had been on the rise (Panepento, 2007). The offenders were primarily employees and volunteers.

Law in the Real World: Rev. Jonathan Wehrle

(Sources: Associated Press, 2018)

In theory, "men of the cloth" (and women as well, as in the examples of priests and nuns) are expected to take a vow of poverty. This does not mean that they are without modest creature comforts. However, not all religious individuals readily believe that as part of their calling, they have to give up a cushy lifestyle. We have already established that in a world of reinterpretation of religious writings, if one is well-off right now, it means that the gods are smiling down on you in this life. No need to wait for heavenly rewards.

The Catholic Church has a long history of opulent architecture, including Vatican City in Italy. Around the world, the church is represented by some of the most magnificent landmarks that have become tourist destinations beyond their original intended uses. One Michigan priest, the Reverend Jonathan Wehrle, wanted to likewise live in opulence himself. Purchasing a 10-acre, 11,000 square foot estate in Williamston with 6 bedrooms, 12 bathrooms, 10 fireplaces, three barns, and a $45,000 indoor swimming pool, this was hardly the home for a man who had taken a vow of poverty. Rev. Wehrle spent an additional $134,000 on landscaping on this estate and on other properties he owned. To put this into perspective, the average suburban home in the U.S. is roughly 2,500 square feet, sitting on about a quarter of an acre of land.

We know from white collar crimes and organized crimes that if someone starts to throw around money on fancy cars and homes, this is a red flag that something is not aboveboard, especially if someone's lifestyle is not in keeping with their salary. When investigated, Rev. Wehrle's attorney claimed that he had personal family wealth at his disposal. He also made the claim that a now-deceased priest gave him permission to use parish funds for his personal residence. At the time of his arrest for embezzlement, Rev. Wehrle hadn't been paying his property taxes and had allowed his homeowner's insurance policy to lapse, both a bit odd considering the amount of money he allegedly had at his disposal.

Arrested and facing both criminal and civil cases, Rev. Wehrle is being accused of embezzling approximately $5 million that authorities are aware of. Having founded St. Martha's Church, he had autonomous control over finances since 1988. When police searched his estate, they found over $63,000 in cash, mostly in bundles of $20 bills, stashed in the ceiling of the basement (Palmer, 2018).

While out on bond, awaiting trial in his embezzlement case, Rev. Wehrle died in March 2020 (Banta, 2020).

Discussion Questions

1. Knowing that some religious leaders make generous salaries, particularly those running *megachurches*, should an opulent lifestyle automatically be a red flag?
2. Though we know that Rev. Wehrle pretty much had free rein in running St. Martha's, what could the Catholic Church have done differently as far as oversight to make sure that embezzlement didn't happen?
3. What do you think was Rev. Wehrle's biggest mistake, beyond his crime of embezzlement?

INCOME TAX EVASION

Organizations that are certified to be religious nonprofits by the IRS do not have to pay income tax, nor do they have to file IRS tax returns. However, they are required to file tax returns on any unrelated business income. For example, if a church is renting out space for non-religious activities, it would have to report this as taxable income.

Income tax evasion within the parameters of religious crimes is more likely to happen when there is an organization whose nonprofit status is being questioned. In that case, the group is required to pay income tax on any money that is generated, if it does not have legitimate tax-exempt status of a nonprofit. For example, the Church of Scientology has spent a number of years fighting to get tax-exempt status and keeping it, as it has been argued to be a self-improvement group rather than an established religion (Frantz, 1997). They have not only had this battle in the United States. They have also argued for tax-exempt status in a number of other countries.

Outside of failing to pay income tax on money earned in non-religious activities, one type of income tax evasion is over-reporting of donations by individuals filing their yearly income tax return. Though U.S. tax laws for deductions have drastically changed beginning in 2018, historically, people who had enough deductions elsewhere (e.g., own a home) could itemize their cash and non-cash charitable donations. This meant that those amounts could be subtracted from taxable income, reducing the overall tax liability for the year the donations were reported. It is precisely due to income tax return fraud that charitable donations should be documented with receipts. As only a small portion of income tax returns get audited by the IRS (approximately 0.5 percent), it is conceivable that the number of falsified donations caught may only be a small portion of false charitable contributions reported (IRS, 2019).

SEDUCING THE FLOCK

Sometimes the attraction to a religion or a sect of a religion has more to do with the personality of the individual leading the flock. Translated into a "neutral" term that could transcend religion and also refer to a magnetic personality in any type of organization, Max Weber described *charisma* as an irrational, personal attraction to a leader (Weber, 1947; Lindholm, 2018). People are drawn to charismatic people not so much for what they know, but by the way they present themselves. We would call these people "charming."

In many respects, a charismatic white collar criminal is one of the most dangerous kind. As Barker (1986) cautions, charismatic leaders can be unpredictable and create their own set of religious rules that followers will blindly adhere to, even when they seem unconventional. This takes into account the demand for members of a religious organization to give up all their worldly goods to prove their devotion, including their life savings.

In the extreme, charismatic leaders demand unwavering loyalty. Whether they convince followers to self-harm, as in the case of Heaven's Gate, or to commit crimes in their name or in the name of religion, the victimization goes beyond the intended targets. There can be collateral damage when taking into consideration family members whose loved ones have joined these questionable religions. Worse yet is when family members are also convinced to join the group, as in our next case of NXIVM.

Law in the Real World: Keith Raniere, NXIVM Leader

(Sources: Associated Press, 2019; Dickson, 2019; Grigoriadis, 2019; Katersky, 2019)

There is perhaps no better example of a tangled web of deceit and crimes associated with pseudo religion than Keith Raniere, the charismatic leader of the cult NXIVM. Raniere trained in IT and after a number of failed (and questionable) ventures, including a pyramid-scheme grocery business in the 1980s, created a cult that represented the intersection of wellness, activism, and feminism. Advertised as a self-help group, NXIVM offered classes to help its female participants overcome a number of life's tragedies, including childhood trauma and divorce.

The organization followed a multi-level marketing plan, similar to direct sales organizations. As we have noted elsewhere in the book, these organizations are legitimate as long as they are not Ponzi schemes, even if their marketing strategies are questionable. Ultimately, NVIXM was determined to be more than a self-help group. It turned out to be a cover for a sex cult.

What makes NVIXM decidedly on the side of other cults found to be based in criminal behavior was level of secrecy surrounding the inner workings of the group that Grigoriadis (2018) describes as "unsavory." Part of appeal of the sales pitch was that women who joined would be admitted to a secret society, a red flag that perhaps something illegal was taking place that new members seemed to ignore.

Raniere, who insisted that followers call him Vanguard, was an unlikely cult figure on the surface. Described as a nerdy, middle-aged Charles Manson, Raniere used a number of tactics to woo female followers, including "those of a pickup artist, like negging [emotional manipulation], with the vernacular of many a modern business." (Grigoriadis, 2019, p. 108). Recruits were promised that by joining and participating in classes, they would become successful in both their personal and professional lives: "[Members] would become stronger, emotionally and physically, or, as some of them called themselves, 'badass.'" (Grigoriadis, 2019, p. 108).

Followers were convinced that Raniere was a highly evolved person, a characteristic of charismatic leaders who are viewed by their flock as otherworldly. In an NPR interview (2018) and her *Vanity Fair* article (2019), Grigoriadis stated that behind the scenes of NXIVM, Raniere had a number of girlfriends who were monogamous to him, living in a number of houses and townhouse in and around Albany, New York, sometimes housed together, sometimes alone.

Raniere seduced some of his followers into recruiting others into the organization, directing them to trendier parts of major cities, including New York and Los Angeles, where there might be more affluent women. This is where Allison Mack, an actress known for her role in the television show, *Smallville* (The WB, The CW), and one of Raniere's recruiters, ran into legal hot water. In actuality, some of the women of NXIVM were hand-selected, Mack included, to conscript unsuspecting victims into a sex slavery scheme that included human trafficking across state and international lines. Once conscripted, the victims were forced to have sex with

Raniere and to participate in a secret initiation where they were crudely branded with his and Mack's initials.

Raniere was not the only person charged or convicted in the case. Though Raniere was considered the mastermind behind NXIVM, Mack was alleged as one of his most active recruiters, pleading guilty to one count of racketeering conspiracy and one count of racketeering. Nancy Salzman, a co-founder of NXIVM, has been accused of illegally logging into NXIVM members' email accounts, tampering with evidence in both the civil and criminal lawsuits. Her daughter, Lauren Salzman, pleaded guilty to two felony counts of racketeering and racketeering conspiracy.

Kathy Russell, the former bookkeeper for NXIVM, pleaded guilty to one charge of visa fraud, as she was instrumental in an attempt to smuggle a woman into the United States using the identification card of a deceased person. Clare Bronfman, an heir to the Seagram fortune, pleaded guilty of perjury, allowing Raniere access to a dead woman's credit card, and harboring an illegal immigrant who worked for her and NXIVM. As part of a plea agreement, Bronfman may face two years in prison and a $6 million judgement when she is expected to be sentenced in January 2020.

In 2019, Raniere was convicted of a number of crimes, including "racketeering, racketeering conspiracy, wire fraud conspiracy, forced labor conspiracy, sex trafficking, sex trafficking conspiracy and attempted sex trafficking." (Katersky, 2019) To date, the case is in the pre-sentencing phase. Separately, Raniere was charged in March 2019 with having sex with underaged girls as well with possession of child pornography. As it stands, Raniere is facing a life sentence for his crimes.

Though NXIVM was identified by prosecutors to be primarily a sex cult, it is important to note that it was possible for followers to part with hundreds of thousands of dollars in order to take the questionable classes and seminars offered, as Raniere preyed on women with substantial means, including Mack.

Discussion Questions

1. As his followers were primarily intelligent, successful women, why might they ignore any red flags while being recruited by Raniere or NXIVM?
2. If solicitation for donations to traditional religious organizations is considered legitimate, why might it be viewed as illegal to collect large sums of money from followers in non-traditional groups like cults?
3. In what ways are the women who help recruit for Raniere victims themselves, even though many of them have pleaded guilty to their own crimes?

We may not consider the case of NXIVM as being a classic case of crimes committed under the guise of religion, but it is important to note that it is not the first to exploit their followers in a cult. The same types of dynamics, including the exploitation of social relationships and preying on the insecurities of potential recruits, are being employed. Though NXIVM has no premise in spirituality, it nevertheless possessed the characteristics of religious cults. The idolization of a charismatic leader can be a cover for fleecing followers and, in the case of Raniere, a means to convince them that sex with the leader is a requirement of membership.

SEX, LIES, AND HUSH MONEY

There are a number of religious leaders who have had extramarital affairs or been convicted of sexual misconduct with minor aged children. Where those objectionable and sometimes criminal acts intersect with white collar crime is when a victim has been paid to stay quiet. More importantly, when someone has been paid to stay quiet with money coming from donations made to a religious organization.

We have already established that religious organizations are also economic organizations. They cannot survive without donations. When there is even a hint of a scandal, donations can dry up quickly. Donors lose faith in the ability of the organization to handle funds, much less their personal affairs (Fleckstein and Bowes, 2000).

Even without scandal, a religious organization can be viewed as an ever-emptying bathtub. Unless you continue to find new members to donate money and keep the organization going (and growing), the natural attrition rate could spell the end of a church, synagogue, mosque, or temple. Members move and pass away. Others become disenchanted. Others yet may find a new place to worship or even a whole new religion to join. When a sex scandal is uncovered it could spell doom, particularly in religions where premarital or extramarital sex is considered taboo.

Case Study ▪ Jim and Tammy Faye Bakker

(Source: Effron et al., 2019)

One cannot have a television ministry without being charismatic and expect to be on the air for long. Jim and Tammy Faye Bakker were the face of the Praise the Lord (PTL) ministries, which became popular in 1970s. Together they became household names on television. Instead of broadcasting from behind a podium, Jim Bakker delivered his sermons and lessons from behind a desk, similar to talk show hosts, promising wealth and deliverance from evil in exchange for donations: "God wants you to be rich" (Effron et al., 2019, retrieved from https://abcnews.go.com/US/scandals-brought-bakkers-uss-famous-televangelists/story?id=60389342). Jim and Tammy Faye Bakker could make people cry and turn over their life savings.

Echoing Rev. Wehrle's lavish lifestyle, the Bakkers had two homes, luxury cars, furs, and jewelry. Jim Bakker even described themselves as being "flamboyant." To fund their operations, they regularly held telethons to raise money and asked for committed monthly donations from their followers in the "PTL Club." As the former PTL security chief Don Hardister explained, other shows asked for money to buy their products in commercials; this was no different. This may have continued indefinitely but for a number of scandals that rocked their PTL ministries.

With the proceeds of their ministry, the Bakkers purchased 2,300 acres of land in Fort Mill, South Carolina, with the intention of building a 500-room hotel, which Jim Bakker envisioned as being a Christian version of Disneyland. The new playground for the faithful would be named Heritage, U.S.A. For $1,000, followers could purchase what was essentially a timeshare in the project, entitling them to annual three-night stays in the Heritage Grand hotel. The problem was that the Bakkers oversold memberships to the point where the hotel would continually have over 100 percent occupancy.

Just as the Bakkers were about to start building a ministry center at the Heritage, U.S.A. site in 1987, Tammy Bakker had an alleged breakdown attributed to drug dependency. Almost simultaneously, *The Charlotte Observer* published an article claiming that Jim Bakker had cheated on his wife six years prior to this with Jessica Hahn, one of PTL's church secretaries. Hahn later described this as a sexual assault, and the ministry paid Hahn more than $200,000 to keep her quiet about the assault. Though Jim Bakker claimed that it was a consensual encounter, the fact that Hahn was paid a substantial amount by the ministry, plus her description, made Bakker's story sound fairly implausible.

It was just a matter of time before the government began investigating PTL's and the Bakkers' finances. Jim Bakker was indicted for 8 counts of mail fraud, 15 counts of wire fraud, and 1 count of conspiracy. For her part, Tammy Faye was not indicted, though many questioned her innocence. This was similar to people's reaction to Bernie Madoff's wife escaping prosecution. In October 1989, Jim Bakker was found guilty on all counts, sentenced to 45 years in prison, plus ordered to pay a $500,000 fine. His attorney immediately filed an appeal protesting the length of sentence. In a 1991 appellate court hearing, the sentence was reduced to 8 years. Jim Bakker did not even serve 5 years in prison, and was paroled in 1994.

Where are they now? Jessica Hahn eventually posed for *Playboy Magazine*. Tammy Faye Bakker filed for divorce while Jim was serving time in prison, marrying Roe Messner, a building contractor. Tammy Faye Messner died in 2007 from colon cancer. After his release from prison, Jim Bakker returned to television, this time streaming *The Jim Bakker Show* with his second wife, Lori, and selling survivor kits for a supposed apocalypse he insists is coming soon.

Discussion Question

1. Why do people give money, sometimes blindly, to religious groups like PTL?
2. We know that extra marital affairs can end careers. Why is the payment of hush money perceived as doubly "criminal"?
3. What reason might there be for Jim Bakker's greatly reduced sentence?

RELIGIOUS FRAUDSTERS

Religious fraud, sometimes called pious fraud or solicitation fraud, is a special kind of crime. The perpetrators use scriptures, supposed miracles, and in some cases, stories of a superior being speaking through them, in order to get followers to donate money. More commonly, this is done through religious television broadcasts.

Of televangelists, the most questionable tend to be faith healers. A very lucrative way to raise funds, as television shows have the potential of reaching many more households than in a physical church, $1 billion a year are given to top television ministries (Barborak, 2014). Of greater concern is when individuals with serious medical conditions turn their backs on conventional medicine to rely solely on faith healing. Though the 1st Amendment of the Constitution promises religious freedom, it is restricted by law that prohibits the practice of faith healing if it is a danger to public health (Rubenstein, 1941). For instance, if there was a communicable disease outbreak ordinarily requiring quarantine of affected individuals, as in the case of the COVID-19 virus, if faith healers claimed that the patient is "cured" and they go out in the community only to infect others, this could prove to be a public health crisis.

RELIGION-BASED EMPLOYMENT DISCRIMINATION

Title VII of the Civil Rights Act of 1964: Religious organizations are allowed to discriminate in employment based on religion. Though this may run counter to the spirit of antidiscrimination laws, Congress and the United States Supreme Court recognized that it would be a challenge to religious organizations if they could not specify the faith of their employees. For example, a private school that is faith-based might require its teachers to adhere to that faith so as to pass on that doctrine to students. Within the *ministerial exception*, religious organizations are protected from certain discrimination lawsuits brought by employees (Williams, 2012). When religious organizations do discriminate on any other basis than religion (e.g., race, sex, disabilities), they run the risk of losing their tax-exempt status. Unlike cases of financial malfeasance, discrimination cases against religious organizations are handled with civil lawsuits rather than in criminal court.

A gray area in discrimination is whether religious organizations in the United States should be allowed to discriminate based on sex. It is important to distinguish between the terms *sex* and *gender* in an age when those definitions are being challenged, and to include the current debates on whether transgender populations can argue discrimination based on sex. As women challenge their traditionally lower statuses in religious organizations, there are increasingly more demands for equality, including the demand for more female representation in religious leadership. As an example, in a number of traditional religions, in particular orthodox religions, women are prohibited from serving in any capacity beyond as laypersons or support staff.

For our purposes, we will define "sex" as the biological markers, including primary and secondary sexual characteristics, though no doubt future debates will include discussions of discrimination based on gender and sexuality, particularly as they relate to religious organizations, as cases make their way through the U.S. court system.

Other types of discrimination that have been challenged by religious organizations include disabilities. One stipulation in The American Disabilities Act (ADA) is that it is against the law to discriminate against individuals with disability in employment. Similar to sex discrimination, here the lines have likewise been blurred, as the ADA relates to religion, demonstrated by our next case study.

Law in the Real World: *Cheryl Perich v. Hosanna-Tabor Evangelical Lutheran Church and School*

(Source: Mann, 2011; Williams, 2013)

If ever there was a situation that looks like the intersection of religious, sex, and disabilities discrimination, it is the case of Cheryl Perich. Initially hired in a faculty support position, she began her career at the Hosanna-Tabor Evangelical Lutheran Church and School in a non-teaching position. Teachers at the school were required to teach religion according the Lutheran Church practices and lead prayers, along with teaching the usual secular curriculum required by law. Perich was eventually vetted to work as a "called teacher[4]," at the 4th grade level at the school, after theological training.

While teaching at the school, Perich was diagnosed with narcolepsy, a disorder that causes people to fall asleep or doze off unexpectedly during the day. The disorder is manageable with medication. In 2004, Perich was granted a disability leave. When she notified her principal that she would be able to return to work in early 2005, she was informed that she had been replaced by a lay teacher for the remainder of the year. According to court documents, the principal expressed concerns that Perich may not be ready to return to the classroom (*Hosanna-Tabor Evangelical Lutheran Church and School v. EEOC*, 565 U.S. 171, 2012). She was asked by the school to resign and offered a portion of her health benefits in return. Perich refused to quit, showing up to work at the beginning of the February term. When asked to leave, Perich in turn sued the church and school for employment discrimination based on religion.

The fuzzy part about this case is that Perich made the claim that in all practicality, her duties and position were similar to that of a minister. The lower court (Sixth Circuit) had ruled in Perich's favor, where in turn the church appealed the case all the way up to the Supreme Court. Though the lower court determined that Perich was not a minister and her firing would not be excluded on the basis of the ministerial exception, this perhaps was her undoing in the case, as The Supreme Court determined that the case should be dismissed on the basis of ministerial exception. The Lutheran Church could fire her as she was not perceived as falling in line with "faith and mission of the church itself" and that any interference by the Court could be viewed as a violation of the ministerial exception (*Hosanna-Tabor Evangelical Lutheran Church and School v. EEOC*, 565 U.S. 171, 2012). In a unanimous vote and in the opinion delivered by Chief Justice Roberts, The Supreme Court ruled that there was no basis in Perich's lawsuit as employment discrimination.

Discussion Questions

1. Conceivably, what types of discrimination might Perich charge, besides religious discrimination?
2. Why might this case be particularly challenging for the Supreme Court to decide?
3. In what ways did Perich's position resemble a minister's job so that her firing was justified, based on the ministerial exception?

---

[4] This is a reference to the teaching position being a religious calling.

As in all cases of discrimination that fall under the Civil Rights Act, we should note that the discrimination can be legislated as unlawful, but prejudice is a much more difficult thing to prove in a court of law as it is based on feelings and not actions. We need to also note that even though discrimination is unlawful, it is only considered criminal in cases of harassment.

GUERILLA RELIGIOUS WARFARE

We do know that religious organizations can be involved in illegal operations, similar to cash-based business and organized crime groups. However, this is less likely to happen here in the United States than overseas. Countries like Nigeria may have money laundering laws in place, but the extent to which they are enforced is another thing all together. In one study, money laundering was found to have become more prevalent in Nigeria due to the proliferation of private schools with religious affiliations and churches (Kingston, 2011).

What is of more serious concern is when an extremist religious group uses violence and property destruction in order to carry out their mission. In this case, there is the argument that religious law, alleged to have been created by a superior being, supersedes state laws created by humans.

In an accounting of religious activism, Bivins (2003, p. 1) writes

> On Ash Wednesday, 1997, a former Josephite priest and five activists illegally boarded the Naval destroyer USS *The Sullivans*. Using hammers, the group enacted the biblical order to "beat swords into plowshares," protesting the military presence in Portland, Maine. Some of the activists poured their own blood on the ship. They were arrested and ultimately convicted of conspiracy and destruction of military property. Their argument in court was, "'God did not provide one reality for governments and another for human beings like you and I. If it is criminal for me to kill, it is criminal for my government to kill."

As we noted at the beginning of this chapter and in our discussions of enforcing the 1st Amendment of the U.S. Constitution, the government hesitates to meddle in religious affairs, even when activities are quasi-religious or objectionable to mainstream society. There is a gap between formal legal policies and actual law enforcement practices (Haklai, 2007). The government will, however, step in when there is obviously criminal activity that is happening, including guerilla activism or financial malfeasance.

SUMMARY

In the United States, there is perhaps no other area of white collar criminal case law as murky as in religious crimes. The 1st Amendment of the Constitution guarantees religious freedom, even if a religion is unorthodox. In the case of consumer crimes, the government does not step in to protect the faithful unless they are clearly being taken advantage of financially. Or in the case where their lives may be in danger.

The most common forms of religious crime are embezzlement and misappropriation. As in the case of any white collar crime, if individuals are living lifestyles that appear to be much more lavish than their incomes could support, it raises the alarm to regulartory agencies, including the IRS. Of course, the same can be said about conventional criminals as well, who might spend their illegally gained money on luxury items. Though it may be a bit odd for religious leaders to live opulent lifestyles in large homes, driving high end cars, Weber would argue that this is in keeping with demonstrating that these leaders must be on the side of righteousness. Otherwise why would they be living such grand lives here on Earth, if they were not blessed by God? Or at least that's the argument.

Sometimes religious leaders will take advantage of the faithful, extracting more than the usual donations. In the case of cults, they may be asked to give up their entire life savings and turn over their personal property, including real estate. In the extreme, they may be asked to sacrifice their lives, as witnessed in the case of Heaven's Gate.

Case Study ▪ The Cult that Created a Town—Rajneeshpuram

Background

In the 1980s, a utopian town sprouted up in Oregon that began as a curiosity for people living in the area and within a few years became cause for serious concerns. As the walled ashram[5] community, Rajneeshpuram, named for its religious founder Bwagwan Shree Rajneesh, increasingly became patrolled by armed guards, questions emerged. Was this a harmless "yuppie"[6] enclave or the home of a dangerous and aggressive cult (Abbott, 2015)? Shortly after establishing itself in Oregon, local residents and members of city government in nearby Antelope came into conflict with the activities of the supposed utopia. Ultimately, Rajneesh and a number of individuals in his inner circle committed a variety of both conventional and white collar crimes. Perhaps all in the name of religion?

There are some conflicting viewpoints as to whether Rajneesh's group could be considered a cult or a New Religious Movement. Cults are generally described as being sinister to outsiders, as in the example of Heaven's Gate or Peoples Temple. On the other hand, New Religious Movements, though

---

[5] An ashram is a spiritual or religious retreat.
[6] The terms "Yuppie" or "Yuppies" referred to young urban professionals with upper mobility. The term was popularized in the 1980s.

non-traditional, are not always viewed as "evil," sometimes looking like completely new religions or like a blend of old and new. For the purposes of our definitions here, we will view the ashram in Oregon and its members as something in between, both a spiritual movement that drew on traditional Eastern religions, as well as a group that was ultimately found to be led by criminals.

Women in particular were attracted to Rajneeshpuram. Not only did Rajneesh exude sexual charisma, the commune offered liberation from conventional roles to both men and women. As Abbott (2015) reports, women outnumbered the men at the commune and were often assertive, taking leadership positions. Taking this into context of the Feminist Movement in the 1970s, for some of these women, it may have been the first time they found their voices.

Two women who joined the movement—Diane Onang, known as Ma Anand Puja within the commune community, and Sheela Silverman, known as Ma Anand Sheela—had checkered pasts like Rajneesh. Puja, more so than Rajneesh or Sheela, came into constant conflict with local residents and county commissioners in Oregon.

It is rare that an extremist New Religious Movement following is so large that it takes over a whole community in the United States. Perhaps the closest equivalent would be the Latter-day Saints (also known as Mormonism) establishments in Utah during the 19th Century. In the case of followers of Rajneesh, bringing a spiritual movement that blended Eastern and Western sensibilities, Oregon seemed to be a place where they could create their own version of utopia. As it turns out, Rajneesh had overstayed his welcome in his native India where he first established his movement and was notorious for getting into conflict with local officials, a behavior that was to be repeated Oregon, escalating into bioterrorism and threats of assassination in the United States.

Beginning with the conversion of a 64,000-acre ranch into a commune, the town of Rajneeshpuram eventually grew to include a strip mall, hotel, disco, airstrip, and public transportation (Oregon Department of Justice, n.d.). Even though Rajneesh's philosophy had fundamental ties to Eastern religions, his planned community was distinctly western (Abbott, 2015). Puja's first run in with authorities was after she arranged for the purchase of the ranch, not fully understanding the Oregon zoning laws (Zaitz, 2019). With the expectation of building housing compounds and bringing business enterprises to the ranch, she allegedly was not aware that in Oregon, the number of people and buildings occupying ranch land is severely limited (Zaitz, 2019). Trying to navigate around this regulation, Rajneeshpurm members pursued the creation of a town out of the ranch land.

As these things sometimes unfortunately go, all was not as it seemed in Rajneesh's utopian dream. On the surface, the guru exposed a lifestyle of free-love, organic farming, and sustainable living before it was fashionable (Urban, 2018), reminiscent of the hippie and commune lifestyles of the 1960s. Rajneesh along with Puja and Sheela and a number of his close inner circle, eventually were accused of a number of crimes. Among these included charges that they executed one of the largest bioterrorism plots in American history.

Defining the Crime(s)

Religious fraud covers a number of schemes that are committed by individuals who are responsible for the spiritual well-being of their congregants. By extension, they are likewise responsible for assuring that any donations made to the religious organization will be used for the purposes that they were intended.

In the case of the town of Rajneeshpuram, it is not simply fraud. Religious fraud is perhaps one of the oldest forms of white collar crime. The people who perpetrate these crimes exploit the human need to connect with spiritual life and a spiritual community. However, there is so much complexity in the Rajneesh case that it would be simplistic to merely chalk the crimes up to religious fraud.

The more serious charges against the group were those of bioterrorism in the form of spreading infectious salmonella bacteria in salad bars and produce stands (Urban, 2018). Puja, reportedly with the help of one of the laboratory technicians from the Rajneesh Medical Corporation located at the ranch, cultured the salmonella bacteria in order to contaminate food products (Haberman and Bernstein, n.d.). The mechanics of the poisoning are documented in a set of notes found at the commune during the investigation into the crimes. The poisonings were allegedly motivated by a conspiracy to disable a significant number of voters so that the Rajneeshees could take control of an upcoming election (Abbott, 2015).

A handful of the elite leadership in the spiritual movement, led primarily by Sheela, were also accused of conspiracy to kill elected officials who questioned the legitimacy of the community which regularly and purposefully ignored local, county, and state regulations. They did manage to succeed in giving salmonella-laced water to county officials, one of whom ended up in the hospital (Abbott, 2015).

Rajneesh was accused, separate from all the other criminal charges that could have been heaped on him, of initially entering the country on a four-month visa and lying when he claimed that he came to the United States to seek medical treatment. In actuality, he intended to stay permanently (*New York Times*, 1986). Immigration fraud covers a number of offenses involving the movement of people across borders. In Rajneesh's case, it was a case of perjuring himself on immigration documents.

More serious yet, the Rajneeshee leadership was suspected of plotting "to fly a bomb laden plane into the county courthouse. . . . 16 years before al Qaeda used planes as weapons." (Zaitz, 2019, retrieved from https://www. oregonlive.com/rajneesh/2011/04/part_one_it_was_worse_than_we.html)

Hence, between the bombing plot and the bioterrorism that they followed through with, at least the leadership at the ashram could be labeled a terrorist group. They were never successful in carrying out their plot.

Puja was separately accused of creating a list of people to wiretap with hidden electronic surveillance devices (Zaitz, 2019). Wiretapping laws can vary from state to state. In some states, it is permissible to record a conversation if only one person consents to having it recorded, known as "one-party consent." Other states are more stringent, requiring that all parties agree to the recording of telephone calls or face-to-face conversations, or the "two-party consent" (MWL, 2019, available at https://www.mwl-law.com/wp-content/uploads/2018/02/RECORDING-CONVERSATIONS-CHART.pdf). Oregon's wiretapping laws are more ambiguous, permitting some types of recordings but not others. However, federal government guidelines are much clearer, under which the Rajneesh followers were charged.

Theories to Explain the Crime

One theory that could explain the appeal of non-traditional religion in the 1970s and 1980s, which made followers ripe for the picking for charlatans, is that it was a period of time in history that seemed to give rise to cult followings. As we noted in the examples of other cults discussed in this chapter, in the 1980s we were still in the grips of the Cold War, we had just survived the Watergate scandal, and we were barely out of the Vietnam War.

Cults historically have been run by charismatic leaders, some who have established them for the sole purpose of exploitation. It is not uncommon in cults that followers are expected to give all their worldly goods, including bank accounts and real estate, over to the organization. There is some evidence of this happening within the Rajneeshpuram community, as reportedly ashram members purchased one Rolls-Royce car after another for Rajneesh, supposedly 93 in total (Zaitz, 2019). There is further evidence of cult-like behavior as Rajneesh's followers in India were encouraged to take part in sexual and violent behavior in group sessions (*Biography*, 2019).

Spiritual well-being is particularly found to be crucial when people are in crisis, whether it is personal strife or community tragedy, as it provides social connectedness to reduce hopelessness (Gaskin-Wasson et al., 2016). There are theories that we tend to see people join cults when their lives are in disarray, though this is not always the case. Research in psychology proposes that the opposite is true. Cult members do not, on average, suffer from mental illness and their psychological well-being prior to joining is within normal limits found in the general population (Buxant et al., 2007). Nor have prospective cult members always been living in financial distress prior to joining. In fact, in the case of Rajneesh's followers, they were primarily more affluent and middle-class, hardly living in conditions of economic hardship. This makes sense when we take into consideration that converts are many times asked to give over their possessions to the cult. More interesting in this case, is that his followers came from all around the world and did not simply represent an exploitation of local converts.

We might turn to Merton's Strain Theory to explain first, why the spiritual movement started, and second, why the group turned to crime to try and achieve their goals. As a refresher of the theory to those who have already had exposure to Merton in a sociology or criminology class, Table 9.1 summarizes his theory. "Institutionalized goals" refers to the goals that society expect people to have. "Institutional means" are the legitimate ways by which we are allowed to achieve those goals. For example, wanting to become a professor is a goal that society generally accepts as being a respectable profession. The only institutional means by which to become a professor is to complete a college education, including with fewer exceptions, post-graduate degrees.

Table 9.1 Merton's Strain Theory

Types	Institutionalized Goals	Institutionalized Means
Conformists	Accept	Accept
Innovators	Accept	Reject
Ritualists	Reject	Accept
Retreatists	Reject	Reject
Rebels	Reject and Replace	Reject and Replace

Source: Merton, 1938, 1968

We might speculate that members of the original India ashram, who, turning their backs on convention, could be labeled "retreatists" within Merton's typologies in Strain Theory. However, in light of the first attempts to work within the existing regulatory system, including attempts to create a town so as to avoid the prohibitions of ranch land in Oregon, they could be more accurately labeled "ritualists." As they moved to more criminal activities, they may be more legitimately labeled "rebels."

Social and Media Responses

Even though Rajneeshpuram dissolved a few decades ago and Rajneesh died in 1990, there has been renewed interest in the cult and its leader in recent years. In 2018 Netflix began streaming a documentary, *Wild Wild Country*, which attempts to explain the appeal of the cult. As one follower stated in the documentary, they felt like they were the "chosen ones," a common theme that runs through mainstream religions as well as cults.

Rajneeshpuram likewise did not escape parody. This far out from the events surrounding the creation of the Oregon town, Rajneeshpuram-like cults have even been loosely spoofed in a Netflix mockumentary, "Batshit Valley" (*Documentary Now!*, Fred Armisen, Bill Haer, Seth Meyers, and Rhys Thomas, executive producers).

Former members of the cult have contradicted the accountings of what really took place in Rajneeshpuram. One follower raised briefly in the town from age 7 to 11 claimed that she had a lot of freedom along with responsibilities, and claims to have had a lot of opportunities to learn new things, including aeronautical mechanics (Silman, 2018). We should note that as this particular follower was a child when the crimes took place, she may not have even been aware they were taking place until she was older and read accounts of them as an adult.

Criminal Justice and Policy Responses

Rajneeshpuram ultimately was a failed experiment. Its demise was largely due to the leaders running into conflict with regulations in the Oregon community, a similar experience to what Rajneesh followers found in India (Abbott, 2015). If it had merely been a question of arguments with local officials, they may have evolved into a commune that followed regulation. When it accelerated into criminal behavior, it made locals even more desperate to get rid of the commune all together, by any legal means possible.

What makes these types of crimes difficult to prosecute in the United States are the protections of religious freedom within the 1st Amendment of the U.S. Constitution. However, legal scholars would argue that individuals who commit religious fraud do not have constitutional protection and they should be criminally prosecuted like any other fraudster (Senn, 1990).

Theoretically, unlike conventional crime, criminal intent can be considered in the case of religious fraud. However, as Senn (1990, p. 336; *United States v. Prince*, 1974) points out, "the fact finder [e.g., prosecutors, judges, juries] is incapable of peering into another's head to discover what lies there in, a defendant's state of mind is rarely capable of being proved by direct evidence." One defense that a religious leader might present is that they were not aware of what they were doing was criminal or that they truly believe in the false narrative that they sell to their congregants. Either way, criminal intent is a difficult thing to prove in crimes associated with religious practices.

Again, the tricky issue is to prove that the fraud was intentional. However, this is where evidence in the form of a paper trail, as well as the testimony of individuals who can dispute the accused's claim of innocence, is beneficial to prosecutors' cases, as we see in the case of Jim Bakker of PTL Club fame.

Ultimately, a federal grand jury indicted several close followers of Rajneesh on charges of wiretapping using electronic bugs. Rajneesh's trusted assistant and spokesperson, Puja, served time in prison, both in Germany and the United States (Zaitz, 2019), for her role in wiretapping. Sheela plead guilty to the charges of attempted murder, electronic eavesdropping (a charge under wiretapping laws), and orchestrating the salmonella plot that reportedly sickened over 750 people at 10 restaurants (Associated Press, 1986). Her concurrent sentences on federal charges required her to serve 4.5 years in federal prison with 1 year suspended (Associated Press, 1986).

In state court, Sheela pleaded guilty to attempted murder as well as arson charges when she caused a fire that destroyed the county planning office (*New York Times*, 1986). Sheela received an additional sentence of 20 years in state prison, was fined $400,000, and ordered to additionally pay approximately $70,000 in restitution for the fire (*New York Times*, 1986).

As far as Rajneesh's criminal charges, he pleaded guilty to charges of immigration fraud, was ordered to pay a $400,000 fine and was ordered to leave the United States (*New York Times*, 1986). He was banned from re-entering the United States without the permission of the United States Attorney General of Oregon (*New York Times*, 1986). Rajneesh returned to India after being denied entry to a number of countries, including Greece, France, Uruguay, and Jamaica (*New York Times*, 1986; *Biography*, 2019). He passed away in 1990, failing in his attempts to resurrect his ashram (*Biography*, 2019).

Unanswered Questions and Unresolved Issues Related to the Case

One of the key features of law enforcement and regulatory agencies is the goal of prevention of crimes. We have already seen throughout this book how difficult this is in white collar crime, much less in conventional crime. What continues to be a sticky subject is that, at least in the United States or other similar countries without a state religion, religious freedom is vigorously defended.

It also begs the question of where to draw the line on religious freedom. In the case of Rajneesh's followers and Rajneesh himself, it was clearly a matter of crossing over into white collar and conventional crimes that have nothing to do with the freedom of religious expression. Do crimes need to become so blatant in religious organizations before they catch the attention of regulators and law enforcement?

Sources

Abbott, C. (2015) Revisiting Rajneeshpuram: Oregon's largest utopian community as Western history. *Oregon Historical Quarterly*. Vol. 116, No. 4: 415-447.

Associated Press. (1986) Ex-aide to guru plead guilty to charges. *Los Angeles Times*. July 23. Retrieved from https://www.latimes.com/archives/la-xpm-1986-07-23-mn-21578-story.html.

Biography. (2019) Bhagwan Shree Rajneesh biography (1931-1990). Oct. 28. Retrieved from https://www.biography.com/religious-figure/bhagwan-shree-rajneesh.

Buxant, C., V. Saroglou, S. Casalfiore, and L. Christians. (2007) Cognitive and emotional characteristics of New Religious Movement members: New questions and data on the mental health issue. *Mental Health, Religion, and Culture*. Vol. 10, No. 3: 219-238.

Gaskin-Wasson, A.L., K.L. Walker, L.J. Shin and N.J. Kaslow. (2016) Spiritual well-being and psychological adjustment mediated by interpersonal needs? *Journal of Religious Health*. Vol. 57: 1376-1391.

Haberman, M. and M. Bernstein. (n.d.) Inside the Rajneeshee secret files. OregonLive, *The Oregonian*. Retrieved from https://www.oregonlive.com/pacific-northwest-news/2018/04/top_secrets_revealed_in_myster.html.

Merton, R.K. (1938) Social structure and anomie. *American Sociological Review*. Vol. 3: 672-682.

Merton, R.K. (1968) *Social Theory and Social Structure*. New York: Free Press.

MWL (2019) Laws on recording conversations in all 50 states. Matthiesen, Wickert and Lehrer, S.C., Attorneys at Law. Oct. 24. Retrieved from https://www.mwl-law.com/wp-content/uploads/2018/02/RECORDING-CONVERSATIONS-CHART.pdf.

New York Times. (1986) Former aides to guru in Oregon plead guilty to numerous crimes. July 23. Retrieved from https://www.nytimes.com/1986/07/23/us/former-aides-to-guru-in-oregon-plead-guilty-to-numerous-crimes.html.

Oregon Department of Justice. (n.d.) Notable department investigations. Media. Retrieved from https://www.doj.state.or.us/media/doj-quick-facts/notable-investigations-achievements/.

Senn, S. (1990) The prosecution of religious fraud. *Florida State University Law Review*. Winter. Vol. 17, Issue 2: 325-352.

Silma, A. (2018) 9 Rajneeshpuram residents on what Wild Wild Country got wrong. The Cut, *New York Magazine*. Apr. 19. Retrieved from https://www.thecut.com/2018/04/9-rajneesh-followers-on-what-wild-wild-country-got-wrong.html.

Urban, H. (2018) Rajneeshpuram was more than a utopia in the desert. It was a mirror of the time: The rise and fall of "Zorba the Buddha" in Oregon. *Humanities*, National Endowment for the Humanities (NEH). Spring. Vol. 39, No. 2. Retrieved from https://www.neh.gov/humanities/2018/spring/feature/rajneeshpuram-was-more-utopia-desert-it-was-mirror.

Zaitz, L. (2019) 25 years after Rajneeshee commune collapsed, truth spills out—Part 1 of 5. OregonLive, The Oregonian. Feb. 5. Retrieved from https://www.oregonlive.com/rajneesh/2011/04/part_one_it_was_worse_than_we.html.

GLOSSARY

1st Amendment, U.S. Constitution   Under the 1st Amendment, as it pertains to religion in the United States, citizens have the rights to freedom of speech and to practice the religion of their choice without interference from the government, within reason.

Affinity fraud   Fraud that is committed by using one's social connections, including those made within religious organizations. Example: Ponzi scheme.

Charlatans   In the context of religion, individuals who fraudulently claim to have a special connection with a superior being, through whom others can only reach through them. Charlatans can also claim that they possess special, sacred information that only they know.

Cults   Religious or quasi-religious groups that operate outside of conventional religion and use aggressive tactics for recruiting new members. Generally the devotion is directed at a charismatic leader.

Establishment and Free Exercise Clauses   As additions to the 1st Amendment, further strengthen the separation of church and state, though they continue to be tested in the courts.

Megachurches   Large, non-denominational churches that have several thousand members and have increasingly become popular alternatives to more traditional Protestant religions.

Ministerial exception   This law allows religious organizations to legally discriminate against people for employment on the basis of religion. For example, a religious school could discriminate against job applicants who do not possess the same religious beliefs.

Misappropriation   Using funds or assets for other than their intended purposes. Example: A religious group using donations that are specifically designated building funds to buy a car for the group's religious leader.

Y2K bug   A computer flaw that was a result of a coding error that if not corrected, would result in computer errors or failure when the date changed from 12/31/1999 to 1/1/2000. Also called the "Millennium Bug," it created some trepidation and gave rise to some "Doomsday" cults who feared that computer failures, plus the end of the 20th century, would result in an apocalyptic event.

REFERENCES AND SUGGESTED READINGS

Associated Press. (2018) Priest accused of embezzling $5 million from his church for lavish estate. *Money*. Mar. 18. Retrieved from http://money.com/money/5223485/michigan-priest-embezzled-from-church/.

Banta, M. (2020) Rev. Wehrle, retired priest charged with embezzlement, died Tuesday, bishop says. *USA Today*. Retrieved from https://www.usatoday.com/story/news/local/2020/03/31/rev-jonathan-wehrle-diocese-lansing-embezzlement-dead/5099438002.

Barborak, N. (2014) Saving the world, one Cadillac at a time: What can be done when a religious or charitable organization commits solicitation fraud? *Akron Law Review*. Spring, Vol. 33, Issue 4: 577.

Barker, E. (1986) Religious movements: Cults and anticult since Jonestown. *Annual Review of Sociology.* Vol. 12: 329-346.

Bivins, J. C. (2003) *The Fracture of Good Order: Christian Antiliberalism and the Challenge to American Politics.* Chapel Hill, NC: The University of North Carolina Press.

Buxant, C., V. Saroglou, S. Casalfiore, and L. Christians. (2007) Cognitive and emotional characteristics of New Religious Movement members: New questions and data on the mental health issue. *Mental Health, Religion and Culture.* May, Vol. 10, No. 3: 219-238.

Dickson, E.J. (2019) A complete guide to the NXIVM trial. *Rolling Stone.* Apr. 22. Retrieved from https://www.rollingstone.com/culture/culture-features/nxivm-trial-whos-who-keith-raniere-alison-mack-salzman-bronfman-825328/.

Dougan, M. (1997) Heaven's Gate survivor kills self. *The Examiner Staff.* May 7. Retrieved from https://www.sfgate.com/news/article/Heaven-s-Gate-survivor-kills-self-3120047.php.

Durkheim, E. (1995; 1912) *The Elementary Forms of Religious Life.* K. Fields, trans. New York: The Free Press.

The Economist. (2012) Affinity fraud: Fleecing the flock. Retrieved from https://www.economist.com/business/2012/01/28/fleecing-the-flock.

Fleckenstein, M. P. and J. C. Bowes. (2000) When trust is betrayed: Religious institutions and white collar crimes. *Journal of Business Ethics.* Jan., Vol. 23, Issue 1: 111-115.

Frantz, D. (1997) The shadowy story behind Scientology's tax-exempt status. *New York Times.* Mar. 9. Retrieved from https://www.cs.cmu.edu/~dst/Cowen/essays/nytimes.html.

Grigoriadis, V. (2019) The horny holy man: Keith Raniere duped followers that power and growth came through submission. *Vanity Fair.* Sept. Published by Condé Nast.

Haklai, O. (2007) Religious-Nationalist mobilization and state penetration: Lessons from Jewish settlers' activism in Israel and the West Bank. *Comparative Political Studies.* June, Vol. 40, No. 6: 713-739.

Katersky, A. (2019) NXIVM founder convicted on all charges in sex cult case. *ABC News.* June 19. Retrieved from https://abcnews.go.com/US/nxivm-founder-keith-raniere-convicted-charges-sex-cult/story?id=63815115.

Kingston, K. G. (2011) Churches and private educational institutions as facilitators of money laundering in Nigeria. Vol. 1, No. 1: 30-38.

Legal Information Institute. (1989) *County of Allegheny v. ACLU,* Greater Pittsburgh Chapter. Cornell Law School. Retrieved from https://www.law.cornell.edu/supremecourt/text/492/573.

Lindhom, C. (2018) Charisma, in *International Encyclopedia of Anthropology.* H. Callan, ed. Wiley Online Library. Sept. 4. Accessed at https://doi.org/10.1002/9781118924396.wbiea1286.

Lindlaw, S. (1997) Some male cult members, including leader, were castrated. *AP News.* Retrieved from https://www.apnews.com/fc9ffd3235d37830cf26da5ad1720b4d.

Mann, B. (2011) Supreme Court asks: Could discrimination claim force female priests? *Catholic News Agency.* May 7. Retrieved from https://www.catholicnewsagency.com/news/supreme-court-asks-could-discrimination-claim-force-female-priests.

National Public Radio (NPR). (2018) Understanding NXIVM, group critics call a "cult." Weekend Edition Saturday. S. Simon, host; V. Grigoriadis, guest. From *Literature Resource Center.*

Palmer, K. (2018) Police: $63K found stashed above ceiling in basement. *Lansing State Journal.* July 18. Retrieved from https://www.lansingstatejournal.com/story/news/local/2018/07/18/father-wehrle-embezzlement-police-find-more-than-63-k-stashed/797883002/.

Panepento, P. (2007) Embezzlement widespread at dioceses, study finds. *Chronicle of Philanthropy.* Jan. 25, Vol. 19, Issue 7.

Rahman, T. (2018) Extreme overvalued beliefs: How violent extremist beliefs become "normalized." *Behavioral Sciences.* Jan., Vol. 8, Issue 1: 10-21.

Rubenstein, I. H. (1941) Criminal aspects of faith healing. *Medicao-Legal and Criminological Review.* July 1, Vol. 9, Issue 3:159-162.

Senn, S. (1990) The prosecution of religious fraud. *Florida State University Law Review.* Winter, Vol. 17, Issue 2: 325.

Spann, D. D. (2017) When the religious fall prey to fraud. *ACAMS Today.* Jan. 17. Retrieved from https://www.acamstoday.org/when-the-religious-fall-prey-to-fraud/.

Supreme Court of the United States. (2012) *Hosanna-Tabor Evangelical Lutheran Church and School v. EEOC*, 565 U.S. 171. October Term, 2011, decided Jan. 11.

U.S. Department of Justice. (2015) Ephren Taylor sentenced to federal prison. Press Release, U.S. Attorney's Office, Northern District of Georgia. March 17. Retrieved from https://www.justice.gov/usao-ndga/pr/ephren-taylor-sentenced-federal-prison.

U.S. Internal Revenue Service. (2019) Enforcement: Examinations. Retrieved from https://www.irs.gov/statistics/enforcement-examinations.

Weber, M. (1947) The nature of charismatic authority and its routinization, in *Theory of Social and Economic Organization*. A.R. Anderson and T. Parson, trans. New York: The Free Press.

Williams, E. Resurrecting free exercise in *Hosanna-Tabor Evangelical Lutheran Church and School v. EEOC*, 132 S. Ct. 694 (2012). *Harvard Journal of Law & Public Policy*. Jan. 1, Vol. 36, p. 391.

Zeller, B. E. (1997) *Heaven's Gate: America's UFO Religion*. New York: New York University Press.

Zillow. (2019) Rancho Santa Fe home prices & values. Retrieved from https://www.zillow.com/rancho-santa-fe-ca/home-values/.

Chapter TEN

Environmental Crime

What harm is a little dumping?

"The most alarming of all man's assaults upon the environment is the contamination of air, earth, rivers, and sea with dangerous and even lethal materials."

—Rachel Carson, Silent Spring

Chapter Objectives

- Introduce the history of environmental protection laws.
- Introduce global efforts to combat environmental crimes.
- Review the economic and political issues surrounding environmental protection.
- Identify some of the common forms of environmental crimes.

Key Terms

Clean Air Act, 1960
Clean Water Act, 1972
Deforestation
E-waste
Eco-terrorism
Endangered Species Act, 1973
Environmental Protection Agency (EPA)

Green criminology
Greenhouse gases
National Environmental Policy Act (NEPA), 1970
Safe Drinking Water Act (SDWA), 1974
Toxic Substances Control Act (TSCA)

INTRODUCTION

With population growth, the environment has increasingly been taxed in a number of ways. Everything from human and domesticated animal waste to materials emitting from machinery and factories has taken its toll. It is only in recent history that societies around the world have come to the realization that not only are many natural resources finite, but also that human activities can have a direct negative impact on the planet. According to a 2019 report to the United Nations from the Intergovernmental Science-Policy Platform on Biodiversity and Ecosystem Services (IPBES), there is overwhelming and alarming evidence that upwards to 1 million species of plants, insects, birds, animals, and microbes are now threatened with extinction (United Nations, 2019).

From the beginnings of industrialization, humans have had an exponentially dramatic effect on the environment. Since the 1970s, when a number of measures were passed to protect the air and waterways, it has been a continued push/pull between the business community and environmentalists' interests. The argument coming from pro-business interests is that attention to environmental issues will somehow stifle economic growth. To a large extent, the politicians responsible for creating laws to protect the environment have been caught in the middle, trying to appease both sides. Environmentalists and their supporters in turn argue that to continue to ignore environmental contaminants may spell doom to all species, including humans.

Along with greater attention to criminal acts against the environment has come the growth of a new branch within criminal justice studies. *Green criminology* takes a multidisciplinary approach to studying environmental crimes, with a focus on creating a defense for basic human and wildlife needs (Mesko and Eman, 2012). With this more contemporary interpretation, we are defining environmental crime in this chapter as

> "every temporary or permanent act or resigned activity, determined and defined as deviant by the (inter)national legislation, which causes any form of harm (an artificial change, worsening, burden, degeneration or destruction) to one or more of the eight elements (air, water, soft soil, mineral materials, human species, animal species, plant species, and microorganisms) that compound the natural environment or interrupt the environments' natural changes." (Mesko and Eman, 2012, p. 80)

In Rachel Carson's 1962 cautionary book, *Silent Spring*, she sounded the alarm on how humans' growing need to eradicate anything that stood in the way of progress has resulted in poisoning ourselves and animals around us in return:

> ".... 500 new chemicals [are created] to which the bodies of men and animals are required to adapt each year, chemicals outside the limits of biological experience.

Among them are many that are used in killing insects, weeds, rodents, and other organisms described in the modern vernacular as 'pests'; and they are sold under several thousand different brand names." (Carson, 1962, p. vi)

Since Carson's cautionary book was published, there have been increasingly more chemical cocktails that have been produced to allegedly make our lives better. When plastics became all the rage in the 1960s, it helped in food preservation, but few envisioned the mounds of trash that would result from these modern day conveniences that take forever (if ever) to naturally recycle back into the earth. Plus, the dangers of plastics to wildlife have been highlighted, as witnessed in attempts to ban six-pack plastic rings. More recently, there have been bans on plastic drinking straws and grocery store bags. Some of these bans were reversed in the face of the COVID-19 crisis in 2020. It was speculated that single-use plastic shopping bags were a safer alternative to people bringing their reusable bags to the store during the pandemic.

Likewise, pesticides and herbicides are advertised as improving our outdoor lives. Some have since been proven to be hazardous to the health of humans, pets, and a number of other living things, including insects that are important to ecosystems. Granted, as in the case of the abatement of malaria-carrying mosquitos, some pesticides have been successful in controlling life-threatening diseases (Aktar et al., 2009). And anyone who has ever visited or lived in Alaska can attest to the fact that the mosquitos are so large and numerous that outdoor activities in the summer are miserable without mosquito control in towns or the use of topical pesticides. However, other than the targeted pests, specifically destructive or stinging, biting insects and weeds in our yards, some pesticides and herbicides have been proven to be deadly, particularly if mishandled. There is also the threat of the chemicals entering the food chain or drinking water.

In thinking about how we can legitimately dispose of harmful substances, use of chemicals that are may be toxic to wildlife, or things like plastic that just won't break down efficiently in the environment once discarded, laws have been created to prevent illegal dumping of toxic materials. In this chapter we focus on the intentional violation of laws, not on accidents or cases of toxic spills due to human error or general carelessness. The case that comes to mind and is not included here is the Exxon *Valdez* oil spill off the coast of Alaska in 1989. The *Valdez*, an oil tanker, spilled roughly 11 million gallons of crude oil when it ran aground. Even though it resulted in the death of untold numbers of fish, birds, and wildlife, it is not classified as an intentional violation or crime. Initially, the captain was reported to have been intoxicated. That was later disproven and hence we probably should not think of the *Valdez* incident as a white collar crime.

In response to growing concerns for the future of the planet, an environmental activist movement sprung up in the late 1960s and early 1970s. With the first official Earth Day on April 22, 1970, there has been a growing demand for accountability when companies contribute to pollution. There has also been an increased demand for consumer goods, including modes of transportation, that are eco-friendly, as witnessed with the push for more electric cars and trains.

To a large extent, activists have been on the front line for changing laws in the United States and around the globe. This can be witnessed by the number of treaties between countries as they realize how essential cooperation is wherever there are shared wildlife and water resources (Society for Conservation Biology, 2019). For example, northern Pacific rim nations (e.g., northern Asian countries and North America) were called upon in 2004 by the United Nations General Assembly to address gaps in fishing conservation and management with the creation of international laws so as to prevent overfishing that could potentially cause the near extinction of some species of fish, particularly those that are important food sources (U.S. Senate Executive Report, 2014). As any astronaut who has travel in space will tell you, when you look back at the earth, there are no political boundaries to be seen and world leaders became increasingly aware towards the end of the 20th century that an environmental disaster in one country can inevitably cross borders into another.

Most, but not all, of the ecological offenders are in the chemical, petrochemical, or energy sectors, though as we will see in this chapter, automotive companies do not always comply with the law as well. We will have additional evidence of careless disregard in some industries in the human tragedy of the Woburn, Massachusetts cancer clusters, where offenders have the financial means to put on substantial defenses in civil courts once caught in the act. This can be emotionally and sometimes financially costly to the attorneys for plaintiffs if they lose the case, so there is little incentive to address environmental complaints. In some cases, the injured parties are not even aware that they have been victimized.

So as to not throw further confusion in the mix when looking at environmental laws, this chapter will focus only on environmental crimes, though in most cases there were no criminal prosecutions. As we will see in the Woburn, Massachusetts case, criminal wrongdoing was handled in civil court with a class action lawsuit. We are not including cases where companies are being sued for potential environmental impact, as in the example where the Sierra Club attempted to block development in the Sierra Nevada Mountains of California near Sequoia National Park (*Sierra Club v. Morton*), or in the case of the Standing Rock Sioux Tribe litigation to prevent the Dakota Access oil pipeline, as valid as these civil lawsuits might be.

Few crimes come close to causing greater widespread harm and misery than environmental crimes. People are more likely to recover from being the victim of a financial crime as compared to being exposed toxic dumping that may irreparably harm their health and that of their children. However, as emotional the concerns for the wellbeing of infants and children are, concerns for the environment runs in cycles and are very much dependent on the political and economic environments. There has generally been more reaction and action taken during and immediately after manmade environmental disasters, rather than preventative measures beforehand. This is similar to most white collar crimes, as witnessed with Enron, the 2008 mortgage banking meltdown, and the Big Pharma introduction of OxyContin, discussed in Chapters 5 and 8.

In studying environmental crimes, it is shortsighted to only look to measures taken in the United States. After all, as we have already mentioned, country borders are human constructs. As the world is one big ecosystem, what happens in one part of the world can have additional impact elsewhere on the planet, as in the example of the Chernobyl and Fukushima nuclear power plant incidents. So as to include the international community, in this chapter we will also explore laws and treaties that are designed to fight environmental crimes globally.

THE PROGRESSIVE CONSERVATION MOVEMENT

For all the push towards industrial progress in the 19th century, there were efforts made to counter the hazardous side-effects of industry and urbanization. One of the primary concerns was that pristine lands would be stripped of both their resources and their beauty. Though primarily lead by the scientific community and not by a general public outcry, the Progressive Conservation Movement (1890-1920) was environmental activism in its infancy. Some of these early struggles to protect natural resources had more to do with debates on who should own them and not as much on conservation, for all the meaning behind the movement's name (Hays, 1999).

It is important to note that not all corporations can be accused of irresponsibly exploiting the environment. Leaders during the Progressive Conservation Movement era came not only from a number of fields in science and technology, but included concerned individuals in industry and political office (Hays, 1999). Theodore Roosevelt, 26th president of the United States, as supporter of the conservation movement, is perhaps best-known today for his efforts in expanding the National Parks system and calling for the protection of public lands.

As an avid hunter, Roosevelt made several visits to the somewhat unsettled West that offered wide open spaces and breathtaking natural landscapes. In his travels and in discussion with local populations, Roosevelt was concerned that there was a blind disregard for thinning herds of bison, elk, and other wildlife due to excessive hunting, plus the practice of overgrazing by domestic animals (National Park Service, 2019). On his return to Washington, D.C. after his adventures out west, Roosevelt turned attention to legislation that would help preserve public lands for future generations. We should also mention, for all the efforts towards conservation, much of these so-called public lands were originally occupied by indigenous people, who were forcibly removed in the 19th century by the U.S government.

To a large extent, Roosevelt can be viewed as the first environmentally conscious president. Up through the 19th century and well into the 20th century, natural resources, including land, were being discovered and exploited. Until the scientific research progressed in the later part of the 20th century to provide a better understanding of the limits of resources and what the environment can withstand, there were few concerns for the impact of human activities on the eco-systems of the planet. The study of global biodiversity didn't even come into its own until the 1980s. Though there was an absence of genuine successful environmental activism until the 1970s, Roosevelt at least paved the wave for conservation. Since the 1970s, there have been several avenues law enforcement can go down to hold companies accountable for environmental crimes.

1970s ENVIRONMENTAL PROTECTION MOVEMENT

There were a number of laws passed by congress in the 1960s and 1970s in an effort to move towards protecting the environment, many of which were strongly objected to by industrial lobbyists. The argument has always been that environmental laws will inhibit progress and cut into profits. Keep in mind that many of these companies are accountable to their shareholders, and the reluctance to change has more to do with an eye on the bottom line than necessarily careless disregard for the environment. Nevertheless, in spite of opposition, the following key acts and laws were passed:

- Clean Air Acts of 1960, 1963, 1970
- National Environmental Policy Act (NEPA), 1970
- Clean Water Act, 1972
- Endangered Species Act, 1973
- Creation of the Environmental Protection Agency (EPA)
- Safe Drinking Water Act (SDWA), 1974
- Toxic Substances Control Act (TSCA), 1976

Since the 1970s, there have been few additions to the list of environmental laws. The 1990s brought growing public concern for a number of issues, including climate change (Clifford, 1998). There have been several attempts to roll back regulation since the 1970s, primarily in response to pressure coming from the fossil fuel industry and special interest groups to deregulate environmental laws. Unfortunately, this leaves regulatory confusion and ambiguity, similar to what we witness in financial crime regulation.

ENVIRONMENTAL PROTECTION AGENCY (EPA)

The *Environmental Protection Agency* is charged with the regulation of a broad range of laws that affect the environment. As we have already noted, the extent to which they do so is a function of the political and economic climate at any given time. Any agency is only as effective as the resources they have at hand, including funding for personnel and research.

The primary responsibilities of the EPA include the following (EPA.gov, 2019):

- Monitor air quality, including emissions and *greenhouse gases.*
- Monitor water quality; manage watersheds, rivers, wastewater, and storm water runoff.
- Monitor and manage landfills and hazardous waste dumps.
- Monitor health-related risks, including effects of pollutants, asbestos removal.
- Regulate the presence of potentially deadly substances in water, soil, and building materials, including formaldehyde and mercury.
- Supervise the safe cleanup of toxic and hazardous spills (e.g., oil spills.)
- Monitor the environmental conditions of states, cities, and communities.
- Provide cleanup and toxic waste dumping facilities.
- Promote green living movement, including education in sustainable energy, transportation choices, and recycling in homes and businesses.
- Provide scientific support in research grants and opportunities.

The EPA is also responsible for ensuring that individuals, residential homes, businesses, and corporations are following environmental laws in the United States. Additional burdens include responsibility for monitoring states, cities, and towns. This requires the EPA to conduct regular inspections — a daunting task — and to be called in when there are suspected violations. When they are required to conduct inspections, they will employ the following methods of evidence gathering during on-site visits (EPA, 2019, available at https://www.epa.gov/compliance/how-we-monitor-compliance):

- Interview facility or site representatives
- Review records and reports
- Take photographs
- Collect samples
- Observe facility or site operations

We should keep in mind some of the basics of human nature when considering the validity of these inspections. If you have taken an introductory psychology course or a research methodology class, you may recall something called the "Hawthorne effect" or "guinea pig effect." Based on a management study conducted at a factory, the premise of the effect is that people will be on their best behavior if they are aware that they are being observed. In the case of any inspection, any behaviors that are within the control of the people who are being scrutinized, such as their compliance with environmental laws, may be altered during the inspection only to return to questionable behavior once the inspectors have left.

INTERNATIONAL EFFORTS

In the earlier part of this century, the environmental movement took a distinctly different approach internationally to tackling the problems of atmospheric greenhouse gases that are threatening the planet. Whatever side of the argument one is on with what is happening with the climate within the past century, describing it as "global warming" or "climate change," average temperatures around the globe have been steadily increasing, oceans have been warming, and sea levels are rising (Boyle, 2018). The problem is increasingly being viewed by the international community as a human rights issue.

With extreme weather, including hurricanes and typhoons[1], there is a real concern for the displacement of populations. For example, as a country bordered by the ocean and less than friendly neighbors, Bangladesh in South Asia, home to a population of nearly 165 million inhabitants, is facing the real possibility of displacement due to flooding and rising sea levels.

The United Nations Paris Climate Agreement of 2015 (or Paris Agreement), with an eye on international environmental law, was to piggyback on earlier efforts to stabilize the climate, including the Kyoto Protocol of 1997 (Boyle, 2018). The goal in both international treaties was to put into practice laws and other ways to help prevent world temperatures from rising any more than an additional 2°C (35.6°F) (Boyle, 2018). The tipping point that has been described by climatologists as the point of no return in global warming is an average rise in temperatures of 4.5°C (40.1°F). In the international agreement, countries have philosophically agreed to slow down or stop human activities that are being blamed for the destruction of ecosystems around the world.

The Paris Agreement and variations created since 2015 have received lukewarm support from the 180 plus countries that have signed the agreement. In a move ordered by President Donald Trump in 2017, the United States withdrew from the climate agreement. To date, there are only 13 countries that have not ratified the agreement (Ayers, 2019), including the United States. Of the 197 countries who have ratified the agreement, few have reportedly complied with the content within the treaty.

As part of efforts to control greenhouse warming effect, there have been calls to reduce *deforestation* and coal production around the world. If Iceland, a volcanic island, is any example, when Nordic explorers arrived on the island in the 9th century, they quickly used up existing trees. In building boats, shelters, and stockpiling for fires in order to keep themselves warm in the harsh climate[2], settlers on Iceland depleted what forest was there. An island that was estimated to

---

[1] Both hurricanes and typhoons are devasting cyclonic storms that originate in the oceans and can cause extreme flooding when they make landfall. When these types of storms occur in the Atlantic or northern Pacific Oceans, they are called *hurricanes*. When they originate in the South Pacific and Indian Oceans, they are called *typhoons*.

[2] If you recall your geography lessons, Iceland is really green for a good portion of the year, with mild summers, but winters can be extremely cold.

be 25-40 percent forest before the Vikings arrived was reduced to an alarming 0.5 percent forest by the early 20th century (Magann, 2019). Even the early settlers had to resort to using peat as heating fuel as trees on the island became scarce. Efforts to reforest Iceland have only been marginally successful, given the example of Hallormsstadaskogur National Forest, populated by the remnants of a birchwood farm. Anyone who has traveled to Iceland will immediately note the overall absence of trees on the island.

Greater concern and efforts in the international community are currently directed at the deforestation of the Amazon. Due to its vastness, scientists have a difficult time quantifying plant diversity (Hopkins, 2007), and some species have yet to be discovered and identified. The plants in the Amazon basin have long had a great importance in producing natural pharmaceuticals for indigenous communities (Vandebroek et al., 2004). Deforestation reduces the number of these plants available. The concerns about losses of rainforests is not only of grave concern to local populations. The Amazon basin contains 10 percent of the world's biodiversity and 15 percent of the world's freshwater supplies (Yale University, 2019).

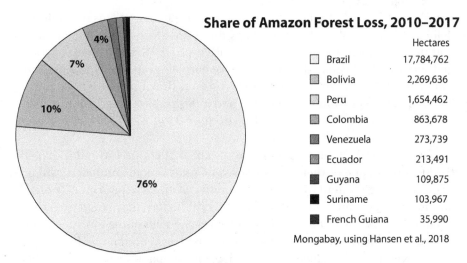

Share of Amazon Forest Loss, 2010–2017

		Hectares
☐	Brazil	17,784,762
▣	Bolivia	2,269,636
▣	Peru	1,654,462
▣	Colombia	863,678
▣	Venezuela	273,739
▣	Ecuador	213,491
▣	Guyana	109,875
■	Suriname	103,967
■	French Guiana	35,990

Mongabay, using Hansen et al., 2018

EXHIBIT 10.1 ‖ **Amazon Forest Loss** *Source:* Mongabay, 2019, https://rainforests.mongabay.com/amazon/amazon_destruction.html.

Most deforestation is illegal in tropical regions, including the Amazon. The primary reason for deforestation in the Amazon has been to make way for cattle ranchers as the demand for animal agriculture, including beef, increases internationally. A secondary industry that is devasting the rainforest, though not to as great extent as animal agriculture, is logging. The means by which deforestation occurs is either by clear cutting, which is a time-consuming method, or by setting fires. Both are injurious to the environment, but of the two, setting fires also creates widespread air pollution as well.

Law in the Real World: Illegal Deforestation in the Amazon

(Source: Wallace, 2019, National Geographic)

Deep in the Amazon rainforest, a battle between the Brazilian Institute of the Environment and Natural Renewable Resources (IBAMA), an environmental regulatory group, and criminal loggers and gold miners has raged on for 30 years. Any commercial removal of timber for any reason within areas of Brazil that are still indigenous is unlawful. In their investigations, the IBAMA has "uncovered elaborate fraud schemes aimed at the theft and clearing of public land for cattle grazing and agriculture." (Wallace, 2019, retrieved from https://www.nationalgeographic.com/environment/2019/08/brazil-logging/#close). But as Wallace (2019) reports, rainforest deforestation is occurring at a pace that is far faster than the IBAMA can control.

Adding to the challenge is the denial of the destruction by current Brazilian President Jair Bolsonaro. In his estimation, satellite photos of rainforest deforestation are fake. His criticism of the IBAMA is harsher yet, claiming that the agency's primary motive is to collect the stiff fines given when criminals are caught illegally deforesting. Bolsonaro also reportedly has plans to roll back existing environmental protections in Brazil in order to open the Amazon to logging, mining, ranching, and industrial-scale agriculture (Wallace, 2019). After taking office, Bolsonaro fired 21 of 27 IBAMA state representatives (Wallace, 2019).

In July 2019, Wallace and a photographer, Felippe Fittipaldi, joined IBAMA during one of their operations. The plan was to conduct a raid on suspected logging activities, with a number of IBAMA personnel, police, and military personnel taking part in the raid. Before they could arrest the offenders, every one of the loggers involved cleared out of the forest. As Wallace (2019) reports, the industry had been tipped off on the raid.

In order to conceal their activities, logging companies will use a number of tactics. Criminal loggers will camouflage their equipment in order to escape aerial surveillance and truck the logs to sawmills at night under the cover of darkness (Wallace, 2019). In the same way that organized crime groups bribe officials, brokers in the logging industry will bribe bureaucrats to falsify documents. In these documents, they state that the loggers have obtained their wood in sustainably managed forests, as they cannot bring illegal lumber to market without certification of where it came from (Wallace, 2019). The sawmills themselves are not held criminally liable unless they are aware that they are processing illegally cut wood (Editor's note, Wallace, 2019).

Using strongarm tactics characteristic of organized crime groups in order to thwart the efforts of the IBAMA, inspectors for the agency have had their lives threatened. As veteran field inspector Givanildo dos Santos Lima describes it, he has been the target of a number of threats spread through social media and cannot travel without police escort (Wallace, 2019).

Even with Bolsonaro undercutting their efforts, including rolling back environmental laws, the president of Brazil won't do away with the IBAMA altogether. This is primarily due to how it might look to the rest of the world. Keep in mind that Brazil is one of the countries that ratified the Paris Climate Agreement. As one IBAMA field agent reported, "He [Bolsonaro] needs IBAMA to show the world that Brazil is taking care of the Amazon." (Wallace, 2019, retrieved from https://www.nationalgeographic.com/environment/2019/08/brazil-logging/#close).

Discussion Questions

1. From what you can tell from this case, how much is Brazil in compliance with the Paris Agreement?
2. In light of the threats made against IBAMA agents, should there be more charges against offenders than simply illegal logging?
3. Besides money, what might be motivating bureaucrats to risk their jobs by issuing false documents in order for logging companies to bring illegal lumber to market?

WATER QUALITY VIOLATIONS

The dependence on water for human life is undeniable. In an emergency situation such as being stranded stranded out in the middle of nowhere, you can live longer without food than you can without water. Since the invention of indoor plumbing, we have complacently assumed that the water pouring from our taps is safe to drink. Along with the combination of two hydrogen atoms and one oxygen atom, water can consist of a number of chemicals and metals — some benign, some toxic to humans and wildlife. Among them are 91 chemicals recognized by the EPA as contaminants (EPA, 2019).

The quest for better water quality is an ongoing challenge. The first line of defense in the United States is the *Clean Water Act*. First passed in 1972 as the Federal Water Pollution Control Act, the legislation has gone under several revisions with amendments. Through the EPA, the Clean Water Act makes unlawful any discharge of pollutants into navigable waters, unless a permit has been obtained (EPA, 2019d). The need to amend the law is necessary to keep current with changes in environmental conditions and discovery of any new threats to the nation's drinking water supply.

The biggest challenge to the EPA is the sheer size of the responsibility to enforce the Clean Water Act. There are approximately 150,000 community water districts throughout the United States that are required to actively monitor contaminant levels (Zivin et al., 2011). Like many government agencies, the degree to which the EPA can effectively do its job is dependent on funding.

Law in the Real World: Woburn, Massachusetts Cancer Clusters

(Source: A Civil Action, Harr, 1996; Kix, 2009)

Beginning in the late 1960s, in a quintessential primarily working-class New England town just outside Boston, Massachusetts, an unusually high number of children were becoming ill. This was not a flu outbreak or other pandemic viruses that routinely run through populations of school-aged children. By 1986, 22 children in Woburn had been diagnosed with childhood leukemia and twelve had died. One adult died of myelocytic leukemia, a rare form of cancer.

In a larger city, this may not be an abnormally high number of cases, but in a town of just over 35,000 residents, it appeared to be more than coincidence. This, along with a number of other inflictions such as birth defects, unusual skin irritations, and rashes, all primarily happening to infants and children, parents began to suspect that there was something in the environment that was causing all the illnesses. There were also an unusual number of cases of kidney cancer.

By 1965, shortly after a new city well started pumping into the water supply, people began to talk about how funny the water tasted coming out of their taps. In 1967, the Massachusetts Department of Health considered shutting some of the wells in the city because of concerns about the water quality. Yet according to the engineer for the Woburn pumping station, chlorine was the culprit, added to the water in supposed safe quantities to kill bacteria. The same engineer certified the water as being safe for drinking.

Charles and Anne Anderson, living in Woburn, had a son being treated for cancer, and had just brought him home after yet another hospital stay. Neighbors and friends gathered to welcome him home. As Harr (1992) reports, it was there that parents started comparing notes on their own children's illnesses. For them, all the pieces of puzzle were starting to fit together and it became abundantly clear that there was good reason to believe that the common denominator was indeed in the water. By 1969, the families formed a committee to pressure the city to have the suspected wells closed. By summer that year, the offending wells were shut down. But in spring of 1970, the wells were opened once again. Now the water not only tasted off, but complaints started pouring into City Councilman Mahoney's office with descriptions of "putrid, ill-smelling, and foul water" coming from taps (Harr, 1992, p. 23).

One of the parents, Donna Robbins, contacted the law firm of Reed & Mulligan in the early 1980s, hoping to find justice for whatever in the water was afflicting children, including her son, who died of cancer in 1981 when he was only nine years old. Prior to contacting Reed & Mulligan, Robbins, a retired nurse, had been visited by researchers from the CDC who were investigating the cancer clusters. They asked her the usual types of questions in cancer cases, including the family's medical histories, exposure to x-rays, and her spouse's occupation.

Robbins, along with seven other families, decided to find resolution through the civil law system as they ran into a number of obstacles working with the city council members and local businesses. Each family had lost at least one child to leukemia. They and others were suspicious that toxic dumping was happening in and around the town, particularly by the Cryovac plant, a subsidiary of the W.R. Grace company, and at the John J. Riley Tannery. Beatrice Foods was later identified in the lawsuit as a co-defendant in the case, as it had purchased the tannery in 1978. Even though they sold the tannery back to the Riley family in 1983, they were still responsible for any of the operations between 1978 and 1983.

Jan Schlichtmann, a personal injury attorney and former employee of Reed & Mulligan, was tasked with visiting the affected families in Woburn. As it was portrayed in the movie *A Civil Action* (1998, Touchtone Pictures), Schlichtmann only visited the families as part of due diligence, but with the understanding that his firm would probably not take the case as it didn't appear, on the surface, to be a case that could be won against companies with deep pockets for legal defense.

Convinced that there was a justifiable case against Cryovac, the tannery, and Beatrice Foods, Schlichtmann eventually took on the lawsuit, against the better judgement of the partners in his law firm. Anyone who has ever read the book *Don Quixote*, may remember the main character's jousting at windmills in his madness. This pretty much describes the uphill battle that Schlichtmann faced and the skepticism from his partners at Schlichtmann, Conway & Crowley law firm as to the sanity of taking on a difficult case that might tax their resources. The plaintiffs were by no means financially well-off. Nonetheless, Schlichtmann was able to convince his partners to take the case.

With a trial that began in 1986, witnesses and evidence pointed to Cryo-vac Plant's dumping of trichloroethylene, a cancer-causing agent used in cleaning industrial equipment. The substance was dumped on ground where it could seep into the water table, eventually reaching the city wells. Management claimed that they had simply ordered employees to get rid of the used cleaning solvent, but without any specific instructions as to how to do so in an ecologically sound way. John Drobinski, a witness for the plaintiffs and manager at Weston Geophysical, a consulting firm, was hired to conduct a survey of the Riley tannery property. Drobinski described in his deposition what he found during his survey of the Riley tannery:

" ... you could smell sweet organic vapor smell in the air, a number of the barrels that we had discovered on the site contained labels on it that would indicate to us that they that [sic] solvents had been used on the site or solvents had been in the barrels. ... " (U.S. States District Court, District of Massachusetts, Civil No. 82-1672-S, Volume 1-23, 1985)

In a separate trial, Beatrice Foods were found liable, with a judgement of $8 million (USD) ruled by Judge Skinner in favor of the plaintiffs. In theory, the law firm of Schlichtmann, Conway & Crowley should have done well financially from the outcome of the Beatrice Foods trial. However, as this was a costly trial with a large number of expert witnesses called, plus the challenge of facing defendants with near limitless legal resources, the trial resulted in the firm going under by crippling debt, and eventually the partnership dissolved.

Even though they were found not liable in the original lawsuit brought against them by the parents, due to a mistrial, W.R. Grace was not off the hook. Once the EPA stepped in, they presented a 50-year plan for land reclamation where the contaminated wells were located. In order to pay for the $69.4 million (USD) project, the EPA filed a lawsuit against W.R. Grace and Beatrice Foods. W.R. Grace was additionally charged by the U.S. Attorney's Office for perjury, as the company lied in statements to EPA.

For any of us who have had the good fortune of meeting Jan Schlichtmann, who eventually became the lead lawyer at the center of one of the biggest environmental cases in the late 20th century, we find a man who is humble and reflective, far from the brash and flashy person he was before he took the Woburn case. As he (and Harr) describes it, the case left him broken, both financially and emotionally:

"Schlichtmann filed for bankruptcy. ... In the Chapter 7 papers filed in bankruptcy in Boston, he listed his assets as fourteen dollars in a checking account, a fifty-dollar cassette radio, one hundred dollars in cash, and five hundred dollars' worth of clothes." (Harr, 1992, p. 491)

As for Schlichtmann, after several failed appeal attempts, he left Massachusetts, escaping to Hawaii. He spent several years there, which he described as his "Wilderness Years" (Harr, 1996). Returning to Boston in 1993, he has spent the subsequent years working on a number of environmental issues.

Discussion Questions

1. What might have motivated Schlichtmann to take a case that he and his law partners suspected would be difficult to win?
2. Why might a company recklessly dump toxic chemicals, even when they are aware of what they are doing is illegal?
3. We have witnessed that companies are more likely to be sued in civil court than be held criminally libel in environmental crimes. What challenges are there in seeking criminal charges in these cases?

Since the Woburn case, as we discussed in our chapter on corporate crime, companies are taking a more active part in protecting the environment. As part of the corporate social responsibility movement of the past couple of decades, plus global consensus on the impact of industry on the environment, a new era has been ushered in where there is more push for global cooperation (Biocanin et al., 2018). It is more difficult for companies to get away with illegally dump toxic waste, at least in the United States, than during the period leading up to the Woburn case. However, the Trump administration ushered in a new era of deregulation, where we may see less compliance.

AIR QUALITY VIOLATIONS

After the *Clean Air Act of 1960* was passed, a number of states passed their own forms of legislation to doubly assure that industries would comply with the new law. For example, Pennsylvania passed its own clean air legislation, the Air Pollution Control Act, in 1960. The legislation gave Pennsylvania's Department of Environmental Protection (DEP) the power to set emission standards for air pollutants and monitor the air quality index in the state (Sharkey, 2009). Companies quickly found that it was an expensive proposition to violate these new laws. They were caught between a proverbial rock and hard place, as many of them had to change their operations or add new equipment in order to comply with air quality standards.

WASTE REMOVAL AND DISPOSAL

Since the inception of contemporary society, humans have produced more trash per capita than can be logically be disposed of without having some impact on the environment. According to the EPA[3], in 2013 Americans created 254 million tons of municipal solid waste, as compared to the 88.1 million tons they produced in 1960 (EPA, 2019e). And this is only including the non-toxic, non-hazardous waste produced in the United States.

In recent decades, one solution to reducing humans' impact on the environment is recycling and reuse. The recycling practices of individuals, whether voluntarily or dictated by their municipalities, has increasingly become popular, with about 35 percent of disposed items being recycled in the United States (EPA, 2019). Recycling rates are higher elsewhere, with the UK reporting a goal of 50 percent recycled waste, but falling short at its current 44 percent (Parveen, 2018).

The removal of waste has become a transnational phenomenon, so much so that organized crime has now gotten in on the business of waste shipping. With a "not in my backyard" mentality, wealthier nations have historically sought ways to ship their garbage (little of which is legal) to poorer nations. This has been at the cost of the inhabitants, including people and wildlife, in those poverty-stricken countries.

Law in the Real World: Waste Trafficking, The Republic of Slovenia

(Source: Mesko and Eman, 2012)

Though this book is primarily about white collar crime, we cannot discount organized environmental crimes, where there is the intersection of seemingly legitimate business with illegal waste trafficking. What makes organized crime groups different from other white collar conspiracies is that they are far more dangerous. Some of the more common types of environmental crimes committed by organized crime groups include "illegal disposal of waste, illegal advertising and criminality associate with rare or wild animal and plant species." (Mesko and Eman, 2012, p. 83). As waste removal has become more profitable, organized crime groups see this as yet another market to exploit.

---

[3] According to the current EPA website, its web archive only reports through 2013 for municipal solid waste.

The country of Slovenia, once a Soviet satellite and part of Yugoslavia, in recent decades has become an ideal transit site between Western and Eastern Europe, and a natural conduit for organized crime. As Mesko and Eman note (2012), Slovenia is uniquely pristine, with vast forests and rich water resources. Posing a threat to this idyllic landscape is the transportation of waste materials, sometimes dumped or stored in places where it can do ecological harm.

Even when there are legitimate attempts to dispose of toxic materials, it can become a convoluted transaction. In the 1993 so-called "Colombia affair," C&G had a 97-ton cargo of toxic waste that was bounced around among and rejected by France, Colombia, Ecuador, and Peru, ending up back in Slovenia. In 1994 the shipment finally made its way to France, where it was destroyed in accordance with environmental standards (Mesko and Klenovsek, 2011).

In an example of Italian organized crime groups illegally disposing of waste in Slovenia, police in the Primorka region of Slovenia found waste unceremoniously dumped in the sinkholes of farmers' pastures. After an investigation, it was discovered that the farmers were being paid by the Italian organized crime groups to unload the waste on their land (Mesko and Klenovsek, 2011).

As Mesko and Eman predict (2012), as long as illegal waste trafficking remains profitable and the risk of penalties remain low, there will be little motivation to stop it. However, the Slovenia government has made efforts within the past decade to put environmental protections in place, including aggressively addressing crimes committed by organized crime groups.

Discussion Questions

1. What might the international community do to prevent the illegal shipping of waste across borders?
2. What role do open borders in the European Union play in the trafficking of waste in Eastern Europe?
3. Why might the countries named in the Colombia affair refuse the waste cargo, even if the C&G company followed all international laws for toxic disposal?

E-WASTE

Not all waste items are easily disposed of or even recyclable. For example, the cell phone that you are carrying contains a number of toxic substances. Even discarded cigarette butts are considered hazardous waste, with the potential of toxins polluting waterways (Barnes, 2011).

We should also reflect on the fact that what are considered to be violations in environmental laws in the United States may not be so in other countries. It is an additional motivation for companies to move to places in the world with little to no environmental protections for financial reasons beyond a cheaper labor force. Of greater concern is the rise of *e-waste* in the age of electronics, where it is a challenge to find solutions to getting rid of toxic chemicals and metals when items become obsolete, only to be tossed and replaced. Some of these toxic substances can be recycled, but they are hazardous to the workers who remove them from the electronics. This and lower operating costs motivate the export of e-waste to other countries than the United States, including China, Nigeria, Pakistan, and Ghana (Sinai, 2017).

Law in the Real World: Brian Brundage, Recycling Executive

(Source: EPA Bulletin, 2019b)

Earlier in this chapter, we noted that as in other types of white collar crime, environmental crimes will more likely end up in civil court, resulting in fines. When environmental crimes are mixed with other types of white collar crime, the offender may not get off so lightly. Brian Brundage, executive and owner of Intercon Solutions Inc. and EnviroGreen Processing LLC, learned this the hard way.

Brundage convinced his customers that he had been responsibly disassembling and recycling materials extracted from discarded electronics. Among his customers were corporations and government agencies. Instead, between 2005 and 2016, Brundage authorized thousands of tons of e-waste to be illegally dumped into landfills, stockpiled, or resold to companies that in turn sent the toxic materials overseas to be recycled. In addition, Brundage profited from these sales and failed to report the earnings to the IRS as personal income. Instead, he reported them as business expenses for his companies and he was eventually investigated for income tax evasion. As we have seen in other cases of greed, Brundage was taking the money to enhance his lifestyle, including paying for the personal services of a nanny and housekeeper, extravagant purchases, and payments to a casino. In total, Brundage owed $743,984 in federal income taxes alone on the money he made in selling e-waste.

Of greatest concern environmentally is his cavalier sale of e-waste that contained dangerous levels of lead. According the EPA case against him, he was well aware that the cathode ray tubes used in the fluorescent screens of televisions and computers were toxic. Cathode ray tubes contain toxins, including lead, that put humans at risk for health problems, including neurological damage to fetuses and small children.

In his plea agreement, Brundage admitted to ordering his employees to sell e-waste to vendors that he knew full well would be selling unscrupulously overseas, leaving untold numbers exposed to toxins. Again, we do have to remind ourselves that the sale of the e-waste to legitimate vendors is not illegal, just the concealment of the income generated from these sales. He also pleaded guilty to wire fraud and income tax evasion.

Brundage was ultimately sentenced to three years in federal prison for his crimes. Special Agent-in-Charge Ryan was quoted as saying that "this sentence should serve as a reminder that HSI [GSA, EPA] will continue to work with its federal, state and local partners to pursue offenders who endanger others by engaging in fraud and deceit." (EPA, 2019b, retrieved from https://www.epa.gov/sites/production/files/2019-05/documents/march-april2019bulletin.pdf.)

Discussion Questions

1. Would Brundage receive any prison time if he had only been held accountable for the illegal dumping of e-waste in landfills?
2. Which offense might be more unethical? Illegal e-waste dumping or income tax evasion?
3. If the dumping of some e-waste is illegal in the United States, why might it be legal to sell it to vendors to recycle (or dump?) overseas?

ECO-TERRORISM

Though not generally discussed in terms of white collar crime, *eco-terrorism* is viewed by the FBI as the most serious domestic threat to the United States (Yang and I-Chin, 2018). We are including eco-terrorism in this book as it is an unusual type of crime that straddles occupational and conventional crime typologies. When activists working for legal or quasi-legitimate environmental groups cross the line into destructive acts, including arson and other types of property damage, it is not simply a nuisance, but also represents financial loss for the industries they target. Some estimated damages include $100 million attributed to the Earth Liberation Front (ELF) and "an estimated $48 million worth of arson and vandalism from 1996 to 2001" by "The Family," another environmental activist group that operates in the shadows. (Yang et al., 2019, p. 1).

Unlike other white collar or occupational crimes, as the crimes themselves are conventional, there are no regulatory agencies that initiate investigations. Generally, these cases fall in the jurisdiction of local law enforcement and the FBI. However, there is some confusion as to whether the targets of eco-terrorist groups, including animal testing facilities, are themselves committing crimes, or at least conducting unethical research. While there are a number of regulations and treaties that protect wildlife, legislation covering the parameters for experimentation on animals is missing (Yang et al. 2019).

ECOCIDE

There are some activists who believe that companies, and in some cases countries, should be held accountable for the willful destruction of whole ecosystems. As there is more movement to address the climate and ecological problems that humankind faces today, there is more demand for criminal prosecution in cases of ecocide. For example, hundreds of dolphins were injured off the shores of France, resulting in their deaths, because of the carelessness of trawler companies who fail to ensure that they don't get tangled in their nets (Monbiot, 2019).

Though not criminally charged, the United States government is being held responsible for the ecological damage done during the Vietnam War. As the war was largely fought in dense jungle terrain, the U.S. military used Agent Orange, an herbicide used to clear foliage, to create better visibility in detecting the North Vietnamese military operations. The herbicide was proven to be an environmental disaster that contributed to number of medical conditions in people exposed to it, including members of the American military. Only recently has the United States contributed to the funding of cleanup efforts in Vietnam (Cusato, 2018). These efforts are largely voluntary. There continue to be international efforts to criminalize any purposeful ecological destruction.

SUMMARY

The most critical resources that need to be protected from ecological crimes and disasters are waterways, reservoirs, air, and food resources, including soil for agriculture production. It has always been a tug-of-war between businesses with a focus on profit and environmentalists. In all fairness, companies themselves may be conflicted as many strive for social responsibility, if for no other reason than it is good for their reputations to be ecologically minded. Politicians are likewise caught in an endless battle of representing their constituents, whether they are powerful corporations or very vocal environmentalists. We certainly have seen these dichotomies play themselves out within the past sixty years.

It is only in recent human history that any attention has been given to the environment. Increasingly, there are greater efforts to create and enforce laws to protect ecosystems. There has also been more civil lawsuits brought against offenders by the EPA and international environmental regulators. We have seen examples of this, such as in our example of toxic dumping in Woburn, Massachusetts.

Of the tools at hand for regulators are a number of environmental laws that have been passed since the early 1960s, including the Clean Air and Clean Water Acts. As the pendulum swings between the needs of the business community and those of the environmentally-focused, we are currently in an era where there are substantial efforts towards deregulation. We have noted that the greatest challenges to enforcement of environmental laws are resources.

Case Study ▪ **Volkswagen—Liar, Liar, Pants on Fire**

Background

Flying into Los Angeles International Airport in the 1960s, there were days when the sky was an unnatural shade of brown, thick with air pollution. Any venturing outside would result in your eyes stinging and your lungs aching. The Los Angeles basin, with the geographical features of the San Gabriel mountains plus a population dependent on cars, became a natural bowl in which smog would settle with nowhere to go when there was no wind. The only relief came on days during the fall and winter months, when Santa Ana winds coming from the east blew the smog out over the ocean. As early as the 1940s, scientists and policymakers in Los Angeles acknowledged that smog was increasingly not only an eyesore (pun intended), but also a serious health hazard.

Even though smog was recognized for a number of decades as being detrimental to one's health, the Environmental Protection Agency (EPA) was not formed until 1970. With its notoriety for smoggy days and smog alerts ordering people indoors, California led the way in the push for better air quality. Since then, the EPA has placed restrictions on auto manufacturers on the amount of pollutants that new cars can emit. Most states have also required emissions inspections of new and used vehicles in order to register cars or to renew registration on used vehicles. In the meantime, auto manufacturers were under pressure to manufacture cars with better gas mileage, particularly during the oil crises of the 1970s.

In 2015, Volkswagen, with automobiles sold worldwide, put on a massive marketing campaign for their diesel cars. In their advertisement, they portrayed the cars as having low emissions, appealing to the global warming/climate change conscious public. It many respects, diesel automobiles have traditionally represented efficiency, with engine parts that last longer than most gasoline-consuming motors, and they generally have better fuel economy. Behind the scenes, VW was falsifying the actual emissions standards of their vehicles, bringing into question their actual fuel economy as well.

Defining the Crime(s)

When it comes to large corporations, it is difficult at times to figure out if what they are doing is crime or simply mismanagement. The lines are not always clear cut. In the case of Volkswagen, they were clearly acting with complete disregard of regulation and environmental protections. The auto industry has been under extreme scrutiny since the environment acts in the 1960s and 1970s, while under extreme pressure from shareholders to bring in, at times unreasonably so, big profits.

If we isolate just the charges against the former chairman of the management board at Volkswagen, Martin Winterkorn, they consisted of conspiracy and wire fraud (U.S. DOJ, 2018). Conspiracy covers a broad range of crimes, including those committed that are characterized as conventional crimes. In order for there to be a criminal conspiracy, the person, or more likely persons, involved are willing to commit a crime. It is classified as an *inchoate* crime, as the crime has not actually been committed as yet, but some steps have been taken in that direction. To use a conventional crime example, if two people plot to murder someone, yet either do not follow through with the crime or are caught before they have committed the crime, they can still be charged with conspiracy to commit murder. No doubt you have seen this plot twist used on a regular basis in television and movies.

Not everyone who has been involved in a conspiracy will be caught. We have to continue to remember that the charges are only as good as the evidence supporting them. In the Winterkorn case, there was enough verification that Winterkorn, along with senior executives at Volkswagen, defrauded customers and violated the Clean Air Act, including evidence that they provided false reports to regulators (U.S. DOJ, 2018).

The second serious charge of wire fraud against Winterkorn is more commonly found in cases of companies that clearly are criminal to begin with. For instance, boiler room operations that temporarily set up shop as telemarketing companies with no intention of providing the goods or services they promise prospective customers never intend to be legitimate. They tend to be fly-by-night operations, meaning they set up and shut down quickly to avoid detection or in order to allude authorities. It is highly unusual for a company as well-respected and well-established as Volkswagen to commit wire fraud.

Wire fraud, like conspiracy, covers a number of types of criminal acts. What is common among wire fraud charges is that the criminal has used any number of types of mediums to commit the crime, including interstate and foreign wholesale or retail business.

Theories to Explain the Crime

Perhaps the best way to describe the case of Volkswagen was that collective greed was part of the culture of the organization. We can point to a number of examples of CEOs who do terrible things, either to their companies or to customers, only to be given handsome exit packages when they gracefully step down from their positions. For example, when the CEO of Boeing, Dennis Milenburg, was fired in the midst of the Boeing 737 Max controversies, he was given a severance package that included a $62 million payout of pay and benefits (Baker, 2020). For those unfamiliar with the Boeing 737 Max stories, there were two fatal accidents involving the aircrafts, allegedly due to problems with sensors in the planes. With the possibility of a substantial severance package, usually written into hiring or promotion contracts, we have to question whether executives really have anything to lose but reputation when they fail on a large scale.

If we examine collective greed among executives or even lower-level employees, the greed acts as a contagion. What might feel on the individual level as being morally wrong, if not criminal, may be justified within a group (Hansen and Movahedi, 2010). As we noted from Hansen and Movahedi's (2010) work in Chapter 2, we ordinarily associate collective greed with the culture of financial institutions. We can equally apply this theory to executives within other industries, including automotive.

We may also consider that the executives may have been acting out of collective fear. If the cost of manufacturing cars to meet environmental standards eats into profits, there might be the very real concern that this will in turn not look good for executives in charge of keeping an eye on the bottom line. And as we know from the culture of financial institutions, envy of one's fellow workers, all placed within a competitive environment, may get the better of them. If we think of this as being similar to kids on the playground trying to outdo one another in some daring feat that has the real potential of physical harm, executives who are lured into conspiracies may be too afraid to speak up. Fortunately, in the Volkswagen case, a whistleblower was brave enough to step forward and disclose the false emissions reports to regulators.

Another question to consider is if fear was a motivating factor for the crimes, and whether it was fear of the market, where decisions may have been made in uncertain times. However, in 2015, environmental laws were far less ambiguous as they are today. As regulatory cycles go, we are currently in an era when EPA laws are influx.

Social and Media Responses

Except in business circles, there was little in the way of immediate, broad social response to the Volkswagen. However, as the news dribbled down to mainstream news media, the more immediate reaction was from investors, some of which unloaded Volkswagen stock, driving the stock price down. Consumers were not completely immune to the news as well.

The *New York Times* (Boudette, 2017) reported that Volkswagen, after an initial drop in sales, began to rebound in 2017. As Boudette's (2017) article suggested, the greatest effect was felt at dealerships. We don't always take into consideration the effect of scandals beyond the parent company. As dealerships act as individual franchises, they were immediately affected, with dealership owners noting that there were weeks when no customers would come in to look at Volkswagens to purchase (Boudette, 2017). We should note that simultaneously at the time overall, car sales had softened overall.

Criminal Justice and Policy Responses

By September 2015, the EPA made claims that the three-liter diesel engine vehicles that Volkswagen sold in the U.S. had software installed that could detect when the cars were being tested for smog emissions. The software would then change the performance of the cars to give the illusion that they were meeting EPA guidelines, thus passing inspection. In truth, the cars were actually spewing out 40 times the recommended emissions of nitrogen oxide pollutants once on the road, exposing children to increased pollution exposure (Joselow, 2019). The EPA estimated that there were approximately 11 million cars worldwide that had been fitted with the deceptive software. After further investigation, it was determined that the actual number of vehicles was 580,000 and that the faked emissions levels were occurring from 2006 through 2015.

The head of VW America, Michael Horn, admitted, "We've totally screwed up" and CEO Martin Winterkorn stated that the company had "broken the trust of our customers and public." (Hotten, 2015, retrieved from https://www.bbc.com/news/business-34324772). Winterkorn resigned as a direct result of the scandal. VW was forced to make the expensive move to recall millions of cars in 2016, and were left with the cost of paying for the removal of software. This was on top of costs of litigation in civil cases, when the company was hit with more than $30 billion in fines, penalties, restitutions in lawsuit settlements. The SEC has additionally charged VW, including Winterkorn, for defrauding U.S. investors, as VW stock plummeted on the heels of the scandal.

Winterkorn has consistently made the claim that the decision to install the deceptive software in cars was being made lower in the chain of command and he was unaware that there was a problem. Winterkorn has just recently been charged, along with a number of other VW executives, and may be facing up to ten years in prison (Jolly, 2019). Taking into consideration that Winterkorn is currently 71 years old, he may be battling this or spending time in prison for the rest of his life, depending on possible conviction and sentencing.

There were seven additional defendants, but complicating matters, some were foreign nationals. Court cases are further complicated when there is a need to extradite defendant even with extradition treaties. Wealthier defendants have the means to drag this process out or move to countries that do not have extradition treaties with the United States. Extradition involves soliciting the country where the individual who has been charged in a criminal case is currently residing, whether they are a citizen of that country or not.

Two Volkswagen engineers, Oliver Schmidt and James Liang, both Germans, pleaded guilty in taking part in the conspiracy to cover up falsified environmental reports, and received seven years and just over three years in prison, respectively (U.S. DOJ, 2018). However, there were five co-defendants who were not apprehended as of 2018, and are believed to be living in Germany, along with former manager of the Audi division of Volkswagen, Giovanni Pamio, who is an Italian citizen.

Volkswagen itself was forced to pay $2.8 billion in criminal penalties in an agreement with the U.S. Department of Justice (U.S. DOJ, 2018). For any company as solidly situated financially as Volkswagen, this was both a public relations debacle and a huge financial blow. Not only were the criminal penalties substantial, Volkswagen stock plunged 50 percent immediately after the scandal was made public (La Monica, 2015).

Unanswered Questions and Unresolved Issues Related to the Case

It is unknown just how much the VW executives knew as far as the fraudulent emission tests.

There is also the question as to why auto companies may at times be quick to put cars out on the market before they have met all safety requirements and regulations. This is not as serious as the Ford *Pinto* case, but certainly from an environmental standpoint, it is offensive, if not simply illegal.

We continue to go back to the question as to why companies take these types of risks when the ultimate costs to reputation and sales outweigh the immediate savings of cutting corners. And this begs the question: when scandals immerge, are we really yet again seeing just the tip of the proverbial iceberg?

Sources

Baker, D. (2020) Did shareholders' benefit by paying Boeing's fired CEO $62 million? Center for Economic and Policy Research. Jan. 16. Retrieved from http://cepr.net/blogs/beat-the-press/did-shareholders-benefit-by-paying-boeing-s-fired-ceo-62-million.

Boudette, N.E. (2017) Volkswagen sales in U.S. rebound after diesel scandal. *New York Times.* Nov. 1. Retrieved from https://www.nytimes.com/2017/11/01/business/volkswagen-sales-diesel.html.

Ewing, J. (2019) VW Executives are charged with market manipulation. *New York Times.* Sept. 24. Retrieved from https://www.nytimes.com/2019/09/24/business/volkswagen-executives-market-manipulation.html.

Hansen, L.L. and S. Movahedi. (2010) Wall Street scandals: The myth of individual greed. *Sociological Forum.* Vol. 25, No. 2: 367-374.

Hotten, R. (2015) Volkswagen: The scandal explained. *BBC*. Dec. 10. Retrieved from https://www.bbc.com/news/business-34324772.

La Monica, P.R. (2015) Volkswagen has plunged 50%. Will it recover? Stockwatch, *CNN Business*. Retrieved from https://money.cnn.com/2015/09/24/investing/volkswagen-vw-emissions-scandal-stock/.

MacDuffie, J.P. and D. Zaring. (2019) Exhausted by scandal: "Dieselgate" continues to haunt Volkswagen. Podcast, Wharton School of Business, University of Pennsylvania. Available at https://knowledge.wharton.upenn.edu/article/volkswagen-diesel-scandal/.

United States Department of Justice (DOJ). (2018) Former CEO of Volkswagen AG charged with conspiracy and wire fraud in diesel emissions scandal. Press Release, Office of Public Affairs. May 3. Retrieved from https://www.justice.gov/opa/pr/former-ceo-volkswagen-ag-charged-conspiracy-and-wire-fraud-diesel-emissions-scandal.

GLOSSARY

Clean Air Act, 1960   First of a number of federal laws targeting air pollution in the United States. Some states have subsequently passed their own laws. The most recent amendment in 1990 was passed in order to address the problem of acid pollution.

Clean Water Act, 1972   Originally called the Federal Water Pollution Control Act, the first federal law regulating the types and amounts of pollutants in lakes, rivers, streams, wetlands, and coastal areas. The act was amended in 1977 and 1987.

Deforestation   The legal or illegal mass removal of trees in the logging, mining, and agricultural industries.

E-waste   Any discarded electronic products, including cell phones, computers, some household appliances, and televisions.

Eco-terrorism   Violent, criminal acts in the name of environmental activism.

Endangered Species Act, 1973   Law that provides the conservation and protection of endangered species and their environments.

Environmental Protection Agency (EPA)   U.S. federal agency charged with enforcing environmental laws.

Green criminology   A fairly new branch of criminal justice and criminological research that focuses on violations of environmental laws.

Greenhouse gases (Greenhouse effect) A number of gases that, when emitted, will result in heat being trapped in the lower hemisphere, raising temperatures at the surface of the planet and contributing to global warming. Some of the greenhouse effect is believed to be natural, whereas some is suspected to be caused by human activity, including the burning of coal.

National Environmental Policy Act (NEPA), 1970 Environmental legislation designed to create the President's Council on Environmental Quality and to support existing environmental laws.

Safe Drinking Water Act (SDWA), 1974 Federal law that sets the standards for drinking water safety, including establishing technical and financial support.

Toxic Substances Control Act, 1976 (TSCA) As another legal arm of the EPA, TSCA calls for the regulation of new and existing chemicals.

REFERENCES AND SUGGESTED READINGS

Aktar, M.W., D. Sengupta, and A. Chowdhury. (2009) Impact of pesticides use in agriculture: Their benefits and hazards. *Interdisciplinary Toxicology*. Vol. 2, No. 1: 1-12.

Ayres, S. (2019) Russia looking to ratify Paris Agreement as U.S. continues withdrawal. *Los Angeles Times*. Feb. 16. Retrieved from https://www.latimes.com/world/europe/la-fg-russia-climate-change-20190216-story.html.

Barnes, R. L. (2011) Regulating the disposal of cigarette butts as toxic hazardous waste. *Tobacco Control*. May, Vol. 20: 145-148.

Biocanin, R. M. Sarvan, and A. Prolovic. (2018) Corporate governance and social responsibility in "fight" against ecological criminality. *Analele Universit ii "Constantin Brâncuşi" din Târgu Jiu: Seria Inginerie*. Vol. 4: 74-91.

Boyle, A. (2018) Climate change, the Paris Agreement and Human Rights. *International and Comparative Law Quarterly*. Vol. 67: 759-777.

Carson, R. (1962) *Silent Spring*. Greenwich, CT: Fawcett Publications, Inc. Reprint.

Clifford, M. (1998) *Environmental Crime: Enforcement, Policy, and Social Responsibility*. Preface. M. Clifford, ed. Gaithersburg, Md.: Aspen Publishers.

Cusato, E. (2018) Ecocide to voluntary remediation projects: Legal responses to environmental warfare in Vietnam and the spectre of colonialism. *Melbourne Journal of International Law*. Vol. 2, Issue 2: 1-27.

Environmental Protection Agency. (2019a) Compliance: How we monitor compliance. Retrieved from https://www.epa.gov/compliance/how-we-monitor-compliance.

Environmental Protection Agency. (2019b) *Environmental Crimes Case Bulletin*. Office of Criminal Enforcement Forensics & Training. Retrieved from https://www.epa.gov/sites/production/files/2019-05/documents/march-april2019bulletin.pdf.

Environmental Protection Agency. (2019c) Facts and figures about materials, waste and recycling. Retrieved from https://www.epa.gov/facts-and-figures-about-materials-waste-and-recycling/national-overview-facts-and-figures-materials#NationalPicture.

Environmental Protection Agency. (2019d) Summary of the Clean Water Act. *Laws & Regulations*. Retrieved from https://www.epa.gov/laws-regulations/summary-clean-water-act.

Environmental Protection Agency. (2019e) Wastes—non-hazardous waste—municipal solid waste. Retrieved from https://archive.epa.gov/epawaste/nonhaz/municipal/web/html/.

Harr, J. (1996) *A Civil Action*. New York: Random House, Inc.

Hays, S.P. (1999) *Conservation and the Gospel of Efficiency: The Progressive Conservation Movement, 1890-1920*. Pittsburgh, PA: University of Pittsburgh Press.

Hopkins, M.J.G. (2007) Modelling the known and unknown plant biodiversity of the Amazon Basin. June 29. *Journal of Biogeography*. Vol. 34, No. 8: 1400-1411.

Jolly, J. (2019) Former head of Volkswagen could face 10 years in prison. *The Guardian*. Apr. 15. Retrieved from https://www.theguardian.com/business/2019/apr/15/former-head-of-volkswagen-could-face-10-years-in-prison.

Joselow, M. (2019) VW emissions cheating scandal increased children's pollution exposure. *Scientific American*. July 17. Retrieved from https://www.scientificamerican.com/article/vw-emissions-cheating-scandal-increased-childrens-pollution-exposure/.

Kix, P. (2009) In the shadow of Woburn. *Boston Magazine*. Sept. 22. Retrieved from https://www.bostonmagazine.com/2009/09/22/in-the-shadow-of-woburn/.

Mesko, G. and A. Klenovsek. (2011) International waste trafficking, in *Understanding and Managing Threats to the Environment in South Eastern Europe*, G. Mesko, D. Dimitrijevic, and C.B. Fields, eds. Dordrecht: Springer, pp. 79-99.

Mesko, G. and K. Eman. (2012) Organised crime involvement in waste trafficking—Case of The Republic of Slovenia. *Criminal Justice Issues: Journal of Criminal Justice and Security*. Issue 5-6: 79-96.

Monbiot, G. (2019) The destruction of the Earth is a crime. It should be prosecuted. *The Guardian*. Mar. 28. Retrieved from https://www.theguardian.com/commentisfree/2019/mar/28/destruction-earth-crime-polly-higgins-ecocide-george-monbiot.

National Park Services. (2019) Theordore Roosevelt and Conservation. Retrieved from https://www.nps.gov/thro/learn/historyculture/theodore-roosevelt-and-conservation.htm.

Parveen, N. (2018) UK's plastic waste may be dumped overseas instead of recycled. *The Guardian*. July 22. Retrieved from https://www.theguardian.com/environment/2018/jul/23/uks-plastic-waste-may-be-dumped-overseas-instead-of-recycled.

Sharkey, E. (2009) Environmental Hearing Board Review: *Eureka Stone Quarry, Inc. v. Department of Environmental Protection*: The rocky results of air quality violations. *Villanova Environmental Law Journal*. Vol. 20, Issue 2: 337-360.

Sinai, M. (2017) Where does e-waste end up? *Recycle Nation*. April 25. Retrieved from https://recyclenation.com/2017/04/where-does-e-waste-end-up/.

Society for Conservation Biology. (2019) Treaties. Retrieved from https://conbio.org/policy/policy-priorities/treaties.

United Nations. (2019) UN report: Nature's dangerous decline 'unprecedented'; Species extinction rates 'accelerating'. *Sustainable Development Goals*. Retrieved from https://www.un.org/sustainabledevelopment/blog/2019/05/nature-decline-unprecedented-report/.

U.S. District Court, District of Massachusetts. (1985) *Deposition, John Drobinski*. Civil No. 82-1672-S.

U.S. Senate. (2014) Convention on the conservation and management of high seas fisheries resources in the North Pacific Ocean (Treaty Doc. 113-2). *Executive Report 113-2*, 113th Congress, 2d Session. Mar. 13.

Wallace, S. (2019). Inside the faltering fight against illegal Amazon logging. *National Geographic*. Retrieved from https://www.nationalgeographic.com/environment/2019/08/brazil-logging/#close.

Vandebroek, I., J. Calewaert, S. De jonckheere, S. Sanca, L. Semo, P. Van Damme, L. Van Puyvelde, and N. De Kimpe. (2004) Use of medicinal plants and pharmaceuticals by indigenous communities in the Bolivian Andes and Amazon. *Bulletin of the World Health Organization*. Vol. 84, No. 4: 243-250.

Yale University. (2019) The Amazon basin forest. *Global Forest Atlas*, School of Forestry & Environmental Studies. Retrieved from https://globalforestatlas.yale.edu/region/amazon.

Yang, S. and J. I-Chin. (2018) An evaluation of displacement and diffusion effects on eco-terrorist activities after police intervention. *Quantitative Criminology*. Vol. 34: 1103-1123.

Yang, S., Y. Su, and J.V. Carson. (2019) Eco-Terrorism and corresponding legislative efforts to intervene and prevent future attacks. *Center for Evidence-Based Crime Policy*, George Mason University. Retrieved from http://cebcp.org/wp-content/onepagers/EcoTerrorismAnd CorrespondingLegislativeEfforts_YangEtAl.pdf.

Zivin, J.G., M. Neidell and W. Schlenker. (2011) Water quality violations and avoidance behavior: Evidence from bottled water consumption. *American Economic Review: Papers and Proceedings*. Vol. 101, No. 3: 448-453.

Chapter ELEVEN

Political White Collar Crime

When clever people do stupid things

"When the President does it, that means that it's not illegal."

—*Richard "Tricky Dick" Milhous Nixon,*
37th President of the United States of America

Chapter Objectives

- Distinguish between types of political crimes.
- Define some of the more common forms of political crime.
- Review the history of political crime in the United States
- Introduce international perspectives on political crime.

Key Terms

Ballot stuffing ("stuffing
 the ballot box")
Clemency
Convictional crime
Corruption
Cronyism
Despots
Eminent domain
Extortion

Impeachment
Kickbacks
Land grants
Nepotism
Non-competitive bidding
"Rent seeking"
Oligarchy
Special counsel
Yellow journalism

INTRODUCTION

Of all the chapters in this book, this is perhaps the timeliest. The events surrounding the Mueller investigation of possible collusion with the Russian government (a historically hostile country towards the United States) were unfolding as this book was being written. This included the release of the redacted[1] Mueller report in April 2019. However, as much as the Mueller investigation was exceptionally interesting to follow for any student of white collar or political crime, it is certainly not the first time that a single person in public office or group of people in power and their allies have been in political and legal hot water.

Throughout history, career politicians and individuals running for office have had every aspect of their lives scrutinized. Whereas American presidents may have had extramarital affairs in the past that went unseen to or ignored by voters, the sexual escapades of politicians in general are more difficult to hide since the era of investigative reporting and social media. Scandals have not been confined to romantic rendezvous. As Basinger and Rottinghaus (2012) note, there are countless stories of politicians' attempts to sell and buy political offices, cheating on taxes, hiring undocumented workers, and embarrassing online communications.

Truly serious political intrigue can read like a John Grisham novel, look like a Netflix series, like *House of Cards* or ABC's *Designated Survivor. Game of Thrones* (HBO) certainly depicts violent jostling for political power. Since the beginning of time, formal and informal leaders emerge whenever people have formed governments, setting the stage for political intrigue and drama.

As illustrated in movies and on TV, political crime is not limited to white collar crime, but can, on occasion, include conventional crime. This includes garden variety burglary or at least the appearance of burglary, as we will see with the Watergate scandal of the Nixon era. It can also mean the occasional bribery of people who possess damaging information about a politician to keep them quiet.

The pursuit of political power can, in the extreme, result in homicide, as in the example of the 1978 murders of San Francisco Mayor George Moscone and Harvey Milk, an elected member of the Board of Supervisors and the first openly gay elected official in California. Milk was killed by fellow city official Dan White, who famously offered the "Twinkie defense" at his trial, blaming his crime on an unhealthy diet, in a diminished capacity plea (Lindsey, 1985). The jury was not swayed by his explanation, convicting him on the lesser charge of manslaughter, which resulted in activist outcry about the leniency (Lindsey, 1985). After serving just over five years in prison, White was released from prison in 1984. In 1985, White took his own life in an apparent suicide that was believed to substantiate his diminished capacity defense (Lindsey, 1985).

---

[1] For those unfamiliar with the term, a *redacted* document released to the public, as in the case of the Mueller Report (2019), has had sensitive information blacked out, sometimes due to national security, sometimes due to ongoing investigations and trials.

Literally killing to gain or maintain political power is also exemplified by mass elimination of rivals, as in the case of Stalin's imprisonment or execution of opponents in the former U.S.S.R. during the late 1930s. He believed the threat of deportation to Siberia or death acted as a deterrent to anyone who might oppose him. British history is also strewn with the corpses of political rivals for power. *Despots*, leaders who lead with fear and intimidation, occupy positions of power in the world today, at times violating the laws of their own countries. However, the attention in this chapter is not so much on the conventional crimes, like homicide, that occasionally happens in politics. The focus will be primarily on white collar crimes involving conspiracy and a wide range of unethical behavior exhibited by people holding public office. As in the case of financial white collar crime, political crimes can undermine public trust in its elected officials and the people these officials surround themselves with.

DEFINING POLITICAL WHITE COLLAR CRIME

Political crime is as difficult to define as white collar crime. Most definitions of political crime are vague and offers a lot of wiggle room for interpretation. For instance, espionage may be viewed as a political crime, but it could also, depending on the circumstances, be considered a matter of national security, as in the case of international spying (e.g., CIA operations).

As we will see later in this chapter, in discussions of Watergate and the Stormy Daniels scandals, what appear on the surface to be conventional crimes later found to be much deeper conspiracies involving white collar crimes. In some cases, the crimes happen in the intersection of a number of government institutions and Wall Street, and are not restricted to only the political machinery. In other words, the conventional crime, if and when a perpetrator is caught, may only be one of many guilty parties.

Broadly, political crime has been defined as any act that undermines the integrity of a political system, including those committed by individuals and administrations. The intention is not always to directly harm the city, state, or country in question, as most definitions of political crime will have you believe. In fact, more often than not it seems that it is simply carelessness and self-centeredness that results in disregard for the political system as a whole. For example, if an individual running for office offers political favors in return for votes or endorsements, that individual does not necessarily take into consideration how this might be damaging to the election process. They may very well believe that the political favors bestowed on supporters may be beneficial as a whole, as in the case of promised tax cuts or promising to award a government contract to a donor, even if laws have been violated.

As Schafer (1971) noted, political crime may be the oldest of crime typologies. If we take into consideration when political crimes are selfish acts, the political white collar criminal has more in common with the conventional criminal than with other white collar criminals. If the crime is based on political ideology or conviction, it can be considered a *convictional crime*, a type of crime that we have yet to explore in this book. In the convictional crime, the motivation is less ego-driven and based on doing what is supposed to be in the best interest of the community as a whole (Schafer, 1972). An example of a convictional political crime would be if the misdeed was committed for the benefit of a particular political party rather than for the individual.

Lately, political crime is being scrutinized more intensely through an international lens. Whereas earlier cases involved squabbling between political opponents leading to political crimes that were contained within the U.S. borders, more frequently now we see reports of interference in political processes coming from outside the U.S. and allegedly, if the Mueller Report is correct, with the blessing of some American politicians. This phenomenon is not unique to the U.S., as in the case of the Clearstream scandal in France, where politicians, including President Nicolas Sarkozy, were suspected of *kickbacks*, as well as money laundering and fraud involving sales of ships to China (*The Economist*, 2008).

Because political crimes are, well, political, the alleged and convicted criminals do not always serve time in prison. In some cases, they have their sentences shortened, as we will see in the case of the Nixon and Blagojevich cases discussed later in this chapter. This can occur due to the appeals process, but more likely to happen in the case of *clemency* or pardons given by presidents (in the United States at least), as part of their executive privileges.

EARLY HISTORY OF POLITICAL CRIME IN THE UNITED STATES

Tammany Hall

In most cases that we see in the news, political crime is being committed by a limited number of co-conspirators. However, there are times when a whole government administration is corrupt. A good starting place to better understand political crime in today's terms is to review the *corruption* coming out of Tammany Hall in New York City. No doubt many of you read about Tammany Hall in either a political science or history class. Tammany Hall emerged out of the early conception of U.S. politics, shortly after the American Revolution in the 18th century.

Tammany Hall was initially created by the need to address a number of social problems of poor immigrants who were struggling in New York City. The Irish, a marginalized immigrant population at the time, fought for inclusion in mainstream American politics during the early part of the 19th century. This was similar to purposes of Hull House in Chicago, founded by Jane Addams and Ellen Starr in the latter part of the 19th century when there was a similar surge of immigrants coming to the United States. Over time, Tammany Hall came to represent primarily the working class and working poor, who were more likely to be affiliated with labor unions.

Initially an organization focused on social welfare, Tammany Hall, also known as the Society of St. Tammany, became a political machine so powerful that its reaches in New York City and beyond spanned three centuries (18th, 19th, and 20th). William M. Tweed, one of the most infamous people associated with Tammany Hall whose name has forever since been associated with greed and corruption in politics, took charge of Tammany Hall in 1858. Unheard of today due to conflicts of interest, Tweed simultaneously held positions as a New York State senator, head of New York City's Department of Public Works, president of the County Board of Supervisors, and acted as the Grand Sachem of Tammany Hall (Kolbert, 2009). Fittingly, Tweed would ultimately be nicknamed "Boss Tweed."

The political machinery of Tammany Hall was not fully dismantled until the election of Mayor Fiorello La Guardia and intervention by President Franklin D. Roosevelt. There has been some speculation that Tammany Hall-like politics made a resurgence in the 1950s and 1980s (Krinsky, 2013). The methods by which political power is concentrated, developed during Tammany Hall, may very well still be in use today, as witnessed in machine politics at certain state levels (e.g., Wisconsin, plagued with alleged corruption) and in Washington, D.C. (Krinsky, 2013).

Unlike Hull House in Chicago, which remained focused on social services until the closing of its doors in 2012, Tammany Hall eventually became synonymous with corruption in city politics. Corruption is a term that loosely describes cases where there is rule or lawbreaking, in many cases involving illicit financial transactions. Financial transactions can take place to silence someone with damaging information or be used in bribery to get individuals to vote or lobby favorably for certain questionable projects, including new construction or policies. Bribery can also be used to halt attempts at legislation or regulation.

Corruption in Tammany Hall included rigged elections, financial crimes involving *extortion* ("*rent seeking,*" Krinsky, 2013), embezzlement, under-the-table kickbacks, and bribes. This was long before the phenomenon of Twitter wars. Much of what people learned about the corruption was heard in the streets in the form of gossip or in *yellow journalism* focused more on sensationalism than factual information. Yellow journalism was the precursor to the tabloid news we see today, currently available on TV, online, or in print media (newspapers, magazines). In today's news, we still see remnants of yellow journalism, but we cannot discount the validity of good, investigative reporting. Even fictional accounts of white collar crime can inform the public. For example, Upton Sinclair's novel *The Jungle* (1906) uncovered the deplorable conditions in meatpacking plants as well as the plight of the working class, resulting in reform, even though Sinclair's book was fiction. As far as the Tammany Hall saga goes, for all the research that has been conducted on the corruption, we may never know the full extent of its reaches. History is only as accurate as those who document it at the time of events.

Teapot Dome Scandal

During the 1920s, the Teapot Dome scandal that tarnished President Warren Harding's administration demonstrated how closely tied the government and the business sector are in a free market system. The oil industry has seen a number of scandals involving government officials or those just on the peripheral, but none so blatantly operated outside ethical boundaries as the then Secretary of the Interior Albert Fall. Fall leased petroleum reserves in Wyoming and California to private oil companies. At the time, a number of petroleum reserves were owned by the government and not by private or publicly traded companies.

The leases themselves were not necessarily unethical. However, the leases were obtained by oil companies in the Teapot Dome Scandal through bribery and *non-competitive bidding*. As the United States government is meant to be run with fiscal efficiency, for any government contract the expectation is that a number of companies will be in the running and will submit proposals, offering their lowest and best estimates. For instance, if Congress approves a public works project, like road repair or construction, the competition among contractors will, in theory, drive the cost down, plus motivate contractors to do their absolute best to finish projects on time. If bidding is non-competitive, *cronyism* or *nepotism* is likely to take place.

Keeping in mind, as we have noted, that the reporting of historical events is only as accurate as the people who document the events, for all of the cases discussed in this chapter, we may not ever know the full extent to which crimes have been committed. We can expect a certain amount of bias in any historical account. This is both a function of the power of elites to hide the full extent of criminal behavior and due to social network dynamics. If you recall in Chapters 2 and 3, we cannot underestimate how much we are unable to see all the members of a criminal network, whether we are talking about terrorists, gang members, or members of a white collar crime conspiracy.

Political crime is not exclusive to city politics. It can take place on the national and international stages. Once it becomes established at any level of government, as long as it remains undetected or ignored, it may eventually become institutionalized within the system and become a difficult thing to stop or discourage. We see, on occasion, similar non-competitive bidding examples in politics today, as witnessed in the Teapot Dome Scandal.

POWER, POLITICS, AND WHITE COLLAR CRIME

In the lyrics for *Absolutely*, written by the British rapper MF DOOM and Madlib, they proclaim, "Absolute power corrupts absolutely" (MF DOOM and Madlib, 2009, track 5). The British duo were not the first to use this expression, but the fact that it has seeped into popular music is a good indication that it has not outlived its usefulness in describing how power can turn the heads of politicians. In the original quote by Lord Acton, borrowed and retooled by MF DOOM and Madlib (2009) in their lyrics, it is implied that people who rise to positions of power may leave their moral compasses behind in the process.

For some people in power, including politicians and monarchs, there is the belief that holding the office or sitting on a throne means that they are above the law. For instance, when a king or queen has inherited the throne of their country, they may believe that they have a divine right to be there. Likewise, in dictatorships, leadership may be passed onto the next generation through nepotism, as witnessed in the succession of Supreme Leader Kim Jong-un in North Korea, who inherited the position from his father, Kim Jong-il.

As we have noted before, once someone has power (or money), they may be motivated by greed or fear (or in some cases, both) to hang on to it at all costs. Certainly, the fear of an uncertain future in the event that one loses political power is real. This is principally true if one's identity is wrapped up in their position, as in the example of a politician who is at a loss as to what to do with their life after they leave office.

Realistically, politicians holding high office have a number of opportunities offered to them in and out of politics once they leave office, even to some of those who have fallen from grace. But as we saw in our chapter on financial crime, even when people have been well-compensated with money, or in the people discussed in this chapter, with power, they may still feel insecure in their ability to hold on to it, in which case they may be willing to cross the line into criminality. We will see this in the case of President Nixon and the Watergate scandal.

Powerful people do not operate in a void. They rely on networks of friends and allies around them to help keep them in power. They can even elicit the help of so-called "frenemies" to assist with the undoing of anyone or anything that might stand in their way of getting and keeping power. Likewise, as in Sutherland's theory of Differential Association, if someone in power surrounds themselves with people who are willing to turn a blind eye to criminal behavior or worse, join in on it, it is difficult to find anyone who might oppose them. In many ways, it is a bit like a bunch of adolescents who are getting away with delinquency because no one is willing to or interested in stopping them.

If charismatic persuasion fails in getting people to do what you want them to do, for some politicians and in political circles, the temptation is to coerce them with money or threats. A good portion of what we are discussing in this chapter is a matter of ethics, including the means by which you get people to do what you want them to do. Some of this unethical behavior may not even cross the line into criminal behavior. For instance, if a politician regularly asks one of their staff to run personal errands, even though it is not in their job description unless they are being compensated in their salary for acting as a personal assistant, this would be unethical. But asking an assistant to run errands would not necessarily be criminal. However, if the same politician is paying that employee under the table in money that goes unreported to the IRS, that would cross the line into criminality for a number of reasons.

Political Crime Typologies

Beyond sex scandals, no other type of crime associated with politicians, at least in the United States, receives more attention than those of people who have committed prosecutable crimes. Even alleged unethical behavior during critical national elections is sometimes overlooked. The fervor surrounding the 2016 presidential election is unmatched in recent history. However, there are a number of ways that elective officials or government employees can commit crimes, beyond those associated with elections, that are still politically motivated.

Like financial white collar crime, political crimes often involve money. Unlike financial white collar crimes discussed elsewhere in this book, political crime is more likely to result from efforts to consolidate power illegally within a government. This again can be motivated either by greed or fear. In some cases, as we will see in the Watergate scandal, it may be motivated by both. Rarely is it the case where someone unwittingly or innocently commits a political crime.

Within the genre of political crimes is state-sponsored crimes. In this instance, it really is more systemic, where one political party or one person in office is not the root cause of crime within in a country's political and economic systems. In state-sponsored crime, including terrorism, there generally is already a history of corruption and abuses of power in a country. In today's global world, any history of corruption in one country will no doubt have an effect on neighboring countries, as indicated by the ongoing drug wars along the U.S.-Mexican border.

Abuse of Political Power

Abuse of political power is exactly what it sounds like. Someone in a political position, either inherited, democratically voted in, or grabbed by brute force, is using their position to further their own political and sometimes financial position. By strict definition, this type of political crime covers a wide range of offenses, whether it is a matter of misconduct or misuse of power by a person who is in position to shape policy and laws.

In the mudslinging and name-calling that takes place in politics, inevitably whichever party is not in power will accuse the other party of abuses of power. In the U.S., the most common office to be accused of abuses of power is the President of the United States and their administration members. For example, in September 2012, a committee within the House of Representatives held a hearing to determine if the Obama administration abused its power within the controversy of immigration laws:

> The Obama administration has abused its power, ignored its duties, evaded responsibilities and overstepped the Constitution's limits on the President.... The Administration has repeatedly, in my view, put its partisan agenda above the rule of law. (Committee on the Judiciary, House of Representatives, 2012)

In this case, as in many other periods of political division, the hearing did not lead to sanctions or other penalties against the Obama Administration.

Case Study ▪ Prime Minister Najib Razak, Malaysia

(Sources: Fullerton, 2019; Griffiths, 2019; Wright and Hope 2019)

It is one thing to ignore financial regulation to benefit your friends. It is another thing to use a state-owned bank as your own personal piggybank. This is exactly how CNN (2019) describes Prime Minister Najib Razak's handling of 1MBD of Malaysia. We are revisiting this scandal that was first introduced in Chapter 4 to examine the political crime aspects of the case. If you recall, in Chapter 4 we focused on Jho Low, the banker who illegally squirreled away billions from an investment fund housed at 1MBD. In this chapter, the focus will be on the abuses of power used by Prime Minister Razak in this case and the part he played in robbing the Malaysian bank.

Within weeks of becoming Prime Minister, Razak used his newly elected power to order the creation of 1MBD with $1.2 billion in assets. Though Malaysia is classified as a democratic society, it also has elements of socialist or communist states, including state-owned banks and businesses. As the bank is state-owned, Razak had greater access to the its funds and investments. Razak stands accused of taking part in stealing $4.5 billion (RM; £ 3.4 billion, $ 1.1 USD) from one of the bank's funds since he took office in 2009. As white collar crimes go, this was one of the most blatant examples of abuses of political in modern history. In total, Razak has been accused of criminal breach of trust, abuse of power, and money laundering. Razak pleaded not guilty to all the charges in Kuala Lumpur High Court. To date, the trial is ongoing.

Discussion Questions

1. How is it possible for a politician in office to abuse their power for a number of years, as in the case of Prime Minister Razak?
2. Why might some politicians risk their reputations, and in this case prison time, by stealing from a state-owned bank?
3. How might a political or economic system prevent leaders from becoming so powerful that they believe they are above the law?

Fortunately, at least in most democratic and socialist societies, there are checks and balances built into the government structure in order to assure that no one person or entity controls all the power. For instance, in the U.S., the Executive Branch, which includes the President of the United States and their cabinet, does not possess more or less power than the Legislative Branch (Congress) or the Judicial Branch (U.S. Supreme Court) by way of the Constitution of the United States. As you may remember from civics class, the three branches hold equal power and are expected, by law, to make sure that there are no abuses of power in any one branch of the government. Where we might run into trouble is if one party somehow controls all three branches, which happens on occasions, though usually temporarily, as people are voted in and out of office.

The same democratic processes cannot be said about dictatorships or autocratic governments. There the power rests either in the hands of one individual or in an *oligarchy* of government insiders. In these types of governments, with only a handful of people in charge of decision-making and laws, there is a greater chance of abuses of power, particularly if there are no opponents to the abuses.

Political Scandals and Impeachment

One solution to political intrigue in the Unites States is the process of *impeachment* as directed in Article II, Section 4 of the U.S. Constitution, as it applies to the removal of individuals elected to federal office. This includes the President of the United States. Impeachment does not mean automatic removal of a person from political office. It is a process that can take a number of months, more likely years, to resolve. It begins with suspected wrongdoing and the call for an investigation into whether it can be confirmed with evidence. There can be a number of reasons why an individual in office might be investigated through the impeachment process.

In the United States, it is the responsibility of the House of Representatives to impeach the suspected official. However, it is the responsibility of the Senate to convict the individual, which effectively removes them from office. It is still unclear as to whether a sitting president can be indicted and convicted of a crime while still in office. The Constitution does not provide transparent guidance and it has yet to be tested. In the event that a president were to be indicted, it would no doubt be a case that would eventually be for the Supreme Court of the United States to decide. This is not to say that a president or any elected official can avoid prosecution once they have left office, whether they resign or are forcibly removed.

Though not considered a political crime per se, a special council was called, under Kenneth Starr, to investigate President Clinton, beginning with a yet to be resolved land development scandal. This was not the first time that President Clinton was accused of possible wrongdoing. While serving as governor for the state of Arkansas, both Bill and Hillary Clinton were suspected in a campaign funding scheme. Known as the Whitewater scandal after the Whitewater Development Corporation, which was involved in a real estate venture, the Clintons and their partners James and Susan McDougal were investigated by federal regulators in the 1980s and 1990s. After a long, protracted investigation, there was no clear evidence of wrongdoing to be found by Starr and his team.

Ultimately the impeachable charges against President Clinton in 1998 while he was in office were not related to the Whitewater scandal, but from his supposed sexual escapades. The charges in the impeachment proceedings included obstruction of justice and lying under oath in his testimony to Congress as to whether he had an affair with then White House intern Monica Lewinsky. When the trial began in the Senate in 1999, it resulted in an acquittal of the charges. Up until 2020 Presidents Trump, Clinton, and Andrew Jackson were the only presidents to have faced formal impeachment proceedings that reached the Senate.

Impeachment is not reserved only for the President of the United States. Anyone holding an elected office, including city mayors, governors, and members of Congress, can be effectively removed from office. The procedures to do so are a bit different and spelled out by the individual cities, states, and the U.S. government, depending on which office the accused is holding. Impeachment does not automatically mean a criminal trial, though in some cases the person kicked out of office will be prosecuted, as in our next case involving the Chicago political machine.

In 2019, the U.S. House of Representatives launched an impeachment investigation of President Trump and his close associates. These accusations were part of an ongoing investigation tied to the Mueller Report. However, no criminal charges have been brought against President Trump or those accused along with him of abuses of power. The televised public hearings began on November 13, 2019.

Those under investigation include former New York City Mayor Rudy Giuliani after a whistleblower came forward with an account of Trump pressuring Ukraine President Volodymyr Zelensky to investigate former Vice President Joe Biden. In exchange, President Trump, according to the *Articles of Impeachment* brought to the Senate floor by the House of Representatives in January 2020, was suspected of using military aid as incentive for opening an investigation on Vice President Biden's son, Hunter Biden. Hunter Biden had served on the board of a Ukrainian natural gas company. Vice President Biden was one of Trump's political rivals in the 2020 Presidential election. Both Vice President Biden and Hunter Biden had been previously scrutinized, both here and abroad in Ukraine. Under the Ukrainian investigation, there had been no evidence to substantiate any claims that either one has done anything legally or ethically wrong. There continues to be as yet unsubstantiated rumors that the Bidens committed some political crimes.

On February 5, 2020, President Trump, a Republican president, was acquitted of both charges in the articles of impeachment that included abuse of power and obstruction of Congress. The vote to acquit was decisively down political party lines, with Congressman Mitt Romney, a Republican representing Utah, as the only voice from the GOP side of the Senate to vote for conviction (*CNN*, 2020). At the time of the impeachment trial in 2020, Republicans held power in the Senate, with majority membership. What makes this a historical impeachment proceeding is that earlier in the trial, the Senate voted down party lines to disallow the introduction of evidence and witnesses, a move that is anticipated to continue a heated debate between both parties in Congress. This has never been the case in impeachment trials in Congress and may very well change future attempts to remove a sitting president from office.

Political Corruption

As well-meaning anyone might be when serving in public office or working for a government, they are unfortunately exposed to a number of opportunities to commit crimes. In some cases, politicians create their own conspiracies. In other cases, they are dragged into it as collateral damage. Corruption is but one of the traps that politicians can fall into, though fortunately, not all will succumb to the temptations.

Anyone who has either read the novel (Kevin Kwan, published in 2013) or seen the movie *Crazy Rich Asians* (Warner Brothers, 2018) cannot walk away from either one without getting the sense that China does not necessarily follow strict Communist ideology. The book and movie, though fictional, mirror the real rise of wealth by individuals in China and other countries in Asia in recent decades, spurred by the technology sector. There is no dispute that much of this wealth was either inherited or honestly earned. But like other countries where those in political office and the military merge to control power and are subject to corruption, the Chinese are no exception.

Fang Fenghui, a high-ranking Chinese general who served as chief of joint staff of the People's Liberation Army, was tried and found guilty of having money that he could not account for, as well as corruption. The 67-year-old is yet another individual who has been investigated, prosecuted, and convicted under China's new anti-corruption campaign (BBC, 2019a). The current efforts have been mostly focused on the military.

The good news is that cases of corruption, when discovered and prosecuted, ultimately result in new models and regulation created to combat corruption. The bad news is that with policy changes and new regulation, government, as a bureaucracy, can get bogged down in the proverbial red tape, or the "Iron Cage of Bureaucracy" that Weber described, while trying to stop corruption. And as in other types of white collar crimes, the criminals can sometimes find ways around new or existing regulations.

LAND SPECULATION AND POLITICS

As we see the controversies play out in the news about the possible dismantling of the National Parks system in the United States to sell portions to private interests, they are presented as being new phenomena. Land that has the potential of yielding natural resources (e.g., oil, minerals) or offers transportation access (e.g., waterways, roads) has always been valuable. No massive real estate transaction, including the sale of public lands, can take place without the blessings of whatever current political environment allows. This was nowhere so apparent as during the 19th century expansion of empires, including the British Empire and North American territories.

Understandably, unless land is lawfully bought, there is always the question of the ethical and moral implication of taking land from inhabitants who are perceived to have no rights to it, as in the case of Native Americans in the U.S. and First Nations people in Canada. In some instances, the original inhabitants of a country will fight back against an empire. The non-violent rebellion and demand for independence from Britain by indigenous people in India is but one example.

What many landowners in the United States may not be aware of is that even with private land ownership, there is the possibility that the government will step in and claim *eminent domain*. Essentially, this gives the government the right to force owners to sell their property for public use. In this case, the government is required to offer payment at fair market value in return for the sale of the land. For example, if a state is planning on building a new highway, the planned route may unfortunately run right through a subdivision of housing. However, payment for land has rarely been the case in expansion of empires, including in the U.S. during the 19th century. Even in the late 19th century, when westward movement in America was underway, some land grabs were found to be so underhanded, politicians and business people were atypically prosecuted for their crimes.

Law in the Real World: Santa Fe Ring Land Grab

(Source: History, Art and Archives, U.S. House of Representatives, n.d.; Caffey, 2015)

Similar to most wars, the Civil War, for all the horror associated with loss of life and the real risk of a country in its infancy falling apart, offered a number of business opportunities. Some of these opportunities present themselves in Western states, such as the gold rush in California and Alaska and the availability of land after the Louisiana Purchase in 1803. One territory that represents the tug-of-war between Mexico and the fairly young

United States is New Mexico. Often mistakenly overlooked as state with an expanse of uninhabitable desert, New Mexico is currently home to approximately 2.1 million people.

In the 1800s, the New Mexico territory, due to its location in the Southwest, was somewhat removed from Washington politics. Before it became a state, there was a divide between Native populations who had been there for millennia and the occupying Anglo businessmen and military officials. In the mix were the wealthy *Hispanos*, rivals of the *nuevomexicano* elites.

Though seemingly far from the battlefields of the Civil War, the war resulted in new business and political opportunities in the Southwest. The New Mexico territory was unable to be completely oblivious to the war. Both Albuquerque and Santa Fe were occupied by the Confederate Army of the West.

After the war, the New Mexico territory represented unexplored resources for politicians, businessmen, cattle ranchers, and mineral prospectors to exploit. Similar to Tammany Hall in New York City, the newly formed partnership between Anglos and Hispanos developed into the powerful Santa Fe Ring. Described as "outsized personalities," key members of the Santa Fe Ring included Stephen Elkins and Thomas Carton, college friends who attended the University of Missouri and were both successful politicians in the New Mexico territory (Archives, U.S. House of Representatives, n.d.).

The Santa Fe Ring was responsible for consolidating political power, using lawyers and judges to grease the wheels in purchasing land within the New Mexico territory. In order to do so, it meant the displacement or suppression of Native American tribes and native New Mexicans. As Plato (1937) observed, each government will bend laws to its advantage.

The land purchases were viewed then and now as theft due to the corrupting influences of the Santa Fe Ring. Similar to what took place in the post-Civil War south, Spanish and Mexican *land grants* that could be questionably (yet legally) purchased by the Santa Fe Ring members were repackaged, driving up the value and prices of the grants. As a result, Elkins and Carton ended up in possession of vast quantities of valuable New Mexican acreage.

As Caffey (2015) discovered in his research on the Santa Fe Ring, the land grab in the 19th century is a story of corrupt and deadly politics, typical in the history of the westward expansion. It also represents the type of social networks that were needed in 19th century land grabs, including lawyers and judges who were willing to compromise morality for greed. However, Caffey (2015) also cautions that without a smoking gun (or in this case, good archival records), it is a challenge to call the Santa Fe Ring a clear case of political corruption. Even so, to this day, the Santa Fe Ring continues to represent the bloody and often criminal birth of statehoods, including New Mexico.

Discussion Questions

1. There is an expression that "war is good business." In what ways can wars offer new opportunities for white collar crime?
2. Who might be the obvious victims in land grabs?
3. What role might the 19th century land grab play in the demographics of New Mexico today, including Native Americans?

FINANCIAL CRIMES IN POLITICS

There is some intersection between financial white collar and political crimes. Corruption may lead to the commitment of other crimes ordinarily associated with organized crime, like money laundering. Plus, corruption often includes bribes. Financial crimes can also involve the withholding of funds or financial aid for political reasons. Any and all financial crimes we introduced in Chapters 4 and 5 can be found in politics.

ELECTION SCANDALS

The current rumblings centered around the 2016 presidential election is certainly not the first time election results have been questioned. *Ballot stuffing* and tampering has been around as long as there has been democratic societies. Just as in the case of white collar crime in general, the amount of tampering that takes place during elections, particularly in this age of social media, is unmeasurable. The interference can come from a number of sources, including political opponents and governments that would like to undermine the political system in a country. Every once in a while, the people who are tampering with an election outcome get sloppy, in which case the election itself becomes suspect when the public finds out. In many respects, this tears at the social fabric of a society more than when a scandal breaks in the private sector.

Law in the Real World: Watergate Office Building Break-In, Democratic National Committee Headquarters

(Sources: Woodward and Bernstein, 2014; Woodward, 2005)

Though we can go back to the Tammany Hall escapades to point to cases of election tampering, in more recent history, the break-in at the Democratic National Committee offices in the Watergate Hotel, in Washington, D.C. prior to the 1972 presidential election has been held up as the "poster child" of political crimes involving a sitting president. Yet at the time, few people took the burglary seriously (Ritchie, 1998).

In 1968, Richard M. Nixon substantially defeated the Democratic Party candidate, Hubert Humphrey, with 301 electoral votes. It was a turbulent time, with the rise of social activism in the 1960s and Vietnam War still lingering on in Southeast Asia after over a decade of American involvement. The country was restless, looking for progressive leadership. In 1971, with Nixon's urging, Congress approved the addition of Amendment 36 of the United States Constitution to lower the voting age from 21 to 18. As we approached the 1972 election and there was still no end in sight to the Vietnam War, plus unrest in the Middle East threatening oil supplies in the United States, Nixon became progressively paranoid as to whether he would be successful in a re-election bid.

In June 1972, just prior to the election, what first appeared to be an ordinary, garden-variety conventional crime of burglary at the Watergate Hotel turned out to be something more sinister. In the FBI investigation that followed, the "burglars" (or so-called "Plumbers") who had been caught in the act of breaking into the Democratic National Committee offices were discovered to be looking for sensitive election information and an opportunity to install surveillance equipment, including bugging telephones. Bob Woodward, who had only been working as a reporter for *The Washington Post* a few months, received a phone call from the city editor of the paper. That phone call would set things in motion for one of the biggest scandals to hit Washington, D.C. to date.

The burglars themselves were viewed as somewhat inconsequential and at the time of the arrest as it seemed like these were conventional burglars. E. Howard Hunt, Gordon Liddy, and James McCord were apprehended during the course of the burglary, along with four other "burglars." It quickly became apparent that this was no ordinary burglary. With Hunt and McCord being former CIA agents, and Liddy a former FBI agent, it was abundantly clear that something more sinister was afoot. Of the Watergate 7, as the burglars became known as, there were only a handful of conventional criminals, more than likely hired for their burglary expertise. Though they were caught in the commission of what looked to be on the surface like an ordinary crime, Hunt, Liddy, and McCord's activities more closely align with definitions of white collar, elite crimes.

McCord was the security coordinator for the re-election committee, also possessing the skills to pull off the burglary. The real culprits were Hunt and Liddy, who at the time were campaign aides for the committee to Re-elect the President. Both were identified as the orchestrators of the burglary.

As these things go, a mistake or two on the part of criminals can result in detection and arrest. However, it took journalists Carl Bernstein and Bob Woodward from *The Washington Post* to uncover the extent to which political espionage and conspiracy was involved in the Watergate break-in. With the use of an informant, "Deep Throat," Bernstein and Woodward were put on the trail of secret campaign funds that were used to pay the Watergate burglars for their services, tying the burglary to the re-election campaign and eventually to Nixon himself, if indirectly.

Key evidence in the Watergate Hotel break-in was the audio tape recordings that Nixon made while talking to his co-conspirators and others, recorded between 1971 and 1973. Specifically, it was what was missing from the tapes that had investigators curious. There was an 18.5-minute missing segment from a conversation with H.R. Haldeman, the White House Chief of Staff, that was allegedly recorded three days after the break-in. In a recording made six days after the break-in, Nixon is heard agreeing with members of his administration who suggested that he should pressure the FBI to stop its investigation into the break-in. This brought about the charge of obstruction of justice in the impeachment inquiries.

Eventually, 21 individuals were discovered to be part of the Watergate scandal and affiliated with both the Nixon administration and the Committee to Re-Elect the President were convicted of their crimes and sent to prison (Ritchie, 1998). Of these, the closest in administrative proximity to Nixon were John N. Mitchell, a former United States Attorney General and director of Nixon election campaign; H.R. Haldeman, the White House Chief of Staff; and John Ehrlichman, who was legal counsel to the president and an assistant in Domestic Affairs. Collectively, these three were sentenced to 2.5 to 8 years in federal prison (Oelsner, 1975).

As part of the investigation into the burglary, the infamous Watergate tapes, recordings that were primarily made in the Oval Office by Nixon himself, were revealed to be a treasure trove of evidence to connect Nixon with the break-ins. On the tapes, Nixon was found to be discussing ways by which the Watergate investigation could be stopped, including a failed attempt to get Attorney General Richard Kleindienst to limit the scope of the investigation (Bernstein, 2012). This was the supposed "smoking gun" (Bernstein, 2012) indicating that Nixon had far greater knowledge of the conspiracy in advance of the burglary than anyone suspected.

Ultimately, faced with the prospect of impeachment that would force him out of office, Nixon resigned from the presidency on August 9, 1974, a full two years and two months after the Watergate Hotel break-in.

As Nixon's vice president, Spiro Agnew, had resigned due to an unrelated charge of income tax evasion, the then-Speaker of the House, Gerald Ford, was sworn in as the 38th President of the United States, as constitutionally mandated. On September 8, 1974, President Ford announced that he would pardon Nixon for his alleged crimes in connection with the Watergate break-in. It is believed he did so with the hopes that the nation would move on and heal politically and spiritually from the scandal, rather than suffer through a possible criminal trial after Nixon left office.

Others in Nixon's circle who were accused of being involved in Watergate were not so lucky. Though Nixon had a number of backdoor deals with his co-conspirators to offer clemency as was his right in his position as President of the United States, ultimately, Nixon was out of office before he could pardon them. The following members of Nixon's administration, the Watergate 7, were prosecuted for conspiracy, among other charges, resulting in prison terms for some:

- Charles Colson, *Special Counsel* (convicted, served seven months in federal prison)
- John Ehrlichman, Counsel, Assistant to the President for Domestic Affairs (convicted, served 18 months in federal prison)
- H.R. Haldeman, White House Chief of Staff (convicted, served one year in federal prison)
- Robert Mardian, Assistant Attorney General (conviction overturned)
- John Mitchell, Attorney General (convicted, served 19 months in federal prison)
- Kenneth Parkinson, Counsel to the Committee to Re-Elect the President (acquitted)
- Gordon Strachan, Aide to H.R. Haldeman (charges dropped)

There are a number of theories as to why Nixon or anyone associated with his re-election campaign would risk everything, including the election, to spy on the Democratic Party. It was particularly confusing as Nixon was already leading in the polls. There has been speculation that Nixon was simply insecure about his chances of remaining in the White House for another term.

As a postscript to the Watergate scandal, the identity of "Deep Throat," the whistleblower in the case, was finally revealed in 2005, some 30 years after the story was first broken by Bernstein and Woodward in *The Washington Post*. At age 91, William Felt, Sr., a career FBI employee, came forward as the informant and whistleblower. Though there were a number of others instrumental in uncovering the details of the break-in and Nixon's involvement, Felt is viewed as the catalyst in the case (Woodward, 2005).

Discussion Questions

1. In 2019, the country faced another round of impeachment hearings in the House of Representatives. In what way is the Watergate scandal different from the alleged election tampering charges associated with the 2016 and 2020 presidential elections?

2. As Nixon's career was essentially ruined as a result of Watergate, what bene-fits were there to Nixon resigning rather taking his chances with a full impeachment process?
3. So much of the evidence in the Watergate Hotel break-in could be found on the tape recordings. What types of evidence might be gathered today in a similar case, now that tape recorders are all but obsolete?

To assure that all materials coming out of the Nixon White House would not be destroyed or altered, The Presidential Recordings and Materials Preservation Act was passed in 1974. The act was only intended to maintain the records spe-cific to the abuses of power within the Nixon White House. On the heels of the Watergate scandals, The Presidential Records Act (PRA) was passed in 1978, requiring that the records of all presidents and vice presidents must be preserved. In 2014, the act was amended to account for electronic records in the Digital Age, providing new provisions for the preservation of records, including emails or elec-tronic transmissions using non-official accounts (National Archives, n.d.). Once a president leaves office, the records are then handed over to the Archivist of the United States National Archives and Records Administration (NARA) (National Archives, n.d.).

The Mueller Report

In 2016, the United States had an election like no other in modern history. Seem-ingly coming out of nowhere in 2015, Donald J. Trump, a television personality (*The Apprentice* and *The Celebrity Apprentice*, NBC) and businessman specializ-ing in real estate, announced that he was running for President of the United States on the Republican ticket. It seemed like a foregone conclusion that his opponent Hillary Clinton, a Democrat, was going to win. Clinton is the wife of Bill Clinton, the 42d President of the United States, and had political experience her-self, having served as a senator for New York (2001-2009) and as Secretary of State under President Barack Obama. On election night in November 2016, a number of people in both dominant political parties[2] were shocked when Trump was elected as the 45th President of the United States.

In an era of social media, the usual political mudslinging that occurs during elections was vicious. There were rumblings during the 2016 election that there was the possibility of Russian interference. Within months of President Trump

---

[2] We cannot discount members of the Independent Party or the Reform Party. However, they have not historically had the numbers to be voted into higher office, as in the case of Ross Perot in the 1992 presidential election, as popular as he was at the time.

taking office, an investigation was opened, led by former FBI Director Robert Mueller, into whether someone within or working for the Russian government had indeed tampered with the presidential election. Of greater concern was whether anyone working for the Trump campaign or within the Trump administration had assisted the Russians. The Trump Organization has a history of business ventures in Russia, including discussions with Russian contacts about building a Trump Tower in Moscow similar to the one in New York City (*BBC*, 2019b).

After nearly two years of investigation, Mueller and his team concluded that the Russian government believed that it would benefit from a Trump presidency. Submitted to then Attorney General William Barr and published as The Mueller Report (*The Washington Post*, 2019), the document included information about confirmed Russian interference in the campaign:

> The first form of Russian election influence and principally from the Internet Research Agency, LLC (IRA), a Russian organization funded by Yevgeniy Viktorovich Prigozhim and companies he controlled. . . . THE IRA conducted social media operations targeted at large U.S. audiences with the goal of sowing discord in the U.S. political system. . . . Using fictitious U.S. personas, IRA employees operated social media accounts and group pages designed to attract U.S. audiences. . . . IRA employees posted derogatory information about a number of candidates during the U.S. presidential campaign. . . . Supporting the Trump campaign and disparaging [Democrat] candidate Hillary Clinton.
>
> (The Mueller Report, p. 14, *The Washington Post*, 2019, p. 72)

Though the Mueller investigation did not come to any conclusions as to whether President Trump had personally been involved in the Russian tampering, Mueller's team did uncover a number of alleged crimes committed by Trump associates. In total, 34 indictments have been handed down as a direct result of the Mueller investigation, including to U.S. and Russian citizens. Of the indictments, there were a number of individuals who closely worked with President Trump on his campaign, some of whom served in his administrations (Gangitano, 2019; Teague Beckwith, 2019; LaFraniere, 2019; Gerstein, 2020; Weiner et al., 2020):

- Paul Manafort, Trump Campaign Manager, Investigated for illegal foreign lobbying. Found guilty on eight criminal counts, including lying on bank loan applications and hiding millions of dollars of income. Sentenced to 7.5 years in prison for financial crimes. While serving time at the Metropolitan Correctional Center, New York.
- Roger Stone, Trump Confident Charged with lying to Congress, sentenced to 40 months in prison in February 2020.
- Michael Flynn, National Security Advisor, Trump Cabinet, Pleaded guilty to lying to the FBI in 2017, agreed to cooperate with investigation. Currently sentencing is indefinitely postponed after original sentence date of

December 18, 2019. There was a question as to whether Flynn will withdraw his previous guilty plea, charges will be dropped by the Department of Justice, under U.S. attorney General William Barr's directions, or whether he may receive a presidential pardon.

- Rick Gates, Manafort's Business Partner, Pleaded guilty in 2018 to lying to investigators and conspiracy, agreed to cooperate with the investigation. Gates was sentenced to three years probation, 45 days in jail, and 300 hours of community service.
- Michael Cohen, Personal Lawyer to President Trump Pleaded guilty to financial crimes, campaign finance violations, and lying to Congress. Instrumental in paying hush-money to Stormy Daniels, a pornographic star, who allegedly had an affair with Trump prior to his taking office. Sentenced to three years in federal prison. Cohen is currently served time in a minimum-security federal prison camp in Otisville, New York and was released to home confinement in May 2020, over concerns of being exposed to the COVID-19 virus while incarcerated (Booker, 2020).
- George Papadopoulos, Trump Campaign Advisor Pleaded guilty to lying to investigators, sentenced to 14 days in a minimum-security prison, one-year probation, and a $9,500 fine.

Not all of the information uncovered in the Mueller investigation involved suspected crimes committed by people associated with President Trump's election campaign. As many pieces of evidence uncovered in the Mueller report are still being sorted through, some of the people investigated were referred to New York prosecutors for possible violations of lobbying laws, including former Obama Administration White House Counsel Gregory Craig and Tony Podesta, the brother of Hillary Clinton's 2016 campaign manager. Craig was acquitted of charges that he lied to investigators. The U.S. Justice Department dropped the investigation on Podesta in late 2019.

POLITICAL AND ECONOMIC CRISIS

It becomes a circular problem as to which came first, an economic crisis or a political crisis. Either way, regardless of whichever happened first, political crime can be the culprit that is causing both crises. Likewise, conventional crimes such as murder can result when both the political and economic environments are eroding. And just like a pebble in the water, there can be ripple effects where the country that is crumbling is not the only one affected. Just as financial crimes can cross borders, so can political crimes spill over, leading to regional and global crises.

Law in the Real World: Nicolas Maduro, Venezuela

(Source: U.S. Senate, 2015)

Since becoming an oil-producing country, Venezuela emerged in the 20th century as one of the richest countries in Latin America with a well-educated population. Venezuela was also one of the first democratic countries in South America. All of this came to a crashing end in the 21st century, when the country fell into the hands of corrupt leaders. The alleged ringleader was Hugo Chávez, who took office as President of Venezuela under a socialist platform. In all reality, though Chávez's regime ushered in an age of state-owned businesses, including in the oil industry, this was in a form that was unrecognizable as being truly socialist, and an oligarchy quickly formed.

Nicolas Maduro became president of Venezuela after the long Chávez era, which had lasted from 1999 to 2013. Hugo Chávez essentially named the then Vice President Maduro to succeed him in the office, though there was an election to make the succession appear legitimate. Maduro inherited an already unstable political climate, as Chávez's power teetered in the last two years he was in office while he was seriously ill. Maduro was almost immediately met with charges of corruption and incompetence, and accused of creating the worsening economic conditions in the country. In Maduro's attempts to right the ship, his regime instead responded by cracking down on dissent and has since been accused by the United Nations of violating the human rights of Venezuelans.

By 2014, the Venezuelan economy all but failed, with inflation rates at an unheard-of 64 percent. To put this in perspective, the United States has run with inflation rates that have been on average close to 2 percent per year for the past decade or so. With the hyperinflation in Venezuela, consumer goods became scarce and murder rates rose quickly in the face of the economic meltdown. Medical supplies, including medicine and equipment, became scarce. Transportation options became unreliable as flights were cancelled in and out of the country, trucking bringing even basic goods was all but halted, and buses could no longer run. At one point in the crisis, Venezuela had the second highest murder rate in the world. The Venezuela National Guard was accused of participating in drug trafficking, further threatening U.S. interests in the region.

As Maduro consolidated his power, conditions continued to worsen in Venezuela for its citizens. A number of alleged abuses began to emerge, including accusations that civilians who protested were met with lethal force by security forces. In one instance, a 14-year-old was shot in the head by national police, only outraging citizens more.

Along with violence and human rights violations, the national bank, Banca Privada d'Andorra, was accused by the U.S. Treasury Department of money laundering $2 billion from the state-owned oil company, PDVSA, which subsequently further laundered the money through U.S. banks. To add insult to injury, the country began to default on foreign loans made to it, including those coming from the U.S. This meant that Venezuela became a poor risk for foreign aid packages and there was no assurance that aid would reach the people who needed it most.

Perhaps the one of the most devastating outcomes of the political and economic crisis is that the Venezuelan public health system is broken, contributing to rising mortality rates (Page et al., 2019). The political and economic crisis has also resulted in a crisis at the borders as Venezuelans attempt to escape an almost impossible situation. Once a country that could boast of an educated, healthy population, Venezuela is rapidly finding itself with an uncertain future as the crisis wears on. It has no doubt additionally worsened in the wake of the COVID-19 pandemic.

Discussion Questions

1. As the Venezuelan crisis wears on, what might this mean for the oil industry and what are the possible effects on a global market?
2. The U.S. has used economic sanctions to try and get things under control. Do economic sanctions work to "punish" political criminals?
3. Is it possible to have a political crisis without an economic crisis, and vice versa?

VIOLENCE IN POLITICAL CRIMES

There is a mistaken idea that white collar crime, including political crime, is somehow victimless. We have certainly disputed that misconception in Chapter 7 regarding consumer crime. In some cases, and certainly in some places in the world, political corruption and malfeasance can result in violent crime. Whistleblowers, journalists, and their loved ones may be threatened. At the extreme, political crime can result in the contracted killing or assassination of individuals who are trying to expose the corruption, as we will see in our next case study.

Law in the Real World: Daphne Caruana Galizia, Journalist

(Source: Kakissis, 2018)

In an online blog, *Running Commentary* (available at https://daphnecaruanagalizia.com/), Daphne Caruana Galizia, an investigative reporter situated in Malta[3], stated that crooks were everywhere and that the situation [in Malta] was getting desperate. It was to be her last posting to the website. Not long after the blog posting, on October 16, 2017, Caruana Galizia was killed in an apparent car bombing, targeting her for her role in uncovering corruption in the Maltese government:

> "He ran towards the burning car barefoot across the field. . . . The explosion had blown the grey Peugeot 108 clear off the road. . . . He couldn't see his own mother, Daphne, whose car it was." (Grey, 2018, retrieved from https://www.reuters.com/investigates/special-report/malta-daphne/)

What was it that Caruana Galizia was investigating that would result in her death? By all accounts, it may have been a number of things that set her assassination in motion. She was known for her biting commentary on Maltese politicians as well as investigating money laundering and fraud at Pilatus Bank, which had been shut down in 2018 by the European Central Bank.

Three men were arrested in 2017 and charged with her murder. Vincent Muscat, Alfred Degiorgio, and George Degiorgio have only recently been indicted. They are accused of being responsible for the car bombing. It is unknown as to the motivation for their involvement, but reportedly Caruana Galizia had been targeted for exposing the alleged corruption among the Maltese political elite (Britton and Ramsay, 2019).

Discussion Questions

1. Why is it a difficult time for journalists throughout the world to report on the news?
2. With the growth of social media, is it more difficult for "bad news" reporting to go away, particularly for public figures like politicians?
3. If Caruana Galizia was investigating more than the political elite in Malta, who else could be suspected in ordering her death?

---

[3] Malta is a small island, a European nation located off the coast of Italy.

STATE-ORGANIZED POLITICAL CRIMES

There is a proverb that a fish will rot from the head down. This alludes to the fact that an organization, or in this case a government, is only as ethical as those who are put in charge of leading it. So far in this chapter, we have been focused primarily on individuals or small groups of individuals who appear to be outliers in their crimes and corruption. Their behavior is extraordinary and the exception, not the rule. Sometimes an entire government is pandemically corrupt, in which case, not only are the leader and their cronies rotten, but the system that got them there in the first place is suspect.

Instead of working with the time-honored tradition of imposing legal embargos and economic sanctions, governments can resort to clandestine operations to unseat a leader or to bring a country to its knees. For instance, if for some reason the United States got into a disagreement with Canada about border security, the U.S. might attempt to upset the trade relations between the two countries, including nullifying the North American Free Trade Agreement (NAFTA) or the more recent United States-Mexico-Canada Agreement (USMCA). As any move from the United States to do so would be public and discussed among the stakeholders, though upsetting, this would be a perfectly legitimate way of applying pressure on a country.

However, once secret forces such as spy networks are involved, there is the very real possibility that state-organized crimes will be committed. We will reserve discussion of state-sponsored crime for Chapter 12, when we discuss the role of white collar crime in funding terrorist acts.

Law in the Real World: Iran-Contra Affair

(Source: Block, 2000)

In the late 1970s, Iran and the United States had an ideological falling out after the Shah, Reza Pahlavi, was deposed in a revolution and replaced with a conservative government built on Islamic religious law. As the Shah's government had been U.S. backed, the U.S. responded by imposing a number of economic sanctions on Iran, including an arms embargo. In the meantime, a revolution had been brewing in the Latin American country of Nicaragua, where the U.S. backed the Contras, a rebel group that opposed the existing socialist government. The two upheavals in Iran and Nicaragua seemed to be unrelated and literally thousands of miles apart from one another, both in ideology and geography.

In 1980, Ronald Reagan was voted into office as the 40th President of the United States. A Hollywood actor who served as the governor in California prior to occupying the Oval Office, Reagan was a well-liked, affable president with a reputation of being a masterful communicator. Easily winning a second term in office in 1984, President Reagan at the time seemed very unlikely to be embroiled in a political scandal, much less a state-organized conspiracy. Yet behind the scenes, there was mischief looming.

In response to the growing unrest in Nicaragua and not wanting to enter yet another protracted police action as witnessed in Vietnam, in 1982 Congress passed the Boland Amendment, which prohibited further funding to the Contras. Reagan, without consulting Congress, quietly supported continued aid to the Contras through Central Intelligence Agency (CIA)-led operations. In a secret deal, the U.S. sold guns to Iran through Israel, which in turn sent the profits to the Contras in Nicaragua.

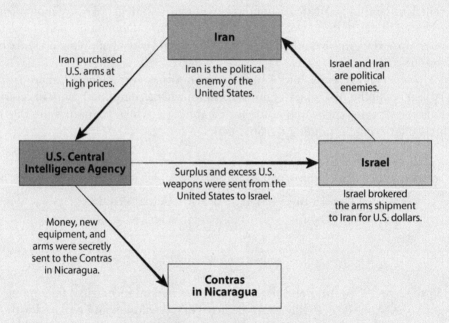

EXHIBIT 11.1 ║ **Iran Contra Affair** (*Source:* https://owlcation.com/humanities/The-Iran-Contra-Scandal-Covert-Affair-in-the-1980s)

Once the scheme was discovered, the Reagan administration hastily made the claim that the illegal arms trade agreements were made in order to free hostages being held in Iran. The American people, and Congress for that matter, had good reason to initially believe this story. During the Islamic Revolution in Iran in 1979, the U.S. embassy in Tehran was taken over, with 52 diplomats and American citizens held hostage until January 20, 1980, not coincidentally released the same day as Reagan took the presidential oath of office at his inauguration.

Nevertheless, Congress launched an investigation into the events leading up to the illegal arms sales to Iran. In testimony given to the Tower Commission, Lieutenant Oliver North, a member of the National Security Council, revealed that he was responsible for at least some of the diversion of funds from the arms sales to Iran to the funding of the Contras. Many believed that Lieutenant North was simply the fall guy. However, testimony uncovered the existence of "The Enterprise," a secret National Security Council group that created and ran the scheme. The Tower Commission findings resulted in the indictment of 14 administration members, some of whom were convicted for their crimes. Of those convicted, all but Thomas Cline avoided spending time in prison (Brown University, n.d., retrieved from https://www.brown.edu/Research/Understanding_the_Iran_Contra_Affair/prosecutions.php):

- Robert McFarlane, National Security Advisor. Charged with four misdemeanor counts of withholding information from Congress. Pleaded guilty to all four counts in plea deal; cooperated with the investigation. Received two years' probation, $20,000 in fines, 200 hours of community service. Pardoned.
- Oliver North, National Security Council. Indicted on 12 counts, including conspiracy and making false statements. Convicted on the charges of accepting a gratuity, aiding in the obstruction of Congress, and destroying documents. Received a suspended three-year prison sentence, two years' probation, $150,000 in fines, 1,200 hours of community service. Court of Appeals vacated his conviction; case was dismissed.
- John Poindexter, National Security Advisor. Indicted on seven felony charges; found guilty of two counts of false statements, two counts of obstructing Congress, and conspiracy. Sentenced to six months in prison for each count, to be served concurrently. Court of Appeals vacated his conviction; case was dismissed.
- Richard Secord, Head of The Enterprise. Indicted on nine counts; pleaded guilty to one felony count of false statements to Congress. Sentenced to two years' probation.
- Albert Hakim, Head of "The Enterprise" Charged with illegally supplementing an official's salary; pleaded guilty to giving money to Oliver North. Sentenced to two years' probation and $5,000 fine.
- Thomas Clines, Businessman in "The Enterprise" Indicted on income tax evasion; pleaded guilty to underreporting earnings, sentenced to 16 months in prison.

- Carl Channell, Fundraiser. Charged with conspiracy to defraud the U.S., pleaded guilty, sentenced to two years' probation.
- Richard Miller, Fundraiser. Charged with conspiracy to defraud the U.S., pleaded guilty, sentenced to two years' probation and 120 hours of community service.
- Clair George, Deputy Director for Operations, CIA. Indicted on ten counts of perjury, false statements, and obstruction. First trial resulted in mistrial; found guilty in two of seven counts during second trial: making false statements and perjury before Congress. Pardoned before sentencing.
- Duane Clarridge, European Division, Chief, CIA. Indicted on seven counts of perjury and false statements, pleaded guilty, sentenced to one year probation and 100 hours of community service. Pardoned.
- Joseph Fernandez, CIA Station Chief in San Jose, Costa Rica. Indicted on five counts of conspiracy to defraud the U.S., obstruction of the Tower Commission, and making false statements. Dismissed in D.C., four-count indictment issued in Virginia, case dismissed.
- Elliot Abrams, Assistant Secretary for Inter-American Affairs, State Department. Indicted on two counts of withholding information from Congress, pleaded guilty, sentenced to two years' probation and 100 hours of community service. Pardoned.
- Casper Weinberger, Secretary of Defense. Indicted on five counts of perjury, making false statements, and obstruction. Pardoned before going to trial.

Dubbed the "Teflon President" in popular media after the non-stick cookware, Reagan was found by the Commission to have not been directly involved in the Iran-Contra Affair. His successor, George H. W. Bush, who served as Vice President under Reagan, was instrumental in getting some of the convictions overturned on appeals, individuals pardoned, or cases dismissed when his administration refused to declassify evidence that could be used in a trail. In one of the most convoluted schemes created to upset an existing government, the Iran-Contra Affair in the 1980s proved to be a colossal embarrassment for the United States.

Discussion Questions

1. This is an unusually long list of defendants as political crimes go. Why might all but one have their cases dismissed or were pardoned, considering the severity of their crimes?
2. As some of the people indicted were convicted but received no prison time, how might they repair their careers after such a big scandal?

3. Why might Lieutenant Oliver North be less culpable in the Iran-Contra Affair, based on his position in the military?

In the bigger scheme of things, the Iran-Contra Affair, though embarrassing, is perhaps not the most offensive state-operated crime. Illegally selling arms is only one type of crime committed by governments. Other state-operated crimes include illegally spying on citizens, including wiretapping; turning a blind eye to officials accepting bribes in drug smuggling operations, and widespread abuses of power within whole administrations or regimes. In the case of state-organized crimes, international laws tend to be violated. The crime operations may not be within the borders of the country, as witnessed by the Iran-Contra Affair. They are often directed at other countries' legitimate governments, however objectionable those governments may be.

SUMMARY

Of all the areas of white collar crime, political crimes come with a wide variety of offenses. Oftentimes, financial crimes intersect with political crimes. Other times, organized crime, as in the case of the Mexican drug cartels, intersect with political crimes. It is not unheard of for political crimes to involve cyberespionage, nor is it surprising to find political crimes overlapping with war crimes. Rarely does political crime live in a vacuum, unrelated to other forms of conventional or white collar crimes.

What makes political crimes unique is that when they are committed due to strong ideological beliefs, they are convictional crimes. By this, we mean that the crimes are being committed due to strong political beliefs. In this, they may have more in common with religious crimes, though those are more likely to happen due to personal greed. With the new age of social media, it is much easier for strong political beliefs to become viral, and this may be one explanation for why there is less public outcry with the 2016 election campaign questions as compared to the outrage expressed during the Watergate scandal in the 1970s. And as convoluted as the Iran-Contra Affair was, nothing seems to have compared in history with the ongoing investigation into whether Russia interfered with (and may still be interfering with) elections in the United States.

As we have seen in this chapter, political crimes are not always nonlethal. But we need to note that the majority of politicians, to the best of their abilities, live within the rule of law, and that some governments around the world are more corrupt than others. However, it is also important to point out that there are some politicians who hang on to their political offices by any means possible. Political opponents can be disposed in a number of ways, including imprisonment and targeted assassination.

Most of the time, what people find distasteful in politics is character assassination, which is difficult to recover from when scandals break in the news. This is regardless of whether the stories have been proven to be true or not. Political power is a formidable aphrodisiac that causes some individuals, and in some cases whole governments, to do anything to stay in power.

Case Study ▪ "Bad Boys" In The "Windy City"—Rod Blagojevich, Governor of Illinois

Background

Chicago has a long, illustrious history of being a wild, political town, much in the same vein as New York City. It came to no surprise to some that when then U.S. Senator Barack Obama, representing the state of Illinois, was elected President of the United States, it would be a political free-for-all in the process of filling his seat in Congress with an appointee. As it happens in these cases, the responsibility to appoint an interim person until an election can be held falls on the shoulders of the governor of the state that the exiting congressperson is from.

At the center of the controversy of replacing President Obama in the Senate was Illinois Governor Blagojevich, a Democrat in his second term in office. He was already in political and legal hot water as he was already suspected of tying his official actions to campaign donations. When the Illinois Congress position became vacant, Jesse White, then the Illinois Secretary of State, refused to endorse Governor Blagojevich's choice, Roland Burris, stating that "Mr. Blagojevich was too tainted by scandal to pick the next senator." (Saulny, 2009, retrieved from https://www.nytimes.com/2009/01/10/us/politics/10illinois.html).

Defining the Crime(s)

The most obvious crime in Blagojevich's case is political corruption. As we will note in our discussion of unresolved issues, the question is whether it is even possible to clean up corruption once it has become institutionalized for so long in a town, city, state, or country. Political corruption is similar to other types of corruption, but is more likely to undermine faith in political systems as all politicians become suspect.

Theories to Explain the Crime

Once corruption is institutionalized, the legal system that is supposed to help prevent it becomes powerless to stop it. As Weeks (1986, p. 123) boldly claimed, Washington, D.C. politics are inevitably corrupt: "Virtually every member of [U.S.] Congress has been compelled to become a crook. Most of them, we can hope, regret the necessity of having had to accept a life of crime, as the price of holding office, but crooks they certainly are. The evidence of the institutionalized corruption of [U.S.] Congress has now become inescapable." If we consider the intersection of Washington, D.C. and Chicago politics, as in the case of Blagojevich, if Weeks (1986) is to be believed, institutionalized corruption is inevitable.

So far, we have not explored the process by which crime become normalized in political circles. Rather than being coincidental, as Charap and Harm (1999) suggested, corruption is systematic and planned. More seriously, kleptocracies may emerge, where government positions are bought and sold to the highest bidder. Though kleptocracies are more likely to be discussed in terms of illicit African governments, the concept can equally be applied to political crime, even in democratic societies. Kleptocracy is basically defined as a government or individual government officials who use their position to exploit power for personal gain.

Social and Media Responses

In Blagojevich's case, the media responses were decidedly different than in most criminal cases.

Unlike most people with criminal charges hanging over them, much less impeachment threats, Blagojevich took to the airways and to the media to plead his case to the public after removal from office and in advance of his federal trial on corruption charges.

His television appearances included live appearances on ABC television network's *Good Morning America* and *The View* (ABC News, 2009). For the second interview, he had his wife at his side, not an uncommon move when accused white collar criminals face television cameras, as this sets up the image of being, as in Blagojevich's case, a solid "family man." Part of the *Good Morning America* interview is available at https://www.youtube.com/watch?v=Kt_5kvPu2vs (Part 1 of 2). He also made appearance on late night interviews, including *The Late Show* (CBS, 2009, available at https://www.youtube.com/watch?v=Blz87f9gSes).

We should note, ironically, that Blagojevich appeared on President Trump's former NBC show, *The Apprentice* (2010). As someone who had exposure to television and the media outside of his official duties, we should not find it unusual for Blagojevich to take his case directly to the public, instead of hiding from the public eye. Unfortunately, his efforts to win over public opinion was for naught, and he was subsequently convicted on corruption charges.

Criminal Justice and Policy Responses

As in the case of impeachment at the federal level, the Illinois State House of Representatives moved to impeach Blagojevich in 2009, which in turn would allow for a trial for his alleged crimes in the State Senate. Within an hour of deliberation, the State House of Representatives voted to impeach Blagojevich in a 114 to 1 vote (Saulny, 2009). The State Senate, in a 59-0 vote, succeeded in voting to remove Blagojevich from office (Berlin and Rumore, 2019).

Once Blagojevich was removed from office, a federal grand jury indicted him on charges of racketeering, wire fraud, and extortion. With Blagojevich, his brother Robert was indicted, along with Chris Kelly, his fundraiser, and John Harris and Alonzo Monk, who had both served as his Chief of Staff while he was in office. In a *Chicago Tribune* article (Pearson and Coen, 2009), the frontpage headline read that Blagojevich's "crew," a term generally reserved for neighborhood-oriented street gangs, ran the state as an organized crime racket. Robert Blagojevich's charges were later dropped after a jury at his trial was deadlocked[4] on the four counts against him.

As we have already noted, white collar criminals are not always allowed a dignified arrest, with their lawyer accompanying them to scheduled booking at the local police station. The narrative of Blagojevich's arrest reads like a classic case of making an example out of an elite criminal with the "perp walk":

> At 6:15 a.m., Gov. Rod Blagojevich is roused from his Ravenswood Manor home [an upscale historical district on the North Side of Chicago], Arrested, handcuffed and hauled before a federal magistrate.... (Berlin and Rumore, 2019, Retrieved from https://www.chicagotribune.com/politics/ct-viz-blagojevich-legal-timeline-htmlstory.html)

Blagojevich pleaded not guilty to the charges. In his June 2010 trial, prosecutors painted a picture of Blagojevich as a selfish man who regularly demanded campaign cash and favors in return for official acts. As in the case of his brother, the jury was deadlocked in the first trial on all but the charge of lying to FBI agents. U.S. District Judge James Zagel declared it a mistrial. Unlike his brother, the prosecutors in turn ordered that he be retried. In the second trial, Blagojevich was found guilty on 17 of the 20 counts he was tried for in connection with his attempt to sell President Obama's senate seat. The conviction resulted in a 14-year sentence in federal prison. Blagojevich was

---

[4] A "deadlocked" or "hung" jury is one in which the members of the jury cannot agree on the verdict for one or more charges against a defendant. The trial can then be declared a "mistrial." A judge and prosecutors have the discretion to order that the defendant be retried with a new jury or dismiss one or more of the charges.

ordered to serve time in the Englewood Federal Correctional Institute, located in Colorado.

In 2019, years after his conviction, the Illinois Bar Association was finally poised to take away Blagojevich's law license. As we have noted in previous chapters, one of the more effective means to punish white collar criminals is to remove their professional licensure. For instance, someone convicted of a crime, operating in the financial industry, will many times be prohibited from holding licenses to sell securities or other investment products. However, being disbarred may not be a deterrent in Blagojevich's case. *Chicago Tribune* writer Jason Meisner (2019) wrote that Blagojevich never did seem to take his law profession seriously. According to Meisner (2019), Blagojevich joked about how during his law school days in California, he was more likely to be on the beaches of Malibu than focused on case law.

In 2019, there were reports that President Trump was considering commuting Blagojevich's sentence. According to television station WGN in Chicago (2019), President Trump backed off from his plans after calls protesting the move flooded the White House switchboards. In 2020, the rumors were confirmed and President Trump extended clemency to Blagojevich. He was released from prison, essentially reducing his 14-year sentence to time served (Klein and Zaslav, 2020).

Unanswered Questions and Unresolved Issues Related to the Case

As in New York City, Chicago has a long history of political scandals dating back to the 19th century. Is it possible to clean up corruption in a city that has institutionalized political crime? Blagojevich's crimes were far from the last to take place in the "Windy City." If the case of Ed Burke is any indication, the possibility of public scandal does not appear to be a deterrence. As dean of Chicago City Council, he found himself re-elected to a 13th term in office in 2019 even though the FBI filed criminal charges against him just prior to the election (Hobson and Bentley, 2019). So what possible deterrence might work when it comes to political corruption?

Corruption is not the only type of crime that Chicago politicians have been accused of. As an example, a member of the Chicago City Council, Alderman Willie Cochran, a former police officer, was sentenced to one year in prison after being convicted of embezzling funds from a charity he founded that was intended to help senior citizens and children (Wall and McAdams, 2019). There is always the question of how many deterrents are in place to prevent these types of crimes to continue to be an issue for the "Windy City."

Has anyone ever been able to make a comeback in politics, after being impeached or having faced a disgraceful scandal, even if they are cleared of the charges? In this day and age of social media, it may be more difficult but not impossible.

Sources

Berlin, J. and K. Rumore. (2019) Rod Blagojevich saga timeline: From arrest to Trump. *Chicago Tribune.* Aug. 8. Retrieved from https://www.chicagotribune.com/politics/ct-viz-blagojevich-legal-timeline-htmlstory.html.

Charap, J. and C. Harm. (1999) *Working paper of the International Monetary Fund: Institutionalized corruption and the kleptocratic state.* African Department, IMF. July.

Hobson, J. and C. Bentley. (2019) How Chicago politics produced a deeply entrenched culture of corruption. *WBUR Radio.* Aired Feb. 28. Available at https://www.wbur.org/hereandnow/2019/02/28/chicago-politics-corruption.

Klein, B. and A. Zaslav. (2020) Trump just granted clemency to 11 people. Here's a look at each. *CNN.com.* Feb. 19. Retrieved from https://www.cnn.com/2020/02/19/politics/trump-pardons-commutations/index.html.

Meisner, J. (2019) State seeks to disbar ex-Gov. Rod Blagojevich from practicing law more than 8 years after conviction. *Chicago Tribune.* Aug. 15. Retrieved from https://www.chicagotribune.com/news/criminal-justice/ct-rod-blagojevich-law-license-20190814-wa6j4ouyhbcjhnz37h75t656cq-story.html.

Patterson, J. (2009) Bringing down Blagojevich. *State Legislatures.* July/Aug., Vol. 35, Issue 7: 38-41.

Pearson, R. and J. Coen. (2019) U.S. says Blagojevich, crew ran state as racket. *Chicago Tribune.* Apr. 3. Retrieved from https://www.chicagotribune.com/news/ct-xpm-2009-04-03-chi-090403blago-feds-story-story.html.

Saulny, S. (2009) Illinois House impeaches governor. *New York Times.* Jan. 9. Retrieved from https://www.nytimes.com/2009/01/10/us/politics/10illinois.html.

Wall, C,. and A. McAdams. (2019) Willie Cochran, former Chicago alderman, sentenced to 1 year in prison. *ABC 7 News.* June 4. Retrieved from https://abc7chicago.com/politics/former-alderman-willie-cochran-sentenced-to-1-year-in-prison/5361219/.

Weeks, J.R. (1986) Bribes, gratuities and Congress: The institutionalized corruption of the political process, the impotence of criminal law to reach it, and a proposal for change. *Journal of Legislation.* Vol. 13, Issue 2: 123-148.

GLOSSARY

Ballot stuffing ("stuffing the ballot box")   The practice of creating fake ballots with votes going to a particular candidate. There are some voting processes that are more vulnerable to ballot stuffing, including the use of paper ballots.

Convictional crime   A crime that is committed because of strong belief that it will be to the benefit of the collective, rather than to the individual. Generally based on strong ideology, as in the case of standing by one's leader or political party, no matter what.

Corruption   Dishonest or fraudulent crimes committed by individuals in power.

Cronyism   The practice of placing one's friends in positions of power, even if they have no experience or qualifications in that position. See *Nepotism.*

Despots   Leaders who demand complete obedience from their citizens and the people they have around them who help them maintain power. Despots use fear and coercion to rule.

Eminent domain   The right for the United States government to purchase private property for public use, even if the property owner does not wish to sell their property. The government is expected to pay fair market value for the property. Example: Purchase of private land in order to build a public highway.

Extortion   Use of damaging information, fear, and/or force to get someone to pay money or give up valuable information.

Impeachment   The process by which a person in an elective office can be removed from the office.

Kickbacks   Illegal "bonus", generally cash, paid to politicians for their vote or policy making that favors an individual or business. Example: Paying a Congress-person money so that they help award a contract to a weapons contractor.

Land grants   Public land that is given or purchased by private individuals, institutions, or businesses. Example: Public land given to help build a university.

Nepotism   The practice of hiring family members without necessarily considering their experience or qualifications. Example in politics: Appointing a family member to serve in a cabinet position. See *Cronyism*.

Non-competitive bidding   In some cases illegal, when a contract is given to a company or contractor without going through a bidding process to hire the best or most cost effective company. Can be related to cronyism and/or nepotism.

"Rent seeking"   Practice of manipulating public policy in order to illegally increase profits.

Oligarchy   Control of a group, organization, or government by a few, elite individuals.

Special counsel   Prosecutor or attorney appointed to oversee the investigation of suspected crimes or malfeasance in the government. Has the power to prosecute or refer individuals to jurisdiction when punishable crimes are uncovered.

Yellow journalism   Sensationalized news reporting that is focused more on profit and selling newspapers than necessarily reporting factual news.

REFERENCES AND SUGGESTED READINGS

Bernstein J. (2012) Nixon's smoking-gun tape and presidency. *Washington Post*. June 22. Retrieved from https://www.washingtonpost.com/blogs/post-partisan/post/nixons-smoking-gun-tape-and-the-presidency/2012/06/22/gJQA0gTlvV_blog.html?utm_term=.de3b7511a630.

Block, A. A. (2000) The origins of Iran-Contra: Lessons from the Durrani Affair. *Crime, Law, and Social Change*. Mar., Vol. 33, Issue 1, 2: 53-84.

Bock Park, D. (2019) The tearful drama of North Carolina's election-fraud hearing. Dispatch, *New Yorker*. Feb. 24. Retrieved from https://www.newyorker.com/news/dispatch/the-tearful-drama-of-north-carolinas-election-fraud-hearings.

Booker, B. (2020) Michael Cohen released from prison due to coronavirus concerns. *NPR*. May 21. Retrieved from https://www.npr.org/sections/coronavirus-live-updates/2020/05/21/860204544/michael-cohen-released-from-prison-due-to-coronavirus-concerns.

British Broadcasting Corporation (BBC). (2019a) Fang Fenghui: China's ex-top general jailed for life. Feb. 20. Retrieved from https://www.bbc.com/news/world-asia-china-47306275.

British Broadcasting Corporation (BBC). (2019b) Four questions about Trump's tower in Moscow that never was. Jan. 18. Retrieved from https://www.bbc.com/news/world-us-canada-46923008.

Britton, B. and M. Ramsay. (2019) Three charged over murder of Maltese journalist Daphne Caruana Galizia. *CNN.com*. Retrieved from https://www.cnn.com/2019/07/17/europe/daphne-caruana-galizia-men-charged-intl/index.html.

Brown University (n.d.) Understanding the Iran-Contra Affair. Prosecutions, *Good Government Project*. Retrieved from https://www.brown.edu/Research/Understanding_the_Iran_Contra_Affair/prosecutions.php.

Caffey, D.L. (2015) *Chasing the Santa Fe Ring: Power and Privilege in territorial New Mexico*. Albuquerque, NM: University of New Mexico Press.

CNN. (2020) READ: Sen. Mitt Romney explains why he'll vote to convict Trump. *CNN.com*. Feb. 5. Retrieved from https://www.cnn.com/2020/02/05/politics/mitt-romney-impeachment-vote-remarks/index.html.

The Economist. (2008) Villepin v Sarkozy: France's Clearstream affair. Dec. 6. Vol. 389, Issue 8609. Retrieved from https://www.economist.com/europe/2008/12/04/villepin-v-sarkozy.

Fullerton, J. (2019) Former prime minister accused over role in looting $4.5 billion sovereign wealth fund. *The Guardian*. Apr. 3. Retrieved from https://www.theguardian.com/world/2019/apr/03/najib-razak-malaysia-former-prime-minister-trial-1mdb-scandal.

Gangitano, A. (2019) Former Podesta lobbyists reap K Street boom. *The Hill*. Sept 4. Retrieved from https://thehill.com/business-a-lobbying/business-a-lobbying/459816-former-podesta-lobbyists-reap-k-street-boom.

Grey, S. (2018) The silencing of Daphne. *Reuters Investigates*. Apr. 17. Retrieved from https://www.reuters.com/investigates/special-report/malta-daphne/.

Griffiths, J. (2019) From Hollywood to Saudi Arabia, Leonardo DiCaprio to Paris Hilton: The scandal that enveloped the world. *CNN World*. Feb. 8. Retrieved from https://www-m.cnn.com/2019/02/08/asia/malaysia-1mdb-trial-najib-intl/index.html.

Kakissis, J. (2018) Who ordered the car bomb that killed Maltese journalist Daphne Caruana Galizia? *NPR*. retrieved from https://www.npr.org/2018/07/22/630866527/mastermind-behind-malta-journalist-killing-remains-a-mystery.

Kolbert, E. (2009) FELLOWship of the ring. In *Today's White Collar Crime: Legal, Investigative, and Theoretical Perspectives*, H.J. Brightman, ed. New York: Routledge.

LeFraniere, S. (2019) Rick Gates, ex-Trump Aide and key witness for Mueller, is sentenced to 45 days in jail. *New York Times*. Dec. 17, Retrieved from https://www.nytimes.com/2019/12/17/us/politics/rick-gates-sentencing.html.

Lindsey, R. (1985) Dan White, killer of San Francisco mayor, a suicide. *New York Times*. Oct. 22. Retrieved from https://www.nytimes.com/1985/10/22/us/dan-white-killer-of-san-francisco-mayor-a-suicide.html.

MF Boom and Madlib. (2009) Absolutely [Recorded by Ape Studio], on *Born Like This*. London: Lex Records. Mar. 24. Track 5.

Oelsner, L. (1975) Mitchell Haldeman, Ehrlichmam are sentenced to 2-1/2 to 8 years, Mardian to 10 months to 3 pears. *New York Times*. Feb. 22. Retrieved from https://www. nytimes.com/1975/02/22/archives/mitchell-haldeman-ehrlichman-are-sentenced-to-2-to-8-years-marmain.html.

Page, K. R., S. Doocy, F. R. G. Barch, J. S. Castro, P. Spiegel, and C. Bevrer. (2019) Venzuela's public health crisis: a regional emergency. Review in *The Lancet*. March, Vol. 393, Issue 10177: 1254-1260.

Pearson, R. and J. Coen. (2019) U.S. says Blagojevich, crew ran state as racket. *Chicago Tribune*. Apr. 3. Retrieved from https://www.chicagotribune.com/news/ct-xpm-2009-04-03-chi-090403blago-feds-story-story.html.

Plato. (1937) *The Republic*. London: William Heinemann.

Schafer, S. (1971) The concept of the political criminal. *Journal of Criminal Law, Criminology, and Police Science*. Northwestern University of Law. Vol. 62, Issue 3: 380-387.

Teague Beckwith, R. (2019) Here are all of the indictments, guilty pleas, and convictions from Robert Mueller's investigation. Politics, Justice, *Time Magazine*. July 24. Retrieved from https://time.com/5556331/mueller-investigation-indictments-guilty-pleas/.

United States House of Representatives. (n.d.) Overview of New Mexico Politics 1848-1898. *History, Art & Archives*. Retrieved from https://history.house.gov/Exhibitions-and-Publications/HAIC/Historical-Essays/Continental-Expansion/New-Mexican-Politics/.

United States House of Representatives. (2012) *Obama Administration's Abuse of Power*. Committee on the Judiciary. 112th Congress, Second Session. Sept. 12. Washington, D.C.: U.S. Government Printing Office.

United States House of Representatives. (2013) *Hispanic Americans in Congress*. The Committee on House Administration of the U.S. House of Representatives. Washington, D.C.: GAO.

United States National Archives and Records Administration (NARA). (n.d.) Presidential Records Act (PRA) of 1978. *National Archives*. Retrieved from https://www.archives.gov/presidential-libraries/laws/1978-act.html.

United States Senate. (2015) Deepening political and economic crisis in Venezuela: Implications for U.S. interests and the Western Hemisphere. *Hearing: Subcommittee on Western Hemisphere Transnational Crime, Civilian Security, Democracy, Human Rights, and Global Women's Issues*. Committee on Foreign Affairs. 114th Congress, First Session. March 17. Washington, D.C.: U.S. Government Publishing Office.

The Washington Post. (2019) *The Mueller Report*. P. Finn, National Security, ed.; R.S. Heldermand and M. Zapotosky, Introduction and Analysis. New York: Scribner.

Woodward, B. (2005) *The Secret Man: The story of Watergate's Deep Throat*. New York: Simon & Schuster.

Woodward, B. and C. Bernstein. (2014) *All the President's men: The greatest reporting story of all time*. Reissue edition. New York: Simon & Schuster.

Wright, T. and B. Hope. (2019) *Billion Dollar Whale: The Man Who Fooled Wall Street, Hollywood, and the World*. New York: Hachette Books.

Chapter TWELVE

White Collar Crime and Terrorism

Follow the money

> "I've never met anyone who wanted to be a terrorist. They are desperate people."
>
> —*John Perkins, Author, Confessions of an Economic Hitman (2004)*

Chapter Objectives

- Define terrorism in the 21st century.
- Identify the types of white collar crimes committed by terrorist groups.
- Highlight the ways that terrorists commit white collar crimes to fund their operations.
- Identify the types of technologies used in terrorist attacks.
- Review legal and law enforcement efforts to combat terrorist white collar crimes.

Key Terms

Aged company
Anomie
Anticybersquatting Consumer
   Protection Act (ACPA)
Bad faith
Cybersquatting
Cyberterrorism
Fraud spree
Front companies
Identity assumption

Identity theft
Improvised explosive device (IED)
Shelf company
Shell company
Smuggling operations
Soft target
Straw buyer
U.S. Customs and Border Patrol
   (CBP)
Weapon of mass destruction (WMD)

INTRODUCTION

We have already established that the fear of conventional crime strikes more fear in the public than white collar crimes. And like conventional crimes, terrorist acts are of greater concern to people than the more real prospect of being victimized by a financial crime or *identity theft.*

The reality is that as much as terrorist acts are horrendous, the probability of being a victim of one, at least in Western countries, is relatively low (Penn et al., 2008). Few people, and researchers for that matter, make the connection between terrorism and white collar crime.

In terrorism studies, one topic that is often neglected is how terrorist acts are funded. Whether a terrorist group is sophisticated and organized or a ragtag bunch of desperate, disillusioned, or delusional people, many of their operations require funding of some kind. With the exception of single-handed terrorist acts using household goods thrown together into an *improvised explosive device (IED)*, events like 9/11 in New York City could not be accomplished without financing and sophisticated planning. As Wall and Kane (2005) note, law enforcement and prosecutors are consistent in reporting that terrorist activities are almost always associated with white collar crimes.

Some of the ways by which terrorist acts are funded are through traditional organized crime operations, like human or drug trafficking. Another tactic is kidnapping tourists and holding them hostage for ransom, either contacting their families or their countries for payment. Even though these are not typically categorized as white collar crimes, the financial proceeds from those activities often have to be laundered through banks or businesses. With ransom money, it has to be made untraceable or it can lead investigators straight to the kidnappers. In this case, the peripheral crimes associated with terrorist acts fall under the umbrella of white collar crime.

There is also the myth that terrorist masterminds are uneducated, "backwards" people. On the contrary, the leaders of terrorist organizations typically have extensive battlefield experience (Van Leeuwen and Weggemans, 2018). Even in the case of the "lone wolves" Boston Marathon bombers in 2013, the Chechen immigrants accused of the crime, brothers Tamerlan Tsarnaev and Dzhokhar Tsarnaev, did not fit the classic stereotype of poor and uneducated converts to violent extremism. The younger brother, Dzhokhar Tsarnaev, was living in the dorms at the University of Massachusetts in Dartmouth, attending college at the time of their plotting and executing the crime.

During the annual marathon, which culminated in downtown Boston, the Tsarnaev brothers set off two homemade devises that exploded, killing three people, including 8-year old Martin Richard, and injuring more than 200 runners and spectators (*CNN Library*, 2019). One primary strength to the arguments about Islamic extremists being far from uneducated is the use of innovation and improvisation, utilizing less advanced, but easily obtained technologies

(Tønnessen, 2017). And the self-educated can be underestimated in their capabilities as well.

The very real concern is that both state and federal law enforcement agencies may not immediately recognize that a white collar crime being committed has ties to terrorist groups. Part of the problem is that these agencies do not necessarily have the resources to devote to thorough investigation and prosecution. Local agencies are even more ill-equipped to investigate white collar crime that might be a cover for terrorist activities. In a 2004 report to the U.S. Justice Department, the National White Collar Crime Center warned that "investigative, enforcement, and prosecuting personnel at these levels [state and local] of government often have limited access to resources, including training, intelligence, and other information." (Kane and Wall, 2004, p. 2). It took the tragic events of 9/11 to bring more attention to the problem and resources to finding solutions.

CHARACTERISTICS OF TERRORISTS

Some of you may have already taken a specialized class covering terrorism. Others may have only studied it in passing in one of your courses. Whatever level of expertise you may have, it is a good idea, before launching into this chapter more deeply, to review what terrorism looks like today.

For our purposes, we could adopt a more current definition of terrorism. Forst et al. (2011, p. xix; Shichor, 2017, p. 255) define terrorism as "the use of force against innocent people, usually with a political or religious motive, and typically aimed at producing wide-spread form of aggression." Where Forst and his fellow researchers fall short in their definition is in failing to include cyberterrorism, where there might not be physical harm done to victims, but the psychological or economic terror is just as real and damaging.

The intent of terrorist acts is to cause widespread fear. It is one thing when soldiers die on a battlefield; it is another thing when civilian populations are targeted. As tragic as any soldier's death might be, it is considered to be an expected risk. Except in some countries where there have historically been somewhat regular incidences of terrorism, as in the example of Israel, most civilian populations, at least in the Western world, do not expect to be victims of terrorism when they go about their daily business of going to work or shopping. By committing an act of terror, the perpetrators are essentially causing civilians to be fearful, which in turn has social, emotional, and as we will see later in this chapter, economic impacts on ordinary citizens.

Few people are recruited to terrorist organizations without some feelings of disfranchisement, whether it is real or imagined. Terrorist attacks are justified by what Durkheim (1897; 1998) termed as *anomie*, where there is a fear that cultural norms and values will be lost with rapid social and economic change. Having lost self-identity and believing that they are economically, politically, and socially exploited, some individuals or populations are at greater risk of being recruited into extremist groups (Morgan, 2017). This is similar to the forces at play that make street gangs attractive to disenfranchised youth in poverty-stricken neighborhoods.

In the last part of the 20th century, much of what we saw in emerging terrorist groups was extreme religious fundamentalism. Before then, the belief was that terrorists would not resort to using *weapons of mass destruction (WMDs)* because those acts would be widely condemned and gain them little sympathy for their cause (Hudson, 1999). However, in more recent decades there is less justification based on social injustice issues and more importance in punishing so-called "non-believers." This can include hate crimes and attacks on members of any religious sect, including Muslims, Jews, and Christians.

In some cases, religious extremism is also an expression of nationalism. For example, a "jihad" in Islamic extremism is described as a struggle against supposed enemies of Islam, as in the ongoing conflict between Palestine and Israel (Dot-Pouillard and Rébillard, 2013). An example would be when improvised suicide missions designed to cause mass casualties are executed, blending both political and religious ideology in this case.

THE COST OF A TERRORIST OPERATION

It is somewhat of a myth that terrorists primarily run their operations with little funding because they are seen as small, localized events, requiring little in the way of financial support. This myth is somewhat supported by the fact that many (but not all) terrorists come from impoverished regions or countries. According to an *NBC News* report, U.S. officials believe that terrorist groups, including Al-Qaeda and ISIS, don't spend lavishly on attacks (Windrem, 2015). This in itself is somewhat disconcerting, as the number of radicalized converts to extremist groups is unknown. With operations ranging in cost from a few hundred to several thousand dollars, it is frighteningly within the means of some groups to pull off attacks with little funding depending on the size, scope, and location of the terrorist act. Others require far more financial support in order to execute their plans.

When we examine the Boston Marathon bombing case, the materials were relatively inexpensive. The Tsarnaev brothers would have been able to purchase the pressure cookers for under $100 each. However, operations like the Kansas City bombing by domestic terrorists in 1995 would have required more funding. With the use of a rental truck and a large quantity of fertilizer, there would be some considerable cost involved, but not impossible for the two perpetrators, Timothy McVeigh and Terry Nichols, to pull off using their personal financial resources.

The UN has estimated that due to the cost of some terrorist operations, they require outside funding. In a 2002 bombing of a Bali nightclub in Indonesia, the estimated cost was $50,000 USD (Kaplan, 2006). This translates to over 700 million Indonesian rupiah (IDR). With relatively low per capita income in Bali, it would be difficult for an organized group to come up with the money needed to execute the 2002 bombing on their own without support coming from outside the country.

Once you reach the scale of a 9/11 terrorist operation with multiple targets, it takes considerable time, planning, and financing. In order to hijack the four planes, it required at least four of the terrorists to be somewhat proficient in flying large commercial jets. Training for commercial jets is no inexpensive proposition. To even become a private pilot, flying a less sophisticated smaller aircraft, the estimates are between $63,000 and $81,000 for training depending on the level of previous flying experience (Airline Career Pilot Program, n.d.).

Some of the terrorists piloting the hijacked planes had allegedly received training at the Flight Safety Academy in Vero Beach, Florida (Fish, 2001). The estimates given by ACPP as to the cost of training does not take into consideration retraining when pilots fail the tests necessary to get licensed the first time. This was the case for at least two of the 9/11 hijackers, who required further training. Realistically, the 9/11 terrorists who flew the four aircraft after they were hijacked did not necessarily have to be licensed, but just have enough training to follow through with their mission. One way or another, flying lessons are expensive.

Added to the expenses of the terrorists prior to the 9/11 tragedy in New York City was their living expenses while they were plotting the operation. A number of them lived in San Diego, California, a relatively expensive city even in more modest quarters. Adding the cost of the first-class airline tickets for 19 hijackers on the four doomed flights, the estimates for the 9/11 operation come in at around $500,000 (USD) (Windrem, 2015).

One of the provisions in the U.S. Patriot Act of 2001, passed after 9/11 with subsequent revisions, is the consideration of the connections between white collar crime and terrorism. The reasoning behind including criminal acts like fraud and financial crimes is that terrorist groups need more than just weapons (Kane and Wall 2005). They also need financing and will use a number of means that are more commonly related to white collar crimes to move cash around. This can include any number of schemes such as smuggling, money laundering, and various frauds.

Needless to say, terrorists cannot simply walk into a bank and ask for a loan to finance their operations. They can, however, ask for a loan to help set up a legitimate business through which terrorist financing can be filtered. They may do so using a *straw buyer*, someone who will either legally or illegally make a purchase or obtain credit on behalf of someone who cannot complete the transaction themself. Terrorist organizations can be dependent on finding legitimate avenues by which to raise money without raising red flags to law enforcement. However, as we examine the specific ways that terrorists raise money, few, if any, means are legitimate.

ROLE OF PROPAGANDA IN TERRORIST ORGANIZATIONS

We cannot underestimate the role of propaganda in raising money or recruitment for terrorist organizations. Similar to other charismatic organizations that attract donations, terrorist groups are dependent on faithful followers who can help finance their operations. Traditionally, the means by which they get attention and appear to be legitimate were the use of print media, including newspapers, pamphlets, and posters to influence the public (Bates and Mooney, 2014). Even television and radio outlets have been exploited, particularly in countries that host terrorism. One method that is more likely to be used today is online forums, including social media.

What is not always reported in the news is the use of distance learning to recruit, train, and inspire would-be terrorists. We ordinarily think of distance learning as an extension of brick and mortar colleges and universities in the form of online classes. In their own "University of Terrorism," jihadist organizations market to potential consumers of their ideology (Bates and Mooney, 2014). Using enthusiastic marketing language, in one brochure, a student of one terrorist "university" boasts:

> "Al-Qaeda is a university that is decentralized, respects no geographic boundaries and does not exist in any one location. And anyone who loves his religion can register. Praise be to God that the Al-Qaeda University graduates [so many] heroes with various specializations... This university has various departments: one for electronic jihad, one for jihad against oneself [to overcome inner resistance], one for the technology of explosives and others!" (Musharbash, 2012; Bates and Mooney, 2014, retrieved from https://www.westga.edu/~distance/ojdla/fall173/Bates_Mooney173.html).

In this way, terrorist organizations can reach vast numbers of potential recruits and donors than if they concentrated their efforts solely on local resources. Distance learning in the guise of an institution of higher learning offers a veneer of legitimacy (save for the terrorist rhetoric). The danger is in the fact that the propaganda is being distributed remotely, making it much more difficult to locate the perpetrators. The problem comes from the anonymity of the perpetrators (Arquilla, 2013). As Arquilla (2013) and Bates and Mooney (2014) all note, no matter how relentless international efforts have been in stopping terrorist propaganda from spreading in cyberspace, the terrorist groups operate unobstructed in their use of this virtual haven through the Dark Web.

Beyond online avenues to spread propaganda, the media is used as a tool to attract attention to terrorist organizations. Terrorist attacks reported in the news act as a lightning rod for possible recruits or donors. Schmid and de Graaf (1982), along with Keinan et al. (2003), argue that instead of acting as negative publicity for terrorists, the victims of their crimes become active consumers looking for up-to-the minute information in this era of 24-hour news cycles. Keinan et al. (2003, p. 150) further argue that terrorists can make

> "unconditional demands for the presence of news reporters or immediate access to broadcasting time.... By the same token, reporters make a 'mad rush' to the site of a terrorist act a persistent attempt to obtain interviews with terrorists or their victims and to provide a maximum number of close-ups or video recordings of terrifying and violent scenes."

In this way, the media becomes the witting or unwitting participant in terrorist propaganda. And with the world connected through cyberspace in most places around the globe, nearly the whole planet becomes witness to terrorist acts. This achieves one of the main objectives of terrorist groups when it comes to propaganda—attention.

CHARITIES

Another means by which terrorist organizations can raise funds is through charities. The charities themselves are represented as being for humanitarian purposes. However, the heads of charities may defraud donors. As we have reviewed in our chapter on religious crimes, nonprofits can have individuals running them who are illegally using some of the donations for their own personal benefit. In the case of charities that are intended to fund terrorist operations through backdoor channels, the managers will hand donations over to terrorist groups. For example, there was a federal indictment of Holy Land Foundation for Relief and Development (HLFRD), suspected of providing over $12 million to Hamas, a Palestinian extremist group primarily operating out of Gaza in Israel (Kane and Wall, 2004).

Law in The Real World: Benevolence International Foundation (BIF)

(Source: Kane and Wall, 2004; United Nations, 2010)

In the case of the Benevolence International Foundation (BIF), what appeared to be a run-of-the-mill charity aimed at humanitarian aid efforts turned out to have ties back to Al-Qaeda and the Taliban. These were the very terrorist organizations that are responsible for the 9/11 attacks on the Twin Towers in New York City and on the Pentagon in Washington, D.C, plus the foiled attempt that resulted in the fourth hijacked plane crashing in Shanksville, Pennsylvania. More disturbingly, the United Nations reported that there was a direct connection from the charity to Usama bin Laden,[1] the then-leader of Al-Qaeda.

Before being incorporated in the United States under the BIF name, the organization was founded in 1987 as *Lajnar al-Birr al-Islamia*, translated as the Islamic Benevolence Committee. The charity was specifically designed to help fund military activities in Afghanistan, including the procurement of a number of types of weapons. Among these weapons were rifles and mortar shells. The charity also aided fighters traveling in and out of Pakistan.

The charity, after rebranding, was moved to the U.S. in order to attract more donations. BIF came under suspicion by the U.S. government in 1993. As an indication of just how slow these types of investigations go, particularly before 9/11, it wasn't until March 2002 that the offices of BIF were searched by Bosnia and Herzegovina law enforcement, at which time they found substantial evidence linking the charity to the activities of Bin Laden and Al-Qaeda. In November 2010, the U.N. reported to the international community that the charity was bogus and nothing more than a coverup for terrorist operations in and around Afghanistan.

In 2011, Bin Laden, along with some of his family members and associates, were killed during a covert military operation after a ten-year search for him through the deserts of Afghanistan and Pakistan.

Discussion Questions:

1. How can donors be assured that the money they give to charity won't end up in the hands of terrorist organizations?
2. What makes charities an attractive way to raise funds for terrorist operations?
3. Where might there be a disconnect between charitable giving, terrorist acts, and some of the supposed religious groups that perpetrate them?

FRONT, SHELF, AND SHELL COMPANIES

We have discussed *shell companies* elsewhere in this textbook. As a reminder, shell companies or corporations serve the purpose of allowing for a well-known company to legitimately move forward with a project before they are ready to

---

[1] Also known as Osama bin Laden. We are deferring to the spelling used in United Nations reports.

announce to the world that they are the originators of the business deal. We used the example of the Walt Disney Company legitimately using shell companies to buy land in Orlando for Walt Disney World and Epcot so as to not to alert land speculators or unwanted businesses to the area. Disney had learned his mistake in Anaheim with the Disneyland project, where to his horror, what he perceived to be tacky stores and hotels started popping up in close proximity to the theme park. Shell companies can either work within legal parameters, as in the example of the Walt Disney Company or can be used for illegal money laundering operations. It is because of this that they are controversial and illegal in some countries.

The purpose of a front company is a bit different than shell companies. *Front companies* are used to avoid negative publicity or lawsuits for the parent company. They can also be used to protect the assets of a parent company. This is similar to why individuals who are self-employed or own small businesses may have their companies listed as "limited liability partnership" (LLP) or as a "limited liability company" (LLC). In this way the business is liable for any judgement that might come from a civil lawsuit, rather than having personal assets of the business owners taken away, including homes, investments, and bank accounts. The problem with a front company, like shell companies, is that it is more likely to be used as a cover for illegal operations.

A *shelf*, "paper," or *"aged" company* is one that is not in operation but in the books as being in existence. Think of it like a sleeper cell in a terrorist organization that is idle until called upon to be useful, though shelf companies do have their legitimate uses. Generally, the purposes of a shelf company is to hold it until it becomes attractive to a potential buyer. One motive for creating a shelf company is that it is easier to set up than a fully functioning corporation or company. For a purchaser, it means buying a company that is already legally established, with a favorable credit rating and potential suppliers.

The problem comes when criminals create or buy any of these types of nontraditional companies. This includes terrorist organizations. For legitimate businesses, they may even have their identities and reputations stolen when a similarly named front, shell, or shelf company impersonates them, deceiving customers, creditors, and suppliers (BusinessIDTHEFT.org, n.d.). This is becoming particularly problematic since the buying and selling of Internet domain names (URLs) in the Computer Age. Companies, similar to fraudulent charities, can be established and disappear before the origins of the company can be detected. Hence there might not be a physical address for the company, but rather a location in cyberspace.

More recently, with the passage of the Uniform Domain-Name Dispute Policy (UDRP) and *Anticybersquatting Consumer Protection Act* (ACPA, United States Senate, 15 U.S. Code §1125, 1999), there has been at least some slowdown of cyberactivity associated with shell, shelf, or aged companies that can potentially be created by terrorists to fund their operations. Sellers of domain names cannot sell one if they have never used the website for commercial use (ACPA, United States Senate, 15 U.S Code §1125, 1999). One of the more important features of the legislations is that people cannot create domain names that are too similar to well-known, well-established businesses. In this way, criminals will not be able to poach customers and suppliers from legitimate companies (ACPA, United States Senate, 15 U.S Code §1125, 1999; Faturoti, 2015). Any person or persons who creates a domain name that could be mistaken for a real company is said to be acting in *bad faith* (Faturoti, 2015).

IDENTITY THEFT

There are a number of ways by which criminals and terrorist groups can steal the identities of innocent people. When it happens, it not only allows criminals to run amok with credit, but it also allows terrorists to conceal their identity and their countries of origin. The Social Security Administration (2018, p. 2) reports a number of ways that thieves can steal personal information:

- Stealing wallets, purses, and mail that contain bank and credit card statements, pre-approved credit offers, new checks, and tax information.
- Stealing personal information provided to unsecured sites online, from work or at home.
- Rummaging through trash, trash of businesses and public trash dumps for personal data.
- Posing by phone or email as someone who legitimately needs information from you (spam and/or phishing).
- Buying personal information from "inside" sources. Example: An identity theft pays a store employee for personal information that appears on applications for goods, services, or credit.

One primary function of identity theft by terrorist organizations is to allow more freedom of movement of recruits and members between countries. For instance, there has historically been a travel ban in place for citizens of North Korea who wish to travel to the United States. By assuming the identity of someone living in a country that is not affecting by the travel ban, like South Korea, potential terrorists may fly under the radar through immigration or in attempts to obtain a visitor's visa. In 2020, under executive orders by President Donald Trump, the following countries were put under a travel ban to the United States:

- Iran
- Libya
- North Korea
- Somalia
- Syria
- Venezuela
- Yemen

There are also "reconsider travel" or "do not travel" advisories for a number of other countries, including Iraq, Afghanistan, Mali, and certain countries in Africa (Bureau of Consular Affairs, n.d.). This means that there is more scrutiny of movement in and out of any of these countries at the borders.

We should also note, as we have noted elsewhere in this book, that in early 2020, the world was hit with a global pandemic. The COVID-19 virus, with no known cure or vaccine at the time, resulted in the closing of borders globally. Scientists and governments around the world were trying to slow down the spread of the virus that appeared to put older populations, as well as individuals with underlying health conditions, at greater risk of death from the illness. In March 2020, President Trump ordered restricted entry to the United States from all countries. This is not to be confused with the earlier travel bans he ordered for suspected terrorist countries or countries that appeared to harbor terrorists.

Identity theft allows individuals who hold citizenship in any of these countries more freedom of movement until they are caught. As Kane and Wall (2005, p. 1) note, "the planning stages of terrorist activities require various acts of deception, such as the creation and use of false identifications to enter the country, gain employment, acquire equipment, and accumulate money and money laundering (to hide the source, destination, use, and amount of money acquired)."

A secondary function of identity theft is to obtain credit or to fraudulently use existing accounts. We will go into greater detail about credit fraud in the next section of this chapter. Before the events of 9/11, Congress passed the Identity Theft Assumption and Deterrence Act in 1998, making it a federal crime (U.S. Senate, 2002). The purpose of the act was to more aggressively prevent identity theft from happening in the first place.

After 9/11, more aggressive measures have been put in place in order to prevent identity theft by terrorists or any criminals. These measures include removal of identifying information from documents, such as including full credit card account information on statements, and streamlining the way by which victims can report fraud (U.S. Senate, 2002). For example, when people used to try and report identity theft, they would have to contact a number of credit reporting agencies along with any financial institution they might have accounts with. However, there was no guarantee that the accounts or credit reports were all flagged for fraud.

Once a fraud has been reported, there is now more synergy between financial institutions and credit reporting companies and suspicious credit card transactions are more readily identified. You may have had the experience of having your credit card company call you while you were in the middle of making an unusual purchase, either because it was for a dollar amount that was much higher than you usually charge or you were traveling out of state or out of the country and trying to use your credit card. These phone calls are a direct result of reforms in how suspected fraud is identified and reported. This is why it is always a good idea to alert your credit card company or bank in advance of making any large purchases or if you plan on using either a credit card or debit card while traveling.

Another preventative measure recommended is to print information about identity theft in a number of languages, as English-speakers are not the only ones to be victimized (U.S. Senate, 2002). The challenge comes in the fact that identities can be stolen more readily in the Internet age. Social Security numbers in particular are being stolen or compromised at an alarming rate, and represents the most common security breach that individuals experience (Social Security Administration, 2018).

For the victims of identity theft, it has been difficult to report the crime, meaning that many cases go undetected or unresolved. The National Center for Victims has stated in the past that victims complained that law enforcement generally would not take reports of identity theft (U.S. Senate, 2000). Unless the victims could identify the exact location of the theft, it was nearly impossible to track down the culprit or culprits. Adding to this difficulty is identifying if the theft has been perpetrated by a terrorist organization.

CREDIT FRAUD

There are any number of ways that credit fraud can be committed. According to Experian, PLC, a credit rating and protection agency, these can include falsifying credit applications, identity theft, *identity assumption*, and *fraud sprees* (Experian, n.d.). Whereas identity theft is generally aimed at short-term fraud, identity assumption involves a long-term commitment to using someone else's identity to cover up or commit crimes.

One of the most common types of credit fraud involves credit cards. Credit cards have only been around since the 1950s, when they were difficult to get approved for. In fact, women had a near impossible time applying for credit in their own name until the Equal Credit Opportunity Act (ECOA) was passed in 1974. According to Stebbins (2019), consumer credit card debt currently surpasses $1 trillion in the United States, with the average American owing $6,354 on bank-issued credit cards. The most common types of credit card scams and frauds include (Bennett, 2018):

- *Application fraud*, which generally happens alongside identity theft. First requires stealing or forgery of the necessary supporting documents to apply for credit, including driver's licenses.
- *Electronic or manual credit card* imprints happen when someone skims the information on the magnetic strip of a card. Also known as credit card skimming, thiefs use a small device, like a "skimmer," to electronically steal the information necessary to make fraudulent purchases.
- *Card not present (CNP) purchases* can happen when a thief has the card number, security code (generally on the back of the card), and expiration date of the card. With this information, fraudulent purchases can be made online or over the phone.

- *Counterfeit card fraud* can be accomplished by skimming devices (See *Electronic or manual credit card*) in order to create a fake card. The magnetic strip or chip on the card doesn't work, but it is often not difficult to convince a merchant that there is something wrong with the card and request that the information be entered by hand.

    We should note that it is difficult and takes skill to create fake cards. This is why the complexity of the security attached to credit cards is becoming more sophisticated.

- *Card ID theft* can happen when card details are known by a criminal and the credit card account is taken over or the criminal uses your name in order to open a new account. This is reportedly the most difficult type of credit card fraud to identify or to recover from.

- *Mail non-receipt card fraud* occurs when someone is expecting a new credit card or replacement in the mail and criminals intercept it. The criminal then registers the card, usually with a phone call, and starts using it in the victim's name.

- *Assumed identity* can happen when a criminal uses a temporary address and false name to obtain a credit card. This, of course, assumes a falsified credit application.

- *Doctored cards* are cards where a strong magnet has been used to erase the data on the metallic strip. This type of card will not work, but the criminal can then convince a merchant to manually enter the information, similarly as in the case of counterfeit cards.

- *Account takeovers* are the most common types of credit card fraud, where a criminal has managed to obtain all the information and relevant documents, often online. They then contact the credit card companies, changing the account address, and replacement cards are sent to that location.

We know that credit fraud is not strictly limited to garden-variety white collar criminals located in the United States. There has been growing evidence for some time that this is a transnational problem. Payment fraud, including the use of credit fraud, has been committed in order to provide material support to terrorist groups in the sum of billions of U.S. dollars (NewsRX, 2019). The biggest concern in trying to make the connection between credit fraud and terrorists is that most victims report the theft or fraud to their financial institution instead of alerting law enforcement (NewsRX, 2019). A second concern is credit and payment fraud is thought of as one cost of doing business by companies, who are themselves not in the habit of reporting compromised accounts or fraudulent charges (NewsRX, 2019).

SMUGGLING OPERATIONS

Parallel to organized crime groups that originate overseas, terrorist groups may smuggle currency into a country where terrorists are planning some sort of attack or disruption. If we take the example of maritime cargo containers, currently only 3.7 percent, or about 400,000, are inspected each year by the *U.S. Customs and Border Patrol (CBP)* (CBP, n.d.). The import/export business is the most logical to be scrutinized, as it is one way to smuggle money into the country to terrorists. However, as we have seen in other agencies, the resources to stop it are just not there, despite calls for a 100 percent scanning policy, as intended after 9/11.

Money is not the only thing that authorities, including the CBP, are concerned with in *smuggling operations*. After 9/11, the fear was that along with money, terrorist organizations could smuggle in weapons and bombmaking components, including those that could be made into a small nuclear device (Kane and Wall, 2005). After the dismantling of traditional Communism during Glasnost in the former U.S.S.R. in the late 1980s, the materials used in making nuclear bombs, including uranium, began to disappear into the black market, much of which has gone unaccounted for (Lavin, 2008). The fear is that even a small "dirty bomb" (e.g., nuclear, chemical, biological) could cause widespread chaos and fear. CBP will open and inspect any container that looks suspicious or scan containers for contents that do not match the manifest (Congressional Budget Office, 2016).

It would be an impossibility to inspect cargo at the country of origin before heading to North America. This is a twofold problem. One, as cargo comes from hundreds of different ports around the world, it would be a monumental undertaking. Not all countries would welcome the interference of American agents to conduct inspections overseas. The second issue is whether foreign agents could be trusted to conduct thorough inspections themselves, even if some policy were to be put in place. We should consider also that smuggling and government corruption may very well go hand-in-hand in some places in the world.

An additional challenge boils down, once again, to funding. With current technology, it is possible to use imaging to see the items in a cargo container without opening it and displacing its contents. In fact, the CBP currently identifies any incoming containers that might be high-risk and inspects them with x-ray or gamma-ray imaging equipment (Congressional Budget Office, 2016). Though not all containers are opened and inspected, all containers coming into the U.S. are scanned for radiation. However, in order to use imaging on all containers coming in, the cost, according to the Congressional Budget Office estimates (2016), would be on average between $150 to $220 per container. This translates to between $22 and $32 billion over the course of ten years (Congressional Budget Office, 2016). The bottom line is scanning all shipping containers, whether they arrive by land, sea, or air, would be costly.

Art, antiques, and antiquities are seemingly unlikely items to smuggle for purposes of funding terrorist groups. Antiquities can include any number of items that are identified as archaeological artifacts. Examples would be oil lamps from Ancient Rome or funerary items from tombs, once upon a time buried in Ancient Egypt. Because of the black market for these items, it is difficult to trace them once they go missing. In many cases, these are items that have been looted during times of war, as in the example of art collections stolen from victims of the

Holocaust that have transferred owners so many times, it is nearly impossible to identify their owners or their descendants (Moskowitz, 2011). There were hundreds of thousands of artifacts taken from ancient sites around the world during the infancy of archaeology in the 19th century, before the discipline became more conservative in excavating sites. Like famous works of art, if not housed in museums, artifacts may be illegitimately held in private collections or in circulation on the black market.

Law in the Real World: Selling Antiquities on Facebook®

(Source: Fernholz, 2019; Swann, 2019)

The social network forum Facebook® has had its hands full trying to keep criminals from using it to sell stolen goods. Private groups in Facebook® have not just restricted themselves to buying and selling stolen artifacts and antiquities. Reportedly, there have also been forums in which there are discussions on how to illegally excavate ancient tombs and archaeological sites.

One of the regions that has been hit hard in recent decades with looting of historical artifacts is the Middle East, particularly Syria and Iraq. Though 70 percent of the antiquities coming out of the region are fake, there is the other 30 percent that have real cultural significance to their countries of origin. As museums around the world are making a concerted effort to return antiquities that were taken from important archaeological sites in the 19th century when excavations were a free-for-all back to their places of origins, modern day thieves are illegally looting more recently discovered sites and selling the items on the black market.

In the Athar Project, a group of anthropologists monitored 95 Arabic-language Facebook® groups from conflict zones in the Middle East, including Syria, Yemen, and Libya, who offered antiquities for sale. One tool they used that you were introduced to in this book was social network analysis. In their released report, they identified a number of extremist groups, including those connected with Al-Qaeda and ISIS, that were benefitting from the sale of the artifacts. The real concern noted by the anthropologists is that antiquities trafficking had long been institutionalized and that Facebook® was merely another forum in order to sell the items looted.

Though Facebook® does make a conscious effort to inhibit illegal activities on its website, it is difficult to monitor. An added complication, according to Fernholz (2019), is that Facebook® has no legal responsibility to prevent the sales of illegally obtained antiquities. Yet the FBI has warned art dealers that any artifacts that were purchased and found to have been stolen by terrorist groups puts them at risk of being held criminally libel (Fernholz, 2019).

Terrorist have not looted without impunity. In 2015, Ahmad Al-Faqi Al-Mahdi, an alleged member of an Islamist terrorist group, was sentenced to nine years in prison for taking part in the destruction of ancient Islamic tombs in Timbuktu (Fernholz, 2019). However, as in the example of cyber-criminals, the face of the terrorist is obscured by the anonymity of online social media, in this case Facebook®. This in turn requires a whole new set of criminal investigation skills, including social network analysis, to identify the perpetrators and locate stolen antiquities and artifacts.

Discussion Questions:

1. Even if the groups are private on Facebook®, why might terrorists take a chance and sell looted goods on the social network site?
2. Should purchasers of stolen antiquities be held accountable for receiving stolen goods?
3. By classic definition, can we consider the looting of archaeological sites as white collar crime? Why? Why not?

Unfortunately, there is little in the way of state or federal efforts to prevent the black market for art and artifacts from flourishing in the United States or in the world. The owners of private collections may or may not know that the items are stolen. As Moskowitz (2011, p. 196) and (Rostomian, 2002) have speculated, "the inconsistency of state law and the absence of any federal regulation, combined with the insufficient resources needed to prevent and prosecute the trade of looted antiquities, enable the black market for terrorist groups, such as the Islamic militant group called the Islamic State of Iraq and Syria ('ISIS')." Beyond the loss for original owners, the illicit antiquities trade represents the theft of cultural heritage as well (Rostomian, 2002).

CYBERTERRORISM

We do not have to go into great length in discussing the means by which terrorists use cyberspace in order to hatch operations and find new recruits. Suffice it to say that many of the means used have already been covered in Chapter 6. What we can focus on here is how the Internet, the Dark Web, and computer systems can be used to terrorize a population or destabilize a government. Terrorists do not have the human resources to fight conventional wars, and as cyberattacks require relatively few fighters, it has become an efficient way for them to operate.

Cyberterrorists are not limited by geopolitical borders or by the limitations of terrain, weather, or any other inconveniences that can cause armies to lose their battles or even their wars. As an example, in *Napoleon's Buttons* (Le Couteur and Burreson, 2004), the authors speculate that the reason why the French emperor's armies failed in their Russian campaign was due to something as simple as the buttons on their uniforms, which were said to have disintegrated because of their molecular makeup when faced with the harsh winters. As if the winters were not bad enough in Russia, the soldiers' uniforms were rendered useless as they could not fasten them.

In the 21st century, though we can still find some localize wars, as in the example of the current Syrian conflict, most of what we see on a global stage are cyberwars. We are less likely to see conventional warfare than we are to see cyber-attacks. The frightening speed of a country's malicious cybercampaign against another makes for a cost-effective, if not deadly, way of waging battles. Besides creating havoc, cyberattacks can result in losses in infrastructure, finance, and/or human life (Albahar, 2019).

Law in the Real World: Ardit Ferizi, Cyberterrorist Suspect

(Source: Infosec, 2016; U.S. Department of Justice, 2016)

The recent history of Kosovo reads like a Kafka novel. Anyone familiar with the Czech writer knows of his dark, brooding literature with depressed characters. As part of the former Ottoman Empire, the Eastern European country has been subject to a number of occupying countries, including the former Soviet Union. Its citizens were able to gain their independence from Serbia in 2008. Tragically, the separation from Serbia did not alleviate ethnic tensions in the country. Out of the conflict of recent decades came the recruitment of anywhere from 100 to 200 Kosovars to ISIS[2] (Infosec, 2016).

One Kosovar recruit, Ardit Ferizi, also known as "Th3Dir3ctorY," was accused of stealing confidential information of approximately 1,300 U.S. military and government personnel. The intent was to use the data to help ISIS members to locate and murder U.S. soldiers (Infosec, 2016). At 20 years old, Ferizi, representing a new kind of terrorist, was accused of illegally accessing a secured government computer. His crimes present a real national

---

[2] Also known as the Islamic State of Iraq and the Levant (ISIL), the preferred name used by the U.S. Department of Justice.

security threat to the U.S. where terrorism is combined with hacking (U.S. Department of Justice, 2016). Ferizi did not have to risk his life to provide material support to ISIS, as he could do this in secret instead of out in the open like a conventional terrorist.

Beginning in 2015, Ferizi passed on the stolen information to Junaid Hussain, an ISIS recruiter and attack facilitator. Hussain, a British national, acted as an English-language cyber influencer during his tenure with ISIS (Hamid, 2018). Hussain was a popular member of ISIS, infamous for his cyber skills as a black hat hacker and his efforts to recruit ISIS sympathizers in the West, urging them to carry out "lone-wolf style" attacks (Infosec, 2016; Hamid, 2018).

Ferizi and Hussain were in discussions on the possibility of publishing the information on the hit list of military and government personnel (U.S. Department of Justice, 2016). According to the U.S. Department of Justice (DOJ), Hussain published a manifesto on the online social media forum, Twitter®, on behalf of the "Islamic State Hacking Division" of ISIS:

> "We are in your emails and social media accounts, we are extracting confidential data and passing on your personal information to the soldiers of the khilafah, who soon with the permission of Allah will strike at your necks in your own lands!" (DOJ, 2016, retrieved from https://www.justice.gov/opa/pr/isil-linked-kosovo-hacker-sentenced-20-years-prison; *The United States of America v. Ardit Ferizi*, 2016)

Even if the manifesto and hit list were not acted on, for anyone in the military and their families or working for the U.S. government overseas, this could at the very least be construed as a psychological terrorist act. In fact, a high priority is placed on psychological warfare, by striking fear in the hearts of targeted victims (Ganor, 2004; Bates and Mooney, 2014).

Ferizi was eventually located in Malaysia, where authorities detained him. Ferizi is alleged to be the first person arrested and charged with cyberterrorism. Ferizi consented to extradition to the U.S. to face charges and pleaded guilty to counts of providing material support to ISIS, as well as accessing a computer without authority (*The United States of America v. Ardit Ferizi*, 2016).

Ferizi has been sentenced to 20 years in prison and is currently serving his term with little hope of a successful appeal or early parole. As in the case of non-citizens who have been convicted of a crime and serving time in U.S. prisons, Ferizi will be deported to his native country, Kosovo, once he has completed his sentence. His accomplice, Hussain, was killed in a U.S.-led drone strike in Raqqa, Syria (Hamid, 2018). Thankfully, not one person on the supposed hit list of military and government personnel was killed in a terrorist attack encouraged by Hussain.

Discussion Questions:

1. We have been living in the Cyber Age since at least the 1980s. Why might it take so long to identify a black hat hacker as a cyberterrorist?
2. How might conditions in Kosovo have influenced Ferizi to join ISIS?
3. Why are cyberattacks so psychologically frightening?

ECONOMIC TERRORISM

Economic or financial terrorism refers to the efforts of a terrorist group or state to attempt to destabilize an economy. Any terrorist act will result in some economic cost to the government or the state that has been targeted (Lutz and Lutz, 2006).

To some extent, the 9/11 terrorist act could have conceivably caused instability of markets, as the events happened close to Wall Street, the epicenter of American and world finance. Certainly, there were a number of tenants in the World Trade Center that were either directly or indirectly connected to the activities of the New York Stock Exchange (NYSE). As soon as it became apparent that the planes flying into the twin towers of the World Trade Center were not a series of accidents and were probable terrorist attacks, the NYSE did not open for trading. The concern was that the market would be sent into a tailspin and as a precaution, trading was halted.

As it is, empirical studies found that only some sectors of the economy were affected by 9/11; for example, there was little effect on the oil sector (Straetmans et al., 2006). This may come as a surprise, considering that the origins of the terrorist group who executed the 9/11 tragedy were oil-producing Middle Eastern countries. Instead of a downward spiral, even though there was some volatility in markets around the world that day, the U.S. markets responded positively with marked increases (Mun, 2005). The stock market recovered relatively quickly after 9/11, returning to business as usual within a couple of weeks (Brounen and Derwall, 2010; Mun, 2005).

What cannot be forgotten is that economies can be affected by emotional, traumatic events. They can also be affected by threats of economic blackmail. In the political rhetoric currently being volleyed back and forth between rival nations, any talk of tariffs on imported products is immediately seen as a form of economic warfare, if not terrorism. However, this is most often simply part of the normal dance in negotiating new trade agreements. Real economic terrorism involves attempts to destabilize, if not overthrow, governments by attacking the economic system and enforcing boycotts or excessive tariffs.

Rarely are targets of terrorist acts randomly chosen. By targeting market-places, restaurants, or any venue where large numbers of people may be gathering, as in the case of a sports or concert event, it results in consumers being concerned enough to stop going to certain places for fear of being victimized. This in turn may result in economic hardships for businesses operating in so-called *"soft target"* locations. Even a perceived threat, however remote the possibility, can have devasting effects on local economies.

In some parts of the world, including the Middle East where there are, relatively speaking, more instances of attacks, the threat of terrorist attacks is ongoing. Using Israel as an example, certain situations are perceived to be more dangerous, including something as simple as running to the market for groceries or to a café for coffee (Cohen-Louck, 2019). In these places, people become fatalistic over time and will go about their daily business without deviating from their plans, but with heightened awareness that there is a higher probability that a terrorist act could happen, as compared to relatively stable areas of the world (e.g. Scandinavian countries). It can also be said that this applies specifically to women as well.

FINANCIAL WAR ON TERRORISM

One means by which to at least slow down terrorist operations is to find an effective way to cut off their funding. Creating regulation that scrutinizes certain financial transaction should in theory decrease the flow of cash to terrorist groups. However, there are some critics to this approach. Warde (2007) believes that we may be underestimating the ability of terrorist groups to raise money, and more importantly measure how successful terrorist groups are in raising support and converts to their mission. In Warde's (2007) estimation, the financial crackdown after 9/11 has had virtually no effect on terrorist groups' operations.

Freezing banks accounts belonging to suspected terrorists in the U.S. and abroad is one obvious solution. This, of course, requires international cooperation, which can be difficult with bank privacy laws. Nevertheless, the National White Collar Crime Center recommends that changes in banking policies, international legislation, and cooperation among nations is only one way to remedy the flow of money to terrorist groups (Kane and Wall, 2004). As in the case of other organized crime groups, terrorist groups will find other means to move cash if conventional ways such as banks and financial institutions are blocked.

SUMMARY

There is no easy way to stem the flow of money in and out of terrorist groups. Like in the case of other organized crime groups, if you stop one illegal enterprise, another will pop up in its place. Keep in mind that not all terrorist acts require sophisticated, expensive planning, and attacks like those committed in 2001 on the World Trade Center in New York City require additional stealth and financial backing.

There are also a lot of myths surrounding what constitutes the "typical" terrorist. Even children have been recruited or forced to take part in suicide bombing attacks, giving credence to the profile of the terrorist as a misguided, naïve person who is generally younger. However, if we look at the ages and expertise of those who have committed bigger, more deadly acts of terrorism, they tend to be older and better educated. Egyptian national Mohamed Atta, a graduate of Hamburg Technical University in Cairo who was the tactical leader and terrorist pilot who hijacked American Airlines Flight 11 out of Boston on 9/11, was 33 when he flew the jet into the North Tower of the World Trade Center (*Biography*, 2019). Atta was not an outlier; there have been a number of older, well-educated terrorists who have led terrorist operations. When we throw in the mix the fact that white collar crimes are many times in themselves sophisticated operations, the media and the public in general underestimate the abilities of the "typical" terrorist.

Though many of the types of white collar crimes that we have been examining in this book can be used by terrorists, there are some that are specific to terrorist groups. Bogus charities can filter money to buy weapons to terrorist groups. Straw buyers can obtain credit for a fee. And like in the case of legitimate business practices, dummy corporations can be created in the form of front, shelf, and shell companies.

Most of the money movement between and to terrorist groups is illegal. Even though legitimate means may be used, like in the case of moving funds from one bank to another, the acts themselves are illegal and more times than not represent money laundering. In this, terrorists have much in common with white collar criminals and with traditional organized crime groups.

Perhaps the most difficult monetary channels to stop are recruitment propaganda and the movement of money through the Dark Web. As fast as authorities detect and identify these activities as illegal, terrorists, along with other criminals, find new means to move funding around. It is an extremely difficult challenge for law enforcement agencies. Part of the problem is a lack of resources in funding and personnel in all fights against terrorism. If we consider that cyber experts can make competitive salaries in the private sector, it may be difficult to recruit "white hats" to work for government agencies that do not historically pay as well to help figure out what exactly terrorists are up to in cyberspace before they create havoc.

One of the few means at the disposal of regulators and law enforcement in combating terrorism is to wage financial war. However, as Warde (2007) cautions, thus far these have not made a dent in stopping terrorist operations from obtaining funding. Besides financial warfare, social network analysis is one way to at least follow a money trail. Though we might not be able to see the whole cast of terrorists in a network, investigators can at least help solve some mysteries that can help shape policies to slow, if not stop, terrorist acts.

Case Study ▪ London Transit Bombing, 2005

Background

In a sprawling city like London, there is a dependency on reliable public transportation. For Londoners, one of the most efficient ways to get around is by subway, otherwise known as "The London Underground" or "The Tube." An alternative to taking the subway or a cab is to take the bus, which in London is often the recognizable red double-decker bus. Few city residents bother owning an automobile, as parking itself can be a constant, expensive burden in most major cities around the world.

Anyone who has ever taken public transportation or driven highways during rush hour in a major city can attest to the fact that it is one big mass of humanity. Commuters during rush hour all have the singular thought of getting to work in the morning or home again in the evening. Yet few commuters think about the larger economic consequences of a whole system forced to shut down, even temporarily; just the inconveniences of scrambling to find alternative transportation or waiting until the system is up and running again.

The United Kingdom, including Northern Ireland, is not immune to terrorist attacks. During the 30-year period of "The Troubles" (1968-1998), when there were clashes between the Catholic minority and the Protestant government in Northern Ireland, the British Isles were accustomed to hearing reports of riots and terrorist acts played out in the streets of Belfast, at times spilling over into London. At the time of the London transport bombing, the U.K. had experienced at least a few years of cautious optimism. But another type of terrorist threat was looming.

On the morning of July 7, 2005, a coordinated terrorist attack was launched against the London subway system. At the time, London was giddy and basking in the glory of having just been announced by the International Olympic Committee as the winner in the competition to host the 2012 Olympics. In the rush hour attack, bombs exploded in three subway trains and one bus. It resulted in the immediate paralysis of the city center, with the entire subway system and bus services shut down. This was necessary so that first responders could tend to the dead, dying, and wounded. It was also necessary as law enforcement were in the middle of determining if additional attacks on the transportation systems were eminent.

Defining the Crime(s)

There is no other way to define this crime except as a terrorist act. By definition, terrorism is orchestrated for the sole purpose of frightening people, which in turn disrupts everyday life. This means that commerce and transportation, at the very least, comes to a halt, as in the case of the London bombings. Secondary fallout from terrorist acts is that victims who do manage to get out alive are more likely to suffer from post-traumatic stress disorder (PTSD). The long-term effects of PTSD are just now being understood by the medical and psychiatric communities.

The bombings were at first only attributed to four Islamic terrorists: Mohammad Sidique Khan, Sidique Khan, Shehzad Tanweer, and Germaine Lindsay. A group that the four terrorists were alleged to be part of, which described itself as being affiliated with Al-Qaeda, took credit for the bombings, taking to an Arabic-language website to make its claims of involvement. It is not unusual for some terrorist groups to lay claim to specific terrorist acts to get attention, even if they did not take part in them. The bombings were supposedly in retaliation for British involvement in the wars in Afghanistan and Iraq. As an ally of the United States, the British offered support after the U.S. invasion of Afghanistan in 2001 and the invasion of Iraq in 2003, both in response to the 9/11 terrorist attack in New York City. There has also been speculation as to whether the U.S. invaded Iraq due to unresolved conflicts between the countries after the first Gulf War in 1990 and 1991, when Iraq invaded Kuwait.

Theories to Explain the Crime

If you recall, we examined the role of social network analysis (SNA) in understanding white collar crime conspiracy. As it turns out, SNA was instrumental in uncovering the way that terrorists send out small groups to execute bombing missions, as is speculated to be the case in the London bombings in 2005. In fact, there is some speculation by researchers as to whether the terrorists in the London bombings themselves used SNA methodology when selecting their underground railway targets (Jordan, 2008; Burcher et al., 2015).

There is some research that supports the theory that terrorists may see themselves as victims of anti-Muslim discrimination. Two Pew Global Attitudes surveys found that feelings of alienation and discrimination in younger Muslims was more likely to increase the probability that for the few who do participate in suicide bombings, the act of harming both others and themselves is justified (Victoroff et al., 2012). Yet this does not explain why the typical suicide bomber is now actually atypical: not necessarily coming from poverty, may very well have a college education, can be either young or middle-aged, married or unmarried, and might have children (Hoffman, 2003). In other words, unlike the earlier days of terrorism, when it was more stereotypically young, uneducated males who committed suicide bombings, there is no "typical" terrorist (Hoffman, 2003).

Criminal Justice and Policy Responses

Through police investigation and SNA, the bombing conspiracy was discovered to have been hatched by more than the four men who actually carried out the bombings. The conspiracy was widespread and included a 2004 trip by Khan and Tanweer to Pakistan, where they met with Rashid Rauf. According to Morgan and Whelan (2015), Rauf claimed that it only took a few days to convince Khan and Tanweer to participate in a suicide mission in London. The ambiguous boundaries of a network illustrates the limitations of using SNA, either by police or researchers. Because the London bombings involved a criminal network, it is almost impossible to fully see all of the criminals involved in the conspiracy (Morgan and Whelan, 2015).

Following the July 7 bombing attack on London transportation, a second coordinated effort was launched on July 12. Five men — Muktar Said Ibrahim, Yassin Hassan Omar, Ramzi Mohammed, and Manfo Kwaku Asieudu — attempted to detonate five more bombs on the London subways, but the bombs failed to explode (Morgan and Whelan., 2015). In total, 12 bombers were identified as part of two cells in the same network (Morgan and Whelan, 2015).

Social and Media Responses

The July 7 bombing had at least a temporary effect on the economy in London and around the world. The 2005 bombings sent negative shock waves through the London Stock Exchange, and consequently through other markets across the globe (Kollias et al., 2013). As in the case of the American stock market after 9/11, the market recovered relatively quickly, and represented only short-term losses to investors. However, the immediate vicinities around where the bombs were detonated no doubt saw a drop in customers at local businesses as panic ensued.

Also taking into consideration that the morning commute was disrupted, the number of employees who failed to report to work that day or even the following days out of fear of a repeated threat represents an untold loss of worker productivity. This in turn represents a financial loss to their employers. If the workers were not compensated for missed work, then they too suffered financial setbacks in lost wages.

Researchers also report that there were persistent negative effects on people's decisions as to whether to take the London subway in the city after the terrorist attacks. Use of the Underground was significantly lower though the end of 2005 (Draca et al., 2011). How much of this is due to a number of Underground stations being closed for repairs is unknown.

One way or another, the 2005 terrorist attack on London transportation represented an economic loss in worker productivity, untold financial loss to local businesses, and loss of revenue for the public transportation systems. In addition to the financial losses to transportation systems and local businesses, Maley (2006) reported in *The Guardian* that visitors were frightened away from London's tourist attractions after the bombings, with the National Gallery seeing 15.2 percent fewer visitors, and the Tate Modern art museum and the London Eye each receiving 12 percent fewer visitors than in 2004. The 2005 bombings in London proved to be, whether it was intended or not, a form of economic warfare.

Unanswered Questions and Unresolved Issues Related to the Case

Besides the economic losses mentioned in the London bombings case, what other economic losses might there be, short-term or long-term? As we know from the 9/11 terrorist acts in the United States, some of the economic impact is still felt today, even if just in how much money is now required to secure airports and other transportation hubs.

Certainly, terrorism has produced a whole new set of career paths in homeland security. A number of security professions that require specialized training have emerged, which in turn creates additional costs that cities and countries did not have to contend with prior to 9/11. Even emergency medical personnel are called upon to assist law enforcement to keep an eye out for suspicious individuals when they are on standby at large events (e.g., stadium football games) (Nixon and Stewart, 2005). Again, the question remains, at what extra cost?

One of the biggest challenges is for law enforcement to reconstruct terrorist acts. Again, this is where social network analysis is useful. But as we have noted elsewhere in this book, it is a difficult task to see the complete network, particularly if network actors are hiding in the shadows. There is always a question of whether there are others who were not caught and may end up being part of sleeper cells that might come out of hiding to commit additional acts of terror.

There is also the question of justice being served for the victims who survive suicide terrorist attacks. As we saw with the conclusion of the terrorist acts in New York City, Pennsylvania, and at the Pentagon in Washington, D.C., the terrorists perished in their suicide missions, whether they fully executed their plans or not. Besides the residual PTSD that victims can suffer, there can also be resentment that there is no opportunity to arrest the perpetrators and see them stand trial for their crimes.

Most importantly, as we have seen with Hoffman's research (2003), if there are no clear characteristics or demographics of suicide bombers, prevention again becomes challenging. We should also note that women have increasingly been recruited to partake in suicide bombings; likewise, children have been coerced as well. Unlike white collar crimes in general, it continues to be a challenge for law enforcement to prevent these types of tragedies.

Sources

Cowell, A. (2005) After coordinated bombs, London is stunned, bloodied and stoic. *New York Times*. July 7. Retrieved from https://www.nytimes.com/2005/07/07/international/europe/after-coordinated-bombs-london-is-stunned-bloodied-and.html.

Draca, M., S. Machin, and R. Witt. (2011) Panic on the streets of London: Police, crime, and the July 2005 terror attack. *American Economic Review*. Aug. Vol. 101: 2157-2181.

Hoffman, B. (2003) The logic of suicide terrorism. *Atlantic Monthly*. June. Reprint by the RAND Corporation. Available at https://www.rand.org/pubs/reprints/RP1187/index2.html.

Maley, J. (2006) Drop in visitors as July 7 effect hits London's tourist trail. *The Guardian*. Feb. 20. Retrieved from https://www.theguardian.com/uk/2006/feb/21/july7.uksecurity.

Nixon, R.G. and C.E. Stewart. (2005) Recognizing imminent danger: Characteristics of a suicide bomber. *Emergency Medical Services*. Feb. Vol. 34, No 2: 74-75.

GLOSSARY

Aged company   Similar to a shell company, but is held onto with the purpose of building reputation and goodwill without actually selling products or services, so as to eventually sell for a profit. Aged companies do not have physical addresses. Same as "shelf company."

Anomie   In the context of terrorism, individuals or groups who feel disconnected from society and believe that they have been treated unfairly, marginalized politically, socially, and economically.

Anticybersquatting Consumer Protection Act (ACPA)   1999 legislation to prevent the intentional use of domain names that may be confused with similar or trademarked names of legitimate companies or businesses.

Bad faith   Entering into a business arrangement or contract with the intention of being misleading or dishonest, or with no intention of fulfilling the obligations.

Cybersquatting   Practice of purchasing a domain (URL) name with no intention of using it in order to drive up the price or to present oneself as being a legitimate company by having a name similar to an established business.

Cyberterrorism   Use of the Internet, including the Dark Web, to organize and fund terrorist organizations or use of cyberspace to threaten individuals, groups, or governments.

Fraud spree   When an individual or group commits several acts of fraud over time, instead of one single act.

Front companies   Companies without physical addresses that can either be legitimate or illegitimate, generally used to protect a parent company.

Identity assumption   When an individual assumes someone's identity and takes over that person's social and financial life for a period of time.

Identity theft   The theft of a number of pieces of information on an individual or group of individuals, including Social Security numbers and bank account information, usually for the purpose of financial gain. The stolen identity is generally only used for a short while so as to allow the criminal to avoid detection. Example: Stolen credit cards used in fraudulent purchases.

Improvised explosive device (IED)   Explosive devices that are thrown together, usually inexpensive and with common materials, not used in conventional military operations.

Shelf company   Similar to a shell company, but is held onto with the purpose of building reputation and good will, without actually selling products or services, so as to eventually sell for a profit. Shelf companies do not have physical addresses. Same as "aged company."

Shell company   Another term for "front company," used to conduct business while protecting a company from bad publicity in the event that a product or service fails. Can be created for legal or illegal purposes. Like "shelf companies" and "aged companies", shell companies do not have physical addresses.

Smuggling operations   Any scheme that is set up to illegally move weapons, money, people, and/or drugs across borders. Can also involve the smuggling of art and artifacts to avoid tariffs or to move and sell stolen items.

Soft target   A terrorist target that is not difficult to attack; an unprotected person or location.

Straw buyer   Someone who for a fee will make purchases or obtain credit for someone else who might not be credit worthy. A straw buyer can be acting legally or illegally. However, there are places in the world where straw buyers are illegal.

U.S. Customs and Border Patrol (CBP)   The agency within the United States government that is responsible for the contents of what comes in and out of the country (e.g., airline passengers' luggage, airfreight, shipping containers) as well as movement of people across the U.S. borders.

Weapon of mass destruction (WMD)   Weapons used by terrorist groups or governments that are designed to do the most damage possible to infrastructure and to the lives of targeted populations. Can be made either out of sophisticated, military grade materials or can be homemade devices. Includes chemical, biological, or radioactive weapons.

REFERENCES AND SUGGESTED READINGS

Airline Career Pilot Program. (n.d.) How much does it cost to become a commercial pilot? Retrieved from https://atpflightschool.com/faqs/pilot-training-cost.html.

Albahar, M. (2019) Cyber attacks and terrorism: A Twenty-First Century conundrum. *Science and Engineering Ethics.* Vol. 25: 993-1006.

Arquilla, J. (2013) Twenty years of cyberwar. *Journal of Military Ethics.* Vol. 12: 80-87.

Bates, R. and M. Mooney. (2014) Distance learning and Jihad: The dark side of the force. *Online Journal of Distance Learning Administration.* Vol. 17, No. 3. Retrieved from https://www.westga.edu/~distance/ojdla/fall173/Bates_Mooney173.html.

Bennett, M. (2018) 11 common types of credit card scams and frauds. *Consumer Protection.* Sept. 28. Retrieved from https://www.consumerprotect.com/crime-fraud/11-types-of-credit-card-fraud-scams/.

Biography.com (eds.). (2019) Mohamed Atta Biography. A&E Television Networks, publisher. Sept. 4. Retrieved from https://www.biography.com/crime-figure/mohamed-atta.

Brounen, D. and J. Derwall. (2010) The impact of terrorist attacks on international stock markets. *European Financial Management.* Aug. 19. Vol. 16, Issue 4: 585-598.

Burcher, M. and C. Whelan. (2015) Social network analysis and small group 'dark' networks: An analysis of the London bombers and the problem with 'fuzzy' boundaries. *Global Crime.* Vol. 16, Issue Vol. 16, Issue 4: 585-598.

BusinessIDtheft.org (n.d.) Shelf corporations and trade rings: Paper companies used for real fraud. Retrieved from http://businessidtheft.org/Education/BusinessIDTheftScams/ShelfCorporationsandTradeRings/tabid/104/Default.aspx.

CNN (2019) Boston Marathon timeline. *CNN Library.* Apr. 9. Retrieved from https://www.cnn.com/2013/06/03/us/boston-marathon-terror-attack-fast-facts/index.html.

Cohen-Louck, K. (2019) Perception of the threat of terrorism. *Journal of Interpersonal Violence.* Vol. 34, No. 5: 887-911.

Dot-Pouillard, N. and E. Rébillard. (2013) The Intellectual, the Militant, the Prisoner and the Partisan: The genesis of the Islamic Jihad Movement in Palestine (1974-1988). *Muslim World.* Jan. Vol. 103, Issue 1: 161-180.

Durkheim, E. (1998) *Suicide.* Originally published in 1897. New York: The Free Press, Simon and Schuster.

Faturoti, B. (2015) Business identity theft under the UDRP and the ACPA: Is bad faith always bad for business advertising? *Journal of International Commercial Law and Technology.* Vol. 10, Issue 1: 1-12.

Fernholz, T. (2019) Terrorists are trafficking looted antiquities with impunity on Facebook. Quartz, Yahoo! Finance. July 3. Retrieved from https://finance.yahoo.com/news/terrorists-trafficking-looted-antiquities-impunity-080045960.html.

Ganor, B. (2004) Terror is a strategy of psychological warfare. Journal of Aggression, Maltreatment, & Trauma. Vol. 9, Issue 1 / 2: 33-43

Hamid, N. (2018) The British hacker who became the Islamic State's chief terror cybercoach: A profile of Junaid Hussain. *CTC Sentinel,* Combating Terrorism Center, West Point. Apr. Vol. 11, Issue 4: 30-37.

Hudson, R. A. (1999) *The Sociology and Psychology of Terrorism: Who Becomes a Terrorist and Why? A Report Prepared under an Interagency Agreement by the Federal Research Division, Library of Congress.* M. Majeska, ed. A.M. Savada and H.C. Metz, project mgrs. Sept. Retrieved from https://fas.org/irp/threat/frd.html.

Infosec. (2016) The Ferizi Case: The first man charged with cyber terrorism. *Security Awareness.* Mar. 9. Retrieved from https://resources.infosecinstitute.com/the-ferizi-case-the-first-man-charged-with-cyber-terrorism/#gref.

Jordan, F. (2008) Predicting target selection by terrorists: A network analysis of the 2005 London underground attacks. International Journal of Critical Infrastructures. Vol. 4, No. 1 / 2: 206-214.

Kane, J. and A. Wall. (2004) *Identifying the Links between White-Collar Crime and Terrorism.* National White Collar Crime Center. Sept. Retrieved from https://www.ncjrs.gov/pdffiles1/nij/grants/209520.pdf.

Kaplan, E. (2006) Tracking down terrorist funding. Council on Foreign Relations. Apr. 4. Retrieved from https://www.cfr.org/backgrounder/tracking-down-terrorist-financing.

Keinan, G., A. Sadeh, and S. Rosen. (2003) Attitudes and reactions to media coverage of terrorist acts. *Journal of Community Psychology.* Mar. 1. Vol. 31, Issue 2: 149-165.

Kollias, C., S. Papadamou, and C. Siriopoulos. (2013) European market's reaction to exogenous shocks: A high frequency data analysis of the 2005 London bombings. *International Journal of Financial Studies.* Vol. 1, No. 4: 154-167.

Lavin, T. (2008) Uranium on the loose. *The Atlantic.* April. Retrieved from https://www.theatlantic.com/magazine/archive/2008/04/uranium-on-the-loose/306729/.

Le Couteur, P.C. and J. Burreson. (2004) *Napoleon's Buttons: 17 Molecules that Changed History.* New York: Penguin Random House.

Lutz, J. M. and B.J. Lutz. (2006) Terrorism as economic warfare. *Global Economy Journal.* Vol 6, Issue 2, Article 2.

Morgan, D. (2017) Inflammatory projective identification in fundamentalist religious and economic terrorism. *Psychoanalytic Psychotherapy.* Sept. Vol. 31, No. 3: 314-326.

Moskowitz, T. (2011) The illicit antiquities trade as a funding source for terrorism: Is blockchain the solution? *Notes, Cardozo Arts and Entertainment Journal.* Vol. 37: 193-228.

Mun, K. (2005) Contagion and impulse response of international stock markets around 9-11 terrorist attacks. *Global Finance Journal.* Aug. Vol. 16, Issue 1: 48-68.

NewsRX LLC. (2019) Payment-card fraud funds terrorism and other transnational crimes. *Lab Law Weekly.* July 12. p 20.

Penn, E.B., G.E. Higgins, S.L. Gabbidon, and K.L. Jordan. (2008) Government efforts on homeland security and crime: Public views and opinions. *American Journal of Criminal Justice.* Vol. 34: 28-40.

Rostomian, P. C. (2002) Looted art in the U.S. market. *Rutgers Law Review.* Fall. Issue 1: 271-299.

Shichor, D. (2017) Adopting a white collar crime theoretical framework for the analysis of terrorism: An explorational understanding. *Journal of Contemporary Criminal Justice.* Vol. 33, No. 3: 254-272.

Schmid, A.P. and J. de Graaf. (1982) *Violence as Communication.* Thousand Oaks: Sage Publishing.

Social Security Administration. (2018) Identity theft and your Social Security number. Pub No. 05-10064. Retrieved from https://www.ssa.gov/pubs/EN-05-10064.pdf.

Stebbins, S. (2019) Where credit card debt is the worst in the US: States with the highest average balance. *USA Today.* Mar. 7. Retrieved from https://www.usatoday.com/story/money/personalfinance/2019/03/07/credit-card-debt-where-average-balance-highest-across-us/39129001/.

Straetmans, S.T.M., W.F.C. Verschoor, and C.C.P. Wolff. (2008) Extreme U.S. stock market fluctuations in the wake of 9/11. *Journal of Applied Econometrics.* Jan.-Feb.: 17-42.

Swann, S. (2019) Antiquities looted in Syria and Iraq are sold on Facebook. British Broadcasting Company (BBC News) May 2. Retrieved from https://www.bbc.com/news/world-middle-east-47628369.

Tønnessen, T. H. (2017) Islamic State and technology—A literature Review. *Perspectives on Terrorism.* Vol. 11, No. 6: 101-110.

United States Congressional Budget Office. (2016) Scanning and imaging shipping containers overseas: Costs and alternatives. June. Retrieved from https://www.cbo.gov/sites/default/files/114th-congress-2015-2016/reports/51478-Shipping-Containers-OneCol.pdf.

United States Customs and Border Patrol (CBP). (n.d.) Cargo security and examinations. Department of Homeland Security. Retrieved from https://www.cbp.gov/border-security/ports-entry/cargo-security.

United State Department of Justice. (2016) ISIL-linked Kosovo hacker sentenced to 20 years in prison. *Justice News*, Office of Public Affairs. Sept. 23. Retrieved from https://www.justice.gov/opa/pr/isil-linked-kosovo-hacker-sentenced-20-years-prison.

United States District Court for the Eastern District of Virginia. (2016) *United States of America v. Adrit Ferizi*. Alexandria Division, Case 1:16-cr-00042-LMB, Document 54. Sept. 16. 19 pp. Available at https://www.justice.gov/opa/file/896326/download.

United States Senate. (1999) *Anticybersquatting Consumer Protection Act* (ACPA) 15 U.S Code §1125. 106th Congress, 1st Session. Aug. 5. Washington, D.C.: U.S. Government Publishing Office. Available at https://www.govinfo.gov/content/pkg/CRPT-106srpt140/html/CRPT-106srpt140.htm.

United States Senate. (2000) Hearing: ID theft: When bad things happen in your good name. Subcommittee on Technology, Terrorism, and Government Information, Committee on the Judiciary. 116th Congress, Second Session. Mar. 7. Washington, D.C.: U.S. Government Printing Office. Available at https://www.govinfo.gov/content/pkg/CHRG-106shrg69821/html/CHRG-106shrg69821.htm#?.

United States Senate. (2002) Hearings: Identity theft. Subcommittee on Technology, Terrorism, and Government Information, Committee on the Judiciary. 117th Congress, Second Session. Mar. 20 and July 9. Washington, D.C.: U.S. Government Printing Office. Available at https://www.govinfo.gov/content/pkg/CHRG-107shrg85794/pdf/CHRG-107shrg85794.pdf#?.

Bureau of Consular Affairs. (n.d.) Travel advisories. U.S. Department of State. Retrieved from https://travel.state.gov/content/travel/en/traveladvisories/traveladvisories.html/

Van Leeuwen, L. and D. Weggemans. (2018) Characteristics of Jihadist terrorist leaders: A quantitative approach. *Perspectives on Terrorism*. Vol. 4, No. 4: 55-67.

Warde, I. (2007) *The Price of Fear: The Truth Behind the Financial War on Terrorism*. Berkeley, CA: University of California Press.

Windrem, R. (2015) Terror on a shoestring: Paris attacks likely cost $10,000 or less. *NBC News*. Nov. 18. Retrieved from https://www.nbcnews.com/storyline/paris-terror-attacks/terror-shoestring-paris-attacks-likely-cost-10-000-or-less-n465711.

Chapter THIRTEEN

The Media and White Collar Crime

Nothing like a juicy scandal to sell ad space

> "Journalism can never be silent: That is its greatest virtue and its greatest fault. It must speak, and speak immediately, while the echoes of wonder, the claims of triumph and the signs of horror are still in the air."
>
> —*Henry Anatole Grunwald*

Chapter Objectives

- Provide a basic understanding of the treatment of white collar criminals in the media.
- Introduce key legal protections for media reporting.
- Identify some of the key effects that the media has on public opinion and juries.
- Explore how famous cases have been reported (or in some cases, not reported) in the news.
- Understand the current distrust that the public has for media sources.

Key Terms

1st Amendment
4th Amendment
6th Amendment
Censorship
Court of public opinion
CSI effect

Libel
Media circus
Perp walk
Slander
Spin doctor

INTRODUCTION

There is an old adage: the higher the hill to climb, the farther to fall. In theory, wealthy and powerful people, particularly those who are assumed to have worked hard to get where they are in life, have more to lose in misbehaving. That in itself should serve as a deterrent.

When people in positions of power are accused of conventional crime, as we recently saw with Hollywood producer Harvey Weinstein, the accusation brings with it strong public reaction as the details unfold in the news and on social media. In fact, the Me Too movement (https://metoomvmt.org/) was born out of public outrage directed at Weinstein and other powerful people in Hollywood, business, and politics who had for some time gotten away with sexual assault and worse. The collective public anger is even greater when the victims are children.

When elite white collar crimes happen and are reported by the press, people are not so much outraged, but confused as to why already affluent people wish to risk their livelihoods, fortunes, or reputations just to further build their wealth or power illegally. Unless the white collar malfeasance affects them directly, as in the mortgage banking crisis in 2008, the public does not have the same level of anger and disgust when powerful people commit ordinary crimes, as we witnessed in the case of convicted murderer Phil Spector, a powerful record producer who shot and killed actress/model Lana Clarkson in his home.

We should also consider that the criminal justice system itself differentiates, to some extent, between celebrity cases and crimes committed by "ordinary" people. The different treatment of defendants is not part of the formal legal system, but rather the informal rules within criminal justice (Walker, 1985). Within the formal legal system, attention is on due process and equal treatment under the law, at least in theory.

Within the informal legal system, treatment of the accused can be decidedly different depending on the financial means and social capital that the defendant possesses. As Walker (1985; Novak, 1986) proposed, the criminal justice system is tiered like a wedding cake ("Wedding Cake Model of Criminal Justice"), where the importance of cases is divided between layers of importance: high-profile cases, serious felonies, less serious felonies, and misdemeanors. At every phase of the process, from jury selection to conviction and sentencing, the outcomes can be completely different depending on the social status of the defendant. Likewise, treatment in the media is tiered.

When O.J. Simpson was accused of brutally killing his ex-wife, Nicole Simpson, and her friend Ron Goldman, there was avid media and public attention. Simpson was acquitted of the murders in 1995 after a lengthy televised trial. He was later found liable in 1997 after being sued in civil court for the wrongful death of his ex-wife and Goldman, and ordered to pay a substantial settlement in the millions. Both the Spector and Simpson cases played out in months of televised reporting. We do not see the same public interest in white collar crime cases.

Ordinarily, white collar crime does not get much attention in mainstream news. When it does prove to be newsworthy, it usually involves high-profile public figures who just cannot be ignored by the media. This was true in Watergate, in major fraud cases like Bernie Madoff's Ponzi scheme, and in the more recent 2019 college admissions scandal discussed as one of our examples in this chapter. Though not a white collar crime case per se, we could also say the same for billionaire Jeffrey Epstein's recent sex trafficking charges. This case has gained more media attention than his previous conviction for having sex with underaged females. The first case resulted in a plea deal. Epstein served 13 months of an 18-month jail sentence in a work release program and was ordered to register as a sex offender, much of which flew under the radar of media or public attention.

The same cannot be said about the more recent sex trafficking charges against Epstein. After his arrest and pleading not guilty in advance of his trail, Epstein was found unresponsive in his jail cell. His death was determined to be a suicide (BBC, 2020). It did not bring an end to the media frenzy around his case, as Ghislaine Maxwell, one of his associates and former girlfriend, has sued Epstein's estate for reimbursement of her own legal fees and security costs (BBC, 2020). The British Royal family has also had to contend with rumors of Queen Elizabeth's son, Prince Andrew, allegedly having a close relationship with Epstein, with stories circulating that Prince Andrew and Epstein vacationed together with younger, possibly underaged women (Osborne, 2019). The British Royal family essentially operates like a corporation and there has been considerable attention to public relation repairs after the alleged relationship between Prince Andrew and Epstein came to media attention.

Where the Epstein case can be discussed within the context of white collar crime or malfeasance is the perception of an unusually light sentence in Florida for the first offenses, arranged by then-U.S. Attorney Alex Acosta. There was no similar public outcry when the sentence was originally was handed down. The media fallout was so great with the recent new charges that Acosta, who had served as Labor Secretary in President Trump's cabinet, felt compelled to resign from that position. Acosta has not been charged with any crime himself, but has been charged and convicted in the *court of public opinion*. Either one can ultimately be detrimental to one's career.

DEFINING MEDIA

For the purposes of this chapter, we will be defining media as any means by which to get information out to the general public. We are talking about formalized avenues, not word of mouth on the streets, at the corner bar, or via Twitter, Instagram, or Facebook. By formalized, we mean information published or broadcasted by news outlets.

Traditionally, the most immediate reporting of news was by way of print media, such as newspapers and magazines that are becoming more obsolete in the digital age. In fact, at one time print media was so slow to get into the hands of readers that by the time it reached them, it was already old news. Imagine what it was like for people living in more rural areas of war-torn countries who may not know for days or weeks that a war had ended. Magazines are even more challenging when it comes to timely news, as the typical publication may only come out once a week or once a month.

The overwhelming majority of people still get their news from television. What is becoming more common is that people who have access to computers are now obtaining news information via the Internet rather than television network news. Increasingly, people are dependent on online media sources to get up to the minute coverage of news stories. We should note that there are still some people who primarily get their news from radio stations, like the National Public Radio (NPR), but they are increasingly less common. Newspaper consumption is even rarer yet, but has yet to disappear completely.

All news outlets, even tiny ones tucked in the corner of some small town, generally have an online presence. For example, Martha's Vineyard, an island off of Cape Cod in Massachusetts with a population of approximately 16,000 full time residents (2010 U.S. Census), has a charming little newspaper, *The Vineyard Gazette*, with a webpage that can be found at vineyardgazette.com. One step further, people are not only getting their news directly from a news outlet website, but through news feed on their social media page (e.g., Facebook®). It is estimated that 38 percent of Americans get their news online, including through social media (Pew Research Center, Mitchell et al., 2016).

Sometimes news stories are so big that they end up hanging around for a long time, especially if updates keep coming. Big cases eventually make it into books, which we will consider part of print media. Because publishers want to get the books out in stores fast while the topic is still buzzing in media circles, some of these books are published fairly quickly. In some cases, the crime is so big that authors are still writing about it years later. An example of media interest in a white collar crime is in the Bernie Madoff case, where books were published shortly after his conviction in 2009, including *The Wizard of Lies: Bernie Madoff and the Death of Trust* (Henriques, 2011, Times Books). Other books came out later, as in the example of the more recently published *Billion Dollar Whale: The Man Who Fooled Wall Street, Hollywood, and the World* (Wright and Hope, 2018, Hachette Books).

Unlike newspaper and magazine articles, books typically take a lot longer to get into the hands of readers. Like the book in your very hands (or on your computer, if a downloaded copy), it takes months, in some cases, years for ideas to go from the imaginations of authors to being published. Because of the time it takes for books to be published, even when the topic is timely, by the time they are published their contents may already have become more history than current events. Many current event books become obsolete in short order and either are largely forgotten or require considerable revision to remain timely as new information emerges.

Other times, stories are so big that they live on in epic television or big screen movies based on true stories. Who doesn't like an edge of the seat, popcorn movie? For those who are interested, some of the Hollywood blockbusters about famous white collar crime cases that made it to the big screen are *The Big Short* (Paramount Pictures), *The Wolf of Wall Street* (Warner Brothers), and *American Hustle* (Sony Pictures). A lesser known film, *A Civil Action* (Touchstone Pictures and Paramount Pictures), depicts environmental crime and is based on the book of the same title by Jonathan Harr (Vintage Publishing, 1996). And of course, there are a number of notable documentary films also based on books as well, including *The Smartest Guys in the Room* (Portfolio Trade, 2003; Magnolia Pictures, 2005), which explores the Enron scandal.

MEDIA AND THE BIRTH OF 24-HOUR NEWS CYCLES

Many of you reading this book today do not remember a time when news was reported on television or radio only a few times throughout the day. When Ted Turner came along in 1980 with a 24-hour news cable television station, CNN, the whole face of news reporting changed. Because television stations depend on advertisers to fund their operations, those 24 hours had to be filled with stories that would grab the attention of viewers.

Evening news shows prior to CNN had to condense stories within an hour or half hour time frame, meaning they only had minutes to report the really important things happening in a day. This meant that news producers had to decide which stories would make it to air. Now, when big stories happen, they have to be reported from a number of viewpoints to fill in all those hours of reporting. When it is a slow news day, it might mean reporting news that in a bygone era we would never see. As Patterson speculated (1996), journalists themselves have become jaded as they report a story for endless hours, days, and sometimes weeks. To some extent, we saw this same phenomenon happening both to reporters and the public in general as the months dragged on during the COVID-19 pandemic in 2020. Patterson (1996) suspected that instead of simply reporting the news as objectively as possible, a trend beginning in the 1990s towards interpretive, subjective reporting, making serious issues secondary to sensational, "good" stories.

Law in the Real World: Operation Varsity Blues

Operation Varsity Blues, an investigation into cheating on SAT and ACT college admissions testing in early 2019, uncovered the underbelly of college admissions frauds (CNN, Levenson and Morales, 2019). The scandal also includes athletic programs, with accusations that students were being accepted to universities to play a sport that they had never even played before and college coaches were receiving bribes to substantiate these falsehoods.

At the writing of this textbook, 50 individuals, including college coaches and consultants who are paid to help high school students with the college application process. Also criminally charged are parents who allegedly used bribes to assure that their offspring would be admitted into schools that they might not ordinarily be admitted to based on their real academic or athletic records. In some cases, people have been accused of hiring "professional" test takers, to take the college admission exams for their clients or their children. In one of the more bizarre schemes reported by the media, college coaches were asked to certify students as being scholarship worthy for sports that the kids were not even playing or competing in.

It has always been more or less taken for granted that the privileged class has deep pockets and back doors to the admissions process at colleges and universities. For instance, how can a college turn down an applicant whose parent has just donated a substantial amount of money to the school? Some would argue that when a wealthy individual donates large sums of money in order to further guarantee their offspring's admission to prestigious institutions of higher learning, the donation is expected to benefit the larger university community in providing scholarships or funds to build much-needed programs and buildings.

The college admissions scandal might have ordinarily taken a back seat to more titillating crime or disaster news, but for two reasons. One explanation is that in recent decades, both students and parents are more acutely aware of the escalating cost of higher education, not to mention the heightened awareness of the type of grades, extracurricular activities, and test scores that students are expected to have in order to be admitted to more competitive schools.

The second reason this case garnered so much media attention is that two of the accused parents are fairly high-profile celebrities. Felicity Huffman, best known for her role on the TV series *Desperate Housewives* (ABC, 2004-2012), along with Lori Loughlin of *Full House* fame (ABC, 1987-1995) and the more recent series *Fuller House* (Netflix, 2016-present) are among the individuals that were investigated and indicted for a number of college admissions frauds. Federal prosecutors are considered whether to include money laundering in the charges. At the time of this writing, Huffman's husband, William Macy — a well-known actor in his own right — has not been named as a suspect. However, Loughlin's husband, famous clothing designer Mossimo Giannulli, has also been implicated and charged in the case (Halleck, 2019). To date, none of the children of accused parents have been criminally charged. Both Loughlin and her husband ultimately decided to enter separate plea agreements in May 2020, assumedly to avoid harsher sentencing if the cases were taken to jury trials (Levenson, 2020).

Yet one of the key defendants, William Singer, who pleaded guilty early on, was a virtual unknown individual in the wider *media circus* of this scandal. According to Andrew Lelling, U.S. Attorney for the District of Massachusetts, Singer pleaded guilty to racketeering and conspiracy, money laundering, defrauding the United States, and obstruction of justice. Singer ran a consulting practice aimed at building high school students' brands for college applications — think of it like Instagram® product marketing, but on a much larger scale.

Singer was the creator of the Key Worldwide Foundation, described as a shady nonprofit with the alleged mission of helping underprivileged high school students into universities. After the scandal broke, there is now an advisory to potential donors that this is a questionable charity (Charity Navigator, 2019). The *New York Times* reported that some school counselors and consultants eyed Singer with suspicion (Bosman et al., 2019).

Discussion Questions

1. How might students who have legitimately made their way through the admissions process to get into college feel victimized by this scandal?
2. Do you think that the case would have received as much media attention if not for a couple of Hollywood actors and their spouses implicated in this case?
3. As high profile scandals go, in what ways does this scandal seem different than when celebrities commit more conventional crimes, as in the examples of domestic violence, or drug offenses?

21ST CENTURY MEDIA SOURCES

In many cases, the general public has very little information about the white collar criminals involved until a news story is broadcast. The names are unfamiliar, as not all powerful people are likewise famous. An individual can have powerful standing within their industry, as in the case of Wall Street moguls, but they are not household names, as compared to high profile celebrities like the Kardashians.

More commonly now, people are getting their news from Internet sources, which is in itself problematic. Google anything and you will find contradicting stories on a number of topics, from politics to health care. Not all media sources on the Internet are reliable or legitimate. This is where it takes a discerning eye to sort out genuine news from fiction. With today's technology, it is not that difficult to create a fictitious website that looks convincingly real.

Some of the news-consuming public confuse fiction with reality as well, particularly in the age of not-so-real reality TV. Screenwriters and producers are able to take creative license in how they portray any criminal case, as the motive is generally to sell advertising or movie tickets, not necessarily to educate the public. Even documentary films can be biased, as much can be done with film editing to present a topic from a particular perspective, and they are rarely presented as objective opinion.

Gone are the days when television news anchors were blandly but authoritatively delivering the news. Most of you reading this will not be familiar with newscasters David Brinkley, Chet Huntley, and Walter Cronkite. Cronkite was instrumental in not only reporting events during the Vietnam War in the 1960s, but delivering the latest news on the Watergate scandal in the 1970s on a nightly basis. Cronkite famously signed off each broadcast with the line, "and that's the way it is." You might want to go to Youtube.com to check out just how different these newscasters were from those we watch today. On the most part, they simply delivered the news with little to no shock tactics.

There is a reason why the attention around some news stories is described as a "media circus." The number of journalists on any given crime story, the amount of news reports generated, and the number of times that the event is covered can sometimes be a distortion of just how truly significant it might be. Think about the attention that some cute homemade video of pets or children get when it goes viral on the Internet, which indicates just how contagious some minor stories can be. Nevertheless, as elite circles are for the most part closed-door and outside the public eye, media is the best means by which the public can become aware of serious white collar crime.

Like other news, when white collar malfeasance is reported in the news today, it is sensationalized and presented as supposedly "normal people" turning to crime for a number of reasons. How many times have we seen when a neighbor is interviewed about their homicidal neighbors, they report, "but they were such good, quiet people"? The news is presented as "infotainment" — information presented as a form of entertainment (Levi, 2006). As Postman (2005) cautioned us, in the 21st century, we are in an era of amusing ourselves to death with the unlimited sources of online and television entertainment, including the news.

There is much discussion about so-called "fake news." What is more important to note is that statistics reported in the news can be deceiving. For instance, if we say that there have been ten homicides in a city, the magnitude of that is dependent on the size of the city. News sources tend to report raw data without comparison to things like population to put it in perspective (Hansen, 2018). When there is a report of one person on Wall Street committing crimes, it is too easy to jump to the conclusion that "everyone is doing it." The reality is that the vast majority of people working in any given profession are following the law to the best of their abilities. By using our homicide example, there is a big difference between a homicide rate of ten people a day in a city of 100,000, as compared to ten homicides a day in a city of over a million residents.

The good news in all this is that we have access to so much more information, so it is more difficult for the "bad guys" to get away with anything. Think about how people can document the commission of a crime on a smart phone that now becomes evidence. The same can be said about emails and social media postings. These have become helpful tools for law enforcement. The bad news that all those sources can be altered or enhanced to create false evidence. The other bad news is that as we have seen in previous chapters, unlike a homicide, the commission of a white collar crime may take years to detect, both by law enforcement and the media.

Of course, fictionalized news is not a recent phenomenon. Any print newspaper from the late 19th and early 20th centuries can be found to have sensational stories loosely based in reality. It is why a good researcher will do something we in methodology call "triangulation," so that information can be verified to be as accurate as possible based on same or similar reporting of news stories on a number of websites, including from overseas news sources like the British Broadcasting Company (BBC).

Beginning in the mid-20th century, there have been fewer and fewer owners of many more available news outlets, whether we are talking about print media, television, or Internet sources. Our mainstream news is now coming to us from a relatively small number of media owners. The main goal of media has historically been, and is still today, to create profits for shareholders.

We should also note that media sources deal in both fiction and reality, in that movie studios and news outlets can be owned by the same media mogul. They may also own media outlets in a number of countries, not just in the U.S. Whether based on facts or fictionalized for television, streaming, or big screen movies, big scandals sell in a number of national and international media outlets and will do so until the next shiny object comes along. As Watergate recedes in public memory, other scandals, as in the case of the Mueller investigation of possible election tampering in the 2016 Presidential election, take the forefront of news headlines.

We are currently in an era when the public distrusts media sources, at least in the U.S. There are distinct differences in people's beliefs as to what constitutes legitimate news sources, largely dependent on what political party one identifies themselves with (Ralph and Relman, 2018). In a survey conducted by the Knight Foundation and Gallup, 62 percent of Americans believe that news sources are biased, with Republicans being less trusting than Democrats (Ralph and Relman, 2018).

Researchers have also found that the type of news being broadcast, either by traditional news outlets or Internet sources, makes a difference in how much people trust the reporting. In the case of economic news, where white collar crime is commonly reported, the more negative the news, the more likely it will be reported (Soroka et al., 2017). For example, more attention is given to high unemployment rates during a recession than positive job reports that indicate that unemployment rates are low in more prosperous times.

MEDIA INFLUENCES ON JURIES IN WHITE COLLAR CRIME CASES

Since most potential jurors have little background in civil or criminal law and procedures, their expectations are shaped by the media that they consume. For some jurors, they expect real life trials to imitate art, as in what they see on television screens in fictionalized legal shows. Reality TV has its share of television judges as well, including *Judge Judy* (CBS Television Distribution). In criminal justice, we call this the *"CSI effect"*:

> "The *CSI effect* refers to the perception commonly held by lawyers, judges, police officers, and even the general public that, due to the apparent availability of forensic evidence on crime televisions shows such as *CSI* [original series airing 2000-2005, CBS], jurors may be either unwilling to convict in the absence of such evidence or overly reliant on it when it is presented." (Maeder and Corbett, 2015, p. 86).

It is doubly challenging in white collar crime cases, as the evidence presented in court by both the prosecution and defense attorneys can be very technical. For instance, in financial crime cases, the evidence presented is coming after forensic accounting investigations. For jurors with little understanding of finance, financial regulations, or general accounting practices, it may be difficult for them to make a connection between the ledgers and crimes committed.

In environmental or medical crimes, the evidence may be grounded in chemistry, biology, and other science disciplines. Though there are greater numbers of people attending college in the U.S. than ever before, not all college students are focused on science, technology, engineering, or math (STEM) curriculums. Nor are they necessarily majoring in criminal justice, though there are growing numbers of students who are doing so in recent decades as more law enforcement agencies are requiring new employees to possess college degrees. Even in homicide cases where sophisticated DNA evidence is presented, as in the O.J. Simpson murder trial in the 1990s, jurors may not fully understand the connection between the evidence and the crime committed.

In some cases, the technical, scientific evidence becomes the media star as victims recede in the background during trials. The Ford *Pinto* exploding fuel system, discussed earlier in this book, is an example where media attention resulted in a number of less than tasteful jokes. Older people may still remember some of these jokes, but not the names of people who died because of faulty and negligent engineering, nor who was ultimately responsible for design decisions. In today's media, insensitive memes can circulate far faster than the Ford *Pinto* jokes did in the 1970s, making the role of public relations spokesperson even more critical ahead of any negative publicity.

WOMEN, THE MEDIA, AND WHITE COLLAR CRIMES

In what we know from crime trends in general, whether we are discussing white collar crime or conventional crime, men commit the vast majority of crimes. Women are underrepresented in white collar crime statistics largely because we think of these crimes as being committed by elite individuals, who are more likely to be older white males in their 50s and 60s (Gottschalk et al., 2015). However, lower-level and younger employees who make modest salaries, including women, can and do at times commit white collar crimes. Granted, these crimes are not on the same scale as the big scandals created by more powerful elites.

Historically women have been treated as both perpetrator and victim in the media. A woman who is victimized in the workplace by a predatory coworker is often times accused of inviting the unwanted attention. Likewise, the homicide of prostitutes is not given the same sympathetic treatment in the media as when a suburban housewife is the murder victim.

In conventional crime, women can sometimes receive harsher sentences for the same offenses committed by males, because they should (in theory) have known better than to commit a crime. This is largely due to gender role socialization, where stereotypically girls should behave themselves but "boys will be boys." Though there is some evidence of a growing trend towards gender-neutral child-rearing practices, even with more egalitarian socialization, parents (and society in general) on average are still more likely to expect traditional gender roles for their children. Female offspring are still expected to be docile, male offspring are expected to be more rough-and-tumble risk-takers (Kollmayer et al., 2018). Gender-specific roles are still reinforced in media, including television, film, and books.

Uniquely, women who commit white collar crimes are few and far between, but there is a question as to whether we know the actual crime statistics. Scholars argue that it isn't a matter of women being underrepresented in white collar crime statistics, but rather that they are misrepresented. If we consider that women have increasingly made up a greater portion of the workforce since the 1970s, it would stand to reason that some would increasingly have more opportunity to commit white collar crimes.

The assumption that women are less opportunistic and more committed to relationships and rules is problematic as it assumes that women are more risk-averse as compared to males (Gottschalk and Smith, 2015; Crompton and Lyonette, 2005, Walklate, 2004;). What is important to note is that part of the perception is due to gender biases in reporting male offenders in the news over female offenders.

The media perception of women is that they take a lesser role in offending, as in the case of co-offending with a spouse who might own the business. In the Bernie Madoff case, it was difficult for the public to believe that his wife, Ruth, had no knowledge of her husband's Ponzi scheme, though he operated it for 26 years before detection. It is also less believable considering that she worked as her husband's bookkeeper for a number of years, during which he was committing financial crimes. When the media do report female offenders, they may leave out some details of the crime, including the offender's name, as a result of misplaced chivalry on the part of the press (Gottschalk and Smith, 2015). This falls in line with the same perception of how law enforcement treats female white collar offenders.

There is also a problem with describing women's work in offices and businesses as "pink collar" rather than "white collar." It implies that women in office work are inevitably in low or moderately paying positions. With more women able to achieve higher positions in business due to a larger number of women completing their college educations, it would stand to reason that we may see more female white collar offenders in elite positions: "The higher the professional positions she has, the more temptation and opportunities for doing crime she gets." (Koshevaliska et al., 2018) It is too soon to say whether law enforcement and the media will continue to treat elite female white collar offenders or offenders' spouses with kid gloves as is currently the case.

THE "PERP WALK"

There are times when law enforcement and media (e.g., TV news reports) work together to make a display, and to some extent a spectacle, of the arrest of a high-profile white collar crime defendant. There is some belief that the embarrassment of public arrest and/or a uniformed police escort to a squad car serves as a deterrent for elite criminals and as a form of shaming. It is also intended to demonstrate transparency in the criminal justice system, much as a televised trial attempts to do the same. This coordinated, uniquely American public display is called the *"perp walk"* (Paciocco, 2013). "Perp" is urban slang for an alleged perpetrator of a crime. It is controversial, as some would argue that it violates the *4th Amendment* prohibiting unreasonable seizures of persons (Paciocco, 2013).

With so many people using smart phones with built-in cameras, it is no longer just journalists capturing photos and video footage of elite offenders' arrests. Photos make their way to social network platforms like Facebook®, Twitter®, and Instagram® as well, both by "citizen" photographers and news outlets. The public shaming is not restricted to arrests. When Michael D. Cohen, former attorney for President Trump, walked himself into a federal court to face arrest for charges of campaign finance law violations, tax evasion and lying to Congress, he did so on his own volition and without handcuffs or escort. Nevertheless, the pathway to the courthouse was lined with media shouting questions and some of the public shouting insults.

When we think of arrests for conventional crimes, we ordinarily think of the ones depicted in police dramas or reality TV series like *Cops* (Paramount Network, 1989 to present). The alleged criminal is taken away in handcuffs, stuffed into the backseat of a police squad car. This is generally the way it happens in real life for serious crimes, as in the case of shoplifting where a store wishes to prosecute, with the arrest often taking place in public.

One concern with the "perp walk" is that when the alleged offender is taken into custody or is publicly shown in handcuffs walking back and forth between the courtroom and jail, the alleged offender already is subliminally believed to be guilty by the viewing public, some of whom may be potential jurors in the case. The alleged offender might very well be presumed guilty until proven innocent in a court of law, which runs contrary to the *6th Amendment* of the Constitution. Or, as sometimes described, they are found guilty in *the court of public opinion*, further enforced with the *"perp walk."*

We have already established that most white collar crimes will be handled in civil court, sometimes in class action lawsuits. After all, if the whole organizational structure is at fault, it is not always practical to arrest everyone involved, nor is it good for shareholders in the case of a publicly traded company. We should also consider that some of the people committing crimes in the organization will testify against others to escape prosecution. Again, most of this is handled discreetly, with little possibility of a "perp walk" occurring.

There is always the possibility of arranging a deal with a prosecutor's office as well, resulting in little to no prison time for many common white collar crime offenses like embezzlement, particularly if legal or media attention will harm the organization financially in the long run. Some employers will not press charges against offending employees because of the reputational damage it might do to the company. In these cases, termination of employment is more commonly the punishment, along with a ruined reputation in the industry. Because there is no law enforcement involvement, these cases rarely get media attention, hence there is no offender to parade out in public.

We have already established that elite white collar criminals are treated differently in the criminal justice system. In some cases, the alleged offender has been notified that an arrest is imminent, either directly by the police or through his or her attorneys. More times than not with wealthier defendants, the alleged offender has the financial means to pay bail money immediately if bail is set, and the arrest and subsequent booking at a police station takes place in fairly short order. This can all be handled discreetly, with little media attention on the actual arrest and booking until it has already taken place.

COLLATERAL DAMAGE TO THE INNOCENT

There is always some collateral damage when an individual or group of individuals in a company go rogue. However innocent others might be, when a crime has been detected, it can have a reverse halo effect on others, where opinions based on a handful of criminals spills over onto the entire company, or even a whole industry. For example, with the Wells Fargo fraudulent account case, it further tarnished the reputation of the banking and finance sectors following on the heels of the system's 2008 meltdown in the U.S. and elsewhere in the world. It also sullied the reputations of those in the company who committed absolutely no wrongdoing and created general distrust in financial institutions, as the Wells Fargo case followed so soon after the 2008 banking meltdown.

There are rare cases when an entire company should be held culpable. We saw this example with the WorldCom fraud case discussed in Chapter 5. In most cases of white collar crime, it is a handful of offenders, at least from a standpoint of who can be sued or prosecuted. In publicly traded companies that have been accused of extraordinary criminal behavior, not only can innocent employees' reputations be damaged and they may lose their jobs and pensions, but shareholders are also at risk of substantially losing some or all of their investment. It requires an extensive public relations effort to resuscitate the goodwill in a company after any major crisis, even those that do not involve criminal wrongdoing.

It is the job of journalists to chase the story down wherever it might lead, under the pressure of deadlines and reporting before any other competitor can. There is generally little regard for the fallout on innocent employees that might happen if a company is exposed for unethical or criminal behavior. As a result, companies and corporations scramble to salvage their reputation when one or more of their employees commits a newsworthy crime.

PUBLIC RELATIONS NIGHTMARES

Rarely is the only role of public relations to merely inform the public of positive or negative events. Cutlip et al. (1994, p. 6; Jo, 2018, p. 1761) defined public relations as "the management function that establishes and maintains mutually beneficial relationships between an organization and the publics on whom its success or failure depends." The key function of public relations is to do damage control in the event that something goes wrong in an organization. This is an important function when white collar crime happens and companies have to scramble to restore their reputations. Most public and private, nonprofit and for-profit organizations either have full-time public relations personnel or hire outside consultants.

As much as it is the job of the media to report news as it is happening, it is the job of government agencies, companies, and corporations to minimize the public relations damage when bad things happen. This is both when they are directly responsible for the event and when it is beyond their control. Some examples that we have already seen in this book are the Ford *Pinto* and *Challenger* space shuttle cases.

Whether they are directly to blame or if an unforeseen disaster occurs, public relations personnel go into high alert in order to salvage what reputation they can of the organizations they work for. For individuals or smaller companies without in-house public relations departments, they may have to hire a consultant from the outside. For instance, if actresses Lori Loughlin and Felicity Huffman have any hope of resurrecting their Hollywood careers, assuming that they do not spend substantial time in prison[1], they may very well have to hire a public relations team to help them to do so after the college admissions scandal in which they faced a number of criminal charges.

One of the roles of public relations professionals is to be the conduit between the organization and the media. Generally, there is a spokesperson whose job is to put the most favorable light on what could be a terrible event. These spokespeople are sometimes referred to as *"spin doctors,"* meaning that they are expected to put a positive spin on even the most negative news.

Law in the Real World: BP Deepwater Horizon Oil Spill

(Source: National Commission on the BP Deepwater Horizon Oil Spill and Offshore Drilling, https://www.govinfo.gov/content/pkg/GPO-OILCOMMISSION/pdf/GPO-OILCOMMISSION.pdf)

For a number of decades, the Gulf of Mexico has been the focus of offshore oil exploration. At times drilling has been running at a fever pitch, with oil companies elbowing their way over the coastal waters of Texas, Louisiana, Mississippi, and Florida.

BP, a global energy business (www.bp.com), is a publicly traded company with a number of operations around the globe. In April 2010, one of their oil rigs off the coast of Louisiana, not far from New Orleans, exploded and spewed millions of gallons of crude oil into the Gulf's waters. Like in many of these cases, ultimately BP, along with Transocean and Halliburton (subcontractors to BP), were accused of a number of cost-saving strategies that resulted in cutting corners, putting humans and wildlife in danger, and the deaths of 11 oil rig workers.

After the explosion and oil spill, BP, Transocean, and Halliburton had their hands full with not only cleanup efforts, but with the subsequent public relations fallout. Because of all the media attention on the accident, the public was alerted to the companies' possible mistakes, shaking the confidence of consumers and investors. The oil spill had widespread environmental and economic consequences, as the spill interfered with normal fishing operations. One of their responses was to air a number of commercials showing their commitment to oil cleanup. This is similar to what Exxon (now Exxon-Mobil, after merger) had to do after the Valdez oil spill, when one of their

---

[1] At the time of this writing, Felicity Huffman has pleaded guilty for her role in the 2019 college admissions scandal, with sentencing pending. Lori Loughlin and her husband, clothing designer Mossimo Giannulli, have pleaded not guilty and are awaiting trial on charges of money laundering through a fake charity as part of the same college admissions scheme.

supertankers ran aground and spilled hundreds of thousands of barrels into the ocean off the coast of Alaska. The commercials were BP's and Exxon's mea culpea public relation responses.

The Deepwater Horizon tragedy was memorialized in the 2016 Oscar-nominated movie, *Deepwater Horizon* (Lionsgate).

Discussion Questions

1. Who might be the target audience for public relations campaigns after humanmade disasters?
2. Why should investors be concerned with isolated, regional accidents if these are large, multinational corporations?
3. What is the most effective way to spread a public relations campaign in this day and age? Why?

LEGAL RIGHTS AND RESPONSIBILITIES OF JOURNALISTS

In recent years, journalists worldwide have been given a bad name. However, the press in the United States is protected by the Constitution and a number of laws. Cited on a frequent basis is the 1st Amendment of the Constitution:

> *Congress shall make no law respecting an establishment of religion, or prohibiting the exercise thereof; or abridging the freedom of speech, or of the press . . . .*

Of course, there are limitations on both freedom of speech and of the press. These limitations include any statement in speech or published in the news that is a threat to government interests or to the legal rights of individuals. This is why there is so much interest in prosecuting Julian Assange, of Wikileaks fame.

Additional limitations include prohibiting threats and words that might prove to be an endangerment to people. For instance, if a credible news source were to report that the planet was in immediate danger of being annihilated by a massive asteroid, threatening life on earth, and it just wasn't so, this could be a criminal offense. If there was malicious intent, the news source could be held responsible for any panic that ensued after the false reporting. Of course, journalists make mistakes in their rush to deliver breaking news and are generally fast to print or report retractions. Much of the grievances over what people say and write are settled in civil court, where the burden of proof is less stringent than in criminal court. Journalists, newscasters, and writers can be sued for *slander* or *libel*.

If we consider that medical and school personnel are required by law to report child abuse to authorities, including to child protective services, why are journalists not held to the same standard when it comes to reporting white collar crimes? Knowing that any crime, but particularly white collar crime, has the potential of causing widespread harm, would it not be the responsibility of anyone who is aware that a crime has been committed to report it? Journalists argue that in order to make sure that they get as much information that they can from sources, they have to be able to offer those sources anonymity, even if in some cases the sources are committing crimes themselves.

Researchers who research crime face the same dilemma of what their responsibilities are when interviewing individuals who have yet to be convicted of any crime (e.g., gang members), who nevertheless divulged that they have committed a crime, including homicide. Alice Goffman, daughter of well-known sociologist Irving Goffman of symbolic interactionist fame, was criticized for protecting individuals she knew or thought had committed crimes while conducting an ethnographic study of young black men in West Philadelphia (Lubet, 2015). Goffman was later criticized for not doing enough within research methodology circles and for not doing enough to protect the identity of her research subjects. Of course, it is much less likely that elite offenders will confess their crimes to reporters, much less researchers, even after they have been indicted.

In order to assure that journalists have the freedom to protect their sources, some states in the U.S. (and some countries) enacted shield laws, similar to client-attorney privilege. Because sources might be unwilling to share vital information without a promise of anonymity, shield laws prevent law enforcement and the courts from forcing journalists to reveal their sources. There is no federal shield law in the U.S. at this time, though there have been several attempts to pass one.

In the same way there are limitations in the *1st Amendment* right of the freedom of the press, shield laws have limitations as well. In *Branzburg v. Hayes*, the U.S. Supreme Court ruled that the 1st Amendment does not prevent journalists from being ordered to testify in a court of law if they have witnessed criminal activity. However, witnessing criminal activity is different than having it reported to a journalist by a source. Nevertheless, there is no real uniformity on which journalists will be threatened with jail time if they do not reveal their sources.

Law in the Real World: Judith Miller, *New York Times* Reporter and the CIA Leak Scandal

(Source: Schmitt, 2005, Retrieved from https://www.latimes.com/archives/la-xpm-2005-jul-07-na-reporters7-story.html; New York Times, 2005, Retrieved from https://www.nytimes.com/2005/07/07/opinion/judith-miller-goes-to-jail.html)

The George W. Bush administration in the early 2000s was fraught with a number of political and military challenges, the least of which was the terrorist attacks on the Twin Towers in New York City on 9/11/2001. The subsequent military action had the goals of removing Saddam Hussein from power in Iraq and dismantling Al-Qaeda in Afghanistan. As the "boots on the ground" military action required intelligence to accomplish these goals, there were CIA operatives working undercover in both countries.

In 2003, in a published article, syndicated columnist Robert Novak identified Valerie Plame, wife to former diplomat Joseph C. Wilson, as a CIA operative with a mission to investigate Iraqi uranium purchases that allegedly took place in Niger. In his article, Novak claimed that his sources were senior administration officials in the Bush White House. The sources of leaked information were traced back to members of President Bush's administration, including I. Lewis "Scooter" Libby, then Chief of Staff for Vice President Dick Cheney, who ultimately was convicted of perjury, obstruction of justice, and making false statements for his part in the leak.

A second journalist, Judith Miller, a Pulitzer Prize winning reporter for *the New York Times*, was sought as a key witness for a federal grand jury investigation into the Bush administration's involvement in publicly identifying Plame as a CIA operative. The leak jeopardized any undercover role she might have then and in the future, as well as put her and her family in harm's way. Miller had yet to write an article on the case, but was believed to be in possession of information that was critical to the prosecution's case. Whether Miller's testimony could prove to be useful or not, in an act of civil disobedience, Miller refused to reveal her confidential sources of possible illegal leaks of a CIA agent's identity.

As a result of Miller's refusal to answer Special Prosecutor Patrick J. Fitzgerald's questions about possible malfeasance committed by members of the Bush administration, U.S. District Judge Thomas F. Hogan ordered Miller to be held in civil contempt of court, imprisoned until she agreed to reveal her sources. Miller's lawyers argued that she should not be sent to jail as she was exercising her 1st Amendment rights.

Another journalist in the same case, *Time Magazine* reporter Matthew Cooper, who was likewise threatened with jail time, agreed to testify at the last minute. Miller, on the other hand, with the support of her newspaper, ultimately served 85 days in jail for her refusal to testify. *the Los Angeles Times* (Schmitt, 2005) reported that in doing so, Miller's intention, beyond protecting sources, was to the extent to which journalists' rights could be protected.

Both criticized and praised by the press for her refusal, Miller ultimately relented and testified that her source was Scooter Libby, but that he had not specifically revealed Plame as a CIA operative. As it turned out, Miller's testimony served little purpose in seeking out the truth about who in the White House actually leaked the information. Miller ultimately was asked to resign from *the New York Times* in 2005 under a cloud of her questionable reporting of other, unrelated news about the Iraqi War, as she claimed disagreement with colleagues as to whether she should have ultimately testified in the Plame case (Seelye, 2005).

Discussion Questions

1. Under what circumstances in white collar crime should reporters be required to reveal their confidential sources?
2. If Miller's testimony offered little information to help the prosecution's case, why might she hold out so long before agreeing to testify?
3. Why might Miller finally agree to testify after 85 days in jail?

What might seem strange to people outside of the United States is that there is no uniformity across the country on what a journalist can or cannot report, or on the extent to which they are obligated to disclose their sources. Because the United States is simply that, a country made up of a number of states, each state can legislate their own restrictions on the 1st Amendment. For example, in theory, unpublished manuscripts, books, news stories, etc. are not considered to be in the public domain until they are published. However, in some states, writers may be compelled by court order to hand over their unpublished work.

ETHICS AND CENSORSHIP IN JOURNALISM

As we have already noted, statistics in the news can be deceiving. The numbers are not necessarily inaccurate, but also not put in perspective for the reader, thus making a case seem more sensational than it actually is. Where there is an ethical concern is news reported on social media platforms. Journalists themselves are not completely guiltless in their omitting important information. In an example given by (Pyatt, 2019, p. 23), the *New York Post* published the following headline:

"World's First Human Head Transplant a Success, Professor Says"

By including a professor in the title, it lends credibility to the authenticity of the story, at least to a number of people. What the *New York Post* failed to include in the headline was that the transplant was successfully conducted on corpses (Pyatt, 2019). There has never been a live human-to-human head transplant.

In this day and age of reading only the headlines, largely a function of an abundance of news information, it is more difficult to discern what is fact and what is fiction. This was nowhere better exemplified as in the misinformation that unfolded on the Internet shortly after news broke about COVID-19, the coronavirus epidemic that spread around the world beginning in late 2019 and early 2020. Rumors flew on social media platforms like Google®, Twitter®, and Facebook® as fast as toilet paper, hand sanitizer, and paper towels flew off the shelves at stores. Though social media companies do make efforts to quickly squash rumors and news that might be a public safety or health threat, Facebook® CEO Mark Zuckerberg reported that removing dangerous misinformation on the social network site was stretching the company to its limits (Lyengar, 2020). Added to this, the company being overwhelmed in its battle to remove fake news surrounding COVID-19, with governments ordering and/or advising citizens to stay home to practice social distancing whether they had symptoms or not, which resulted in a surge in use of Facebook® as a means to keep connected with people.

Unfortunately, news agencies have to waste valuable media space dispelling myths, as in the case of Tito's® brand vodka, which was reported through social media as a substitute for hand sanitizer. Even the Center for Disease Control (CDC) had to post on Twitter® that hand sanitizer needs to contain at least 60 percent alcohol, as compared to Tito's® vodka that contains 40 percent (Asmelash, 2020). This is the least of rumors surrounding COVID-19 precautions. Of even greater concern is the rise of white collar crime and fraud associated with the pandemic, some of which will be perpetrated on the Internet through social media, that may not be fully uncovered until after the crisis has passed.

In a global market, we now have to consider the validity of any news we may consume, including crime reports. Responsibility for ethical reporting no longer is limited to the local population. However, journalism today requires ethical practices that take into consideration an audience scattered across the globe (Ward, 2005).

We should also consider that journalistic ethical standards are not uniform around the world. There is relative freedom of the press in some countries, whereas there are restrictions in others, like in the example of North Korea. So as much as some white collar crimes are sensationalized in both traditional and social media sources, they may be altogether absent from others, even though white collar crimes too big to ignore may be occurring. We cannot assume that one country has a bigger propensity for any crimes, including white collar crimes, based solely on the news accounts. *Censorship* is variable around the world, mostly for politically and ideological reasons.

MEDIA AS A WHITE COLLAR CRIME RESEARCH TOOL

It has always been a challenge to collect research data on white collar crime. Any research, or criminal investigation for that matter, involving otherwise well-respected individuals is problematic. In research circles, there are few guidelines on how to interview elite members of society who are not generally willing to participate in studies (Harvey, 2015). However, journalism has offered one way to effectively study, from a historical perspective, major white collar crime cases.

The researcher should be cautioned that it is not sufficient to rely on one or two news stories in order to be confident that what they are reading is accurate. There is a very handy strategy in research methodology, called triangulation, mentioned earlier in this chapter, where the researcher verifies information in a number of journalistic sources that report the same news. It is also critical to sift through varying viewpoints as news outlets are inevitably biased, with some being more so than others.

We should note that because court records in many cases are part of the public record, researchers in white collar crime can find many details outlined in court documents. What is limiting with public records is that there might be a number of pieces of evidence that, while interesting, may not be admissible in court. If this is the case, there might be some valuable information lost to a researcher that can only be gathered via other methodologies, including face-to-face interviews.

SUMMARY

For better or worse, media sources are one of the best ways (and perhaps the only way) for the public and white collar crime scholars alike to find stories on elite crimes. It is clear that white collar criminals with the financial means to hire the best legal representation are treated differently in the criminal justice system compared to conventional criminals. In some cases, individuals and companies who have committed white collar crimes may be sued in civil court rather than prosecuted in criminal court. Of course, there are times when individuals or companies are both sued and prosecuted, as in the example of a wrongful death civil case, where the offender has also been convicted of negligent homicide.

It is also clear that elite criminals are also treated differently by the media. This does not always work in their favor, as they may be required to take the "perp walk" and be publicly shamed before they have even been convicted. Wealthier individuals who have been accused of a crime have more means, including access to skilled lawyers, to prevent their cases from becoming part of a media circus. However, law enforcement and media at times work together to make an example of an alleged offender by putting on display their arrest and transport in a police vehicle.

Television and radio are no longer the only sources for news. People are increasingly relying on Internet sources to get their news. Because there are so many more news sources available online, including in social media feeds, there is a greater likelihood that the news being reported, at least from some sources, is inaccurate. One of the main goals of the Mueller investigation into Russian meddling in the 2016 Presidential election was to determine to what extent that they had infiltrated social media in order to plant fake election-related news.

Beyond journalists, media sources can be valuable tools for the white collar crime researcher. Though not preferable to examining attitudes toward white collar crime and malfeasance in "real time" with surveys and face-to-face interviews, historical reports are helpful, along with public records like court proceedings, to help piece together theories. Researchers face the same ethical issues as journalists when they are aware of unreported crimes. Journalists are somewhat protected in some states with shield laws, so they are not required to reveal their sources. Researchers do not have the same protection or luxury.

Case Study ▪ To Perp Walk or Not to Perp Walk? That Is the Question

In this chapter, we again deviate, as we did in Chapter One, on the format of our case study. Since the media is not on trial here, we will be discussing the merits of one of the least understood rituals in publicly exposing people who are suspected of committing a white collar crimes or any crime for that matter—the so-called "perp walk." For the uninitiated, non-criminal justice majors, and/or those of you who do not watch cop shows on television or streaming services, "perp" is short for perpetrator — the person who is alleged to have committed a crime. If we take the literal meaning of the word "perpetrator," it is someone who is already assumed to have committed a crime or other serious wrongdoing. Therefore, the perp walk could assumedly create a reverse halo effect for the alleged criminal, trying them in the court of public opinion. The purpose of arresting a white collar criminal, or any criminal for that matter, in a public way so as to allow the media to capture the moment is to subject the accused to public shaming in advance of their judgment in a court of law. As Village Voice writer Nat Hentoff observed (Haberman, 2018, retrieved from http://www.nytimes.com/2018/12/02/us/perp-walk.html), "'even Mother Teresa would look extremely suspicious, especially if her hands were cuffed behind her back.'" We should note that individuals who are forced to take the perp walk are sometimes allowed to have their wrists handcuffed in front of them, sometimes with the cuffs camouflaged with a coat draped over the hands or with a coat thrown over their head as they run the gauntlet of reporters. Either way, the supposed crime perpetrator is often accompanied by a battery of detectives or police officers.

A perp walk can also take place when the accused is arriving or leaving the courthouse, as we more recently saw when we saw Harvey Weinstein, on trial for sexual assault, using a walker and looking frail. For the defendant, this can also be an opportunity to put on display their alleged vulnerability.

Background

For those of us who study white collar crime, it seems to be arbitrary as to which white collar criminals will be subject to a raid of their home or business with the intent to arrest them. Not far from the truth is the fact that there is no real rhyme or reason as to why some elite criminals can quietly check themselves in at the local police station and while others will be publicly shamed.

There are a number of reasons why law enforcement prefers to have a defendant turn themselves in. Shlarsky, a former assistant U.S. attorney in Illinois, claims that there is less paperwork involved and there are not the same safety concerns with the process of taking someone into custody when the person turns themselves in, as compared to when there is a surprise arrest (Ward, 2019). Logically, it also frees up detectives and officers on the street.

Public humiliation is not limited to the arrest of a suspect. There can also be dramatic raids by law enforcement, including by the FBI, that can make headlines. An example from organized crime would be the arrest of Whitey Bulger, a crime boss who had operated out of Boston and was at one point an FBI informant. After evading arrest for RICO charges for a number of years, he was arrested in Santa Monica, California on a public street, his condominium raided in plain sight of the media as the FBI gathered possible evidence from his apartment.

Perhaps one of the more dramatic raids made in recent history that immediately became part of the media frenzy is that of Trump's former lawyer, Michael Cohen. We were first introduced to Cohen in Chapter 11, in our discussions of political crime. Similar to the perp walk, any publicly display of intrusion into a home by law enforcement, however warranted, can also serve as a form of social punishment, humiliating the individual in front of family, friends, and the whole neighborhood.

Theories to the Explain the "Perp Walk"

In order to understand the perp walk, we have to look to the history of the public display of alleged or guilty criminals. Historically, punishment that wasn't being conducted in a dungeon somewhere would take place in the public square for all the locals to witness.

Parading the accused or the condemned has not been limited to more recent history, where television cameras and smart phones can be used to capture the moment. Perhaps the most famous early account of a perp walk goes back some 2,000 years ago, when a Nazarene was reportedly forced to march through the crowd-filled streets of Jerusalem with a crown of thorns and carrying the very cross he would later be crucified on (Haberman, 2018). Public humiliation of alleged criminals has evolved through the centuries, limited only by the imagination of the public, law enforcement, and media.

Take the example of the stocks in Colonial America. Stocks were wooden or metal scaffolding in which the accused would be forced to sit or stand with either their hands or legs restrained. Not only was it a physically uncomfortable punishment, but the resulting humiliation as townspeople walked by was psychological misery. In some cases, townspeople were encouraged to pelt the individual with food. More sinisterly, in some locations, people were encouraged to throw objects more dangerous than food at the heads of those locked up in the stocks.

More dire forms of punishment in public included executions by hanging, beheading, or, in France, by the guillotine. This required the accused to take an additional walk of shame to their death. The public execution would become a free-for-all, sometimes resulting in people taking time away from their occupations to attend. Northern Ireland mythology alleges that the term "hangover" was used to describe how 19th century employers having to give their employees the day off following an execution in order to recover from the alcohol consumption during a public hanging. It may very well be just a story that tour guides like to tell visitors.

The perp walk was also popularized in the 1930s, during the heyday of probation and organized crime. Similar to the paparazzi chasing down a famous actor to photograph, preferably in a compromising situation, the media would cluster around the police and the accused in one massive mob (Haberman, 2018). In the 1960s, we witnessed on television the media mob surrounding Lee Harvey Oswald, who was accused in the assassination of President John F. Kennedy. Unfortunately, the crowd, which consisted of law enforcement, curious onlookers, and the media, also shielded from view Jack Ruby, who in an instant stepped forward from the crowd and shot Oswald, who later died never having stood trial for the death of President Kennedy.

In more contemporary usage, the term "perp walk" became popularized in the 1980s by the media. There are a number of television shows and movies that have used the term as they depict the arrest of an alleged criminal. Originally reserved for the shortcut specialized language used by police officers, it has now crept into mainstream conversations.

Some theorists believe that the purpose of the perp walk is not so much to humiliate the accused, but rather to give the impression that law enforcement are doing their job. In fact, depending on the political climate, some studies suggest that law enforcement should use the perp walk prudently, dependent on whether their primary goal is to gain more public support (Lageson, 2018; Van Slyke et al., 2018).

Social and Media Responses

Sometimes the perp walk has political purposes. During the 1980s, when Rudy Giuliani served as a prosecutor in New York City, he was very public about his interest in cleaning up white collar crime on Wall Street. Part of his political strategy while running for mayor of New York was to routinely initiate the perp walk when arresting white collar criminals or when they were arriving or leaving court during their trials (Haberman, 2018).

It goes without saying that the media salivates for the next juicy story. The public is practically insatiable when it comes to public scandals. It becomes particularly titillating when the alleged criminal does not hang their head in shame. When they have their head held high and stare defiantly into the camera lenses, this is described as a "perp strut" rather than a perp walk. We are less likely to see this in the case of white collar criminals.

One more notable perp strut was that of John Gotti, the notorious mobster and head of the Gambino crime family. Instead of hanging his head in shame, he faced the media defiantly (Haberman, 2018). More commonly, the cuffed individual looks sheepish and sometimes in a rumpled state, depending on when and where the arrest takes place.

Unanswered Questions and Unresolved Issues with the "Perp Walk"

The biggest question we have to ask ourselves is whether it is fair to put the accused on display before a trial. There is twofold concern. The first is that, at least in U.S. law, the accused is presumed innocent until proven guilty in a court of law. Realistically, making an arrest public, including stuffing the accused into the backseat of a police squad car, gives the impression, however untrue the case may be, that this is indeed a guilty individual. Why else would the police be arresting them?

A second concern is that by making someone's arrest a public spectacle, it begs the question of whether the defendant or defendants can receive a fair trial. This was certainly questioned with all the publicity surrounding the Rodney King beating case and the murder case of Laci Peterson and her unborn son in Northern California, where her husband, Scott Peterson, was arrested, found guilty, and subsequently sentenced to death. In both of these examples, even before the widespread use of the Internet to spread news, they were so well publicized that there was a lot of doubt surrounding whether the defendants in either case could be fairly tried with an impartial jury that had not been exposed to the news.

Sources

Haberman, C. (2018) For shame: a brief history of the perp walk. *New York Times*. Dec. 3. Retrieved from https://go-gale-com.wne.idm.oclc.org/ps/i.do?v=2.1&u=mlin_w_westnew&it=r&id=GALE%7CA564106965&p=GPS&sw=w.

Lageson, S. (2018) The politics of public punishment. *Criminology and Public Policy*. Vol. 17, Issue 3: 635-642.

Van Slyke, S.R., M.L. Benson, and W.M. Virkler. (2018) Confidence in the police, due process, and perp walks: Public opinion on the pretrial shaming of criminal suspects. *Criminology and Public Policy*. Vol. 17: 605-634.

Ward, S.F. (2019) To perp or not: When do white collar defendants get to surrender peacefully? *ABA Journal*. Nov. 26. Retrieved from http://www.abajournal.com/web/article/perp-walk-white-collar-arrests.

GLOSSARY

1st Amendment (1789, revised 1992)   As it pertains to journalism, Congress shall make no laws that prohibit or abridge the freedom of speech or of the press.

4th Amendment   Cited as to the unconstitutionality of the "perp walk," it is the right of the people to be secure in their persons and prohibits unreasonable searches and seizures.

6th Amendment   The accused has the right to a speedy and public trial by an impartial jury in the state (or federal) jurisdiction. Critics of the media argue that it is difficult to find an impartial jury when there is high media attention on a case.

Censorship   As censorship relates to journalism, it is the suppression or prohibition of the publication of any news that might be politically unacceptable or controversial.

Court of public opinion   The opinions people form by reading media accounts of crimes as to the guilt or innocence of the accused.

CSI effect   With the popularity of television series and movies that depict police procedures, including evidence gathering and testing techniques, there is an alleged effect on the expectations of jury members as to what is considered to be adequate evidence to convict or exonerate the accused of their criminal charges.

Libel   A published false statement that damages an individual's or organization's reputation.

Media circus   The increased media attention surrounding high-profile criminal cases, including journalists, paparazzi, and civilians who sell photos and stories to news outlets.

Perp walk   The walk that an alleged offender takes, usually handcuffed, to a waiting police squad car or when traveling from jail to courtroom during a trial.

Slander   Spoken false statement that damages an individual's or organization's reputation.

Spin doctor   Public relations spokesperson who is tasked with reducing the damage done when there is negative publicity. The spokesperson can represent an individual, a group of individuals, or the whole organization.

REFERENCES AND SUGGESTED READINGS

Asmelash, L. (2020) Tito's tells customers to not use their vodka for hand sanitizer. CNN. Mar. 19. Retrieved from https://www.cnn.com/2020/03/05/us/titos-vodka-coronavirus-trnd/index.html.

Bosman, J., S.F. Kovalesky, J.A. Del Real. (2019) "Pied piper" of college admissions: Scam had all the answers. *New York Times*. Mar. 18. Retrieved from https://www.nytimes.com/2019/03/18/us/william-rick-singer-admissions-scandal.html.

British Broadcasting Company. (2020) Ghislaine Maxwell sues Jeffrey Epstein's estate over legal fees. Mar. 19. Retrieved from https://www.bbc.com/news/world-us-canada-51955675.

Charity Navigator. (2019) Key Worldwide Foundation CN Advisory. Mar. 21. Retrieved from https://www.charitynavigator.org/index.cfm?bay=search.summary&orgid=17998.

Crompton, R. and C. Lyonett. (2005) The new gender essentialism—domestic and family choices and their relationship to attitudes. *The British Journal of Sociology*. Vol. 56, No. 4: 601-620.

Gottschalk, P. and R. Smith. Gender and white collar crime: Examining representations of women in media? *Journal of Gender Studies*. Vol. 24, No. 3: 310-325.

Halleck, R. (2019) Who's been charged in the college admissions cheating scandal? Here's the full list. *New York Times*. Mar. 12. Retrieved from https://www.nytimes.com/2019/03/12/us/felicity-huffman-lori-loughlin-massimo-giannulli.html.

Hansen, L.P. (2018) Applied Analytical Methods Survival Guide. Revised 1st edition. Dubuque, IA: Kendall Hunt Publishers.

Harvey, W.S. (2015) Strategies for conducting elite interviews. *Qualitative Research*. Open Research Exeter: 1-20.

Iyengar, R. (2020) The coronavirus is stretching Facebook to its limit. *CNN Business*. Mar. 18. Retrieved from https://www.cnn.com/2020/03/18/tech/zuckerberg-facebook-coronavirus-response/index.html.

Jo, S. (2018) In search of a causal model of the organization-public relationship in public relations. *Social Behavior and Personality*. Vol. 46, No. 11: 1761-1770.

Kollmayer, M., M. Schultes, B. Schober, T. Hodosi, and C. Spiel. (2018) Parent's judgements about the desirability of toys for their children: Association with gender role attitudes, gender-typing of toys and demographics. *Sex Roles*. Vol. 79: 329-341.

Koshevaliska, O., B. Tashevska Gavrilovic, and E. Maksimova. (2018) Criminological aspects of pink collar crime. *Balkan Social Science Review*. June. Vol. 11, Issue 11: 51-64.

Levenson, E. and M. Morales. (2019) Wealthy parents, actresses, coaches, among the charged in massive college cheating admission scandal, federal prosecutors say. CNN.com. Mar. 13. Retrieved from https://www.cnn.com/2019/03/12/us/college-admission-cheating-scheme/index.html.

Levenson, E. (2020) Lori Loughlin and Mossimo Guiannulli agree to plead guilty in college admissions scam. CNN.com. May 21. Retrieved from https://www.cnn.com/2020/05/21/us/lori-loughlin-guilty/index.html.

Levi, M. (2016) The media construction of financial white collar crimes. *British Journal of Criminology*. 46: 1037-1057.

Lubet, S. (2015) Ethnography on trial: Alice Goffman's acclaimed book *On the Run* tells a compelling story. But can we trust it? *New Republic*. Sept./Oct. Vol. 246, No. 9/10: 38-43.

Maeder, E.M. and R. Corbett. (2015) Beyond frequency: Perceived realism and the CSI effect. *Canadian Journal of Criminology & Criminal Justice*. Vol. 57, Issue 1: 83-114.

Mitchell, A., E. Shearer, J. Gottfried, and M. Barthel. (2016) Pathways to news. *Pew Research Center, Journalism & Media*. July 7. Retrieved from https://www.journalism.org/2016/07/07/pathways-to-news/.

New York Times. (2005) Judith Miller goes to jail. July 7. Retrieved from https://www.nytimes.com/2005/07/07/opinion/judith-miller-goes-to-jail.html.

Novak, D.R. (1986) Normative and interpretive conceptions of human conduct: Decision-making, criminal justice, and parole. *Washington and Lee Law Review*. Vol. 43, Issue 4, Article 3: 1243-1253.

Osborne, L. (2019) Prince Andrew and Jeffrey Epstein: What you need to know. *The Guardian*. Retrieved from https://www.theguardian.com/uk-news/2019/dec/07/prince-andrew-jeffrey-epstein-what-you-need-to-know.

Paciocco, P. (2013) Pilloried in the press: Rethinking the Constitutional status of the American perp walk. *New Criminal Law Review: An International and Interdisciplinary Journal*. Vol. 16, No. 1: 50-103.

Patterson, T.E. (1996) Bad news, bad governance. *The Annals of the American Academy*. 546: 97-108.

Postman, N. (2005) *Amusing ourselves to death: Public discourse in the Age of Show Business*. New York: Penguin Books.

Pyatt, R. (2019) Studies show … or maybe they don't: Misinterpreted data and unsubstantiated conclusions plague press and social media. What can journalists do to stop them? *Society of Professional Journalists*. Winter, Vol. 107, Issue 4: 22-27.

Ralph, P. and R. Relman. (2018) These are the most and least biased news outlets in US, according to Americans. *Business Insider*. Sept. 2. Retrieved from https://www.businessinsider.com/most-biased-news-outlets-in-america-cnn-fox-nytimes-2018-8.

Schmitt, R. B. (2005) Journalist jailed for not revealing sources in court. *Los Angeles Times*. July 7. Retrieved from https://www.latimes.com/archives/la-xpm-2005-jul-07-na-reporters7-story.html.

Seelye, K. Q. (2005) Times and reporter reach agreement on her departure. *New York Times*. Nov. 9. Retrieved from https://www.nytimes.com/2005/11/09/business/times-and-reporter-reach-agreement-on-her-departure.html.

Soroka, S., M. Daku, D. Hiaeshutter-Rice, L. Guggenheim, and J. Pasek. (2018) Negativity and positivity biases in economic news coverage: Traditional versus social media. *Communication Research*. Oct. Vol. 45, Issue 7: 1078-1098.

U.S. Constitution, Amendment I. (1789, rev. 1992).

Ward, Steven J.A. (2005) Philosophical foundations for global journalism ethics. *Journal of Mass Media Ethics*. Vol. 20, No. 1: 3-21.

Walker, S. (1985) *Sense and Nonsense About Crime*. Florence KY: Wadsworth, Inc.

Walklate, S. (2004) *Gender, crime and justice*. Cullompton: Willan Publishing.

Chapter FOURTEEN

Investigating and Prosecuting White Collar Crime

When it pays to have a good defense attorney on retainer

"It's not about the money—it's about the game."

—*Gordon Gekko, Wall Street: Money Never Sleeps*
(2010, 20th Century Fox)

Chapter Objectives

- Introduce readers to the white collar crime "watchdogs" and regulatory agencies.
- Identify the agencies that are responsible for white collar crime investigations.
- Introduce a number of financial and fraud crime detection professions.
- Reinforce the understanding of the differences between civil and criminal proceedings.
- Distinguish the differences between the prison system for conventional criminals, as compared with the prison experience for white collar criminals.

Key Terms

4th Amendment	Circumstantial evidence
Audit	Compliance
Certified Compliance Officer	Comptroller
Certified Financial Forensic Accountant (CFFA)	Direct evidence
	Extradition
Certified Financial Accountant (CFA)	Forensic accounting
Certified Public Accountant (CPA)	General Accountability Office (GAO)

Prisoner's Dilemma

Recidivism (rates)

Subpoena

Third-party subpoena

Truth in sentencing laws

Wiretapping

INTRODUCTION

Never is it more true as in white collar crime investigations that in order to catch the criminals, you have to follow the trail of money. Most of the mistakes made by white collar criminals, even when they are very clever, are due to not covering up their tracks or, in the case of Bernie Madoff, building their scheme with a house of cards that comes tumbling down when there are market changes.

The most obvious avenue by which investigations start is when victims step forward. However, unlike conventional crime, the victims of white collar crime may not even be aware that they have been victimized. It is not like a homicide where there is a body. If victims do detect something, they may blame themselves for their own naivety or might be embarrassed to report their supposed stupidity. Their victimization is viewed part of "business as usual," as in the case of illegal usury, with justice believed to be beyond their grasp. In cases where a company is the victim, there is fear that reporting the victimization might cause sales or stock prices to plummet.

Many times, it takes the coordinated efforts of both regulatory agencies and law enforcement to bring white collar criminals to justice. Other times, white collar malfeasances are first brought to light in class action lawsuits handled in civil courts. In white collar crime, it can be a fine line between the unethical and the truly criminal. We have discussed this in previous chapters, but will go into more in depth on how these court processes are different in white collar crime cases.

In this chapter, we also treat examples a little differently. As the focus of this chapter is on regulation and investigations, we will spend less time on discussing the criminals so we can introduce more detail about crimes themselves and the agencies that investigated the criminals. Like in previous cases in this book, we reveal what penalties they paid once caught, whether they were civil or criminal charges or both.

Finally, we will spend a bit of time discussing what prison life is like for white collar criminals who are sentenced to time in a correctional facility. Though *truth in sentencing* laws (existing since the 1980s) require that an individual sent to prison for their crimes is to serve a substantial amount of the sentence before they are paroled, the length of the sentence, plus the prison where time is served, is a function of whether a judge wishes to set an example of a white collar criminal or not. Prison life is difficult for any convict, but the extent to which it is more tolerable is dependent on what facility the criminal is sent to. We will also discuss how *recidivism* rates are different for white collar criminals, as compared to conventional criminals sentenced to time in prison.

COMPLIANCE

Within organizations, there are a number of people responsible for the financial well-being of the company or corporation. Until recent decades, there was inconsistency in who was to blame in an organization if financial wrongdoing was discovered. Since the age of Enron, officers of a company cannot claim the same ignorance as they could once upon a time, even if they are completely clueless that a white collar crime is being committed. The Sarbanes-Oxley Act of 2002, discussed earlier in this book, held officers responsible for company crimes, though there have been some efforts in recent years to try and dismantle the act. The act is argued to put the direct costs of enforcing it disproportionately on the shoulders of small businesses (Coates and Srinivasan, 2014). Additional criticism is that there is continued ambiguity in research as to whether the Sarbanes-Oxley Act is really a preventative measure in corporate white collar crime (Coates and Srinivasan, 2014).

One growing field within finance coming out of the early 2000s is in the area of *compliance. Certified Compliance Officers* within financial institutions have traditionally been attorneys who are responsible for determining risks for white collar crime or any other possible financial irregularities that might violate regulations. Compliance officers function differently than comptrollers, who are more focused on accounting principles and practices. As legal counsel, compliance officers offer guidance on existing and new laws as they relate to the industries they work in. To do so, not only do compliance officers have to thoroughly understand the law and regulations, they also have to have a thorough understanding of their companies and the possible risks they face.

We will see in the next (and last chapter of this book) that employers and compliance officers have to understand the informal structures and social dynamics within their companies, not only the formal structure. To some extent, they need to have a good grasp of sociology, psychology, and human nature. Many compliance officers have to possess thorough knowledge of international laws as they apply to multinational corporations or if their company has international dealings. Like other white collar crime prevention professions described in this chapter, compliance officers are required to have advanced degrees and certification specific to the industry they work in.

THE REGULATORS

Regulatory agencies play a critical role in curbing white collar criminal tendencies. In fact, as Gunningham claims (2016, p. 503), "Regulation is one of the most important mechanisms used to curb white collar and corporate crime.... through statutory schemes administered by specialist agencies. The limitation of regulatory agencies is that they do not act like the police; they can only act to enforce rules and laws." And in some cases, as we have seen earlier in this book, some of these regulations are purposely ambiguous so as to not to interfere with the function of the economy (Gunningham, 2016). At least, in theory.

We have already established that professional associations are one of the best lines of defense for enforcing industry standards and laws. The American Bar Association (ABA) and American Medical Association (AMA) go a long way in protecting the integrity of the legal and medical professions. Even though some organizations, like the ABA or the AMA, and their boards have the power to strip misbehaving members of their licenses to practice their professions, they have to rely on various government agencies and prosecutors' offices in order to hold criminals accountable.

Employees within regulatory agencies are employed by either the federal or state governments in the United States. This is similarly so in other countries as well because of regulators' roles in enforcing existing laws. Regulatory agencies are required to function in a much more specialized way than conventional law enforcement agencies, and even conventional law enforcement departments will have divisions that will specifically investigate homicides, organized crime, property crimes, or sex crimes. In the case of regulatory agencies, for example, the SEC can hardly be asked to regulate and protect the environment. That is the responsibility of the United States Environmental Protection Agency (EPA). The SEC strictly enforces the laws and regulations surrounding the selling, buying, and trading of a wide range of investment products, including stocks and bonds.

In the financial industry, the Securities and Exchange Commission's (SEC) main function is to protect investors, as well as monitor markets so that they are fair and efficient, without inhibiting a free market system (U.S. SEC, 2019). We should keep in mind that the SEC's role is to primarily monitor U.S. markets, but as we currently have a global economy to contend with, the SEC is dependent on the cooperation of their counterparts in other countries and vice versa. When one market is stumbling in an advanced economy, it can spell doom, or at least serious setback, in world markets. For example, at one time Japan appeared to be the next global financial giant. During the 1990s, when the United States was stumbling financially, it resulted in a domino effect in Japanese markets as well as others.

In addition to the SEC, the Financial Industry Regulator Authority (FINRA), though a non-governmental group, has been instrumental in regulation and investigations. The partnership between the public and private sector is critical in addressing any changes in technology that has an effect on securities trading (U.S. Senate, 2016). Once upon a time, stock purchases and sales were verbal orders to brokers, either in person or by phone call. Fax machines sped up this process. Now, once stock sales, purchases, or trades are ordered, they are instantaneously executed using computers, which creates a whole new set of risks to the market.

One of the key agencies that acts as a watchdog for government is the *General Accountability Office (GAO)*. The GAO holds the profound responsibility of *auditing* every aspect and agency of the United States government. The GAO acts as an arm of the legislative branch of the government and is often described as the "congressional watchdog" under the direction of the *Comptroller* General (GAO, 2019, retrieved from https://www.gao.gov/about/).

The GAO was instrumental in investigating the questionable spending of the Department of Defense in the 1980s. Under President Reagan, the Department of Defense received one of the largest budgets in its history, targeted at fulfilling "weapons-driven" requests, including on research and development (Adams, 1986). In the process of justifying the inflation of the budget, unusual spending was uncovered with a finger pointed at military defense contractors. As the *Los Angeles Times* reported, a division of Litton Industries was accused of defrauding the U.S. government by charging exorbitant prices, such as $285 each for ordinary screwdrivers and $74,165 each for aluminum ladders (Smith, 1986).

Beyond financial regulatory agencies, there are a number of other agencies that are devoted to investigating and reporting companies that are in noncompliance. One agency that we have yet to discuss in this book is the Occupational Safety and Health Administration (OSHA). A product of the OSHA Act of 1970 and under the guidance of the Department of Labor, the function of OSHA is to regulate and enforce safe working conditions that are required in both public and private organizations (OSHA, 2019). Unfortunately, companies may not always operate within OSHA guidelines and regulations after inspectors finish investigations and file their reports.

OSHA-Approved State Plans

OSHA-approved state plans (private sector and public employees)

Federal OSHA (private sector and most federal employees)

OSHA-approved state plans (for public employees only; private sector employees are covered by Federal OSHA)

EXHIBIT 14.1. **Map with State OSHA Plans** *(Source:* https://www.osha.gov/Publications/all_about_OSHA.pdf, p. 7).

Some states have their own versions of the federal agency, as in the example of Cal/OSHA in California. Most states simply require that companies comply with OSHA's regulations. The arguments for having separate OSHA programs include the need to be more responsive to local needs, as in the example of a state whose economy is agriculture-based or states where employees are more likely to be working outside in extreme weather conditions, such as extreme winter conditions in northern states and Alaska or extreme heat during the summer months in many southern states. State programs have to be certified and approved by the federal OSHA (OSHA, 2019).

Whether we are examining OSHA or an OSHA-endorsed state program, agencies are in charge of making sure that both public and private companies provide workers with safety equipment. Companies are also required to provide training to protect employees from being exposed to the following hazards and more (OSHA, 2019):

- Toxic and hazardous materials
- Fall hazards
- Machinery
- Blood or airborne pathogens
- Communicable diseases

Employers are required by law to provide safety equipment at the cost of the company, though if we use the example of steel-toed shoes worn in construction or lab coats worn by some hospital employees, workers may have to incur some of the costs of their safety equipment. Like other whistleblower protections, the law also prevents employers from firing, demoting, transferring, or using any other forms of retaliation against workers who report safety hazards (OSHA, 2019).

Law in the Real World: OSHA and Material Handling Systems/MHS Technical

(Source: United States Department of Labor, OSHA, 2019; Schneider, 2016)

Mail handlers and mail carriers face a number of hazards in their professions. From fending off dogs on postal routes to lifting heavy packages, these can be physically demanding jobs. But we sometimes forget that hazards might await in the facilities themselves, not simply on the street, and it is not only the employees of the United States Postal Service (USPS) who might face work hazards if facilities are unchecked. Employees working for private mail and package delivery services can also be exposed to workplace dangers.

In 2015, a United Parcel Service (UPS) facility in Addison, Illinois was inspected by OSHA and found to have a number of possible violations on a construction project being completed by Material Handling Systems/MHS Technical Services. Material Handling Systems/MHS Technical Services is a company that specializes in conveyor belt systems to move objects along quickly and efficiently within a building, as in the example of packages at the UPS facility. The private package delivery company was working on a project to replace the conveyer system at UPS with a new high-speed system. Material Handling Systems/MHS Technical Services, the company contracted to do the work, had previously been cited for similar violations at a Keasby, New Jersey construction site in 2014.

In their investigation, OSHA found three willful violations (as opposed to simply unintended oversight), including exposing workers to the risk of falling more than six feet in the facility. OSHA also cited the company for not providing safety training for workers, as well as failing to provide safeguards like guardrails or safety nets. There were also citations admonishing Material Handling Systems/MHS Technical Services for exposing workers to combustible materials in the tarps used to protect them from welding sparks. According to the Bureau of Labor Statistics (BLS), falls are the leading cause of fatal and nonfatal injuries in the construction industry (OSHA, 2019; BLS, 2019). The financial penalties of the conveyer belt company's violations totaled $92,400.

Four months after being cited for the violations by OSHA, Matt Cienkus, an employee of Material Handling Systems/MHS Technical Services, fell 22 feet to his death. Cienkus was in the process of dismantling equipment at the time of his accident.

Discussion Questions

1. Why might a company ignore the worker safety recommendations made by OSHA?
2. If financial penalties do not work to stop worker safety violations, as in the case of Material Handling Systems/MHS Technical Services, what other strategies could OSHA take in order to get compliance?
3. If you were CEO of UPS, how might you put your own safety measures into practice, even if a contracted construction company is ultimately responsible for workers' health and safety?

When an offense is so big that the penalty goes beyond civil or professional sanctions and fines, regulatory agencies have to closely coordinate their efforts with more conventional law enforcement agencies, including the FBI. Though agencies may open investigations, the arrests and criminal charges are the responsibilities of conventional law enforcement departments and local state or federal prosecutors' offices.

The unfortunate reality is that regulatory agencies are dependent on the political whims of whomever is in office, both on the state and federal levels. The United States is not alone in this conundrum. For example, in the U.K., financial supervisors within the British government had responsibilities for regulation shifted to their central banks due to political pressures because of a shadow banking system where risky investments were being managed under practices outside of banking norms (Isaac, 2018). The shadow banking sector is so profitable, U.K. politicians are at a loss as to how to fully regulate it (Isaac, 2018).

In many respects, regulatory agencies, either pre-existing or newly formed, will only be called upon to react with strong arm tactics after a major crisis. In the U.S., the Consumer Financial Protection Bureau was only created after the 2008 financial crisis, starting with taking a critical look at unethical mortgage lending practices.

On the topic of international efforts, imagine the challenges in regulating commerce within the European Union (EU). Since its inception in the early 1990s, 28 countries have joined, creating economic alliances that made trade and travel between member states more efficient. But this also meant that there had to be the creation of some regulatory uniformity as well. The main challenge was to monitor trade between countries without taking away their autonomy (Groenleer and Gabbi, 2013). Using the example of food safety, the European Food Safety Authority (EFSA), headquartered in Italy, was formed in 2002 in order to assure that any food and animal feed that crossed EU borders would maintain health standards that member countries could agree on (Groenleer and Gabbi, 2013).

THE INVESTIGATORS

In some respects, investigators need to possess the same skill set as the criminals—it may very well take thinking like a criminal to catch a white collar criminal. For example, the skills of an identity thief include social skills, intuitive skills, technical skills, and system knowledge (Copes and Vieraitis, 2017), expertise that help investigators who likewise possess them in catching criminals. Investigators can only uncover the motive and means by which white collar criminals commit their crimes if they understand the mechanics of how the crimes are committed in the first place.

Most investigations in the United States inevitably involve federal agencies. This is for logical reasons, as white collar crimes tend to be interstate, with the offender located in one jurisdiction and victims covering several geographical areas, crossing state lines (Bazely, 2008). This does not mean that state or local law enforcement agencies won't cooperate with federal investigators, but local authorities can only directly investigate and detain suspects who have allegedly committed crimes within their jurisdictions. This isn't to say that they are not allowed to assist in federal cases when it is appropriate.

Increasingly, white collar crime investigators in the U.S. are required to work with international authorities. This in itself has its fair share of risks to a successful prosecution. The International Criminal Police Organization (INTERPOL) was established in order to promote more intergovernmental cooperation in capturing criminals who offend across international borders. INTERPOL currently has 194 member countries and is not limited to EU members as the agency pre-dates the creation of the EU. As INTERPOL investigates both conventional and white collar crime, they are regularly involved in investigating financial crimes, including those that are committed online and offline (INTERPOL, 2019).

When looking at cooperation across domestic or international agencies, there may not be agreement as to how much disclosure there should be of investigatory findings (Dervan, 2011). With more criminals disregarding international boundaries and laws, *extradition* becomes more vital (Caruso, n.d.). Negotiations with international governments are not always successful if extradition is necessary to bring a suspected white collar criminal to prosecution in the United States or elsewhere in the world. The challenge is in having both parties agree that the crime is extraditable (Caruso, n.d.).

As we will see shortly in our discussion of accounting audits, financial crime investigation is not always done by law enforcement agencies. Financial crime investigation is a growing field within the private sector when there are suspicions of corruption, financial malfeasance, embezzlement or other financial crimes (Gottschalk, 2015). There are a number of reasons why a company wants to keep financial crime investigations out of the hands of law enforcement. Most commonly, it is because the company doesn't want its reputation publicly damaged, if at all possible.

FORENSIC ACCOUNTING

Most accounting irregularities will be found in audits. Organizations generally have a process by which they conduct an internal assessment of their accounting and bookkeeping practices on a regular basis to make sure there are no errors. Some organizations are too small to require a full department dedicated to accounting. In those cases, they may engage the services of an outside accounting firm. Even larger organizations will hire outside consultants to take a closer look at their ledgers. In some cases, a company can be court-ordered to hire an external auditor, if irregularities are suspected. In others, it may be a professions' oversight organization, as in the example of the American Bar Association, that will require an audit of accounting practices, if an individual is suspected of financial wrongdoing.

One of the most demanded skills in white collar crime investigation is *forensic accounting*. It requires an expertise beyond basic accounting training and *Certified Public Accountant (CPA)* licensing. Though CPAs are very adept at catching what is off in ledgers, forensic accounting demands a developed sixth sense, plus training on how to detect intentional financial malfeasance in accounting practices. In order to become a forensic accountant, a person must have either a specialized degree or a master's degree in accounting. Increasingly we are seeing college programs, both in the undergraduate and graduate levels, offering degrees in forensic accounting. At the very least, many colleges and universities offer courses in forensic accounting.

Forensic accountants have two important roles. They can be instrumental in investigating possible financial crime. They can also use their skills to prove a crime has been committed and testify to that fact in court. Of course, they can also uncover evidence that might exonerate a suspect or defendant.

There are a few additional professions within forensic accounting that are worth mentioning for any budding investigators. As fraud is a common white collar crime, certified fraud examiners are experts in the prevention and detection of fraud and fraud risk. Coming as no surprise, certified fraud examiners have their own professional organization to keep them current on developments in the field (and to keep them honest, like similar associations). The Association of Certified Fraud Examiners is an international organization that provides anti-fraud training and education (available at https://www.acfe.com/).

Certified financial forensics accountants similarly uncover fraud, but they are also experts in income tax evasion and money laundering. Forensic accountants and *certified financial accountants* are asked by law enforcement or by court order to come in after a crime is suspected, whereas certified fraud examiners are more anticipatory, recommending strategies to prevent fraud, though they will be called in after the fact as well.

Forensic accounting has become such an integral part of white collar crime investigation that even in FBI job advertisements, forensic accounting is at the forefront of skills that the agency is looking for in their applicants (available at https://www.fbijobs.gov/). The job outlook for accountants and auditors in general is promising, with an anticipated 6 percent growth in openings within the next decade (Available at https://www.bls.gov/ooh/business-and-financial/accountants-and-auditors.htm). The outlook for professionals specializing in forensic accounting is even better, with an anticipated 10 percent growth through 2026 (available at https://www.forensicscolleges.com/careers/forensic-accountant).

Law in the Real World: Fraud in Toshiba

(Source: Caplan et al., 2019; Hass et al., 2018)

Toshiba is a diversified electronics manufacturing firm located in a suburb of Tokyo, Japan, with a 140-year history. Like many Japanese firms, they operated on a clan model of worker management, with people staying in the same division of the company from their hiring date until the day they retire (Ouchi, 1980). The premise of the clan model is to hire someone fresh out of school and socialize them in the culture of the company in hopes of gaining loyalty. It also saves time and money to not have to continually train new employees when there is any turnover. Employees can be rewarded with raises for non-performance criteria, like major life events (marriage, birth of children, care of elderly parents, etc.) (Ouchi, 1980). Toshiba's management practices were in keeping with traditional Japanese culture that expects efforts to be directed at what is good for the collective instead of towards individual pursuits or ambitions as what we see in Western cultures. By the late 20th century, the clan model of management became obsolete in the face of growing global competition.

In 2006, Toshiba purchased Westinghouse Electric Corporation, an American company that was founded in 1886, first based in Pittsburgh, Pennsylvania. As the saying goes, timing is everything. The purchase of Westinghouse was made in advance of the worldwide financial crisis of 2008. As Westinghouse became a financial liability, management started cooking the books to cover their losses. As Spitzer (2015) noted, it was the lack of internal controls, on top of the culture of deference to management, that resulted in supervisors operating unchecked (Hass et al., 2018).

Japan has its own Whistleblower Protection Act (April 2006), creating an internal notification system for public firms. As is typical in the electronic age, the Toshiba fraud was first brought to light by a whistleblower at the Japanese Securities and Exchange Commission (JSESC) (Hass et al., 2018; Nikkei, 2015). Subsequently, Toshiba employees began to come forward as well. In 2015, Toshiba announced that they would release new financial reports to correct the previous statements. However, in the process, new suspicious accounting practices were uncovered (Nikkei, 2015).

As accounting irregularities became too big to ignore, the accounting firm Ernst & Young ShinNihon was called in to conduct an audit of the Westinghouse books. Eventually Japan's SEC counterpart, the Securities and Exchange Surveillance Commission (SESC), was called in to investigate, along with the Financial Services Agency (FSA). During their investigations, they found four major fraud schemes committed by Toshiba. Toshiba deceived investors and filed fraudulent financial reports in its scramble to make up the deficits created by acquiring Westinghouse. The frauds are described as "window dressing" (Hass et al., 2018, pp. 268-269):

- Overstatement of sales and understatement of expenses
- Profits overstated by fraudulently adjusting profits and losses
- Overstatement of product values
- Failure to eliminate overstated inventory costs

It is important to note that there was a disagreement between Japan's public prosecutor's office and the SESC as to how to proceed in holding Toshiba accountable for their fraudulent accounting practices. The prosecutor's office wasn't sure if the accounting irregularities warranted criminal charges against the three former presidents of Toshiba, who were ultimately responsible for the fraudulent practices even if they were unaware of management's malfeasance.

After Ernst & Young ShinNihon, the accounting firm hired to conduct the internal audit, were convicted of negligence themselves, the firm was fined ¥17.3 million ($17.3 million USD). The venerable name of Westinghouse was dragged through the mud and they filed for bankruptcy protection in 2017. Toshiba sold Westinghouse in 2018.

Discussion Questions

1. One takeaway from this case is that when there are accounting irregularities, there are a number of agencies and outside accounting firms that can be called in to investigate. Who should be responsible for the cost of the investigation?
2. Why might it take more than a handful of accountants to ultimately uncover accounting frauds?
3. How might Japan's clan model of management result in less reluctance to come forward as a whistleblower if an employee discovers some serious accounting problem?

We should note that it is in a company's best interest to keep its financial house in order, especially if it is a publicly traded corporation. Any whiff that financial malfeasance is happening will make investors skittish. It is to their advantage to first conduct private investigations by internal auditing and only resort to calling in outside auditors when it is beyond their capability to take corrective action. As they can be held accountable by regulators, companies may have to call for inspections by the appropriate agencies in order to remain in compliance. For example, a food processing plant will ultimately be required to call in a Food and Drug Administration inspector if there has been any contamination detected.

CYBER INVESTIGATORS

As in the case of forensic accountants, cyber investigators are required to have skills beyond basic computer science or information technology training. In many cases, it takes a cybercriminal to catch a cybercriminal. We have discussed the difference between the "white hat," "black hat," and "gray hat" hackers in our cybercrime chapter, and sometimes the distinction between them is a fine line. Generally, the people who go into the business of investigating cybercrime are "white hats" who have dedicated their careers to the detection of cybercrimes and undoing the harm that is done. And clearly, the motive of "black hats" is to steal information or create havoc in computer systems. The "grey hats" and their role in detecting crime is unclear. They can either help or hinder the efforts of cyber investigators.

As far as actual investigations go, the FBI is the leading agency in investigating cyberattacks that affect U.S. citizens, the government, or commerce. Their primary investigation targets are cyberattacks that are perpetrated by criminals, overseas adversaries (unfriendly nations or "frenemy" nations), or terrorists (FBI, 2019a). In doing so, the FBI has to coordinate their efforts with divisions or memberships within the agency, including the U.S. Intelligence Community (USIC) and the National Cyber Investigative Joint Task Force (NCIJTF) (FBI, 2019b).

Law in the Real World: First Cyber Bank Robbery

(Source: FBI, 2014)

If you think of the classic bank robbery, you think of one or more masked people running into a financial institution with guns as their primary weapon used to intimidate. Bank tellers and managers nervously hand over the contents of their cash drawers or the bank vault. There might be a security guard, but they are either shot early in the robbery (at least in Hollywood depictions), found on the ground cowering, or bumbling around in some fashion. This is far from reality and this image of a bank robbery is largely exaggerated in Hollywood movies.

Bank robbers do not always carry weapons and may simply pass a note over to a teller with the claim that they have a gun, at which point the teller hands over the contents of the cash drawer, which generally has one bundle of cash called "bait money". The bait money, when removed from a teller's drawer, triggers a silent alarm. In some banks, there is a silent alarm button under each teller's station. In many cases, the bait money has a hidden dye pack, that, when disturbed by the robber, will explode and scatter dye all over the cash and the perpetrator, making it impossible to spend the money without people being suspicious. Plus, it makes it easier to figure out who the bank robbers are in a crowd when the dye gets all over their hands and clothing as they run, walk, or drive away from the crime scene. Generally, we do not find that bank robbers are successful when trying to rob a brick and mortar bank with today's security features.

Unfortunately, we now have to contend with cybercriminals who don't even have to leave their home to rob a bank. They don't need a note, mask, or weapon, only their computers. In July 1994, in what was believed to be the first cyber bank robbery, the FBI was alerted by bank managers at a major U.S. bank that money was disappearing electronically. Several of their corporate customers were collectively missing $400,000 from their accounts. In their investigation, the FBI soon discovered that a hacker or hackers had infiltrated the bank's electronic cash management system. The system allowed for customers to move their funds around between global banks.

In their investigation, the FBI found that the cybercriminal or criminals were gaining access through a telecommunications network, which in turn compromised user IDs and passwords.

Instead of closing or freezing the accounts, the FBI worked with the bank to monitor the accounts and were able to identify approximately 40 additional illegal transactions, totaling to more than $10 million in theft.

During the investigation, the FBI was able to determine that money transfers within the U.S. were being generated out of San Francisco, which is, next to NYC, the second biggest financial center in the U.S. By focusing on San Francisco, FBI investigators were able to identify bank accounts owned by a married Russian couple. As soon as the couple was identified as probable perpetrators of the cyber robberies, the wife was arrested as she attempted to withdraw funds from the San Francisco bank. Her husband was arrested shortly afterwards and both cooperated with the FBI. In their interviews, they told investigators that the hacking operations were based in a St. Petersburg, Russia computer firm. They also identified a Russian, Vladimir Levin, who they answered to.

Once the Russian couple had been identified and arrested, and Levin was pointed to as the possible mastermind, the FBI worked with Russian authorities to obtain evidence against Levin. Two additional Russian nationals were also identified in the investigation and arrested. In March 1995, Levin was lured to London and subsequently arrested and extradited to the U.S. Levin pleaded guilty in January 1998.

Due to media attention and the scope of the robberies, the FBI described this as a wakeup call to financial institutions that might be vulnerable to other cyber robberies. Since 1994, cybersecurity has become far more advanced, but as we noted in Chapter 6, cybercriminals are many times a few steps ahead of cybercrime investigators.

Discussion Questions

1. Why might it have taken so long for a cybercriminal to attempt to rob a bank (1998), considering that the Computer Age began in the 1950s?
2. What challenges might there be in conducting a cyber investigation into a bank robbery?
3. Why does it seem like, at least from the news we hear, so many cyberattacks on the United States (and other western countries) appear to be initiated by people living in Russia?

Because so many white collar crimes are done by using computers, through the Internet and the Dark Web, there is a continued demand for cybersecurity experts. Cybersecurity positions pay more than other information technology jobs because of the additional skills that employees need. As Ackerman (2019) predicted, currently there is a shortage of cybersecurity experts in the private sector alone, discounting the additional needs in the U.S. government. It is one reason why there is such high demand for cybersecurity experts at the FBI, as the primary agency to investigate cybercrimes.

WHITE COLLAR CRIME DEFENSE ATTORNEYS

White collar crime defense attorneys have to be specialized in their field, like defense attorneys for other types of crimes. For instance, if you are suspected of committing a homicide, assuming you had the money to do so, you would want to hire the best defense attorney with experience and successes in defending clients against murder charges. In the case of white collar crime, the more complex the case, the greater the need for an attorney who understands the intricacies of the case. As in the situation of anyone indicted of a crime, it may be necessary to hire a whole team of defense attorneys, again, assuming that you have the funds to pay them or at least friends with deep pockets who are willing to pay for your criminal defense.

It is not unusual for former prosecutors of white collar or conventional crimes to end up on the other side of the courtroom as defense attorneys or working in compliance. In order to be an effective defense attorney, it is extremely helpful to understand how the prosecutor's office works. Defense attorneys may also join the private sector, working for law offices specializing in white collar crime investigations. For example, take Charles M. Carberry, who was instrumental in investigating and debriefing Ivan Boesky during the insider trading scandals in the 1980s, for the U.S. Southern District of New York City. Carberry, who was at the time an assistant federal district attorney, left the department to join a private law firm (Cuff, 1987) and continues to investigate white collar crimes. Some public prosecutors, having a better understanding of prosecutorial strategies, go on to work as defense attorneys in white collar crime cases.

Of course, we have to acknowledge that a good portion of white collar crimes are low level, primarily involving the embezzlement of funds or merchandise from employers. In these cases, generally the defendant is not a person of means and will only be able to hire the defense attorney they can afford if indicted. In many of these cases, the defendant will have to rely on a public defender, much as the alleged conventional criminal.

CRIMINAL INTENT IN WHITE COLLAR CRIME CASES

It is easier to demonstrate criminal intent in conventional crime. In a first-degree, premeditated homicide conviction, the evidence generally points to the murderer as clearly intending to harm their victim. Prosecutors are not in the habit of pressing charges against suspects, unless they think they can win the case based on the evidence they have in their possession. In some white collar crimes, premeditation is equally clear, as in the example of embezzlement.

In other cases, it is a bit more difficult to determine whether the white collar criminal intended to hurt anyone. In our political crime chapter, as we explored in discussions of illegal campaign contributions, did the donor clearly intend to commit a public harm, or was the donor merely trying to give their candidate an unfair advantage? Intent is a bit clearer if the donor obviously expects a political favor in return.

As Ann Fitz, a Florida criminal defense attorney, contends (2019), criminal intent is both important and difficult to prove in a court of law. Fitz (2019) notes that the burden of proof lies at the prosecutor's doorstep, and that in order to prove guilt, the following has to be demonstrated:

- The criminal intended to commit or conceal a crime AND
- The criminal acted purposely, knowingly, recklessly, or negligently

It is hard to say whether someone is really guilty or simply afraid to face possible prosecution, even though they might be innocent, when they attempt to flee justice. Some white collar criminals have the means to relocate to countries without extradition treaties. One example of an individual who has managed to elude arrest is 58-year-old Jorge Iglesias[1]. He has been accused of defrauding Medicare for an estimated $1 million in Puerto Rico. In 2008, a federal arrest warrant was issued in Puerto Rico (FBI, 2019c). Iglesia is still wanted by the FBI and is at large in an unknown location (FBI, 2019c). Fleeing an arrest warrant, regardless of whether the individual is innocent, at the very least gives the impression of criminal intent and criminal guilt.

---

[1] Iglesias has several aliases, including Jorge Iglesias-Vazquez, Jorge Iglesias Vazquez, and Jorge Islesias Vazquez (FBI, 2019c).

EVIDENCE IN WHITE COLLAR CRIMINAL CASES

We need to first distinguish between *direct* and *circumstantial* evidence. It is the difference between "facts" and reasonable, logical "speculation." An example would be if you went for a hike in the woods and spotted a bear, you are an eyewitness to the wildlife and can testify in court, "I saw a bear." This would be direct evidence. On the other hand, assuming that you are a wildlife expert, you could go on a hike and identify a set of bear tracks. The only conclusion you can come to is that there was a bear in the woods, even though you didn't actually see it. If you had to testify to this in court, it would be considered circumstantial evidence.

In white collar crime cases, generally there is a smoking gun, or more accurately, a paper trail that can serve as direct or circumstantial evidence. For example, you suspect someone of committing insider trading. Was the person's timing on buying stock a brilliant, intuitive decision, or did they have information that they should not act on because it is against the law? If you witnessed the individual placing the trade, knowing full well that what they were doing was criminal, then it would be direct evidence. If you are looking at financial documents and know that the only person who could place the trade was the suspect, then you have circumstantial evidence.

The most obvious evidence in white collar crime cases are financial records. These can include income tax returns, bank statements, and financial contracts. For suspected companies, it includes investigating all financial records, including profit and loss statements, plus all documentation of transactions. In publicly traded companies, public documents like the required quarterly and yearly statements to the IRS (10Q and 10K reports, respectively) are important evidence in cases when what companies are reporting to the government does not match the actual financial picture.

The biggest concern is in the gathering of information that is protected by privacy laws. As the example given by Applegate (1982) in prosecuting a bank robber, the financial records of a bank are not required. However, if a bank employee is suspected of embezzlement, not only are the bank records likely to be needed in order to prosecute the individual, but it might be necessary to review the private financial records of all bank employees who are suspected to be involved. However, defense attorneys will argue that obtaining these records, even with *subpoenas*, violates *4th Amendment* rights protecting people from unreasonable searches and seizures. Subpoenas are not automatic and there can be expensive, months-long, or, in some cases, years-long efforts to obtain the requested documents. A current example is the New York State prosecutors' subpoena of President Trump's personal and business corporate income tax returns that is expected to go through a number of appeals. To date, it is unknown if the president will ever actually be required to hand over the documents.

Financial records are not limited to the documents of companies. In many investigations, the targets of investigation include personal employee financial records. As in the example of insider trading discussed in Chapter 4, the suspicion of criminal behavior may start with a financial institution. As the real offenders are discovered through company records, it may mean inspecting the personal bank statements of suspected employees. If not willingly surrendered in an investigation, investigators may have to go to court to request a subpoena in order to obtain the documents.

Of course, what we have seen in previous chapters is that the difficulty in getting an accurate picture of an individual's financial standing is complicated by the use of offshore accounts. Even with companies, the use of shell companies to hide financial transactions becomes problematic. It is even more problematic if the company is keeping two sets of books, one with supposedly legitimate transactions and a second one that has actual transactions. Of course, in most cases, the "books" are likely to be maintained and stored electronically.

Tangible assets are also used as evidence in white collar cases. If we consider that it is always suspicious when someone is appearing to live beyond their means (e.g., salary, investment income), it may be necessary to assess the value of personal assets, including homes, investment property, and automobiles. Of course, there are those individuals who are termed "house poor" where they pay an unusually high percentage of their income on their homes. It is a red flag that an individual may be in over their head with mortgage payments.

Even investments in art are suspicious if individuals are buying works by famous artists and do not appear to have legitimate income to pay for these purchases. And as in the case of drug dealers, it becomes a big red flag to investigators if someone is driving around in a high-end automobile (e.g., something like a Ferrari) while living in a lower- or middle-class neighborhood. Of course, here we get into the sticky issue of profiling, but one way to keep up the appearances of being successful is to drive a flashy car. Like buying a large home and living at the edge of what you can comfortably afford to do so, some people prioritize investment in automobiles that they may just barely be able to afford.

Beyond records of tangible and financial assets, there are other documents that are helpful in investigations. Business and personal travel records can be telling as well. As in conventional crime cases, if you can place the alleged perpetrator at the scene of the crime by examining travel documents, including airline tickets, car rental contracts, or credit card records showing hotel accommodations or restaurant receipts, this can be valuable evidence in court cases.

DIGITAL EVIDENCE

Though following the money is critical in any white collar crime case, there are several other pieces of evidence that can be used to indict suspects or to help prove liability in civil cases. For obvious reasons, the most concrete evidence is a paper trail, but can also include emails and other cyber records that point to wrongdoing. Increasingly, as we witnessed in the Ukrainian scandal within the U.S. House of Representatives' impeachment inquiry into President Trump, even text messages are offered up as evidence. Though we have not readily seen this as yet, and certainly not in the impeachment trial of President Trump where no evidence was admitted in that case, it may only a matter of time before a suspect's statements on Twitter® will be held up as evidence.

Like in ordinary criminal cases, prosecutors in white collar crimes are increasingly becoming dependent on digital evidence. However, unlike other types of evidence, digital evidence can be substantial in quantity in any given case, creating challenges for both prosecutors and defense attorneys. As Turner (2019, p. 237) notes in regards to digital discovery,

> " ... the volume, complexity, and cost of digital discovery will incentivize the prosecution and the defense to cooperate more closely in cases with significant amounts of electronically stored information (ESI)."

Because of the sheer sums of ESI that individuals accumulate digitally, for both criminal and civil cases it becomes an almost impossible task to sift through evidence. This is similar to financial data where the investigator may have to sort through mounds of meaningless information to get to meaningful evidence.

There is always the question of whether privacy laws are broken in the gathering of electronic evidence. Like in the case of private bank records, these pieces of evidence can be difficult to obtain.

WIRETAPPING IN WHITE COLLAR CRIME INVESTIGATIONS

Legally (or illegally) eavesdropping on the conversations of criminals has been around for a number of decades. *Wiretapping* is an investigative tool that has been used in the investigation of organized crime. Since the 2008 financial crisis, it is increasingly being used in investigations of white collar crimes (Atkins, 2013).

It is against federal law to record private conversations without the parties' consent. This is similar to recording of interviews with research subjects without first having them sign a consent form. In white collar crime investigations, the Supreme Court, in *Katz v. United States* (1968), determined that it is illegal to wiretap a suspect without a court-ordered warrant as a violation of the 4th Amendment. This is not limited to conventional crime investigation and warrants are required in order to wiretap a white collar crime suspect.

Similar to other types of search warrants, investigators are required to demonstrate to the court that there is probable cause. According to Morvillo and Anello (2011), there are approximately 2,000 wiretaps legally placed each year. With new means of communication, wiretapping laws are not limited to telephone conversations and apply to any means of communication conducted by wire, including electronic or oral communications (Morvillo and Anello, 2011).

There are a lot of complexities to wiretapping laws. Investigators are required to provide to the court a statement spelling out the suspected offense, the identity of the suspected offender, the device or location that will be intercepted, and the nature of the conversations (Morvillo and Anello, 2011). The reality is that some or all of that information may have eluded the investigators and it would take wiretapping to obtain it, which puts serious restrictions on what investigators can legally do. In the Wiretap Act (U.S. Code §2511), the types of electronic communications that can be wiretapped is a rather limited list (Legal Information Institute, 2019).

Wiretapping is not limited to criminal cases, as in the example of insider trading investigations by the SEC, in civil enforcement proceedings (Atkins, 2013). Regulators in civil cases seeking warrants for wiretapping are held to the same standards required for criminal investigation. As we have already noted, there are a number of obstacles to legally obtaining a warrant to wiretap a suspect.

Law in the Real World: Raj Rajaratnam Wiretaps

(Source: Henning, 2011; Wachtel, 2011; Dugan and Harbus, 2019)

In 2019, 62-year-old Raj Rajaratnam, former hedge fund manager at the Galleon Group, was spotted leaving a $17.5 million townhouse in Manhattan, presumably his own. Rajaratnam's previous residence was an eight-by-ten prison cell he called home for eight years. The former billionaire and convicted insider trader had just been released from prison. For all of his financial resources, Rajaratnam couldn't escape an investigation into a $70 million insider trading scandal.

The road to convicting Rajaratnam was a bumpy one for investigators. Ultimately the most powerful piece of evidence was the wiretaps that captured conversations between Rajaratnam and sources of his insider information via three separate calls taking place in 2008 (Wachtel, 2011, retrieved from https://www.businessinsider.com/listen-to-the-raj-rajaratnam-wiretaps-2011-3):

1. In the first call, Rajaratnam and Rajiv Goel (former Intel official) discussed how the stock price of PeopleSupport, a business process outsourcer, was down on the heels of bad press. However, Rajaratnam had insider information, which he disclosed, about PeopleSupport putting millions in escrow, thus making it attractive to buy.
2. In the second call, Rajaratnam is speaking with Anil Kumar, a former McKinsey executive, who gave a tip about a deal that had not been publicly announced involving AMD, a global semiconductor company:

    AK: So yesterday they agreed on . . . at least, they've shaken hands and said they're going ahead with the deal.
    RR: So, can I buy now?
    AK: Go ahead and buy.

3. In the third call recorded in a wiretap, Rajaratnam is speaking with Adam Smith, a former trader who worked for him at Galleon. In the

call, they talked about Vishay, another semiconductor and electronics firm. In the conversation, Smith indicated, based on insider information he had, that the company looked like a winner to buy stock in despite its public reputation.

The wiretaps were permissible in court and the jury was allowed to hear the recordings where Rajaratnam could be found giggling during his phone calls, almost like a guilty schoolboy. Smith had turned state's evidence, testifying against Rajaratnam, in return for not being prosecuted for destroying computer records and documents. Goel also turned state's evidence, in return for leniency in his sentencing, resulting in two years probation and fine, as well as forfeiture of $266,000 (McCool, 2012).

Discussion Questions

1. Besides the 4th Amendment, why are there so many difficulties in obtaining a wiretapping warrant?
2. Why might criminals use communication methods that can so easily be used to gather evidence against them, including cell phones?
3. If Goel and Smith were the ones providing insider information, why was Rajaratnam the target of investigation?

COOPERATIVE WITNESSES

When there are a number of defendants in a white collar crime case, prosecutors are hoping that witnesses will come forward to help build the state's case. In some cases, the best witnesses are some of the defendants themselves. In order to persuade defendants to turn state's evidence against fellow defendants, it generally requires prosecutors to offer a plea deal. According to the *New York Times*, 97 percent of federal cases and 94 percent of state cases end up in plea bargains with defendants pleading guilty to lesser charges in order to receive more lenient sentencing (*New York Times*, 2012) as we saw with Goel in our wiretapping example. We also saw this with the actress Felicity Huffman's case of college admissions test fraud, where she pleaded guilty to the charges in return for receiving a lighter sentence of two weeks in prison. Other defendants in the same case, including actress Lori Loughlin and her husband, have more recently pleaded guilty and there is speculation that they will receive much harsher sentences than Huffman.

It is very much a case of the *Prisoner's Dilemma* of game theory fame, where defendants will be pitted against each other in order to get as much evidence possible as well as getting cooperative witnesses to testify for the prosecution.

WHITE COLLAR CRIME AND THE CIVIL COURT SYSTEM

As we have noted, in civil court, the burden of proof of liability is not as stringent as in a criminal court of law. In the United States, a person is convicted in criminal cases "beyond a reasonable doubt." In civil court, there only needs to be enough proof that the person being sued is at fault or liable; or as it is termed, a "preponderance of the evidence." One benefit of taking the civil court route in white collar crime cases is that it is much easier to demonstrate that the respondent ("offender" in a criminal case) is at fault. In civil court, the person who is suing is called the "plaintiff," whereas the person who is being sued is the "respondent." This is also the language used in family court (e.g., child custody, divorce), rather than criminal court, which has the more severe sounding label of "defendant" for the person suspected of wrongdoing.

In a civil case, unless there are corresponding criminal charges, the respondent is not arrested or indicted. There is no bail and the respondent is free to live their lives with the expectation that they will show up in court when their trial or hearing has been scheduled on the docket. They will be served court documents beforehand by a process server that indicates that they are being sued. Judges can require the respondent to pay a fine or offer other types of restitution if they rule in favor of the plaintiff.

WHITE COLLAR CRIME AND THE CRIMINAL COURT SYSTEM

One way to find justice for white collar crimes, at least in terms of retribution for a state, federal government, or foreign government, is to indict, arrest, and convict a white collar criminal. This is great in theory, until we consider that the burden of proof rests on the shoulders of the prosecution. Depending on how technically complex the execution of the crime is, it may be difficult to convince a jury of guilt if evidence is not clearly explained.

In criminal proceedings, the accused will be arrested and formally indicted. There is no exception as far as treatment of suspected white collar criminals when it comes to their arrest and arraignment. However, depending on the wealth of the individual, the severity of the crime, and the leniency of the courts, white collar criminals are far more likely to be allowed to stay out of jail in advance of their trials. Depending on the severity of the crime, the defendant may only have to report to a police station to be booked and fingerprinted if their lawyers have already arranged for bail or the defendant is ordered released on their own recognizance. This basically means that the defendant has agreed to show up to court. For obvious reasons, they are not to reoffend while released pre-trial, or they will be arrested and may have to remain in jail until their trial. If they have a passport, they are required to surrender it if they are out on bail or otherwise released before trial.

The tricky part is when criminal behavior crosses jurisdictional boundaries. For instance, someone can commit a financial crime that is not only prohibited in the United States, but elsewhere in the world. For example, Julian Assange, an Australian citizen of Wikileaks fame, has been in legal hot water in the United States, the U.K., and Sweden. The charges in Sweden are unrelated to his intelligence leaking and involves an alleged rape. Which the Swedish government is no longer looking to prosecute at this time. All said and done, depending on the criminal, it can be a prosecutorial tug-of-war across international borders.

WHITE COLLAR CRIMINALS IN THE PRISON SYSTEM

As we have established elsewhere in this textbook, white collar criminals are not generally viewed as a physical threat to society. Even though their crimes might involve stealing millions upon millions of dollars, as nonviolent offenders, they are generally sentenced to low- to minimum-security correctional facilities. Some of the federal facilities do not look like standard prisons and are set up as dormitory-style campuses (similar to what some of you may be living in while attending college). In these "looser" facilities there are no fences or barbed wire and prisoners are not locked into their rooms, as in the example of Otisville Prison Camp in New York state (Cantrell, 2018) where President Trump's former attorney and fixer, Michael Cohen, served a portion of his three-year sentence, before being released early due to concerns for his safety in the face of the COVID-19 pandemic.

Once in a while, a judge will want to set an example with a convicted white collar criminal and send them to a maximum-security prison to serve time alongside convicted rapists and murderers. But this is generally the exception. The type of prison that a white collar criminal is sent to can be part of a plea agreement as well.

While low-security prisons have the reputation of being somewhat fun and easy like summer camp, this is no longer the case in most facilities. They gained reputations for going too easy on the convicted, with nicknames like "Club Fed." "Camp Cupcake" was the name given to the facility where Martha Stewart was incarcerated, which was described as being America's "cushiest" prison (Fuchs and Tzatzev, 2013). In the early 2000s, Congress passed laws to toughen the federal penalties for committing white collar crime, calling for longer sentences of white collar criminals (Carney, 2013). This also meant that the Federal Bureau of Prisons in turn reoutfitted prison camps to look more like higher-security facilities (Carney, 2013). Gone were the swimming pools and tennis courts that existed at some low-security prisons in the past.

While prisoners in a supermax correctional facility will spend up to 23 hours a day in their cells, prisoners in low- or minimum-security prisons have more freedom of movement during the day. We do know that, on average, the cost of putting someone in a maximum-security prison is assumed to be higher than in low- or minimum-security prisons. However, because of the use of private prisons to supplement government-run facilities in the United States, there is no real way of knowing whether they are really more cost effective (GAO, 2007).

Another option that judges have available at their discretion is to allow convicts to participate in a work release program. This means that convict that has a low risk for escaping or reoffending and is a nonviolent offender who can be employed and working during the day. However they are required to stay at a jail or prison facility at night and weekends. By utilizing this option, it offers a greater chance for the convict to be reintegrated into society after they are no longer incarcerated. It also represents lower costs for incarceration for the prison.

The challenge in work release programs for white collar criminals is that many were employed in positions of responsibility, as in the example of a bank manager who is caught embezzling. Most (if not all) of these types of more elite offenders will have been fired from their jobs and it is difficult for them to find white collar employment, at least in the short term. If self-employed, the white collar criminal may have been stripped of all their licensing and certification that allowed them to practice their profession, as in the example of an attorney who has been disbarred by the American Bar Association (ABA) or a doctor who loses his medical license.

No matter what the sentence or where it is served, the stigma of being convicted follows the white collar criminal through the remainder of their days. Many lose their spouses and friends after their conviction. Some may become estranged from their family members, including their children. Michael Kimelman, a convicted insider trader, describes adjusting to life after prison (Cantrell, 2018, retrieved from https://www.institutionalinvestor.com/article/b18b7g0qjk5pwb/ Surviving-Prison-as-a-Wall-Street-Convict):

> 'I don't think judges, prosecutors, or even defense lawyers understand what happens once the gavel comes down at the end of the trial. Right now we're pretending that you learn a lesson, you rehabilitate, you go on and live a life … we have done everything we can in the last 20 years to make sure that you keep paying that price over and over again.' For example, his [Kimelman's] record comes up when he fills out school applications for his kids or if he want to coach their Little League teams.

Punishment extends past the convicted themselves, affecting families, friends, and even coworkers, similar to what we see with conventional criminals. White collar criminals have a difficult time adjusting to life after prison, even when they have the financial means to get back on their feet. If they are shunned by their neighbors and community, they can live in their own self-imposed prisons for the rest of their lives, as in the example of hedge fund manager Joseph "Chip" Skowron III.

When Skowron was released from prison after being convicted of insider trading, he returned to his Greenwich, Connecticut community. He found that in spite of being surrounded by the luxury of his home in an upscale neighborhood, he was likely to encounter former friends and neighbors who were still living the type of successful life he led before he was convicted (Pomorski, 2019). It was a painful reminder of the lifestyle, power, and prestige he lost, along with his career as a hedge fund manager. On the bright side, Skowron was able to reinvent himself after prison. Since being barred from working in securities, he has been able to purchase ownership stakes in a number of businesses. He also speaks to audiences, including to Wall Street professionals, about his fall from grace and redemption (Pomorski, 2019).

CORRUPTION WITHIN THE CRIMINAL JUSTICE SYSTEM

The criminal justice system itself is not immune to its own cases of white collar crime. For anyone who has taken a policing class, you are no doubt familiar with the names for police officers who take bribes. The "grass eaters" are the ones who take small favors in return for police protection or other services that officers are already paid for with their salaries. For example, if a police officer accepts a free lunch every day from a restaurant in return for keeping an extra eye out for crime around the premises, this is a case of bribery, but far less offensive than if the officer is accepting large sums of money from the restaurant owner to allow illegal activities to take place there. In our restaurant example, if a police officer is taking a share of the money made in drug deals that are happening in the parking lot and turning a blind eye to the crimes, they would be termed a "meat eater."

Likewise, though most judges do their utmost best to maintain a fair courtroom, it isn't always the case. There have been a number of instances where judges have been investigated for questionable practices in sentencing. It is in many ways much easier to monitor unfair sentencing after the federal sentencing guidelines enacted in the late 1980s helped to reduce the amount of disparity from one court room to the next. For instance, prior to the sentencing reform, two defendants could receive the same guilty verdict on the exact same crime or crimes but, depending on the judge in the case, have completely different outcomes in sentencing. Though there are still some discrepancies, these are mostly found on the state and not on the federal level.

SUMMARY

In this chapter, we have by no means exhausted all of what goes into white collar crime investigation. It is meant to give a broad range of options for regulators and prosecutors' offices. Certainly, as much as we don't like to see white collar crimes committed, this chapter also gives a good sampling of the career opportunities for students who are interested in pursuing work in this field. Some of these career paths include compliance officers, cybersecurity experts, and forensic accountants and fraud specialists.

There are two first lines of defense against white collar crime. Professional organizations can go a long way in keeping their members honest, particularly if they require licensing, as in the cases of doctors and lawyers. Much time and money has been spent by these individuals to get the education necessary for these professions, as well as for licensure. This in itself should be a form of deterrence. In this way, the profession is self-regulating.

The second line of defense, no less important than professional organizations, is regulation through legislation. Regulatory agencies have the power to enforce laws and fine individuals and companies when they violate or ignore regulation. Regulatory agencies have some limitations. First, they are often understaffed and underfunded, dependent on whatever political culture is prevailing. Second, even if the regulatory agencies (e.g., EPA) conduct periodic inspections, there is no guarantee that people will stay in compliance once the inspectors leave. As we saw in the case of the conveyer belt company and UPS, even after they were fined, yet another person died due to faulty employee safety measures.

As we have discussed in other chapters, white collar criminals can be criminally prosecuted. More often, however, they are sued in civil court. The good news in going the civil court route is that a good portion of the financial judgement goes to the victims, as compared to criminal court where fines go to the state, though there are cases when a criminal court will sentence both fines and restitution. However, most companies would prefer to keep cases of white collar crime out of criminal court if possible, as it can be more damaging to a company than civil cases, as much as those can be equally detrimental to their financial health.

Historically, when white collar criminals have been sentenced to jail or prison time, they have been primarily sentenced to serve in low-security level federal prisons. The reason for this is twofold in that they are not generally viewed as violent offenders and these federal prisons had a reputation of "going soft" on convicts, with swimming pools and tennis courts at some facilities. However, after the blatant disregard for the law witnessed first with Enron and later during the 2008 financial crisis, Congress and the public demanded more parity between prisons for conventional criminals and those that housed low-level offenders, including white collar criminals.

White collar crimes are more likely to be committed across state lines in the United States, placing the crimes in federal jurisdiction. When they cross international borders, it will take the coordinated efforts of international agencies, including INTERPOL, and cooperation between countries if the criminal has to be extradited to the United States or elsewhere in the world.

At best, we can say that regulatory agencies, the courts, and the corrections systems do their best to ensure that white collar criminals are made to pay for their crimes. Realistically, except in the case of publicized scandals too big to ignore, the public does not make the same demands for justice as in conventional crimes. However, when white collar criminals are brought to justice in the current environment, they may serve far more time than they ever expected to serve for their crimes, even with the best criminal defense that money can buy.

Case Study ▪ *People v. Lomma et al.,* 2012

Background

New York City is always bustling with construction, to the chagrin of its residents. Like any major city in the world, there is never a time when there are no cranes to be seen on the city skyline. In 2008, at a construction site located on 51st Street in Manhattan, a construction crane collapsed, resulting in the deaths of the crane operator and a man working on the ground, and injuring a third person. In many of these cases, it is human error or unsuspected faulty equipment. This particular crane accident was deemed preventable and the State of New York built a case for second degree manslaughter against the company that owned the crane and its head mechanic, and against James Lomma and J.F. Lomma, Inc. Lomma was owner on record of both the crane company, New York Crane and Equipment Company, and of J.F. Lomma, Inc. at the time of the accident.

When the Occupational Safety and Health Administration (OSHA) weighed in on the accident, they concluded that without the necessary support, the crane mast essentially became a freestanding structure and an accident waiting to happen. The supporting slings used could not adequately or safely hold the mast in place (Ayub, 2008).

Defining the Crime(s)

The premise of the manslaughter case against the defendants was that J.F. Lomma, Inc. had purchased a replacement part for the crane from a Chinese company that sold it to Lomma for half the cost and with faster delivery promised (Marsh, 2017b). The prosecutors' argument was that the replacement part was known to not meet acceptable safety standards for cranes operated in the U.S., and therefore merited a manslaughter charge.

In legal terms, manslaughter is a lesser charge than murder. In order for a crime to be considered first degree murder, the prosecutor generally has to prove that there was a purposeful goal to cause the death of a person. In New York Penal Law §125.27, a person has to knowingly and intentionally cause the death of another person in order to be charged with first-degree murder, the most serious charge involving a death of a person (New York State Unified Court System, n.d.). To be proven, a number of criteria have to be met. For instance, a contract killing is treated more seriously than a garden variety homicide. New York State does not have a death penalty at this time, and therefore no convictions on first-degree murder with special circumstances. It is reasonable to say that unless the death was directly intentional, it is difficult to make the argument for first-degree murder in an industrial accident.

It is not uncommon to charge individuals and companies accused of wrongdoing in an industrial accident with the lesser charge of manslaughter, as was the case with the crane accident. Lomma was charged with felony manslaughter, which in terms of New York Penal Law reflects more negligence on the part of the crane company than intentional, willful homicide (New York State Unified Court System, n.d.). Similarly, a charge of negligent homicide, brought against the mechanic who installed the faulty replacement part into the crane, implies that the individual did not willingly cause the death of someone. However, this is not to imply that it is simple human error.

Theories to Explain the Crime

When we examine industrial accidents due to negligence, we have to depend more on economic theories or theories on business practices in order to understand why they happen. They are better explanations than our standard criminological theories, though we do not have to dismiss criminological theories altogether.

There is continued debate over whether the cause of industrial accidents lies at the feet of deregulation. The argument against regulation is that it inhibits economies and in turn stifles profits (Steinzor, 2012). So far in this book, we have primarily discussed regulation in terms of financial markets. When we start talking about regulations around workers' safety, it is a far more emotional subject. If this is the case, then we need explanations for why companies may ignore regulations and take the risk of harming their employees.

Of all occupations, people working in what are classified as blue collar jobs are most at risk to being exposed to a number of hazards. As Fang et al. (2015, p. 1) and Fang and Wu (2013) note, "Construction is one of the most dangerous industries all over the world, where large numbers of accidents result in workers' deaths, injuries, work-related illness, as well as other direct and indirect losses." According to Heinrich et al. (1950), accident causation theory places blame for accidents on individual behavior, including the extent that supervisors are focused on worker performance, offering intervention and instruction when worker safety is being called into question.

In construction, as in most organizations, larger operations require several layers of supervision. A construction project specifically is proposed to have three main strata: (1) strategic management lead by a project manager, (2) tactical layer that acts as middle management, and (3) the frontline operational layer, as in the example of foremen who have direct supervisory responsibility of workers to assure good safety practices (Fang et al., 2015). Any bad decision or neglect by individuals, either intentionally or accidentally at any of these levels, can result in injury or death to workers.

Workers themselves may be afraid to come forward to report unsafe conditions because they fear retaliation. Even though there have been more whistleblower protection laws in recent years, both at the federal and state levels, not all companies have anonymity protections for their employees. The most effective means for whistleblowing to work in the construction industry is to provide protection for whistleblowers, including the use of anonymous reporting channels, as in the example of hotlines by used by police departments for anonymous crime tip reporting (Oladinrin et al., 2016).

Social and Media Responses

Unlike some industrial accidents, when there is a construction accident in New York City, or in any large city for that matter, it brings things to a standstill, at least in the area where it happens. East 51st Street is right in the heart of midtown Manhattan. It is not an exaggeration that New York City is described as the city that never sleeps. To have a major accident like this happen where it did, it was impossible to hide the accident from the public eye, no matter how jaded New Yorkers are perceived to be. However, media focus was primarily localized to New York City and the northeastern part of the United States.

Most of the media attention to the accident was on Lomma's responses after the civil judgement. Dubbed the "Crane King" in the tabloid media, he was portrayed as callously refusing to pay the families, even though his net worth was reportedly $200 million at the time of the accident (Marsh, 2017a). In earlier accounts, Lomma is noted as refusing to sell his personal airplane, a $4.6 million Pilatus PC-12 turboprop, claiming that the sale would result in tax consequences of $480,000 (Eustachewich, 2016). Whether there is any truth in the reporting or not, Lomma is not painted as a sympathetic character, a businessman who had no idea that his mechanic was buying faulty parts.

Criminal Justice and Policy Responses

In gathering evidence, prosecutors for the State of New York served a subpoena for the personal financial records of Lomma. In doing so, they did not give notice to Lomma. As soon as Lomma became aware that his records were being subpoenaed, Lomma's attorneys argued that neither the defendants nor the courts received notice as required by law from the prosecutors. Furthermore, because of the alleged illegality, the defense attorneys argued that the subpoena should be altogether nullified, meaning that if the courts ruled in Lomma's favor, the records could conceivably never be obtained by prosecutors.

The prosecutors made the argument that as this was a *third-party subpoena*, they were not required to notify the defendant or the courts. The court agreed with the prosecutors and ruled that they were not required to provide notice of the subpoena. The court came to this conclusion based on the differences between serving subpoenas for criminal cases as compared to civil cases. The requirement to notify defendants did not apply in this case, as it was a criminal trial.

For those of you who are curious about the outcome of the criminal case, it resulted in only a partial win for the prosecutors. The head mechanic, Tibor Varganyi, pleaded guilty to one count of criminally negligent homicide and avoided prison time in exchange for testifying against Lomma (Buettner, 2012). Lomma, owner of the crane companies, was acquitted of all charges in 2012. In an unusual move, the judge, Justice Daniel P. Conviser, heard Lomma's case without a jury. As Eligon (2012) rightfully noted, it is difficult to prove criminal liability in construction accidents.

Lomma did not escape a civil lawsuit, as noted in our section on the media responses to the crime. The families of the two men who were killed sued Lomma and his companies, resulting in an initial civil jury award of $96 million to be paid to the families of the victims of the accident, forcing him to file Chapter 11 bankruptcy (Gleason, 2016). In 2017, the Manhattan appeals court reduced the award to $35 million (Marsh, 2017b).

Unanswered Questions and Unresolved Issues Related to the Case

This was an unusually large settlement for a civil case. As tragic as the accident was, the casualties were far less than in other crane accidents in and around NYC. A question remains: Why might the jury award such a large amount to be paid to the victim's families in this particular civil case? We have to ask ourselves if this has anything to do with the ability to pay for really good legal representation, whether in criminal or civil cases.

This case also begs the question, to what extent should companies be criminally liable when one of their employees commits a crime, unbeknownst to supervisors or management? If the head mechanic was ultimately to blame for ordering a defective part, logically we might presume that only the person making a bad decision should be held accountable. This is something that is not uniformly followed from court to court, and much has to do with the tenacity of prosecutors, as well as what evidence there is that someone other than the guilty party knew what was going on.

Finally, as in this case, we might question why prosecutors have more subpoena power in criminal cases compared to civil lawsuits. There is, at least on the surface, reasonable explanation for this discrepancy. In criminal cases, the defendant or defendants, including companies, have to be proven guilty beyond the shadow of a doubt. Not so in civil cases. As a reminder, the person accused of wrongdoing in a criminal case is called a defendant, while in civil cases, they are the respondent. There only needs to be enough evidence for juries and judges to believe that there is a pretty good chance that the respondents are liable of some wrongdoing. Juries and judges do not have to be 100 percent sure in civil cases.

Sources

Ayub, M. (2008) Investigation of the March 15, 2008 fatal tower crane collapse at 303 East 51st Street, New York, New York. Occupational Safety and Health Administration, U.S. Department of Labor. Sept. Retrieved from https://www.osha.gov/doc/engineering/2008_r_02.html.

Eligon, J. (2012) Crane owner is cleared of all charges in fatal collapse. *New York Times*. Apr. 26. Retrieved from https://www.nytimes.com/2012/04/27/nyregion/james-lomma-acquitted-of-all-charges-in-crane-collapse.html.

Eustachewich, L. (2016) "Crane King" won't sell plane to pay accident victims' families. *New York Post*. Oct. 17. Retrieved from https://nypost.com/2016/10/17/crane-king-wont-sell-plane-to-pay-accident-victims-families/.

Heinrich, H.W., D. Petersen, and N. Roos. (1950) *Industrial Accident Prevention*. New York: McGraw-Hill.

Marsh, J. (2017a) "Crane King" who hasn't paid accident victims' families worth $200M: lawyers. *New York Post*. Mar. 21. Retrieved from https://nypost.com/2017/03/21/crane-king-who-hasnt-paid-accident-victims-families-worth-200m-lawyers/.

Marsh, J. (2017b) Appeals court slashes record verdict awarded to families of crane collapse victims. *New York Post*. Sept. 12. Retrieved from https://nypost.com/2017/09/12/appeals-court-slashes-record-verdict-awarded-to-families-of-crane-collapse-victims/.

Oladinrin, O., C. Man-Fong Ho, X. Lin. (2016) Critical analysis of whistleblowing in construction organizations: Findings from Hong Kong. *Journal of Legal Affairs and Dispute Resolution in Engineering and Construction*. Vol. 2, No. 2: 0451612.

Steinzor, R. (2012) The Age of Greed and the sabotage of regulation. *Wake Forest Law Review*. Vol. 503: 503-536.

Supreme Court, New York County. (2012) *The People of the State of New York v. Lomma et al.* May 16. Retrieved from http://courts.state.ny.us/Reporter/3dseries/2012/2012_22023.htm.

GLOSSARY

4th Amendment   As it applies to evidence, law enforcement must not illegally search or seize evidence without first obtaining a court-order to do so.

Audit   An accounting practice that can be conducted by people working within an organization (e.g., bank) or by an independent consultant, company that specializes in audit. In an audit, all accounts are reviewed along with any supporting documents; for example, an IRS audit of an income tax return.

Certified Compliance Officer   An individual, most likely to be an attorney, who is licensed to investigate possible violation of laws or regulations in a company and advises in preventative measures to assure that laws are not broken.

Certified Financial Accountant (CFA)   A Certified Public Accountant (CPA) with advance degrees and/or specialized training in the investigation of financial crimes or suspected malfeasance.

Certified Financial Forensic Accountant (CFFA)   See *Certified Financial Accountant.*

Certified Public Accountant (CPA)   An accountant who has passed the Certified Public Accountant exam to be licensed and is required to continue to take course work in order to remain certified.

Circumstantial evidence   Evidence that brings the investigator to certain conclusions, even though there might not be physical evidence or an eyewitness to a crime being committed.

Compliance   The extent to which laws and regulations are being followed by individuals and organizations where they apply to specific industries (e.g., financial institutions).

Comptroller   A title used for individuals who serve as financial officers (e.g., CFOs) or auditors in their companies.

Corporate violence   Injury or death that happens to customers, employees, or civilians as a result of calculated neglect, usually as a cost-saving measure, by a company or corporation.

Direct evidence   Verifiable physical or firsthand eyewitness evidence in a criminal case.

Extradition   In a criminal case where the suspect is not physically present (e.g., in another state or country), they are returned to the jurisdiction where there is an arrest warrant out for them and where they are being charged with a crime.

Forensic accounting   A specialized area of accounting where CPAs are trained to look for mistakes, omissions, or criminal entries in accounting files of individuals or organizations.

General Accountability Office (GAO)   Part of the legislative branch of the U.S. government, the GAO is an independent and non-partisan office that is responsible for the monitoring and review of government spending and reports their findings to the United States Congress.

Prisoner's Dilemma   Part of Game Theory, the Prisoner's Dilemma proposes that if co-defendants are separated from one another and each given the opportunity to turn state's evidence in exchange for lesser charges or even dismissal of charges, there is a certain probability, depending on a number of factors, that they will take the deal and confess their crime or take their chances with a not guilty plea and not sell out their co-offenders.

Recidivism (rates)   The rate at which convicts, once released from prison or if on probation or parole, will reoffend and be arrested again, starting the cycle all over again through the criminal justice system. The recidivism rate for reoffending is approximately 35 percent within one year of release from prison, approximately 66 percent within five years of release.

Subpoena   A court ordered demand that evidence is turned over in a civil or criminal case.

Third-party subpoena   A court ordered demand for documents from people or organizations who have possible evidence pertaining to an individual who has been indicted or is being sued. An example would be the bank statements of a defendant in an embezzlement case that would have to be requested from the bank and not directly from the individual who is being accused of the crime.

Truth in sentencing laws   Laws enacted in the 1990s to assure that offenders would serve a large portion of their sentence in prison, instead of being granted an unusually early release.

Wiretapping   The legal or illegal practice of listening in on a telephone or Internet-based conversation. Investigators are required by law to obtain a court order allowing them to wiretap a suspect or suspects.

REFERENCES AND SUGGESTED READINGS

Ackerman, R. (2019) Too few cyber professionals is a gigantic problem for 2019. *Techcrunch.* Jan. 17. Retrieved from https://techcrunch.com/2019/01/27/too-few-cybersecurity-professionals-is-a-gigantic-problem-for-2019/.

Applegate, J.S. (1982) The Business Papers Rule: Personal privacy and white collar crime. *Articles by Mauer Faculty, Mauer School of Law: Indiana University.* Vol. 16 No. 2: 189-241.

Cantrell, A. (2018) Surviving prison as a Wall Street convict. *Institutional Investor.* Dec. 13. Retrieved from https://www.institutionalinvestor.com/article/b18b7g0qjk5pwb/Surviving-Prison-as-a-Wall-Street-Convict.

Caplan, D.H., S. K. Dutta, and D.J. Marcinko. (2019) Unmasking the fraud at Toshiba. *Issues in Accounting Education.* Vol. 34, No. 3: 41-57.

Carney, J. (2013) Is Raj Rajaratnam really living like a prison king? CNBC. Aug. 27. Retrieved from https://www.cnbc.com/id/100991730.

Caruso, C.A. (n.d.) Overcoming Legal Challenges in Extradition. *Asia Law Initiative, American Bar Association.* Available at https://www.americanbar.org/content/dam/aba/directories/roli/raca/asia_raca_charlescaruso_overcoming.authcheckdam.pdf.

Coates, J.C. and S. Srinivasan. (2014) SOX after ten years: A multidiscipline review. *Accounting Horizons.* Vol. 28, No. 3: 627-671.

Copes, H. and L. Vieraitis. (2017) Identity theft: Assessing offenders' motivations and strategies, in *In Their Own Words*, M.L. Birzer and P. Cromwell, eds. 7th edition. New York: Oxford University Press. Ch. 8.

Cuff, D.F. (1987) Business people; Insider prosecutor to join law firm. *New York Times.* July 15. Retrieved from https://www.nytimes.com/1987/07/15/business/business-people-insider-prosecutor-to-join-law-firm.html.

Dervan, L.E. (2011) International white collar crime and the globalization of internal investigations. *Fordham Urban Law Review*. Vol. 39, Issue 2: 361-390.

Fitz, A. (2019) Why intent is so important in white collar crime cases. Law office of Ann Fitz. Aug. 22. Retrieved from https://palmbeachfederaldefense.com/blog/2019/08/why-intent-is-so-important-in-white-collar-crime-cases/.

Fuchs, E. and A. Tzatzev. (2013) Camp Cupcake: Take a tour in America's cushiest prison. *Business Insider*. June 6. Retrieved from https://www.businessinsider.com/take-a-tour-of-americas-cushiest-prison-2013-6.

Gleason, S. (2016) James Lomma, owner of crane in 2008, files for bankruptcy. Jan. 7. Retrieved from https://www.wsj.com/articles/james-lomma-owner-of-crane-in-2008-collapse-files-for-bankruptcy-1452191914.

Gottschalk, P. (2015) Private investigations of white collar crime suspicions: A qualitative study of the Blame Game Hypothesis. *Journal of Investigative Psychology and Offender Profiling*. Vol. 12: 231-246.

Groenleer, M. and S. Gabbi. (2013) Regulatory agencies of the European Union as international actors. *European Journal of Risk Regulation*. Jan. 1. Vol. 4, Issue 4: 470-492.

Gunningham, N. (2016) Regulation: From traditional to cooperative, in *The Oxford Handbook of White-Collar Crime*. New York: Oxford University Press. Ch. 24.

Hass, S., P. Burnaby, and M. Nakashima. (2018) Toshiba Corportion—How could so much be so wrong? *Journal of Forensic and Investigative Accounting*. Vol. 10, Issue 2, Special Issue: 267-280.

Henning, P.J. (2011) The pitfalls of wiretaps in white collar crime cases. *New York Times*. Mar. 25. Retrieved from https://dealbook.nytimes.com/2011/03/25/the-pitfalls-of-wiretaps-in-white-collar-crime-cases/.

International Criminal Police Organization (INTERPOL). (2019) Financial crime threatens people in every aspect of their lives: at home, at work, online and offline. *Financial crime*. Retrieved from https://www.interpol.int/en/Crimes/Financial-crime.

Isaac, A. (2018) UK shadow banking sector worth at least £2.2 trillion. *The Telegraph*. July 2. Retrieved from https://www.telegraph.co.uk/business/2018/07/02/uk-shadow-banking-sector-worth-least-22-trillion/.

Kleibl, J. (2013) The politics of financial regulatory agency replacement. *The Journal of Politics*. Apr. 9. Vol. 75, No. 2: 552-566.

Legal Information Institute. (2019) U.S. Code §2511. Interception and disclosure of wire, oral, or electronic communications prohibited. Cornell Law School. Retrieved from https://www.law.cornell.edu/uscode/text/18/2511.

McCool, G. (2012) Ex-Intel exec Rajiv Goel avoids jail in Rajaratnam case. *Business Week, Reuters*. Sept. 24. Retrieved from htpps//www.reuters.com/article/galleon-goel-rajaratnam-idINDEE88N0GK20120925.

Morvillo, R.G. and R.J. Anello. (2011) Overview of federal wiretap law in white collar cases. *New York Law Journal*. Feb. 1. Vol. 245, No. 21: 1-2.

Nikkei. (2015) There are a lot of whistler's rights after the announcement of the delay of financial reporting at Toshiba. Sept. 1. Retrieved from https://www.nikkei.com/article/DGXLASDZ31I27_R30C15A8TI1000/.

Ouchi, W.G. (1980) Markets, bureaucracies, and clans. *Administrative Science Quarterly*. Mar, Vol. 25, No. 1: 129-141.

Pomorski, C. (2019) Look homeward, hedgie. *Vanity Fair*. Aug., pp. 62-65; 92-93.

Schneider, G. (2016) Local company faces $320K fine in worker death. *Courier Journal*. Aug. 7. Retrieved from https://www.courier-journal.com/story/money/companies/2016/08/07/local-company-faces-320k-fine-worker-death/88338482/.

Smith, J. (1986) $37 screws, a $7,622 coffee maker, $640 toilet seats: suppliers to our military just won't be oversold. *Los Angeles Times*. July 30. https://www.latimes.com/archives/la-xpm-1986-07-30-vw-18804-story.html.

Spitzer, K. (2015) Toshiba accounting scandal in Japan could speed corporate reforms. *USA Today*. July 24. Available at https://www.usatoday.com/story/money/business/2015/07/24/toshiba-accounting-scandal-japan-could-speed-corporate-reforms/30612009/.

Turner, J.I. (2019) Managing digital discovery in criminal cases. *The Journal of Criminal Law & Criminology*. Vol. 209, No. 2: 237-311.

United States Bureau of Labor Statistics. (2019) Injuries, illness, and fatalities. U.S. Department of Labor. Retrieved from https://www.bls.gov/iif/.

United States Federal Bureau of Investigations (FBI). (2014) A byte out of history: $10 million hack 1994-style. *News*. Jan. 31. Retrieved from https://www.fbi.gov/news/stories/a-byte-out-of-history-10-million-hack.

United States Federal Bureau of Investigations (FBI). (2019a) Cyber crime. *What We Investigate*. Retrieved from https://www.fbi.gov/investigate/cyber.

United States Federal Bureau of Investigations (FBI). (2019b) Addressing threats to the Nation's cybersecurity. *Documents*. Retrieved from https://www.fbi.gov/file-repository/addressing-threats-to-the-nations-cybersecurity-1.pdf/view.

United States Federal Bureau of Investigations (FBI). (2019c) Most wanted. *White Collar Crimes*. Retrieved from https://www.fbi.gov/wanted/wcc/jorge-iglesias-vazquez.

United States General Accountability Office (GAO). (2007) Cost of prisons: Bureau of Prisons needs better data to assess alternatives for acquiring low and minimum security facilities. Report to the Subcommittees on Commerce, Justice, and Sciences, Senate and House Appropriations Committees, *Highlights of GAO*. Oct. Washington, D.C.: U.S. GAO.

United States Occupational Safety and Health Administration (OSHA). (2019) About OSHA. United States Department of Labor. Retrieved from https://www.osha.gov/aboutosha.

United States Occupational Safety and Health Administration (OSHA). (2019) State plans. U.S. Department of Labor. Retrieved from https://www.osha.gov/dcsp/osp/.

United States Occupational Safety and Health Administration (OSHA). (2019) Worker falls 22 feet to death, 4 months after OSHA cites employer for same job site: Louisville employer faces $320K in fines for serial disregard of fall protection. *OSHA News Release—Region 5*. Retrieved from https://www.osha.gov/news/newsreleases/region5/08012016.

United States Senate General Accountability Office (GAO). (2019) About GAO: Overview. Retrieved from https://www.gao.gov/about/.

United States Senate. (2016) Regulatory reforms to improve equity market structure: hearing before the Subcommittee on Securities, Insurance, and Investment of the Committee on Banking, Housing, and Urban Affairs, United States Senate, One Hundred Fourteenth Congress, second session, on examining recent efforts by the SEC and FINRA in aiding the function and stability of the equity markets, and identifying key issues under consideration to reduce market complexity, increase operational stability, and promote efficiency, competition, and capital formation, Mar. 3, 2016. Monograph, U.S. Government Publishing Office.

United States Securities and Exchange Commission. (2019) What we do. Retrieved from https://www.sec.gov/Article/whatwedo.html.

Wachtel, K. (2011) Listen to the Raj Rajaratnam wiretaps. *Business Insider*. Mar. 14. Retrieved from https://www.businessinsider.com/listen-to-the-raj-rajaratnam-wiretaps-2011-3.

Chapter FIFTEEN

Diagnosis and Treatment of White Collar and Corporate Crime[1]

Eating the elephant one bite at a time

"An incident is just the tip of the iceberg, a sign of a much larger problem below the surface."

—*Don Brown, Vice President and Director,*
BasicSafe, Inc.

Chapter Objectives

- Explore areas where employers can help in preventing white collar crime.
- Review concepts presented earlier in the book, including the formal and informal structures of the workplace.
- Characterize additional triggers for white collar criminality, including drug and alcohol abuses.
- Identify the roadblocks in white collar crime prevention.

Key Terms

Boiler room operation
Cold calling
Corporate Social Responsibility (CSR)
Garnishment

Moral appeal
Penny stocks
Pump and dump
Rogue employees

---

[1] An earlier version of this chapter was published as "Corporate Financial Crime: Social Diagnosis and Treatment" in the *Journal of Financial Crime* (2009, Vol. 16, No. 1).

INTRODUCTION

As we started our journey through this book, we identified early on that white collar crime just isn't on the radar of law enforcement and the public in general, except in the case of high-profile defendants. Even after the flurry of crimes being committed in the financial sector during the 1960s, 1980s, and more recently the 2000s, it is as if there is collective amnesia. We might be morally horrified for a moment, but then the next big conventional crime happens (e.g., serial killings). The public tends to wring their hands over crimes that, except for a select few, have no direct impact on them. And yet, as we noted early on, most of us will be affected by white collar crime sometime in our lives.

By necessity, because regulatory systems are dependent on the political environment, this chapter is more focused on theories of controlling white collar crime. As these suggestions are theoretical, they are by no means the only routes to crime-free workplaces, nor do we suggest that any of these theories are used in practice today. It is merely one roadmap, along with regulation, that might curb white collar crime in a number of different professions.

First and foremost, the biggest challenge to curbing white collar crime is the culture in business within the past few decades. As Strickler (2019, p. x) has warned, "Today the world is dominated by an idea I call 'financial maximization'. The belief that in any decision, the right choice is whichever option makes the most money. This is the default setting that runs most of the world." Prior to the 1970s, what drove markets was the effort to build the middle classes, which in turn would contribute to a post-industrial consumer economy. Owning a home in the "right" neighborhood, driving the "right" car for your social status, and having the economic power to keep up with the Joneses[2] was an unfortunate side effect of shifting to a consumer-driven economy. We can assume that the need to give the outward appearances of affluence may motivate some individuals to cross the line and commit white collar crimes. This, to a large extent, is motivation driven by greed, and an explanation for the white collar crimes we have discussed throughout this book.

We have also discussed in some detail about how fear can drive people to commit crimes as well, whether we are talking about white collar crimes or conventional crimes. Piquero (2012) suggests that the fear of falling (fear of falling hypothesis) or more accurately, the fear of failing, may motivate some people to commit crimes if they believe that they may lose everything they have worked for. The potential of losing financial security, coupled with the opportunity to commit a crime, may make for a perfect recipe for white collar offending.

If there is nothing to prevent the crime from happening, as suggested in Cohen and Felson's (1979) Routine Activities Theory, it may be a foregone conclusion that a crime will be committed. If you will recall, Routine Activities

---

[2] The expression "keeping up with the Joneses" refers to the desire to keep up with or outdo your neighbors in the appearances of material wealth.

Theory proposes that if there is a motivated offender, no one around to stop the crime, and a potential victim or victims, there is far greater probability that a crime will be committed. In this case, we may look to the intersection of Piquero's (2012) fear of falling hypothesis, along with Routine Activities Theory, in order to find some solutions to white collar crimes.

One of the first strategies in combating white collar crime is to raise public awareness. It can be challenging, as a large percentage of the public only have a vague understanding of what white collar crime is. Even in criminology and criminal justice programs, it may get passing attention (Wright and Friedrichs, 1991; Friedrichs, 2009). It is only recently that politicians have publicly chastised corporations for unethical, if not criminal, practices, as demonstrated by Senator Elizabeth Warren's continued campaign for finance and consumer protection reform. To a large extent, politicians can't be wholly blamed for their inattention. To go after corporations requires biting the hand that feeds you, as those running for public office seek out donations from the public and private sectors.

There is an age-old question of "how do you eat an elephant." The answer is that you have to eat it, or in this case, tackle the overwhelming problem of white collar crime, one bite at a time. With no easy solutions, it takes the coordination and cooperation of lawmakers, regulatory agencies, and the business world. As we have noted throughout this book, these separate entities are not always on the same page, or even on the same side of the law.

In this chapter, we explore some possible tools to diagnose and treat crime in the workplace. Using a synthesis of existing theories in economic sociology and criminology, we explore some of the flaws that might be corrected. We will additionally explore concrete strategies and policy changes that regulators and corporate decision makers might consider. The key goal is to discover ways by which organizations can increase their social responsibilities while promoting policy and regulatory change in the current economic climate.

Unless you are notably victimized with your life savings erased due to financial crime, there is generally not the same collective cry for justice and reform as in the case of conventional crimes. We have also noted that for all the lack of interest in reform, at least within the general population, white collar crime results in more financial loss to individuals as compared to street crime. White collar crime is rarely broadcasted (and rebroadcasted) on television or Internet news.

As we have already seen throughout this book, corporate malfeasance and social indiscretions are handled more frequently as civil matters, not as criminal offenses. This may only result in modest fines, comparatively speaking, and little in the way of retribution for the victims. In most cases, the offenders are not contrite. Even if white collar criminals land in criminal court, like most conventional crimes, it results in plea-bargaining (Shapiro, 1984), as we saw for some of the defendants in the "Varsity Blues" college admissions scandal and as we will see in the last case in this chapter of Jordan Belfort, "the Wolf of Wall Street."

As white collar and corporate crime is rarely committed by all members of an organization and we can frequently point to an individual or a small group that is the only offender, we need to reexamine individual behavior and revisit the competitive structure of corporate life in order to "diagnose" and "treat" corporate crime. As in understanding disease in medicine, by "diagnosing" the root causes of corporate crime, it offers us better opportunities to find successful "treatments." The focus in this final chapter of this book is on exploring solutions to white collar criminality.

Perhaps the biggest roadblock to implementing preventative measures is that researchers in the social sciences do not always come to an agreement on solutions, nor are they necessarily listened to by policy and lawmakers. To a large extent, it is the proverbial Tower of Babel. For those less familiar with the biblical tale, the Tower of Babel (Genesis 11:1-9) was a story about how people who speak different languages will not be able to effectively communicate with one another. As Sutherland (1973) observed, just as economists do not look at business through the criminological lens, criminologists are much less likely to look at crime through the business lens. Likewise, there can be a divide between criminologists and individuals with practical experience in the criminal justice professions.

We will not be able to address the larger issue of cybersecurity or how to prevent terrorism and political crime. It is a practical fact that prevention measures are rapidly changing. In this chapter we will focus only on the social dynamics that can be monitored. This in itself can be challenging to try and do so without intruding on the personal lives of workers. We will also focus on some practical business solutions that might help to prevent or at least reduce incidences of white collar crime in the workplace.

DIAGNOSING INDIVIDUAL WHITE COLLAR CRIME AND MALFEASANCE

The concern with looking at the characteristics of the individual white collar criminal is that we are too quick to impose a stereotype. As we have witnessed in this textbook, there is a wide range of individuals, in a variety of professions, who have committed crimes. It would be difficult to come up with a single set of characteristics, like poverty or drug addiction, as in conventional crimes. For example, it is difficult, if not impossible, to compare the insider trading crimes committed by Dennis Levine and his cronies with the crimes committed by President Nixon and some members of his administration. There are, however, a number of theories that can be applied to white collar criminals that can bridge the crime types themselves.

One core theory to explain white collar crime and perhaps be valuable in creating a diagnosis, is self-control theory. Except in rare cases, like those discussed in Chapter 5 on corporate crime, not all elites within a given organization or industry will commit crimes. We saw examples of widespread malfeasance in the cases of Dennis Levine, the Lincoln Savings and Loan scandal, and Enron, which were examined in examples given in this book. But for all of the Dennis Levines out there committing white collar crime, millions of others in the same industry are not doing so.

Self-control theory helps to explain elite crimes committed by individuals, whereas social bonding theory is a better explanation for lower-level employees, as in the case of petty embezzlement. Self-control theories are pretty self-explanatory—people commit crimes because they cannot control their compulsion to commit a crime. In social bonding theory, applied to white collar crime, the individual is less likely to commit a crime if they have faith in their employer or place of business, they are committed to their jobs, and are actively involved in day-to-day operations (Akers, 2000).

As an alternative theory, one might consider that the social bonding theory (Hirschi, 1969) would be a good explanation for white collar malfeasance. However, since the premise of the theory is that there are weak social bonds, it is a more difficult theory to endorse as an elite white collar crime explanation. On the contrary, elite criminals are very committed to those they are participating in schemes with.

If we look at the example of lower-level white collar crimes, as in the example of a cashier embezzling from their employer, it makes social bonding theory a much more plausible explanation. The cashier might feel like they are being treated unfairly by their boss or the company they work for, and feel entitled to dip into the cash drawer from time to time. It is a more difficult leap to use the social bonding theory to explain why laypersons help count out the money from the church collection plate, only to pocket some of the bills for their personal use. It is assumed that people join religious organizations in order to create social bonds with people who share the same faith, which is in itself a form of social cohesion.

Social bonding theories cannot be completely dismissed even if we are looking at elite criminals and if we look at modern society. As we inched our way towards an industrial society, and certainly in our post-industrial age, people moved from being connected with, and committed to, a small group of people, to living in impersonal cities where there is less commitment to community. To further complicate matters, people change jobs much more frequently today than ever before. According a Bureau of Labor Statistics study conducted in 2015, younger Baby Boomers (born between 1957 and 1964) changed their jobs an average of 11.7 times between ages 18 and 48 (BLS, n.d.). That does not foster a sense of loyalty to any one organization or to fellow employees. There may not be the same urgency to build trust if one already has one foot out the door, ready to jump onto the next job opportunity.

The reality in most organizations is that opportunities to advance in one's career are limited. There are only so many advancement prospects when examining the typical corporate or organizational ladder, yet this is part of the mantras and myths in capitalist societies — "if you work hard, you will most definitely get ahead" and "the deserving will be promoted". As we have discussed in other chapters, workers today are finding advancement by making lateral or horizontal moves to better paying positions in other companies once they are feeling that they are stagnating in their current job. Again, this does not foster loyalty to any one company. With mid-life career changes, it may not represent loyalty even to a particular profession.

In light of the limited opportunities to move up the corporate ladder, as well as the stiff competition for those positions, workers may feel compelled to commit any number of indiscretions to advance in their careers (Ermann and Lundman, 1996). When they do move up the ladder with promotions, they are more likely to identify with their jobs and the organization they work for (Collins, 1975). At this point, criminal behavior, if any, might move from being good for the individual to being good for the company. Upper management positions offer rewards in better salaries as well as bestowing more power and prestige on the manager. This also comes with more responsibility to stakeholders.

We should caution that middle management jobs have been rapidly vanishing since the 1990s. In fact, by some accounts, they are virtually extinct (Finkelstein, 2015). The traditional career ladder is practically nonexistent, with the workload itself remaining. This begs the question, where does work land if middle managers are no longer there? The answer is that beginning in the 1990s, work became more automated with technology, plus some of the work of middle managers was being moved down to lower level employees. This coincided with changing the labels we use for positions. Where a salesperson used to be called a "sales clerk," now they may be called a "sales associate," a name that carries the suggestion that the position is more important and part of a team. Secretaries and file clerks may now be called "administrative assistants" or "executive assistants." Yet incomes overall have stagnated since the 1990s with little compensation, save the new titles, for the additional workloads placed on the shoulders of lower-level employees.

Workers began to be told in the 1990s that they were "empowered" to make decisions for themselves, including quality control that had been passed over to technology. For example, tax preparers used to have to have the income tax returns they filled out for their clients reviewed by a quality control team in some of the larger tax preparation companies. Once technology took over that role in the form of computer software, flagging the tax returns automatically for any discrepancies, quality control departments were no longer needed. Though it streamlined operations in tax preparation offices, this resulted in quality control professionals being displaced.

If promotion is no longer an incentive to be on one's best behavior, then what other positive reinforcements could be used? Some companies began offering the Employee Stock Option Programs (ESOPs), while others employed team building exercises. Unfortunately, the most effective way of controlling some workers is with the threat of firing or, when there is a downturn in the economy, as in the case of a recession, or more recently with the COVID-19 pandemic, the threat of layoff.

IDENTIFYING ROGUE EMPLOYEES

The use of the term *rogue employees* is more commonly used in the information technology sector (IT). However, it is an apt name for employees who are, by their actions, disruptive to an organization. Whether operating out in the open or covertly, the rogue employee will not follow rules and may be responsible for upending the work environment either by resentment or by generally embracing anarchy and nonconformity.

The difficulty in hiring professionals and experts in a particular field is that they may also know how to fly under the radar when they are deviant or criminal. For instance, a corporate spy will have to have the expertise to get hired at a rival company, as well as knowing strategies on how to not get caught. Sometimes the criminal is right under the nose of authorities, hiding in plain sight.

In other cases, the rogue employee may be openly contemptuous of their workplace and is most dangerous when they are on the way out the door, either with an anticipated firing or voluntary resignation. In extreme, and thankfully rare, cases an ex-employee will return to their former place of employment after being fired, seeking revenge. They do so with a mission to commit workplace violence that can result in a number of fatalities. In many cases, they will take their own lives in the process. As workplace violence is underreported, the best estimates for the Bureau of Labor Statistics is that around 78 percent of workplace homicides are attributed to shootings (BLS, 2013). Many of these homicides are committed by disgruntled employees, some of whom are suffering from mental illnesses.

According to Grimes (2015), a columnist for InfoWorld, an information technology media company, there are seven signs to look for in identifying rogue employees (available at https://www.infoworld.com/article/2888470/7-warning-signs-rogue-employees.html):

1. *Unexpectedly fails a background check.* In some more sensitive fields, it is not "one-and-done" background check at hiring. There may be periodic background checks, including into personal finances.
2. *States that past employers didn't trust them.* Someone who plays the "victim card" without taking responsibility for their own mistakes can be a potential liability.
3. *Knows information that they shouldn't.* Concern here is how they accessed the information in the first place. Are they regularly eavesdropping on conversations that are confidential? Have they been accessing files that they do not have the authority to see?
4. *Says that they can hack a coworker or company systems.* This item is more specific to the IT industry, but can apply to any company that is using computer technology. In this day and age, we would be hard pressed to find a company that isn't keeping their records digitally.

5. *Switches screens away from company assets as you walk up.* It is not unheard of to pop into a coworker's office or cubicle to have them quickly close out the Facebook app, Internet shopping site, or solitaire game. Workers who have time on their hands can be embarrassed about their non-productive activities if they are not given specific permission to use their free time in whatever way they see fit as long as they get their work done. However, if an employee is working on a company website or database that they do not have the authority to review, this requires investigation into why they are doing so.

6. *They never take vacation time.* Let's face it: the West, along with some Asian countries, is populated with workaholics. People will work insane hours to get ahead or to prove their worthiness, particularly in some industries like finance. However, the individual who *never* takes vacation time may be afraid to do so because they are constantly covering up their tracks so they don't get caught. In fact, they may be eager to cover for other employees when they take time off so that they have access to more company information.

7. *Leaves the company angry.* There is a reason why firings or layoffs are more likely to happen at the end of the day on Friday. Generally, firings and layoffs come as a surprise to employees, even if there are rumors. In this way the situation is somewhat defused, as the ex-employee has the weekend to cool off. However, there is concern if the employee has access to sensitive company information that they can download on their way out the door, or if they have had a lot of company privileges.

Law in the Real World: Bruce Bagley, Money-Laundering Expert

(Source: Romo, 2019; U.S. Department of Justice, 2019)

We are always surprised when one of the "good guys" turns out to be one of the "bad guys." In the case of Bruce Bagley, renowned expert on organized crime, it turned out that the saying, "it takes one to know one" is pretty darn apt. In November 2019, Bagley, a professor in the International Studies program at the University of Miami, was arrested and charged with conspiracy to commit money laundering and money laundering (U.S. DOJ, 2019a).[3]

---

[3] NOTE: These are two separate charges. One for planning it, the other for actually following through with money laundering.

EXHIBIT 15.1 | Among Bruce Bagley's More Popular Books Is *Drug Trafficking, Organized Crime, and Violence in the Americas Today*

At 73 years old, Bagley had long established himself as a researcher in the area of organized crime. Among his more popular books is *Drug Trafficking,*

Organized Crime, and Violence in the Americas Today (Bagley and Rosen, 2017), one of his recent publications.[4]

Bagley is being accused of taking part in a fraud scheme involving millions of dollars. Allegedly, he has been laundering money for corrupt foreign nationals who were accepting bribes and embezzling from a public works project in Venezuela (Romo, 2019). He was essentially laundering money that had been stolen from the Venezuelan people, who are already living in difficult times due to political and economic upheaval in recent years.

According to Bagley's indictment, he was able to do so by opening a bank account on behalf of a bogus company that he owned and operated. Through this phony company, he was able to funnel money from corrupt officials. The money was attributed to contracts that authorities claim were fraudulent. For his part in the scheme, Bagley is said to have pocketed approximately 10 percent of the $3 million in funds stolen, or about $300,000 (U.S. DOJ, 2019a).

To put this in perspective, the website *Glassdoor* reports that the average salary of a full-time professor at the University of Miami is $230,269 a year (glassdoor.com, 2018). Considering that Bagley served as an assistant dean at one point in his career at University of Miami, it is conceivable that he was making even more income than average in a legitimate job. To put this further into perspective, the average yearly salary for a full-time professor in the United States, according to the American Association of University Professors (AAUP), is just over $100,000 (Flaherty, 2018).

Considering Bagley's income as a professor, added to what royalties he might have earned for his books and other writings, it seems unfathomable that someone who knew the dangers and consequences of getting caught would take such a risk. Why would he risk his career and reputation when he was already assumed to be making an income that placed him, at the very least, in the upper middle class? Yet for whatever compulsion driving him, Bagley risked everything for an amount of money that may equal only around one year's worth of his legitimate income. We should note that at age 73, Bagley likely was close to retiring, though there is generally no set retirement age for those working in academia.

There is the real possibility that if he is convicted, with his advanced age, Bagley will spend the rest of his life in prison. FBI Assistant Director-in Charge William F. Sweeney Jr. stated that, "About the only lesson to be learned from Professor Bagley today is that involving oneself in public corruption, bribery, and embezzlement schemes is going to lead to an indictment." (U.S. DOJ, 2019a, retrieved from https://www.justice.gov/usao-

---

[4] Bagley's books are still available on Amazon.com, so it can be assumed that he will still be making money on royalties while under indictment, though those funds may ultimately go to legal fees and possibly restitution fines.

sdny/pr/professor-international-studies-charged-international-money-laundering-scheme). As we should note in all of these cases, and as the U.S. Department of Justice (2019) reminds us, the accused is, in theory, presumed to be innocent unless or until convicted of their charges.

Discussion Question

1. We have asked this question before in context of "respectable" people working in the financial sector. Why would a well-respected expert in organized crime take the chance of getting involved in any crime?
2. Since Bagley is a so-called expert in organized crime, even if his research is solid, how credible will his research be considered, even if he is not convicted of his crimes?
3. As we asked in the beginning of this case, does it "take one to know one"? In other words, do these type of criminals have to understand both sides of the law in order to successfully get away with their crimes?

We should not be looking for criminals in every expert out there. However, as we cautioned in Chapter 2 on how real organizations work, organizations should not resort to ceremonial evaluations, as described by Meyer and Rowan (1977). Many times, the experts, those with more knowledge or technical skills, are evaluated by managers who know little about what the experts actually do. They may not readily catch general bad practices, much less unethical or criminal behavior.

It is perhaps the best course of action to have experts evaluate experts. Certainly, any companies that are started by experts for purposes other than consulting may do with closer inspection, at least by regulators. Even consulting companies could be hiding more sinister motives. However, any type of monitoring of experts may be unrealistic given that most companies, as we have already noted, do operate aboveboard, and regulatory agencies are notoriously short-handed.

DIAGNOSING WHITE COLLAR CRIME AND MALFEASANCE COMMITTED BY GROUPS

So where does the impulse to commit crimes, even if there is the risk of detection and the ruination of one's professional reputation, come from? If we borrow from economics, exchange theory helps to explain why groups of people will make the decision to collectively commit crimes. Exchange theory, as classically defined in economics and sociology, proposes that in order for a transaction to take place, there has to be value to both parties in the exchange (Turner, 2002). Georg

Simmel (1997; Turner, 2002, p. 259) proposed that there are four characteristics in social exchange:

1. The desire for a valued object that one does not have (e.g., the buyer);
2. The possession of the valued object by an identifiable other (e.g., the seller);
3. The offer of an object of value to secure the desired object from another (e.g., the seller); and
4. The acceptance of the offer (from the buyer) by the possessor (seller) of the valued object.

To put this in more concrete terms, say you had a car to sell. You would only be able to sell that car if (a) there was an interested buyer and (b) you could agree to the terms of the sale. The same can go for transactions between white collar criminals. In an episode from the Network show *Better Call Saul* (Gilligan and Gould, 2015, Season 1), there was a pharmaceutical employee who stole prescription drugs from his employer. He did so with the intention of selling them to a drug dealer in exchange for a considerable amount of cash. Before that transaction could be successfully executed, the pharmaceutical employee had to be satisfied that he got the right amount of money (by counting it) and the drug dealer had to make sure that he was receiving the pharmaceuticals he had ordered (by inspecting the bottles). We should note that in this fictional example, we had both white collar and conventional crime taking place. Had there not been a satisfactory exchange, as the episode implied, there could be bloodshed.

White collar crimes involving some sort of exchange are generally not so gruesome as our *Better Call Saul* example. Remember we are not discussing conventional theft, burglary, or drug-related crimes that are largely explained by the need for money or drugs or both. In white collar crime, the endgame may not be money, but power. In exchange theory, the benefit of entering into a conspiracy with others outweighs the possibility of being detected.

If we also look at exchange theories in sociology, combined with social network theories that we discussed earlier in this book, they offer additional reassurance that we might be on the right track of figuring out why and how white collar criminals find each other within a company or industry. In fact, more contemporary exchange theories include discussions of social network theory (Turner, 2002).

You would think that if one person in a group of professionals started talking conspiracy, the rest would jump in and tell them that this is a bad idea. But it may be the very processes of competition in business that has them egging each other on instead of trying to prevent them from making what might be the biggest mistake of their lives. These are the very characteristics that Blau, an exchange theorist in sociology, talked about: how it is the attraction to one another in a group, friendly competition, and the possibility of exchanging and combining talents that is the glue that helps to keep members of the group together (Turner, 1991). The same can be said about the white collar crime conspiracy.

Many times, it is simply more lucrative to pull off a financial crime as a group, with a false sense of security that there is safety in numbers, more so than if they tried to commit crimes on their own. An example of this is in an insider trading ring (see Chapters 3 and 4) that views trading information for information or information for money as a fair exchange. Just think of how valuable a player in a network you might be if you possess all the juicy information that can make you and others wealthy, even if it is illegally. But as we already indicated earlier in the book, the more people who are in on the secret, the more likely that secret will get out.

Law in the Real World: HealthSouth

(Source: CFO.com, 2017; Abelson and Freudenheim, 2003; FBI, 2003)

On the heels of the rising health care costs, companies that provide insurance and health care are increasingly looked upon as nothing more than money-making propositions in the United States. Profit for shareholders, which we have already demonstrated, is the driving force behind many business decisions in publicly traded companies. It becomes the number one concern of management, who may themselves be watching out for their jobs. Health insurance is viewed as a necessary evil, even for the healthiest of individuals. Simply put, you as the holder of an insurance policy are gambling that you will get sick. Insurance companies, on the other hand, are gambling that you will continue to be healthy, not needing to use the insurance you have paid for. However, those who need medical attention want faith that their health care providers, at the very least, are not primarily operating on a financial motive.

HealthSouth, a company founded in 1984, initially offered outpatient health care, and later primarily owned and operated rehabilitation hospitals. The rehabilitation hospitals eventually attracted celebrity patients from the sports world, including Shaquille O'Neal, Michael Jordan, and Roger Clemens, with their "hip and young" vibe (Abelson and Freudenheim, 2003). HealthSouth was based out of Birmingham, Alabama, but quickly grew into a national company with rehabilitation hospitals in a number of states plus Puerto Rico. In 1986 HealthSouth went public, inviting investors to purchase stock in the company. This was unusually fast for a company in its infancy. On the face of things, it looked like there was no way that the company could fail. But under the slick surface, HealthSouth accounting practices were none too healthy.

The founders, among them Richard Scrushy, who started the company on a reported $55,000, were millionaires overnight. Along with the founders, top management also had personal stock investments in company.

This is not an unusual practice, but the exponential rise of the value of the stock is. As former CFO Aaron Beam explains it, he went from having a net worth of less than $100,000 to having the ability to pay cash for a Mercedes Benz and plunk down $30,000 for Hermes ties (CFO.com, 2017).

Unfortunately for investors, the actual income that was being generated by the company fell far short of financial analysts' predictions. Instead of coming clean with the disappointing numbers, Scrushy falsified approximately $2.6 billion in income in financial reports. Not only were financial documents falsified, there were false medical claims filed with Medicare.

When authorities caught up with him, Scrushy became one of the first executives to be charged under the Sarbanes-Oxley Act. If you recall, the act was passed in response to Enron, and executives could no longer claim innocence of bad accounting practices in their firms. In total, the federal government charged Scrushy with 85 criminal counts. The FBI (2003, retrieved from https://archives.fbi.gov/archives/news/stories/2003/november/health_110403) stated that among the charges were:

- Leading a scheme that inflated the company's earnings by an estimated $2.7 billion; covering tracks with phony financial statements and filings;
- Using stock options, bonuses, and salary payments from inflated results to pad his own bank account by some $267 million [USD];
- Using that money to buy real estate, aircraft, boats, luxury cars, jewelry, and other items;
- Doling out large compensation packages to fellow conspirators to keep them quiet about the scheme; and
- Deliberately making false public statements about HealthSouth's growth and profitability.

Though Scrushy appeared to be the ringleader, he had a number of accomplices. Senior employees at HealthSouth came to dread Monday morning meetings with Scrushy, who had a reputation of being somewhat of a bully. (Abelson and Freudenheim, 2003). Scrushy ruled with intimidation, which can partially explain the complicity of Scrushy's co-conspirators. Federal prosecutors believed that the financial records of HealthSouth had been falsified from the time the company went public in 1986.

As for Scrushy, founder and former CEO of HealthSouth, he was forced to give up the lavish lifestyle that he had so carefully cultivated. He served nearly six years in federal prison after receiving a reduced sentence handed down in appeals in 2012 (Pavlo, 2012). In total, 15 HealthSouth employees, including Scrushy, pleaded guilty to various charges of fraud. Of the 15 that pleaded guilty, 14 cooperated with the federal government in the Health-South case. Hannibal Crumpler, HealthSouth's comptroller, did not take a plea bargain, to his detriment. Instead, he stood trial and was found guilty of his charges, including the falsification of financial statements. Crumpler ultimately received the harshest sentence, eight years in federal prison.

HealthSouth senior executives were not the only ones caught up in the financial scandal. Former Alabama Governor Don Siegelman was released from federal prison after serving five years for convictions of bribery and obstruction of justice (Lyman, 2019). Siegelman, who had served as governor from 1999 to 2003, had been accused of receiving $500,000 from Scrushy. In return, Scrushy would be given a seat on the Certificate of Need board, which has the responsibility of oversight on hospital improvements and expansions (Lyman, 2019).

Siegelman's defense was that the exchange of money between himself and Scrushy was "normal in the course of politics." (Lyman, 2019, retrieved from https://www.montgomeryadvertiser.com/story/news/2019/06/14/don-siegelman-wins-release-supervision/1454948001/)

At the time of the downfall of most of its senior executives, HealthSouth was the biggest provider of outpatient surgery, diagnostic imaging, and rehabilitation services (FBI, 2003). After the scandal, HealthSouth was subsequently rebranded in 2017 as Encompass Health, shifting to providing inpatient and home-based care, including rehabilitation services, with an entirely new management team (Encompass Health, n.d.). Mark Tarr, the current CEO, stated that the name change helped to create a seamless transition, though the name change cost the company between $25 and $35 million to accomplish (AP, 2017).

The Encompass Health Corporation, in good faith, has also agreed to pay $48 million to settle disputes over Medicare fraud allegation against HealthSouth under the False Claims Act (U.S. DOJ, 2019b). By doing so, the company did not have to be dismantled, no doubt saving investors further losses in the long term, as well as preserving some of the jobs and reputations of innocent HealthSouth employees.

Discussion Questions

1. As big as this scandal was, why might whistleblowers be afraid to come forward?
2. Is there something about the health care industry that might lend itself to scandals involving a number of people, rather than the "lone wolf" offender?
3. Besides investors, who else might have lost confidence in the health care industry after the HealthSouth scandal?

When caught, there is always the risk that everyone in a white collar conspiracy will start pointing fingers at one another in order to cut a deal with prosecutors. This is bad for the crime ring, great for prosecuting attorneys, and better for society in general. We certainly saw evidence of this in the college entrance exams and admissions scandal, where co-conspirators have turned on one another. We have also seen this in the arrests, convictions, and plea bargaining around the Russian election meddling scandal in the 2016 Presidential election, outlined in the Mueller Report (2019).

We cannot discount that when a group of people commit elite crimes together, there is a chance that corporate crime is justified as being for the "social good" of the organization. If a publicly traded company is covering up some type of misadventure or crime, management may be thinking about the broader consequences of it being disclosed to the public or to regulators. Not only can it cost the company money, but it might result in the loss of customers and investors. Covering up the problem may save jobs and help preserve investors' portfolios, as misguided as that line of thinking might be.

LOOKING FOR THE INFORMAL STRUCTURE

We have already established that the informal structure, in this case the social network, might be more influential in getting people to do their jobs or, more sinisterly, commit crimes. Though there are rules in most companies and corporations on dating between coworkers, there are really no rules on who you can hang out with outside of work. Employers could hardly mandate who you become friends with in the workplace.

Nevertheless, employers can dictate certain aspects of your social life at work. For example, coworkers who are dating may be required to sign disclosure statements in their human resources department to avoid any possible sexual harassment claims. Many employers have within their company rules that coworker dating is forbidden altogether, often called "non-fraternization" policies (Camp, 2010). Though there have been some lawsuits over the legality of these company policies, for the most part, state legislation has done little to ban non-fraternization policies (Camp, 2010).

As much as employers can, to some extent, dictate your romantic life at work, they cannot dictate who you make friends with through your professional connections. What is of greatest concern is when activities between coworkers outside of work interferes with getting their jobs done during the work week. More serious to consider is if work-related relationships result in collective white collar crimes, as we have seen in a number of chapters of this book.

THE DRUG AND ALCOHOL ADDICTION CONNECTION

Though there has been little research on the types of drugs used by people working in the banking industry on Wall Street, there are a number of substantiated rumors that it "snows on Wall Street," particularly during the heyday of 1980s mergers and acquisition frenzy. One can only surmise that there might have been a number of addicts working in finance jobs at that time. With cocaine being a relatively expensive drug compared to other stimulants, addiction to this drug, or any drug, may result in criminal behavior to pay for the habit. In this, white collar workers who believe they require the consumption of street drugs to maintain their "edge" in business have this in common with some sex workers. For example, a study of Cambodian sex workers found that one prevalent drug of choice was amphetamine-like stimulants, presumably to keep up with the late hours of their profession (Carrico et al., 2016).

More recently, white collar workers in high-stress careers that require long days on the job have turned to prescription drugs to keep them alert. Swab (2014) reported that Adderall, a drug used to treat attention deficit disorders (ADD, ADHD), has replaced cocaine among investment bankers. According to Swab (2014), any first-year analyst can expect to work long hours doing tedious work in the post-2008 crash environment of Wall Street. Like college students, who have reportedly been abusing the drug Adderall at alarming rates (Rolland and Smith, 2017), the competitive nature of Wall Street has some employees turning to Adderall to keep up with the pace.

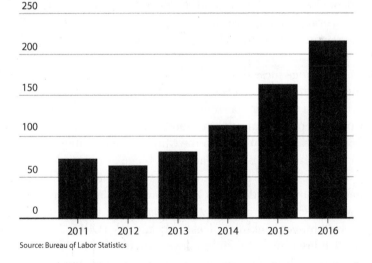

Ominous Trend

Deaths in the workplace from unintentional overdoses have nearly tripled in six years, amid a worsening opioid crisis in the U.S.

Fatalities from non-medical use of drugs or alcohol at work

Source: Bureau of Labor Statistics

EXHIBIT 15.2 ‖ Fatalities from Non-Medical Use of Drugs or Alcohol at Work

Being that street drugs, including prescription drugs on the black market, are illegal and carry the risk of incarceration, the more socially acceptable drug of choice is alcohol. Of course, alcohol has the opposite effect of stimulants, in that it acts as a depressant. The danger is when alcohol consumption becomes part of the culture of "doing business as usual." Clients and potential customers are often wined and dined, sometimes to the detriment of the people trying to secure sales or contracts or those on the receiving end of the wooing. Alcohol-related illnesses can ultimately result in loss of productivity and in some cases, the loss of a career for the alcoholic. Again, there is the real possibility that excessive alcohol consumption will result in poor judgement, including criminal behavior.

In the 1990s, there was a rash of workers' compensation cases filed that were alcohol-related. A study of these cases (Spain and Ramsey, 2000) found that there was a particular danger in sales-focused careers. Sales positions can often require travel and, as we have already noted, wooing clients and customers with alcohol-fueled meals or business discussed over cocktails. From Spain and Ramsey (2000, p. 264) and West (1999), the following are a sample of the cases coming out of the mid-1990s involving accidents attributed to alcohol consumed during business meetings:

- An inebriated saleswoman was killed on her way home after lunch meeting. (*Balk v. Austin Ford Logan, Inc.*, New York, 1995)
- An inebriated car sales manager driving a company car was killed on his way home after a dinner meeting. (*Beattie v. Industrial Commission*, Illinois, 1995)
- An inebriated service manager was injured driving a company car during a workday. (*Bridges v. Reliable Chevrolet*, Missouri, 1997)

Hence, alcohol-related injuries and deaths are not only costly to employers, but to states' workers' compensation systems. Even if there is no judgement awarded to the petitioner, court costs alone can be staggering.

We should note that there is less encouragement to indulge in alcoholic beverage at business meetings these days, especially if the attendees are driving. Stricter drunk driving laws since the 1980s would, in theory, prevent people from getting behind the wheel of a car after consuming alcohol. However, the U.S. Department of Transportation reports that approximately one person dies from an alcohol-related car accident every 50 minutes in the United States (National Transportation Traffic Safety Administration, n.d.). In addition, binge drinking, defined as the consumption of an average of seven drinks in one sitting, has significantly increased within the past decade. According to a 2015 study by Centers for Disease Control and Prevention (CDC), approximately 17.1 percent of U.S. adults 18 years old and over reported binge drinking at least once a week (CDC, 2020). Companies are at risk for liability if one of their employees injures themselves or others while under the influence of drugs or alcohol during work-related activities.

When employers are faced with employees with drug or alcohol problems, particularly in the United States, the first instinct is to let them go. The good news, if any, is that problem drinking is often noticeable before the individual is an alcoholic by clinical definition (Spain and Ramsey, 2000). Human resources departments, at least in some industries, are now more likely to provide referrals to health care providers and counseling services when employees come forward with drug or alcohol issues that are interfering with their work. Increasingly employers are enforcing drug-free zones at work, as it is the responsibility of human resources personnel to ensure the safety of all employees (U.S. Substance Abuse and Mental Health Services Administration, n.d.)

FINANCIAL COMPENSATION AND INCENTIVES

There is much to be said about making a small fortune, though for many people, happiness does not come with money. However, for those who are driven by the financial compensation for their labors, it can be the biggest motivator for their work performance. In other words, they are working to live, and who they are is wrapped up both in their profession and the income it generates. For others, the thrill of the possibility to amass a fortune may result in "cooking the books"[5], much as we saw in the HealthSouth case.

One way to help stem employee malfeasance is for employers to supply them with financial compensation and competitive incentives packages. They should adequately pay them for their education, expertise, and years of experience. If employees are only paid just enough to keep the roof over their heads, resentment may be bubbling under the surface. For instance, certain housing markets have boomed where the tech industry has moved in with well-paid employees, making rent and mortgages out of the reach of those working in other industries whose wages are not keeping up with inflation. This, of course, is not the fault of the employers, but as the cost of living rises, the so-called "cost of living adjustments" (COLAs) should be regularly reviewed and, if possible, given to employees. These should not be advertised to employees as actual raises based on job performance, but rather the employer's acknowledgement that the cost of living has gone up while wages may not necessarily do the same. Being told a COLA is a raise, rather than keeping wages current with inflation, may result in employee resentment.

The challenge is in convincing for-profit and publicly traded companies who are beholden to shareholders that employee compensation packages should be regularly reviewed. This also includes audits to assure that employees who have been in a company longer and may have stagnant wages are being fairly compensated, as compared to newer employees who may be receiving more competitive salaries to attract them in the first place. As Strickler (2019) cautioned, in recent decades, employees may be more likely to act in self-interest. More alarmingly, Strickler (2019) notes that pay raises often go into paying off college loans and consumer debt, further justifying regular review of any changes in the cost of living for employees.

---

[5] "To cook the books" refers to falsifying financial records, usually to cover up criminal behavior or mistakes being made by a company.

WATCHING OUT FOR WALL STREET PREDATORS

Imagine being fresh out of "B-school" (undergraduate major or MBA program in business management) and you are being recruited to work for a financial institution located on or near Wall Street in Manhattan, New York. You could not help but think that you have managed to land right in the center of the excitement of financial markets. For most of those fresh out of university business schools, this translates to 72+ hour work weeks. For some, they burn out within the first few years. This means that they may have to step back to work at less prestigious banks or brokerage firms, likely taking a cut in pay.

For some of those who can make it through the grueling hours, they thrive, at least for a short time, in the highly charged atmosphere of Wall Street. Like skilled athletes, they hone their craft, climbing up corporate and financial ladders. For the stars in this industry, they will come out the other end of this trial by fire period with corner offices and handsome salaries. Others may ultimately come by their *real* income by abusing the system and committing any number of financial crimes. This may result in defrauding investors and employers. What is alarming is that the ones who are caught might be speculated to be only the tip of the iceberg, as Brown suggests in the opening quote to this chapter.

The lesson to be learned from the "Wolf of Wall Street" story is that if an employee's sales seem to be too good to be true, the employer might want to take a closer look at their sales strategies, particularly in brokerage houses. Investors should likewise be suspicious of promises of quick riches to be made by investments.

Prospective employers should also question why prospective brokers left their previous place of employment. The employee might be bringing in a lot of money to the firm in new business, but if the transactions are not aboveboard, it invites scrutiny and possible investigation by the SEC and/or by the U.S. Attorney's office of the Department of Justice. Even if the offender is the only criminal in the company, it can be damaging to the reputation of a brokerage firm and send investors fleeing. The responsibility of a brokerage firm is to protect itself and to protect its investors.

MORAL APPEALS

One somewhat effective and inexpensive way to combat white collar crime is to launch a *moral appeal*. Mason and Mason (1992; Friedrichs, 1996) conducted a study in which they examined the effectiveness of using mass media to extract tax-payer compliance. The more successful media campaigns focused on fairness, rather than threats of punishment for under-reporting income or other ways of cheating on income tax returns (Friedrichs, 1996; Mason and Mason, 1992; Schwartz and Orleans, 1967). More recently, the same type of media campaign was launched in some states to encourage participation in the 2020 Census, appealing to the usefulness of the information for funding of public programs. Similarly, companies to get people to wear masks appealed to the idea of "we are all in this together", collective good, during the COVID-19 pandemic.

The threat of sanctions does not seem to adequately prevent people from committing white collar crimes. Because there is the perception that the criminal justice system goes easy on white collar criminals, the legal penalties do not appear to stop the crimes from happening. Chambliss (1967; Paternoster and Simpson, 1996) argued that threats of formal punishment should be enough to deter white collar crime, as people employed in elite professions are supposedly not committed to a criminal lifestyle, but we nevertheless have seen a number of cases where this is simply not true. We certainly see this in the case of Belfort, "the Wolf of Wall Street" covered at the end of this chapter. It seems that in many of the cases we have seen within the past few decades, when white collar criminals are caught, their preoccupation is with committing the crimes, not with their professions.

The most obvious form of social control through moral appeals comes from religion. As most Western countries operate with a plurality of religions within their borders, it would be difficult to utilize religious doctrine to keep people from committing crimes. In addition, as we saw in our chapter on religious crimes, even the so-called devoted can dip their hands into the collection plate for their own purposes. The reality is that morality is better served with ethical codes of conduct that are secular. Though there are standards set out by professional organizations, as in the examples of the American Bar Association and American Medical Association, there are a number of professions that do not have similar watchdogs.

The fact that white collar crimes like income tax evasion, insider trading, etc. tend to be nonviolent crimes creates a moral dilemma in itself. Since the harm done is diffused, the victims themselves are often hard to identify (Green, 2014). As such, with the laws themselves vague as to the definitions of social harm, it becomes a challenge for prosecutors to charge white collar criminals on moral grounds. There is some talk in the legal professions that there should be more effort to clearly define the ethical and moral consequences of white collar criminality (Green, 2014).

CORPORATE SOCIAL RESPONSIBILITY (CSR)

Corporate social responsibility (CSR) is a fairly new approach to management. CSR is a form of self-regulation where companies are more than just financially responsible to employees and customers. It is a means by which larger companies are also socially responsible to the community in general, taking up positions on social issues from gun control to climate change (Cresanti, 2019).

The CSR model is far from being a perfect solution to malfeasance. One criticism of the CSR model is that in implementing it, a company can be perceived as "warmer" (approachable) and therefore more competent, regardless of whether it is or not (Shea and Hawn, 2019). Just like a perceived "good child" can have the room fooled, in presenting themselves as somehow more self-aware, the company might be able to hide its flaws.

A second problem is whether smaller companies have the means by which to incorporate principles of social responsibility. Small businesses can equally be vulnerable to white collar crime and malfeasance, though having fewer employees means it might be easier to detect when things go wrong. The social glue that might informally hold small businesses to high standards is that they tend to be more closely tied to a community. As they are dependent on local commerce, there might be less temptation to harm customers financially or otherwise. As Cresanti (2019) discovered, small business leaders, having to focus on local business, will often build tight bonds with their local community through civic engagement. In many respects, small businesses can seem more authentic in their moral compass than larger, impersonal corporations.

SUMMARY

It is not always a question of looking at individual criminal behavior. There are far too many examples of conspiracies that include a number of individuals to ignore the role of social networks in white collar criminality. Employers can take a number of preventative measures, including being aware of any signs of unhappiness among employees. Employees will talk to one another, particularly if they have a grievance, like salary structure, in common. Though for-profit companies are more driven to meet the demands of shareholders and stakeholders, salary and compensation packages, including cost of living adjustments, should be reviewed on a regular basis.

Like in conventional crime, we cannot discount the role that drug and alcohol abuse plays in white collar crime. Depending on the type of drug addiction, it can result in the need to supply a habit that is beyond the means of one's salary, putting addicted employees at risk of committing white collar crimes. Alcohol consumption is associated with risk-taking behavior, when inhibitions drop under the influence.

Controlling transnational companies is particularly problematic, taking into consideration regional and cultural differences. This is largely due to the absence of powerful international regulations and inconsistent national legislation (Hansen, 2009; Gerber and Jensen, 2000). There is argument that transnational companies should self-regulate as much as possible, within the framework of localized laws. The cost to prosecute transactional corporations is cost-prohibitive, with challenges in securing criminal convictions (Hagan, 1988). Adding to the cost is when witnesses have to be brought in from all over the country, or all over the world, to testify (Hagan, 1988).

White collar and corporate crime prevention cannot be localized in the 21st century. With varying applications of corporate social responsibility (CSR), there is no consistency in self-regulating in organizations. Certainly, the degree to which CSR is being utilized is dependent on regional business cultures. Matten and Moon

(2008) concluded that there are stark contrasts on either side of the Atlantic and Pacific Oceans in the attention given to CSR. Since the 2000s, American corporations appear to be leading the trend in self-awareness of risks for crime and malfeasance. Foreign corporations have only recently entered the CSR trend (Matten and Moon, 2008).

Whether change is desired or not, it is important to note that it is more cost-effective in the long run to invest in preventative measures, including employee and manager training. Research bears that the change has to occur at the organizational level to be effective, rather than by state or federal regulation (Schnatterly, 2003). Unfortunately, as in the case of conventional crime, white collar criminals may easily adapt to changes and modify their behavior so that they can continue their criminal activities by altering their modus operandi.

Case Study ▪ The Wolf of Wall Street, Jordan Belfort

Background

If ever there was a "poster child" for greed in the investment industry, Jordan Belfort would fit the bill. Brash and unashamedly lavish in his tastes, Belfort started out as an entry-level broker at L.F. Rothschild. Within six years, he co-founded Stratton Oakmont with Danny Porush in Long Island, New York in 1989. This was at the tail end of a decade of virtual debauchery on Wall Street, which resulted in the arrests and convictions for financial crimes of Ivan Boesky (depicted in the movie *Wall Street*), Michael Milken, and Dennis Levine, among others.

Belfort and Porush's brokerage firm was not Wall Street royalty, but it was in close enough spitting distance to the financial hub to have some prestige rub off on it[6]. Belfort's way of getting clients resembled a *boiler room operation*, where brokers used strongarm tactics to sell stocks, including *pump and dump* schemes and *penny stock* sales. One annoying, yet legal tactic that boiler room operations employ is *cold calling*. Cold calling means that unsolicited calls are made to potential clients or customers, in order to convince them to buy a product that they haven't asked for in the first place, in this case, questionable stock investments. Cold calling generally includes high-pressure sales techniques.

Whatever illegal schemes he and his brokers carried out was seemingly justified by the lawlessness of Wall Street firms at the time (Belfort, 2007, p. 72):

"It was ironic, I thought, how America's finest and supposedly legitimate financial institutions had rigged the treasury market (Salomon Brothers);

---

[6] Somehow, "The Wolf of Long Island" doesn't have the same ring to it.

bankrupted Orange County, California (Merrill Lynch); and ripped off grandmas and grandpas to the tune of $300 million (Prudential-Bache). Yet they were all still in business—still thriving. . . ."

An admitted consumer of drugs (Quaaludes and cocaine) and prostitutes' services, Belfort began to make millions from his brokerage firm and divorced his first wife, as can be the cliché all too often when someone begins with nothing and rises quickly within the ranks of their profession. Perhaps, as Bocanegra (2013) speculates, Belfort found prostitutes easier to deal with than his wife, who reportedly could be manipulative herself. Boldly living a life of excess with abandon, Belfort and his second wife began purchasing the usual things we regularly see with the *nouveaux riche*[7]: Luxury homes in upscale neighborhoods, yachts, and fancy automobiles. These can be red flags to authorities when the income supporting these luxury items is coming from questionable sources.

Defining the Crime(s)

Setting criminal activities in motion, some of the brokers at Stratton Oakmont, with Belfort and Porush's blessings, began a penny stock scheme. They sold low-valued stocks, primarily to small, middle class investors, with outrageous brokerage fees. By selling the stocks in large volumes, it drove up the price of the stocks ("pumping"), which Belfort and others could turn around and sell at an obscene profit ("dumping"). Ultimately, it cost their customers millions of dollars, triggering a number of criminal investigations.

Belfort and Porush's legal problems were only beginning. In the early 1990s, they were under investigation by the SEC for engaging in fraudulent sales practices, including making baseless price predictions (*SEC v. Stratton Oakmont, Inc.*, 1995). This was followed by an FBI investigation, and ultimately by federal charges. By 1996, Stratton Oakmont was shut down permanently by federal authorities.

Theories to Explain the Crime

If ever an argument could be made for collective greed and Sutherland's differential association theory, perhaps Belfort and Porush's crimes are textbook examples. As we noted earlier in the book, individual greed is largely a myth (Hansen and Movahedi, 2010). The concept of greed, in economic terms, dates back to Adam Smith in his description of the "invisible hand" in *The Wealth of Nations*, though he does not specifically use the term "greed" (Jin and Zhou, 2013). The "invisible hand" refers to the unseen forces that creates demand in markets.

---

[7] Nouveaux riche, or the "newly rich," historically have different spending patterns than "old money," where people who have more recently acquired money are more likely to spend it on status goods (Bronsert et al., 2016).

In Belfort and Porush's world, it may very well be a more visible and obvious hand that drove them to commit crimes. Wall Street tycoons generally wish to display their success and wealth with material goods, like flashy cars and expensive homes.

To a large extent, greed is contagious. Even in theoretical math models, greed breeds greed, similar to the gambler who sits at a slot machine, throwing in money in hopes of making it big. If we also take into consideration social network theory, greed may very well breed greed within elite circles.

Additionally, feelings of economic deprivation are relative. You can live in an upscale neighborhood, but if you have the least expensive house on the block, you may envy your neighbors. Worse yet, there is a tendency to spend more money when you associate with people who have more money than you do. For example, you may go shoe shopping with one of your wealthier friends. If they pick out an expensive pair to purchase, you may be tempted to do the same, even though you may have to forgo paying rent that month to do so.

Both Belfort and Porush may very well have been chasing after wealth with any means possible, including criminal, in order to keep up with the proverbial Joneses[8] on Wall Street. There would always be those in the finance industry that had far more money than they did, whether from hard work or, in many cases, inheritance.

We should not confuse greed or wealth with happiness. As we will see, money certainly didn't buy Belfort happiness in his married life. In some studies, wealth is meaningless without social connection, meaning that people with money will not be happy if they are socially isolated (Sarracino, 2011).

Social and Media Responses

One immediate social response to the crimes was personal, as Belfort's life began to crumble around him. As he notes in his 2007 autobiography, he had hoped that his arrest would bring the craziness to an end, including the drug abuse. Belfort instinctively knew that he could not keep up the pace forever. Instead of relief from the manic pace of keeping the conspiracy under wraps, he was extremely disappointed when his bail was set at $10 billion. Subsequently, his second wife announced that she did not love him, "dropping the D-bomb" and asking for a divorce from Belfort on the courthouse steps (Belfort, 2007).

Belfort's bunkmate in prison at Taft Correctional Institution in California was Tommy Chong of Cheech and Chong, the popular comedic duo from the 1970s (Weisman, 2014). Chong was serving time in prison for selling drug paraphernalia. As Chong was himself writing a book, he encouraged Belfort to do the same, resulting in the 2007 bestseller *The Wolf of Wall Street* (Random House).

---

[8] The expression "Keeping up with the Joneses" refers to the need in some people to appear to be as wealthy as those around them, even though they might not have the means to do so.

The book was subsequently made into a movie, starring Leonardo DiCaprio as Belfort and with Martin Scorsese directing (Paramount Pictures and Red Granite, 2013). If you recall, we previously reviewed the 1MDB case in Malaysia, a company that helped fund the movie *The Wolf of Wall Street*. So, in many respects, this was a case of art imitating life imitating art. It is ironic that a movie about a white collar criminal was allegedly funded by a white collar crime conspiracy.

Both book and film proved to be lucrative deals for Belfort, even though he was required to pay 50 percent of his gross income in court-ordered restitution (Lynch and Schwartz, U.S. DOJ, 2013). We might add that the royalties that Belfort received for these were made legitimately. Belfort also serves as a consultant and motivational speaker, continuing to publish books on sales strategies.

In spite of the sizable financial judgement against him, Belfort's current net worth is allegedly in the range of $100 million (Wealthy Gorilla Staff, n.d.; Sorbello, 2019). There is even a song commemorating Belfort's excesses, by Wes Walker and Dyl (Atlantic Records, available at https://www.lyrics.com/lyric/32188133/Dyl/Jordan+Belfort).[9]

"Jordan Belfort

Jordan Belfort

I been getting dirty money Jordan Belfort

Stacking penny stocks while I'm flipping these birds

Sipping on Ciroc, trip 'em up with words. . . ."

(*Jordan Belfort*, Wes Walker and Dyl, released August 2015)

In the long run, Belfort's case, by all appearances, being a Wall Street predator has paid off handsomely in terms of both notoriety and his bank account.

Criminal Justice and Policy Responses

Belfort's legal case only became more threatening when prosecuting attorneys informed him that unless he pleaded guilty to the charges, his soon-to-be ex-wife would be charged as well. As she was the mother of Belfort's children, even though she was filing for divorce, he did not want to see her dragged into the indictments. His attorney also informed him that if he went to trial, he could spend up to 30 years in prison if found guilty by a jury on all charges.

Belfort pleaded guilty in 1999, with Porush following suit in 2002, to charges of stock manipulation, securities fraud, and money laundering.

---

[9] WARNING: Explicit language, including sexual and drug references.

Belfort only served 22 months of a 42-month sentence in a federal prison camp, as is typical for white collar convictions. Porush served a 20-month sentence. A number of others connected to the stock fraud case were also indicted, some serving more time than Belfort and Porush. Turning State's witness, Belfort helped to convict Danny Gaito, an accountant who assisted with money laundering in the scheme. Gaito received the more severe penalty of a ten-year sentence at his conviction.

In Belfort's sentencing, he was ordered to pay $110.4 million in restitutions and fines. The U.S. government sued Red Granite in a civil lawsuit in order to *garnish* money that Belfort made on the movie for restitution (Vaswani, 2016). The original publishing house, Simon and Schuster, was also required to garnish payments to Belfort.

As a postscript, Belfort's partner, Danny Porush, went into the medical supply business after he was released from prison and placed on probation in 2004. He evidently did not learn his lesson while in prison. In 2014, Porush, along with others, were sued for alleged Medicare fraud in connection with Med-Care Diabetic & Medical Supplies, Inc., under the False Claims Act, after a whistleblower came forward (Baynes, 2014).

Unanswered Questions and Unresolved Issues Related to the Case

In light of the media attention, including a film about his life, we have to ask ourselves whether Belfort learned any lessons from the high-profile Wall Street crimes that were being successfully prosecuted in the 1980s. Likewise, in light of Porush's re-offending, he appeared to fail to learn lessons from his earlier criminal indictment for the Stratton Oakmont scandals.

Is it possible for white collar criminals of this magnitude to ever be reformed? We can look to other white collar criminals who seem to turn their lives around after conviction. For example, Michael Milken of junk bond fame, though prohibited from selling securities again in his lifetime, was able to take his finance experience and turn his attention to philanthropic work through the Milken Family Foundation (available at https//www.mff.org).

In Belfort's case, he has a number of critics, many of whom do not believe that he has reformed at all. In a 2018 article, he was accused of being a deadbeat who was avoiding paying restitution to his victims, though he profited from books sales (Hurtado and Smythe, 2018). So far, we have not brought up the point that in some cases, restitution ordered in either criminal or civil court can at times seem excessive, where it may be near impossibility to make a commitment to full payment. Of course, the ability to do so is dependent on the financial means of the convicted, plus potential for future earnings. The question continues to be what price can be placed on the emotional and financial burden suffered by white collar crime victims that can realistically be paid back.

Sources

Baynes, T. (2014) Health fraud lawsuit echoes "Wolf of Wall Street." *Reuters*. Feb. 21. Retrieved from https://www.reuters.com/article/us-fraud-wolfofwallstreet/health-fraud-lawsuit-echoes-wolf-of-wall-street-idUSBREA1K1W120140221.

Belfort, J. (2007) *The Wolf of Wall Street*. New York: Random House, Bantam Books.

Bocanegra, T. (2013) Book review: *The Wolf of Wall Street* by Jordan Belfort. *Booked Solid*, Blog, Dallas Public Library. Sept. 14. Retrieved from https://www.bbc.com/news/business-36852755.

Hansen, L.L. and S. Movahedi. (2010) Wall Street scandals: The myth of individual greed. *Sociological Forum*. Vol. 25, No. 2: 367-374.

Hurtado, P. and C. Smythe. (2018) "Wolf of Wall Street" Jordan Belfort isn't paying his debts US says. *Bloomberg*. May 16. Retrieved from https://www.bloomberg.com/news/articles/2018-05-16/-wolf-of-wall-street-belfort-isn-t-paying-his-debts-u-s-says.

Jin, H. and X. Y. Zhou. (2013) Greed, leverage, and potential losses: A Prospect Theory Perspective. *Mathematical Finance*. Jan. Vol. 23, No. 1: 122-142.

Sarracino, F. (2011) Money, sociability and happiness: Are developed countries doomed to social erosion and unhappiness? *Social Indicators Research*. Vol. 109, No. 2: 135-188.

Vaswani, K. (2016) 1MDB: The United States v The Wolf of Wall Street. *BBC News*. July 21. Retrieved from https://www.bbc.com/news/business-36852755.

Weisman, A. (2014) How Jordan Belfort's prison bunkmate—Tommy Chong—inspired him to write "Wolf of Wall Street." *Business Insider*. Feb. 28. Retrieved from https://www.businessinsider.com/jordan-belforts-prison-bunkmate-was-tommy-chong-2014-2?r=US&IR=T&IR=T/.

Wealthy Gorilla Staff. (n.d.) Jordan Belfort net worth. *Wealthygorilla.com*. Retrieved from https://wealthygorilla.com/jordan-belfort-net-worth/.

Wright, R.A. and D.O. Friedrichs. (1991) White collar crime in the criminal justice curriculum. *Journal of Criminal Justice Education*. Vol. 2: 95-119.

GLOSSARY

Boiler room operation   Investment schemes that involve high-pressure sales tactics, usually involving calling potential clients or current clients by "cold calling." The investments marketed by boiler room operations are usually questionable with no legitimate promises of return to investors.

Cold calling   Contacting clients or potential clients who have not requested to be called. Businesses that practice cold calling will sometimes use customer lists or bases that they have purchased. It is not necessarily an illegal practice, but commonly used by criminals who are attempting to defraud individuals with bogus merchandise or investments.

Corporate Social Responsibility (CSR)   A fairly recent practice of businesses, particularly large corporations, to engage in civic activities that do not directly generate income, but creates good will for companies.

Garnishment   Court order withholding of a portion of someone's income in order to pay a judgement against them in a civil or criminal court case.

Moral appeal   Use of ethics in order to get employees to agree to a standard of what is right or wrong.

Penny stocks   Common stock that is near worthless (<$1 USD) and carry high probability of low or no return on investment. Penny stocks are not illegal per se, but are regulated under strict guidelines of the SEC.

Pump and dump   Through aggressive marketing, brokers will boost the sale of nearly worthless investments (see Penny stocks), and by sheer volume, commonly with false information to investors, raise the market value ("pump"). They will in turn sell off the stock at the higher price ("dump"). The brokers themselves often own shares in the stock, thus making a handsome (but illegal) profit.

Rogue employees   Employees who either obviously or covertly do not follow, nor believe in the rules or practices of a company or a profession.

REFERENCES AND SUGGESTED READINGS

Abelson, R. and M. Freudenheim. (2003) The Scrushy mix: Strict and so lenient. *New York Times*. Apr.20. Retrieved from https://www.nytimes.com/2003/04/20/business/the-scrushy-mix-strict-and-so-lenient.html.

Associated Press. (2017) Alabama-based HealthSouth changing name. *Associated Press News*. July 11. Retrieved from https://apnews.com/19abdc5561334b97a220f3581ce7d9b5

Bagley, B.M. (2017) *Drug Trafficking, Organized Crime, and Violence in the Americas Today*. J.D. Rosen, ed. Gainesville, FL: University Press of Florida.

Bronsert, A., A. Glazer, and K.A. Konrad. (2016) Old money, the nouveaux riches and Brunhilde's marriage strategy. *Journal of Population Economy*. Vol. 30: 163-186.

Bureau of Labor Statistics (BLS). (2013) Fact Sheet: Workplace Homicides from Shootings. United States Department of Labor. Jan. Retrieved from https://www.bls.gov/iif/oshwc/cfoi/osar0016.htm.

Camp, A.C. (2010) Cutting Cupid out of the workplace: The capacity of employees' constitutional privacy rights to constrain employers' attempts to limit off-duty intimate associations. *Hastings Communications & Entertainment Law Journal* (COMM/ENT). Vol. 32, Issue 3: 427. Retrieved from https://repository.uchastings.edu/cgi/viewcontent.cgi?article=1702&context=hastings_comm_ent_law_journal.

Carrico, A. W., E. Nil, C. Sophal, E. Stein, M. Sokunny, N. Yuthea, J.L. Evans, S. Ngak, L. Maher, and K. Page. (2016) Behavioral interventions for Cambodian female entertainment and sex workers who use amphetamine-type stimulants. *Journal of Behavioral Medicine*. Vol 39:502-510.

Centers for Disease Control and Prevention (CDC). (2020) Morbidity and Mortality Weekly Report: Trends in total binge drinks—United States, 2011-2017. Jan. 17. Retrieved from https://www.cdc.gov/mmwr/volumes/69/wr/mm6902a2.htm?s_cid=mm6902a2_w.

CFO.com. (2017) Two CFOs tell a tale of fraud at HealthSouth. Mar. 27. Retrieved from https://www.cfo.com/fraud/2017/03/two-cfos-tell-tale-fraud-healthsouth/.

Cohen, L.E. and M. Felson. (1979) Social change and crime rate trends: A routine activity approach. *American Sociological Review*. Vol. 44: 588-608.

Collins, R. (1975) Conflict theory of organizations. *Conflict Sociology: Toward an Explanatory Social Science*. New York: Academic Press. pp. 286-347.

Encompass Health. (n.d.) Our Purpose. Retrieved from https://www.encompasshealth.com/home-office-ehc.

Ermann, D.M. and R.J. Lundman (Eds). (1996) *Corporate and Governmental Deviance: Problems of Organization Behavior in Contemporary Society*. New York: Oxford University Press.

Federal Bureau of Investigation (FBI). (2003) Crime in the suite: Former HealthSouth CEO indicted in $2.7 billion case of corporate fraud. *Stories*. Nov. 4. Retrieved from https://archives.fbi.gov/archives/news/stories/2003/november/health_110403.

Flaherty, C. (2018) Faculty salaries up 3%. *Inside Higher Ed*. Apr. 11. Retrieved from https://www.insidehighered.com/news/2018/04/11/aaups-annual-report-faculty-compensation-takes-salary-compression-and-more.

Finkelstein, S. (2015) The end of middle management? *BBC Worklife*. June 24. Retrieved from https://www.bbc.com/worklife/article/20150624-the-end-of-middle-management.

Friedrichs, D.O. (2009) *Trusted Criminals: White Collar Crime in Contemporary Society*. 4th ed. Belmont, CA: Wadsworth Publishing Company.

Gilligan, V. and P. Gould. (2015) *Better Call Saul*. AMC. Season 1.

Glassdoor.com. (2018) University of Miami Professor salaries. Dec. 7. Retrieved from https://www.glassdoor.com/Salary/University-of-Miami-Professor-Salaries-E33297_D_KO20,29.htm.

Green, S.P. (2014) Moral ambiguity in white collar criminal law. *Notre Dame Journal of Law*. Vol. 18, Issue 2. *Symposium of Criminal* Punishment: 501-519.

Lyman, B. (2019) Former Gov. Don Siegelman wins release from supervision. *Montgomery Advertiser*. June 14. Retrieved from https://www.montgomeryadvertiser.com/story/news/2019/06/14/don-siegelman-wins-release-supervision/1454948001/.

Lynch, L.E. and B.P. Schwartz. (2013) Correspondence to Judge Gleeson; Re: *United States v. Belfort*, Criminal Docket No. CR-98-0859 (E.D.N.Y. Jun. 11, 2014).

U. S. Department of Justice, United States Attorney, Eastern District of New York. Oct. 11. Retrieved from https://www.abc.net.au/mediawatch/transcripts/1419_dojcase.pdf.

Mason, L. and R. Mason. (1992) A moral appeal for taxpayer compliance: The case of a mass media campaign. *Law & Policy*. Vol. 14: 381-399.

Meyer, J.W. and B. Rowan. (1977) Institutional organizations: Formal structure as myth. *American Journal of Sociology*. Sept. Vol. 83, No. 2: 340-362.

Paternoster, R. and S. Simpson. (1996) Sanction threats and appeals to morality: Rational Choice Model of corporate crime. *Law and Society Review*. Vol. 30, No. 3: 549-583.

Pavlo, W. (2012) Former HealthSouth CEO, Richard Scrushy, gets prison sentenced [sic] reduced. *Forbes*. Retrieved from https://www.forbes.com/sites/walterpavlo/2012/01/26/former-healthsouth-ceo-richard-scrushy-gets-prison-sentenced-reduced/#3bc3439338e2.

Piquero, N.L. (2012) The only thing we have to fear is fear itself: Investigating the relationship between fear of falling and white collar crime. *Crime and Delinquency*. Vol. 58, No. 3:362-379.

Romo, V. (2019) U.S. arrests money-laundering expert for laundering money. NPR. Nov. 19. Retrieved from https://www.npr.org/2019/11/19/780877837/u-s-arrests-money-laundering-expert-for-laundering-money.

Shapiro, S. P. (1984) *Wayward Capitalists*. New Haven, CT: Yale University Press.

Shea, C. T. and O. Hawn. (2019) Microfoundations of corporate social responsibility and irresponsibility. *Academy of Management Journal*. Vol. 52, No. 5: 1609-1642.

Schwartz, R.D. and S. Orleans. (1967) On legal sanctions. *University of Chicago Law Review*. Vol. 34: 274-290.

Simmel, G. (1997) *The Philosophy of Money*. D. Frisby, ed., Bottomore and D. Frisby, trans. New York: Routledge.

Sorbello, A. (2019) Jordan Belfort net worth, quotes, and story. *Astrogrowth.com*. Retrieved from https://www.astrogrowth.com/blog/jordan-belfort-net-worth/.

Spain, J. and R. Ramsey. (2000) Workers' Compensation and Respondeat Superior Liability legal cases involving salespersons' misuse of alcohol. *Journal of Personal Selling & Sales Management*. Fall. Vol. 20, Issue 4: 263-269.

Swab, A. (2014) Adderall not cocaine: Inside the lives of the young wolves of Wall Street. *PBS News Hour*. Feb. 18. Retrieved from https://www.pbs.org/newshour/economy/adderall-cocaine-inside-lives-young-wolves-wall-street.

Turner, J. (2002) *The Structure of Sociological Theory*. 7th ed. Belmont, CA: Wadsworth Publishing Company.

United States Bureau of Labor Statistics (BLS). (n.d.) Number of jobs held in lifetime. *National Longitudinal Studies*. Retrieved from https://www.bls.gov/nls/nlsfaqs.htm#anch41.

United States Department of Justice (U.S. DOJ). (2019a) Professor of International Studies charged in international money laundering scheme. Press Release, U.S. Attorney's Office, Southern District of New York. Nov. 18. Retrieved from https://www.justice.gov/usao-sdny/pr/professor-international-studies-charged-international-money-laundering-scheme.

United States Department of Justice (U.S. DOJ). (2019b) Encompass Health agrees to pay $48 million to resolve False Claims Act allegations relating to its inpatient rehabilitation facilities. Published in Legal Monitor Worldwide. July 16. http://www.syndigate.info/.

United States Department of Transportation. (n.d.) Drunk driving: Overview. National Highway Transportation Safety Administration. Retrieved from https://www.nhtsa.gov/risky-driving/drunk-driving.

United States District Court for the District of Columbia. (1995) *SEC v. Stratton Oakmont, Inc.*, 878 F. Supp. 250 (D.D.C. 1995). Feb. 28. *Justia*. Retrieved from https://law.justia.com/cases/federal/district-courts/FSupp/878/250/1439881/.

United States Substance Abuse and Mental Health Services Administration (SAMHSA). (n.d.) Drug-free workplace programs: Prepare your workplace. Retrieved from https://www.samhsa.gov/workplace/toolkit/plan-implement-program/prepare-workplace.

GLOSSARY

1st Amendment   Under the 1st Amendment, as it pertains to religion in the United States, citizens have the rights to freedom of speech and to practice the religion of their choice without interference from the government, within reason.

As it pertains to journalism, Congress shall make no laws that prohibit or abridge the freedom speech or of the press.

4th Amendment   As it applies to evidence, law enforcement must not illegally search or seize evidence without first obtaining a court order to do so. Cited as to the unconstitutionality of the "perp walk," it is the right of the people to be secure in their persons and prohibits unreasonable searches and seizures.

6th Amendment   The accused has the right to a speedy and public trial by an impartial jury from the state (or Federal) jurisdiction. Critics of the media argue that it is difficult to find an impartial jury when there is high media attention on a case.

Administrative court   The civil court that specializes in administrative matters, as in the case of malfeasance with public hospital administration.

Affinity fraud   Fraud that is committed by using one's social connections, including those made within religious organizations. Example: Ponzi scheme.

Aged company   Similar to a shell company, but is held onto with the purpose of building reputation and goodwill, without actually selling products or services, so as to eventually sell for a profit. Aged companies do not have physical addresses. Same as "shelf company."

Agency   The extent to which an individual is acting in their own best interest.

Alienation of workers   A topic that is particularly popular among Marxist and Neo-Marxist scholars, proposes that the nature of work in contemporary life creates workers who are not connected with the work they produce.

Anomie   In context of terrorism, individuals or groups who feel disconnected from society and believe that they have been treated unfairly and marginalized politically, socially, and economically.

Apps Applications, or "apps," as they are more commonly known as, are software that can be installed on a computer or mobile phone.

Audit An accounting practice that can be conducted by people working within an organization (e.g., bank) or by an independent consultant, company that specializes in audit. In an audit, all accounts are reviewed along with any supporting documents; for example, an IRS audit of an income tax return.

Autocrat Leadership in which the manager, supervisor has absolute power over workers.

Bad faith Entering into a business arrangement or contract with the intention of being misleading or dishonest, or with no intention of fulfilling the obligations.

Ballot stuffing ("stuffing the ballot box") The practice of creating fake ballots with votes going to a particular candidate. There are some voting processes that are more vulnerable to ballot stuffing, including the use of paper ballots.

Bank Secrecy Act of 1970 (BSA) Enacted by Congress in order to prevent money laundering, requiring businesses to keep records and file reports to regulatory agencies with transparency of cash flow, income sources, etc.

Bankruptcy Lacking the necessary funds or finances to repay debt; sometimes results in filing for bankruptcy with civil court in order to consolidate, reduce, or eliminate debt.

Barter system An economic system where goods or services are exchanged instead of currency.

Belmont Report A 1970s report written by the National Commission for the Protection of Human Subjects of Biomedical and Behavioral Research that provides ethical guidelines in conducting research on human subjects.

Big Pharma The nickname for the pharmaceutical industry.

Black market The illegal economic system that functions underground. Law enforcement and regulatory agencies are aware of its existence but find it difficult to prevent. Example: the illegal prescription drug market.

Blockchain A supposedly incorruptible digital ledger of economic transactions.

Boiler room operation Investment schemes that involve high-pressure sales tactics, usually involving calling potential clients or current clients by "cold calling."

The investments marketed by boiler room operations are usually questionable with no legitimate promises of return to investors.

Botnet   A network of private computers infected with malicious software and controlled as a group without the owners' knowledge. Example: Email spamming from infected computer.

Bounded rationality   First identified by Herbert Simon (1982), the bounded rationality model proposes that decisions are made on the limited amount of information and time available to make those decisions.

Broker   An individual who is between two actors who do not have ties in a network, or acts as a conduit between two separate networks.

Bureaucracy   Described by Max Weber as a merit-based, impersonal organizational structure that is characterized by written rules, organizational hierarchy, and the promise of promotion within a career for the deserving.

Bureaucratic control   A system by which an organization is impersonally organized, where workers' behavior and employers' expectations are controlled through formal rules.

Censorship   As censorship relates to journalism, it is the suppression or prohibition of the publication of any news that might be politically unacceptable or controversial.

Certified Compliance Officer   An individual, most likely an attorney, who is licensed to investigate possible violation of laws or regulations in a company and advises on preventative measures to ensure that laws are not broken.

Certified Financial Accountant (CFA)   A Certified Public Accountant (CPA) with advanced degrees and/or specialized training in the investigation of financial crimes or suspected malfeasance.

Certified Financial Forensic Accountant (CFFA)   See *Certified Financial Accountant.*

Certified Public Accountant (CPA)   An accountant who has passed the Certified Public Accountant exam to be licensed and is required to continue to take coursework in order to remain certified.

Chain of command   Synonymous with hierarchy, ranks or positions make clear as to who are in leadership positions (e.g., CEO, midlevel managers) and who is subordinate (e.g., entry-level employees).

Chapter 11 bankruptcy   A bankruptcy option for corporations or partnerships that are in financial trouble, giving them time to reorganize and work with creditors so as to ensure that their companies can survive.

Charlatans   In the context of religion, individuals who fraudulently claim to have a special connection with a superior being whom others can only reach through them. Charlatans can also claim that they possess special, sacred information that only they know.

Children's Online Privacy Protection Act (COPPA)   Legislation passed by the U.S. Congress in 1998 to give parents more control of what information can be collected from children who are using the Internet.

Circumstantial evidence   Evidence that brings the investigator to certain conclusions, even though there might not be physical evidence or an eyewitness to a crime being committed.

Class action lawsuits   Civil cases where a number of people who have been harmed or defrauded by a company can sue the company collectively instead of suing individually.

Clean Air Act, 1960   First of a number of federal laws targeting air pollution in the United States. Some states have subsequently passed their own laws. The most recent amendment in 1990 was passed in order to address the problem of acid pollution.

Clean Water Act, 1972   Originally called the Federal Water Pollution Control Act, the first federal law regulating the types and amounts of pollutants in lakes, rivers, streams, wetlands, and coastal areas. The act was amended in 1977 and 1987.

Clique   A subgroup of a network, made up of three or more closely connected individuals.

Coercive isomorphism   Dimaggio and Powell's (1983) term to mean the social and economic pressure to conform to an industry standard not because of choice, but due to competition.

Cold calling   Contacting clients or potential clients who have not requested to be called. Businesses that practice cold calling will sometimes use customer lists or bases that they have purchased. It is not necessarily an illegal practice, but commonly used by criminals who are attempting to defraud individuals with bogus merchandise or investments.

Compliance   The extent to which laws and regulations are being followed by individuals and organizations where they apply to specific industries (e.g., financial institutions).

Comptroller   A title used for individuals who serve as financial officers (e.g., CFOs) or auditors in their companies.

Computer coding   Also program coding; a set of instructions forming a computer program, which is executed by a computer.

Computer Fraud and Abuse Act, 1986   United States cybersecurity bill that is an amendment to existing computer fraud as part of the Comprehensive Crime Control Act of 1984.

Computer Hacking   To use a computer to gain unauthorized access to data in a system.

Computer worms   Malware computer program that replicates itself in order to spread to other computers, much like a computer virus.

Conglomerate   A number of companies in different industries that are under one corporate entity. Example: Johnson & Johnson products include pharmaceuticals, baby products, and over the counter medications.

Conservatorship   A court-appointed family member or guardian who oversees the personal and business affairs of individuals. Those individuals are deemed by the court to be temporarily or permanently mentally or physically limited and cannot care for their own affairs.

Consumer Financial Protection Bureau (CFPB)   Created in 2011, the CFPB has the responsibility of assuring that credit cards, mortgages, and other loan products are fair and transparent for consumers so that they can make informed. choices in their financial decisions. See https://www.consumerfinance.gov/.

Control fraud   Any financial malfeasance or criminal act that is committed by a person who is highly placed in an organization, including a company, corporation, nonprofit, or government office or agency, for personal gain.

Controlled substances   A list of drugs and substances that the U.S. government identify as either having no medical use and/or have some level of risk for addiction. Doctors are only allowed to prescribe a limited number of doses to patients of prescription drugs identified as controlled substances. Patients are required to show ID in order to purchase these drugs.

Convictional crime   A crime that is committed because of strong belief that it will be to the benefit of the collective, rather than to the individual. Generally based on strong ideology, as in the case of standing by one's leader or political party no matter what.

Corporate espionage   Also called industrial espionage and corporate spying, it is the act of either infiltrating a company or working for a company to steal trade secrets and intellectual property that can be used by competitors or sold on the black market to foreign governments.

Corporate espionage   Also referred to as industrial espionage; intellectual property theft committed for commercial purposes, increasingly includes foreign countries infiltrating commercial enterprises.

Corporate Social Responsibility (CSR)   A business model that is a fairly new trend where companies self-regulate their activities so that they are in the best interest of employees, customers, and business partners. Viewed as a smart part of the public relations functions of companies.

Corporate violence   Injury or death that happens to customers, employees, or civilians as a result of calculated neglect, usually as a cost-saving measure, by a company or corporation.

Corruption   Dishonest or fraudulent crimes committed by individuals in power.

Court of public opinion   The opinions people form by reading media accounts of crimes as to the guilt or innocence of the accused.

Cronyism   The practice of placing one's friends in positions of power, even if they have no experience or qualifications in that position. See *Nepotism*.

CSI effect   With the popularity of television series and movies that depict police procedures, including evidence gathering and testing techniques, there is an alleged effect on the expectations of members of juries as to what is considered to be adequate evidence to convict or exonerate the accused of their criminal charges.

Cults   Religious or quasi-religious groups that operate outside of conventional religion and use aggressive tactics for recruiting new members. Generally, the devotion is directed at a charismatic leader.

Cyber Fraud   Fraud committed by using the Internet as a means by which to perpetrate online scams.

Cybercrime   Criminal activities that are cared out by means of computers or the Internet.

Cybersquatting   Practice of purchasing a domain (URL) name with no intention of using it in order to drive up the price or to present oneself as being a legitimate company by having a similar name to an established business.

Cyberterrorism   Use of the Internet, including the Dark Web, to organize and fund terrorist organizations, or use of cyberspace to threaten individuals, groups, or governments.

Dark Web   World Wide Web content that exists on overlaying networks that use the Internet but require specific software, configurations, or authorization to access. Users and crimes committed on the Dark Web are difficult to detect.

Deforestation   The legal or illegal mass removal of trees in the logging, mining, and agricultural industries.

Density   In social network terms, the density of a network is measured by how many actual social ties there are between the actors in it.

Despots   Leaders who demand complete obedience from their citizens and the people who help them maintain power. Despots use fear and coercion to rule.

Differential Association Theory   Edwin Sutherland's (1939, 1947) theory that criminal behavior is learned when people associate with criminals.

Direct evidence   Verifiable physical or firsthand eyewitness evidence in a criminal case.

Directional ties   Social network ties between actors where things may flow in one direction between them. Example: Information.

Dodd-Frank Act of 2010   Also known as the Dodd-Frank Wall Street Reform and Consumer Protection Act, it helped create the CFPB and was intended to address many of the problems in the financial industry, including mortgage lending, that resulted in the 2008 financial crisis in the United States.

Earned income   Income you make by selling your labor, either as an independent contractor or employee, often subject to state and federal taxes depending on income level.

Eco-terrorism   Violent, criminal acts in the name of environmental activism.

Electronic Crime Task Force (2001)   One function of the United States Secret Service tasked to provide surveillance of illegal activity on the Internet, as part of the USA Patriot Act, 2001.

Embeddedness   Within a social network, the degree to which people are connected on the individual level. Can also refer to the extent that two or more social networks are connected to one another through mutual ties.

Embezzlement   Theft of property or money by employees, trustees, or other individuals who are paid to safeguard them.

Eminent domain   The right of the United States government to purchase private property for public use, even if the property owner does not wish to sell their property. The government is expected to pay fair market value for the property. Example: Purchase of private land in order to build a public highway.

Employee Stock Option Plan (ESOP)   Plans that became popular beginning in the 1970s, giving employees stock shares in the company they work for. The philosophy behind ESOPs is that a worker will work harder if they own part of the company.

Endangered Species Act, 1973   Law that provides the conservation and protection of endangered species and their environments.

Endowment   Generally charitable donations in the form of money or property given to nonprofit causes. Endowments can be given while donor is alive or can be bequeathed in a will after their death.

Environmental Protection Agency (EPA)   U.S. federal agency charged with enforcing environmental laws.

Espionage Act of 1917   United States bill passed to make it a punishable offense to speak, write, or act against the government or military, including submitting false reports or interfering with war efforts. The bill was passed while the United States was still involved in WWI.

Establishment and Free Exercise Clauses   Additions to the 1st Amendment that further strengthen the separation of church and state, though they continue to be tested in the courts.

E-waste   Any discarded electronic products, including cell phones, computers, some household appliances, and televisions.

Extortion   Use of damaging information, fear, and/or force to get someone to pay money or give up valuable information.

Extradition In a criminal case where the suspect is not physically present (e.g., in another state or country), they are returned to the jurisdiction where there is an arrest warrant out for them and where they are being charged with a crime.

Extrinsic rewards Rewards that can be measured in salary, income, bonuses, or material goods that might motivate workers to be more productive in their jobs.

Federal Deposit Insurance Corporation (FDIC) Created after the Great Depression, the Federal Deposit Insurance Corporation insures deposits in banks, credit unions, and thrifts that are insured by the FDIC that is backed by the U.S. government. Depositors are insured up to $250,000 per account, with some exceptions. See https://www.fdic.gov/deposit/deposits/brochures/deposit-insurance-at-a-glance-english.html for more details on FDIC insurance.

Federal Drug Administration (FDA) The U.S. agency that is charged with the responsibility of regulating prescription distribution and safety, as well as the safety of medical devices.

Federal Trade Commission One of the key U.S. agencies charged with protecting consumers.

FICO® credit score The Fair Isaac Company (FICO®) provides creditors with credit scores of potential borrowers to demonstrate credit worthiness, typically ranging from 300 (poor) to 850 (excellent).

Fiduciary responsibility An individual's responsibility through their occupation, whether employed or self-employed, to secure the finances and/or material goods, including intellectual property, of clients, customers, and their employer.

Fiduciary responsibility The responsibility of an individual to act in the best interest of their employer or client while entrusted with their money or other assets, including property.

Financial markets Used to buy and trade a number of securities and futures, along with other types of financial investments. Examples of securities are stocks, bonds, precious metals that have monetary value. Future markets are places where individuals can invest in, and to some extent gamble on, goods that will have true market value at a future date. An example of a future investment would be an agricultural crop that will not have a specific monetary value until it is harvested.

Forbidden triad Condition identified by Granovetter (1973) where in a triad of three people, if there are two strong ties between two of the actors, a third will inevitably form and all three actors will be connected.

Forensic accounting   A specialized area of accounting where CPAs are trained to look for mistakes, omissions, or criminal entries in accounting files of individuals or organizations.

Forgery   A forgery is any fake replication or reproduction of signatures, currency, checks, or works of art without legal permission.

Formal organizational structure   Any organizational structure that has been formally adopted, generally with all aspects of how the organizations is to be operated written down in mission statements, employee handbooks, and company charters.

Formal social networks   These are the generally sanctioned social networks that are part of an organization. Examples: Chain of command, hierarchy.

Fraud   Criminal deception that is intended to obtain money from unsuspecting victims, with no compensation of goods or services.

Fraud spree   When an individual or group commits several acts of fraud over time instead of one single act.

Free-rider   An individual who benefits from the work of a group or network, without putting in the same efforts as other members of the group.

Front companies   Companies without physical addresses that can either be legitimate or illegitimate, generally used to protect a parent company.

Garnishment   Court order withholding of a portion of someone's income in order to pay a judgement against them in a civil or criminal court case.

Gender politics   The ongoing politics and debate about roles people are supposed to have in and out of the workplace depending on their biological sex.

General Accountability Office (GAO)   Part of the legislative branch of the U.S. government, the GAO is an independent and non-partisan office that is responsible for the monitoring and review of government spending and reports their findings to the United States Congress.

Green criminology   A fairly new branch of criminal justice and criminological research that focuses on violations of environmental laws.

Greenhouse gases (Greenhouse effect)   A number of gases that when emitted will result in heat being trapped in the lower hemisphere, raising temperatures at the surface of the planet and contributing to global warming. Some of the greenhouse effect is believed to be natural, whereas some is suspected to be caused by human activity, including the burning of coal.

Hegemony   The degree to which an individual or a group of individuals has power in a network, generally measured by the number and quality of social ties they possess.

Hierarchy   Synonymous with chain of command, the hierarchy is a clear organizational chart indicating who gives orders in an organization and who follows orders. An example of a hierarchy or chain of command is the organizational structure in the military.

Hippocratic Oath   Written by Hippocrates, who was a medical practitioner in 4th century B.C.E. Some physicians still take a modification of this oath when they graduate from medical school, essentially promising to put their patients first and to practice medicine ethically.

Identity assumption   When an individual assumes someone's identity and takes over that person's social and financial life for a period of time.

Identity theft   The theft of a number of pieces of information on an individual or group of individuals, including Social Security numbers and bank account information, usually for the purpose of financial gain. The stolen identity is generally only used for a short while so as to allow the criminal to avoid detection. Example: Stolen credit cards used in fraudulent purchases.

Impeachment   The process by which a person in an elective office can be removed from the office.

Improvised explosive device (IED)   Explosive devices that are thrown together, usually inexpensive and with common materials; not used in conventional military operations.

Informal organizational structure   The friendships, alliances, and enmities that form between workers outside of the formal, written structure, which may enhance or undermine an organization.

Informal social networks   The natural social network that forms within formal social networks due to friendship, mutual dependency, or expediency.

Informed consent   A form that research subjects sign that spells out the purposes of the study, possible risks, confidentiality, and the participant's rights.

Insider tipping   Telling someone information that has not been made public about a publicly traded company that might result in their stock going up or down.

Insider trading   Selling or buying stocks or other market investments on information that has not been made public. Example: A pharmaceutical executive buys stock in a company before there is FDA announcement that a new drug will be approved.

Institutional Review Board (IRB)   A committee charged with making sure that any research conducted at their institution is following the principles in the Belmont Report.

International Monetary Fund (IMF)   Created in 1945 on the heels of WWII, the IMF was formed to create financial stability around the world. See https://www.imf.org/external/index.htm

Intrinsic rewards   Unlike extrinsic rewards, there is no monetary value attached to them; includes feelings of accomplishment and wellbeing in the work one does or the position one has in an organization.

Iron Cage of Bureaucracy   Weber's (1922) cautionary tale about the downside of bureaucratic structures where they become so rule-bound, nothing gets accomplished.

Isolate   An individual who is technically part of a network, but has no tie to others in the network. Example: A new student in a classroom who has become part of that class but has not formed any friendships with anyone yet.

Jurisdictional roles   Within the formal structure of a bureaucratic organization, written instructions that spell out exactly what work that each employee is responsible for. Jurisdictional roles can many times be found in employee handbooks or the organizational chart showing the chain of command.

Kickbacks   A bride or payment usually paid to someone who is a co-conspirator in a scheme. Within political crimes, a kickback is an illegal "bonus," generally cash, paid to politicians for their vote or policy making that favors an individual or business. Examples: Paying regulators a bride to turn a blind eye to malfeasance or crime; paying a congressperson money so that they help award a contract to a weapons contractor.

Land grants   Public land that is given or purchased by private individuals, institutions, or businesses. Example: Public land given to help build a university.

Libel   A published false statement that damages an individual's or organization's reputation.

Malfeasance   Any ethical or illegal wrongdoing by an individual or organization.

Malpractice   Any type of misconduct, neglect, or harm committed by a health care provider that results in harm or death to a patient.

Malware   Software that is intended to damage or disable computers.

Markets   Generally associated with, but not limited to, free market economies where investments, goods, and services are bought and sold.

Media circus   The increased media attention surrounding high profile criminal cases, including journalists, paparazzi, and civilians who sell photos and stories to news outlets.

Medicaid   U.S. health care program that provides government assistance to lower income individuals or families. Was part of health care reform in the 1960s.

Medicare   U.S. health care program that provides government assistance to senior citizens aged 65 and older.

Megachurches   Large, non-denominational churches that have several thousand members and have increasingly become popular alternatives to more traditional Protestant religions.

Micromanagement   Leadership style where the manager takes charge of every aspect of day-to-day operations.

Mimetic isomorphism   The phenomenon identified by Dimaggio and Powell (1983) where people or companies will start looking like one another by imitating each other's structure.

Ministerial exception   This law allows religious organizations to legally discriminate against people for employment on the basis of religion. For example, a religious school could discriminate against job applicants who do not possess the same religious beliefs.

Misappropriation   Using funds or assets for other than their intended purposes. Example: A religious group using donations that are specifically designated building funds to buy a car for the group's religious leader.

Mobile Medical Applications (MMAs)   Applications that can be downloaded to a computer or mobile device to provide users with medical and health care information. MMAs are regulated by the Federal Drug Administration to ensure that the information is accurate and that they are legitimate sources.

Monopolies   Companies that have essentially squashed any competitors with the intention of controlling products or trade in a specific industry. Side note: The goal of the board game *Monopoly* (Parker Brothers) is to own as much property as possible so that other players go broke paying you rent on the properties you own (e.g., railroads, real estate).

Moral appeal   Use of ethics in order to get employees to agree to a standard of what is right or wrong.

Multinational corporation   A company or corporation that has an international presence, with factories, stores, or restaurants throughout the world. Examples of a multinational corporation would be Coca Cola® or McDonald's® fast food restaurants.

Mutual funds   An investment fund that trades in a diversified portfolio and is managed by a certified financial professional.

National Environmental Policy Act (NEPA), 1970   Environmental legislation designed to create the President's Council on Environmental Quality and to support existing environmental laws.

Nepotism   The practice of hiring and promotion practices of family members or friends, not necessarily on merit, qualifications, experience or credentials. Example: Appointing a family member to serve in a cabinet position in a federal government. See *Cronyism*.

Network boundaries   The extent to which we can identify all members belonging to a social network.

Network noise   Events or false information that disrupt the flow of factual information through a social network.

Node   Another term for "actor" in SNA that can refer to a thing (e.g., a company) or a person.

Non-competitive bidding   When a contract is given to a company or contractor, in some cases illegally, without going through a bidding process to hire the best or most cost-effective company. Can be related to cronyism and/or nepotism.

Normative isomorphism   The type of conformity that is expected within a profession (Dimaggio and Powell, 1983).

Oligarchy   Control of a group, organization, or government by a few elite individuals.

Organizational death   Conditions where internal or external forces result in the end of an organization, company, or corporation.

Peer pressure   The pressure to conform to the behaviors and expectations of a group of people that you consider to be your equals.

Penny stocks   Common stock that is near worthless (<$1 USD) and carry high probability of low or no return on investment. Penny stocks are not illegal *per se*, but are regulated under strict guidelines of the SEC.

Perp walk   The walk that an alleged offender takes, usually handcuffed, to a waiting police squad car or when traveling from jail to courtroom during a trial.

Phishing   The fraudulent practice of sending emails purporting to be from reputable companies or individuals in order to obtain personal information, including passwords and credit card numbers.

Ponzi schemes   Pyramid schemes that often offer unrealistic returns on investments where people who first invested in them are being paid dividends from new investors' contributions rather than from a legitimate investment product.

Price gouging   When a seller raises the prices of products or services higher than is considered to be fair or ethical.

Price hiking   An increase in prices of products or services, usually measured by a percentage. See *price gouging*.

Prisoner's Dilemma   Part of Game Theory, the Prisoner's Dilemma proposes that if co-defendants are separated from one another and each given the opportunity to turn state's evidence in exchange for lesser charges or even dismissal of charges, there is a certain probability, depending on a number of factors, that they will take the deal and confess their crime, or take their chances with a not guilty plea and not sell out their co-offenders.

Provenance   Documents that provide proof of authenticity of artwork and history of ownership.

Pump and dump   Through aggressive marketing, brokers will boost the sale of nearly worthless investments (See *penny stocks*), and by sheer volume, commonly with false information to investors, raise the market value ("pump"). They will in turn sell off the stock at the higher price ("dump"). The brokers themselves often own shares in the stock, thus making a handsome (but illegal) profit.

Pyramid sales structures   All Ponzi schemes are pyramid schemes, but not all pyramid marketing structures are Ponzi schemes that are illegitimate. See *Ponzi schemes*.

Racketeering   Broad category of crimes that involve deceptive or fraudulent business transactions. First used in prosecution of organized crime figures, now commonly used in charging white collar criminals.

Recidivism (rates)   The rate at which convicts, once released from prison or if on probation or parole, will reoffend and be arrested again, starting the cycle all over again through the criminal justice system. The recidivism rate for reoffending is approximately 35 percent within one year of release from prison, approximately 66 percent within five years of release.

Reciprocal ties   Social ties where the action/feelings/transaction are identifiably going in both directions between actors. Example: One broker will offer information on possible leads to another broker in exchange for information, an exchange that is beneficial to both parties.

Refund Anticipation Loans (RALs)   Popular in the 1980s and 1990s, RALs offered tax filers the opportunity to receive their income tax refunds faster than the IRS could process the return and send out a check. The loans provided payment out of the tax refund for tax preparation services. They have been replaced with Refund Anticipation Check (RAC) programs.

Rent seeking   Practice of manipulating public policy in order to illegally increase profits.

RICO Act of 1970   The Racketeer Influenced and Corrupt Organizations Act (RICO) is a federal law that was initially passed to target organized crime, allowing for greater criminal or civil penalties if crimes are committed as part of an established criminal enterprise. In recent decades, it is used to prosecute street gangs and white collar criminals.

Robocalls   Automated phone calls, typically from telemarketing companies.

Rogue employees   Employees who either obviously or covertly do not follow or believe in the rules or practices of a company or a profession.

Safe Drinking Water Act (SDWA), 1974   Federal law that sets the standards for drinking water safety, including establishing technical and financial support.

Sarbanes-Oxley Act of 2002   Federal law passed in response to the Enron scandal intended to tighten auditing and financial regulations for publicly traded companies (i.e., companies that sell stock to investors).

Securities   Tradable and sellable investments that can result in profit or loss for owners and are not insured by the FDIC, like bank deposits. Example: stocks.

Shelf company   Similar to a shell company, but is held onto with the purpose of building reputation and goodwill without actually selling products or services, so as to eventually sell for a profit. Shelf companies do not have physical addresses. Same as "aged company."

Shell company   Companies that do not have a physical location, employees, or assets, but are used to raise money, conduct hostile takeovers, start a new business, or add additional businesses to an already established company. Shell companies are not illegal per se, but can be used to hide criminal activities.

Shell company   Another term for "front company," used to conduct business while protecting a company from bad publicity in the event that a product or service fails. Can be created for legal or illegal purposes. Like "shelf companies" and "aged companies," shell companies do not have physical addresses.

Sherman Antitrust Act of 1890   First law in the United States to outlaw monopoly companies.

Simple control   Type of worker control found in smaller operations, like a family-owned restaurant. Rules and roles for employees may not be written down and could be arbitrary, personal.

Slander   Spoken false statement that damages an individual's or organization's reputation.

Smuggling operations   Any scheme that is set up to illegally move weapons, money, people, and/or drugs across borders. Can also involve the smuggling of art and artifacts to avoid tariffs or to move and sell stolen items.

Social contagion   Any piece of information, whether factual or falsehood, that is passed around quickly within and between networks.

Social network actor   Another name for an individual who is a member of a social network.

Social Network Analysis (SNA)   A set of theories and research methodologies that are grounded in mathematical and qualitative sociology within criminology that helps in understanding how individuals, organizations, and things are socially connected.

Social network tie   A definable connection between actors within a social network.

Soft target   A terrorist target that is not difficult to attack; an unprotected person or location.

Span of control   The number of employees that a supervisor has working directly below them and that they are responsible for.

Special counsel   Prosecutor or attorney appointed to oversee the investigation of suspected crimes or malfeasance in the government. Has the power to prosecute or refer individuals to jurisdiction when punishable crimes are uncovered.

Spin doctor   Public relations spokesperson who is tasked with reducing the damage done when there is negative publicity. The spokesperson can represent an individual, a group of individuals, or the whole organization.

Stocks   Investments in companies that give the investor the potential to share in the profits of those companies. There is also the risk of losing some or all of the investment if a company goes out of business with no takeover or buyer.

Straw buyer   Someone who, for a fee, will make purchases or obtain credit for someone else who might not be creditworthy. A straw buyer can be acting legally or illegally. However, there are places in the world where straw buyers are illegal.

Structural hole   The gap between two actors, identified by Burt (1992) as being a competitive edge, where there is a broker who connects the two actors together where they are not personally connected to one another. Example: The buyer and seller of a home do not ever meet and the transaction between them is handled by a real estate agent.

Subpoena   A court-ordered demand that evidence is turned over in a civil or criminal case.

Technical control   A company that has the control of workers built into the physical structure. Examples would be offices with cubicles that discourage workers from socializing or factory assembly lines.

Telemarketing   Generally unsolicited telephone calls to potential customers. These can be automated calls or "cold calling" by operators at telemarketing companies.

Third-party subpoena A court-ordered demand for documents from people or organizations who have possible evidence pertaining to an individual who has been indicted or is being sued. An example would be the bank statements of a defendant in an embezzlement case that would have to be requested from the bank and not directly from the individual who is being accused of the crime.

Tort law Civil law that is used to measure the degree to which an individual has been harmed or injured and the monetary reward that is considered fair compensation.

Toxic Substances Control Act, 1976 (TSCA) As another legal arm of the EPA, TSCA calls for the regulation of new and existing chemicals.

Truth in sentencing laws Laws enacted in the 1990s to assure that offenders would serve a large portion of their sentence in prison instead of being granted an unusually early release.

U.S. Customs and Border Patrol (CBP) The agency within the United States government that is responsible for the contents of what comes in and out of the country (e.g., airline passengers' luggage, airfreight, shipping containers) as well as movement of people across the U.S. borders.

Unearned income Income that is generated by investments, including stock dividends, and profits made in the sale of assets, including stocks, real estate, collectables (e.g., art works).

Upfront fee A fee charged by a company in advance of a product or service being provided to a customer. The fee can be a deposit towards final payment or a separate fee for providing a product or service in advance of payment.

Usury lending The practice of illegally charging unusually high interest rates on personal and consumer loans.

Weapons of mass destruction (WMDs) Weapons used by terrorist groups or governments that are designed to do the most damage possible to infrastructure and to the lives of targeted populations. Can be made out of sophisticated, military grade materials or can be homemade devices. Includes chemical, biological, or radioactive weapons.

Whistleblower Protection Act (WPA), 1989 Along with the False Claims Act passed by Congress, these acts assure that whistleblowers cannot be retaliated against or fired when they come forward to report mismanagement, malfeasance, or crime in the organization they work for. The act also provides the whistleblower with anonymity and immunity from prosecution.

Whistleblowers   Individuals who bring activities within their organizations that might be unethical or illegal to the attention of management or the public.

White collar crime   First identified in Edwin Sutherland's 1939 address at the annual conference of the American Sociological Association, defined as a crime that is committed by individuals with respectable and high social statuses within their occupations.

White collar malfeasance   Ethical or illegal wrongdoing within the context of white collar occupations (e.g., attorneys, accountants, doctors).

Wire fraud   Any financial fraud where telecommunications, including cable, telegraph, or information technology, is used to commit the crime.

Wiretapping   The legal or illegal practice of listening in on a telephone or Internet-based conversation. Investigators are required by law to obtain a court order allowing them to wiretap a suspect or suspects.

Workers' compensation   Insurance policies that provide employees who have been injured or fall ill as a direct result of their job with medical benefits and income while recovering, required by law to be provided by employers with five or more employees. Workers' compensation does not have to be provided for independent contractors hired by a company.

World Bank (WB)   International banking group that provides loans and funding to poorer, developing countries.

Y2K bug   A computer flaw that was a result of a coding error that, if not corrected, would result in computer errors or failure when the date changed from 12/31/1999 to 1/1/2000. Also called the "Millennium Bug," it created some trepidation and gave rise to some "Doomsday" cults that feared that computer failures, plus the end of the 20th century, would result in an apocalyptic event.

Yellow journalism   Sensationalized news reporting that is focused more on profit and selling newspapers than necessarily reporting factual news.

TABLE OF REFERENCES

Abelson, R. and M. Freudenheim. (2003) The Scrushy mix: Strict and so lenient. *New York Times.* Apr. 20. Retrieved from https://www.nytimes.com/2003/04/20/business/the-scrushy-mix-strict-and-so-lenient.html

Abolafia, M. Y. (1996) *Making markets: Opportunism and restraint on Wall Street.* Cambridge, MA: Harvard University Press

Ackerman, R. (2019) Too few cyber professionals is a gigantic problem for 2019. *Techcrunch.* Jan. 17. Retrieved from https://techcrunch.com/2019/01/27/too-few-cybersecurity-professionals-is-a-gigantic-problem-for-2019/

Adam, S., L. Arnold, and Y. Ho. (2018) The story of Malaysia's 1MDB, the scandal that shook the world of finance. *Bloomberg.* Dec. 17. Available at https://www.bloomberg.com/news/articles/2018-05-24/how-malaysia-s-1mdb-scandal-shook-the-financial-world-quicktake

Agarwal, N. and M. Sharma. (2014) Fraud risk prediction in merchant-bank relationship using regression models. *Vikalpa: The Journal of Decision Makers.* July-Sept., Vol. 39, Issue 3: 67-75

Airline Career Pilot Program. (n.d.) How much does it cost to become a commercial pilot? Retrieved from https://atpflightschool.com/faqs/pilot-training-cost.html

Aktar, M. W., D. Sengupta, and A. Chowdhury. (2009) Impact of pesticides use in agriculture: Their benefits and hazards. *Interdisciplinary Toxicology.* Vol. 2, No. 1: 1-12

Albahar, M. (2019) Cyber attacks and terrorism: A Twenty-First Century conundrum. *Science and Engineering Ethics.* Vol. 25: 993-1006

Alsup, D. and D. Simon. (2017) Couple raises thousands for homeless veteran to thank him for selfless act. *CNN.* Nov. 24. Retrieved from https://www.cnn.com/2017/11/24/us/couple-raisesmoney-for-homeless-man/index.html

Amaral-Garcia, S. (2019) Medical malpractice appeals in a civil law system. Do administrative and civil courts award noneconomic damages differently? *Law and Society Review.* June, Vol. 23, Issue 2: 386-419

American Cancer Society. (2014) The study that helped spur the U.S. stop-smoking movement. Jan. 9. Retrieved from https://www.cancer.org/latest-news/the-study-that-helped-spur-the-us-stop-smoking-movement.html

American Museum of Tort. (2019) The Ford Pinto. *Famous Cases.* Retrieved from https://www.tortmuseum.org/ford-pinto/

Amore, A. M. (2015) *The Art of the Con.* New York: St. Martin's Press

Applegate, J. S. (1982) The Business Papers Rule: Personal privacy and white collar crime. *Articles by Mauer Faculty, Mauer School of Law: Indiana University.* Vol. 16 No. 2: 189-241

Arquilla, J. (2013) Twenty years of cyberwar. *Journal of Military Ethics.* Vol. 12: 80-87

Asmelash, L. (2020) Tito's tells customers to not use their vodka for hand sanitizer. CNN. Mar. 19. Retrieved from https://www.cnn.com/2020/03/05/us/titos-vodka-coronavirus-trnd/index.html

Associated Press. (2017) Alabama-based HealthSouth changing name. *Associated Press News.* July 11. Retrieved from https://apnews.com/19abdc5561334b97a220f3581ce7d9b5

Associated Press. (2018) Priest accused of embezzling $5 million from his church for lavish estate. *Money.* Mar. 18. Retrieved from http://money.com/money/5223485/michigan-priest-embezzled-from-church/

Ayer, M. and S. Glover. (2018) California's largest utility provider's role in wildfires is under scrutiny. *CNN.* Dec. 19. Retrieved from https://www.cnn.com/2018/12/19/us/camp-fire-pge-invs/index.html

Ayres, S. (2019) Russia looking to ratify Paris Agreement as U.S. continues withdrawal. *Los Angeles Times.* Feb. 16. Retrieved from https://www.latimes.com/world/europe/la-fg-russia-climate-change-20190216-story.html

Bagley, B. M. (2017) *Drug Trafficking, Organized Crime, and Violence in the Americas Today.* J.D. Rosen, ed. Gainesville, FL: University Press of Florida

Banta, M. (2020) Rev. Wehrle, retired priest charged with embezzlement, died Tuesday, bishop says. *USA Today.* Retrieved from https://www.usatoday.com/story/news/local/2020/03/31/rev-jonathanwehrle-diocese-lansing-embezzlement-dead/5099438002

Barborak, N. (2014) Saving the world, one Cadillac at a time: What can be done when a religious or charitable organization commits solicitation fraud? *Akron Law Review.* Spring, Vol. 33, Issue 4: 577

Barker, E. (1986) Religious movements: Cults and anticult since Jonestown. *Annual Review of Sociology.* Vol. 12: 329-346

Barnes, R. L. (2011) Regulating the disposal of cigarette butts as toxic hazardous waste. *Tobacco Control.* May, Vol. 20: 145-148

Bartash, J. (2019) Prescription drug prices aren't rising—they're falling for the first time in 47 years. Market Watch. March 12. Retrieved from https://www.marketwatch.com/story/prescriptiondrug-prices-arent-rising-theyre-falling-for-the-first-time-in-47-years-2019-03-12

Bates, R. and M. Mooney. (2014) Distance learning and Jihad: The dark side of the force. *Online Journal of Distance Learning Administration.* Vol. 17, No. 3. Retrieved from https://www.westga.edu/distance/ojdla/fall173/Bates_Mooney173.html

Bauman, Z. (1993) *Postmodern ethics.* Cambridge, U.K.: Polity Press

Belk, D. (2019) True cost of healthcare. *Malpractice statistics.* Retrieved from http://truecostofhealthcare.org/malpractice_statistics/

Benediktsdóttir, S., G. B. Eggertsson, and E. Þórarinsson. (2017) The rise, fall, and resurrection of Iceland: A postmortem analysis of the 2008 financial crisis. *Brooks Papers on Economic Activity.* Fall: 191-308

Bennett, J. and D. O'Donovan. (2001) Substance misuse by doctors, nurses, and other healthcare workers. *Current Opinion in Psychiatry.* Vol. 14, Issue 3: 195-199

Bennett, M. (2018) 11 common types of credit card scams and frauds. *Consumer Protection.* Sept. 28. Retrieved from https://www.consumerprotect.com/crime-fraud/11-types-of-credit-card-fraud-scams/

Bernstein, C. (2005) *The secret man: The story of Watergate's Deep Throat.* New York: Simon and Schuster

Bernstein, J. (2012) Nixon's smoking-gun tape and presidency. *Washington Post.* June 22. Retrieved from https://www.washingtonpost.com/blogs/post-partisan/post/nixons-smoking-gun-tape-and-the-presidency/2012/06/22/gJQA0gTlvV_blog.html?utm_term=.de3b7511a630

Bilton, N. (Host) (2019, Nov. 22) Can a whistleblower really bring down Trump? *Inside the Hive by Vanity Fair* [Audio podcast] Retrieved from https://podcasts.apple.com/us/podcast/inside-the-hive-with-nick-bilton/id1232383877

Bindley, K. (2012) Internet romance scams cost victims $50 million in 2011. *Huffington Post.* Retrieved from https://www.huffingtonpost.com/2012/05/15/online-romance-scams-cost-50-million-in-2011_n_1518162.html

Biocanin, R. M. Sarvan, and A. Prolovic. (2018) Corporate governance and social responsibility in "fight" against ecological criminality. *Analele Universit ü "Constantin Brâncusi" din Târgu Jiu: Seria Inginerie.* Vol. 4: 74-91

Biography.com (eds.). (2019) Mohamed Atta Biography. A&E Television Networks, publisher. Sept. 4. Retrieved from https://www.biography.com/crime-figure/mohamed-atta

Bivins, J. C. (2003) *The Fracture of Good Order: Christian Antiliberalism and the Challenge to American Politics.* Chapel Hill, NC: The University of North Carolina Press

Black, W. K. (2005) *The Best Way to Rob a Bank is to Own One.* Austin, TX: University of Texas Press

Block, A. A. (2000) The origins of Iran-Contra: Lessons from the Durrani Affair. *Crime, Law, and Social Change.* Mar., Vol. 33, Issue 1, 2: 53-84

Bock Park, D. (2019) The tearful drama of North Carolina's election-fraud hearing. Dispatch, *New Yorker.* Feb. 24. Retrieved from https://www.newyorker.com/news/dispatch/the-tearful-drama-of-north-carolinas-election-fraud-hearings

Bone, E. (2017) 'Truffle oil' without any actual truffles. *The New York Times.* Sept. 15. Retrieved from https://www.nytimes.com/2017/09/15/opinion/truffle-oil-chemicals.html

Booker, B. (2020) Michael Cohen released from prison due to coronavirus concerns. *NPR.* May 21. Retrieved from https://www.npr.org/sections/coronavirus-live-updates/2020/05/21/860204544/michael-cohen-released-from-prison-due-to-coronavirus-concerns

Bosman, J., S. F. Kovalesky, J. A. Del Real. (2019) "Pied piper" of college admissions: Scam had all the answers. *New York Times.* Mar. 18. Retrieved from https://www.nytimes.com/2019/03/18/us/william-rick-singer-admissions-scandal.html

Bosse, D. A. and R. A. Phillips. (2016) Agency theory and bounded self-interest. *Academy of Management Review.* Vol. 4, No. 2: 276-297

Bossler, A. M. and G. W. Burruss. (2011) The general theory of crime and computer hacking: Low self-control hackers? *Corporate hacking and technology-driven crime: Social dynamics and implications,* T. J. Holt and B. H. Schell, eds. UK: IGI Global

Boyle, A. (2018) Climate Change, the Paris Agreement and Human Rights. *International and Comparative Law Quarterly.* Vol. 67: 759-777

British Broadcasting Corporation (BBC). (2019a) Fang Fenghui: China's ex-top general jailed for life. Feb. 20. Retrieved from https://www.bbc.com/news/world-asia-china-47306275

British Broadcasting Corporation (BBC). (2019b) Four questions about Trump's tower in Moscow that never was. Jan. 18. Retrieved from https://www.bbc.com/news/world-us-canada-46923008

British Broadcasting Corporation (BBC). (2020) Ghislaine Maxwell sues Jeffrey Epstein's estate over legal fees. Mar. 19. Retrieved from https://www.bbc.com/news/world-us-canada-51955675

Britton, B. and M. Ramsay. (2019) Three charged over murder of Maltese journalist Daphne Caruana Galizia. *CNN.com.* Retrieved from https://www.cnn.com/2019/07/17/europe/daphne-caruana-galizia-men-charged-intl/index.html

Broadhurst, R., P. Grabosky, M. Alazab, B. Bourhours, and S. Chon. (2014) Organizations and cyber crime: An analysis of the growing nature of groups engaged in cyber crime. *International Journal of Criminology.* Vol. 8 (1): 1-20

Bronsert, A., A. Glazer, and K. A. Konrad. (2016) Old money, the nouveaux riches and Brunhilde's marriage strategy. *Journal of Population Economy.* Vol. 30: 163-186

Brooke, D., G. Edwards, and T. Andrews. (1993) Doctors and substance misuse: types of doctors, types of problems. *Addiction.* Vol. 88: 655-663

Brounen, D. and J. Derwall. (2010) The impact of terrorist attacks on international stock markets. *European Financial Management.* Aug. 19. Vol. 16, Issue 4: 585-598

Brown University (n.d.) Understanding the Iran-Contra Affair. Prosecutions, *Good Government Project.* Retrieved from https://www.brown.edu/Research/Understanding_the_Iran_Contra_Affair/prosecutionsphp

Bryman, A. (2004) *The Disneyization of society.* London: Sage Publishing

Buchanan, M. (2002) *Nexus: Small worlds and the groundbreaking science of networks.* New York: W.W. Norton and Co., Inc

Burcher, M. and C. Whelan. (2015) Social network analysis and small group 'dark' networks: An analysis of the London bombers and the problem with 'fuzzy' boundaries. *Global Crime.* Vol. 16, Issue Vol. 16, Issue 4: 585-598

Bureau of Consular Affairs. (n.d.) Travel advisories. U.S. Department of State. Retrieved from https://travel.state.gov/content/travel/en/traveladvisories/traveladvisories.html/

Bureau of Labor Statistics (BLS). (2013) Fact Sheet: Workplace Homicides from Shootings. United States Department of Labor. Jan. Retrieved from https://www.bls.gov/iif/oshwc/cfoi/osar0016.htm

Bureau of Labor Statistics (BLS). (2019) Injuries, illness, and fatalities. U.S. Department of Labor. Retrieved from https://www.bls.gov/iif/

Bureau of Labor Statistics (BLS). (n.d.) Number of jobs held in lifetime. *National Longitudinal Studies.* Retrieved from https://www.bls.gov/nls/nlsfaqs.htm#anch41

Burgess, R. and R. L. Akers. (1966) A differential association-reinforcement theory of criminal behavior. *Social Problems.* Vol. 14: 363-383

Bush, M. (2014) 10 CEOs brought down by greed. *MSN News.* Oct. 23. Retrieved from https://www.msn.com/en-ca/news/other/10-ceos-brought-down-by-greed/ss-BBaHOLt

BusinessIDtheft.org (n.d.) Shelf corporations and trade rings: Paper companies used for real fraud. Retrieved from http://businessidtheft.org/Education/BusinessIDTheftScams/ShelfCorporationsandTradeRings/tabid/104/Default.aspx

Buxant, C., V. Saroglou, S. Casalfiore, and L. Christians. (2007) Cognitive and emotional characteristics of New Religious Movement members: New questions and data on the mental health issue. *Mental Health, Religion and Culture.* May. Vol. 10, No. 3: 219-238

Caffey, D. L. (2015) *Chasing the Santa Fe Ring: Power and Privilege in territorial New Mexico.* Albuquerque, NM: University of New Mexico Press

Camp, A. C. (2010) Cutting Cupid out of the workplace: The capacity of employees' constitutional privacy rights to constrain employers' attempts to limit off-duty intimate associations. *Hastings Communications & Entertainment Law Journal* (COMM/ENT). Vol. 32, Issue 3: 427. Retrieved from https://repository.uchastings.edu/cgi/viewcontent.cgi?article=1702&context= hastings_comm_ent_ law_journal

Cantrell, A. (2018) Surviving prison as a Wall Street convict. *Institutional Investor.* Dec. 13. Retrieved from https://www.institutionalinvestor.com/article/b18b7g0qjk5pwb/Surviving-Prison-as-a-Wall-Street-Convict

Caplan, D. H., S. K. Dutta, and D. J. Marcinko. (2019) Unmasking the fraud at Toshiba. *Issues in Accounting Education.* Vol. 34, No. 3: 41-57

Carney, J. (2013) Is Raj Rajaratnam really living like a prison king? CNBC. Aug. 27. Retrieved from https://www.cnbc.com/id/100991730

Carrico, A. W., E. Nil, C. Sophal, E. Stein, M. Sokunny, N. Yuthea, J. L. Evans, S. Ngak, L. Maher, and K. Page. (2016) Behavioral interventions for Cambodian female entertainment and sex workers who use amphetamine-type stimulants. *Journal of Behavioral Medicine.* Vol. 39: 502-510

Carson, R. (1962) *Silent Spring.* Greenwich, CT: Fawcett Publications, Inc. Reprint

Caruso, C. A. (n.d.) Overcoming Legal Challenges in Extradition. *Asia Law Initiative, American Bar Association.* Available at https://www.americanbar.org/content/dam/aba/directories/roli/raca/asia_raca_charlescaruso_overcoming.authcheckdampdf

Census Bureau. (2019) Quarterly retail e-commerce sales, 12st quarter 2019. U.S. Department of Commerce. May 17. Retrieved from https://www.census.gov/retail/mrts/www/data/pdf/ec_current.pdf

Center on Media, Crime, and Justice, John Jay College. (2019) 15% of pharmacies bought nearly half of opioids. *Crime and Justice News,* The Crime Report. Aug. 13. Retrieved from https://thecrimereport.org/2019/08/13/15-of-pharmacies-handled-nearly-half-of-opioids/

Centers for Disease Control and Prevention (CDC). (2019) Opioid overdose. Retrieved from https://www. cdc.gov/drugoverdose/data/statedeaths.html

Centers for Disease Control and Prevention (CDC). (2019) U.S. Public Health Service Syphilis Study at Tuskegee. Retrieved from https://www.cdc.gov/tuskegee/timeline.htm

Centers for Disease Control and Prevention (CDC). (2020) Morbidity and Mortality Weekly Report: Trends in total binge drinks—United States, 2011-2017. Jan. 17. Retrieved from https://www. cdc.gov/mmwr/volumes/69/wr/mm6902a2.htm?s_cid=mm6902a2_w

CFO.com. (2017) Two CFOs tell a tale of fraud at HealthSouth. Mar. 27. Retrieved from https://www.cfo.com/fraud/2017/03/two-cfos-tell-tale-fraud-healthsouth/

Charity Navigator. (2019) Key Worldwide Foundation CN Advisory. Mar. 21. Retrieved from https://www.charitynavigator.org/index.cfm?bay=search.summary&orgid=17998

The Christian Century. (2009) Church embezzlers also rob congregations of trust. Sept. 22, Vol. 126, Issue 19: 16

Christie, B. (2014) Swindler Keating dies at 90. *Associated Press, Daily Hampshire Gazette.* April 10. Retrieved from https://www.gazettenet.com/Archives/2014/04/keating-hg-040214

Chung, D. E. (2018) When bureaucracy is actually helpful, according to research. *Harvard Business Review.* Jan. 3. Retrieved from https://hbr.org/2018/01/when-bureaucracy-is-actually-helpful-according-to-research

Clifford, M. (1998) *Environmental Crime: Enforcement, Policy, and Social Responsibility.* Preface. M. Clifford, ed. Gaithersburg, Md.: Aspen Publishers

Clifton, J. (2017) The world's broken workplace. *Gallup.* Retrieved from https://news.gallup.com/opinion/chairman/212045/world-broken-workplace.aspx

CNN (2019) Boston Marathon timeline. *CNN Library.* Apr. 9. Retrieved from https://www.cnn.com/2013/06/03/us/boston-marathon-terror-attack-fast-facts/index.html

CNN (2020) READ: Sen. Mitt Romney explains why he'll vote to convict Trump. *CNN.com.* Feb. 5. Retrieved from https://www.cnn.com/2020/02/05/politics/mitt-romney-impeachment-vote-remarks/index.html

Coates, J. C. and S. Srinivasan. (2014) SOX after ten years: A multidiscipline review. *Accounting Horizons.* Vol. 28, No. 3: 627-671

Cohen, L. E. and M. Felson. (1979) Social change and crime rate trends: A routine activity approach. *American Sociological Review*. Vol. 44: 588-608

Cohen-Louck, K. (2019) Perception of the threat of terrorism. *Journal of Interpersonal Violence*. Vol. 34, No. 5: 887-911

Coleman, J. W. (1985) *The criminal elite: The sociology of white collar crime*. New York: St. Martin's Press

Collins, R. (1975) Conflict theory of organizations. *Conflict Sociology: Toward an Explanatory Social Science*. New York: Academic Press. 286-347

Congressional Budget Office. (2016) Scanning and imaging shipping containers overseas: Costs and alternatives. June. Retrieved from https://www.cbo.gov/sites/default/files/114th-congress-2015-2016/reports/51478-Shipping-Containers-OneCol.pdf

Copes, H. and L. Vieraitis. (2017) Identity theft: Assessing offenders' motivations and strategies, in *In Their Own Words*, M. L. Birzer and P. Cromwell, eds. 7th edition. New York: Oxford University Press. Ch 8

Cornwell, B. and F. A. Dokshin. (2014) The power of integration: Affiliation and cohesion n a diverse elite network. *Social Forces*. Vol. 93, No. 2: 803-832

Crompton, R. and C. Lyonett. (2005) The new gender essentialism—domestic and family choices and their relationship to attitudes. *The British Journal of Sociology*. Vol. 56, No. 4: 601-620

Cuff, D. F. (1987) Business people; Insider prosecutor to join law firm. *New York Times*. July 15. Retrieved from https://www.nytimes.com/1987/07/15/business/business-people-insider-prosecutor-to-join-law-firm.html

Cunningham, L. (2015) In a big move, Accenture will get rid of annual performance reviews and rankings. *The Washington Post*. July 21. Retrieved from https://www.washingtonpost.com/news/on-leadership/wp/2015/07/21/in-big-move-accenture-will-get-rid-of-annualperformance-reviews-and-rankings/?utm_term=.b7bff359321a

Cusato, E. (2018) Ecocide to voluntary remediation projects: Legal responses to environmental warfare in Vietnam and the spectre of colonialism. *Melbourne Journal of International Law*. Vol. 2, Issue 2: 1-27

Customs and Border Patrol (CBP). (n.d.) Cargo security and examinations. Department of Homeland Security. Retrieved from https://www.cbp.gov/border-security/ports-entry/cargo-security

Dalins, J., C. Wilson, and M. Carman. (2018) Criminal motivation on the dark web: A categorization model for law enforcement. *Digital Investigation*. Vol. 24: 62-71

Dangremond, S. (2018) The most famous victims of Bernie Madoff's Ponzi scheme. *Town and Country*. Nov. 20. Retrieved from https://www.townandcountrymag.com/society/money-and-power/g13797624/bernie-madoff-victims/

Dashineau, S. C., E. A. Edershile, L. J. Simms, and A. G. C. Wright. (2019) Pathological narcissism and psychosocial functioning. Personality Disorders: Theory, Research, and Treatment. July 1. Advance online publication. http://dx.doi.org/10.1037/per0000347

Date, S. V., J. Rokade, V. Mule, and S. Dandapannavar. (2014) Female sterilization failure: Review over a decade and its clinicopathological correlation. *International Journal of Applied Basic Medical Research*. July-Dec., Vol. 4, No. 2: 81-85

Davies, Barrell, Will, Lewellyn and Edwards, PLC. (2016) $1.8 million jury award in wrongful pregnancy case. *Firm News*. August. Retrieved from https://www.dbwle.com/firm-news/2016/august/-1-8-million-jury-award-in-wrongful-pregnancy-ca/

Davis, J. L., B. L. Green, and R. V. Katz. (2012) Influence of scary beliefs about the Tuskegee Syphilis Study on willingness to participate in research. *ABNF Journal*. Summer, Vol. 23, No. 3: 59-62

Department of Health and Human Services. (2019) *National Health Expenditures 2017 Highlights*. Centers for Medicare and Medicaid Services. Retrieved from https://www.cms.gov/Research-Statistics-Data-and-Systems/Statistics-Trends-and-Reports/NationalHealth ExpendData/downloads/highlightspdf

Department of Justice. (2015) Ephren Taylor sentenced to federal prison. Press Release, U.S. Attorney's Office, Northern District of Georgia. March 17. Retrieved from https://www.justice.gov/usao-ndga/pr/ephren-taylor-sentenced-federal-prison

Department of Justice. (2016) ISIL-linked Kosovo hacker sentenced to 20 years in prison. *Justice News*, Office of Public Affairs. Sept. 23. Retrieved from https://www.justice.gov/opa/pr/isil-linked-kosovo-hacker-sentenced-20-years-prison

Department of Justice. (2018) Two Chinese hackers associated with the Ministry of State Security charged with global computer intrusion campaigns targeting intellectual property and confidential business information. Press release, Office of Public Affairs. Dec. 20. Retrieved from https://www.justice.gov/opa/pr/two-chinese-hackers-associated-ministry-state-securitycharged-global-computer-intrusion

Department of Justice. (2019) Doctor charged for prescribing narcotics to non patients ordered detained until trail. *Press release*, Office of Public Affairs, The U.S. Attorney's Office, Southern District of Georgia. Jan. 28. Retrieved from https://www.justice.gov/usao-sdga/pr/doctorcharged-prescribing-narcotics-non-patients-ordered-detained-until-trial

Department of Justice. (2019) Encompass Health agrees to pay $48 million to resolve False Claims Act allegations relating to its inpatient rehabilitation facilities. Published in Legal Monitor Worldwide. July 16. http://www.syndigate.info/

Department of Justice. (2019) Former defense intelligence officer pleads guilty to attempted espionage. Press Release, Office of Public Affairs. Mar. 15. Retrieved from https://www.justice.gov/opa/pr/former-defense-intelligence-officer-pleads-guilty-attempted-espionage

Department of Justice. (2019) Medical device maker ACell Inc. pleads guilty and will pay $15 million to resolve criminal charges and civil false claims allegations. Press Release, Office of Public Affairs, The U.S. Attorney's Office, U.S. District Court, Maryland. Retrieved from https://www.justice.gov/opa/pr/medical-device-maker-acell-inc-pleads-guilty-and-will-pay-15-million-resolve-criminal-charges

Department of Justice. (2019) Professor of International Studies charged in international money laundering scheme. Press Release, U.S. Attorney's Office, Southern District of New York. Nov. 18. Retrieved from https://www.justice.gov/usao-sdny/pr/professor-international-studies-charged-international-money-laundering-scheme

Department of Justice. (2019) South Florida health care facility owner convicted for role in largest health care fraud scheme charged by The Department of Justice, involving $1.3 billion in fraudulent claims. Press Release, Office of Public Affairs. Retrieved from https://www.justice.gov/opa/pr/south-florida-health-care-facility-owner-convicted-role-largest-health-care-fraudscheme-ever

Department of Justice. (2020) Department of Justice announces disruption of hundreds of COVID-19 related scams: Hundreds of domains disrupted through public and private sector cooperative efforts. *Justice News*, Office of Public Affairs. April 22. Retrieved from https://www.justice.gov/opa/pr/department-justice-announces-disruption-hundreds-online-covid-19-related-scams

Department of Justice. (n.d.) Information about the Department of Justice's Attorney General China Initiative, AAG Demers bio and compilation of China related criminal cases since Jan. 2018. Press release. Retrieved from https://www.justice.gov/opa/press-release/file/1179321/download

Department of Justice, United States Attorney, Eastern District of New York. Oct. 11. Retrieved from https://www.abc.net.au/mediawatch/transcripts/1419_dojcase.pdf

Department of Transportation. (n.d.) Drunk driving: Overview. National Highway Transportation Safety Administration. Retrieved from https://www.nhtsa.gov/risky-driving/drunk-driving

Dervan, L. E. (2011) International white collar crime and the globalization of internal investigations. *Fordham Urban Law Review*. Vol. 39, Issue 2: 361-390

Dewar, R. D. and D. P. Simet. (1981) A level specific perdition of spans of control examining the effects of size, technology, and specialization. *Academy of Management Journal*. Vol. 24, No. 1: 5-24

Diamond, S. (1985) The Bhopal disaster: How it happened. *The New York Times*. Jan. 28

Dickson, E. J. (2019) A complete guide to the NXIVM trial. *Rolling Stone*. Apr. 22. Retrieved from https://www.rollingstone.com/culture/culture-features/nxivm-trial-whos-who-keith-ranierealison-mack-salzman-bronfman-825328/

Dimaggio, P. J. and W. W. Powell. (1983) The iron cage revisited: Institutional isomorphism and collective rationality in organizational fields. *American Sociological Review*. Vol. 48, No. 2: 147–160

Dipert, R. R. (2010) Ethics of cyberwarfare. *Journal of Military Ethics*. 9(4): 384-410

Domscheit-Berg, D. (2011) *Inside WikiLeaks: My time with Julian Assange at the world's most dangerous website.* London: Jonathan Cape

Dot-Pouillard, N. and E. Rébillard. (2013) The Intellectual, the Militant, the Prisoner and the Partisan: The genesis of the Islamic Jihad Movement in Palestine (1974-1988). *Muslim World*. Jan. Vol. 103, Issue 1: 161-180

Dougan, M. (1997) Heaven's Gate survivor kills self. *The Examiner Staff.* May 7. Retrieved from https://www.sfgate.com/news/article/Heaven-s-Gate-survivor-kills-self-3120047php

Durkheim, E. (1995; 1912) *The Elementary Forms of Religious Life.* K. Fields, trans. New York: The Free Press

Durkheim, E. (1998) *Suicide.* Originally published in 1897. New York: The Free Press, Simon and Schuster

Durney, M. and B. Proulx. (2011) Art crime: A brief introduction. *Crime, Law, and Social Change.* Sept. 56: 115-132

Dykeman, A. and MoneyBuilder. (2011) Are online banks safe? *Forbes.* Retrieved from https://www.forbes.com/sites/moneybuilder/2011/03/30/are-online-banks-safe/#15ced1ac5017

Eaton, L. (2004) The Martha Stewart verdict: The overview; Stewart found guilty of lying in sale of stock. *The New York Times.* March 6. Retrieved from https://www.nytimes.com/2004/03/06/business/martha-stewart-verdict-overview-stewart-found-guilty-lying-sale-stock.html

The Economist. (2008) Villepin v Sarkozy: France's Clearstream affair. Dec. 6. Vol. 389, Issue 8609. Retrieved from https://www.economist.com/europe/2008/12/04/villepin-v-sarkozy

The Economist. (2012) Affinity fraud: Fleecing the flock. Retrieved from https://www.economist.com/business/2012/01/28/fleecing-the-flock

Edwards, R. (1979) *Contested terrain.* New York: Basic Books (Hachette Books)

Ekmekci, P. E. (2016) Main ethical breaches in multicenter clinical trials regulation in Turkey. *Medicine and Law.* Vol. 35: 491-508

Encompass Health. (n.d.) Our Purpose. Retrieved from https://www.encompasshealth.com/homeoffice-ehc

Environmental Protection Agency. (2019a) Compliance: How we monitor compliance. Retrieved from https://www.epa.gov/compliance/how-we-monitor-compliance

Environmental Protection Agency. (2019b) *Environmental Crimes Case Bulletin.* Office of Criminal Enforcement Forensics & Training. Retrieved from https://www.epa.gov/sites/production/files/2019-05/documents/march-april2019bulletinpdf

Environmental Protection Agency. (2019c) Facts and figures about materials, waste and recycling. Retrieved from https://www.epa.gov/facts-and-figures-about-materials-waste-and-recycling/national-overview-facts-and-figures-materials#NationalPicture

Environmental Protection Agency. (2019d) Summary of the Clean Water Act. *Laws & Regulations.* Retrieved from https://www.epa.gov/laws-regulations/summary-clean-water-act

Environmental Protection Agency. (2019e) Wastes—non-hazardous waste—municipal solid waste. Retrieved from https://archive.epa.gov/epawaste/nonhaz/municipal/web/html/

Ermann, D. M. and R. J. Lundman (Eds). (1996) *Corporate and Governmental Deviance: Problems of Organization Behavior in Contemporary Society.* New York: Oxford University Press

Fallick, B., C. A. Fleischman, and J. B. Rebitzer. (2006) Job-hopping in Silicon Valley: Some evidence concerning the microfoundations of high-technology cluster. *The Review of Economics and Statistics.* Vol. 33, No. 3: 472-481

Faturoti, B. (2015) Business identity theft under the UDRP and the ACPA: Is bad faith always bad for business advertising? *Journal of International Commercial Law and Technology.* Vol. 10, Issue 1: 1-12

Feder, B. J. (2003) John Sidgmore, 52, dies; Headed WorldCom. *The New York Times.* Dec. 12. Retrieved from https://www.nytimes.com/2003/12/12/business/john-sidgmore-52-diesheaded-worldcom.html

Federal Bureau of Investigation (FBI). (2003) Crime in the suite: Former HealthSouth CEO indicted in $2.7 billion case of corporate fraud. Stories. Nov. 4. Retrieved from https://archives.fbi.gov/archives/news/stories/2003/november/health_110403

Federal Bureau of Investigations (FBI). (2014) A byte out of history: $10 million hack 1994-style. News. Jan. 31. Retrieved from https://www.fbi.gov/news/stories/a-byte-out-of-history-10-million-hack

Federal Bureau of Investigations (FBI). (2019) Addressing threats to the Nation's cybersecurity. *Documents.* Retrieved from https://www.fbi.gov/file-repository/addressing-threats-to-the-nations-cybersecurity-1.pdf/view

Federal Bureau of Investigations (FBI). (2019) Cyber crime. *What We Investigate.* Retrieved from https://www.fbi.gov/investigate/cyber

Federal Bureau of Investigations (FBI). (2019) Most wanted. *White Collar Crimes*. Retrieved from https://www.fbi.gov/wanted/wcc/jorge-iglesias-vazquez

Federal Drug Administration (FDA). (2019) Is the product a medical device? Device Regulation. Retrieved from https://www.fda.gov/medical-devices/classify-your-medical-device/productmedical-device

Federal Trade Commission. (2014) FTC alleges Amazon unlawfully billed parents for millions of dollars in children's unauthorized in-app charges: No password or other indication of parental consent was required for charges in kids' apps; internal e-mail referred to situation as "house on fire." Press release, July 10. Retrieved from https://www.ftc.gov/news-events/pressreleases/2014/07/ftc-alleges-amazon-unlawfully-billed-parents-millions-dollars

Federal Trade Commission. (2016) Federal Court finds Amazon liable for billing parents for children's unauthorized in-app charges. Press release, April 27. Retrieved from https://www.ftc.gov/news-events/press-releases/2016/04/federal-court-finds-amazon-liable-billing-parentschildrens

Federal Trade Commission. (2019) How to donate wisely and avoid charity scams. Retrieved from https://www.consumer.ftc.gov/features/how-donate-wisely-and-avoid-charity-scams

Fernholz, T. (2019) Terrorists are trafficking looted antiquities with impunity on Facebook. Quartz, Yahoo! Finance. July 3. Retrieved from https://finance.yahoo.com/news/terrorists-trafficking-looted-antiquities-impunity-080045960.html

Field, R. I. (2011) The malpractice crisis turns 175: What lessons does history hold for reform? *Drexel Law Review*. Vol. 4: 7-39

Fielding, N. G. (2017) The shaping of covert social networks: Isolating the effects of secrecy. *Trends in Organized Crime*. 20: 16-30

Finkelstein, S. (2015) The end of middle management? *BBC Worklife*. June 24. Retrieved from https://www.bbc.com/worklife/article/20150624-the-end-of-middle-management

Fischer, S. (2007) *When the mob ran Las Vegas: Stories of money, mayhem, and murder.* New York: MJF Books. 3d ed.

Fitz, A. (2019) Why intent is so important in white collar crime cases. Law office of Ann Fitz. Aug. 22. Retrieved from https://palmbeachfederaldefense.com/blog/2019/08/why-intent-is-so-important-in-white-collar-crime-cases/

Flaherty, C. (2018) Faculty salaries up 3%. *Inside Higher Ed*. Apr. 11. Retrieved from https://www.insidehighered.com/news/2018/04/11/aaups-annual-report-faculty-compensation-takes-salary-compression-and-more

Fleckenstein, M. P. and J. C. Bowes. (2000) When trust is betrayed: Religious institutions and white collar crimes. *Journal of Business Ethics*. Jan., Vol. 23, Issue 1: 111-115

Flemma, R. J. (1985) Medical malpractice: A dilemma in the search for justice. *Marquette Law Review*. Winter, Vol. 68, Issue 2: 237-258

Frantz, D. (1997) The shadowy story behind Scientology's tax-exempt status. *New York Times*. Mar. 9. Retrieved from https://www.cs.cmu.edu/dst/Cowen/essays/nytimes.html

Freeman, J., G. R. Carroll, and M. T. Hannan. (1983) The liability of newness: Age dependence in organizational death rates. *American Sociological Review*. Oct. Vol. 48, No. 5: 692-710

Friedman, J. S. (2006) Whiskey and the wires: The inadvisable application of the wire fraud statute to alcohol smuggling and foreign tax evasion. *The Journal of Criminal Law and Criminology*. Vol. 96, No. 3: 911-945

Friedrichs, D. O. (2009) *Trusted Criminals: White Collar Crime in Contemporary Society*. 4th ed. Belmont, CA: Wadsworth Publishing Co.

Fuchs, E. and A. Tzatzev. (2013) Camp Cupcake: Take a tour in America's cushiest prison. *Business Insider*. June 6. Retrieved from https://www.businessinsider.com/take-a-tour-of-americas-cushiest-prison-2013-6

Fuller, J. R. (2017) Seven ways to tell if your olive is fake. *Epicurious*. May 25. Retrieved from https://www.epicurious.com/ingredients/seven-ways-to-tell-the-difference-between-real-andfake-olive-oil-article

Fullerton, J. (2019) Former prime minister accused over role in looting $4.5 billion sovereign wealth fund. *The Guardian*. Apr. 3. Retrieved from https://www.theguardian.com/world/2019/apr/03/najib-razak-malaysia-former-prime-minister-trial-1mdb-scandal

Gangitano, A. (2019) Former Podesta lobbyists reap K Street boom. *The Hill.* Sept. 4. Retrieved from https://thehill.com/business-a-lobbying/business-a-lobbying/459816-former-podestalobbyists-reap-k-street-boom

Ganor, B. (2004) Terror is a strategy of psychological warfare. Journal of Aggression, Maltreatment, & Trauma. Vol. 9, Issue 1 /2: 33-43

Garcia-Carmona, M., M. D. Marin, and R. Aguayo. (2019) Burnout syndrome of secondary school teachers: A systematic review and meta-analysis. *Social Psychology of Education.* Vol. 22: 189-208

Garcia Sigman, L. I. (2017) Narcotrafico en la Darkweb: Los criptomercados. *URVIO.* Dec. (21): 191-206

Geisst, C. R. (2018) *Wall Street: A history.* New York: Oxford University Press

Georgia Department of Law. (2019) Telemarketing fraud. Consumer Protection Division. Retrieved from http://consumer.georgia.gov/consumer-topics/telemarketing-fraud

Gerber, J. (2000) On the relationship between organized and white collar crime: Government, business, and criminal enterprise in post-Communist Russia. *European Journal of Crime, Criminal Law, and Criminal Justice.* Apr. Vol. 8, No. 4: 327-342

Gilligan, V. and P. Gould. (2015) *Better Call Saul.* AMC. Season 1

Giroux, G. (2008) What went wrong? Accounting fraud and lessons from recent scandals. *Social Research.* Winter, Vol. 75, Issue 4: 1205-1238

Gist, N. P. (1938) Structure and process in secret societies. *Social Forces.* Vol. 16(3): 349-357

Glassdoor.com. (2018) University of Miami Professor salaries. Dec. 7. Retrieved from https://www.glassdoor.com/Salary/University-of-Miami-Professor-Salaries-E33297_D_KO20,29.htm

Gleason, S. (2016) James Lomma, owner of crane in 2008, files for bankruptcy. Jan. 7. Retrieved from https://www.wsj.com/articles/james-lomma-owner-of-crane-in-2008-collapse-files-for-bankruptcy-1452191914

Gonzales, R. (2019) New York AG says Sacklers transferred $1 billion from Pharma accounts to themselves. *NPR.* Retrieved from https://www.npr.org/2019/09/13/760688886/new-york-agsays-sacklers-transferred-millions-from-pharma-accounts-to-themselves

Gorman, T. (1999) Bookkeeper in estate fraud case enters guilty plea. *Los Angeles Times.* Nov. 11. Retrieved from https://www.latimes.com/archives/la-xpm-1999-nov-11-me-32277-story.html

Gottschalk, P. (2015) Private investigations of white collar crime suspicions: A qualitative study of the Blame Game Hypothesis. *Journal of Investigative Psychology and Offender Profiling.* Vol. 12: 231-246

Gottschalk, P. and R. Smith. Gender and white collar crime: Examining representations of women in media? *Journal of Gender Studies.* Vol. 24, No. 3: 310-325

Government Accountability Office (GAO). (2007) Cost of prisons: Bureau of Prisons needs better data to assess alternatives for acquiring low and minimum security facilities. Report to the Subcommittees on Commerce, Justice, and Sciences, Senate and House Appropriations Committees, *Highlights of GAO.* Oct. Washington, D.C.: U.S. GAO

Government Accountability Office (GAO). (2019) About GAO: Overview. Retrieved from https://www.gao.gov/about/

Granda, C. (2019) Embezzlement suspect accused of stealing more than $88,000 from Girl Scout troops, Beverly Hills Cancer Center. *ABC Channel 7.* Retrieved from https://abc7.com/woman-accused-of-embezzling-more-than-$88k-from-nonprofits/4285406/

Granovetter, M. S. (1973) The strength of weak ties. *American Journal of Sociology.* May, Vol. 78, No. 6: 1360-1380

Green, S. P. (2014) Moral ambiguity in white collar criminal law. *Notre Dame Journal of Law.* Vol. 18, Issue 2. Symposium of Criminal Punishment: 501-519

Greenberg, J. A. (2008) Hysteroscopic sterilization: History and current methods. *Reviews in Obstetrics and Gynecology.* Summer, Vol. 1, No. 3: 113-121

Grettisson, V. (2018) 36 bankers, 96 years in jail. *The Reykjavík Grapevine.* Feb. 7. Retrieved from https://grapevine.is/news/2018/02/07/36-bankers-96-years-in-jail/

Grey, S. (2018) The silencing of Daphne. *Reuters Investigates.* Apr. 17. Retrieved from https://www.reuters.com/investigates/special-report/malta-daphne/

Grier, P. (2010) George Steinbrenner spent big on politics, too. *The Christian Science Monitor.* Retrieved from https://www.csmonitor.com/USA/Politics/Decoder/2010/0716/George-Steinbrenner-spent-big-on-politics-too

Griffiths, J. (2019) From Hollywood to Saudi Arabia, Leonardo DiCaprio to Paris Hilton: The scandal that enveloped the world. *CNN World*. Feb. 8. Retrieved from https://www-m.cnn.com/2019/02/08/asia/malaysia-1mdb-trial-najib-intl/index.html

Grigoriadis, V. (2019) The horny holy man: Keith Raniere duped followers that power and growth came through submission. *Vanity Fair*. Sept. Published by Condé Nast

Groenleer, M. and S. Gabbi. (2013) Regulatory agencies of the European Union as international actors. *European Journal of Risk Regulation*. Jan. 1. Vol. 4, Issue 4: 470-492

Guardado, J. R. (2018) Medical professional liability insurance premiums: An overview from 2008-2017. *Policy Research Perspectives*, American Medical Association. Retrieved from https://www.ama-assn.org/sites/ama-assn.org/files/corp/media-browser/public/government/advocacy/policy-research-perspective-liability-insurance-premiumspdf

Gunningham, N. (2016) Regulation: From traditional to cooperative, in *The Oxford Handbook of White-Collar Crime*. New York: Oxford University Press. Ch 24

Haklai, O. (2007) Religious-Nationalist mobilization and state penetration: Lessons from Jewish settlers' activism in Israel and the West Bank. *Comparative Political Studies*. June, Vol. 40, No. 6: 713-739

Halleck, R. (2019) Who's been charged in the college admissions cheating scandal? Here's the full list. *New York Times*. Mar. 12. Retrieved from https://www.nytimes.com/2019/03/12/us/felicity-huffman-lori-loughlin-massimo-giannulli.html

Hamid, N. (2018) The British hacker who became the Islamic State's chief terror cybercoach: A profile of Junaid Hussain. *CTC Sentinel*, Combating Terrorism Center, West Point. Apr. Vol. 11, Issue 4: 30-37

Handelman, S. (1999) Russia's rule by racketeers. *The Wall Street Journal*. Sept. 20

Hansen, H. and J. Netherland. (2016) Is the prescription opioid epidemic a white problem? *American Journal of Public Health*. Dec. Vol. 106, Issue 12: 2127-2128

Hansen, L. L. (2009) Corporate financial crime: Diagnosis and treatment. *Journal of Financial Crime*. Vol. 16, No. 1: 28-40

Hansen, L. L. (2011) Les coûts sociaux des délits d'initiés sur les marchés financiers *(à traduire)* (Tearing at the Social Fabric: Social Costs of Insider Trading as Informal Economy) in *Shadow Economies and Their Paradoxes*. N. Barbe and F. Weber, eds. Paris: Editions de la Maison des Sciences de l'Homme

Hansen, L. L. and S. Movahedi. (2010) Wall Street scandals: The myth of individual greed. *Sociological Forum*. Vol. 25, No. 2: 367-374

Hansen, L. P. (2018) Applied Analytical Methods Survival Guide. Revised 1st edition. Dubuque, IA: Kendall Hunt Publishers

Harr, J. (1996) *A Civil Action*. New York: Random House, Inc.

Harris, J. G. and A. E. Alter. (2014) Corporate culture: California dreaming. Accenture *Outlook*, retrieved from https://www.accenture.com/t20150522T061601Z__w__/us-en/_acnmedia/Accenture/Conversion-Assets/Outlook/Documents/1/Accenture-Outlook-California-Dreaming-Corporate-Culture-Silicon-Valley.pdf#zoom=50

Harvard Health Publishing. (2009) Premature heart disease. *Harvard Men's Health Watch*, Harvard Medical School. Retrieved from https://www.health.harvard.edu/heart-health/prematureheart-disease

Harvey, R. (2002) *A few bloody noses: The realities and mythologies of the American Revolution*. New York: Abrams Books

Harvey, W. S. (2015) Strategies for conducting elite interviews. *Qualitative Research*. Open Research Exeter: 1-20

Hass, S., P. Burnaby, and M. Nakashima. (2018) Toshiba Corportion—How could so much be so wrong? *Journal of Forensic and Investigative Accounting*. Vol. 10, Issue 2, Special Issue: 267-280

Haworth, J. (2019) 41 charged in opioid ring allegedly responsible for distribution of 23 million pills. ABC News. Retrieved from https://abcnews.go.com/US/41-charged-opioid-ring-allegedlyresponsible-distribution-23/story?id=65265173

Hays, C. L. (2004) Martha Stewart's sentence: The overview; 5 months in jail and Stewart vows, "I'll be back." *The New York Times*. July 17. Retrieved from https://www.nytimes.com/2004/07/17/business/martha-stewart-s-sentence-overview-5-months-jail-stewart-vows-ll-be-back.html

Hays, S. P. (1999) *Conservation and the Gospel of Efficiency: The Progressive Conservation Movement, 1890-1920*. Pittsburgh, PA: University of Pittsburgh Press

Heller, R. (2003) Parmalat: A particularly Italian scandal. *Forbes*. Dec. 30. Retrieved from https://www.forbes.com/2003/12/30/cz_rh_1230parmalat.html#49f969d95162

Helmer, J. B., Jr. (2013) False Claims Act: Incentivizing integrity for 150 years for rogues, privateers, and patriots. *University of Cincinnati Law Review*. Vol. 81, Issue 81: 1261-1282

Henning, P. J. (2011) The pitfalls of wiretaps in white collar crime cases. *New York Times*. Mar. 25. Retrieved from https://dealbook.nytimes.com/2011/03/25/the-pitfalls-of-wiretaps-in-white-collar-crime-cases/

Hofverberg, E. (2014) Iceland: Icelandic bankers jailed for fraud. *Global Legal Monitor, The Law Library of Congress*. July 30. Retrieved from https://www.loc.gov/law/foreign-news/article/iceland-icelandic-bankers-jailed-for-fraud/

Hookway, N. (2018) The moral self: Class, narcissism and the problem of do-it-yourself moralities. *The Sociological Review*. Vol. 66(1): 107-121

Hopkins, M. J. G. (2007) Modelling the known and unknown plant biodiversity of the Amazon Basin. June 29. *Journal of Biogeography*. Vol. 34, No. 8: 1400-1411

Horowitz, I. L. (2003) The cult of dictatorship vs. the culture of modernity. *Society*. Jul/Aug, 40, 5: 9-19

Horsley, S. (2006) Enron founder Kenneth Lay dies of heart attack. *NPR*. July 5. Retrieved from https://www.npr.org/templates/story/story.php?storyId=5534705

Howell, E. (2019) Columbia disaster: What happened, what NASA learned. *Spaceflight, Space.com*. Feb. 1. Retrieved from https://www.space.com/19436-columbia-disaster.html

Hubbell, C. (1965) An input output approach to clique identification. *Sociometry*. 28(4): 377-399

Hudson, R. A. (1999) *The Sociology and Psychology of Terrorism: Who Becomes a Terrorist and Why? A Report Prepared under an Interagency Agreement by the Federal Research Division, Library of Congress*. M. Majeska, ed. A.M. Savada and H.C. Metz, project mgrs. Sept. Retrieved from https://fas.org/irp/threat/frd.html

Hutchings, A. (2014) Crime from the keyboard: organized cybercrime offending, initiation and knowledge transmission. *Crime, Law and Social Change*. Vol. 62 (1): 1-20

Inez Guzman, A. (2019) Faked out: Counterfeit Native jewelry, has flooded the market, fooling buyers and harming authentic makers. *New Mexico Magazine*. July. Pp 38-45

Infosec. (2016) The Ferizi Case: The first man charged with cyber terrorism. *Security Awareness*. Mar. 9. Retrieved from https://resources.infosecinstitute.com/the-ferizi-case-the-first-man-charged-with-cyber-terrorism/#gref

Internal Revenue Service. (2019) Enforcement: Examinations. Retrieved from https://www.irs.gov/statistics/enforcement-examinations

International Criminal Police Organization (INTERPOL). (2019) Financial crime threatens people in every aspect of their lives: at home, at work, online and offline. *Financial crime*. Retrieved from https://www.interpol.int/en/Crimes/Financial-crime

Isaac, A. (2018) UK shadow banking sector worth at least £2.2 trillion. *The Telegraph*. July 2. Retrieved from https://www.telegraph.co.uk/business/2018/07/02/uk-shadow-banking-sector-worth-least-22-trillion/

Isaacson, W. (2011) *Steve Jobs*. New York: Simon and Schuster

Iyengar, R. (2020) The coronavirus is stretching Facebook to its limit. *CNN Business*. Mar. 18. Retrieved from https://www.cnn.com/2020/03/18/tech/zuckerberg-facebook-coronavirus-response/index.html

Javers, E. (2011) Secrets and lies: The rise of corporate espionage in a global economy. *Georgetown Journal of International Affairs*. Winter-Spring, 12 (1): 53-60

Jo, S. (2018) In search of a causal model of the organization-public relationship in public relations. *Social Behavior and Personality*. Vol. 46, No. 11: 1761-1770

Jolly, J. (2019) Former head of Volkswagen could face 10 years in prison. *The Guardian*. Apr. 15. Retrieved from https://www.theguardian.com/business/2019/apr/15/former-head-of-volkswagen-could-face-10-years-in-prison

Jones, C. M. (2014) Why persistent offenders cannot be shamed into behaving. *Journal of Offender Rehabilitation*. 53: 153-170

Jordan, F. (2008) Predicting target selection by terrorists: A network analysis of the 2005 London underground attacks. International Journal of Critical Infrastructures. Vol. 4, No. 1 /2: 206-214

Jorna, P. (2016) The relationship between age and consumer fraud victimization. *Trends and Issues in Crime and Criminal Justice.* Nov. Issue 519: 1-16

Joselow, M. (2019) VW emissions cheating scandal increased children's pollution exposure. *Scientific American.* July 17. Retrieved from https://www.scientificamerican.com/article/vw-emissions-cheating-scandal-increased-childrens-pollution-exposure/

Joseph, A. (2019) 'A blizzard of prescriptions': Documents reveal new details about Purdues's marketing of OxyContin. *Boston Globe, STAT.* Jan. 15. Retrieved from https://www.statnews.com/2019/01/15/massachusetts-purdue-lawsuit-new-details/

Kakissis, J. (2018) Who ordered the car bomb that killed Maltese journalist Daphne Caruana Galizia? *NPR.* retrieved from https://www.npr.org/2018/07/22/630866527/mastermind-behind-malta-journalist-killing-remains-a-mystery

Kandel, E. and E. P. Lazear. (1992) Peer pressure and partnerships. *The Journal of Political Economy.* Aug. Vol. 100, No. 4: 801-817

Kane, J. and A. Wall. (2004) *Identifying the Links between White-Collar Crime and Terrorism.* National White Collar Crime Center. Sept. Retrieved from https://www.ncjrs.gov/pdffiles1/nij/grants/209520pdf

Kaplan, E. (2006) Tracking down terrorist funding. Council on Foreign Relations. Apr. 4. Retrieved from https://www.cfr.org/backgrounder/tracking-down-terrorist-financing

Katersky, A. (2019) NXIVM founder convicted on all charges in sex cult case. *ABC News.* June 19. Retrieved from https://abcnews.go.com/US/nxivm-founder-keith-raniere-convicted-chargessex-cult/story?id=63815115

Katz, L. (1947) On the matric analysis of sociometric data. *Sociometry.* 10: 233-241

Keating, E. K. and P. Frumkin. (2003) Reengineering nonprofit financial accounting toward a more reliable foundation for regulation. *Public Administration Review.* Jan.-Feb. Vol. 63, Issue 1: 3-16

Keinan, G., A. Sadeh, and S. Rosen. (2003) Attitudes and reactions to media coverage of terrorist acts. *Journal of Community Psychology.* Mar. 1. Vol. 31, Issue 2: 149-165

Kelly, H. (2018) Facebook says attack exposed info of 50 million users. Retrieved from https://money.cnn.com/2018/09/28/technology/facebook-breach-50-million/index.html

Keneally, M. (2019) Man who spent 36 years in prison for stealing $50 from a bakery to be freed. *ABC News.* Aug. 29. Retrieved from https://abcnews.go.com/US/man-spent-36-years-prisonstealing-50-bakery/story?id=65264675

KGO-TV. (2019) PG&E Chapter 11 Bankruptcy: Here's how it will affect customers, employees, and shareholders. Jan. 29. Retrieved from https://abc7news.com/business/pg-e-bankruptcy-hereshow-itll-affect-customers-employees-shareholders/5076360/

Kingston, K. G. (2011) Churches and private educational institutions as facilitators of money laundering in Nigeria. Vol. 1, No. 1: 30-38

Kinsella, E. (2017) Leonardo DiCaprio surrenders $3.2 million Picasso and $9 million Basquiat to US government. *Art and Law, artnet®news.* Retrieved from https://news.artnet.com/artworld/leonardo-dicaprio-gives-pack-jho-low-picasso-basquiat-996377

Kix, P. (2009) In the shadow of Woburn. *Boston Magazine.* Sept. 22. Retrieved from https://www.bostonmagazine.com/2009/09/22/in-the-shadow-of-woburn/

Kleibl, J. (2013) The politics of financial regulatory agency replacement. *The Journal of Politics.* Apr. 9. Vol. 75, No. 2: 552-566

Kolbert, E. (2009) FELLOWship of the ring. In *Today's White Collar Crime: Legal, Investigative, and Theoretical Perspectives,* H.J. Brightman, ed. New York: Routledge

Kollias, C., S. Papadamou, and C. Siriopoulos. (2013) European market's reaction to exogenous shocks: A high frequency data analysis of the 2005 London bombings. *International Journal of Financial Studies.* Vol. 1, No. 4: 154-167

Kollmayer, M., M. Schultes, B. Schober, T. Hodosi, and C. Spiel. (2018) Parent's judgements about the desirability of toys for their children: Association with gender role attitudes, gender-typing of toys and demographics. *Sex Roles.* Vol. 79: 329-341

Kopfstein, J. (2013) Hacker with a cause. *The New Yorker.* Nov. 21. Retrieved from http://www.newyorker.com/tech/elements/hacker-with-a-cause

Koshevaliska, O., B. Tashevska Gavrilovic, and E. Maksimova. (2018) Criminological aspects of pink collar crime. *Balkan Social Science Review.* June. Vol. 11, Issue 11: 51-64

Krause, R., Z. Qu, G. D. Bruton, and S. Carter. (2019) The coercive isomorphism ripple effect: An investigation of nonprofit interlocks on corporate boards. *Academy of Management Journal.* Feb. Vol. 62, Issue 1: 283-308

Latiff, R. (2018) Malaysian fugitive Jho Low, four others hit with fresh 1MBD charges. *World News,* Reuters. Retrieved from https://www.reuters.com/article/us-malaysia-politics-1mdb-financier/malaysian-fugitive-jho-low-four-others-hit-with-fresh-1mdb-charges-idUSKBN1O40AW

Lau, C. (2015) IBM's stagnation is ending. *IT World Canada.* April 28. Retrieved from https://www.itworldcanada.com/blog/ibms-stagnation-is-ending/374115

Lavin, T. (2008) Uranium on the loose. *The Atlantic.* April. Retrieved from https://www.theatlantic.com/magazine/archive/2008/04/uranium-on-the-loose/306729/

Lazarus, A. (2016) There's an app for that (but it might be fake). U.S. Federal Trade Commission Consumer Information. Dec. 22. Retrieved from https://www.consumer.ftc.gov/blog/2016/12/theres-app-it-might-be-fake

Le Couteur, P. C. and J. Burreson. (2004) *Napoleon's Buttons: 17 Molecules that Changed History.* New York: Penguin Random House

LeFraniere, S. (2019) Rick Gates, ex-Trump Aide and key witness for Mueller, is sentenced to 45 days in jail. *New York Times.* Dec. 17. Retrieved from https://www.nytimes.com/2019/12/17/us/politics/rick-gates-sentencing.html

Legal Information Institute. (1989) *County of Allegheny v. ACLU,* Greater Pittsburgh Chapter. Cornell Law School. Retrieved from https://www.law.cornell.edu/supremecourt/text/492/573

Legal Information Institute. (2019) U.S. Code §2511. Interception and disclosure of wire, oral, or electronic communications prohibited. Cornell Law School. Retrieved from https://www.law.cornell.edu/uscode/text/18/2511

Levenson, E. (2020) Lori Loughlin and Mossimo Guiannulli agree to plead guilty in college admissions scam. CNN.com. May 21. Retrieved from https://www.cnn.com/2020/05/21/us/lori-loughlin-guilty/index.html

Levenson, E. and M. Morales. (2019) Wealthy parents, actresses, coaches, among the charged in massive college cheating admission scandal, federal prosecutors say. CNN.com. Mar. 13. Retrieved from https://www.cnn.com/2019/03/12/us/college-admission-cheating-scheme/index.html

Levi, M. (2016) The media construction of financial white collar crimes. *British Journal of Criminology.* 46: 1037-1057

Lichtenberg, P. A., M. A. Sugarman, D. Paulson, L. J. Ficker, and A. Rahman-Filipiak. (2015) Psychological and functional vulnerability predicts fraud cases in older adults: Results of a longitudinal study. *Clinical Gerontology.* Vol. 39, No. 1: 48-63

Lindhom, C. (2018) Charisma, in *International Encyclopedia of Anthropology.* H. Callan, ed. Wiley Online Library. Sept. 4. Accessed at https://doi.org/10.1002/9781118924396.wbiea1286

Lindlaw, S. (1997) Some male cult members, including leader, were castrated. *AP News.* Retrieved from https://www.apnews.com/fc9ffd3235d37830cf26da5ad1720b4d

Lindsey, R. (1985) Dan White, killer of San Francisco mayor, a suicide. *New York Times.* Oct. 22. Retrieved from https://www.nytimes.com/1985/10/22/us/dan-white-killer-of-san-francisco-mayor-a-suicide.html

Long, A. L. (2012) Profiling hackers. SANS Institute. Retrieved from https://www.sans.org/readingroom/whitepapers/hackers/profiling-hackers-33864

Lubet, S. (2015) Ethnography on trial: Alice Goffman's acclaimed book *On the Run* tells a compelling story. But can we trust it? *New Republic.* Sept./Oct. Vol. 246, No. 9/10: 38-43

Lutz, J. M. and B. J. Lutz. (2006) Terrorism as economic warfare. *Global Economy Journal.* Vol. 6, Issue 2, Article 2

Lyman, B. (2019) Former Gov. Don Siegelman wins release from supervision. *Montgomery Advertiser.* June 14. Retrieved from https://www.montgomeryadvertiser.com/story/news/2019/06/14/don-siegelman-wins-release-supervision/1454948001/

Lynch, L. E. and B. P. Schwartz. (2013) Correspondence to Judge Gleeson; Re: *United States v. Belfort,* Criminal Docket No. CR-98-0859 (E.D.N.Y. Jun. 11, 2014)

Lyons, D. (2015) "White Hat/Black Hat," Silicon Valley. HBO. Season 2, Episode 8

Maeder, E. M. and R. Corbett. (2015) Beyond frequency: Perceived realism and the CSI effect. *Canadian Journal of Criminology & Criminal Justice.* Vol. 57, Issue 1: 83-114

Mann, B. (2011) Supreme Court asks: Could discrimination claim force female priests? *Catholic News Agency.* May 7. Retrieved from https://www.catholicnewsagency.com/news/supremecourt-asks-could-discrimination-claim-force-female-priests

Marjoua, Y. and K. J. Bozic. (2012) Brief history of quality movement in US healthcare. *Current Reviews in Musculoskeletal Medicine.* Dec. 5 (4): 265-273. Retrieved from https://www.ncbi.nlm.nih.gov/pmc/articles/PMC3702754/

Mason, L. and R. Mason. (1992) A moral appeal for taxpayer compliance: The case of a mass media campaign. *Law & Policy.* Vol. 14: 381-399

McCool, G. (2012) Ex-Intel exec Rajiv Goel avoids jail in Rajaratnam case. *Business Week, Reuters.* Sept. 24. Retrieved from htpps//www.reuters.com/article/galleon-goel-rajaratnam-idINDEE88N0GK20120925

McDonald, G. (2017) Flying cars are (still) coming: Should we believe the hype? All Tech Considered, NPR. April 25. Retrieved from https://www.npr.org/sections/alltechconsidered/2017/04/25/525540611/flying-cars-are-still-coming-should-we-believe-the-hype

McLean, B. and P. Elkind. (2006) The guiltiest guys in the room. *CNN Money.* July 5. Retrieved from https://money.cnn.com/2006/05/29/news/enron_guiltyest/

McLean, B. and P. Elkind. (2006) *The Smartest Guys in the Room: The Amazing Rise and Scandalous Fall of Enron.* New York: Penguin Books

Mejia, L. (2019) Santa Clarita Girl Scout treasurer charged with embezzlement returns to court. Radio station *KHTS.* March 2019

Mello, M. M., A. Chandra, A. A. Gawande, and D. M. Studdert. (2010) National costs of the medical liability system. *Health Aff.* Sept. Vol. 29, No. 9: 1569-1577

Memmott, M. (2011) Michael Jackson's doctor gets four-year sentence. *NPR.* Nov. 29. Retrieved from https://www.npr.org/sections/thetwo-way/2011/11/29/142895015/michael-jacksonsdoctor-gets-4-year-sentence

Mesko, G. and A. Klenovsek. (2011) International waste trafficking, in *Understanding and Managing Threats to the Environment in South Eastern Europe,* G. Mesko, D. Dimitrijevic, and C.B. Fields, eds. Dordrecht: Springer, 79-99

Mesko, G. and K. Eman. (2012) Organised crime involvement in waste trafficking—Case of The Republic of Slovenia. *Criminal Justice Issues: Journal of Criminal Justice and Security.* Issue 5-6: 79-96

Meyer, J. W. and B. Rowan. (1977) Institutional organizations: Formal structure as myth. *American Journal of Sociology.* Sept. Vol. 83, No. 2: 340-363

MF Boom and Madlib. (2009) Absolutely [Recorded by Ape Studio], on *Born Like This.* London: Lex Records. Mar. 24. Track 5

Micallef, J. V. (2018) What's in your cellar? Counterfeit wines are a multi-billion dollar business. Forbes. Dec. 1. Retrieved from https://www.forbes.com/sites/joemicallef/2018/12/01/whatsin-your-cellar-counterfeit-wines-are-a-multi-billion-dollar-problem/#7ae741ac1c83

Miceli, M. P. and J. P. Near. (1994) Relationships among valued congruence, perceived victimization, and retaliation against whistleblowers. *Journal of Management.* Vol. 20 No. 4: 773-794

Michel, C. (2018) Cognitive dissonance resolution strategies after exposure to corporate violence scenarios. *Critical Criminology.* Mar. Vol. 26, No. 1: 1-28

Mims, J. H. (2017) The Wells Fargo scandal and efforts to reform incentive-based compensation in financial institutions. North Carolina Banking Institute. Article 21, Vol. 21, Issue 1: 428-467

Mintzberg, H. (2001) The yin and yang of managing. *Organizational Dynamics.* Spring, Vol. 29, Issue 4: 306-312

Mitchell, A., E. Shearer, J. Gottfried, and M. Barthel. (2016) Pathways to news. *Pew Research Center, Journalism & Media.* July 7. Retrieved from https://www.journalism.org/2016/07/07/pathways-to-news/

Monbiot, G. (2019) The destruction of the Earth is a crime. It should be prosecuted. *The Guardian.* Mar. 28. Retrieved from https://www.theguardian.com/commentisfree/2019/mar/28/destruction-earth-crime-polly-higgins-ecocide-george-monbiot

Monthe, P. (2007) How Nick Leeson caused the collapse of Barings Bank. *NextFinance.* Retrieved from https://www.next-finance.net/How-Nick-Leeson-caused-the-

Morgan, D. (2017) Inflammatory projective identification in fundamentalist religious and economic terrorism. *Psychoanalytic Psychotherapy*. Sept. Vol. 31, No. 3: 314-326

Morvillo, R. G. and R. J. Anello. (2011) Overview of federal wiretap law in white collar cases. *New York Law Journal*. Feb. 1. Vol. 245, No. 21: 1-2

Moskowitz, T. (2011) The illicit antiquities trade as a funding source for terrorism: Is blockchain the solution? *Notes, Cardozo Arts and Entertainment Journal*. Vol. 37: 193-228

Mueller, T. (2011) *Extra Virginity: The Sublime and Scandalous World of Olive Oil*. New York: W.W. Norton & Co

Mun, K. (2005) Contagion and impulse response of international stock markets around 9-11 terrorist attacks. *Global Finance Journal*. Aug. Vol. 16, Issue 1: 48-68

Nash, R., M. Bouchard, and A. Malm. (2018) Twisting trust: Social networks, due diligence, and loss of capital in a Ponzi scheme. *Crime, Law, and Social Change*. 69: 67-89

National Archives and Records Administration (NARA). (n.d.) Presidential Records Act (PRA) of 1978. *National Archives*. Retrieved from https://www.archives.gov/presidentiallibraries/laws/1978-act.html

National Council on Aging (2019) Top ten financial scams targeting seniors. Retrieved from https://www.ncoa.org/economic-security/money-management/scams-security/top-10-scamstargeting-seniors/#intraPageNav8

National Park Service. (2019) Theodore Roosevelt and Conservation. Retrieved from https://www.nps.gov/thro/learn/historyculture/theodore-roosevelt-and-conservation.htm

National Public Radio (NPR). (2018) Understanding NXIVM, group critics call a "cult." Weekend Edition Saturday. S. Simon, host; V. Grigoriadis, guest. From *Literature Resource Center*

Near, J. P. and M. P. Miceli. (1996) Whistle-blowing: Myth and reality. *Journal of Management*. Vol. 22, No. 3: 507-526

NewsRX LLC. (2019) Payment-card fraud funds terrorism and other transnational crimes. *Lab Law Weekly*. July 12. p 20

New York Daily News. (2016) Yankees owner George Steinbrenner is pardoned by Ronald Reagan in 1989 for his illegal contributions to Nixon. Originally published Jan. 20, 1989, M. Santini. Retrieved from https://www.nydailynews.com/sports/baseball/yankees/george-steinbrennerpardoned-ronald-reagan-article-1.2478639

New York Times. (2005) Judith Miller goes to jail. July 7. Retrieved from https://www.nytimes.com/2005/07/07/opinion/judith-miller-goes-to-jail.html

Nikkei. (2015) There are a lot of whistler's rights after the announcement of the delay of financial reporting at Toshiba. Sept. 1. Retrieved from https://www.nikkei.com/article/DGXLASDZ31I27_R30C15A8TI1000/

Novak, D. R. (1986) Normative and interpretive conceptions of human conduct: Decision-making, criminal justice, and parole. *Washington and Lee Law Review*. Vol. 43, Issue 4, Article 3: 1243-1253

Nowicki, D. and B. Muller. (2018) John McCain gets into 'a hell of a mess' with the Keating Five scandal. *The Republic*. April 2. Retrieved from https://www.azcentral.com/story/news/politics/arizona/2018/04/02/john-mccain-keating-five-scandal-arizona-senator/538034001/

Occupational Safety and Health Administration (OSHA). (2019) About OSHA. United States Department of Labor. Retrieved from https://www.osha.gov/aboutosha

Occupational Safety and Health Administration (OSHA). (2019) State plans. U.S. Department of Labor. Retrieved from https://www.osha.gov/dcsp/osp/

Occupational Safety and Health Administration (OSHA). (2019) Worker falls 22 feet to death, 4 months after OSHA cites employer for same job site: Louisville employer faces $320K in fines for serial disregard of fall protection. *OSHA News Release—Region 5*. Retrieved from https://www.osha.gov/news/newsreleases/region5/08012016

Oelsner, L. (1975) Mitchell, Haldeman, Ehrlichman are sentenced to 2-1/2 to 8 years, Mardian to 10 months to 3 years. *New York Times*. Feb. 22. Retrieved from https://www.nytimes.com/1975/02/22/archives/mitchell-haldeman-ehrlichman-are-sentenced-to-2-to-8-years-marmain.html

Office of the Inspector General. (n.d.) Whistleblower Protection Act (WPA). United States Consumer Product Safety Commission. Retrieved from https://www.cpsc.gov/About-CPSC/Inspector-General/Whistleblower-Protection-Act-WPA

Olick, D. (2018) Mortgage fraud is getting worse as more people lie about their income to qualify for loans. *CNBC*. Oct. 3. Retrieved from https://www.cnbc.com/2018/10/03/mortgage-fraud-isgetting-worse-as-more-people-lie-about-their-income.html

Olmsted, L. (2017) *Real Food/Fake Food: Why You Don't Know What You're Eating and What You Can Do About It.* New York: Algonquin Books

Osborne, L. (2019) Prince Andrew and Jeffrey Epstein: What you need to know. *The Guardian.* Retrieved from https://www.theguardian.com/uk-news/2019/dec/07/prince-andrew-jeffreyepstein-what-you-need-to-know

Ouchi, W. G. (1980) Markets, bureaucracies, and clans. *Administrative Science Quarterly.* Mar. Vol. 25, No. 1: 129-141

Paciocco, P. (2013) Pilloried in the press: Rethinking the Constitutional status of the American perp walk. *New Criminal Law Review: An International and Interdisciplinary Journal.* Vol. 16, No. 1: 50-103

Page, K. R., S. Doocy, F. R. G. Barch, J. S. Castro, P. Spiegel, and C. Bevrer. (2019) Venzuela's public health crisis: a regional emergency. Review in *The Lancet.* March, Vol. 393, Issue 10177: 1254-1260

Palmer, K. (2018) Police: $63K found stashed above ceiling in basement. *Lansing State Journal.* July 18. Retrieved from https://www.lansingstatejournal.com/story/news/local/2018/07/18/fatherwehrle-embezzlement-police-find-more-than-63-k-stashed/797883002/

Panepento, P. (2007) Embezzlement widespread at dioceses, study finds. *Chronicle of Philanthropy.* Jan. 25, Vol. 19, Issue 7

Parveen, N. (2018) UK's plastic waste may be dumped overseas instead of recycled. *The Guardian.* July 22. Retrieved from https://www.theguardian.com/environment/2018/jul/23/uks-plastic-waste-may-be-dumped-overseas-instead-of-recycled

Paternoster, R. and S. Simpson. (1996) Sanction threats and appeals to morality: Rational Choice Model of corporate crime. *Law and Society Review.* Vol. 30, No. 3: 549-583

Patterson, T. E. (1996) Bad news, bad governance. *The Annals of the American Academy.* 546: 97-108

Paul, R. G. (1984) Damages for wrongful pregnancy in Illinois. *Loyola University Chicago Law Journal.* Summer, Vol. 15, Issue 4: 799-842

Pavlo, W. (2012) Former HealthSouth CEO, Richard Scrushy, gets prison sentenced [sic] reduced. *Forbes.* Retrieved from https://www.forbes.com/sites/walterpavlo/2012/01/26/former-healthsouth-ceo-richard-scrushy-gets-prison-sentenced-reduced/#3bc3439338e2

Pearson, R. and J. Coen. (2019) U.S. says Blagojevich, crew ran state as racket. *Chicago Tribune.* Apr. 3. Retrieved from https://www.chicagotribune.com/news/ct-xpm-2009-04-03-chi-090403blago-feds-story-story.html

Penn, E. B., G. E. Higgins, S. L. Gabbidon, and K. L. Jordan. (2008) Government efforts on homeland security and crime: Public views and opinions. *American Journal of Criminal Justice.* Vol. 34: 28-40

Peterson, H. (2020) Nordstrom is permanently closing 16 stores in 9 states. Here's the list. *Business Insider.* May 8. Retrieved from https://www.businessinsider.com/nordstrom-will-close-16-stores-list-2020-5

Phelps, T. (2016) Why hackers want your medical records. NetStandard. 17 Nov. Retrieved from http://www.netstandard.com/hackers-want-medical-records/

Pierce, O. and M. Allen. (2015) How Denmark dumped medical malpractice and improved patient safety. *ProPublica.* Retrieved from https://www.propublica.org/article/how-denmarkdumped-medical-malpractice-and-improved-patient-safety

Piquero, N. L. (2012) The only thing we have to fear is fear itself: Investigating the relationship between fear of falling and white collar crime. *Crime and Delinquency.* Vol. 58, No. 3: 362-379

Plato. (1937) *The Republic.* London: William Heinemann

Polfeldt, E. (2017) This crime in the workplace is costing US businesses $50 billion a year. *CNBC.* Sept. 12. Retrieved from https://www.cnbc.com/2017/09/12/workplace-crime-costs-usbusinesses-50-billion-a-year.html

Pollman, E. (2019) Corporate disobedience. *Duke Law Journal.* Jan. Vol. 68, Issue 4: 709-765

Pomorski, C. (2019) Look homeward, hedgie. *Vanity Fair.* Aug. 62-65; 92-93

Postman, N. (2005) *Amusing ourselves to death: Public discourse in the Age of Show Business.* New York: Penguin Books

Pratt, T. C., K. Holtfreter, and M. D. Reisig. (2010) Routine online activity and internet fraud tartgeting: Extending the generality of Routine Activity Theory. *Journal of Research in Crime and Delinquency.* Vol. 47, No. 3: 267-296

Preskorn, S. H. (2014) Clinical psychopharmacology and medical malpractice: the four Ds. *Journal of Psychiatric Practice.* Sept., Vol. 20, No. 5: 363-368

Pyatt, R. (2019) Studies show . . . or maybe they don't: Misinterpreted data and unsubstantiated conclusions plague press and social media. What can journalists do to stop them? *Society of Professional Journalists.* Winter, Vol. 107, Issue 4: 22-27

Rahman, T. (2018) Extreme overvalued beliefs: How violent extremist beliefs become "normalized." *Behavioral Sciences.* Jan. Vol. 8, Issue 1: 10-21

Ralph, P. and R. Relman. (2018) These are the most and least biased news outlets in US, according to Americans. *Business Insider.* Sept. 2. Retrieved from https://www.businessinsider.com/most-biased-news-outlets-in-america-cnn-fox-nytimes-2018-8

Ramseyer, J. M. (2010) The effect of universal health insurance on malpractice claims: The Japanese experience. *Journal of Legal Analysis.* Vol. 2: 621-686

Recovery Worldwide, LLC. (2019) Substance abuse in healthcare. Addiction Center. Retrieved from https://www.addictioncenter.com/addiction/medical-professionals/

Reep-van den Bergh, C. M. M. and M. Junger. (2018) Victims of cybercrime in Europe: A review of victim surveys. *Crime Science.* 7 (1): 1-15

Richards, M. (2016) *83 Minutes: The Doctor, The Damage, and the Shocking Death of Michael Jackson.* New York: Thomas Dunne Books

Rishikof, H. and K. Lunday. (2011) Corporate responsibility in cybersecurity: Building international global standards. *Georgetown Journal of International Affairs.* Vol. 12 (1): 17-24

Ritzer, G. (2011) *The McDonaldization of society.* Thousand Oaks, CA: Pine Forge Press. 6th ed.

Roberts, J. (2004) Enron traders caught on tape. *CBS Evening News.* June 1. Retrieved from https://www.cbsnews.com/news/enron-traders-caught-on-tape/

Romo, V. (2019) U.S. arrests money-laundering expert for laundering money. NPR. Nov. 19. Retrieved from https://www.npr.org/2019/11/19/780877837/u-s-arrests-money-laundering-expert-for-laundering-money

Rosenberg, J. M. (2017) After a Katrina or Harvey, businesses suffer long after water recedes – many never recover. *Associated Press, NOLA.com.* Sept. 6. Retrieved from https://www.nola.com/news/business/article_06c0e4bb-0061-5a30-b099-c40e8519231b.html

Rosoff, S., H. Pontell, and R. Tillman. (2013) *Profit without honor: White collar crime and the looting of America.* New York: Pearson Education. 6th ed.

Rostomian, P. C. (2002) Looted art in the U.S. market. *Rutgers Law Review.* Fall. Issue 1: 271-299

Rubenstein, I. H. (1941) Criminal aspects of faith healing. *Medicao-Legal and Criminological Review.* July 1, Vol. 9, Issue 3: 159-162

Rubio, P. F. (2010) *There is always work at the Post Office: African-American Postal workers and the fight for jobs, justice, and equality.* Chapel Hill: University of North Carolina Press

Rubio, P. F. (2018) After the storm: Postal politics and labor relations following the 1970 U.S. Postal wildcat strike, 1970-1981. *Employee Responsibilities and Rights Journal.* March 1. Vol. 30: 65-80

RxList. (2019) Diprivan: Side effects. Retrieved from https://www.rxlist.com/diprivan-drug/patientimages-side-effects.htm

Satgunam, P. N. and L. Chindelevich. (2017) Vision screening results in a cohort of Bhopal gas disaster survivors. *Current Science.* May 25. Vol. 112, No. 10: 2085-2088

Schafer, S. (1971) The concept of the political criminal. *Journal of Criminal Law, Criminology, and Police Science.* Northwestern University of Law. Vol. 62, Issue 3: 380-387

Schmid, A. P. and J. de Graaf. (1982) *Violence as Communication.* Thousand Oaks: Sage Publishing

Schmitt, R. B. (2005) Journalist jailed for not revealing sources in court. *Los Angeles Times.* July 7. Retrieved from https://www.latimes.com/archives/la-xpm-2005-jul-07-na-reporters7-story.html

Schneider, G. (2016) Local company faces $320K fine in worker death. *Courier Journal.* Aug. 7. Retrieved from https://www.courier-journal.com/story/money/companies/2016/08/07/local-company-faces-320k-fine-worker-death/88338482/

Schneier, B. (2017) Who are the Shadow Brokers? *The Atlantic.* May 23. Retrieved from https://www.theatlantic.com/technology/archive/2017/05/shadow-brokers/527778/

Schwartz, R. D. and S. Orleans. (1967) On legal sanctions. *University of Chicago Law Review*. Vol. 34: 274-290

Scutti, S. (2018) At least 8 million IVF babies born in 40 years since historic first. *Health, CNN*. July 3. Retrieved from https://www.cnn.com/2018/07/03/health/worldwide-ivf-babies-born-study/index.html

Secret Service. (2018) Cyber operations. United States Government. Retrieved from https://www.secretservice.gov/investigation/#

Securities and Exchange Commission (SEC). (2003) SEC charges Martha Stewart, broker Peter Bacanovic with illegal insider trading. Press Release. Retrieved from https://www.sec.gov/news/press/2003-69.htm

Securities and Exchange Commission (SEC). (2006) SEC settles litigation with former Chief Corporate Counsel of Tyco International Ltd. *Litigation Release No. 19678*. May 1. Retrieved from https://www.sec.gov/litigation/litreleases/2006/lr19678htm

Securities and Exchange Commission (SEC). (2018) Annual Report. *Division of Enforcement*. Retrieved from https://www.sec.gov/files/enforcement-annual-report-2018pdf

Securities and Exchange Commission (SEC). (2019) SEC awards $50 million to two whistleblowers. Press Release. March 26. Retrieved from https://www.sec.gov/news/press-release/2019-42

Securities and Exchange Commission (SEC). (2019) What we do. Retrieved from https://www.sec.gov/Article/whatwedo.html

Seelye, K. Q. (2005) Times and reporter reach agreement on her departure. *New York Times*. Nov. 9. Retrieved from https://www.nytimes.com/2005/11/09/business/times-and-reporter-reach-agreement-on-her-departure.html

Seiberg, J. (1996) Fed to order more audits of foreign banks in wake of Daiwa and Barings scandals. *American Banker*. Vol. 161, Issue 45: 3

Senn, S. (1990) The prosecution of religious fraud. *Florida State University Law Review*. Winter, Vol. 17, Issue 2: 325

Shapiro, S. P. (1984) *Wayward Capitalists*. New Haven, CT: Yale University Press

Sharkey, E. (2009) Environmental Hearing Board Review: *Eureka Stone Quarry, Inc. v. Department of Environmental Protection:* The rocky results of air quality violations. *Villanova Environmental Law Journal*. Vol. 20, Issue 2: 337-360

Shea, C. T. and O. Hawn. (2019) Microfoundations of corporate social responsibility and irresponsibility. *Academy of Management Journal*. Vol. 52, No. 5: 1609-1642

Sherchan, W., S. Nepal and C. Paris. (2013) A survey of trust in social networks. *ACM Computing Surveys*. Aug. Vol. 45, No. 4, Article 47: 1-33

Shichor, D. (2017) Adopting a white collar crime theoretical framework for the analysis of terrorism: An explorational understanding. *Journal of Contemporary Criminal Justice*. Vol. 33, No. 3: 254-272

Simko-Bednarski, E. (2019) Homeless man in GoFundMe case arrested. *CNN*. Jan. 10. Retrieved from https://www.cnn.com/2019/01/09/us/gofundme-bobbitt-arrest-warrant/index.html

Simmel, G. (1906) The sociology of secrecy and of secret societies. *American Journal of Sociology*. Vol. 11(4): 441-498

Simmel, G. (1997) *The Philosophy of Money*. D. Frisby, ed., Bottomore and D. Frisby, trans. New York: Routledge

Simon, H. A. (1982) *Models of bounded rationality*. Cambridge, MA: MIT Press

Sinai, M. (2017) Where does e-waste end up? *Recycle Nation*. Apr. 25. Retrieved from https://recyclenation.com/2017/04/where-does-e-waste-end-up/

Skogstad, A., J. Hetland, L. Glasø, and S. Einarsen. (2014) Is avoidant leadership a root cause of subordinate stress? Longitudianl relationships between laissez-faire leadership and role ambiguity. *Work & Stress*. Oct.-Dec. 28, 4: 323-341

Skyes, M. and D. Matza. (1947) Techniques of neutralization: A theory of deviance. *American Sociology Review*. Vol. 22, No. 6: 664-670

Smaili, N. and P. Arroyo. (2019) Categorization of whistleblowers using the whistleblowing triangle. *Journal of Business Ethics*. Vol. 157: 95-117

Smallridge, J. L. and J. R. Roberts. (2013) Crime specific neutralizations: An empirical examination of four types of digital piracy. *International Journal of Cyber Criminology*. Dec., Vol. 7, No. 2: 125-140

Smith, A. (2018) More employers ditch performance appraisals. SHRM. May 18. Retrieved from https://www.shrm.org/resourcesandtools/legal-and-compliance/employment-law/pages/moreemployers-ditch-performance-appraisals.aspx

Smith, J. (1986) $37 screws, a $7,622 coffee maker, $640 toilet seats: suppliers to our military just won't be oversold. *Los Angeles Times.* July 30. https://www.latimes.com/archives/la-xpm-1986-07-30-vw-18804-story.html

Social Security Administration. (2018) Identity theft and your Social Security number. Pub No. 05-10064. Retrieved from https://www.ssa.gov/pubs/EN-05-10064.pdf

Society for Conservation Biology. (2019) Treaties. Retrieved from https://conbio.org/policy/policy-priorities/treaties

Sorbello, A. (2019) Jordan Belfort net worth, quotes, and story. *Astrogrowth.com.* Retrieved from https://www.astrogrowth.com/blog/jordan-belfort-net-worth/

Soroka, S., M. Daku, D. Hiaeshutter-Rice, L. Guggenheim, and J. Pasek. (2018) Negativity and positivity biases in economic news coverage: Traditional versus social media. *Communication Research.* Oct. Vol. 45, Issue 7: 1078-1098

Spain, J. and R. Ramsey. (2000) Workers' Compensation and Respondeat Superior Liability legal cases involving salespersons' misuse of alcohol. *Journal of Personal Selling & Sales Management.* Fall. Vol. 20, Issue 4: 263-269

Spann, D. D. (2017) When the religious fall prey to fraud. *ACAMS Today.* Jan. 17. Retrieved from https://www.acamstoday.org/when-the-religious-fall-prey-to-fraud/

Spector, M. and J. DiNapoli. (2019) Exclusive: OxyContin maker prepares 'free-fall' bankruptcy as settlement talks stall. *Business News*, Reuters. Sept. 3. Retrieved from https://www.reuters.com/article/us-purdue-pharma-opioids-exclusive/exclusive-oxycontin-maker-prepares-freefall-bankruptcy-as-settlement-talks-stall-idUSKCN1VO2QN/

Spitzer, K. (2015) Toshiba accounting scandal in Japan could speed corporate reforms. *USA Today.* July 24. Available at https://www.usatoday.com/story/money/business/2015/07/24/toshiba-accounting-scandal-japan-could-speed-corporate-reforms/30612009/

Srinivasan, M. (2005) Southwest Airlines operations – A strategic perspective. *Airline Industry Articles.* Retrieved from http://airline-industry.malq.net/southwest-airlines-operations-a-strategic-perspective/

Stebbins, S. (2019) Where credit card debt is the worst in the US: States with the highest average balance. *USA Today.* Mar. 7. Retrieved from https://www.usatoday.com/story/money/personalfinance/2019/03/07/credit-card-debt-where-average-balance-highest-across-us/39129001/

Stevens, L. (2017) Amazon, FTC end legal battle, clearing the way for up to $70 million in refunds. *The Wall Street Journal.* Apr. 4. Retrieved from https://www.wsj.com/articles/amazon-ftc-endlegal-battle-clearing-the-way-for-up-to-70-million-in-refunds-1491337565

Straetmans, S. T. M., W. F. C. Verschoor, and C. C. P. Wolff. (2008) Extreme U.S. stock market fluctuations in the wake of 9/11. *Journal of Applied Econometrics.* Jan.-Feb.: 17-42

Substance Abuse and Mental Health Services Administration (SAMHSA). (n.d.) Drugfree workplace programs: Prepare your workplace. Retrieved from https://www.samhsa.gov/workplace/toolkit/plan-implement-program/prepare-workplace

Sukumaran, T. (2018) What's the deal with Jho Low, Malaysia's most wanted man? *South China Morning Post.* Nov. 2. Retrieved from https://www.scmp.com/news/asia/southeast-asia/article/2171428/whats-deal-jho-low-malaysias-most-wanted-man

Supreme Court of the United States. (2012) *Hosanna-Tabor Evangelical Lutheran Church and School v. EEOC*, 565 U.S. 171. Oct. Term, 2011, decided Jan. 11

Swab, A. (2014) Adderall not cocaine: Inside the lives of the young wolves of Wall Street. *PBS News Hour.* Feb. 18. Retrieved from https://www.pbs.org/newshour/economy/adderall-cocaine-inside-lives-young-wolves-wall-street

Swann, S. (2019) Antiquities looted in Syria and Iraq are sold on Facebook. British Broadcasting Company (BBC News) May 2. Retrieved from https://www.bbc.com/news/world-middle-east-47628369

Sweeney, P. (2002) The travails of Tyco. *Financial Executive.* June. Vol. 18, Issue 4: 20-22

Tapscott, D. and A. Tapscott. (2016) *Blockchain revolution.* Brilliance Audio (MP3), May 2

Taunton, Y. (2020) Coronavirus and cybercrime – hackers use COVID-19 as phishing bait. UAB News, The University of Alabama at Birmingham. April 3. Retrieved from https://www.uab. edu/news/research/item/11219-coronavirus-and-cybercrime-hackers-use-covid-19-asphishing-bait

Taylor, L. (2011) How to deal with "multiple boss madness": Learn "multiple boss mastery" and reduce job stress. *Psychology Today*. Feb. 23. Retrieved from https://www.psychologytoday. com/us/blog/tame-your-terrible-office-tyrant/201102/how-deal-multiple-boss-madness

Teague Beckwith, R. (2019) Here are all of the indictments, guilty pleas, and convictions from Robert Mueller's investigation. Politics, Justice, *Time Magazine*. July 24. Retrieved from https://time. com/5556331/mueller-investigation-indictments-guilty-pleas/

Teitelman, R. (2016) Michael Milken and the birth of junk bonds. *Mergers and Acquisitions: The Dealermaker's Journal*. May. Vol. 51, Issue 5: 44-50

Tønnessen, T. H. (2017) Islamic State and technology—A literature Review. *Perspectives on Terrorism*. Vol. 11, No. 6: 101-110

TRAC Reports, Inc. (2019) White collar crime prosecutions for April 2019. Syracuse University. Retrieved from https://trac.syr.edu/tracreports/bulletins/white_collar_crime/monthlyapr19/fil/

Tran, M. (2002) WorldCom accounting scandal. *The Guardian*. Aug. 9. Retrieved from https://www. theguardian.com/business/2002/aug/09/corporatefraud.worldcom2

Treasury Department. (2018) *National Terrorist Financing Risk Assessment*. Retrieved from https:// home.treasury.gov/system/files/136/2018ntfra_12182018pdf

Tressler, C. (2020) COVID-19 contact tracing text message scams. Consumer Information, Federal Trade Commission. May 19. Retrieved from https://www.consumer.ftc.gov/blog/2020/05/ covid-19-contact-tracing-text-message-scams?utm_source=govdelivery&fbclid=IwAR3z GRvy1b0ZWXDTwYw5wEqVZwEY7-5fJniyuqu11ksnjkI4vaZcNks8wDU

Tucker, G. (2018) Sarbanes-Oxley is suffocating our essential capital market. *Real Clear Markets*. May 11. Retrieved from https://www.realclearmarkets.com/articles/2018/05/11/ sarbanesoxley_ is_suffocating_our_essential_capital_markets_103255.html

Turner, J. (2002) *The Structure of Sociological Theory*. 7th ed. Belmont, CA: Wadsworth Publishing Co.

Turner, J. I. (2019) Managing digital discovery in criminal cases. *The Journal of Criminal Law & Criminology*. Vol. 209, No. 2: 237-311

United Nations. (2019) UN report: Nature's dangerous decline 'unprecedented'; Species extinction rates 'accelerating.' *Sustainable Development Goals*. Retrieved from https://www.un.org/ sustainabledevelopment/blog/2019/05/nature-decline-unprecedented-report/

United States Bureau, Department, or other agency. *See name of specific agency without U.S. or United States preceding it*

United States Congress. (2004) *Hearing Before the Committee on Banking, Housing, and Urban Affairs, United States Senate*. June 3. 108 Congress, Second Session

United States District Court for District of Columbia. (1995) *SEC v. Stratton Oakmont, Inc.*, 878 F. Supp. 250 (D.D.C. 1995). Feb. 28. *Justia*. Retrieved from https://law.justia.com/cases/ federal/district-courts/FSupp/878/250/1439881/

United States District Court for District of Massachusetts. (1985) *Deposition, John Drobinski*. Civil No. 82-1672-S

United States District Court for Eastern District of Virginia. (2016) *United States v. Adrit Ferizi*. Alexandria Division, Case 1: 16-cr-00042-LMB, Document 54. Sept. 16. 19 pp. Available at https://www.justice.gov/opa/file/896326/download

United States District Court for Southern District of New York. (2018) *United States v. Zhu Hua, a/k/ a/"Afar," a/k/a "CVNX," a/k/a "Alayos," a/k/a "Godkiller," and Zhang Shilong, a/k/a "Baobeilong," a/k/a "Zhang Jianguo," a/k/a "Atreexp."* Dec. 1, file date. https://admin.govexec. com/media/china_casepdf

United States House of Representatives. (2009) Meeting on assessing the Madoff scheme and the need for regulatory reform. Committee of Financial Services. 111 Congress, First Session. Jan. 5

United States House of Representatives. (2012) *Obama Administration's Abuse of Power*. Committee on the Judiciary. 112th Congress, Second Session. Sept. 12. Washington, D.C.: U.S. Government Printing Office

United States House of Representatives. (2013) *Hispanic Americans in Congress*. The Committee on House Administration of the U.S. House of Representatives. Washington, D.C.: GAO

United States House of Representatives. (n.d.) Overview of New Mexico Politics 1848-1898. *History, Art & Archives.* Retrieved from https://history.house.gov/Exhibitions-and-Publications/HAIC/Historical-Essays/Continental-Expansion/New-Mexican-Politics/

United States Senate. (1999) *Anticybersquatting Consumer Protection Act* (ACPA) 15 U.S. Code §1125. 106th Congress, 1st Session. Aug. 5. Washington, D.C.: U.S. Government Publishing Office. Available at https://www.govinfo.gov/content/pkg/CRPT-106srpt140/html/CRPT-106srpt140htm

United States Senate. (2000) Hearing: ID theft: When bad things happen in your good name. Subcommittee on Technology, Terrorism, and Government Information, Committee on the Judiciary. 116th Congress, Second Session. Mar. 7. Washington, D.C.: U.S. Government Printing Office. Available at https://www.govinfo.gov/content/pkg/CHRG-106shrg69821/html/CHRG-106shrg69821.htm#?

United States Senate. (2002) Hearings: Identity theft. Subcommittee on Technology, Terrorism, and Government Information, Committee on the Judiciary. 117th Congress, Second Session. Mar. 20 and July 9. Washington, D.C.: U.S. Government Printing Office. Available at https://www.govinfo.gov/content/pkg/CHRG-107shrg85794/pdf/CHRG-107shrg85794.pdf#?

United States Senate. (2014) Convention on the conservation and management of high seas fisheries resources in the North Pacific Ocean (Treaty Doc. 113-2). *Executive Report 113-2*, 113th Congress, 2d Session. Mar. 13

United States Senate. (2015) Deepening political and economic crisis in Venezuela: Implications for U.S. interests and the Western Hemisphere. *Hearing: Subcommittee on Western Hemisphere Transnational Crime, Civilian Security, Democracy, Human Rights, and Global Women's Issues.* Committee on Foreign Affairs. 114th Congress, First Session. March 17. Washington, D.C.: U.S. Government Publishing Office

United States Senate. (2016) Regulatory reforms to improve equity market structure: hearing before of the equity markets, and identifying key issues under consideration to reduce market complexity, increase operational stability, and promote efficiency, competition, and capital formation, Mar. 3. Monograph, U.S. Government Publishing Office. Subcommittee on Securities, Insurance, and Investment of the Committee on Banking, Housing, and Urban Affairs, United States Senate, One Hundred Fourteenth Congress, second session, on examining recent efforts by the SEC and FINRA in aiding the function and stability

U.S. Constitution, Amendment I. (1789, rev. 1992)

Vandebroek, I., J. Calewaert, S. De jonckheere, S. Sanca, L. Semo, P. Van Damme, L. Van Puyvelde, and N. De Kimpe. (2004) Use of medicinal plants and pharmaceuticals by indigenous communities in the Bolivian Andes and Amazon. *Bulletin of the World Health Organization.* Vol. 84, No. 4: 243-250

Van Leeuwen, L. and D. Weggemans. (2018) Characteristics of Jihadist terrorist leaders: A quantitative approach. *Perspectives on Terrorism.* Vol. 4, No. 4: 55-67

Van Vugt, M., S. F. Jepson, C. M. Hart, and D. De Cremer. (2004) Autocratic leadership in social dilemmas: A threat to group stability. *Journal of Experimental Social Psychology.* Vol. 40: 1-13

Van Zee, A. (2009) The promotion and marketing of OxyContin: Commercial triumph, public health tragedy. *American Journal of Public Health.* Feb. Vol. 22, No. 2: 221-227

Vaughn, D. (2016) *The Challenger launch decision: Risky technology, culture, and deviance at NASA.* Chicago: The University of Chicago Press

Voiskounsky, A. E. and O. V. Smyslova. (2004) Flow-based model of computer hacker's motivation. *CyberPsychology and Behavior.* July, 6(2): 171-180

Voronin, Y. (1997) The emerging criminal state: Economic and political aspects of organized crime in Russia. In *Russian Organized Crime: The New Threat?*, P. Williams, ed. London: Frank Cass Publishers. pp. 53-62

Wachtel, K. (2011) Listen to the Raj Rajaratnam wiretaps. *Business Insider.* Mar. 14. Retrieved from https://www.businessinsider.com/listen-to-the-raj-rajaratnam-wiretaps-2011-3

Walker, S. (1985) *Sense and Nonsense About Crime.* Florence KY: Wadsworth, Inc

Walklate, S. (2004) *Gender, crime and justice.* Cullompton: Willan Publishing

Wallace, S. (2019) Inside the faltering fight against illegal Amazon logging. *National Geographic.* Retrieved from https://www.nationalgeographic.com/environment/2019/08/brazil-logging/#close

Wall Street Journal (online). (2020) The Michael Milken pardon: Trump's act of clemency recalls an era riff with the politics of envy. Feb. 19. *ProQuest.* Web. 23 Feb. 2020

Wansink, B., G. Cordua, E. Blair, C. Payne, and S. Geiger. (2006) Wine promotions in restaurants: Do beverage sales contribute or cannibalize? *Cornell Hotel and Restaurant Administration Quarterly.* Nov. Vol. 47, Issue 4: 327-336

Ward, Steven J. A. (2005) Philosophical foundations for global journalism ethics. *Journal of Mass Media Ethics.* Vol. 20, No. 1: 3-21

Warde, I. (2007) *The Price of Fear: The Truth Behind the Financial War on Terrorism.* Berkeley, CA: University of California Press

Washington Post. (2019) *The Mueller Report.* P. Finn, National Security, ed.; R.S. Heldermand and M. Zapotosky, Introduction and Analysis. New York: Scribner

Wasserman S. and K. Faust. (1994) *Social network analysis: Methods and applications.* Cambridge University Press

Weber, M. (1922, 2013) Bureaucracy. *Economy and Society.* Vol. 2. Oakland, CA: University of California Press. Ch 11

Weber, M. (1947) The nature of charismatic authority and its routinization, in *Theory of Social and Economic Organization.* A.R. Anderson and T. Parson, trans. New York: The Free Press

Weeke, S. (2019) Parma's god falls from the sky: An Italian city mourns as a dynasty collapses over financial scandal. *World News on NBCNEWS.com.* Retrieved from http://www.nbcnews.com/id/4030254/ns/world_news/t/parmas-god-falls-sky/#.XXp0_utKjOQ

Weimann, G. (2015) Going dark: Terrorism on the dark web. *Studies in Conflict and Terrorism.* Vol. 39(3): 195-206

Wells Fargo Bank. (2019) History of Wells Fargo. Retrieved from https://www.wellsfargo.com/about/corporate/history/

Whitmire, N. (2015) Julian Assange, Wikileaks, and the trickster: A case study of archetypal influence. *ReVision.* Winter, Vol. 32, Issue 2/3: 84-93

Wigand, J. S. (1995) Testimony transcript, *The State of Mississippi v. Brown and Williamson.* June 25, 2019. Retrieved from http://www.jeffreywigand.com/pascagoulaphp

Williams, E., Resurrecting free exercise in *Hosanna-Tabor Evangelical Lutheran Church and School v. EEOC,* 132 S. Ct. 694 (2012). *Harvard Journal of Law & Public Policy.* Jan. 1, Vol. 36, p 391

Williams, L. (2002) Tyco CEO receives $1.65 mln salary. *Market Watch.* Jan. 28. Retrieved from https://www.marketwatch.com/story/tyco-ceo-kozlowski-gets-hefty-salary-bonus-hike

Windrem, R. (2015) Terror on a shoestring: Paris attacks likely cost $10,000 or less. *NBC News.* Nov. 18. Retrieved from https://www.nbcnews.com/storyline/paris-terror-attacks/terror-shoestring-paris-attacks-likely-cost-10-000-or-less-n465711

Woods, C. D. M. (2014) Do campaign finance violations warrant jail time? A question of ethics. *Roll Call.* Retrieved from https://www.rollcall.com/news/do-campaign-finance-violations-warrantjail-time-a-question-of-ethics

Woodward, B. (2005) *The Secret Man: The story of Watergate's Deep Throat.* New York: Simon & Schuster

Woodward, B. and C. Bernstein. (2014) *All the President's men: The greatest reporting story of all time.* Reissue edition. New York: Simon & Schuster

Wright, T. and B. Hope. (2019) *Billion Dollar Whale: The Man Who Fooled Wall Street, Hollywood, and the World.* New York: Hachette Books

Yale University. (2019) The Amazon basin forest. *Global Forest Atlas,* School of Forestry & Environmental Studies. Retrieved from https://globalforestatlas.yale.edu/region/amazon

Yang, S. and J. I-Chin. (2018) An evaluation of displacement and diffusion effects on eco-terrorist activities after police intervention. *Quantitative Criminology.* Vol. 34: 1103-1123

Yang, S., Y. Su, and J. V. Carson. (2019) Eco-Terrorism and corresponding legislative efforts to intervene and prevent future attacks. *Center for Evidence-Based Crime Policy,* George Mason University. Retrieved from http://cebcp.org/wp-content/onepagers/EcoTerrorismAndCorrespondingLegislativeEfforts_YangEtAlpdf

Zaki, M. (2014) The ethical issues in the relationship between the psychologist as therapist and the patient. *Medicine and Law.* Oct. Vol. 33, No. 3: 3-12

Zeller, B. E. (1997) *Heaven's Gate: America's UFO Religion.* New York: New York University Press

Zhang, S. (2019) A decades-old doctor's secret leads to new fertility fraud law. *The Atlantic.* May 7. Retrieved from https://www.theatlantic.com/science/archive/2019/05/cline-fertility-fraud-law/588877/

Zillow. (2019) Rancho Santa Fe home prices & values. Retrieved from https://www.zillow.com/rancho-santa-fe-ca/home-values/

Zivin, J. G., M. Neidell and W. Schlenker. (2011) Water quality violations and avoidance behavior: Evidence from bottled water consumption. *American Economic Review: Papers and Proceedings.* Vol. 101, No. 3: 448-453